THE PRACTICAL GUIDE TO
KAYAKING CANOEING & SAILING

THE PRACTICAL GUIDE TO
KAYAKING CANOEING & SAILING

INCLUDES EXPERT ADVICE, GUIDELINES AND INFORMATION COVERING
EVERY ASPECT OF EACH SPORT, WITH OVER 1500 IMAGES INCLUDING
STEP-BY-STEP PRACTICAL INSTRUCTIONAL SEQUENCES THROUGHOUT

Bill Mattos and Jeremy Evans

LORENZ BOOKS

This edition is published by Lorenz Books, an imprint of Anness Publishing Ltd Hermes House, 88–89 Blackfriars Road, London SE1 8HA; tel. 020 7401 2077; fax 020 7633 9499

www.lorenzbooks.com; www.annesspublishing.com

Anness Publishing has a new picture agency outlet for images for publishing, promotions or advertising. Please visit our website www.practicalpictures.com for more information.

UK agent: The Manning Partnership Ltd; tel. 01225 478444; fax 01225 478440; sales@manning-partnership.co.uk
UK distributor: Grantham Book Services Ltd; tel. 01476 541080; fax 01476 541061; orders@gbs.tbs-ltd.co.uk
North American agent/distributor: National Book Network; tel. 301 459 3366; fax 301 429 5746; www.nbnbooks.com
Australian agent/distributor: Pan Macmillan Australia; tel. 1300 135 113; fax 1300 135 103; customer.service@macmillan.com.au
New Zealand agent/distributor: David Bateman Ltd; tel. (09) 415 7664; fax (09) 415 8892

Publisher: Joanna Lorenz
Managing Editors: Linda Fraser, Conor Kilgallon, Judith Simons
Senior Art Manager: Clare Reynolds
Compendium Editor: Lucy Doncaster
Project Editors: Sarah Ainley, Mariano Kälfors, Polly Willis
Text Editors: Richard Rosenfeld and Paul Grogan
Photographers: Helen Metcalfe, Ocean Images
Designers: Gowers Elmes Ltd, Nigel Partridge
Illustrators: Creative Byte, J. B. Illustrations
Production Controller: Steve Lang

ETHICAL TRADING POLICY
At Anness Publishing we believe that business should be conducted in an ethical and ecologically sustainable way, with respect for the environment and a proper regard to the replacement of the natural resources we employ.
As a publisher, we use a lot of wood pulp to make high-quality paper for printing, and that wood commonly comes from spruce trees. We are therefore currently growing more than 500,000 trees in two Scottish forest plantations near Aberdeen – Berrymoss (130 hectares/320 acres) and West Touxhill (125 hectares/305 acres). The forests we manage contain twice the number of trees employed each year in paper-making for our books.
Because of this ongoing ecological investment programme, you, as our customer, can have the pleasure and reassurance of knowing that a tree is being cultivated on your behalf to naturally replace the materials used to make the book you are holding.
Our forestry programme is run in accordance with the UK Woodland Assurance Scheme (UKWAS) and will be certified by the internationally recognized Forest Stewardship Council (FSC). The FSC is a non-government organization dedicated to promoting responsible management of the world's forests. Certification ensures forests are managed in an environmentally sustainable and socially responsible basis. For further information about this scheme, go to www.annesspublishing.com/trees

Previously published in two separate volumes, *The Practical Guide to Kayaking and Canoeing* and *The Practical Guide to Sailing*

Disclaimer
Even though some of the photographs in this book show people sailing or paddling without a life jacket (personal flotation device), helmet or buoyancy aid, the author and publisher wish to stress that they strongly advise their use for all sailing and paddling situations. In most cases there are no laws or regulations regarding the use of lifevests, although they are invariably mandatory for dinghy racing and at sailing schools, and both sailing and paddling are about taking responsibility for your own decisions and actions.

CONTENTS

KAYAKING & CANOEING 6

KAYAKING & CANOEING

INTRODUCTION

Taking Up Paddling

The words "canoeing" and "kayaking" describe two similar but different types of small boat paddling. Collectively, they represent an activity that has a longer history than people now imagine, predating the invention of the wheel.

Thousands of years ago, primitive peoples hollowed out logs to make vessels for hunting, fishing and transport. Others such as the Inuit found ways to make boats from skins, bones, and driftwood. As they fashioned these simple craft, they could have no idea that they were developing designs for today's paddlers, or that their craft would one day be executed in space-age materials.

While canoeing and kayaking have existed for millennia, it was only during the recreation explosion of the twentieth century that these paddle sports experienced a meteoric rate of growth. It has touched the lives of the thousands of people who enjoy the outdoors, and in particular, the unrivalled pleasure of simply messing about in boats.

Spirit of Adventure

There is something about the simplicity of paddling a boat with a free blade – that is, a paddle unattached to the boat – that captures the imagination. Few who have tried paddling can deny that it is amazing fun, and that you can get a real sense of freedom even if it is your very first day on the water. Best of all is the fact that, providing you know the limits of your ability and have a responsible attitude towards personal safety, you don't need expert knowledge or any specialist skills to enjoy yourself.

Once you have dabbled at paddling for a while, you will start to get restless when you are away from the water for any length of time. In the words of the late Bill Mason, American canoe guru and author of many inspirational texts on the subject, "Before you get serious about canoeing, you must consider the possibility of becoming totally and incurably hooked on it." What first starts out as fun can quickly become addictive.

ABOVE *Children don't always concentrate on correct grip or posture – they're too busy having fun! These two are warmly dressed, correctly equipped, and having a fine time.*

LEFT *With the right boat and equipment, a day on the water will be a relaxed and happy affair.*

How to Use This Book

The purpose of this book is to provide the beginner with a lively and accessible guide to taking up kayaking and canoeing, and is a seminal reference work for anyone who cares about making the most of their early paddling experience in a kayak or a canoe. We will look at the best way to prepare yourself for paddling in order to have fun and to avoid taking risks. There is advice on choosing a suitable boat, and on getting the best from your gear and from your body. The essential equipment you will need for comfort, safety and performance is covered in detail, as are the physical skills and strokes which are described in depth to enable you to understand and master them with practice. These are covered in the order in which you are likely to need them, so that you can work your way through this section over time.

The emphasis is on helping you to make decisions and acquire skills safely and responsibly. There is also detailed information on safety and first aid issues that any paddler should know about.

Although you will undoubtedly benefit from reading this book right through before you try canoeing or kayaking, it is designed to be the sort of book you can continue to refer to as you progress. You should of course be aware of the basic do's and don'ts before you take to the water, and of the safety issues involved that may affect you. But don't feel that the theory is more important than the practice. There is nothing like time on the water – get paddling!

ABOVE *Two paddlers in a sit-on kayak making smooth and harmonious progress.*

BELOW *A kayaker enjoying bright sunshine and calm seas – the perfect conditions for a day on the water.*

The Origins of Paddling

The design and appearance of kayaks and canoes have undergone a revolution since trees were first hollowed out by early tribesmen. Today's models are fast and lightweight, and tough enough to survive the most extreme water conditions.

Kayaking and canoeing share the same goal – to propel a craft over water by the simplest and most versatile means possible. Unlike rowing, there is an almost unbroken tradition in which the paddler faces the direction of travel, and this has helped make paddling a more versatile way of negotiating difficult water and overcoming changeable conditions. Rowing, on the other hand, is often a more efficient way of powering your way across water but, except in a race or a long journey across open water, power is worth little without the control provided by a free blade and a clear view ahead.

ABOVE *Canoe design developed out of need. Here, Native Americans use a dugout canoe to transport fruit to store.*

LEFT *This painting shows an English ship meeting hostile natives on land and in kayaks in the waters off Greenland.*

Early Boats

The first canoes were logs, paddled by hand or propelled with makeshift poles made from strong, stout branches. It can not have taken early tribes long to realize that a better and more stable alternative was a hollowed-out log. Depending upon the type of trees and tools available, the log was either scraped out or had a fire lit on top, burning out a hollow. There is archaeological evidence of both techniques. The one big problem with a craft fashioned from a solid log was the difficulty of transporting the heavy craft over land for any distance.

Kayak and Canoe Design

Eventually, people acquired the necessary tools and skills to construct a more manageable boat from scratch, using a variety of smaller components, and this is when the now distinct and quite separate forms of kayak and canoe first appeared.

The kayak was invented by the aboriginal Inuit peoples of the Arctic and sub-Arctic regions, probably because a single blade could not generate enough power in the rough seas in which the Inuit hunted and travelled. The kayak paddler, who always sits, uses a paddle with a blade at each end. A shortage of large pieces of wood or bone meant that ancient kayak paddles would have been shorter and thinner than they are today.

The canoe was developed in response to the needs of the native peoples of North America several thousand years ago. The boat is propelled using a single-blade paddle or a pole that is not attached to the boat, in which the paddler sits or kneels facing the direction of travel.

Inuit kayaks and North American canoes were first made from wood bark and bone frames with animal skins stretched over them. In other parts of the world, canoes resembled dugouts made from solid wood, except in South-east Asia, where bamboo was sometimes used.

Recreational Boats

Both kayaks and canoes were conceived out of necessity, and their form continued to follow their intended function. One of the first examples of a boat created purely for recreation was that of John MacGregor, nicknamed Rob Roy, a nineteenth-century English adventurer. MacGregor built his kayak in order to tour the inland waterways of Europe. His book, *A Thousand Miles in the Rob Roy Canoe*, may be the prime reason why many people still use the word "canoe" as a generic term for kayak or canoe. He designed his boat to fit in a railway carriage for easy transportation – modern kayaks are often small enough to fit into a family car!

ABOVE *John MacGregor's kayak, the Rob Roy. The boat was made using the clinker construction of traditional boatbuilding.*

BELOW *MacGregor encounters a herd of cattle swimming a river.*

ABOVE *A Thousand Miles in the Rob Roy Canoe by John MacGregor. The illustration shows the author seated and using a two-bladed paddle: his craft is therefore a kayak, despite the book's title.*

RIGHT *MacGregor gets a huge welcome from the Swiss town of Bremgarten.*

The Evolution of Kayaks and Canoes

For thousands of years the basic form of kayaks and canoes changed little, but 200 years ago came the introduction of modern materials, including mass-produced woven fabrics and smooth-planed wood. While there are still a few Inuit hunting boats made from sealskins, the traditional boats have now been superseded.

In an effort to create lighter boats in the nineteenth and twentieth centuries, boats were given a canvas skin over a wooden frame. Light fold-up frames, such as the Klepper, were designed for easy transportation. While some canoes from the Victorian era made from wood construction methods, such as clinker (overlaying planks and/or woodstrip), have survived, the more common canvas boats of that time have not. Further changes came when the skins of kayaks and canoes were replaced by newer manmade fabrics, such as plywood.

RIGHT *The Klepper folding kayak mimics the construction style of skin-on-frame boats but now uses modern materials.*

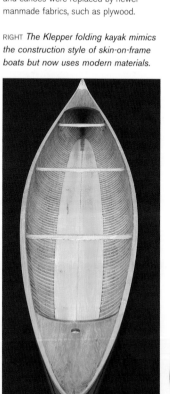

Plastic Fantastic

During the latter half of the twentieth century, kayaking and canoeing received a dramatic boost from new technology. In the 1950s, the prevalent form of construction was still canvas over a wooden frame, and the paddles were made exclusively from wood. But, within 20 years, fibreglass (or glass-reinforced plastic) had totally revolutionized boat construction, and most boats were now made this way. For the first time it was possible to make more rounded shapes, and countless new designs soon flooded the paddling world.

In the 1980s, fibreglass and even more advanced composites, such as carbon fibre and Kevlar™, were dramatically overshadowed by plastic. The advent of plastic suddenly made it possible to mass-produce cheap and durable kayaks or canoes whose performance could almost rival the more expensive and fragile composite boats.

ABOVE AND LEFT *This woodstrip boat is a traditional Victorian courting canoe, dating from the late nineteenth century and used for recreational purposes only.*

BELOW *The Percy Blandford Kayak, or PBK, is an example of a wood and canvas boat from the 1950s. The construction method used is similar to the early Inuit kayaks.*

ABOVE *Wooden battens line the floor of the PBK to protect the boat's fragile canvas skin when the paddler steps in.*

RIGHT *The first fibreglass kayaks were not so different from their wood and canvas forebears. This 1960s example is more manoeuvrable because of its shorter length.*

RIGHT *The next progression in general-purpose kayak design was to make the boats slightly wider behind the cockpit and higher in front, for better rough-water handling. This boat was used on extreme white water during the Descent of Everest Expedition in 1975.*

ABOVE *For steep descents in heavy white water, boats became rounder, to give more control, and bigger in volume, with end grabs and foot rests.*

Introducing the Kayak

The modern general-purpose kayak is so strong and versatile that even moderately experienced practitioners can tackle difficult feats. That is one reason why kayaking has recently become so popular, with many disciplines that provide all the thrills and spills of surfing.

Changing Shape and Form

Canoes might have remained largely unchanged while they were used primarily as a means of transport, but the design of kayaks for sport gradually deviated from their original look. Those used for recreation have become unrecognizable from the original Inuit style, which is now only retained by sea kayaks designed for open-sea use.

The kayak became a recreational and sporting boat in the twentieth century, and quickly adapted two forms. The flat water touring and racing kayak shape has derived from the rowing shell or skiff and, as the rowing boat became narrower and more rounded, so did the kayak. By the 1930s, the general-purpose and white water kayak had settled into a fairly widely accepted form, about 4m (13ft) long and 60cm (2ft) wide across the beam. The ultimate derivatives of these boat designs were seen in slalom and white water racing competitions, and for most of the late twentieth century they were the driving force behind the new look of the kayaks and decked canoes.

At about the same time, slalom racers realized that the boats performed much better if they were very low in volume, with thin pointed ends that could dip under the hanging poles, and slice better through the water to save time as they raced down the course. This development resulted in the invention of many of the techniques that have shaped the sport as it is today, and changed the way kayaks and decked canoes look forever.

The Influence of Plastic

The widespread introduction of mass-produced plastic boats in the 1980s brought further changes, both to the look of kayaks and the way in which they were used. Before then, boats belonged either to the high-performance competitive market and featured sleek, low-volume craft handmade from space-age composite materials, or they were recreational designs, typically more rounded, general-purpose boats made of plastic. Then, technological developments began to produce plastic boats that had many of the performance characteristics of the handmade models, combined with greater durability, and because they were cheaper to make, they were relatively inexpensive.

This change marked the end of slalom and river racing as the pinnacle to which every white water paddler aspired; both now became marginalized by the very different activities that the new plastic boats had made possible.

New Disciplines

The plastic revolution enabled even paddlers of intermediate ability to attempt white water descents that would have been impossible even for the most skilled paddler in the older, composite boats. This was partly because the new boats were more likely to bounce off rocks without mishap, and because they were shorter and more manoeuvrable.

Front deck
The top of the whole front half of the kayak (or decked canoe).

Bow or end grab
This can be used for carrying the boat, tying it to a roof rack or trailer, recovering the boat in the water, and in rescue situations. On a white water kayak this would be strong enough to hold 1000kg (2200lbs) or more.

Footrests
Kayaks should always have some kind of footrest; pressing on this with the feet is an important part of the paddling technique. Most footrests are adjustable.

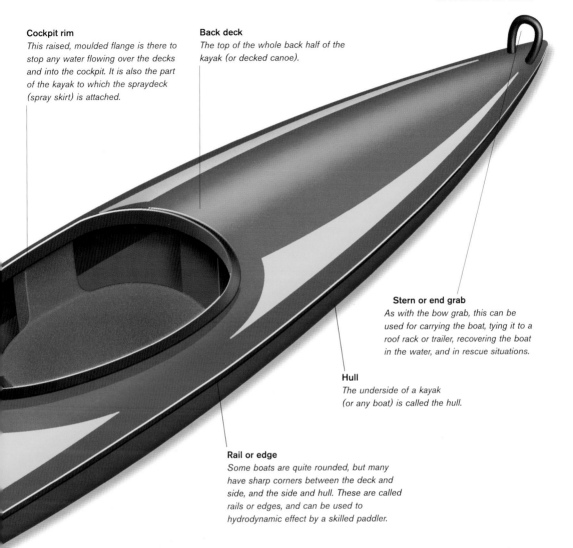

Cockpit rim
This raised, moulded flange is there to stop any water flowing over the decks and into the cockpit. It is also the part of the kayak to which the spraydeck (spray skirt) is attached.

Back deck
The top of the whole back half of the kayak (or decked canoe).

Stern or end grab
As with the bow grab, this can be used for carrying the boat, tying it to a roof rack or trailer, recovering the boat in the water, and in rescue situations.

Hull
The underside of a kayak (or any boat) is called the hull.

Rail or edge
Some boats are quite rounded, but many have sharp corners between the deck and side, and the side and hull. These are called rails or edges, and can be used to hydrodynamic effect by a skilled paddler.

Initially, short boats were frowned upon by the more conservative, traditional paddlers, but the designers kept creating even shorter models. The stage has now been reached whereby the boats cannot get any shorter because the paddlers' feet are so close to the end of the boat. This development, more than any other, has altered white water paddling for ever. It has also meant that many of the skills and strokes practised today are unique to the newer boats now in common use.

Plastic boats made descents of extreme white water possible for the first time, and enabled white water

boaters to perform demanding, high-energy manoeuvres that would previously have smashed a lightweight competition boat. In short, plastic led to the sport of freestyle kayaking, where paddlers perform acrobatic tricks on white water and create complex routines to be judged on style and technical ability.

Meanwhile, the flat water touring and competition scene continued largely unaffected by the plastic revolution. The competitive side is best seen at the Olympics, and features very long, narrow and unstable sprint boats. They, and other similar boats, can also be used for fast

inland touring. Touring boats with better rough water handling have been designed for less sheltered conditions and coastal use, while the Inuit-style sea kayak is extremely popular for more demanding estuary and ocean paddling.

Paddling on the sea taught kayakers how to handle their craft in surf and waves, which in turn led to the popular sport of kayak surfing. A number of kayak styles can be used to ride waves like surfers do, and to perform tricks and manoeuvres. Competitions for kayak surfing judge paddlers on the style and quality of their rides, as with freestyle kayaking.

Introducing the Canoe

Many canoes today look remarkably similar to their traditional Native American ancestors. Some, such as those used for racing, slalom and freestyle, look entirely different. All have benefited from the advances in materials technology that changed kayaking forever, but there are still many canoe paddlers who prefer to adhere to tradition.

The canoe remained largely unchanged in shape and concept while it was used as a means of transport. Apart from the Polynesian canoes and outrigger boats that were used for fishing and inter-island sailing, the prevalent form has always been the open boat with an upswept bow and stern associated with the North American hunters and trappers. Once the canoe became a recreational and sporting boat in the twentieth century, new developments began.

Open Canoes

Many of today's open canoes look much like the traditional models. Materials and construction techniques may have altered, but in form and function they remain virtually unchanged. While these boats are unsuitable for open sea touring, there is and always will be a tradition of using open boats for inland touring. There are many traditionalists who prefer to paddle an open canoe, using air bags or buoyancy tanks to stop the boat sinking in heavy water. For the family and recreational user, the relatively low purchase price and durability of the open canoe make it an extremely practical choice of boat for general-purpose use.

Decked Canoes

Decking in the top part of the boat is a logical move to keep the paddler dry in rough water conditions. Decked boats were initially designed for performance and the more extreme disciplines.

Decked boats were best seen in action in slalom and white water racing competitions, and for most of the latter part of the twentieth century the needs of these disciplines were the driving force behind much of the commercial development in canoes. The single-seater competition canoe, known as the C1, became, for all intents and purposes, like a kayak in design, except for the kneeling position and the smaller cockpit. The two-seater competition canoe, or C2, had cockpits at either end, although competitive racing meant that the cockpits were moved as close to the centre of the boat as possible, to provide sharper manoeuvrability.

At about the same time, slalom racers realized – as with kayaks – that the boats performed much better if they were less buoyant (very low in volume), with thin, pointed ends that could pass underneath the vertical hanging poles of the slalom course, and carve a quicker passage through the water. The move towards low-volume boats led, in turn, to the development of many of the handling techniques seen in the sport today.

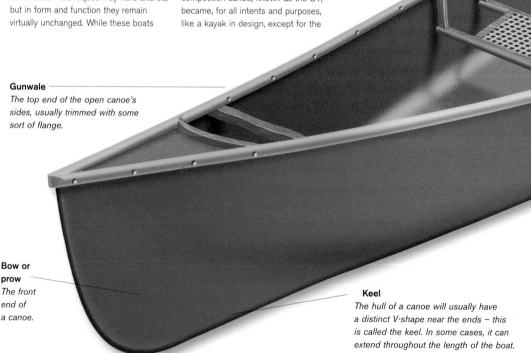

Gunwale
The top end of the open canoe's sides, usually trimmed with some sort of flange.

Bow or prow
The front end of a canoe.

Keel
The hull of a canoe will usually have a distinct V-shape near the ends – this is called the keel. In some cases, it can extend throughout the length of the boat.

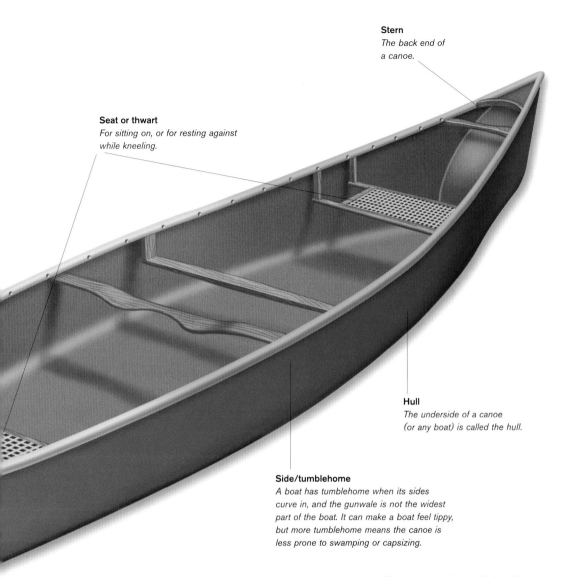

Stern
The back end of a canoe.

Seat or thwart
For sitting on, or for resting against while kneeling.

Hull
The underside of a canoe (or any boat) is called the hull.

Side/tumblehome
A boat has tumblehome when its sides curve in, and the gunwale is not the widest part of the boat. It can make a boat feel tippy, but more tumblehome means the canoe is less prone to swamping or capsizing.

Modern Materials

The arrival of plastic boats in the 1980s had huge repercussions on the sport. Before then the canoe world had two very distinct groups. At the top end of the scale were the expensive low-volume decked boats used by the high-performance competitive scene, which were handmade from the latest materials. Meanwhile, the recreational scene was still dominated by general-purpose open boats made of fibreglass or wood. By the 1970s, technological developments led to plastic boats that could rival the handmade ones; they were tougher and less expensive, and allowed white water paddlers to have bigger aspirations than slalom and river racing. The plastic boats of the 1980s gave an extra edge to the competitive world of canoeing, changing it completely.

The new plastic canoes, like the new kayaks, were becoming so manoeuvrable they could perform increasingly aggressive moves. This led to the sport of freestyle canoeing, where paddlers take turns to perform elaborate tricks on white water.

The plastic revolution enabled paddlers of intermediate ability to attempt descents (not always safely) that would have been beyond even skilled boaters in the older, composite boats. The new boats were tough and could withstand knocks against rocks, and they were highly manoeuvrable. While there were dramatic developments in white water canoeing, flat water touring, slalom and competitions continued largely unaffected. The Olympic Games is still the focus for long, narrow and unstable sprint canoes.

Different Types of Canoes and Kayaks

While everyone has a mental picture of what is meant by them, the words "canoe" and "kayak" encompass such a wide spectrum of designs that it can be difficult to know where to start. Canoes are in a sense easier, since although there are many types, the more common ones you are likely to come across as a beginner all look much the same, however many subtle differences they may harbour. Kayaks, on the other hand, are now commonly found in such a bewildering variety of shapes and sizes that the beginner will almost certainly need advice from someone experienced before getting involved.

Types of Canoes

Open canoes fall into two broad categories – those used for flatwater and those for white water. The white water ones can be identified by their airbags and complex internal fittings, and are best avoided by beginners if only because they are so difficult to paddle in a straight line! Almost any other open boat is suitable for beginners, as long as it has a fairly flat bottom in the middle part of the hull. Some of the more rounded designs can be a bit wobbly!

Canoes are available in various lengths and with a variety of seating positions, some intended for solo use, some double or more. Most are versatile and can be paddled solo even if large enough to accommodate a small family and picnic. You should be aware that a large boat can be too heavy to carry unaided.

There are also decked canoes, which are for all intents and purposes the same as kayaks, but paddled in a kneeling position with a canoe blade.

Types of Kayaks

Kayaks come in a wider variety of designs. A surprising number of them are suitable for beginners, but you might need to seek expert advice before investing in one.

Sit-on Kayaks are eminently suitable for beginners. These plastic or foam kayaks do not enclose your legs, and are blissfully free of unnecessary encumbrances. These surprisingly versatile boats are great fun, stable, and cannot fill up with water or sink. The only disadvantage is that if you become more advanced you may find you want to be better attached to the boat than is easily achievable with a sit-on-top. Solo and double versions are available. Don't mistake a wave-ski for a sit-on kayak – they look similar but wave-skis are made for advanced paddlers to use in the surf.

General-purpose Kayaks are usually about 3m (10ft) long and 60cm (2ft) wide, and made of plastic. These kayaks have a deck enclosing your legs and a cockpit opening which can be sealed with a spraydeck. They are usually fairly stable and quite easy to paddle in a straight line, but you need to be confident about getting out if you capsize.

Touring Kayaks are usually about 4m (13ft) long, sometimes more. They are very stable and very easy to paddle in a straight line. In fact they can be slow to turn for a beginner, unless fitted with a rudder. They are closed deck boats, but they usually have such a big cockpit that it isn't at all hard to get out. They can be made from plastic or glassfibre-type composite materials, and are easily identified by their high, ship-like bow and stern.

ABOVE *A specialist closed cockpit touring kayak with shockcord on the deck for maps or accessories.*

LEFT *This general purpose kayak is suitable for any type of paddling if it is correctly outfitted for the purpose. For example fit a skeg for touring, or a creek boat outfitting for challenging white water.*

Sea Kayaks are normally over 4.5m (15ft) long. They are similar to touring boats but usually have distinctive upswept bow and stern. They are often characterized by rope decklines and other specialist fittings such as hatches and compass mountings. Often made of plastic but more commonly glassfibre, these boats are suitable for beginners but are specially designed for sea trips and aren't terribly versatile. They are less stable and harder to steer than most other types of boat.

Racing/Fast Touring Kayaks are usually 4.5m (15ft) long, low and narrow, and wider behind the cockpit than in front. They look appealing to beginners because of their rakish lines and big cockpits, but they are terribly wobbly and not a suitable first boat at all. White water kayaks can be identified by their short length (under 3m/10ft) and rounded ends. Made from plastic, they are actually fine for beginners to use, but they are quite expensive and have a lot of features that are only intended for use on rapids. They are very stable, and very easy to turn. Perhaps they are a little too difficult to paddle straight for some people, but many find it acceptable. If you intend to take up white water paddling at some point, you could do worse than start with a boat like this.

ABOVE *A two-person, open cockpit kayak is a good compromise between the closed cockpit boat and the sit-on – the paddlers sit inside the boat and stay fairly dry, but their legs are not really under the deck, so it's much easier to get in and out.*

BELOW *A sit-on kayak has the advantage that the paddler's legs are not inside the boat. This style of kayak is the best type for beginners.*

White Water Playboats are extremely short (usually sub-2.1m or 7ft) and have a wide, flat hull. This makes them very stable, and they are quite easy for a beginner to control on flat water. However, they often have aggressive internal fittings that make it hard to get in and out, and are painfully slow, so they are not a suitable choice of first boat.

White Water Creek Boats are designed for extreme white water. Their short length (2–2.5m or 6.5–8.2ft) and rounded ends are for manoeuvrability and for bouncing off rocks in white water. They also have many safety features designed to enhance their strength and safety, but otherwise they are very like the general-purpose kayak.

GETTING STARTED

GOING PADDLING FOR THE FIRST TIME

There are a wide variety of paddle sports, ranging from the placid to the frankly insane, and it pays to be sure that you know what you are getting into. Most people take the gentle approach, and learn to paddle on completely safe, flat, sheltered water. Even so, many kayaks and canoes seem initially unstable, and for most people that is exactly what distinguishes these craft from more solid dinghies and rowing boats.

The possibility of being capsized means that you have to take certain precautions. Being able to swim at least 50m (170ft) in clothing is a prerequisite, and wearing a buoyancy aid (personal flotation device, or PFD) is important, particularly when you start because you might fall into the water quite often. What is more often overlooked is the need to think through what will happen if you do end up in the water. Will the boat float? Will you be able to get ashore quickly? Is there land close by?

These considerations are covered in this chapter. The important point when starting out is to think about your personal safety; do not just jump into a boat and paddle off. Canoeing and kayaking are not dangerous, but a cavalier approach most certainly is.

LEFT *Two kayakers in traditional Inuit-style boats cruising up a beautiful estuary.*

BELOW *Paddlers getting organized in plastic general-purpose boats.*

Where and When to Paddle

Boating is great fun, but it pays to be careful. Stick to the elementary rules and always put safety first. A few minutes' careful checking before you get into the water is all that is required.

Suitable Waters

Until you have achieved the level of self-sufficiency that sets a kayaker or canoeist apart from someone just "having a go", it is best to seek out safe, predictable environments to paddle in, where there is help at hand if required.

You should learn to paddle on still water, although this is often surprisingly hard to find. Non-tidal rivers and lakes in calm weather, or reservoirs where public access to the water is allowed, would be suitable, but make sure there is good bank access in case you have to swim ashore. Beaches are generally safe for beginners as long as the waves are less than 2m (6½ft) and the wind is not blowing offshore. Find out about the character of the stretch of beach you plan to use in advance, and make sure there are no strong currents you cannot see.

ABOVE *The points to consider on a beach are wave size, wind and water currents.*

LEFT *Sheltered inland waterways such as this river are ideal for safe paddling.*

BELOW *For novices in search of trouble-free water, inland lakes are best of all.*

Where Not to Paddle

There are a number of situations that are unsuitable for paddling. Some situations can present difficulties, while others are dangerous. It pays to know what to avoid.

Do not paddle where the wind or current can carry you away faster than you can paddle or swim. In fact, avoid fast currents when learning; it is far easier to learn if the conditions are in your favour.

Do not paddle where it might be difficult to get out of the water. Remember that you might be cold and tired after capsizing. Avoid any obstacle that might present a problem, such as steep banks, deep mud and slippery rocks, which can be a nightmare to the tired paddler with a boat full of water.

If there is a current, avoid paddling where there are rocks, trees, pontoons or obstructions in the water. A barely visible current can be enough to pin a boat or a person against the upstream side of an obstruction, and this is a common cause of paddling accidents.

Always stay away from weirs. Do not approach them either from above or below. Not all weirs are dangerous, but it takes experience to be able to tell a friendly weir from a dangerous one, and even friendly weirs have minor hazards. The only safe policy is to give them a wide berth unless you are an experienced and confident white water paddler who chooses to accept the risk. To beginners, weirs represent a genuine threat to safety and should be avoided at all costs.

BELOW *Beware of water flowing beneath low bridges, such as this. Although the water here is fairly slow-moving, it could easily pull you along with it. If your boat were to jam under the low bridge, you could find yourself in trouble very quickly.*

ABOVE *Do not paddle on fast-flowing water until you have learned a range of skills.*

BELOW *Weirs can be extremely dangerous for paddlers, and it is always advisable to stay away from them.*

Serious Hazards

Some situations can and do prove fatal. It is imperative that you are aware of the dangers involved with any of the following.

River Levels

Be aware that river levels can rise and fall very suddenly. This might only affect your access to or exit from a river, but it could turn a friendly stream into a lethal one.

Rivers rise because of the amount of rainfall or because of snow melt. Many mountain rivers rise very dramatically in the afternoon because the sun melts the snow or ice, and the water produced reaches the river a few hours later.

ABOVE *The mud banks and reeds here would make it very difficult to get out of the river with your boat.*

LEFT *Compare these two pictures, taken on the same day. The water level has risen 1m (3½ft) and turned a meandering stream into a potentially lethal torrent after several hours of rain.*

BELOW *Beware when paddling upstream of any obstruction in the river, especially if the water can flow through or under it, as in the case of this log-jam. The current could very easily force you into or under such an obstruction.*

In addition, many very steep rivers are dammed for hydro-electric power. When the turbines are required, the dam will be opened and a lethal wall of water can be sent hurtling down the valley.

Strainers and Siphons

These are usually found on white water rivers, but they can occur anywhere the water is flowing at a significant speed.

A barrier through which water flows, such as a fallen tree or log jam is called a strainer because it lets water pass through but will catch anything solid. These are very dangerous. Do not risk being swept into the upstream side of one.

Even more dangerous is the siphon, where water disappears underground. Get too close and you will be sucked down too, and possibly jammed stuck.

Preparing to Paddle

When first learning to paddle, it is best to practise in a familiar area, within sight of a reliable launching and landing place, instead of attempting any kind of journey. As you build up your experience, and become more familiar with the boat and the basic manoeuvring techniques, you will be able to go further afield and use your boat to explore.

Once you have become hooked on boating, it is very easy to become complacent and to imagine that you are more experienced and more capable than you really are. Beware of asking too much of yourself too soon. Remember your own limitations and, just as importantly, those of the other members of your group. A failure to do this can seriously compromise your safety, and no amount of fun will justify this risk.

Are You Up To It?
It is vital that you have a realistic idea of the kind of distance you can paddle, and that you know your own limitations in terms of ability, fitness and strength: some people are surprised at how quickly they become tired in a boat out on the water. Remember, too, that you could get hot, cold, tired, hungry or dehydrated according to the weather conditions. While this might not be any different from when going for a long walk, if any of these conditions affect you severely

CHECKLIST
If the answer to any of the following questions is "No", reassess your plan before you set out on the water.
• Is everyone in the group capable of looking after themselves? If not, will some be able to look after the others?
• Do you have all the appropriate equipment for today's trip?
• Does everyone know how many hours they will paddle for?
• Are you sure that you can get to where you intend to go in that time?
• Does someone on land know where the group is going and what time they are expected to finish?

while you are on or near the water, the consequences can be far more serious. Consider this before you set out, and make sure that you are properly equipped.

Advance Planning
It always pays to be prepared for likely eventualities. Make it a key part of your preparation routine to plan the route of your journey, using an up-to-date Ordnance Survey 1:50,000 map. If your group can all do this together, so much the better. Listen to a detailed weather report for the area on the day of your trip and consider how the weather is likely to affect the water conditions. If you know what to expect, you will be able to make an informed choice to continue with the trip, to resort to the contingency plan or

ABOVE *Paddlers will often "raft up" to give themselves a rest if anyone in the group is feeling tired.*

to put the whole thing off for another day in order to avoid anything too severe that might cause you problems. Check that you have the right type of clothing and equipment for the conditions, and enough food and drinking water to see you through to the end of your trip. Finally, consider the needs of the weakest member(s) of the group and adapt your preparation plan accordingly, allowing more time for the journey and more provisions as necessary. Your plan must take account of all levels of expertise if everyone is to have an enjoyable time.

Exposure to the Elements

Whether you are boating on an inland stream or out at sea, you are generally more exposed to the elements than when you are on land. It is necessary to take precautions since the effects of heat and cold, and sudden changes of wind direction, can strike very suddenly.

Sun

When you are out on the water, the effects of the sun are greater than normal, and ultimately these may dictate how long you can stay out. It is quite possible to get severe sunburn in as little as 30 minutes on the water on a day when you could sunbathe on the shore for much longer. It is extremely important that you always take with you an

adequate sunscreen for your face, neck, arms and legs. If you are not wearing a helmet, protect your head and the back of your neck with a sunhat or baseball cap to minimize the risk of sunstroke.

Wind

The effects of wind are also much more pronounced when you are on the water. A light breeze ashore, which necessitates no more than a thin summer shirt, might cause serious wind chill when you are afloat. As a general guide, there are few days when you will not need a windproof top plus at least one thermal layer, even when the sun is out and the weather is hot. If you are wet after a swim, these potential problems will all be magnified.

Always take with you a selection of clothes that allow you to adjust your level of insulation during the course of the trip.

Never go paddling during a gale. High winds make it almost impossible to control a kayak or canoe, and you will struggle to hang on to your paddle. In addition, the water will become rough and unpredictable. You won't be able to make forward progress against anything more than a stiff breeze but, bizarrely, it is a following wind or a crosswind that make the boat hardest to control. Accept that strong winds and paddling just don't mix, unless you are equipped to sail your boat.

Rain

It can be very pleasant to paddle in the rain if you are sensibly dressed. On the other hand, it can be a miserable experience if you aren't. Being cold and wet at the same time is uncomfortable and it can become a real problem if the temperature is low. If rain is likely, make sure you pack a waterproof garment. A woollen hat or a hood on your jacket or cagoule can make a huge difference to how you feel. Reducing the heat loss from your head is an effective remedy when you are cold, and in the rain, headgear will stop water constantly running down your face, which can become very uncomfortable.

Lightning

Although it is a lot more rare than a situation involving strong currents or a sudden change in the weather, lightning is one of the most dangerous weather phenomena for paddlers. On the land you are unlikely to be struck by lightning. On open water, it is a different matter. Anything sticking up out of the water is in danger, and that means you. You also have a long pole (your paddle) in your hands to add to the effect. On land, the people most likely to be struck by lightning are golfers because they stand in the middle of open spaces holding golf clubs that serve as

LEFT *Paddlers out at sea are exposed to sun, wind chill and salt spray.*

conductive objects. As a boater, you are taking the lightning attractor concept several stages further because lightning is more likely to strike a solitary object on water than on land. If the weather report suggests storms, don't go out at all; if a storm blows up while you are on the water, get ashore as quickly as possible.

Extreme Hot and Cold

Luckily, you are unlikely to experience extreme heat and cold in the same location. However, if you go paddling in an extreme climate, your usual paddling clothing may not be appropriate, and you will need to consider other safety issues.

In hot climates, apart from the dangers of sunburn and sunstroke, there is a real danger of dehydration and heat stroke. The most important thing is to keep drinking water. If you feel thirsty, you are already dehydrated. If you cannot quench your thirst, or have a limited water supply, you need to get into the shade and cool down. One of the problems with very hot, tropical environments is the humidity. The air is so saturated that the process of sweating does not cool you down, although your body doesn't realize and carries on sweating. This is why you get dehydrated even though you may be soaking wet the whole time.

ABOVE *Taking a rest in the hot midday sunshine. This paddler would be at risk without his drinking water, sunscreen and protective hat.*

BELOW *Make sure you are equipped for all weather conditions before you set out.*

In very cold air or water, the key is to dress to be both warm and dry. If you get soaked in a freezing environment you only have a few minutes to get warm and dry before you start to suffer from hypothermia. For practical reasons, then, a dry suit is needed for severely cold conditions. This will ensure that you don't get wet from immersion. Wear gloves or mitts on your hands: they will prevent the pain of frozen fingers.

Managing Body Temperature

By far the best way to control your body temperature is to wear good quality thermal base layers, which will work with your body's inherent control mechanism. A versatile cagoule with adjustable seals will allow you to adjust your temperature by opening and closing the neck or rolling up the sleeves. If you wear conventional manmade fabrics, you will find yourself endlessly putting on extra clothes and taking them off as your body heats and cools down too rapidly.

Basic Safety and Rescue

It might be tempting to think that you are quite experienced, and can cope with any potential danger, but the rule is, always, "Beginners beware!" Make sure you and your group are up to the challenge.

Safety in Numbers

When out on the water, there should always be at least three people in the group. In the event of an accident or a medical emergency, one person can stay with the victim and the other can go for help. It is even better if there are four or five people, so that no one has to deal with emergencies alone, but if there are too many in the group then other logistical problems arise, even when things are going smoothly. Experienced paddlers may choose to ignore this basic safety rule, but they only do so when they feel totally confident about taking risks. Beginners should always stick to the rule.

Assessing your Group

You must be sure that the group is capable of taking care of itself as a unit, and can sort out any problems as they arise. Everyone should be able to swim 50m (170ft) in their clothing, and flotation aids should always be worn when afloat. But what if a boat has filled with water? Will the group be able to empty it and get the paddler back in? Or tow the victim back to shore? And what if the location turns out to be trickier than imagined, or the distance greater? Will the group have the skills required to get a tired paddler back to safety if they cannot paddle alone?

These are crucial questions. If the answers to any of them are "No", then you should restrict your paddling to safe locations, such as a beach or small lake, where everyone could make it ashore, and there are no significant safety threats.

ABOVE *The husky tow, in which one paddler is pulled by two, is used for long distances.*

BELOW *Assisted tow. A tired paddler is helped and towed by her companions.*

CHECKLIST

Some of the following safety gear is optional but what you choose to carry should be dictated by conditions. If in doubt, or if the conditions are variable, take it anyway.

- Bivvy bag
- Drinking water and a hot drink (optional)
- First aid kit
- Repair kit
- Diver's knife or folding saw
- Spare paddle (optional)
- Throw line (optional)
- 1:50,000 map
- Torch
- Whistle
- Tow line
- Flares if at sea or on a very large lake (optional)

Rescue Procedures

Although you may be unfamiliar with paddling a canoe or kayak, let alone rescuing one, it is a good idea to know what to expect if you find yourself in need of a tow because of tiredness or injury, or if you are swimming in the water after a capsize. If you are already an accomplished paddler, these techniques can be used to help a fellow boater in the event of a mishap.

What to do in the event of a capsize is covered in detail at the beginning of the chapters on kayaking and canoeing skills. If you are unable to roll your boat, your priority is to get out. Once out, you can be carried back to shore on the front or back of another paddler's boat, or you can be helped back into your own boat while it is still afloat, using a X-rescue or, for a larger boat, a H-rescue. If you need a pull because of tiredness or injury, your fellow paddlers can use a husky tow or an assisted tow to help you back to shore.

Practising basic rescue skills is an important part of becoming a competent paddler. If everyone in your group is familiar with the rescue skills shown opposite, the group will be self-sufficient, as well as safer and more confident.

X-rescue

1 Drag the boat across the rescuer's deck, and rock it to and fro to empty it of water. Constantly reassure the victim, who may be in shock.

2 Put the empty boat back in the water, the right way up and alongside, and with the stern next to, the rescuer's bow. Place both paddles across the decks.

3 The victim can lift his legs up out of the water and over the paddles, keeping an equal amount of body weight on each boat. Keep reassuring the victim.

4 The rescuer holds the victim's boat to stop the two boats floating apart. The victim shuffles forward until he is able to put his feet into his boat.

5 Shifting the weight across, the victim is now entirely back on his own boat, and is ready to climb back in. The rescuer can hold his boat steady as he does this.

6 With the rescued paddler now securely back in his boat, he can take his paddle and push off from the rescuer's boat to continue the trip.

Alternative Rescue Techniques

LEFT AND ABOVE *One paddler tows the empty boat, while another paddler carries the swimmer on the back of their boat.*

LEFT *Heavier larger boats can be difficult to empty using the X-rescue. Some paddlers use a H-rescue, which involves two boats, as shown here.*

RIGHT *Another way to transport a swimmer is on the front of the boat like this. It is slower than on the back deck, but the rescuer can see the victim.*

EQUIPMENT AND PREPARATION

From a sport that, in the 1980s, had little in the way of specialized equipment, kayaking and canoeing have certainly come a long way. The clothing and safety equipment, and the boats and paddles, are now quite sophisticated and high-tech. This is thoroughly appropriate because sport on water is physically quite demanding.

When you first start boating, you will not need much in the way of specialist gear. If you only intend to splash about on flat water near to land, and never go far or encounter difficult conditions, the bare minimum may be perfectly adequate. If, on the other hand, you decide to progress, and try more demanding water conditions, you will find that there is an ever-increasing array of equipment that you must consider.

LEFT *Sea kayakers wearing comprehensive paddling gear and in well-equipped boats.*

BELOW *A kayaker stretching in preparation for a session out on the water.*

Kayaks

A huge range of kayaks are now available, and it is important that you check the following features. When buying a kayak, talk to the sales staff: ask the right questions, based on the following criteria, and make sure you are happy with the answers. If you are unable to find out what you want to know, you could contact kayak manufacturers for more information about their products.

• A kayak must have sufficient buoyancy to float when full of water, and provide you with something to hold on to if you are swimming alongside after capsizing. The buoyancy should be distributed so that the kayak floats level when swamped.

• It must have a seat, and a footrest to brace against, otherwise you will not be able to paddle it properly.

• Not advisable the first time out because it makes entry and exit more difficult, but beneficial thereafter, is padding either

ABOVE *This touring kayak is an all-round boat and a good first-time buy.*

LEFT *This boat has been fitted out to a high standard with hard-foam padding to hug the hips and legs, and make the paddler an integral part of the kayak.*

BELOW *Adjusting the backrest. This kayak has a modern fit system that allows you to fine-tune your position while you are seated in the boat.*

side of the hips. Without this, your body movements will not be transmitted to the boat and the boat's movements will not be felt by you. Much of your body's energy is also delivered to the boat by your knees, so it is particularly important that the knees are held firmly in position. This is usually achieved by some sort of built-in grips or mouldings to hold the legs in place under the deck. Without these, the boat will not respond well to you or you to it.

• All kayaks, except those used for competition or the more specialist disciplines, need to have end grabs, which give you something to hold on to if you need to tow the boat, or a capsized paddler in the water, to the shore.

• Be confident that you can get out of the kayak easily before you agree to use it on the water. Your paddling will not be very good if you are constantly worried that you will not be able to free yourself if the boat capsizes.

Spraydecks

A spraydeck (spray skirt) fits around your waist and over the cockpit to stop water getting into the boat. Spraydecks are not generally needed on flat water, where the water is calm, with little or no splashing.

Nylon spraydecks are commonly used for teaching beginners, but these can let in water because they are only really designed to be splash-proof. Neoprene ones are much drier and warmer, but they are more expensive and more difficult to fit and detach. You may not use a spraydeck at first, but if you do it is important that you can attach and remove it easily, without help. This can take quite a bit of practice.

Fitting a Spraydeck

Whichever type of spraydeck you use, you should be wearing it around your waist before you get in the kayak. Once you are sitting comfortably, and have made sure that you are not sitting on any part

CHECKLIST

• Are you confident about the idea of wearing a spraydeck (spray skirt)? If not, don't agree to use one.

• Is the spraydeck the correct size for the boat? They do vary, so ask someone experienced to check.

• Is the spraydeck adjustable at the waist? If so, make it tight enough to hold up around the chest but without being uncomfortable.

• Is the release handle securely sewn on to the spraydeck? Never put one on a boat without checking this.

• Can you find the release handle with your eyes shut while sitting in the boat with the spraydeck fitted? If not, you are unlikely to be able to do it underwater. Practise until you know exactly where it is.

of the spraydeck, reach back with both hands and put the shock cord, or other attachment, under the cockpit rim at the back. Now feed the hands outwards, keeping some tension on the spraydeck, until you can pull forwards with both hands and fit the spraydeck over the front of the cockpit. Make sure that the release strap is outside and not trapped within. Familiarize yourself with where it is: you will need to find it quickly if you capsize.

To release the spraydeck, take the release strap in your hand and pull firmly upwards. It is usually better to pull a little

ABOVE *A nylon spraydeck (spray skirt) might be used by a beginner on flat water.*

forwards at the same time, rather than back. Once the spraydeck has been released from the front of the cockpit, run your hands under it right the way round to make sure it is totally free. It is annoying to start getting out of the boat and then come to an abrupt halt as the spraydeck pulls tight.

As a beginner you need a spraydeck that is easy to put on and release. It may not be very waterproof compared to other models on the market, but it will keep the kayak from filling up, and this is as much as you will need on flat water.

Fitting your Spraydeck

1 Get into the kayak wearing the spraydeck (spray skirt). Fit the spraydeck under the cockpit rim at the back of the boat.

2 Feed the hands forward, keeping the spraydeck under tension so that it stays hooked under at the back.

3 Hook it over the front of the cockpit, making sure the release handle is outside and can be reached easily.

Canoes

There are some basic features that you should check for when choosing a canoe.
• Make sure you know which end is the front. Some models appear symmetrical at both ends but all have a bow and a stern.
• Consider whether you want to sit or kneel in your canoe and choose a model in which you feel comfortable doing that.
• Solo and double open canoes are available, as well as boats for three or more people. Doubles can be paddled by one person, but putting two people in a solo canoe is a recipe for a swim.
• End grabs may not be necessary because you can hold the seat or even the gunwale (upper edge of the hull).
• Padding around the seat is rarely needed because your legs can brace against or under the seat and on the inside of the boat, making your position more secure.

RIGHT *The design of the open canoe has changed very little since its invention.*

BELOW *An open canoe fitted with suitable equipment for use on white water.*

Paddles

Kayak paddles have a blade at each end. Canoe paddles, in contrast, have only one blade and a T-grip at the other end, which is held in the top hand. Both kayak and canoe paddles come in a huge variety of shapes and sizes, and can be made from many different combinations of materials.

• The cheapest paddles will have plastic blades and a metal alloy shaft. They are commonly used for teaching beginners because they are inexpensive and fairly durable when used for low power, low-stress paddling. They are, however, heavy and invariably more difficult to use when compared with more expensive paddles.

• Wooden paddles can feel very nice, but they are rather high maintenance, since once the varnish is chipped they soak up water and become damaged. They are also fairly heavy, unless you buy one of the extremely expensive models.

• Composite paddles (carbon or moulded fibreglass) are light and strong, and they feel exquisite, but they are very expensive. They are probably the only type of paddle to deliver a really good flex pattern: this means the paddle is designed to flex enough to absorb shocks caused by impact with the water, but not enough to bend in a way that wastes energy or diminishes control. Most paddlers prefer stiff blades with some flex in the shaft.

Paddle Blades

When choosing a paddle you will find yourself faced with a range of shapes and sizes that may seem bewildering until you know what you are looking at.

Some paddles have "dihedral" faces, which means they have a raised spine on the drive face, sloping back either side. This adds strength and stiffness, but is mainly intended to stabilize the blade by allowing water to flow evenly off the face at each side. These paddles tend to be more powerful than spoon-shaped ones.

CLOCKWISE FROM TOP LEFT : *paddle with reinforced metal edges used for white water paddling; asymmetrical paddle used for touring or racing; wing paddle used for racing; symmetrical paddle for general-purpose use.*

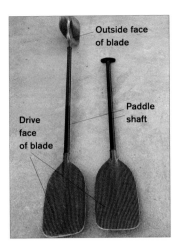

Outside face of blade

Drive face of blade

Paddle shaft

ABOVE *General-purpose kayak paddle (left) and the shorter canoe paddle.*

ABOVE *Nineteenth-century wooden kayak paddle with no feather.*

Paddles can have either symmetrical or asymmetrical blades. Asymmetrical blades are designed to enter the water more cleanly when forward paddling. They don't offer any significant benefits apart from this, and the disadvantage is that you can't use them either way around (you can use either side of a symmetrical blade). Beginners should choose a symmetrical blade.

In addition, a paddle can be feathered or unfeathered. Feather is the term used to describe the angle between the two blades on a kayak paddle. Many paddles are set at 90°, but the trend nowadays is for lesser angles of around 45°. The original reason for feather is so that the blade that isn't in the water doesn't present wind resistance. Hence, sea kayakers and racers use more feather.

Paddle Length

For beginners and general recreational paddling, the right length of paddle for you is determined by your height, and hence, your reach. The best way to check the length of a kayak paddle is to stand it up, level with your foot, and reach up and grasp the top blade. You should be able to do this comfortably with your arm only slightly bent.

With experience, paddlers tend to increase or decrease this length to suit their favourite type of paddling. White water paddles can be up to 20cm (8in) shorter than the general-purpose flat water kayak paddle, to give the paddler greater manoeuvrability. Open water and sea touring and racing paddles can be up to 10cm (4in) longer in order to give more power to each stroke.

A general-purpose canoe paddle is always shorter than a kayak paddle because it only has one blade. The T-grip of the canoe paddle should reach somewhere between your shoulder and your chin when the paddle is standing upright, level with your foot.

Paddle Shaft

Usually the shaft of the paddle will be round, but some paddles have an oval section where the hands go, so that you can immediately feel which way the blade is facing. Canoe paddles achieve this by having a T-grip at the top, but the shaft

ABOVE *A bent paddle shaft (left) shown alongside a straight shaft.*

is often oval-shaped in the area used by the bottom hand. Kayak paddles can be oval at the point where one or both of the hands take hold.

BELOW *Typical length of a general-purpose kayak paddle for flat water.*

BELOW *Typical length of a white water kayak paddle: shorter for more control.*

BELOW *Typical length of a single-bladed flat water canoe paddle.*

ABOVE *These lightweight white water paddles are extremely strong, and superior to heavier models.*

ABOVE *Laminated wooden paddle. The wooden paddle can still compete with paddles made from man-made materials.*

ABOVE *Split (break-down) paddles can be stored inside the kayak as spares in case of loss or breakage.*

Some expensive paddles have bent shafts, which apply less stress to the wrists by loading them in a way that is more anatomically sound. Many paddlers used to straight-shafted paddles find that this feels a bit strange at first, but the concept is gradually gaining acceptance across all paddling disciplines.

Whichever type of paddle you first learn with, you will probably find that your personal style and anatomy, and your preferred type of paddling, dictate that you will soon want a longer or shorter paddle than these guidelines suggest.

Boaters will often be fiercely protective of their paddles, but if you are able to borrow the paddle of a friend before you buy your own, it will give you a better idea what differences a longer or shorter paddle, and the wide choice of shapes and constructions, can make to your paddling. If you are a member of a paddling club that supplies equipment, take the opportunity to test out different models. The sooner you can identify what works well for you and have a paddle that is exactly what you need, the faster your stroke skills will progress. But don't rush

into it. Make sure you are comfortable with a paddle before you buy. Paddles can be expensive, and it is a good idea, if you can, to put off buying one for as long as possible. When you are sure what kind of paddling you want to practise, and have learned the basic strokes, you will be in a much better position to choose.

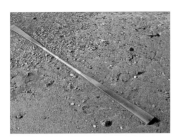

ABOVE *A replica of a traditional Greenland paddle, based on the Inuit style.*

RIGHT *Traditional wooden canoe paddles. One has a reinforced square tip; the other is more suited to deep water.*

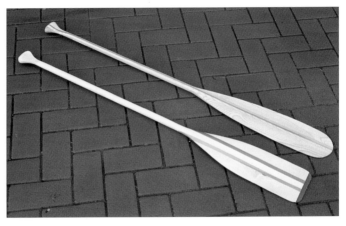

Transporting your Boat

Most people need to move their boat about on land before they can use it on the water. How you do this will depend on the type of craft and how far you have to carry it. Broadly speaking, there are two options: carrying the boat manually, or mechanically.

Carrying the Boat

Many beginners will carry a boat between two people, using the end grabs. Two boats together can also be carried in this way. However, once you have become more familiar with carrying your boat, you might find it easier to carry a kayak or a light canoe on your shoulder. Carrying boats by holding on to the ends is the usual method for heavily laden craft.

When carrying a boat on your shoulder, you can either carry the paddle in your free hand, or you can put the paddle in the cockpit and carry the boat and the paddle together.

Boats that are too heavy to lift, such as a loaded sea kayak, can be moved short distances using a trolley. The trolley can be dismantled and transported in the boat while afloat.

ABOVE *A fold-up trolley is useful for moving large boats to the launching point. The trolley can be dismantled and stowed on the boat during the trip.*

RIGHT *Kayaks and canoes are now made from such lightweight materials that most adults are able to carry their boat on their back for short distances.*

BELOW *Two paddlers carry their loaded sea kayaks down to the water. Hold the boat's end grabs, one in each hand.*

Transporting Your Boat

Over longer distances, you may have to transport your boats by car or van, boat or aeroplane. The key here is to be sensible, and to think about whether your boat will get damaged, or could cause damage to other people's property.

A cockpit cover will allow you to put additional gear inside your boat. This is by far the best way to carry paddles and bulky safety and rescue equipment.

You will need a good roof rack if you are going to carry your boat on top of your car. Make sure the roof bars are securely attached to the car; if in doubt, tie the boat to the car as well.

Pad your roof rack with pipe lagging or proper pads bought for the purpose, and tie down the boat, using webbing roof straps with metal buckles. If you plan to carry more than two boats, it is worth getting upright bars to attach to the roof rack to enable you to carry up to six boats.

Don't be afraid to take your boat on a commercial flight or passage. Most companies will carry one piece of sports equipment per passenger free of charge. You just have to check the boat in with the rest of your luggage, and then take it over to the oversized baggage area. Always make sure it is well wrapped.

TOP RIGHT *Kayaks are best transported on their side, strapped firmly to the bars and uprights. It is much better to use proper roof straps than to tie the boat on with rope.*

BELOW *A strong roof rack is essential. This one has uprights bolted to it, which are ideal for transporting kayaks.*

ABOVE *Do not tie kayaks on to roof racks right side up. They are unaerodynamic this way, and they will quickly fill with water if it rains.*

BELOW *The roof bars and uprights can be padded with proprietary roof bar pads or with pipe lagging, to protect the boats from damage during transit.*

ABOVE *The correct orientation for a single kayak if you are not using uprights on the roof rack. If carrying more than one boat, store them sideways.*

BELOW *Make sure the boats are sensibly positioned and roughly centred fore and aft on the roofrack.*

Essential Clothing

The right clothing is vital when you are on the water, not least because if you fall in and the conditions get cold, you could suffer remarkably quickly.

Before you get into a boat, you must consider what you should be wearing, some of which might be provided by your instructor. This will, to an extent, depend on the weather, but as a general rule you need to think about thermal insulation, in addition to footwear and flotation.

Insulation

Your insulation requirements will depend on the weather conditions you can expect to experience on the day you are boating. Always check the weather forecast before you set out, and adapt your level of clothing accordingly.

• If the climate is tropical and the water is warm, you do not need any insulation. You could paddle in a swimming costume, but some degree of sun protection is recommended. If the weather is balmy, you should have a T-shirt and shorts, and something warmer in case you capsize or swim, and get drenched. Whatever you wear should not get heavy when soaked; items made of polyester or polypropylene

ABOVE *Tight-fitting thermals are the best base layer in cold weather.*

ABOVE *A thermal top worn with board shorts is ideal for warm weather.*

BELOW *A correctly fitting cagoule: close-fitting but allowing full upper body motion.*

BELOW *This cagoule is too big. It would be cold and difficult to swim or paddle in.*

BELOW *A flotation aid worn over the top of a cagoule and board shorts.*

ABOVE *A correctly fitting wetsuit. The suit should fit close like a second skin.*

ABOVE *An incorrectly fitting wetsuit. The baggy suit will not feel comfortable.*

ABOVE *Waterproof trousers and a cagoule over thermals is an alternative to a wetsuit.*

are better for warmth when wet than cotton. Board shorts, popular with surfers, are ideal for boating because they are durable for sliding in and out of the kayak or canoe, but do not soak up much water.
• If the water temperature is less than pleasant for dangling your fingers and toes in, or the air is a little too chilly for a T-shirt, then a thermal base layer is necessary. Choose one made from polyester fleece or polypropylene thermal

material, or wear a wetsuit over your thermal layers. The wetsuit should be as close fitting as possible without being restrictive.
• If wind chill is an issue, you can add a wind- and spray-proof shell top over your thermals for upper body warmth. There is a wide variety available from water-sports suppliers, including wind-tops, spray-tops, paddling jackets or cagoules (also known as cags); different manufacturers give

their products different names. The features to look for are waterproof fabric, neoprene cuffs, comfortable neck seal and an adjustable or elasticated waist.

Protective Headgear

Helmets are not a legal requirement but they should be worn whenever your experience and the conditions dictate that they are necessary. You are always safer wearing a helmet: if in doubt, wear one.

BELOW *A correctly fitting helmet sits snugly on the head without sliding forward.*

BELOW *A helmet that is too small exposes the temples, giving no protection.*

BELOW *A helmet that is too big will expose the base of the skull and can impair vision.*

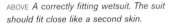

ABOVE *Technical sandals: lightweight and comfortable, and widely available.*

ABOVE *Wetsuit boots make ideal footwear and will keep feet warm even when wet.*

ABOVE *Specialist water-sports shoes make a good alternative to wetsuit boots.*

Footwear

You cannot paddle well if you are wearing heavy, cumbersome footwear, although bare feet are not ideal either.

In most water environments it is a good idea to wear something on your feet. Old trainers (sneakers) or running shoes are often recommended, but they can be bulky and the rubber soles can jam on the inside of the boat.

If the weather is warm, technical sandals may be appropriate. These are comfortable, and are light enough to swim in should you capsize. They are also relatively inexpensive.

Otherwise, wetsuit boots are best, although they will add to the cost of kitting yourself out. Wetsuit boots are

good to walk, scramble and swim in, they are unlikely to come off accidentally, and are warm as well as lightweight.

Specialist water-sport shoes are a good alternative to wetsuit boots. These have non-slip soles that are ideal for wet surfaces, and are padded and reinforced in all the right places. They often have straps to keep them firmly on the feet during a swim. Again, though, this is specialist footwear and not necessary for beginners starting out.

Flotation

A buoyancy or flotation aid (personal flotation device, also known as a PFD) is a vital piece of paddling equipment. Over-confident beginners might think

that the buoyancy aid is surplus to their requirements, but no matter how strong a swimmer you are, you should always wear one when you are on the water. It is extremely rare for anyone to drown while kayaking or canoeing with a buoyancy aid; but unfortunately it does happen to those without them.

There are many different styles on the market, but the important thing is that it should be a buoyancy aid and not a life jacket, and that it should allow you to wave your arms about freely. It should fit well enough so that it does not pull up and off when you are in the water – check this does not happen by pulling up, or getting someone else to pull up, the shoulders. Also check that all the straps and fasteners do up properly.

In many countries there are stringent standards for what may be sold as a buoyancy aid. In Europe, look for the CE EN393 Approved Buoyancy Aid, and in the United States, the US Coastguard Approved Personal Flotation Device.

Flotation Maintenance

It is worth remembering that a buoyancy aid that is a few years old may not provide the expected level of flotation. It really does pay to look after your buoyancy aid correctly. Whether you are using your own buoyancy aid or one belonging to your paddling club, do not stand on it, sit on it or do anything else that might compress the foam, and make it less effective. Although wearing a buoyancy aid is never an absolute guarantee of your safety, it is essential that the buoyancy aid you wear will perform exactly as you expect it to.

BELOW *A correctly adjusted flotation aid should fit snugly to the body.*

BELOW *Check the flotation aid cannot come off accidentally by pulling firmly upwards.*

ABOVE *A reinforced neoprene spraydeck (skirt) for white water paddling. It has a tight-fitting body tube that is pulled right up to prevent water getting in.*

BELOW *A nylon spraydeck suitable for flat water paddling, but not rough water.*

ABOVE *A cagoule is worn over the spraydeck to prevent water from splashing up and entering down the body tube.*

RIGHT *A nylon spraydeck worn over a light sweater and board shorts is perfectly adequate for flat water paddling.*

TIP

Spraydecks (skirts) are not needed on flat water because you are not likely to get a soaking from splashing water. However, if you do use one, it is essential that you know how to attach and remove it without help.

Fitness and Personal Skills

As with most sports, the fitter you are the more success you will have. When it comes to boating, being relatively fit and a competent swimmer are even more important for the sake of personal safety. You must also be able to set yourself clearly defined, achievable goals.

You need very little in the way of skills when you first begin to paddle, but the one essential is the ability to swim. You should be able to swim at least 50m (170ft) in the clothing you will be wearing when you paddle the boat. Only if reliable, trained rescue cover is forewarned and constantly at hand should a paddler who can not meet these basic standards go paddling, unless practising in the shallow end of a swimming pool.

Personal Fitness

One of the important activities most commonly overlooked by paddlers is their physical preparation for the demands of the sport. The demands will obviously be to a much higher degree if you are doing white water freestyle, but even if you are paddling around gently you need some kind of preparation. It will dramatically enhance the amount of fun you get from paddling, while simultaneously reducing the likelihood of injury and tiredness. After all, why tend aching muscles and stiff joints the day after you paddle, when you can so easily avoid them?

As you attempt more and more demanding kinds of paddling, or paddle further and in more exposed situations, you should have a level of strength and fitness commensurate with the challenge you are undertaking. This can only be acquired by practice and experience. Even extremely strong and athletic people find that they struggle when attempting to use their strength and fitness in unfamiliar ways or conditions.

Mental Fitness

Sportsmen and women now realize that their state of mind is as important as their physical condition. It does not matter what level they are at, whether professional or amateur, they still want to perform to the best of their ability.

The secrets of a good state of mind are feeling confident and positive, and clearly visualizing yourself realizing a set of achievable goals. Unless you believe you really can realize these goals, you will make it much harder for yourself to do so. Have a clear picture in your mind of what you plan to do. And having achieved those goals (or not!), set the next ones with an equal degree of realism.

The final stage of mental fitness is remembering to listen and be receptive. That does not just mean listening to your instructor. The most important thing is to listen to your body, and to be aware of yourself and the water. Never become so obsessed with what you have been told, or what you have read, that you focus on that more than upon vital, first-hand experience.

ABOVE *The ability to swim 50m (170ft) in the clothing you paddle in is essential.*

Special Needs Paddlers

Paddlers with disabilities (mental or physical) have particular needs that must be met if they are to realize their potential on the water with minimal risk and full enjoyment. The aim is to enable the special needs paddler to participate as far as possible with the same equipment and the same objectives as anybody else, with any modifications being made as required for that person. The key factor is good communication between the experienced paddler(s) leading the group, the paddler with special needs, his or her parents, and any medical and care staff. This will produce a paddling programme tailored to meet the needs of the individual.

Out-of-water Training

Knowing the ins and outs of keeping fit, and avoiding injury, apply as much to paddlers as to any other sportsmen and women. Being fit also enables you to achieve your goals; you cannot paddle if your muscles are aching and tired.

All-body Workouts

Many people use paddling as their main form of exercise, and paddling vigorously or over a long distance is certainly an excellent, all-body workout. Despite the fact that your legs do not appear to be doing much, they are actually contributing quite a lot of the power, provided you have a good paddling technique. If you want to progress with your boating skills, however, you may want to do extra, non-paddling exercises to tone your muscles and increase body strength.

BELOW *Cycling is good training for the quads, the powerful muscles in the thighs.*

ABOVE *Running is good cardiovascular exercise, but beware of impact.*

ABOVE *Swimming provides an excellent body workout without straining muscles.*

Any fairly vigorous physical activity benefits the cardiovascular system and hence your general fitness. Swimming is an excellent form of fitness training because it exercises the whole body, while making you an even stronger swimmer at the same time, which is exactly what you want. Practise the backstroke and butterfly, because the back and shoulder muscles are important for paddling, and are difficult to exercise by other means.

Cycling and running are good for improving all-round fitness, and are especially good for the quadriceps (the big thigh muscles), which are used a surprising amount when paddling. Much of the torso rotation in a forward paddling stroke comes from the quadriceps.

Many paddlers favour either climbing or snowboarding as a second sport, whether because of a love of the outdoors or because they are extremely complementary disciplines. Whatever cross-training you choose to do, use it in moderation and aim for a good all-round level of fitness. Regular gentle exercise – every day, if possible – will help you avoid illness and injury.

Targeted Action

If you have access to a gym, then a professionally planned regime can target the muscle groups you need to exercise.

Avoid concentrating too much on the arm muscles because the quadriceps, abdominals, shoulder and back muscles do most of the work when you are in the boat. The arms mainly provide fine motor control, and gain more from activities such as juggling than from lifting weights.

Press-ups, pull-ups and crunches are the best simple non-gym exercises to prepare you for paddling, and these are all something you can do at home.

Avoiding Injury

Whichever exercises you do, remember that it is vitally important to warm up first, and then to stretch, or you might strain or pull a muscle. It is also important to make sure that your posture is correct when exercising. Kayakers, in particular, are prone to lower back problems if they fail to keep their spinal curvature correct.

After any form of exercise you must also stretch again and warm down. This helps keep injuries at bay. It might seem

BELOW *Diagonal crunches (elbow to knee) are excellent training for paddling.*

ABOVE *The press-up is an exercise to build short, powerful muscles in the pectoral, bicep and tricep areas of the body.*

wholly unnecessary, but it pays dividends. It also gives you time to focus on how you have performed, and how you can improve next time. Mental visualization is extremely important, and will make more difference to your paddling than almost any other single factor.

Good Habits

If you can integrate exercise into your daily life it will save you a lot of time and money that you might otherwise spend on fitness clubs and sports equipment. Simply being more aware of your body will help you enormously. For example, by knowing which muscle groups are

ABOVE *You may find that by supporting your weight with your knees, you will find it easier to do more repetitions.*

working to perform different actions, you may find yourself doing a mini workout just walking up the stairs.

Maintaining a good body posture at all times, whether exercising, at work in the office or watching television at home, will also make a difference. Your posture can affect both your performance as a paddler and your overall well-being. Not only will you find it easier to make more effective strokes in your boat, you will also reduce the risk of injury, particularly damage to your back.

BELOW *Pull-ups mimic paddling well and help to promote arm strength.*

Warming Up

You should always warm up before you do any kind of strenuous activity. Warming up is essential to prepare your body for sudden exertions and to minimize the risk of injury. Your body will then be much more flexible and able to absorb shocks and over-extensions. Even stretching should not be attempted until you have warmed up thoroughly.

Establish a Routine

It is important to formulate a pre-paddling routine for yourself, and to make a habit of following it as a precursor to going out on the water.

Start with some light warm-up exercise for at least 15 minutes. Depending on how often you go out paddling, you might want to include a selection of activities in your routine, so that you don't become bored with the same one.

Once you have warmed up, it is time for some gentle stretching. This can improve the performance of your muscles and tendons enormously and, at the same time, it will dramatically reduce the likelihood of injury.

Practise the body stretches given over the following pages to achieve a good all-round level of flexibility. Do not bounce to increase your range of movement, but

extend yourself gently to the limit of comfort and hold each stretch for about 15 seconds before relaxing.

Next, get into your boat, still on land, and continue with the boat stretching exercises. You can then take the boat stretches one step further by going out on to the water. This will ensure that everything has been stretched in the right way, and that there are no problems with your range and freedom of movement.

After paddling for a while, it is often beneficial to stop your boat and repeat the in-boat stretches. Remember, too, that it is important to warm down and stretch once again after you have finished paddling and are back on land.

LEFT *Simulated paddling action on land can make sure everything is moving properly without any undue strain.*

ABOVE *Gentle jogging, especially through water, is a great way to warm up.*

How to Warm Up

The best way to warm up is with gentle exercise. This could take the form of walking briskly, particularly uphill, with your arms swinging. If the water is warm, then you could have a warm-up swim. Some people like to play with a frisbee, and this sort of group activity can be a lot of fun, and adds to the enjoyment of the whole occasion.

In fact, any activity is fine, provided you actually feel yourself getting warm, and your heart rate is raised significantly. You should be able to sense this without taking your pulse. Do not go for a fast run to warm up though, or do anything that involves impact because it could be counter-productive.

Body Stretches

Light stretches are a vital part of your warm-up routine. They help fine-tune the body, can be done in the home or on the river bank or beach, and are a good way of building up team spirit when done in a group. There are a variety of simple stretches you can do to ensure that you have extended every muscle group in your body, and you will not require any props or assistance to do them.

RIGHT *Gentle neck rotation to the left and to the right is a good way to start off your stretching routine.*

ABOVE *Neck flexion. Bend the head forward from the neck, but do not rotate or roll the head, as it is is bad for the spine.*

ABOVE *Spine extension.*

BELOW *General arm and shoulder stretch.*

ABOVE *Hamstring, tricep and shoulder stretch.*

BELOW *Trunk rotation stretch.*

ABOVE *Quadriceps and hamstring stretch.*

BELOW *Side stretch.*

Stretching in the Boat

After your initial stretches on land, it is time to get seated in the boat and continue your warm-up routine with exercises that simulate more closely your movements while out on the water.

Before Getting Afloat

Exercises performed in the boat while you are still on land serve a dual purpose. First, you will be getting all the usual benefits of stretching, but specifically geared to the range of motion you have in the boat. Second, you are checking that you have good freedom of movement in the boat and in your paddling kit. If something is hurting, chafing or digging into your ribs when you do these stretches, get out now and solve the problem immediately.

On the Water

Once you have warmed up, stretched, and are afloat, it is a good idea to go for a bit of a paddle to settle into your boat, and then do some more stretching, perhaps using the paddle as an additional prop. There are a number of useful exercises that anyone can do without risk of capsizing, and they are all good confidence-building tools for new or nervous paddlers.

Having done all this preparation, you are now ready to paddle more skilfully and effectively than someone who jumps straight into the boat without first warming up and stretching. Typically, the whole process would take about 30 minutes, but it is time well spent. Without this pre-paddling routine, you probably would not be able to spend as much time on the water, and your skill and fitness levels might well stagnate.

TIPS

• Always stretch gently and progressively; never bounce.
• Only use your muscles to stretch; do not use weights or external forces, which will cause muscle strain and possible injury.
• If you stretch to the point that it hurts, you have over-reached yourself and should stop the stretch.

Boat Stretches on Land

1 Make sure you can reach the right-hand side of the stern with your left hand.

2 Repeat the same stretch on the other side of the boat, using your right hand.

3 Extend fully backwards, so that you are stretching over the back deck.

4 Then, extend fully forwards, so that you are stretching over the front deck.

Boat Stretches on Water

1 Press the left blade against the right-hand side of the bow and vice versa.

2 Press the left blade against the right-hand side of the stern and vice versa.

3 Stretch forward in the boat as far as you can and hold for a few seconds.

4 Stretch backwards in the boat as far as you can and hold for a few seconds.

KAYAKING SKILLS

Kayaking and canoeing are accessible to most people because the skills required to get in the boat and have fun are not specialized. If, however, you want to progress in one area of the sport, or want to paddle for longer distances or look after friends and family while they, too, enjoy their paddling, you ought to acquire some new skills.

This section outlines the basic skills and strokes that will help you to use the boat in a skilful manner. The exercises are described in approximately the order in which they tend to arise, although some instructors may prefer a different order.

When you are learning how to do each technique, try not to progress too fast. Make sure you have the right skills in place before you move on. Equally, though, it is a bad idea to practise a technique badly. If something is not working and you do not know why, change to a different skill until you can find out how to deal with your problem. Sometimes just going away and trying again much later is all it takes.

Choose a sheltered piece of flat water near to the shore to try out these skills. Put safety first, and make sure you are confident that you can swim to a safe landing place and rescue your equipment. This is a simple point, but so often overlooked.

LEFT *A group of paddlers under instruction, using short general-purpose kayaks.*

BELOW *Practising a reverse sweep stroke. Head and body rotation are part of good technique.*

Getting into the Kayak

The first thing to learn is how to get into your kayak when it is afloat. If it is a sit-on or an open cockpit boat, this is a simple enough matter, but a closed cockpit kayak (where your legs are under the deck) can be more difficult. You can practise on dry land if your boat is reasonably sturdy, but sooner or later you'll have to try it on water.

Find a place to launch where the bank or jetty is not too much higher than the gunwale of your kayak. Place the boat on the surface of the water here, making sure that the water is sufficiently deep that you will still be afloat after you get in! If it is deep enough to capsize, ensure that it is also deep enough to get out of the boat when upside down.

Don't be tempted to tether the boat to the bank, which would make things very difficult if you capsized. It may be possible to step into the boat while holding on to the bank, simply pick up your paddle, and paddle away, but this can often be tricky. A useful technique is to place your paddle across the boat at the back of the cockpit, and hold on to it and the cockpit rim at the same time. The paddle blade will then be resting on the bank, and this will stop the boat floating away, as well as supporting the back deck of the boat – some kayaks are not strong enough to be sat on without a little reinforcement.

Don't attempt this if the bank is much higher than the kayak, or you just will tip yourself in: find another launch place.

Now that the boat is afloat and you are holding on to it and the paddle, place one foot in the bottom of the boat, and make sure it is right in the middle before you put any weight on it. Transfer all your weight on to that foot and, still holding on to boat and paddle with one hand, place your other foot right inside the footwell of the boat and sit down on the back deck. Take a moment to get settled.

You may now need to change hand positions, but from here you should be able to lift yourself up again and move forward to sit down on the seat. With luck or practice you are still holding the paddle behind you, and have your other hand free to help you stabilize your position without being cast adrift. Sit centrally on the seat and arrange your clothing and equipment in an orderly fashion.

Finally, get your legs into position in the cockpit. Now you are ready to use your free hand to hold on to the bank, and can bring your paddle around in front of you ready to paddle away.

Getting into the Kayak

1 Place the boat in the water as close to the river bank as possible. Keep hold of the cockpit to stop the boat drifting off.

2 Place the paddle across the back of the cockpit. Continue to hold on to the front of the cockpit with your left hand.

3 Put one leg at a time into the boat. Steady yourself and the boat by holding on to the bank and the boat.

4 Slide forward into the cockpit and get both legs in. You should still be holding on to the paddle and the river bank.

5 Bend your knees to get both your legs stretched out beneath the front deck. Continue to hold the paddle and the bank.

6 Adjust your position so that you are sitting comfortably on the seat. Bring the paddle to the front and you are ready.

Seating Position

Sloppy posture is bad at any time, but doubly so when paddling because it puts a strain on your back, and can lead to all sorts of problems, some of which can mean long-term damage. The following tips spell out exactly how you should sit to avoid injury.

In most kayaks there will be a seat, which, with the position of the backrests and footrests, will dictate which way you are supposed to face. What is not so obvious is the correct posture.

Maintaining good spinal posture means keeping your back straight and shoulders back, so that your spine is curved like the letter S: imagine you were sitting on an upright chair. If you do not, you will not be able to paddle properly. If your kayak is equipped with a back strap, the strap will give support and will encourage you to sit up properly. Even without this support though, you should be able to maintain a good, upright posture.

A common mistake is to slouch against the back of the cockpit. New paddlers often do this from the start, and even after you know how to sit there is a tendency to do this when tired. But if you cannot sit up properly in the boat, it is time to get out. By slouching, you make every stroke more difficult and less effective, and it is very bad for your back.

In most kayaks you will sit with your knees under the deck and your legs bent, so that pressing the feet against the

BELOW *Correct seating position in a kayak. The knees are under the deck, and the body is upright and central.*

ABOVE *Incorrect seating position. The knees should not be bent up in this particular type of kayak.*

footrest will push your knees up and out to maintain a firm grip on the boat. In some racing and fast touring boats the paddler will sit with the knees straight up, but in the majority of kayaks this does not afford good control.

Sometimes people worry that they will not be able to get out of the boat if they capsize because their legs are under the deck. This is not actually a problem, but worrying about it is, so practise getting out until you have allayed your fears.

RIGHT *Correct seating position for a narrow, racing kayak, which is designed to be paddled with the knees up.*

BELOW *Correct posture. The body is upright, maintaining a defined spinal "S".*

BELOW *Incorrect posture. Slouching backwards may cause spinal injury.*

BELOW *The release handle of the spraydeck (spray skirt) should be within reach.*

Capsize Drill in a Kayak

You cannot get into a boat unless you accept that you may capsize. Hence, you also need to learn the escape drill. It is a simple skill, but the sooner you learn it the better. Losing the fear of capsizing means you will enjoy paddling a lot more.

Most people realize that a kayak, by its very nature, is prone to capsize. Although this can be avoided, the beginner will not know how, and that is why everyone should know how to capsize.

If you try to get out of a kayak while it is in the process of capsizing, you run the risk of injuring yourself or ending up in a position where your head is underwater, but you cannot free yourself. It is better to wait until the boat has capsized and stopped moving, and then get out. It is quite hard to visualize what you will do when you are upside down, but do not worry. When you are in the water you will not be aware of being upside down.

Everything will look and feel exactly as it does when upright, except, of course, that you will be holding your breath.

First, remove your spraydeck (spray skirt), if you are wearing one, by pulling up the release handle and letting go. Then, bang on the bottom or sides of the boat to attract attention. Lean forwards and push yourself out by placing your hands either side of the cockpit. You will naturally do a somersault in the water, breaking surface in front of the cockpit.

If you come up directly under the boat, do not worry because kayaks are so narrow that there is no way you will be stuck underneath. If you can open your eyes it helps, but you can easily escape blind. If possible, try to keep hold of your paddle, but this is often difficult. As soon as your head breaks surface, take hold of the boat and paddle or swim to the bow or stern. From there you can swim the

boat ashore. Alternatively, someone may rescue you and help you back to land, or put you back in your boat so that you can continue paddling.

You should practise the capsize drill every time you go kayaking, until you are extremely confident. Most people do it at the end of a session because emptying a boat is tiring, and you need to be fully warmed up before you do it. If you get cold doing a capsize drill at the end of a session, imagine what it would have been like to capsize at the beginning.

With practice, you may be able to keep hold of the boat with one hand, and the paddle with the other. This can be very useful to rescuers, or if you need to try to get back in the boat on your own. In practice, however, a paddler with these skills will be ready to learn how to roll as an alternative to capsizing, and will be determined to stay in the boat.

Capsize and Get Out (underwater view)

1 Locate the spraydeck (skirt) release handle and pull off the spraydeck.

2 Bring your knees together, place your hands on each side and tuck forwards.

3 Push firmly away with your hands and you will fall out of the boat easily.

4 From the cockpit, turn to one side. Hold on to the boat and paddle if you can.

TIPS
• Wait until the boat has capsized completely before you try to get out of the boat.
• Pull off your spraydeck (spray skirt) as a matter of urgency, using the handle at the front of the boat.
• Make sure your spraydeck has been released all the way around the cockpit before you attempt to move, or you risk getting caught up in it.
• Free both of your knees from under the deck at the front of the boat.
• Tuck your body forwards, with your knees pulled up to your chest in a foetal position; don't try to lie across the back deck.
• Aim to keep hold of your boat with one hand as you come up to the surface of the water.
• Don't try to get your head above the surface of the water until your legs are completely out of the boat because you risk getting into a tangle that could prove dangerous: learn the stages of a capsize in one sequence and keep to it.

Capsize and Get Out (above water view)

1 You are on flat water and are ready to begin the capsize drill. Keep your hands by your sides and take a deep breath.

2 Lean over to one side and capsize. At first, you may have to resist your body's natural instinct to right itself.

3 Remain sitting upright, at 90° to the boat, as you go over. It may help to place your hands on the sides of the boat.

4 It will help to keep hold of the sides of the boat as your head hits the water and goes under.

5 Wait in this position until the boat stops moving. You will feel it settle when you are completely upside down.

6 Once completely inverted, bang on the bottom or sides of the boat. This makes a loud noise and attracts attention.

7 RIGHT Once out of the boat, go to one end and hold on to the grab handle. Swim the boat to the shore or towards the rescuer.

TIPS

• Only practise the capsize drill when there is an instructor or experienced rescuer on hand to help you in case you get into difficulties.
• Make sure the water is at least 1.2m (4ft) deep. It is tempting to stay in shallow water, but this can lead to entrapment or injury.

Holding the Paddle

How the paddle is held is critical if you are going to use it properly. This is because the correct grip enables the paddler to apply the maximum amount of force with the minimum effort. It is also important to hold the paddle in the same way every time you pick it up. Reacting to the signals the paddle sends you from the water is an important part of paddling, and you can only learn to interpret that feedback if you have a consistent grip.

Almost all kayak paddles are feathered (one blade at an angle to the other), which means that with each stroke you will turn the paddle to put the other blade in the water. One hand will be your control hand and will grip the paddle at all times. Allow the paddle shaft to turn in the other, non-control hand, gripping it only as you make the stroke on that side.

Find your best hand position by putting the middle of the paddle shaft on your head and shuffling your hands until your elbows make 90°, making sure that your hands are still equidistant from the blades when you have finished.

Hold the paddle out in front of you with your arms straight and horizontal, knuckles up. Grip the paddle with your control hand so that the blade on this side is vertical, and the drive (concave) face is forward. If it is your paddle, you can mark the hand positions with tape. Now you are ready to paddle.

Never be tempted to change your grip on the paddle once you've got it right. There are no significant advantages to shifting your grip, and you will find that any changes hamper the learning process. Learning is feedback-related. You do something, you feel the effect; you do it a bit differently, and you feel a different effect. Changing your grip means you have to start out all over again.

You will get used to the feather angle of your paddle. Beginners often ask why kayak paddles can't be flat: the reason is so that the blade that isn't in the water doesn't give wind resistance as it goes through the air. Once you are used to it, a change in feather will feel strange to you. This is one reason why you should try to use the same paddle if you can.

ABOVE *A good way to find the correct grip is to put the paddle on your head, with your hands equidistant from each end and your elbows at 90°.*

TIPS

• The control hand's grip on the paddle never changes during a stroke; instead, the wrist of the control hand is flexed.
• The slip hand loosens between strokes to allow the shaft to rotate.

BELOW *Make sure that when your arms are pointing straight up, the blade on the control side is facing down towards the water.*

ABOVE *Incorrect hold. You should never hold the paddle shaft off-centre.*

BELOW *Incorrect hold. Here, the hands are too close together on the shaft.*

Using the Paddle

There is more to paddling than building up a fantastic set of arm muscles, and thrashing about. Good paddling is an art, and that means following certain rules.

With all paddle strokes you should aim to put the whole of the blade in the water, but no more. There is no advantage to the blade being deeper in the water, and it will not work properly if it is only half in. The whole blade should be just immersed.

When you make a stroke, you should always try to rotate your shoulders to give you as much reach as possible. This also means that much of the power for the stroke will come from your leg and torso muscles, leaving your relatively smaller arm muscles to provide control and react to feedback during the stroke. It is a misconception to think that kayaking is exclusively about using your arms. In fact, with good technique, a vigorous workout is much more likely to leave you with tired and aching legs and stomach muscles.

The other point that a kayak paddler should concentrate on is head rotation. Before making a stroke you should make sure your head is facing in the direction

ABOVE *Using the paddle properly is vital to make each of your strokes count.*

BELOW *Correct technique: the paddle blade is submerged just deep enough to start a forward stroke.*

you want the boat to move in. So, for forward paddling, you must be looking at the horizon. If you want to turn the boat to the left or right, you should first turn your head to look that way. This helps the whole of your body make the strokes. It also tends to inhibit various bad practices, such as looking at the paddle blades or the end of your boat, neither of which are any help and will encourage bad posture, which can lead to injury.

ABOVE *Blade too deep in the water – the paddler's hand is too low.*

BELOW *Blade too shallow in the water – only half the blade would come into play.*

Forward Paddling

A good forward paddling stroke is a basic requirement, but it is not the easiest stroke to master. The main aim is to propel the boat forward while applying as little turning force as possible. Normally, if you make a stroke on one side, the boat will move forwards while turning away from the paddle blade that made the stroke. In order to minimize this effect, you should make the stroke as close to the boat as possible, with the paddle shaft as upright as possible.

Reach forward as far as you can, leaning from the hips but without bending your spine forward. You should be able to put the blade in the water about 2.5cm (1in) from the boat, near your feet, and drive face back. When the blade is fully immersed, pull it back using your shoulders and torso, straightening up your top arm to push the "air blade" to the side of the boat that the stroke is on. This will make the paddle vertical and a lot more comfortable for you.

Continue to pull the paddle blade through the water until it is level with the back of the seat. Try to resist the urge to pull with your bottom arm for as long as possible. When your arm finally does bend at the elbow, it will be time to extract the blade from the water. Keep this blade the same distance from the boat throughout the stroke.

As soon as the blade is out of the water, rotate your body the other way to make the next stroke on the other side. As you do so, you will have to rotate the shaft with your control hand; drop in the blade with the drive face pointing the same way as before.

Forward Paddling Technique

1 Begin the forward stroke by placing the blade as far forward in the water as you comfortably can do.

2 Drop the whole of the blade into the water and start to push away from you with your top hand.

3 The blade in the water follows the side of the boat, and the bottom arm stays fairly straight.

4 As the water blade passes your body, the top arm should be coming across in front of your face.

5 Finally, as you reach the end of the stroke, the air blade starts to come down towards the water.

6 Continuing this motion recovers the water blade, and you are ready to place the opposite blade in the water.

ABOVE *Excellent body rotation, as the paddler is about to place the left blade in the water for another stroke.*

ABOVE *About to make a stroke. Note that the top arm is bent, ready to punch the top blade forward.*

ABOVE *Good forward paddling technique. The paddle is quite vertical and the blade is submerged.*

BELOW *Forward paddling on flat water in a general-purpose kayak.*

Backward Paddling

Paddling backwards is in principle no different from paddling forwards, but it is more difficult to get the hang of.

Do not change your grip on the paddle: this is a classic mistake made by most beginners. Always back-paddle using the back of the blade. There is no need to turn the paddle around since its curvature actually helps you to make the back stroke, and because it is bad practice to change your grip.

It is not possible to keep the paddle shaft as vertical as you do for forward paddling, or to keep the blades so close to the boat, but this is what you should aim for. Make a big effort to rotate your shoulders as far as you can to place the blade behind you – this also helps you to glance behind and see where you are going. Push your paddle forward through the water with your arms fairly straight, and make the stroke as long as you can.

Most boats will turn during the back stroke so that you zig-zag a little. Find somewhere where you will not crash into anything, and see how long you can keep going backwards in a straight line. It will teach you excellent control over the boat.

ABOVE *Incorrect method. Do not turn the paddle around like this.*

> ### TIPS
> • Think before you back-paddle: it may be quicker and easier to turn your boat and paddle forwards.
> • Look over your shoulder at least every other stroke to avoid a crash.
> • Pick out a feature behind you in the direction of travel, and focus on it whenever you turn around.

Backward Paddling Technique

1 Rotate as far as you can to one side, and place the blade quite far back in the water behind the boat.

2 Drive the blade forwards through the water using your torso; do not use your arms for strength.

3 As you come around to face the front, straighten your arms, keeping the blade as close as you can to the boat.

4 Try to keep looking behind you as you finish the stroke. This may seem difficult at first but it will come with practice.

5 The stroke should end with the bottom arm straight and the blade in the area of the boat next to your feet.

6 As the blade comes out of the water, you can continue rotating to place the blade behind you on the other side.

Stopping

Learning how to stop the boat quickly is important. Use this stroke if you are in danger of hitting something.

Begin by moving the boat forwards at a good pace. To stop, jab one blade into the water next to your body, as if to paddle backwards. The drive face should be pointing backwards with the shaft perpendicular. Resist the force on the blade, but as soon as you tense against that force and the boat begins to turn, jab the other blade in quickly on the other side. Repeat on the first side, and by the time you make your fourth jab, the boat should have stopped. Do the jabs quite aggressively, and switch sides when you feel the pressure on the back of the blade.

RIGHT *Stopping quickly in a fast racing kayak requires sharp jabs in the water.*

Stopping Technique

1 Jab the paddle in on one side, at 90° to the kayak rather than as you would for a normal stroke.

2 Pull the paddle out again as soon as you feel the pressure of the water on the blade and the boat begins to turn.

3 Drop the opposite blade in on the other side. Resist for a little longer this time, until the boat is pointing straight again.

4 Back on the side of the boat on which you started, make a longer back stroke this time.

5 Moving backwards this time, make a final stroke to straighten up the boat.

6 At the finish, you should be pointing in the same direction you were at the previous step, except with the boat still.

Forward Sweep Stroke

The forward sweep is the most useful turning stroke in the kayaker's repertoire. It will turn the boat on the spot, and can be used to turn the boat through 180°. By inserting just one sweep stroke, you can also change or correct your direction while paddling forwards, without breaking your rhythm.

Start by placing the blade in the water as far forward as possible, with the shaft fairly low and the drive face pointing away from the boat. Rotate your head and shoulders, so that they are facing the direction of travel. Keeping your bottom arm straight, sweep the paddle in as wide an arc as you can. When you have turned as far as you need to, or the blade is coming close to hitting the back of the boat, lift the blade straight out of the water – don't let it hit the boat.

It helps considerably if you can "edge" the boat slightly, so that the side opposite your stroke is raised a little for the first half of the stroke. Level the boat again as the paddle passes perpendicular to the kayak, or you may catch the paddle.

ABOVE *The forward sweep stroke is the most valuable turning stroke. It can be used to spin or to change direction.*

TIPS
- Practise edging the boat by lifting up one of your knees.
- The bigger the arc, the more effectively you will turn the boat.
- Think about the difference between a forward paddling stroke (vertical paddle, close to the boat) and a sweep stroke (low paddle, wide arc).
- Use the forward sweep if you want to turn while travelling forwards.

Forward Sweep Technique

1 Place the paddle in the water as far forward as you can reach, with the blade facing away from the boat.

2 Keeping your lower arm straight, swing your paddle blade away from the front of the boat.

3 Looking in the direction you want to turn, continue to sweep the blade in the widest arc you can make.

4 Still looking where you want to go, continue to sweep until the blade is swinging in towards the stern.

5 At this point, quickly flip the blade up out of the water before it catches on the back of the boat and trips you up.

6 If you keep the boat stable and the blade out of the water, you'll carry on turning even after the stroke is finished.

Reverse Sweep Stroke

As the name implies, the reverse sweep stroke is the exact opposite of the forward sweep. It is a much more powerful turning stroke, but it should not be used while moving forwards unless you want to turn and head back in the other direction because it will arrest all forward motion.

Start with the paddle blade as far back as you can reach, on the side you want to turn towards. Rotate your head and shoulders in this direction. Drop the blade into the water with the drive face towards the boat, then sweep the blade forwards in the widest arc you can, until you are pointing the right way, or until the blade is about to hit the front of the boat. Lift the blade straight up out of the water.

Keep your bottom arm as straight as you can throughout the stroke, and try to keep the boat level in the water.

ABOVE *Incorrect technique: don't turn the paddle around. Use the back of the blade for all reverse strokes.*

It should be easy to turn most general-purpose boats through 180° with one reverse sweep. Once the blade is out of the water, the kayak will continue to spin for further rotations. Practise spinning

using alternate forward and reverse sweep strokes. Go forward on the left and reverse on the right to turn clockwise. Go forward on the right, then reverse on the left to spin in the opposite direction.

TIPS

• Use the back of the paddle blade and don't change your grip.
• Use a reverse sweep stroke when you need to make a powerful turn.
• Keep the boat fairly level in the water for a reverse sweep stroke.
• Remember, a reverse sweep stroke will arrest forward progress.
• Practise combining forward sweep strokes and reverse sweep strokes on opposite sides of the boat.

Reverse Sweep Technique

1 Rotate your body and look where you want the boat to be pointing. Place the blade in the water close to the stern, with the drive face towards the boat.

2 Sweep the blade out and forward, keeping the bottom arm straight. Note how the body hasn't actually moved but the boat has.

3 Complete the arc, leaning your body forward over the front deck to extend your reach as far as you can at the front of the boat.

4 Lift the paddle blade out of the water before it reaches the boat, or you will risk catching your paddle under the boat.

5 Keep the boat level and the blade out of the water, and keep looking where you want to go!

6 The boat continues turning on its own. It is usually possible to complete a 180° turn like this in general-purpose boats.

Draw Stroke

This stroke moves the boat through the water sideways, and although you can get by without being very good at it, learning to do it well will help you to improve many of your other skills. The draw stroke is, curiously, a fairly obscure technique that many paddlers never learn to do properly.

Place the blade in the water as far from the side of the kayak as you can reach, with the drive face pointing towards the boat. Push your top arm out as far as you can, so that the paddle shaft is as vertical

as possible. Lift the edge of the kayak with your knee on the stroke side, and pull the blade towards your body. This should pull a general-purpose boat about 50cm (20in) sideways.

As the blade approaches, cock your wrists back quickly to rotate the blade 90°, then slice it back to where it started. If you do not, and the blade hits the boat, you may be knocked off balance or fall in. If you try to stop the stroke before it hits the hull, the same may happen.

From the starting position, straighten your wrists so that the paddle is pointing towards the boat, and repeat the stroke. If the boat turns rather than moves sideways, the stroke is being made too far towards the front or the back of the boat. If the bow starts to turn towards the paddle, move the stroke back a little, or vice versa for the stern. It can be very useful to make this happen deliberately though, so practise doing draw strokes towards the bow or stern.

Draw Stroke Technique

1 Rotate your body to face the way you want to move. Place the blade as far out to the side as you can, with the drive face towards the boat.

2 Pull the blade towards the boat, keeping the paddle as vertical as you can. Lifting your knee on the paddle side of the boat will help you achieve this.

3 Continue to pull smoothly until the paddle blade is just about to reach the boat at a point level in the water with your hip.

4 Turn your wrists sharply through 90° to change the angle of the blade before it hits the boat.

5 Move the paddle away from the boat by slicing the blade out sideways to where it first started.

6 Flick your wrists back to their original position, so that the drive face is towards the boat. Repeat as required.

Sculling Draw

Like the draw stroke, the sculling draw will move the boat sideways. It has the advantage, however, of being more useful in a confined space. For instance, when you are close to a jetty and want to move closer, the draw stroke may be difficult to execute. The sculling draw is also a lot less likely to tip you in, although it is more difficult to do effectively.

Start with the paddle blade next to your hip, 20cm (8in) from the boat, with the shaft vertical and the drive face towards the hull. Cock your wrist so that the blade rotates 20°, opening out towards the bow.

Keep the shaft vertical and move the paddle forwards as far as you can. Keep the paddle 20cm (8in) from the boat, resisting its tendency to slice away from the hull. If anything you will be pulling it inwards, which is where the sideways

motion of the boat is generated. When the blade is as far forward as you can get it, keep the shaft vertical and rotate your wrist the other way to angle the drive face 20° towards the stern. Then pull the blade back through the water as far as you can. At this point, quickly rotate again to push forward, maintaining enough pressure on the blade face to keep it the same distance from the boat at all times.

As you push and pull the paddle to and fro, the boat will move towards the side where you are paddle stroking. It helps to lean towards the paddle and to edge at the same time, so that the leading edge (the one nearest the paddle) of the boat is lifted. It is also possible to do this with the blade angles reversed, so that the pressure is on the outside (back) face of the paddle. The boat will then move

ABOVE *A sculling draw. Note how the boat moves quickly sideways, creating a wave.*

sideways away from the paddle. This is a sculling pushover. In this case the leading edge is the one opposite to the paddle.

Sculling further forward will move the boat sideways with the bow ahead of the stern, while sculling behind will mean the tail leads. In this way, sculling can move and turn the boat at the same time.

Sculling Draw Technique

1 Start as for a draw stroke, but with the blade only 20cm (8in) from the hull. Bend your wrists back so that the drive face is facing slightly towards the bow.

2 Move the blade forwards as far as you can reach without leaning, keeping it vertical and exactly the same distance from the side of the boat.

3 Quickly cock the wrists so that the paddle blade is pointing slightly towards the stern. (Note: the paddle is shown partly out of the water for teaching only).

4 Move the paddle back, keeping the pressure on the blade so that it stays equidistant from the hull.

5 When the paddle is as far back as is comfortable, cock the wrists back again to open the drive face towards the bow.

6 Move the paddle forwards as before, keeping the pressure on at all times. Repeat as necessary.

Stern Rudder

Sometimes it is desirable to make subtle direction changes, or to keep a kayak running in a straight line while in readiness for a turn. For this the stern rudder is extremely useful.

As the name of the stroke suggests, the paddle blade is used as a rudder at the stern of the boat. Place the paddle in the water, with the drive face towards the boat and the paddle shaft at a low angle. The back arm will probably be fairly straight. If the boat is not moving this will have no effect at all, but if you have some forward momentum the boat will probably turn slightly towards the paddle. If you move the paddle away from the hull, the turn will become more pronounced; closer to the hull and there will be less effect. If you bring it really close to the boat you may even start to turn the other way, away from the paddle.

BELOW *Textbook stern rudder. The body is rotated to help place the blade as far back as possible, while the paddler looks ahead to where he is going.*

A good exercise involves getting the boat up to speed, and then placing your stern rudder in the water, letting you experiment with pushing and pulling, and getting the boat to veer to and fro until it runs out of momentum, without taking the blade out of the water. This is a useful way to get used to feedback from the paddle.

A handy technique is to approach a landing place perpendicular to the shore, using a stern rudder to keep the boat pointing straight at the spot where you want to land. At the last moment, before the bow touches the bank, sweep your stern rudder forward in a reverse sweep to turn the boat 90° and kill your speed. You will finish up stationary and parallel to the shore, close enough to get out.

When deciding how to make a turn, ask yourself what you are trying to achieve apart from turning the boat. If you want to stop and turn, the reverse sweep may be better. The stern rudder does not propel you, and has little effect on speed except for interrupting your paddling.

It is possible, when paddling backwards, to do a sort of stern rudder at the bow of the boat, with the paddle placed as for the beginning of a forward sweep, the drive face pointing away from the hull. This is sometimes called a front rudder, and should be regarded as a rudder for going backwards.

TIPS

• Use a stern rudder sparingly. Think of it as a stroke to control steering, rather than to change direction.
• A stern rudder will impair forward movement, so you may prefer to use a forward sweep instead.
• Always have the drive face of the blade pointing towards the boat.
• Remember that your blade is acting as a rudder to steer the boat, and not as a brake to stop it.
• The stern rudder is used most when surfing waves, but practise it anyway, even if you don't need it just yet.

Bow Rudder

Expert paddlers seem to use bow rudders for everything, and can make complex manoeuvres while appearing just to stick in a bow rudder and lean on it. The bow rudder is in fact the fastest and most attacking turning stroke of them all, and it is the signature stroke of demanding white water paddling for this reason.

The bow rudder, unlike the stern rudder, can be a very difficult stroke to learn. It seems appropriate to mention it now, but you may find it difficult to make it work until you have mastered all the other strokes in this section. It relies on an excellent feel for what the paddle is doing in the water, as well as the draw stroke skills already covered.

The bow rudder is a compound stroke, which is to say it is a collection of smaller movements rather than one single stroke. It can make the boat spin dramatically, or it can turn the boat in a long, powerful sweep. It can be applied to great effect when the boat is turning with the current. It can also be used without any current, if you have sufficient forward speed.

While moving forwards, place the paddle vertically in the water 30cm (12in) from the side of the bow, about level with your feet, with the drive face of the blade towards the boat. Experiment with rotating your wrists to turn the blade out slightly, but resist any forces that act on the blade in the water. You will find that there is a position with the blade face almost parallel to the side of the boat when the boat does not tend to slow or turn, and you cannot feel any pressure on the blade. Roll your wrist back and turn the blade out to face the bow, and the boat will start to turn towards the paddle. The more you roll your wrist back to open out the blade, the more you will turn, but there will be a lot of force on the blade and the boat will quickly stop.

You can increase the effect by letting the pressure take the blade away from the boat, then pulling it back towards the bow in a modified draw stroke. There are many ways in which you can control the boat with the paddle blade in this mode, so experiment, noting what happens when you go with the water or oppose it.

ABOVE *It is not easy to see how the bow rudder works by watching it. The boat can spin around the paddle up to 180° while the paddler seems only to hold his blade vertically in the water.*

Don't be discouraged by your first attempts to perform the bow rudder. You will need a lot of practice to build up the strength, mobility and feel for the water that is necessary to execute the stroke properly and to make full use of it when you are paddling, and this can be very demanding on your strength and patience. But once you have it, you'll love it.

TIPS

• In manoeuvrable kayaks the bow rudder is very versatile.
• Familiarize yourself with how it feels when you rotate the blade in the water while the boat has some speed.
• Imagine running along a street and grabbing hold of a lamppost. You would swing around it, wouldn't you? This is how the bow rudder works.
• Most boats have a turning centre somewhere near your calves. Next to or slightly in front of this is where the bow rudder works best.

Low Brace

A low brace is a support stroke on the back of the blade, and it is used to keep you upright when you find yourself side-on to a wave that is trying to capsize you. All bracing or support strokes require quite a leap of faith. It is difficult to believe that you can trust your weight to your paddle blade, but this is exactly what you must do. The force that you commit to the paddle is exactly how much support you will get from it in return.

Place the blade on the surface with the drive face up. If you are moving, you must angle the leading edge up to stop it diving. It is easier to low brace with the blade behind you, but the further the blade is from the boat while flat on the surface, the better the technique will work.

Committing your weight to the blade will support you and stop you capsizing until the blade sinks too far into the water to keep it flat. If using the low brace to avoid a capsize, you must use your legs to level the craft before the paddle sinks. If the boat is moving, a low brace can be used to turn the boat, while giving some support. This is called a low brace turn.

ABOVE *The low brace is an important stroke that can be as useful to a white water aficionado as it is to a beginner.*

BELOW *The low brace is the best way to support your weight while leaning over, thereby preventing a capsize. If you are moving forwards, it will also make the boat turn towards the paddle.*

High Brace

The high brace works on the same principle as the low brace, but with the drive face of the paddle downward, and the bracing blade in the water rather than flat on the surface. This a support stroke, used to keep you upright – for instance, when a wave threatens to tip you in.

A high brace is more powerful than a low brace, and should be avoided if the latter is possible because of the huge force it exerts on the shoulders, which can lead to injury. However, as the paddle is already in the high position as you stroke, it can be more convenient to turn that stroke into a high brace when a wave is about to turn you over, rather than change your paddle position for a low brace.

Because the drive face is pointing down, high bracing demands that your elbows are below the paddle shaft. This usually means that the water is higher than the boat, either because of a wave or because you have tipped over a long way.

Keep your weight on the paddle until you can right the boat with your legs and hips. Move the weight of your body back over the boat to regain your equilibrium.

TIP
• Do not use the high brace in any powerful water feature, including river rapids. The blade may get jerked down without warning, and if the opposite arm is held too high it can be forced even higher, increasing the likelihood of a shoulder dislocation.

ABOVE *When taken to the extreme, the high brace over-extends the shoulders and there is a significant risk of dislocation or other, often very serious, injuries to the shoulders and upper back.*

BELOW *The high brace is more powerful than the low brace because you can reach further out for more leverage, and use the drive face of the paddle.*

CANOEING SKILLS

Canoeing is accessible to most people because the skills for getting in and out of the boat, and having fun, are not specialized or demanding. If, however, you plan to progress to a specialist area or want to paddle longer distances, or look after friends and family while they, too, enjoy their paddling, it is time to acquire new skills.

This section outlines the basic skills and strokes that will help you use the canoe in an effortless and skilful manner. The exercises are tackled in approximately the order in which they tend to arise, although some instructors may prefer a different order.

When you are learning the following skills, choose a suitable place to practise them, and try not to progress too fast. Make sure you have mastered them before you move on. If something is not working and you do not know why, take a break and then have another go. If there is still a problem, get expert advice. Also remember that until you can do most of the strokes, you will not be able to paddle the boat to the desired location, and that is why it is vital that you know you can swim to a safe landing place.

LEFT *Two paddlers charging along a flat water river in a tandem open canoe.*

BELOW *Swimming with an upturned canoe after a capsize, keeping hold of the boat and paddle.*

Getting into the Canoe

The first key lesson while the canoe is floating on the water is to get into the boat. It is much trickier than it looks, but it will come with practice.

It is best to start by finding a launching site where the river bank or jetty is low enough to let you step into the canoe without having to jump or climb in. Place the boat on the surface. The water should be deep enough to keep the craft afloat with your weight. If the water is deep enough to capsize in, make sure that it is deep enough for getting out of the boat when it is upside down.

Also consider how you are going to stop the canoe from floating away while you climb in. Do not be tempted to tether the boat to the bank, as this will make things difficult if you capsize. It may be possible to step into the boat while still holding on to the bank, just pick up the paddle beside you, and paddle away. Often, however, this is quite tricky. A useful technique is to place your paddle on the ground next to the boat, and keep one hand on it as you climb in. This is often easier than clinging on to a grass bank.

When the boat is afloat and you are holding on to it and the paddle, you are ready to get in. Place one foot in the bottom of the boat, and make sure it is right in the middle before you put any weight on it. Now gradually transfer all your weight on to that foot, and still holding on to the paddle if necessary, place your other foot right inside the footwell of the boat and gently sit or kneel down. Get comfortable and stable, and pick up the paddle if you have not already done so. Finally, get into your preferred sitting or kneeling position.

Getting into the Canoe

1 Put the canoe in the water close to the bank and keep hold of the nearside gunwale, so that the canoe cannot stray.

2 Make sure the canoe is floating freely, and that it won't touch the bottom when you get in. Lay the paddle across.

3 Holding on to both gunwales and the paddle, put one foot in the middle of the canoe and transfer your weight on to it.

4 When you feel confident that the canoe is balanced and stable, bring your other foot into the boat, still holding the paddle.

5 Supporting your weight on your hands, and holding on to the paddle, sit or kneel down in the bottom of the canoe.

6 Settle yourself into your preferred paddling position, still holding the paddle. You are now ready to set off.

Sitting or Kneeling?

Finding the right seating position is a fundamental part of canoeing. It is not just a matter of comfort, but a way of helping you control the craft.

You can sit on a seat in a canoe, or you can kneel in the bottom of the boat with your feet under the seat, resting your bottom against it. The latter is more stable because your weight is lower, and because you can brace your knees against the sides of the boat for better control. If you prefer to sit, find a way of bracing your legs because it is hard to balance the canoe if you are perched on the seat as if on a kitchen chair.

ABOVE *Kneeling correctly, with buttocks resting on the seat and knees apart.*

BELOW *Kneeling down and slouching is bad posture, and provides little control.*

Whether sitting or kneeling, you should always maintain good spinal posture, with your back straight. This is important for comfort, control and to prevent back pain or injury. It might seem easier to slouch at first, but this is a very bad idea.

Seating Position

The next step is called trimming the boat, which means sitting in the right position so that the boat performs well in the water. This means trying to keep the boat level or slightly bow up. A single paddler should sit in the middle, and two paddlers should sit so that the lighter paddler is in the bow.

The advantage of trimming slightly bow up is that less of the keel will be in the water, making the boat turn more easily, but you will sacrifice some speed. A level boat will be faster, but will be more difficult to turn unless it is flat-bottomed.

ABOVE *Sitting on the seat, with the knees against the sides, gives good control.*

ABOVE *Sitting off-centre on the seat, or with the knees together, should be avoided.*

Capsize Drill in a Canoe

If you are going to paddle a canoe it is important that you know what to do if it capsizes. The ability to swim is obviously important, but how you get out of the boat and handle yourself from there is a safety issue that should be addressed as soon as possible.

With some skill and practice you will be able to salvage almost any situation without capsizing, but sometimes it is unavoidable. When it does happen, you have a surprisingly long time to react. The question is, do you get out of the boat as it goes over, or wait until it has capsized before getting out?

If you try to get out of a canoe while it is capsizing, you run the risk of a gunwale cracking you on the head, or getting in a muddle as you try to get out. It is far better to get out once upside down, when the boat has stopped

moving. Push away from the gunwale with your hands and, if possible, try to keep hold of your paddle. As soon as your head breaks surface, take hold of the boat and swim to one end. You can then either swim the boat ashore, or try to turn it over.

A reasonably athletic canoeist can often right the boat and get back in unaided. Get alongside the upturned canoe, and take hold underneath. Push it up until the gunwales are about to break the surface, keeping it level. Tread water to maintain upward force. Finally, allow yourself to sink into the water and, as you come up again, push up harder on one side than the other, flipping the canoe over with the minimum of water inside. With a really light boat it is possible to throw it into the air and land it upright. Having righted the boat, push down the

side nearest to you, and reach across to the opposite gunwale to haul yourself in.

The technique for capsizing, escaping and recovering is one every canoeist should learn, but there is an advanced method that can be used to avoid the danger of being caught under the boat. When you realize a capsize is otherwise inevitable, you can jump over the side; pushing off from both gunwales as you do so ensures that the boat levels out and remains upright. Your paddle, still held in the bottom hand grip, can be used as a brake; slap it down hard on the surface as you go in, and you should be able to keep your head above water, boat in one hand, paddle in the other. This is, of course, a very safe and controlled way to exit the boat. From this position, you can swim ashore or re-enter the boat as described above.

Capsize and Get Out

1 To practise the capsize sequence, start from your usual paddling position, sitting or kneeling upright in the canoe.

2 Let go of the paddle with one hand and take hold of the gunwale of the boat.

3 Lean over to one side until the boat overbalances. Continue to keep hold of the paddle as you go over.

4 Allow the boat to capsize, still holding on to the gunwale and the paddle.

5 Wait until you are completely upside down and the boat has stopped moving.

6 Kick away from the boat and surface – ideally, still holding the boat and paddle.

Jump Out of the Boat

1 When you realize the boat is going to capsize, reach across to the lower gunwale with your opposite hand.

2 Keep hold of the paddle in your other hand and jump out. Keep holding on to the gunwale.

3 By holding the paddle blade flat you can often prevent your head from going under the water.

TIPS

• If you know the boat is going to capsize, it is worth getting out if you have enough time.
• Only jump out of the boat if you are able to do so before it flips over.
• By kicking off from the high side of the boat, you can often stop the canoe turning over.
• If you jump out before a capsize, you will be able get back in without the difficulty of righting and emptying the canoe.

RIGHT *Watching experienced paddlers acting out a capsize situation is a very useful exercise. All beginners should learn to capsize as soon as they first start out on the water, and most paddle club instructors make this a priority.*

Go to the Front and Swim

1 Swim your way to the front of the boat, keeping hold of the canoe and the paddle if at all possible.

2 Take hold of the front of the canoe, leaving it upside down.

3 Using the paddle, if you can, and your arms and legs, swim the canoe to the shore or to other paddlers in your group.

Right Boat and Re-enter

The technique for righting the boat and climbing back in is well worth learning and practising until you are confident you can do it. The technique makes the canoeist fully self-sufficient and able to cope with almost any eventuality on the water. Once you are confident that you can do it in any reasonable weather (high winds and waves make it more difficult) you will be happy to jump out of the boat rather than to capsize, which is, in many circumstances, a much safer thing to do.

Beware, however, of becoming too reliant on your powers of self-rescue. With this technique, as with the ability to roll, there is a danger that you will simply give up and capsize or get out in a situation that may in fact have been recoverable using a decent support stroke. Obviously, you will be safer, drier and more in control if you can stay upright in your canoe.

BELOW *Properly trained canoe paddlers can have great fun on white water, even when there is a risk of capsize.*

Although the open canoe is in a sense more vulnerable to capsize than a kayak and is far more likely to take in water, we can see from the solutions illustrated that the canoe is just as capable a craft as the kayak, and in some ways it is more versatile. Although it is possible to re-enter a capsized kayak, it is rare to see it done successfully, and the paddler nearly always has to contend with a boat that is full of water. The canoeist can quite often avoid this. The disadvantages of the open boat are that you cannot simply roll without bailing out, unless your boat is fully kitted out with airbags or similar buoyancy (flotation), and that a canoe loaded with gear can be almost impossible to right from the water.

If there are two paddlers, or another canoeist is able to assist, then have one person hold the gunwale down on the side opposite that on which you're getting in. The trick is to hold it firmly enough so that the canoe doesn't capsize or ship any water, but not to keep the boat so level that the person trying to get in cannot pull themelves up.

TIPS

• Lift the boat slowly. The pocket of air between the hull of the boat and the water surface creates some buoyancy, which will help to support you. This shouldn't be broken until the last possible moment.
• Focus on forcefully throwing the boat upwards, not on flipping it over.
• You will need both hands to right the boat, so leave your paddle on the water between you and the canoe.
• Put your paddle into the boat as soon as the boat is righted.
• Climb into the boat carefully: to mess up this part and fall back into the water is exhausting, and you need to preserve your energy.
• If you were paddling tandem when you capsized, one of you can hold on to the far gunwale while the other climbs into the boat.
• With every capsize you bring water into the canoe: remember to bring a sponge or a small bucket next time!

Right Boat and Re-enter

1 Practise the righting sequence from any starting position in the water. Swim alongside the middle of the canoe.

2 Treading water to keep yourself afloat, take hold of both gunwales in the middle of the boat.

3 Holding the gunwales, lift the boat as high as you possibly can, then push it up and away from you so that it rights itself.

4 Keep holding the boat up out of the water as much as possible. Be prepared for your head to go under as you put all your strength into holding up the boat.

5 The boat turns over and lands right side up, with a minimum of water inside. You will have had to let go of the boat to turn it, so now get hold of the gunwale again.

6 Hold on to the nearest edge and throw all of your weight on to it. This should tip the boat towards you until you can take hold of the far gunwale.

7 Holding on to the far gunwale, haul yourself across the canoe, trying not to tip the boat so far with your weight that you take on even more water.

8 Get all of your weight across the boat, with both hands on the far gunwale. Then, bring one knee up and inside the boat. This will level out the boat.

9 Flip yourself around so that you can get into your paddling position. If your paddle has floated away, ask someone in your group to retrieve it for you.

Holding the Paddle

It may look easy, but there is a definite knack to holding a canoe paddle correctly. If you think paddling a canoe means grabbing the nearest paddle and roughly holding it, you will have no hope of mastering canoe techniques.

You can only use a paddle properly if you are holding it correctly in the first place. This is because the correct grip enables the paddler to apply the maximum amount of force with the minimum effort. It is also important to hold the paddle in exactly the same way every time you use it. This is the only way for you to become familiar with – as quickly as possible – the feel of the paddle in the water, and how to learn to interpret the feedback you get from it. This is key to becoming a good paddler.

Canoe paddles have only one blade, with a T-grip at the other end. It is important to hold this T-grip with your top hand knuckle up and thumb under, and the shaft of the paddle with the other hand. If the paddle has a curved blade, you should grip the paddle with the bottom hand so that the blade has the drive (concave) face towards you. Hold the T-grip in one hand; place the other hand so that if the paddle is held horizontal in front of you, your hands are slightly further apart than your shoulders.

Which Side to Paddle On?

Early on in your canoeing career, you are going to have to decide whether you are a leftie or a rightie – that is to say, whether you will paddle on the left-hand

ABOVE *Incorrect technique. The top hand is not over the T-grip and the bottom hand is upside down.*

LEFT *Good paddle hold. The top hand is over the T-grip, the bottom hand is above the gunwale height (thumb at the top), and the paddle shaft is vertical and close to the boat.*

side of the boat or on the right. Most people are able to paddle on either side, but have a preferred side. The only way to find out is by trial and error; whether you are right- or left-handed has very little bearing on the matter.

What is certain is that whichever side you are paddling on, you should try to keep to that grip. It is the principle of canoe paddling, as opposed to kayaking, that you should be able to do everything from one side of the boat, without changing sides. Expert paddlers use cross-bow strokes to put the blade in on the opposite side from their normal paddling side without altering their grip, although some purists claim that even to put the blade in the water on the "off" side is nothing short of bad form. Ultimately, do whatever works for you, but the easiest and most stylish technique is to paddle on the on-side where possible, using a cross-bow stroke or two if necessary.

Using the Paddle

Beginners often find what they imagine to be the easiest tasks actually the trickiest. Using the paddle is a very good example but, by following the guidelines below, and establishing good habits from the start, you should have no problems.

For all paddle strokes you should aim to put the whole of the blade in the water, but no more. There is no advantage to the blade being deeper in the water, and it will not work properly if it is only half in. Put the blade in until it is totally immersed; keep the paddle shaft visible.

When you make a stroke, you should lean forwards to give you as much reach as possible. This also means that much of the power for the stroke will come from your leg and torso muscles, leaving your arm muscles to provide control and react to feedback from the water. It is a misconception to think that canoeing is all about using arm muscles. If your technique is good, a vigorous paddle is more likely to leave you with tired, aching legs and stomach muscles.

The next point that a canoe paddler must concentrate on is head rotation. Before making a stroke, make sure your head is facing in the direction you want to move in. So, with forward paddling, you must look straight ahead at the horizon. If you want to turn the boat to the left or right, first turn your head and shoulders

to look that way. Such movements mean that the whole of your body is part of the stroke-making process. This also helps eliminate bad practices, such as looking at the blade or the end of your boat, neither of which will help your technique.

ABOVE *Paddling with a correctly immersed blade. The whole of the blade area is completely covered but only just, and the paddle shaft is almost vertical. The hand is well clear of the water.*

BELOW *Blade not fully immersed. This will not give you enough grip on the water.*

BELOW *Paddle too deep. Never put the shaft in the water, and certainly not your hand!*

BELOW *Dynamic forward movement starts with good paddling technique. Holding the paddle correctly is a part of this.*

Forward Paddling

A correct forward paddling stroke is a basic requirement if you want to be a good canoeist, but it is not the easiest stroke to master. In addition to the technique for moving forwards, you will inevitably have to learn how to paddle backwards, stop and steer. Learning to combine these techniques is a useful discipline that teaches you control and the ability to respond to feedback from the water. In turn, this will help to make you a really good forward paddler.

The main aim of forward paddling is to propel the boat forwards. It is important to apply as little turning force as possible, since by turning you are making your forward stroke less effective. Normally, if you make a stroke on one side, the boat will move forwards but it will also turn away from the paddle blade that made the stroke. In order to minimize this effect, you should make the stroke as close as you can to the boat, with the paddle shaft as vertical as possible.

If you are paddling a canoe alone, you will also have to use a special technique to keep the boat in a straight line. This is called the J-stroke. If two people are paddling tandem, their paddles will be on opposite sides of the boat, and the J-stroke will not be necessary because their turning effects on opposite sides will cancel each other out.

BELOW The lighter paddler should sit in the front of the boat when paddling tandem.

Tandem Forward Stroke

Begin with both paddlers reaching forwards as far as they can, leaning from the hips without bending the spine forwards. Both should put the blade in the water as far forward as possible, with the drive face pointing back. When the blade is fully immersed, it should be pulled back firmly, using the shoulders and torso, straightening the top arm, and

ABOVE *With a paddle on each side of the boat when tandem paddling, it is easy to propel the canoe in a straight line.*

keeping the T-grip on the side of the boat that the stroke is on. This will make the paddle as vertical as is comfortable.

Continue to pull the blade through the water until it is level with your seat. Try to resist the urge to pull with your bottom arm for as long as possible. When it finally does bend at the elbow, it will be to extract the blade from the water. Aim to keep the blade the same distance from the boat throughout the stroke.

As soon as the blade is out of the water, lean forwards smoothly to begin another stroke. The less time the paddle is out of the water the more control you have, but if you lunge forwards too sharply it will stop the canoe in its tracks.

Canoeists generally paddle on one side of the boat only. There is a stroke that involves reaching across to paddle on the other side, without changing grip, called cross-bow paddling, but this is usually the preserve of white water canoeists.

The J-stroke

This is the cornerstone of canoe paddling. Unless there are two people paddling the canoe on opposite sides, or you have an extremely straight-running craft, you will need this stroke to keep the boat going in a straight line.

The principle of the J-stroke is to perform a normal forward stroke but, at the end of the stroke, when the bottom arm is starting to bend, you must rotate your top hand outwards to point your thumb down. As a result, the drive face of the blade will then turn away from the hull of the canoe. This turns the stroke into a strong rudder, which arrests any turning force you may have inadvertently applied during the stroke. If you hesitate for a moment with the blade in this position, you will also be able to make fine adjustments to your course, by pushing or pulling the blade relative to the hull.

Although this may seem impossible at first, you should practise looking straight ahead in the direction of travel when making the J-stroke, rather than at the paddle itself.

It takes a while to master the J-stroke. Initially it may not seem to work, but persevere and learn to respond to the feedback from the blade. If, once you can do the J-stroke effectively, you find that some boats or conditions still make it difficult to paddle straight, there is a more powerful variation called the C-stroke. This is a J-stroke with a sharp pull of the drive face towards the hull at the very beginning, so that the blade creates a C rather than a J-shape. See the Draw Stroke for more help.

J-stroke Technique

1 Put the paddle in the water as far forward as possible, leaning forward to increase your reach.

2 Push with the top hand rather than pull with the bottom, and use your body as well as your arms.

3 As the blade passes your body, twist the paddle shaft so that your thumbs are pointing down. Unlike this paddler, you should aim to look straight ahead of you.

4 Keep the pressure on the paddle until the end of the stroke or else it won't work. It's a stroke with a twist, not a stroke followed by a stern rudder.

TIPS

• Practise the J-stroke for as long as it takes you to feel comfortable with it: it's key to the good handling and control of a solo canoe.

• Use the J-stroke to keep yourself in line when you are happy with your general direction.

RIGHT *This paddler is using a J-stroke to keep his white water open canoe on course as he moves downstream.*

Backward Paddling and Stopping

Paddling backwards is in principle no different to going forwards, but it is a bit more difficult. Beginners will often try to change their grip on the paddle, which is a mistake – always keep the same grip.

The first thing to note is that you back-paddle using the back of the blade. There is no need to turn the paddle around because any curvature actually helps you do the back stroke. It is bad practice to change your grip. It is not possible to keep the paddle shaft as vertical as you do for forward paddling, or to keep the blade so close to the boat, but you should try to do so as much as possible. Make a big effort to rotate your shoulders as far as you can to place the blade behind you; this also gives you an opportunity to look behind you to see where you are going.

Push your paddle forwards through the water with your arms fairly straight, and make the stroke as long as you can. Most boats will turn during the stroke, so you may have to turn the back face of the

BELOW Look where you are going when paddling backwards in tandem!

blade out at the end of the stroke in a sort of reverse J-stroke, unless there are two of you paddling the canoe. Find somewhere safe where you will not crash into anything, and see how long you can keep going backwards in a straight line. It teaches you excellent control.

Don't be disappointed if you can't paddle backwards very far. It is a difficult technique to pick up, and can take a while to learn properly. Try to be as good at it as you can, but bear in mind that it is usually easier to turn the boat around and paddle forwards instead.

Stopping

Getting an open boat to stop in a straight line is almost impossible because the boat will always turn towards the paddle. If you have room to let the boat turn sideways this will be the safest way to stop. If not, stick the paddle in the water as a brake, and, when the boat turns, use a sweep or pry manoeuvring stroke to keep the boat straight. Repeat as many times as it takes until you are still. Once you have learnt the pries and bow rudder strokes, this will seem a lot easier.

ABOVE *Rotating the shoulders as you place the blade behind you will help you make a more effective back stroke.*

Forward Sweep Stroke

The forward sweep stroke is the simplest and most useful manoeuvring stroke of all. It is used either to turn the boat on the spot, or to make adjustments to your course while moving forwards.

Unlike the technique for forward paddling, sweep strokes are intended to turn the boat as much as possible. Proceed by placing the blade as far forwards as you can, but with the shaft fairly low, and the drive face looking away from the boat. Then rotate your head and shoulders so that they are facing the direction you want to go. Now, keeping your bottom arm straight, sweep the paddle in as wide an arc as your reach allows. When you have turned enough, or the blade is close to hitting the back of the boat, lift it straight out of the water. It helps if you can edge the boat a little, using your legs, so that the side opposite your stroke is raised a little, just for the first half of the stroke.

Unlike a kayak, which can be turned through an angle of 90° or more on the spot, a canoe will only turn between 30° and 40° per stroke. It can also be used to change or correct direction while paddling forwards, by simply inserting one sweep stroke without otherwise breaking the rhythm of your strokes.

RIGHT *Here, the stern paddler is using a sweep stroke to change the direction of the boat on white water. The bow paddler maintains his forward stroke technique.*

Forward Sweep Technique

1 Place the paddle blade as far forward as you can, with the drive face pointing away from the canoe.

2 Look over your shoulder in the direction you want to go, and sweep the blade in a long wide arc.

3 When the blade gets to the back, lift it out of the water before it gets caught and your boat trips over it.

Reverse Sweep Stroke

As the name implies, the reverse sweep stroke is the exact opposite of the forward sweep. In fact, it is a much more powerful stroke, imparting more turning force, but it should not be used while moving forwards unless to turn around and head back in the other direction, because it will effectively arrest all forward motion.

Start with the paddle blade as far back as you can reach, on the side you want to turn towards. Rotate your head and shoulders in this direction. Drop the blade into the water with the drive face towards the boat this time, and then sweep the blade forwards in the widest arc you can make, until you are pointing the way you want to go, or until the blade is about to hit the front of the boat. Lift the blade out of the water.

Again, keep your bottom arm as straight as you can throughout the stroke. It helps to lean dramatically towards the stroke because it simultaneously lifts the keel and extends your reach.

It should be very easy to turn most canoes through more than 45° with one reverse sweep. You will find that once the blade is out of the water, the canoe will continue to rotate.

RIGHT *The reverse sweep is a powerful stroke. It turns the boat so well that it halts all forward progress.*

Reverse Sweep Technique

1 Begin the reverse sweep stroke by leaning back and placing the paddle blade in the water near the stern. The drive face of the blade should be pointing towards the boat.

2 Lean your body towards the paddle and sweep the paddle forward in a big arc towards the front of the boat. Use your body, specifically your torso muscles, not your arms to make the stroke.

3 Continue to lean over towards the paddle, and get all of your weight behind the blade as you push it forward to make the turn. Brace your legs against the sides of the boat to help keep your balance.

Draw Stroke

Few people learn to master this way of moving the boat through the water sideways. While you can manage without being very good at it, learning to do it well helps you master many other skills.

Begin by placing the blade in the water as far from the side of the canoe as you can reach, with the drive face pointing towards the boat. Push your top arm out as far as possible so that the paddle shaft is almost vertical. Now lift the edge of the canoe, using your legs, on the side you are making the stroke, and pull the blade straight towards your body. This should pull the boat sideways about 30cm (12in) in an all-purpose boat, less in a longer boat or one with a deep keel.

Do this gently at first because, as the blade approaches the boat, you need to cock your wrist back quickly to rotate the blade through 90°, and slice it away through the water back to its starting position. If you fail to do this and the blade hits the boat, you may fall in or become unbalanced. If you try to stop the stroke before it hits the hull, the same thing will happen. That is why it is important that you give yourself the time to execute the final part of the stroke.

When the blade has sliced out of the water, and is in the starting position, you can turn your wrist so that the paddle faces the boat as before. Then repeat the stroke. If the boat tends to turn rather

ABOVE *The draw stroke involves pulling the paddle sideways towards the boat.*

ABOVE *Applying a twist to a bow draw can turn the boat and move it sideways.*

than move sideways, it is because the stroke is being made too far towards the front or back of the boat. If the bow turns towards the paddle, move the stroke back a little, or vice versa for the stern. It will improve your skills if you make this happen deliberately; practise doing draw strokes, alternating with the bow or stern pointing forwards.

The draw stroke, also known as a hanging draw support, is very good for giving you support in the event of

a wobble or imminent capsize. When you have some purchase on the water with the blade, level the boat, and pull the boat into position beneath your body.

The technique needs to be practised over and over again, otherwise, by the time you will have thought about it, it will be too late to use it; you need to be able to use it reflexively. Being able to control your boat in three dimensions is very satisfying. Mastering these strokes will really set you on your way as a canoeist.

Draw Stroke Technique

1 Reach out as far to the side as you can, with the blade facing the boat. Bend at the waist to increase your reach. Leaning the boat away from the paddle actually helps, but it is very unstable.

2 Pull the paddle firmly towards you, keeping the blade fully immersed in the water. Continue to lean the boat away from the paddle if you feel confident enough to maintain your balance.

3 Lean the boat back towards the paddle. If your body weight is not inside the boat by the time the blade gets level with the hull, you could fall into the water. Twist the blade 90° and slice away from the boat.

Stern Rudder

The stern rudder, and also the bow rudder, will change the direction of your boat. Both strokes require the boat to be moving in order to be effective.

Sometimes it is desirable to make small direction changes, or to keep a canoe going in a straight line in readiness for a turn. For this, and many of the more advanced skills, the stern rudder is a very useful stroke.

As the term implies, the paddle blade is used as a rudder at the stern of the boat. Place the paddle in the water as for the start of a reverse sweep stroke, with the drive face pointing towards the boat and the paddle shaft at a low angle. Both your arms will probably be fairly straight. If the boat is not moving this will have no effect at all, but if you have some forward momentum the boat will probably turn slightly towards the paddle.

When you move the paddle away from the hull, the turn will become more pronounced; bring it closer to the hull and there will be less effect. By pulling it in towards the boat you may even start to turn the other way, away from the paddle. If you get up to speed, and then place your stern rudder in the water, you

BELOW *The stern rudder is a passive stroke that is used to correct direction and to keep the boat running straight.*

can experiment with pushing and pulling, and get the boat to veer to and fro until it runs out of momentum, without taking the blade out of the water. You will find this a very useful way to get used to the feedback from the paddle.

A handy technique is to approach a landing place perpendicular to the shore, using a stern rudder to keep the boat pointing at the spot where you want to land. Seconds before the bow touches the bank, sweep your stern rudder forwards in a reverse sweep to turn the boat 90° and kill your speed. You will end

ABOVE *The canoe needs to be moving for the stern rudder to be effective.*

up stationary and parallel to the shore, close enough to get out with ease.

Always think about the next strokes you need to make. When going forwards followed by a turn, use strokes such as the forward sweep that will not impede your forward motion. If trying to stop and turn, the reverse sweep may be better. Note that the stern rudder does not propel you, and has little effect on your speed except to interrupt your paddling.

Bow Rudder

The bow rudder, unlike the stern rudder, is a very difficult stroke to learn. It is appropriate to mention it now, but you may find it difficult to make it work until you have mastered all the other strokes in this section. It relies on an excellent feel for what the paddle is doing in the water, and the draw stroke skills that have already been covered. The bow rudder is only effective if the boat is already moving forwards.

Place the paddle in the water about 30cm (12in) from the side of the canoe, about level with your knees and with the drive face pointing towards the boat. Experiment, rotating your wrists to turn the blade slightly, but resist any forces that act on the blade in the water. You will

ABOVE *A bow rudder while moving fast, requires commitment and a willingness to resist the force of the water against the paddle blade.*

LEFT *Wrapping the top arm around in front of the paddle helps to rotate the paddle blade to face the bow.*

find that there is a position with the blade face almost parallel to the side of the boat in which the boat does not tend to slow or turn, and you cannot feel any pressure on the blade.

Next, turn the blade to face the bow, and the boat will start to turn towards the paddle. Bring your top hand and T-grip back until it is near your opposite shoulder. The more you roll your bottom wrist back to open out the blade, the more you will turn, but there will be a lot of force on the blade and the boat will quickly stop.

Bow Draw

You can increase the effect of the bow rudder by letting the pressure take the blade out, and then pulling it back towards the bow in a modified draw stroke. This is called a bow draw. It is a versatile canoe stroke whether you are moving or stationary. By experimenting, you will find that you can control the boat in many subtle ways, either by going with the water or by opposing it.

Sculling

The sculling strokes are refinements of the basic strokes, and will allow you much more subtle control of your boat.

Sculling Draw

The sculling draw, like the draw stroke, moves the boat sideways. It has the advantage, however, of being more useful in a confined space. For instance, when you are close to a jetty, and need to get even closer, the draw stroke may be difficult to execute. The sculling draw is also a lot less likely to tip you in.

Start with the paddle blade next to your hip, about 20cm (8in) from the boat, the shaft vertical and the drive face towards the hull. Cock your wrist back so that the blade face rotates 20° and opens out a little towards the bow.

Keep the shaft vertical and move the paddle forwards as far as you can, but keep it 20cm (8in) from the boat, and

ABOVE *You need to put the whole of the blade in the water for a sculling draw. A blade that is only half immersed just won't work at all.*

ABOVE *Sculling right next to your body, as here, will move the boat sideways. Sculling slightly behind you will turn the boat away from the paddle.*

Sculling Draw Technique

1 With your wrist rolled back, push the blade forwards through the water.

2 Take the stroke as far forwards as is comfortable for you.

3 Now, cock your wrist the other way and bring the blade backwards.

4 Push the blade back to the start position and repeat until the boat moves sideways.

resist its tendency to slice away from the hull. If anything, you will be pulling it inwards, which is where the sideways motion of the boat is generated. When the blade gets as far forward as possible, keep the shaft vertical, rotate your wrist the other way to angle the drive face 20° towards the stern, and pull the blade back as far as you can. At this point, rotate again to push forward, maintaining enough pressure on the blade to keep it equidistant from the boat at all times.

As you move the paddle, the boat will move sideways towards the stroke. It helps to lean towards the paddle and to lift the leading edge of the boat.

Sculling Pry

Reversing the blade angles, so that the pressure is on the outside (back) face, moves the boat sideways away from the paddle in a sculling pry. Like the sculling draw, the sculling pry exerts a continuous sideways force. Unlike the draw, the pry pushes the boat away from the blade. Sculling further forward will pull the boat bow-first in the direction of travel, while sculling further back will bring the stern around first. In this way, you can move and turn the boat at the same time.

Pry Stroke

A pry is a stroke that pushes the blade away from the canoe. It is so-called because it usually involves resting the paddle shaft against the gunwale of the boat, using it as a fulcrum or pivot as you lever the blade up and out. The basic pry is the opposite of the draw stroke, and pushes the boat through the water, away from the paddle.

Start with the blade next to the hull, the drive face in and the shaft in a vertical position. Then jam the paddle shaft against the boat and lever the blade away from you. As with the draw, when the stroke reaches the limit of its motion, you must rotate the blade 90° in order to slice it back to where it started. The sculling pry is a continuous version of the basic pry. It is used to push the boat sideways away from the paddle.

In the same way that a draw stroke can lend support, you can use a pry as a support stroke to lever the high (opposite) side of the boat down if there is going to be an imminent capsize on the side away from the paddle. This is very useful when you remember that you only paddle on one side, and you will not always capsize conveniently towards the paddle.

ABOVE *Using a pry. Although it may be difficult at first, try to look where you are going, and not at the prying blade.*

Go carefully when you first start to use pries. Until you have learnt excellent edge control, using your legs and knees, there will be a tendency to overdo it and lever yourself right into the water. You need to balance the boat, so that the power of the stroke is turned into a lateral motion and not a capsizing one.

TIPS
• Proceed cautiously at first.
• Concentrate on keeping the boat level with your legs.
• Experiment with prying at different parts of the boat to get used to the turning effect.
• Look in the direction of the turn and not at the blade or you risk catching the blade on the boat.

Pry Stroke Technique

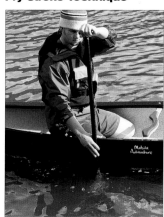

1 To begin the stroke, wedge the paddle shaft flush against the side of the boat. The blade should be just immersed in the water.

2 Lever the blade away from the boat, bracing your legs against the sides and edging the boat to keep the canoe level in the water.

3 Turn the paddle blade in the water through 90° to slice it back to the start point. Repeat until the boat has moved to face the direction you want.

Low and High Brace

The low and high brace are support or recovery strokes that are used to help you regain your balance when you are about to capsize. All support strokes require a willing suspension of disbelief. It is initially difficult to believe that you can trust most of your weight to a paddle blade, but this is exactly what you must do. The weight that you commit to the paddle is exactly how much support you will get in reaction to it.

Low Brace

The low brace gives support from the back of the blade. Place the blade on the surface with the drive face pointing up. If you are moving, angle the leading edge up slightly to stop it diving. It is usually easier to low brace with the blade just behind you, but the further it can be from the boat while staying fairly flat to the surface, the better the result.

Commit your weight to the blade and it will support you, and stop you from capsizing on that side, until the blade sinks too far into the water to keep it flat. When using the low brace to prevent a capsize, you must use your legs to level the boat before the paddle sinks, then recover the blade. If the boat is moving,

a low brace can be used instead of a stern rudder to turn the boat, while also providing some support.

High Brace

This works on the same principle as the low brace, but with the drive face pointing downward. Because of this, your elbows are below the paddle shaft, which implies that the water is higher than the boat, either because of a wave or because you are in danger of capsizing. In a canoe this means that water will be entering the boat, so it is an extreme measure. The high brace is a powerful stroke, but should be avoided if a low brace is possible because of the

ABOVE *The canoe has tipped over until it is in danger of shipping water, and the paddler will recover using the support of the blade in a low brace.*

huge force it exerts on your shoulders, which can lead to serious injury.

As with any support stroke, keep your weight on the paddle until you can right the boat with your legs, then move your body back over the boat. Don't allow the paddle to take your weight if it is above your head because you risk an injury. It is better to capsize and recover by rolling.

BELOW *Bracing in white water. The recovery is often so extreme that it is almost a roll.*

Tandem Manoeuvres

Open canoes are ideally suited to being paddled by two or more canoeists. Tandem paddling removes a lot of the problems of steering and straight paddling. Communication is the key, however, and a constant dialogue is necessary to keep things running smoothly. Usually, the paddler at the back is in command because the back paddler can see what the front paddler is doing, and needs this information. The stern paddler will also have more effect on steering.

When forward paddling, both canoeists should paddle on opposite sides, so there is no need for J-strokes. Concentrate on keeping the strokes in time. This also applies when going back, when the stern paddler will have to look alternately over his shoulder (to check the direction) and back (to keep time with the other paddler).

Turning In Tandem

1 While the canoe is moving forward, the front paddler plants a bow rudder stroke in the water.

2 As the boat turns, the rear paddler uses a forward sweep stroke to maintain the momentum of the turn.

3 The front paddler keeps leaning on the bow rudder, and can if required turn it into a bow draw.

4 The rear paddler can either finish with a stern draw stroke, or can start forward paddling again, as appropriate.

ABOVE *A tandem turn towards the front off-side can be done while the boat is stationary or going forwards.*

To turn a canoe in tandem, a rudder stroke at the back can be combined with a bow draw at the front to bring the boat around quickly. If turning on the spot, the front paddler can do a forward sweep and the back paddler a reverse sweep on the opposite side, or vice versa.

TIPS

• Agree who is in charge before you get into the boat: squabbling about it mid-route is guaranteed to cause you difficulties. If the bow paddler is making the turning decisions, the stern paddler should follow and complement those decisions, and vice versa.
• The strokes of a tandem pair need to complement each other. To understand the importance of each paddler's strokes, it is a useful exercise to spend some practice time swapping positions, so that both paddlers can be aware of the needs of their other half at the opposite end of the boat.

KAYAK AND CANOE ROLLING

Rolling is the art of righting a kayak or canoe unaided while still inside it. Only 20 years ago, any paddler who could complete an Eskimo roll would be regarded as an expert boater. Nowadays, rolling has become a basic skill learnt by almost everybody who goes out in a boat, even before they are very skilled at anything else.

It is possible to roll almost any canoe or kayak that you can grip well enough with your legs to ensure that you do not fall out, but clearly this skill is only of use if the boat will still be paddleable afterwards. There is little point in rolling an open boat without airbags, or a kayak without a spraydeck, because you will not be able to paddle (or indeed, balance) until you have emptied out the water.

Most paddlers learn to roll in a kayak, but there is no technical reason why you cannot learn with a single blade if canoe paddling is your one and only interest. The techniques may be quite different, but the essential principle is just the same.

LEFT *An open-boat canoeist finishing a roll in turbulent white water.*

BELOW *Preparing to roll an open canoe. This is the typical start position for a canoe roll.*

The History of the Roll

If it was not for the Inuit tribesman, who needed to right his boat without exiting to avoid swimming in icy seas, we might have had to wait a lot longer before rolling caught on.

Righting a capsized boat by rolling, without having to get out, was exclusively a kayak skill until the latter part of the twentieth century. It was invented by the Inuit tribes of sub-Arctic regions who paddled in such extremely cold seas that, had they tried to swim for safety from a capsized kayak, they would have almost certainly died. By wearing a kayaking jacket (tuvilik) of sealskin, laced on to the boat, with only hands and face exposed, the hunters could survive immersion if capsized, provided they could quickly roll up again. For this reason the skill was often called the Eskimo roll, though that term has now been abbreviated to the roll.

The first written account of rolling, by a missionary in 1765, lists about ten different techniques and drills, and is interesting because it cites a flick of the hips as the means used to right the kayak in each case. This trick is the key to effective rolling, and was overlooked by Europeans until as late as 1965.

The first non-Inuit paddler who learnt to roll was probably a curate named Pawlata, a Christian missionary to the Inuit in 1927. The Inuit had a wide variety of advanced rolling techniques that they would practise during the summer months to ensure survival in the freezing winter conditions. The skills Pawlata acquired were very basic and his technique was crude, but he took the idea of rolling back with him to Europe, and the method of kayak rolling known as the Pawlata roll is still used today as a stepping stone

to more involved rolling techniques.

Rolling did not become a viable skill for white water paddling until the mid-1960s and the introduction of the more robust kayaks. Until then, spending any time upside down in white water damaged the kayak. With the advent of fibreglass craft, however, reliable rolling became the goal for any adventurous kayak paddler or decked canoeist. Before long, airbags in open boats in white water made rolling also practical for open canoeists.

Now regarded as an essential skill for anything more advanced than placid water paddling, the roll has been refined to the point that it surpasses even the skills of the Inuit. The latest innovations in boat design have led to a degree of

BELOW *Rolling up in a capsized sea kayak, using the screw roll technique.*

ABOVE *Rolling up from a capsize in an ultra-low-volume kayak. With good technique you can roll any canoe or kayak.*

RIGHT *Rolling a hi-volume general purpose kayak – notice that the head stays in the water until the boat is almost upright.*

control and body fit that could barely have been imagined even a decade ago, and this has aided the development of some of the rolling skills that follow.

In the chapter that follows, we look at how to learn to roll. The hip-flick concept is constantly reiterated because it is a key element in any roll. Described thereafter are a number of different rolling styles, in roughly the order of difficulty that dictates how they should be tackled. Conspicuous by their absence are many of the "extended grip" techniques that were at one time the most usual starting point. These are not so relevant now that better rolling methods have been developed.

Learning to Roll

The indispensable, essential roll may look quite daunting, and even dangerous, but once you have grasped the basic technique, it is actually surprisingly easy.

The best place to learn to roll is in warm, clean, calm water, where a helper or instructor is able to stand waist-deep beside your boat. A swimming pool is often the best place, although repeatedly capsizing in chlorinated water may become unpleasant. If it is possible to learn in warm sea or fresh water, do so.

Unlike the majority of paddling skills, rolling is not particularly reliant on feedback from the paddle. Instead, you must master a special sequence of actions that need to be timed correctly. As with learning to juggle, each action flows on to the next. With regular practice it becomes second nature. You just think "Roll!", and you are up.

There are a few key tips of which you need to be aware before you start to practise rolling. First, successful rolling is never about heaving yourself up with the paddle. Second, the point of the exercise

RULES OF ROLLING — 5 KEY TIPS

• Never try to get your body up out of the water first. Concentrate on righting the boat with your hips and legs.
• Your head should always be the last part of your body to emerge out of the water.
• Go with the flow. As a general rule, always roll up on the downstream side in moving water, or on the upwave side if you are sideways on to a wave in the surf.
• Have a sense of urgency, and roll quickly, as soon as you can. If it does not work, switch sides straight away because you are probably turning the wrong way.
• If you nearly succeed with a screw roll, it is the perfect moment to dive into a reverse screw roll the other way. The reverse screw roll is nearly always the best exit from a convoluted screw roll, but not vice versa.

is to right the boat, not get your head out of the water. Third, the more of you that is in the water, the more support you will get from your natural buoyancy, so right the boat first, then let your body follow. Your head will always come out last.

Initially, your desire to breathe and perhaps your determination to succeed will make you try to get your head up out of the water. This is quite natural. Your instincts and reflexes are programmed to get your head above water at all costs. You need to stop being a human in a boat, and imagine yourself as a different creature with a hull instead of legs.

The whole principle of rolling is that, with a little support from the paddle (in the manner of a high or low brace or a sculling technique), you will be able to turn the boat up the right way using your legs. Once the boat is righted, it is a simple matter for you to sit upright and paddle away. But you must right the boat before you can afford to worry about getting your body out of the water.

There are different ways of rolling, and which one you use should be decided by your position under the water, and where your paddle has ended up. It is definitely worth trying to learn all the techniques described here, but the best roll to master first is the screw roll. This is the one roll that no paddler can do without; in fact, many paddlers don't ever learn anything else.

ABOVE *When a capsize is inevitable, a paddler sets up a reverse screw roll as he tips over.*

ABOVE *Rolling up on the downstream side. The boat is righted with the hips and legs.*

BELOW *As the boat rolls up, the body barely moves and the head comes out last.*

Kayak Rolling Drills

The best way to become proficient at rolling is to practise the following six drills. The drills are aimed at beginners, and will take you through each stage, building your confidence and improving your technique until you are ready to attempt the screw roll, which is the one key roll that no paddler can do without.

The fundamental principle of rolling is that you can right the boat by flicking it upright with your hips. This movement is known as the hip flick, or snap, and it is the most important part of any roll. In fact, the motion really comes from the waist. If you bend rapidly to one side, your body will stay still and the boat will twist the other way. That is the secret of rolling.

It is extremely difficult to roll a boat if you do not fit it properly. If borrowing a boat, try to acquire some padding in the form of foam or a purpose-made padding kit. Make sure there is a footrest, too, because it is difficult to brace without one. And do not forget your spraydeck!

Drill 1: Familiarization

This drill helps counter confusion when you are upside down, but you will need an experienced guide to assist you. The helper should stand beside the boat in waist-deep water. You sit in your kayak, and put your hands by your sides. Then capsize, and your helper will grasp the far side of the boat and pull you upright. Do this until you feel completely comfortable, and then progress to the next stage.

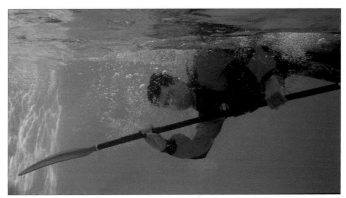

TOP *An underwater view of a screw roll. The paddler bends his trunk to get his head near the surface, but he stays in the boat until it is righted.*

ABOVE *An underwater view of a reverse screw roll. The paddler is about to start the roll by sweeping the paddle blade forwards towards the camera.*

Familiarization

1 Start off sitting upright with your hands on either side of the boat. Next, capsize towards your helper.

2 Once you are upside down, the helper reaches over the boat and flips it upright. Do not try to move your arms and legs.

3 After a few attempts, you will find that you are not disorientated by flipping 360°, and can progress to drill 2.

Drill 2: Hip Flick

The next step is to hold on to the pool rail or a partner's hands or paddle for support, and practise righting the boat with the hip flick. This allows you to concentrate on the flick movement, without worrying about holding your paddle.

Practise rotating your hips from side to side, making sure that you feel quite free and will not hurt yourself. Get a good grip on whatever you are using for support, capsize and relax your arms so that they are not supporting your weight. Bend your body up towards your hands as far as possible without using your arms.

You must now try to turn the boat up the right way using your hips and legs, without trying to lift your body out of the water. Remember, no matter what else happens, keep your head in the water until the boat is upright and capable of supporting your weight.

Hip Flick Practice Using the Pool Rail or Side

1 Holding on to the pool rail, position your body just under the water surface rather than hanging straight downwards.

2 Flick the boat upright with your knees and hips, leaving your head in the water. Repeat several times.

Hip Flick Practice with a Helper

1 Holding on to the hands of your helper, practise flicking the boat upright using your legs. Keep your head submerged.

2 At the end of the manoeuvre, the boat should be completely righted but your head should still be in the water, as here.

ABOVE *Practise the rolling drills as often as necessary to build your confidence.*

Drill 3: Using a Float

The next step is to repeat the same technique, using a swimming float or life jacket that affords much less support. This will show you whether you are really righting the boat with a hip flick from the waist, or whether you are relying too much on your arms. When you can right yourself using only a float, it is time to try rolling with a paddle.

TIPS

• Practise using whatever resources you have at your disposal on the day.
• Never practise alone: there should be someone to help in an emergency.
• If using a fixed platform, make sure you can't get stuck underneath it.
• If you are not able to practise with a swimming float you can skip drill 3, but make sure your other drills emphasize righting the boat only with the hips and legs, and not the arms.
• Do each drill perfectly ten times before you move on.
• If you are not proficient at one of the drills, go back two stages and start again from there.

Drill 4: Bow Rescue

This final confidence-building exercise is excellent rolling practice, and a useful technique when recovering from an accidental capsize if you fail to roll or lose your paddle.

First, capsize. When you are under the water, tuck your body forward into a safe position. Bang your hands on the bottom or sides of the boat to attract attention. Then push your hands up as far as possible out of the water on both sides of the boat, and sweep them forward and back to indicate that you are hoping to be rescued. A rescuer in a boat should now approach, their bow touching the side of your boat. One of your sweeping arms will make contact with the rescuer's boat. Grab it with both hands, and then use a hip flick to recover.

RIGHT *The bow rescue technique will save you from an uncomfortable swim in the event of a rolling mishap, which can happen to anyone from time to time.*

Bow Rescue Technique

1 The paddler is capsizing and unable to roll. This is a problem situation and the paddler needs to be helped.

2 Upside down, the paddler bangs on the boat to attract attention, then sweeps his hands to and fro on both sides of the boat.

3 A rescuer approaches and slowly moves the bow of their boat into the path of the sweeping hands.

4 On making contact with the rescue boat, the upside-down paddler grips the bow with both hands.

5 He then uses a hip flick to right the boat, putting as little weight as possible on the rescuer's boat.

6 The paddler then sits up, ready to retrieve his paddle and continue with the trip down the river.

Drill 5: Using a Paddle with an Instructor Helping

Now it is time to try to use one of the rolls described in the following pages. Some older books suggest learning to roll with a different grip on the paddle from the one you normally have when upright. This may have some advantages, but modern boats and paddles are not really suitable. And remember, rolling relies on the hip flick concept, not on the paddle. If you cannot roll using your normal paddling style, there is something wrong with your hip flick, and there is no point in practising a bad technique masquerading as a success.

Begin by asking someone to stand in shallow water and help you, and then decide which of the rolls you are going to try. For the screw roll, which most people learn first, place the paddle in the set-up position and capsize.

ABOVE *The set-up position for a screw roll. This is the position you will need to get into under water, from which to start.*

As you bring the paddle into position to start the roll, the helper will take hold of the blade and keep it on the surface while still allowing you to move it. You can then roll up according to your chosen method, with your helper's primary task being to ensure that you will make it if it goes wrong, and to work out whether the way you are moving the paddle is helping or hindering you. It is no use you trying to work out what you did with your paddle, because you were under the water, holding your breath, and you don't know what it is supposed to feel like anyway. An experienced helper will be able to tell you what to concentrate on. The most common problems are that the paddler is pulling on the paddle with their arms, which never works; or that the paddler is sweeping the blade correctly but the blade is angled in a way that doesn't offer much support.

Rolling with Help Using a Paddle

1 From the starting point of the set-up position, capsize with your helper standing on the other side from your paddle set-up.

2 The helper can give you a push to make sure you capsize quickly.

3 Bring the paddle into the start position. The helper takes hold of the paddle blade to add a little support.

4 Get your body as near to the surface of the water as you can without needing any support from the helper. Do not use the paddle for support.

5 Start your roll from this position, with the helper holding on to the blade but providing only as much support as is absolutely necessary.

6 The helper will be ready to catch you if you fall back into the water, but with a bit of luck you will finish the roll perfectly on your own, like this.

Drill 6: Using a Paddle Unaided

This is the stage that you are aiming for on the open water, but for now you still need to have a helper standing by to flip you up if required. Do not try to visualize the whole roll but get into the correct position, and then flick the boat upright. Everything else will happen naturally. If it does not, either your set-up is not right or your hip flick is not good enough: keep practising the early drills.

TIPS

• Get into the start position, pause, then do the hip flick: don't think about anything else.
• If it doesn't work at first, go back to basics and make sure you can do drills 1 to 5 in turn. Try drill 6 again.
• Ask your helper to guide your paddle blade through the sweep.
• If you succeed, well done, but make sure you are rolling using your body and not your paddle, or else the roll won't work when you need it.

RIGHT *Rolling an inflatable kayak, or "duckie", relies more on the paddle because the paddler is less secure than in a rigid kayak.*

Rolling Unaided Using a Paddle

1 First you need to capsize, ready to roll on your own. You may find the capsize quite slow. Just keep the paddle close to the boat and wait.

2 Rolling up for the first time. The paddle has gone very deep without support from the helper, but the boat is coming up and the head is still in the water.

3 Completing the roll. Because the body language was good, the roll has worked despite the poor paddle action. This has been a very good first attempt.

Screw Roll

This is the most common practical roll of all. Many very proficient paddlers find they can get along using this as their only roll.

Begin the roll by placing the paddle in the water, along the side of the boat, with the water blade at the bow. The water blade is the blade in the water, used for the rolling stroke, while the other is the air blade. If you are rolling up on your right, the water blade will be the right blade. Tuck your body forward and up, facing the surface of the water on the side that the paddle is on. Next, push the air blade up out of the water as far as possible and then wrap your back arm around the hull of the boat.

This might push the water blade down below the surface, but it does not really matter. Try to keep the blade as near to the surface as possible. This starting position virtually guarantees you a good blade presentation as you roll.

ABOVE *Once underwater, tuck your body forwards and up, facing the surface.*

Sweep the blade away from the boat, without pulling down on the blade. As the blade comes to the perpendicular, bend from the waist to throw your upper body into the water, and continue to sweep backwards. Continue with the bend – do not stop. You will come up leaning back, with the blade near the back of its arc.

ABOVE *Push the air blade up out of the water as far as you can.*

The screw roll is very reliable because the blade gives you plenty of lift for a long time. It is also a good roll to use if you are tired. However, the set-up from which you start is time-consuming and you rarely capsize with your blades in this position. The final position is not possible in a weight-sensitive, modern short boat.

Screw Roll Technique

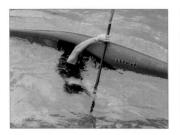

1 To practise the screw-roll, set up with your top arm straight and the paddle along the side of the boat like this.

2 Capsize on the paddle side of the boat. Wait until you are completely upside down and the boat has stopped moving.

3 Wrap your back arm (which is on the left here) around the boat. You should still be holding the paddle with both hands.

4 Sweep the paddle blade in a big sweeping arc across the surface of the water, reaching as far as you can.

5 Arch your back to try to throw your head downwards, and right the boat with your legs only.

6 Keeping your head down in the water, continue to sweep the blade back until you are sure you are upright again.

Reverse Screw Roll

This is a favourite with freestyle paddlers and surfers because it begins on the back deck, which is where you will often end up after being hit by a big wave. Surprising as it may seem, you can still find yourself in the set-up position after falling over your blade while trying to do something dynamic.

Start by lying on your back as shown, and wrap your back (water blade) arm around in front of your face so that the paddle lies along the deck. Remember to keep your water blade to the stern and your air blade to the bow, which is the hard part of this roll. Now, capsize in that position so that you are lying face down in the water.

Next, twist your body out to that side, pushing the water blade out as far as you can, and try to get the air blade up and out of the water. Bending from the waist, use your body to sweep the water blade

forward. As this happens, snap your body downwards to the right of the boat. You will have to cock your water-blade wrist back slightly to stop the blade diving during the stroke. Continue the sweep forwards, and you will emerge on the front deck, with lots of support from the paddle, which will now be beneath you.

Since you may often find yourself in the start position by accident, you may as well use this roll. It is immensely powerful if you do it correctly, and you can get away with rolling at a bad time or in a bad place. Be careful, though, because this roll exposes your face to submerged objects. From a freestyle point of view, lying on the back deck in a big water feature will either ruin your manoeuvre, give you a good thrashing, or both.

RIGHT *This should be the position of your paddle and body when capsized.*

Reverse Screw Roll Technique

1 To practise the reverse screw, wind your arms and paddle up like this and capsize towards the paddle.

2 Use your body to sweep the water blade away from the boat.

3 It helps to wrap the air blade arm around the hull of the boat like this as you sweep the water blade.

4 Drive the water blade forward using your body, and flick the boat upright with both of your legs.

5 Bend your head and body downwards as you come back up to the surface of the water.

6 When you come out of the roll you should be leaning forward with your head tucked down. You are ready to paddle off.

Put Across Roll

Also known as the combat roll, the put across roll is far more solid than the previous two rolls, but unfortunately you really need to learn the others first. Once you've mastered all three, you'll probably find yourself using the put across (combat) roll in combination with some elements of the others, according to your circumstances.

Begin by pushing the air blade out of the water. Swing the water blade away from the boat until it's as perpendicular to the kayak as possible. Do not lean forwards or back, just bend sideways until your body is as near the surface as possible. Now, do a hip snap – hurl your upper body down into the water, and snap the boat upright with your legs. Keep your head down, face down.

If your body was bent to the left at the start, you just have to bend it as far to the right as you can, and as fast as you can.

Do not do anything with the paddle except keep the drive face down, and do not move fore or aft. You will be up in a sudden snap, on a really solid brace.

It is quite hard to keep your paddle near the surface for this roll, but it does not matter. Even coming up on a vertical blade is acceptable, and often puts you in an excellent position for paddling again.

This is an exceptionally quick, powerful roll, and enables you to stay in the centre of the boat. It is good for a position in a hole, and means you are ready for another move if freestyle paddling. Since the paddle position is not critical, you can roll straightaway without having to flail around underwater. The power of the roll is especially suited to today's wide white water boats, in which you need to do the roll quickly or you will not succeed. You do need quite a bit of sideways flexibility, but with practice that is achievable.

You can modify this freestyle roll to make it a super combat roll. Just lean ridiculously far forwards, so that your nose is on the deck. Keep your arms and paddle forward, too, and do the roll across the front deck without sitting up until you are upright. It is more of an upper body snap than a hip flick, but if you can do the freestyle version you will not find it hard to master this one. It is nearly as powerful, and protects your face from any impact in shallow water.

If you are in a position to start a screw roll, the combat roll is just the same without the sweeping of the paddle, and with the body modified to move across the boat only. If, on the other hand, you are on the back deck, as for a reverse screw roll (this is much more common), then you can begin as for a reverse screw and convert to a put across roll as you get the paddle to the perpendicular.

Put Across (Combat) Roll Technique

1 Begin from the same set-up position as for a screw roll. Capsize with the paddle along the side of the boat.

2 When you are completely upside down and the boat has stopped moving, push the paddle up above the water.

3 Bend your body up sideways, so that you are as near to the surface as you possibly can be.

4 Plant the paddle so that the drive face is pointing down, then bend your body aggressively down on the other side.

5 Concentrate on levelling the boat by bracing your legs. Your head will come out of the water as the boat levels off.

6 Finish upright, and keep both your hands on the paddle if you are not practising in a swimming pool.

Hand Rolling

The following rolls are quite sophisticated, and can only be approached when you have acquired all the preceding skills.

The front and back deck hand rolls have a variety of benefits, the main one being that they will hone and fine-tune your paddling skills for more advanced future techniques. Hand rolls are a useful and advanced skill. Many instructors would claim that you should never have to use a hand roll, but it can save you a long and unpleasant swim if you are unfortunate enough to drop your paddle.

Furthermore, it is an excellent training exercise to ensure that your roll is not over-reliant on the paddle. This is a weakness in many people's rolling technique, and can mean that when tired or in very turbulent water their roll will fail them just when they need it most. It is a good idea, therefore, to work on a solid hand roll in both the forms described

here, thereby improving your technique for the main types of paddle rolls.

The best way to learn to hand roll is to build up to using less and less support. In the same way that you built up the six drills when you first learnt to roll, practise initially by holding on to the pool rail or a partner's hands, focusing on putting less and less weight on the hands and righting the boat just with your hips. Then try with a flotation device in your hands, and after that, a swimming float, until you can right yourself with your only support being your cupped hands in the water.

Back Deck Hand Roll

This is the easiest way to hand roll. Lean back and out to the side as you would for a reverse screw roll, and reach out to the same side with both hands, palms facing downwards. Bend up to the surface as much as you can. When you are fully

extended in this position, sweep your hands downwards to lend support, and simultaneously hip flick as hard as you can. Arch your body back as you do so, keeping your centre of gravity as near to the boat as you can. Since your top arm will not be able to remain in the water for the whole move, throw it across to the other side as you come up, and this will help balance the boat in the slightly tenuous finish position.

The back deck hand roll is easier to perform in many boats than the front deck variant, mainly because lying on the back deck gives you such a low centre of gravity. It is possible to succeed even if you are quite lazy about it. However, as with the screw roll, the finish position of the back deck hand roll is rather unstable, and the slightly more difficult front deck hand roll will be much more practical in a genuine emergency situation.

Back Deck Hand Roll Technique

1 Start the manoeuvre by capsizing into the water, leaning back a little, with your body leaning to one side.

2 Keep your body turned to face the water as you go over.

3 Maintaining this position under the water, reach out to the side with your cupped hands.

4 Sweep your hands downwards and keep them together, and use hip rotation to right the boat.

5 Arch your back and throw your top arm across the boat for balance as the boat rights itself.

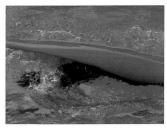

6 Finish the roll by leaning back on the deck, with a hand in the water on each side of the kayak.

Front Deck Hand Roll

This very useful hand roll relies on the hip flick, mobility and timing. It utilizes the technique used for the put across roll.

Bend up to the side to bring your head as close to the surface as possible, but do not lean back. Rotate your upper body so that you are facing downwards. Reach out to the side as far away from the boat as you can, hands cupped and palms down. Then sweep the hands down into the water using your torso as well as your arms, and hip flick aggressively. This time you will come up with both hands still in the water on the same side of the boat, but it may help to switch one hand across right at the end to help you keep your balance.

With this and the back deck hand roll, even more than rolling with your paddle, it is essential that your head stays in the water until the roll is effectively finished. This demands commitment and a good

level of flexibility, but the roll will never work if you have to support the weight of your upper body as it gets out of the water – your hands simply do not provide enough lift.

It is fairly easy to hand roll narrow boats such as those used for slalom and polo, and some fast sea kayaks. However, the modern general-purpose kayak is wide and flat-bottomed, and is generally hard to right only using your hands. It is best, therefore, to learn in a pool using an easy boat such as the polo kayak.

With either the front or back deck hand rolls, you will find that the more complex hand movement is better than slamming the hands straight down. Imagine that you were swimming in a "doggy paddle" style: this helps you to reach out further and sweep a more efficient arc. In addition, if one hand paddles slightly after the other, this extends the amount of time that you have support during the roll. Try sweeping

ABOVE *Underwater shot of the start position for the front and back deck hand rolls.*

the top arm first, which makes sense, since as you roll up the top arm won't be able to reach the water. Alternatively, you can try sweeping the bottom arm first and getting in three strokes with your hands (bottom, top, bottom). Remember to hip flick as soon as the first stroke gets a hold of the water.

Front Deck Hand Roll Technique

1 Start the maneuvre by turning your whole body to one side of the boat to face the water and capsizing.

2 As soon as you are underwater, you need to reach out as far as you can away from the boat.

3 Sweep both your hands downwards and hip flick hard to rotate the boat.

4 Keep both your hands moving downwards and continue the hip flick for as long as you can.

5 Drop your head forward on to the spraydeck (spray skirt).

6 Complete the roll with your head and body tucked forward, as shown. Your arms should be wrapped around the boat.

Canoe Rolling

The technique for rolling a decked canoe would be essentially the same as for a kayak, but using a canoe paddle means you can only use the normal rolls on one side. Many canoe paddlers change their grip if they need to roll on the other side, but this has several disadvantages, especially in turbulent water. It would be very easy to lose the paddle, and a better solution is to learn a cross-bow roll. In this roll you flip over the paddle blade in mid-roll to keep it flat on the water, a useful skill that eradicates much of the vulnerability of canoe paddling. If you are learning to roll an open boat, some of the positions are a little different because it is not possible to reach over the hull of the boat. It is also difficult to finish the roll because the boat is very wide and unstable when it is on its side.

ABOVE *Underwater view of the start position for a canoe roll.*

ABOVE *Rolling up: the canoe is on its side but the paddler's body is underwater.*

Most open canoe paddlers use a roll that is somewhere between a reverse screw roll and a put across roll, because to finish leaning forwards is a more tenable position in an open boat. If you are paddling a decked canoe, any kayak roll would be suitable. Once you are confident rolling on your "on" side, start experimenting with a cross-bow roll. Visualize the start and finish positions. You will have to flip the blade over at some point, or you'll get twisted up!

Canoe Rolling Technique

1 You can set up for a canoe roll with the paddle straight in front of you. Lay the blade of the paddle flat on the deck.

2 Capsize your boat and reach out to one side with your paddle. Extend the paddle as far as you can.

3 Use hip rotation to roll the boat upright. Keep the paddle extended as you roll the boat towards the surface.

4 Press down in the water with the paddle and lean forward as your body comes up out of the water.

5 Tuck your head down low and keep holding the paddle in the water in this rather unstable final part of the roll.

6 When you finish the roll you should be upright, with the paddle in your hand. You are ready to paddle off.

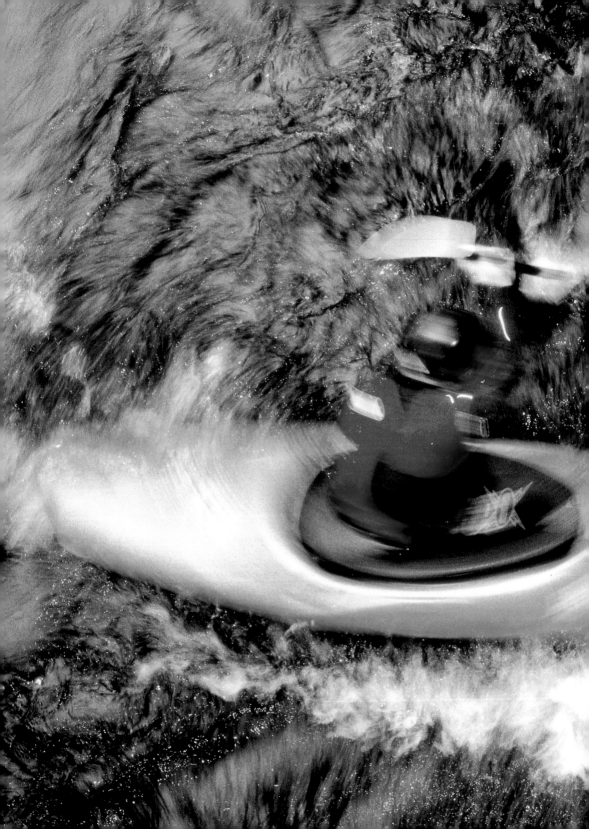

ON MOVING WATER

WHITE WATER PADDLING

Kayakers and canoeists with an adventurous streak gravitate towards white water paddling. The plastic revolution and the subsequent trend towards short boats have made the turbulent waters of steep rivers and creeks accessible to more people, and spawned the explosion of white water sport that emerged in the late twentieth century.

But what is white water, sometimes described as wild water? The terms describe any water, usually in a river, that has rapids with fast-flowing sections where the shape of the river bed causes waves and currents that are chaotic and unpredictable. When the turbulence is pronounced, the water becomes aerated, as if air is being vigorously beaten into the water, creating its white and bubbly appearance.

A fairly mild current or a small wave is enough to cause problems for a paddler without experience of moving water. Once you understand the behaviour of the water, however, it is possible to cope, and indeed play, with white water rapids that look terrifying to the uninitiated. There is always an element of danger though. A moment's loss of concentration could prove fatal if the proper precautions are not observed.

LEFT *White water river features demand concentration and proficient paddling skills.*

BELOW *An open-boat canoeist and two kayakers navigate their way around a white water river.*

White Water Hydrology

Rapids have a relatively small number of components that always behave in much the same way. Once you can identify and understand these components you are well on the way to being able to master white water paddling.

When you look at a rapid, try not to see it as a whole. The non-paddler looks at white water as one big chaotic mass, when it is in fact made up of separate areas of water that are all fairly constant in their behaviour.

Currents

The water in a river flows predominantly downstream, but there are some parts moving faster than others, and sometimes water even moves upstream. Water in the centre of the river flows quite a bit faster

RIGHT *A medium-volume and steep white water rapid, Grade (Class) 4.*

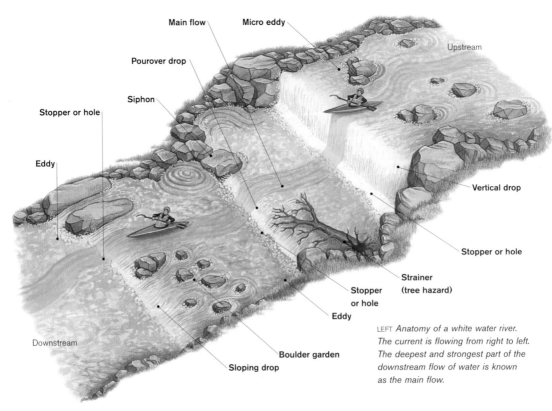

Main flow

Micro eddy

Upstream

Pourover drop

Siphon

Stopper or hole

Eddy

Vertical drop

Stopper or hole

Strainer
(tree hazard)

Stopper
or hole

Eddy

Downstream

Boulder garden

Sloping drop

LEFT *Anatomy of a white water river. The current is flowing from right to left. The deepest and strongest part of the downstream flow of water is known as the main flow.*

than water near the banks because of friction with the bank, and because the river is generally deeper in the middle than the shallow margins.

As the river goes around a corner, the fastest part of the current will move towards the outside of the bend. There will still be a zone of slower moving water right next to the outside bank, but it will be narrower, and the slow zone on the inside will be consequently wider.

If the river goes round a very sharp bend, the water cannot flow smoothly around it. This means that the fastest part of the current will collide with the bank on the outside of the bend, and then rebound and continue downstream. Aim to stay in the slower part, which will move in a much more predictable way.

ABOVE *A kayaker reaches over a breaking wave and punches his way through.*

LEFT *Paddling in a large eddy on a pool-drop river. Although the paddler is in relatively calm, or slack, water, it still swirls and moves around him.*

Eddies

If the bank protrudes, a rock breaks the surface, or there is a sharp corner, the water will flow around it and re-circulate upstream to form a sheltered area behind the protrusion or corner. This is called an eddy. It can be flat and calm, or it can rotate strongly, depending on the shape of the feature and the strength of the current. All but the most savagely swirling eddies are good places for kayaks and canoes to rest, regroup, or look for the best route downstream.

Green Water V-shapes

When you look at a rapid you can see that the water flowing between the rocks forms a green water V-shape with its apex pointing downstream. This shows you the path of the deepest and least turbulent current. You can paddle down these Vs, and they are usually the safest route. If this feature is a downstream V, then the V-shaped wakes caused by the rocks are upstream Vs. An upstream V has an obstruction or shallow water at its apex, and should usually be avoided by taking the middle of the downstream V.

The waves that form on either side of the V will meet at the apex and fold over each other to form what is known as a folded or V wave. Since your boat may capsize if you plunge directly into a folded wave, it is sometimes better to leave the V before you hit the apex.

Waves and Hydraulics

If the water flows over a ledge or rock on the bottom of the river, it will cause a disturbance on the surface. What this disturbance looks like to the paddler depends on the shape of the rock, and the depth of water flowing over it.

The more powerful the vertical re-circulation of a water feature, the more it will tend to hold a buoyant object, such as a boat, preventing it from passing through and carrying on downstream. Some people try to differentiate between wave types, but they are all similar phenomena with a profile that varies according to the velocity of the current and the resistance it meets.

When a hydraulic becomes powerful enough to hold a boat, it is often called a stopper or a hole. In extreme cases they can even re-circulate a swimmer. An unbroken wave can also stop a boat if it is big and steep enough, but because it has no component moving upstream, it will never hold a swimmer.

Sometimes the energy of a hydraulic water feature means that instead of one wave, there will be a whole series of them, getting progressively smaller as you go downstream. This is called a wave train, and is usually a bouncy but safe line to take down a rapid. The waves are nearly always pyramidal rather than river wide, and you will get a drier ride by paddling over the corners of waves, so avoiding the deeper middle.

Falls

These are a more dramatic example of the previous phenomena of waves and hydraulics. Where the river drops dramatically, the water will hit the bottom

and rebound upwards. What it does then is dependent on the depth and the steepness of the drop. The more re-circulation and the longer the towback, the more difficult it is for the boater to escape the clutches of the hydraulic.

Back-cut Drops

Certain geological features allow falls to erode in such a way that the water re-circulates behind, as well as downstream of the falls. This forms a double hydraulic from which it may be almost impossible to escape.

Cushions

Where the current rebounds directly off an object in its path, some of the water is forced upwards and some upstream. This forms what is known as a cushion (pillow). Far from being hazardous, these features will usually prevent you from colliding with rocks and walls. However, they can still capsize the unwary, and you should always approach them with caution.

Running a Downstream V

1 When approaching a rapid, look between the rocks and you will see a green water V shape, or "downstream V".

2 A downstream V is where the currents flowing around the rocks converge. This is the least turbulent part of the current.

3 The best route is usually to paddle down the apex of the V, as if it were an arrow pointing out the safest line.

4 There may be extremely turbulent water at the very apex of the V, if it is formed by two waves, as is the case here.

5 Even if the water looks fierce at the apex, this will still be your best route. The water at either side is much worse.

6 This paddler is safely through the V. Downstream Vs rarely point to anything nasty, but be aware that they can.

ABOVE *On enormous white water the severity of water features is magnified.*

Boils and Seams

Water sometimes wells up from the bottom of the river as it rises to find its way downstream. This forms a feature that would look to a fish's eye like a mushroom, but appears on the surface as an area of elevated, bubbly water that moves outwards from the centre and down at the edges. This is called a boil. Where two or more boils meet, the join, also known as the seam, can be quite accentuated. It can be powerful enough to suck down a swimmer or even an entire boat, but in all but the biggest water this is usually only temporary, and both swimmer and boat will resurface without difficulty after a few seconds.

Whirlpools

The whirlpool is perhaps the most evocative white water feature, but it is also over-rated. It is not nearly as exciting or as dangerous as it seems: only on enormous white water will the whirlpool have the power to do anything more than snatch at the boat, and cause a bit of a wobble, although for paddlers new to

white water they are best avoided. Whirlpools occur in areas of adjoining, extremely different phenomena, where there is a high current differential – for instance, along the boundary between an eddy and a strong current. Whirlpools are, unusually, rarely stable features, and they tend to appear at the top of such a boundary and whirl downstream for a few seconds before disappearing altogether.

TIPS FOR THE UNWARY

With the exception of whirlpools, the aforementioned white water features will be static on the rapid. The actual water is moving, but features such as waves, holes, and eddies will be standing still. If the river is higher than its usual level, it may begin to surge a little so that the features constantly change slightly in appearance in a rhythmic cycle, but they still will not move much. Because of this, a white water rapid is very predictable to an experienced boater, and in this chapter we will show how to make the best use of these static forms.

If the river has flooded badly and its course has completely altered, there may be some visibly moving features. Since the river bed and the banks will not have eroded to provide a smooth passage for the current, there will be some instability that causes waves to move around and to surge, explode and disappear. This is quite rare, however and is, in any case, a scenario that is best avoided because of its unpredictability and the likelihood of other dangers, such as trees, debris and low bridges.

BELOW *Probably one of the biggest whirlpools ever captured on camera.*

Grading Rivers

It is vitally important that you know how to accurately assess a white water river, and how to fully appreciate someone else's verdict on its safety level. In very extreme cases, it could be the difference between life and death. Always make sure you know your grades.

Grading or classifying white water rivers is essential if you are to assess their severity, and hence their suitability, for your level of paddling. There is a widely accepted international system

BELOW *A group of paddlers getting out to scout a Grade (Class) 4 rapid on an otherwise Grade 2 or 3 section of river.*

available to all paddlers. However, it is a subjective system that can be open to misinterpretation. As in other areas of paddling, what really counts is your own experience of rivers and your ability to judge a particular river for yourself.

Grades of River

Grade (Class) 1 This is flat water. If the water is moving at all, it has so little energy that the currents can be ignored and they will not affect the boat unduly. Grade 1 rivers are suitable for beginners unless extreme weather has affected the water conditions – for example, if heavy rain has caused flooding.

Grade 2 There may be water currents strong enough to prevent you paddling upstream, or through waves and eddies, but whichever route you take, the rapid will be safe if you have good basic paddling skills.

Grade 3 The waves, currents and eddies will be more pronounced, and there may be obstructions and/or drops that necessitate a particular route down the rapid in order to remain safe and in control of the boat. On Grade 3 water, the safe route should always be obviously visible to the experienced paddler while on his way down the rapid.

Grade 4 There is a safe route down the rapid, but it is not obvious from the boat. The size of the waves and the drops, and the complexity of the rapid, usually dictate that the paddler must first inspect it from the bank in order to plan a safe line and remain in control.

Grade 5 The size and severity of the features, and the complexity of the rapid, has increased to the point where, although there may be a best line through, even that route is not entirely safe, and the paddler can expect to lose control. The rapid is so turbulent and powerful that it is dangerous even for the highly experienced, skilled paddler. Often, swimming in this type of water would result in injury or drowning.

Grade 6 This has always been defined as the upper limit of practicality. There is no safe line to take through the water, and to swim would prove fatal.

BELOW *A big volume Grade 3 rapid such as this calls for experienced handling.*

ABOVE *This fairly straightforward rapid is Grade 4 because of the volume and severity of the water.*

Is the System Perfect?

Over time, as boats and skills have constantly improved, many rapids that were once Grade 6 have become widely regarded as a less severe Grade 5; many Grade 4 rapids are now classed as Grade 3, and so on. These revisions make for some confusion in the system.

A number of paddlers have modified the international grading system in an attempt to improve it. Some use a + or − symbol to create more increments, so that 3+ means a difficult Grade 3 river and 5- means a relatively straightforward Grade 5. Some paddlers prefer to add a letter, so that the number indicates the difficulty of paddling the rapid and the letter the level of danger. So 5a would mean "Incredibly hard, but if you swim you will be fine," and 4d would mean "Fairly hard but any kind of mistake would be very dangerous."

None of these alternative, modified systems has gained universal acceptance, however. The original system may have

its problems, but everyone understands it, and it gives a good indication of what you can expect to find. The most important point is that you are able to look at a rapid and accurately assess it, knowing the likely consequences of tackling it given your paddling ability and that of the rest of your group.

Tackling White Water

Before you attempt to tackle white water, you must understand the river grading system. If you are new to paddling rapids, do not attempt anything over Grade 2, particularly until you have learnt to roll. As you gain confidence, you can build up to more difficult rapids, but it should be a progressive development. You will also need all the strokes that will be outlined in this section. Being able to roll well is important as you are likely to capsize, but you are unlikely to roll successfully every time (initially, at least), so be prepared for a swim. Above all, be confident: an anxious boater is never a good boater. Facing and overcoming challenges is part of any adventure sport, but you should not attempt anything if you are not comfortable with the possible outcome.

BELOW *This massive waterfall is ungradeable because of its power. To run it would probably result in death: the paddler's skill and route would make no difference.*

WHITE WATER EQUIPMENT

The minimum equipment you need for tackling white water will include a boat, paddle, spraydeck (spray skirt), if paddling in a kayak, flotation device and helmet. You should also have a throw-line, and a knife that can be used to cut the throw-line in an emergency. Many people paddle with only the minimum amount of equipment, and find their paddling all the more enjoyable for not being weighed down with extraneous items, some of which they are unlikely to ever need.

On the other hand, there are many other pieces of equipment that can be useful, important or even essential, depending on the conditions you are likely to encounter on the water. In the following chapter, we outline the types of equipment that are commonly used by white water paddlers today, and discuss when they are required and why. Deciding how much equipment you need is a personal choice, and it should always be based on your own needs and experiences.

LEFT *A well-equipped paddler in a modern white water kayak.*

BELOW *Airbags lashed in place on a modern white water open canoe.*

Kayaks for White Water

A kayak for white water paddling will usually be made of plastic, unless it is designed for a specialist discipline such as slalom, white water racing, or squirt boating. It should have enough buoyancy to float well even when completely full of water. If there is any significant risk that, when full of water, you might end up swimming out of your boat (and there is a risk unless you are highly skilled), you should also fit airbags inside the boat to minimize the amount of water that can enter. Airbags are inflatable PVC bags designed to keep water out of the boat in the event of swamping.

Choosing a Kayak

Most people are now introduced to white water in a boat that is about 2.5m (8½ft) long, and fairly flat-bottomed. Many older books and some instructors still regard boats that are 4m (13ft) long and round-hulled as more suitable, but beginners and experienced paddlers alike will benefit from the responsiveness of a short boat. Also, the more volume the boat has, the better it will respond in white water, but it should not be so huge that the paddler can not properly reach the water when seated.

The boat must have strong footrests with some shock absorption system, and a back strap to support the back and maintain a spinal "S". The boat should also be equipped with end grabs strong enough to take a 1,000kg (2,200lb) load,

ABOVE *A heavy-duty, reinforced white water paddle with a symmetrical blade. This is a good, affordable solution as a first white water paddle.*

and should be padded inside as much as is necessary to fit the paddler exactly. A boat that does not fit you is no fun at all.

Kayak Paddles

White water paddles are shorter than flat water paddles – a typical length is 1.9–1.98m (6ft 2in–6ft 7in). Many older books recommend longer paddles, and in 1975, white water kayakers were using paddles 2.1–2.2m (6ft 10in–7ft 2in) long, but they were also using 4m (13ft) kayaks. Things have changed since then. In today's short

ABOVE *A lightweight carbon fibre white water paddle with an asymmetrical blade. Lighter and stronger, this is the choice of the white water expert.*

boats, shorter paddles mean faster paddle strokes and therefore more responsive paddling.

The paddle must be strong enough to survive being smashed against rocks, and it should be stiff enough to provide good feedback from the water. Good models can be expensive, but their superior performance and durability justify the cost.

ABOVE *This boat has been fitted with thigh grips, a back strap and foam padding to ensure the paddler fits snugly and cannot move inside the boat.*

ABOVE *A modern white water kayak suitable for beginners. However, an expert could tackle all but the most extreme white water in this boat with further outfitting.*

RIGHT *The Perception Dancer, an early modern white water kayak, first built in 1979. At 3.7m (12ft) in length, this boat changed the widely held belief that kayaks needed to be 4m (13ft) long. In fact, 4m (13ft) was originally a slalom kayak dimension designed to limit performance, not to enhance it.*

RIGHT *This 3m (10ft) Pyranha kayak is short enough to be versatile but long enough for touring. Hence, it represents the modern general-purpose kayak, suitable for white water if correctly equipped.*

RIGHT *The modern playboat is as short as can accomodate the paddler's legs (typically around 1.9m (6.2ft)) and has a flat hull, sharp rails and chines. While these boats are designed for high levels of performance, they are still only suitable for use on white water that is within the paddler's ability, because they are slow and difficult to control unless you have expert skills. For beginners or for more challenging runs, a longer, more rounded kayak with appropriate safety features would be a much better choice.*

RIGHT *The modern extreme white water kayak is often known as a "creek" boat. 2–2.5m (6.6–8.2ft) long, it features a more rounded hull than the playboat in order to maximize secondary stability and reduce impact when landing flat off drops (boofing). The ends are rounded to resist entrapment, and there will be a safety features, such as high-strength attachment points on the deck, structural pillars and a full plate shock-absorbing footrest.*

RIGHT *This inflatable kayak may look less functional, but it is suited to running hard rapids. With the aid of thigh straps you can lock yourself in.*

Canoes for White Water

Canoes for white water paddling have more variations in design than kayaks. Open boats can be made from fibreglass, but are more usually polyethylene plastic or a sandwich of plastics with a core. The latter can give incredible durability with excellent stiffness and low weight.

On an easy stretch of white water, open canoeists might risk paddling without any special equipment, ensuring only that the boat has enough buoyancy to float when it is full of water. More often, though, every bit of the boat not occupied by the crew will be filled with airbags or rigid buoyancy barrels (very good for storing additional gear), which are lashed in place with cords or webbing. The conventional canoe seat or thwart can be replaced by a foam saddle, which might even have thigh straps to hold you in place. This enables the open canoe to be rolled like a decked boat should it capsize.

ABOVE *An open-boat canoe is packed with air bags, which will keep it afloat when swamped with water.*

ABOVE *A white water canoe paddle, made from Carbon-Kevlar™ and fibreglass.*

RIGHT *A white water freestyle canoe. This boat is designed for play paddling, but could be used as well for running rapids.*

RIGHT *A typical white water canoe is characterized by its short length, rounded ends and continuous rocker.*

ABOVE *On white water, every bit of space in the boat is filled with airbags, which are lashed in place with cord.*

LEFT *All white water canoes feature saddle seats, as well as footrests behind the seat for use when kneeling.*

Open boaters often carry throw-lines attached to the ends of the boat. In the event of a swim, which is very likely because open canoes are quite hard to roll, the paddler can swim to the bank holding the end of the line, and then brace himself until the boat swings into the bank. This can be better than trying to swim with such a large boat in the rapid.

Open or Decked?

The first decision is whether to choose a decked or open canoe. The decked canoe is basically a kayak with a seat, footrest, and its back rest replaced by a saddle and straps. There are very few purpose-built decked canoes today, except for hand-built composite slalom boats. Most recreational and freestyle white water paddlers use a kayak shell which they transform to a canoe.

Often the body position in a decked canoe is further forward than it would be in the equivalent kayak, because the paddler's legs are in a kneeling position and not in front of him. This can mean that the canoeist needs a special spraydeck (spray skirt) made with the body tube further forward. Always check that the hole for your waist is in the right place for the seat in your boat!

Canoe Paddles

Just like kayak paddles, canoe paddles for white water need to be strong, light, and stiff enough to provide good feedback. A little flexibility is important because it allows the paddle to absorb shocks and prevent muscle strain; too much flexibility, on the other hand, will be counter-productive to your efforts.

Nowadays most canoe paddles are made from composite materials such as fibreglass, carbon or Kevlar™. There are traditionalists who prefer the warmth and feedback that comes from a wooden paddle, but wooden paddles are very high maintenance in a white water environment. The cheapest paddles have ABS plastic blades on a metal tubular shaft. These will certainly do the job for a quarter of the price of some models, and would be suitable for beginners who may not progress far with white water. However, they don't deliver much power or feedback from the water. They can also snap easily, especially in cold conditions.

BELOW *A tandem open canoe breaking into the current on a white water river.*

Accessories and Clothing for White Water

On white water you need heavy duty gear to keep you dry in turbulent water, and to protect you from injury and drowning.

Spraydecks
Spraydecks (spray skirts) for kayaks and decked canoes are absolutely essential in rough water. Spraydecks are invariably made from neoprene, the same material that is used for wetsuits. Fabric spraydecks used for flat water are splash-proof rather than waterproof, and will not be adequate for white water.

A good neoprene spraydeck will keep out every drop of water, and will not come off the cockpit rim unless you pull hard on the release strap, which is usually located at the front. Some basic spraydecks are available for the less confident paddler, which will come free if you kick and twist them, but that means they will probably come off in a roll or heavy waves. To see how secure the spraydeck is, put it on your empty boat, then put your hand in through the tube and under the deck, and lift up the boat by the spraydeck. If it stays on, it can be used on serious white water.

Whichever spraydeck you get, make sure that you can release it easily using the strap provided: practise doing this on white water as well as flat. When putting the spraydeck on, always check that the release strap is not trapped inside.

Flotation
Make sure that the flotation you use is intended for white water. For severe white water, some paddlers use special aids with a quick-release chest belt in case they need to be rescued. However, you should only get one of these if you know how to use one. Otherwise it is more likely to endanger than save you.

White water flotation aids can be minimal and slimline, as favoured by freestyle and play paddlers, or bulky and more buoyant, for tackling extreme rapids. The choice is determined by the likelihood of being capsized. The freestyle aids will allow more freedom, and you will be able to paddle better, but they might not afford you enough support if you are swimming in heavily aerated water.

ABOVE *This reinforced white water buoyancy aid (personal flotation device) is fitted with a chest belt for use in a rescue situation. The belt should only be used by paddlers who have been trained in white water rescue.*

BELOW *A white water play paddler equipped for summer: note the short-sleeved shell and wetsuit shorts. The flotation device, helmet and high-performance spraydeck (skirt) should be worn in all weathers.*

BELOW *A reinforced white water spraydeck made from neoprene, the minimum quality material for white water paddling. The tight-fitting body tube is pulled right up to prevent water getting into the boat.*

BELOW *A white water river running outfit. With the harness flotation aid, wetsuit trousers and a long-sleeved drytop, this paddler is equipped for extreme white water in any weather.*

Helmet

All white water paddlers are advised to wear helmets because of the high risk of finding yourself in the water, and knocking your boat or yourself against rocks. Choose a good-quality model that will protect your temples and forehead. Make sure the helmet fits well and will not come off, fall over your eyes, or expose the base of your skull to an impact. Remember, too, that the bigger the helmet, the more it can wrench your head around when you are upside down.

There used to be a fashion for having drainage holes in a helmet to let out any water that gets in during a capsize or roll.

BELOW *Some people use all-in-one drysuits for cold weather paddling, but the zipper can be an encumbrance and the suit lacks many of the features of the drytop.*

Many books still in circulation recommend that you only use a helmet with drainage holes. However, modern helmets are now padded with closed-cell foam. This stops the water getting in, and it means there is less chance of anything (such as an overhanging tree branch) poking through one of the holes. Foam-lined helmets are also warmer.

Clothing

In hot weather, the main purpose of clothing on the upper body is to keep water from entering the spraydeck tube, and protect you from the sun. In colder climes or on cold water, you may need several layers of clothing to keep warm.

Most boaters today use a specially designed paddling jacket, called a cagoule or cag. For warmer weather, there is a short-sleeve version. Cags

usually have a seal at the neck and wrists to keep out water, the ultimate being an efficient latex dry seal. Good cags have a double waist system that sandwiches your spraydeck. They are made from a breathable, waterproof fabric, which will cut down on perspiration.

How much insulation you wear under your paddling jacket is up to you, but you will not need much. White water boating is extremely vigorous, and if you wear a thick fleece you will overheat in no time. One or two light to midweight layers should suffice, even in cold weather.

Wetsuits

Beginners to white water often wear wetsuits to keep them warm and protect them from knocks. A popular wetsuit is the long-john design, which allows the upper body freedom of movement. More confident paddlers may find this wetsuit too restricting, preferring wetsuit shorts, wetsuit trousers, or thermal leggings with dry or semi-dry over-trousers, according to the weather and water conditions.

Footwear

Your choice of footwear for white water paddling needs to have a good sole for scrambling about on wet, slippery rocks. Some paddlers choose wetsuit boots, some prefer special watersports shoes, and others wear technical sandals, with or without wetsuit socks. Be aware that anything that is not strapped firmly to your feet is likely to get sucked off during a white water swim.

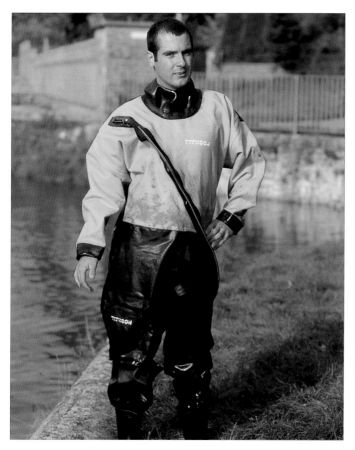

FREESTYLE

Some freestyle boats are so slimline that you cannot get in wearing bulky footwear. Yet these boats are paddled on white water, so what do freestylers wear on their feet? The point here is that you would only be paddling the more vulnerable freestyle boat in the first place if you were an experienced paddler and within your personal limits. Freestyle boaters usually wear either wetsuit socks or go barefoot, with a pair of sandals or shoes tied in the back of the boat for when they are back on shore.

Safety and Rescue Equipment

There are a number of pieces of rescue equipment that are specially designed for white water use, and all kayakers who intend to paddle rapids should have a basic understanding of their use. There are four essential pieces of equipment that you require.

Throw-line

A throw-line is an invaluable piece of white water equipment. Practise with it until you are confident you could use it in an emergency: the throw-line is next to useless unless it is deployed correctly.

A throw-line is a rescue rope. It consists of a length of rope that will float tied to a bag. The bag will often have some foam buoyancy to keep it afloat as well.

In order to rescue someone who is swimming after a capsize, take your throw-line, open the bag and grasp the loose end of the rope, and throw the bag to the victim. Modern throw-lines are superbly designed so that they fly a

BELOW A throw-line is attached to a rescue belt flotation aid using a karabiner.

BELOW The throw-line is an essential piece of rescue equipment.

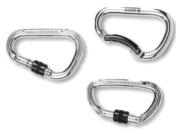

long way with the rope running out smoothly behind. Aim to land the bag beyond the swimmer, so that the rope falls across him, and he can grab it and be pulled to safety.

In theory, this would appear simple, but it can be a tricky procedure when the water is moving fast, particularly if the victim panics. This is why it is imperative that all paddlers practise being both victim and rescuer, and are able to throw and catch the line. Always read the instructions that come with the throw-line.

Flotation

A buoyancy aid (personal flotation device) used for flat water is not appropriate for white water. White water models are sometimes fitted with a rescue belt, which can be an advantage to the trained user in extremely severe rescue situations.

The purpose of the quick-release rescue belt is to allow for a line to be attached to the back of the buoyancy aid, so that the wearer can attempt a rescue with someone holding the other end of the rope. Because the rescuer might also get into difficulties, it is essential that he can release himself using the quick-release buckle fitted to the front of the belt.

The line is attached to the back of the rescue belt. This is so that the wearer would remain the right way up, and able to breathe, if held in a fast-flowing current at the end of a line. Bear in mind that not all white water flotation aids are well designed. Take care when faced with a selection of models: choose one that you know works well for rescues.

Another common problem is that white water flotation aids often rely on the rescue belt to give them a good fit. Before you buy, make sure the aid fits well when the chest belt is unfastened. Otherwise, you may find yourself swimming in an ill-fitting buoyancy aid, just when you need it most.

Slings, Karabiners and Pulleys

A sling can be used as a towing aid and for securing boats. Made from reinforced nylon webbing, slings

ABOVE Karabiners: the chunky screw-gate (here, the pink ones) and the quicker but less secure snap-gate (the blue).

BELOW Climbing slings are very useful for towing and securing boats and paddles.

BELOW *A pruning saw is a fantastic tool on the river. This cheap garden tool will cut through quite large branches and strong plastic with equal ease. Be careful to get one that can be locked closed, as the blade is dangerous if not kept securely.*

LEFT *A typical folding river knife. This one has a serrated part to the blade for hacking at difficult jobs, such as tree branches.*

Knives and Saws

Whenever you take a rope with you as part of your safety and rescue equipment, you should also take a knife to cut it with. Small folding knives are the best because they are extremely sharp, but are still small enough to be carried in the pocket of most buoyancy aids. Some white water paddlers carry fixed-blade diving knives, but these can easily cause accidental injuries, and because they are much heavier they will quickly sink if you drop them in the water.

An ordinary garden pruning saw does not weigh too much, and is invaluable for cutting away branches of trees, which are the white water paddler's worst nightmare. They can also be used in more extreme cases – for example, to free a boater who has become trapped by a fallen tree branch.

are extremely strong but occupy very little space in the boat. If you also have a karabiner – a lightweight alloy coupling link – it will make the sling easier to deploy for securing and towing boats. Karabiners can have a screw-gate or a snap-gate fastening, and you should try to include one of each. Some karabiners are big enough to close around a paddle shaft: these are the most useful because you can use them to secure or tow paddles.

If you have a sling and a couple of karabiners you can use them together to make a pulley for your throw-line rope. In some situations, such as when a boat has become lodged between rocks after a capsize, a pulley system, operated from the river bank, will be your best chance of recovering the boat. Special pulleys for white water rescue are available, and they are more effective, but your boating will be turning into quite an operation if you get to this stage. For advice on how to work a pulley system, see *White Water Safety and Rescue.*

TOP RIGHT *The throw-line can be stowed inside the kayak or decked canoe.*

RIGHT *On an open canoe, the throw-line can be attached to the ends.*

Using a Throw-line

1 Get to the shore and out of your boat. Standing on the river bank, undo the bag of your throw-line and pull out about 2m (6½ft) of rope.

2 Identify where the swimmer is and throw the bag (NOT the rope) to them. Aim for somewhere behind them, so that the rope falls over their head.

3 Bring the rope from the swimmer, around the back of you and over your shoulder. Lean back and take the strain as the swimmer swings into the bank.

WHITE WATER SKILLS

This chapter provides a guide to the fundamental skills required to paddle through rapids. There are a few basic tips that can make a big difference to how well you cope with the transition from flat water to rapids. Having read the section on white water hydrology, you will understand that many forces are acting on the boat. Anticipation is the key to remaining in control. If you react to the water, your actions will always be too late. You must lean, edge and use the paddle, anticipating what the water will do. This comes only with experience.

Where you look is where you go. If you want your boat to change direction, rotate your body and look at your new goal to make it easier to turn the boat. The exception to this is rolling, when the body will follow the boat out of the water.

To be successful you also need to be aggressive. White water does not reward defensive behaviour. If you shy away from a wave or a rock, it will tip you in. Turn your shoulder and lean aggressively towards it, and you will survive the problem.

Finally, do not start doing something if you have not got a fixed goal. If you leave the safety of an eddy, you should know where the next safe place is, and be confident that you can get there. If you head down river without a plan, you are likely to run into trouble.

LEFT *A group of experienced paddlers enjoying big and bouncy white water rapids.*

BELOW *Novice kayakers learning their first white water skills under expert supervision.*

Planning Your White Water Trip

Before you paddle on white water it is extremely important to know and understand what you are getting into. You can at best have a bad day, and at worst come to some serious harm if you misinterpret its nature and severity.

In the enthusiastic rush to get on the water, it is very tempting to overlook certain basic safety requirements. These include making sure everyone in the group knows the plan for the trip, who is carrying what in terms of safety and rescue equipment, provisions and maps, and where the dry clothes are at the end of the journey.

Pre-trip Preparation

Everyone going out on the water should understand the basic principles of white water hydrology and the international grading system. Someone in the paddling group (preferably everyone, but this is not always possible) must be experienced enough to be able to judge the grade of water, and whether it is suitable for everyone in the party. Finally, if parts of the river are too difficult for people in the group, will they be able to stop, get out and walk around the section?

BELOW *Preparing for a trip on white water. Lay out the equipment on the ground, and check off everything you will need.*

ABOVE *Before you get afloat, make sure everyone knows the plan for the trip.*

Everyone should also know how long the trip is going to last, so that they can bring appropriate amounts of food, drink and equipment. It might be a quick 20-minute blast down an exciting section of river, or a trip lasting a few days with camping on the river bank. The type of provisions and extra clothing needed will also depend on the weather, so listen to a reliable daily weather report for the area before you set out.

Shuttles

A white water trip is usually a one way journey because the water flows too fast for there to be any possibility of paddling back to the starting point. Your group may be fortunate enough to be delivered to the put-in and collected from the take-out (also known as the egress), but more usually the group will have to give some thought to the procedure known as the "shuttle". Here is how it works.

The group convenes at the put-in to unload their boats and the equipment they will need on the river. All the dry clothes and anything that will not be required until the end of the trip, including towels and hot drinks, is loaded into one or more vehicles, which are driven to the get-out point. The drivers of these vehicles now need to get back to the put-in, so one extra vehicle will have to accompany them and bring everyone back, unless you are lucky enough to have the help of a non-paddling driver, known to boaters as a "shuttle-bunny".

It may be practical to walk back to the put-in, which means that no vehicles are left at the top of the river and you won't need to return there afterwards. Otherwise, when the trip is over, someone will have to take the shuttle driver back to his car. Remember, all the dry clothes should remain at the get-out point until everyone has finished the trip.

If you don't have a shuttle-bunny at the get-out, it is essential that the paddlers carry with them the keys for all cars left there. It is all too common to leave the keys in the car left at the put-in, and then have to go on a long and arduous mission to recover them at the end. This can be extremely unpopular with a group of cold and tired paddlers whose warm clothes are safely locked away!

Safety Measures

Make sure that everyone knows the plan, and who is responsible for what during the trip. In a group of experienced paddlers who know each other well, there will not be any formalities because everyone knows what to do, but in a mixed-abilities group, it is important to have a preliminary talk before you set out.

An experienced group member must run through the procedure for the trip, emphasizing where you will re-group, who will go first and last, and who has the essential safety equipment. Typically the strongest and/or most experienced paddlers will go first and last, taking the basic items of rescue equipment. At least three members of the party (if not everyone) should carry throw-lines.

Finally, the entire group should warm-up and stretch at the same time. This means that everyone is ready together and you won't have some getting cold and stiff while others are still getting ready.

Communication

Hand signals can be used between paddlers for communication. This should not be attempted while paddling, but it is useful if paddlers have stopped in separate eddies because the noise of the river can preclude verbal communication. Some books describe a "correct" signalling procedure, but different groups use different signals. Discuss the signals the group will use during the pre-trip talk.

RIGHT *A group of paddlers get out of the water for a meeting in a remote gorge.*

BELOW *These paddlers are discussing the plan for the next section of their trip.*

CHECKLIST
• What is the strength and ability level of the group?
• What is the aim of the trip?
• Will there be a support party?
• What equipment will the group need and who will carry it?
• Are there any special points to include in the group's briefing?
• How will the weather and water conditions be checked? By whom?
• Are any permissions required for access points or stretches of water?
• How will the group be organized on the water? Who will lead the group?
• What are the transport and shuttle arrangements?

Launching into White Water

There are several options when it comes to launching a boat, including techniques for entering the water from banks 10m (33ft) high. Build up your launching skills gradually. If you attempt an ambitious technique you are not ready for, you are likely to get hurt.

Getting into the water can be trickier than you might think. Unless there is an area of slow-moving flat water at the put-in, it will be impossible to get into the boat by the usual means. Kayak paddlers will find it difficult to put on their neoprene spraydecks (spray skirts) while afloat, and it will be difficult for anyone to get settled in the boat and not get swept away while trying to arrange their equipment. One of several techniques will be required.

Launching in an Eddy

If there is a convenient eddy at the put-in, it may be possible to put your boat in the water, get in, and put on spraydecks before pushing off. However, even the gentlest eddies are not usually stationary, and the water will be trying to carry you upstream and feed you into the current before you are ready. You will therefore need someone to hold your boat while you get in and put on your deck, making sure that your paddle does not float away.

RIGHT *Seal launching a kayak off a low river bank on to flat water.*

BELOW *Getting into a white water open canoe on a section of slack water.*

Seal Launching

Because getting into the boat in an eddy is sometimes impossible, and since most paddlers prefer to be independent, it is normally better to get into the boat and get everything in place on dry land, and then launch yourself into the water. This technique is called a seal launch. No-one seems to know whether this refers to the way a seal slides into the sea from a rock, or the fact that the paddler is sealed in the boat as it is launched.

How you launch is determined by the bank, the depth of the water, and the nature of the river downstream. If there is a gently shelving slope into the water, you can get in the boat at the water's edge and push yourself into the water. If the water is moving fast, it may be better to launch backwards because the current will spin the boat around, pointing it upstream as you go in. This is a better orientation for getting away from the bank.

If there is a vertical drop from the bank to the water that is not too big, it is often better to shuffle to the edge sideways, and then lean out until you can bump the boat off the ledge with your hips, landing flat in the water. It takes practice to do this without falling in, so try it in deep, safe water at first. It is not comfortable or safe to use this method from a height of more than 1m (3½ft), unless the water is extremely aerated.

ABOVE *A canoe can be seal launched off a bank as easily as a kayak.*

BELOW *Launching sideways off a low wall. This is a better solution if the water is too shallow for a vertical dive.*

BELOW *Making an enormous vertical seal launch. This kind of thing should only ever be attempted out of necessity.*

If the drop from the river bank is larger than 1m (3½ft) or not quite vertical you will have to launch forwards. This may involve free-falling, bow first, into the water, so you will need to make sure that the water is deep enough. Stick your paddle into the water to measure the depth: if it is less than 1m (3½ft) deep you risk injury from hitting the bottom. Push yourself to the edge using the paddle on one side and your free hand on the other, then launch yourself off the bank with a shove, bringing the other hand on to the paddle as you fall.

The push off is important because if you topple slowly you will over-rotate, and might land on your head. Sit fairly upright, and do not hold the paddle in front of your face in case it hits you in the nose. People have been known to seal launch safely from heights of up to 18m (60ft) this way, but try it initially from no more than 3m (10ft) because it can be difficult to maintain the correct posture while performing the manoeuvre.

ABOVE *Getting a group into their boats on a rock ledge. When they are all ready to go, they will slide off into the rapid.*

If you have to launch from a great height but the water is not deep enough for a vertical entry, you still have a few options. You can either shove off hard from the bank, or get someone to give you a push, so that you enter the water at a shallower angle; this can be tricky. Or you can drop into the water sideways and land flat, provided you feel that your fitness or the aeration of the water means that you can exceed the 1m (3½ft) rule without injuring yourself; this is more risky. Or you can drop in sideways, letting the boat land on its side if you have the skill to do this. If you attempt this, do not land with a lot of force on your paddle blade. Even if the paddle does not touch the bottom you can hurt your shoulder, and you might break the paddle. It is better to capsize than to find yourself stranded or injured.

Breaking Out Techniques

The break out is a manoeuvre that allows you to move the boat out of the current and into an eddy whenever you want to take a break from the fast-moving water.

The eddy will be divided from the main flow of the river by an eddy-line. This is a distinct line or interface between the water moving downstream and the water in the eddy, which is stationary or is moving more slowly upstream.

As the boat crosses the eddy-line the current will try to spin the boat around and tip it over. In order to counter this it is important to lean the boat upstream, i.e. into the turn, as it crosses the line.

It is usually advisable to paddle into the eddy while pointing downstream, and allow the current to spin the boat to face upriver. This makes it easy to enter the top of the eddy, a relatively safe and predictable place, and to leave it again to proceed downstream. However, it is

ABOVE *Two canoeists negotiate their way down the river from one eddy to another.*

Breaking Out using a Bow Rudder

1 Aim to get the bow into the top of the eddy at an angle of 45°.

2 Plant the bow rudder firmly in the eddy and lean the boat upstream.

3 Hang on the bow rudder until the boat is completely in the eddy.

4 Turn the rudder into a power stroke to pull you back up the eddy, if required.

possible to paddle into the eddy across the current, or even while pointing upstream if necessary. The crucial point is to maintain that upstream lean once in the eddy.

It is best to approach the eddy at some speed, and to perform a powerful sweep stroke on the downstream side as you cross the eddy-line to ensure that you cross it properly and do not hang about at the interface, which can be a difficult place even for experts. As the boat turns into the eddy and you apply or increase your lean, you should support yourself with a low brace for stability, and to ensure that the boat carries on turning the right way. You should finish up well inside the eddy-line, facing upstream, and with the bow of the boat close to the top of the eddy.

With a good technique it is possible to enter the eddy without doing any strokes at all, just relying on the edges and carving performance of the boat to give you the necessary drive and turning force.

Exactly what type of stroke you use to break out is up to you. You should be

Breaking Out using a Low Brace

1 Aim the bow into the top of the eddy at 45°, and low brace on the upstream side.

2 As the boat begins to turn, lean on the low brace fairly hard.

comfortable with all the strokes by the time you venture out on to white water for the first time, so with any luck it will come naturally. Remember, though, that it is the difference in current as you cross the eddy-line that turns the boat and not your stroke.

The advantage of a low brace as you cross the eddy-line is that it will provide the greatest support. It is also an easy stroke to apply in what is (to the novice) an uncertain situation; as a result it is quite common to see paddlers new to white water using the low brace.

The advantage of using a bow rudder stroke is that it can be feathered to apply only as much braking force as required (which means it need not slow the boat), yet it still provides support to the confident paddler, and can feather into a forward stroke to take you deeper into the eddy as you come to a halt. The bow rudder would be the stroke of choice for experienced paddlers when breaking in or out of a current on white water.

To break out with no paddle strokes is good practice and helps you to feel the effect the water has on the hull, uncluttered as you are with feedback from the paddle. When you are entirely confident at moving around on a rapid, breaking with no brace can be used as a training exercise to maintain your concentration and control.

Breaking Out with No Brace

1 Attack the eddy at 45°, as when using a low brace.

2 Lean upstream a little before you start to turn the boat.

TIPS
• Think of the break-out technique as a sequence of three actions:
1. Position the boat
2. Achieve a balanced turn
3. Use an appropriate stroke
• Be decisive when you spot an eddy and decide with conviction to go for it or not. If you are not sure you can make it across the eddy-line, avoid it.

GO WITH THE FLOW
A white water river is primarily made up of water currents and eddies. It is up to the paddler to use these forces to manoeuvre and stop the boat. Entering currents, stopping the boat in case of a problem, to take a rest or to look at something interesting, and navigating your way across a river are vital skills that you need to learn to stay in control of your boat, and to enjoy your time on white water.

3 Hold the lean and keep believing it is going to work!

4 Finish facing upstream, and don't level the boat until you have stopped turning.

Breaking In Techniques

The technique for entering the river current from an eddy and proceeding downstream is known as breaking in. It is precisely the opposite of beaking out.

Paddle into the current while pointing slightly upstream, and with enough speed to ensure that you make it completely into the flow. As with breaking out, use a powerful forward sweep on the upstream side to drive the bow into the current and initiate the turn. Then use a low brace or similarly supportive turning stroke on the downstream side to complete the turn. Clearly, the forces here are acting the other way, so the current will be trying to tip you upstream. You must lean quite decisively downstream, again into the turn, supporting yourself with your turning stroke, until you are well into the current.

If there are waves in the main flow, you will do better to enter the current in a trough rather than on the peak of a wave.

As with the breaking out technique, there are a number of ways that you can achieve your goal of crossing the eddy-line into the current. The safest and most reliable way at first, when you are first learning to break in, is to use a low brace. Start off by paddling up the eddy fast enough to allow you to make it across the eddy-line: you need to do your low brace as, or slightly before, the boat

crosses the line and starts to turn. If you are paddling too slowly, you will spin around to face the downstream right on the eddy-line, and you will probably fall into the water. However, it is incorrect to paddle across the eddy-line and then turn. This feels all wrong, and it doesn't put you in a good position in the rapid either.

ABOVE *The important thing about breaking in is to make it into the flow, where you can establish a safe line downstream.*

More experienced paddlers tend to do exactly the same thing but using a bow rudder stroke in place of the low brace. This has the advantage that if you are not going quite fast enough, or if you

Breaking In using a Low Brace

1 Paddle up to the top of the eddy-line. Make your last stroke on the current side.

2 Your next stroke will be a sweep to drive you into the flow and start the turn.

3 Place the low brace on the downstream side for support as you make the turn.

turn too much, your paddle blade is ready for a forward stroke, sweep stroke or support stroke, responding to what the current is doing and making sure you complete the turn while making it into the flow of the current. The only difference is that you should reach forwards to place the bow rudder in the current because this stroke will not always slice cleanly

across the eddy-line without snagging in the water or tipping you right in.

Experienced paddlers may break into the current without using a turning/bracing stroke. This is rather like the technique for breaking out with no brace, which is not a stroke but an exercise. In the case of breaking in, the paddler would appear to paddle across the

ABOVE *Breaking in below a small drop and immediately lining up for the next one.*

eddy-line, which is bad technique. A paddler with excellent balance and control may be able to cross the eddy-line and turn, while appearing to paddle forwards, but do not attempt this until you have the skill and experience to do it well.

Break In using a Bow Rudder

1 Paddle out of the top of the eddy at 45°, lifting the upstream edge of the boat.

2 Make a bow rudder on the downstream side and lean on the stroke.

3 Hold the stroke until you are pointing downstream, then start paddling again.

Ferry Glide

Sometimes you will want to paddle across the current without turning downstream, often from an eddy to a point on the other side. This is known as a ferry glide, named after the ferry boats that used to cross rivers attached to a fixed wire. This does not involve a wire, but you have to paddle fast enough to stop being swept away. The skill of maintaining the correct angle is just the same as the ferryman's.

Ferry gliding is a very useful skill for crossing fast rivers, and for moving into a better position in the current. It can also be done in reverse, so that you move across the current while still facing downstream as you look for the best line down a rapid.

You need to keep the boat pointing upstream. The faster the current and the more its speed varies across the flow,

the more directly upstream you will need to aim. Rather than keeping it on track by using forward sweeps on the downstream side to stop the boat from spinning around, you should lift your upstream edge. Use your knee rather than leaning your body downstream, and keep paddling hard enough so that you move across the current without being carried downstream. If you are entering an eddy on the other side, you will need to release your edge and lean slightly upstream as you cross the eddy-line.

If you find that the boat tries to turn downstream, you were not pointing upstream enough. Forward sweep the bow aggressively back into line to recover. However, anticipation is always better than reaction. It tends to go wrong only because you didn't set the correct

angle of attack. Getting the angle exactly right only comes with experience. Initially, the rule of thumb is to set off pointing as directly upstream as you can while still allowing you to get across the eddy-line.

Reverse Ferry Glide

The ferry glide can also be done in reverse, so that you move across the current while still facing downstream, as you look for the best line down a rapid. The reverse ferry glide is an essential skill in white water paddling because many rivers have sections that can only be paddled in reverse. Unlike many reverse skills, it is actually easier in many ways to keep the boat tracking across the current than it would be when ferry gliding forwards, although all paddlers have less boat control when paddling backwards.

Ferry Glide Technique

1 As you leave the eddy, point as far upstream as you can while still making it across the eddy-line.

2 Lift the upstream – eddy side – edge of the boat as you cross the eddy-line into the main current.

3 Keep paddling, adjusting your angle across the current as needed.

4 As you reach the other side of the eddy, change edges as you cross the eddy-line by lifting the downstream edge.

5 Enter the other eddy in the same way as you would if you were breaking out.

6 You can now continue to paddle your way up the eddy.

S-cross

If the current is too fast to ferry glide, and the eddy-line is too difficult to negotiate, or the target eddy is a little downstream from your starting point, you can try a modified ferry glide called a cross. This involves letting the boat turn enough so that you ensure a fast transit across the current, at the expense of being carried downstream a short distance. In extreme cases this becomes an S-cross; the boat is allowed to break in until it is travelling directly across the current, then you immediately change to a break out to enter the target eddy, making an S shape across the river.

The S-cross as a set piece is used more for practice than anything else. However, learning to S-cross accurately from one eddy to another on a rapid will give you a lot of confidence in your ability

to navigate white water, and will help you combine your repertoire of different skills and manoeuvres into a seamless flow. You will find this technique extremely useful when eddy-hopping your way down an unknown rapid, when you want to get from one safe eddy to another without having to think too hard about how to go about it.

If you attack the eddy-lines at speed, the boat can be made to plane and jet across narrow currents very quickly indeed. It will need practice and excellent reflexes to change edges at just the right time. If you cross a wider current like this, the boat will quickly stop planing and you will be in a conventional ferry glide. If this is not what you want, make sure you attack wider jets without too much speed, or at a less acute angle.

S-cross Technique

1 Break into the current at about 45°, using your normal breaking-in technique.

2 Start paddling fast before you are facing downstream.

3 Charge forcefully across the current, and keep leaning the boat downstream as you do so.

4 Cross the opposite eddy-line. Aim to keep the boat moving at speed as it crosses the narrow current.

5 Change edges, using your legs, and begin the break-out sequence. This relies on excellent timing: practice is all.

6 You should finish the manoeuvre facing upstream in the other eddy.

Eddy Use and Etiquette

Now that we know the basics of getting into, out of and between eddies, it is time to learn a little about how they should be used. As has been explained, an eddy is an important river feature and the right etiquette and protocol should always be observed when using one.

Eddies are primarily used as a place to stop, rest and look ahead before running rapids. They vary in size; many are large enough for a whole group to stop and chat, whereas others might only be big enough for a single boat. Some people call very small eddies like this "micro eddies". In fact, they might be so tiny that only an expert paddler would ever notice them, let alone be able to land a boat in one in the middle of a powerful rapid.

This means that paddlers must think about the whole group when entering and leaving eddies. If an eddy fills up, one or more paddlers might have to carry

ABOVE *A paddler in a large eddy and another approaching from upstream. This eddy is so big that etiquette isn't really an issue.*

Entering a Micro Eddy

1 Attack the eddy-line more perpendicular than you would with a normal eddy.

2 Brake to reduce speed as you go across the eddy-line.

3 Level the boat early so that you don't spin back into the rapid.

4 Finish as close to the banks as you can without bouncing off the current.

on downstream without a plan. Before leaving an eddy, therefore, everyone should know where they are next going to eddy out – i.e. make their next stop.

Whoever is first into an eddy should back down or move away from the eddy-line so that the next paddler can also enter at the top. It is much better for everyone to break out as high up the eddy as they can; if someone misses they still have a chance to catch the eddy further down. The trouble is, sometimes this means that the person who was first into the eddy has to be the last out. This is one of the many reasons for having your best paddlers positioned first and last on the river.

In a very safe place where paddlers are playing on the rapid, it may not be necessary or appropriate to back away from the top of the eddy. Sometimes, other paddlers will be queuing to leave the top of the eddy, and it would be rude and unnecessary to jump to the front of the line. If you see that this is the case, join the back of the eddy queue like everyone else. If, on the other hand, you are anxious or out of control, aim for the top of the eddy – it is up to more experienced paddlers to recognize your problems and make room for you.

When you are ready to leave an eddy, make sure that there is no one paddling downstream who will end up too close to you, or who might be aiming for the part of the eddy that you are leaving. It is too easy on white water to miss what other people are trying to do, but being considerate is very important.

Eddy-hopping

It is important that a group of paddlers leaves an eddy knowing that they will be able to catch one another within the distance that they can see (or know from experience) is safe. This way of running a river from one eddy to the next is called "eddy hopping". However, it may not be possible for everyone to make the same eddy, so before you leave, look ahead and consider where you and everyone else in the group will break out next. In small eddies, it may be necessary for the paddlers to swap the lead.

ABOVE *An open canoe joins the top of an eddy. The kayakers have made room at the top to give him safer access.*

BELOW *Group dynamics in an eddy. The expert paddlers at the top and back of the eddy will leave first and last.*

Running Rapids

Many rapids have hydraulic and/or rock features that can be hazardous, and you need to know how to avoid them, or deal with them if they are unavoidable.

Waves and Holes

The nature of hydraulics changes with the depth and flow of the water. Unbroken waves are usually no problem because you can paddle over them. If they get very big or are really close together, it may be sensible to take a diagonal route over them. However, a wave that is breaking hard can stop and hold the boat. In extreme cases, it will hurl the boat end over end, disorientating the paddler. You will learn from experience whether you're likely to punch through a wave or not.

As the depth reduces, the drop into the breaking pile becomes more pronounced, and the re-circulating water pours back into the depression. This hydraulic will hold the boat, and it is only safe if you can see that the ends are pointing downstream to allow you to escape.

ABOVE *This kayaker is on the towback of a powerful hydraulic, and the water is so aerated that his kayak barely floats. He must keep moving downstream to avoid being sucked back in.*

BELOW *This rapid is full of big waves, although the water is too deep for them to form retentive "stoppers" or "holes", and the paddler's approach is dictated by comfort more than by safety.*

Reducing the depth of the water further turns this hole into a pourover. Pourovers are nearly always unpleasant because they do not allow the boater to ride comfortably on the front of the pile – there is too much water falling on the upstream side of the boat. Sometimes you can jump over the towback by paddling right through the pourover, but it is better to skirt around it.

Whenever you look at a hydraulic, try to imagine what will happen to the boat if you are held sideways in its grip. It takes experience to read the water in this way, and there is no better test than watching what someone else does. You will quickly learn to spot the little tongues of water that can provide a passage downstream, and to recognize whether the pile helps you towards an exit through which you can escape, or constantly pushes you away from it. Practise as much as you can by playing in holes that are small and safe, gradually moving on to more difficult ones. Once you can go into a hole, and come out again unscathed, you are well on the way to confidently running rapids.

ABOVE *This is a particularly unpleasant scenario. A lot of water is falling steeply into a re-circulating stopper or hole. The white water is flowing back upstream from as far as 5m (16ft) downstream. A paddler or swimmer caught in this hydraulic would be swamped with water and would not be able to escape. In this example it is just about possible to sneak past the hole on either side, but the only sane route is on the bank.*

BELOW *Although this stopper has a big breaking foam pile, it is friendly because the drop into it is not too steep. It is very powerful and will hold the boat indefinitely, but a skilful paddler can remain in control and can effect an escape by simple paddling out of the end of the pile. The hole is safe because if you were to swim, you would be flushed downstream. This feature is called an elevated pile.*

Running Drops

If you want to try paddling over a drop of any significant size, you need to know what the water below is like. It is likely that you will not have a good view of the water from your boat. Vertical drops have different characteristics from sloping drops, but both present significant dangers to the paddler. They should always be inspected to check for rocks or trapped trees. On a vertical drop you can often measure the depth with a paddle.

Sloping Drops

A sloping drop will usually have a big hydraulic at the bottom that you may have to paddle through. Look for any gaps in the pile, or any sign of a downstream V. This will be the best spot. If the water going down the ramp is not flat but consists of two or more flows crossing over each other, you need to be on the top flow. The other(s) would carry you under the top one, and might flip your boat as it goes over the drop.

BELOW *This man is using a kayak paddle to check the depth of the pool below a small 1m (3½ft) waterfall. He can also make sure that there are no trees or other obstructions under the water that might entrap the submerged kayak when he runs the drop.*

ABOVE *A kayaker is attempting a meltdown on a sloping drop where he had no chance of jumping the hydraulic.*

BELOW *Running a sloping drop into an eddy. The kayaker can take a diagonal line across this drop to get to the eddy.*

ABOVE *Running any kind of drop can be a serious undertaking and should not be attempted without careful thought. A huge white water rapid such as this is for experts only.*

Vertical Drops

Waterfalls usually have a deep and very strong hydraulic re-circulation system at the bottom, but you will usually land downstream of it. If the fall is so big that you cannot do this, consider the sanity of the undertaking. If going ahead, the main consideration is the height of the drop. Can you survive the impact uninjured, and is the water deep enough? Whatever the profile of the fall, there are basically two ways of running it.

Meltdown

A meltdown is a way of taking the drop so that your hull stays in contact with the green water all the way down, and you then go through, or under, the re-circulating hydraulic. It was invented by squirt boaters in the 1980s, and has revolutionized vertical drops in all but the most high-volume boats. Just paddle normally towards your chosen spot on the lip of the drop, keeping your weight forward. As you drop into the pile, tuck your head right forwards and down,

and put the paddle along the boat as if preparing for a roll. You may well need to roll, anyway, but the main reason for doing this is to prevent the pile from snapping the paddle across your chest.

If the drop is vertical, do not paddle too fast; drop over the edge at your current speed, or a little faster to retain some control. This will ensure you do not go out too far. Do not lean back as you see the water below because the boat may

over-rotate, and this may hurt. However, if the drop is sloping, the faster you are going when you hit the pile, the better your chance of sliding through. Just make sure the nose of the boat goes under the pile, not up the face of it.

Boof

A boof is the opposite way of taking a fall. This involves paddling hard off the lip of the drop, and keeping the weight back just before take-off, so that the boat shoots downstream a long way and lands flat on the hull. It helps if you make your last stroke right at the lip, and use your whole body to heave back the blade. This means that the boat is projected forwards, and your weight will be at the back as you start to fall. Throw yourself dynamically forward as soon as you are in freefall because this keeps the bow up, which helps the boat land flat and prevents the nose from plunging deep into the pile.

Boofing allows you to remain dry and in control, and you can land in shallow water if you get it right. Never boof high vertical drops unless the water below is very aerated, or you risk spinal compression. On a sloping drop, it is only possible to boof diagonally into an eddy – generally, you cannot get enough speed to clear the hydraulic unless it is a vertical fall.

BELOW *Launching out from a waterfall in order to boof into the water below.*

White Water Safety and Rescue

There are three main areas of risk that you need to protect yourself from while out on the water. Ultimately, the main threat is drowning, and you need to focus on the likely causes that can occur on white water.

Entrapment

The main killer of white water paddlers is entrapment. This can happen in rapids because they are typically fairly shallow, and filled with obstructions. The power of the water can easily pin a kayak against a rock, tree or even the river bed in such a way that you are powerless to dislodge it or escape from the boat. If you are trapped in this way with your head below the water, you will drown in a matter of seconds; rescuers do not have long to get you out and resuscitate you.

Fortunately, most people who venture on to white water are aware of this danger, while the relatively inexperienced will be strictly monitored by an instructor. There are many rapids on which you can practise where the danger of entrapment is minimal. As a general rule, note that entrapments are nasty and sudden, so take great care if you think there is the remotest chance of one happening.

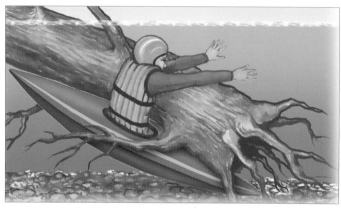

LEFT *If the bow of your kayak hits the bottom when negotiating a drop, you can get vertically pinned like this. The force of the water on your back makes it impossible to get out of the kayak. Sometimes you can shake the boat free or push off the bottom with your paddle, but the rule is, if you can breathe, don't move in case you make it worse. Rescuers can assist you by pulling the boat upwards to free the bow.*

The upstream side of any rock is a potential danger spot, where you can be pinned against an obstruction, often one that is submerged under the water level. Sometimes, if the water makes a cushion wave, you will not be trapped, but you cannot rely on that happening. A fallen tree or any object that has become embedded in the river bed can be a fatal hazard: avoid at all costs.

TOP *You can get into serious trouble if any part of your body becomes stuck between rocks on the river bed.*

ABOVE *If you hit the upstream side of a tree in moving water, this is how it can end. Even if you were on the surface when you hit the tree, the current will quickly force you below water level, and there is no escape. Avoid trees at all costs.*

If you do hit some type of obstruction and you get pinned against it, you must act quickly. There will be a brief moment of just a couple of seconds before things may start to take a turn for the worse. Throw your weight downstream towards the obstruction, and use every bit of your strength to lift the upstream edge of the boat before the water flows over you. With luck, you may then be able to drag

ABOVE *This paddler has been swept into a rock in the middle of a rapid. By leaning on to the rock, he is holding the upstream edge of his boat above water, which saves him from disaster.*

yourself around the obstruction and release the boat from the pressure pinning it to the obstruction. If not, you are in trouble. If you can get right out of your boat and on to the rock or other obstruction, do it. These situations have a habit of deteriorating rapidly.

If you fail to hold the upstream rail up, the boat will angle down and become inextricably pinned. It may even start to fold up under the pressure of the water. You may be held in the boat by the force of the water, and might be unable to keep your head up. It is easy to say "Don't panic," but you have only got seconds to find a solution. Wriggle the boat around, and fight to get out. If you do get out, try to kick off in a direction that will take you around the obstruction and away.

Other entrapment dangers include vertical, shallow drops. It is possible to be rescued from this situation, but only if your fellow paddlers can get to you quickly, or are in position already,

ABOVE *If the paddler can't lean downstream quickly enough, the current will flip the boat upstream and pin it in a position from which there may be no escape.*

ABOVE *In this instance, things have gone wrong. The boat is pinned on the rock, but the paddler is able to get out and on to the rock to await rescue.*

ABOVE *If a boat is pinned to a rock by the current, you need to mount a serious recovery operation from the shore, using ropes, to get the boat free.*

ABOVE *Here, the paddler is using an elevated pull to lift the boat up from the rocks. The throw-line can then be used to drag the boat back to the shore.*

monitoring your progress. As a rule, a boat or person pinned to an obstacle by the current can only be released in the direction from which they came – usually upstream. If you cannot release the boat and have to extract the paddler, take care that the force of the water as he exits does not cause leg or other injuries.

Undercut rocks or cliffs are extremely dangerous. They are undercut because the current flows under them, and you can easily get trapped against the rocks. There may also be trees and other debris that has accumulated next to the rocks. If the water flows right up against a rock or bank, but there is not much of a cushion or pressure wave, assume that most of the current is flowing underneath the water surface: never paddle here.

Release and Recovery

If a boat is pinned by rocks, use one of the following pulls to dislodge it and/or drag it back to the shore.

A shoulder belay – in which the rope passes from the boat around your shoulders – is much more powerful than simply using your arms. The elevated pull is designed to lift the boat to reduce friction and water pressure while the boat is dragged away horizontally from the water. For the vector pull, tie a rope from the pinned boat to a tree or rock, then pull at 90° to the rope to reduce pressure on the boat and pull it free.

BELOW *Using a vector pull to free a boat from entrapment on rocks in the water.*

Hydraulics

There are certain hydraulic wave features on white water that can stop and hold a kayak. In extreme cases, particularly on weirs and below waterfalls and pourovers, hydraulics are able to hold a swimmer and re-circulate him indefinitely. This is a potentially life-threatening situation.

The endless cycle of being submerged, surfacing, then being sucked upstream and submerged again rapidly leads to exhaustion. A swimmer in this situation can be rescued with a throw-line, or sometimes an experienced paddler can approach from downstream in a boat and pull him out. Self-extraction is extremely difficult, and impossible to practise safely. Prevention is always the best answer.

ABOVE *Wrapping the rope around your shoulders in a shoulder belay will make more effective use of your strength when recovering a boat from the water.*

White Water Swimming

Swimming down a rapid after a capsize has plenty of hazards besides the danger of entrapment. You are usually safer if you keep hold of your upturned boat because it will tow you through the hydraulics, and you can use it as a fender. If you have to make a choice between holding on to the paddle or the boat, choose the paddle: the boat will be easier to find later.

Position yourself so that you are upstream of the boat to avoid getting pinned. Face downstream and keep your legs up, pointing downstream, in what is known as the defensive swimming posture. You can use your feet to push yourself away from boulders, but be aware of the danger of getting your feet caught between rocks.

Keep holding on to your boat and paddle, and concentrate on conserving your energy. Wait for an opportunity to swim ashore, then head straight for the bank. If you still have the boat, ditch it if you are in any doubt about making it to safety. If you do not make it, the water will return you to the centre of the river and the attempt will have been wasted. You have limited reserves of energy, so choose your moment carefully.

RIGHT *A paddler caught in a hydraulic can be rescued with a throw-line from the shore, or by another paddler towing him to safety. However, the rescuer must be careful not to be sucked into the hydraulic himself.*

FOOT ENTRAPMENT

This is a very real threat. As soon as the foot is caught, the victim will fall down and the force of the current may hold him down and drown him. If you find your foot trapped, kick it upstream and upwards as hard as you can – yanking at it as you fall downstream will make things worse. To avoid foot entrapment, make it a rule never to stand in moving water more than 30cm (1ft) deep.

Using a Throw-line

A swimmer in the defensive posture can usually be rescued with a specialist rescue rope called a throw-line.

To rescue someone from the water, take your throw-line, open the bag and grasp the loose end of the rope. Throw the bag (NOT the rope) to the victim. Aim to land the bag beyond the swimmer, so that the rope falls across him, and he can grab it and be pulled to safety.

Throwing the bag and line can be tricky in fast moving water, particularly if the victim panics. All paddlers should practise throwing and catching the throw-line until they are confident they can use it.

BELOW *The defensive swimming posture. Float with your feet up and facing downstream to avoid entrapment.*

BELOW *When the time is right, turn on to your front and swim as hard as you can for the river bank.*

LEFT *This man is trying to swim his way out of a powerful hydraulic after a capsize. Although the river is flowing from top to bottom in the picture, the man is being sucked back upstream by the re-circulating water and submerged again by the water pouring over the drop. The enormous force of the water means that with every attempt to move, the swimmer is becoming exhausted and less able to act decisively. If he can't find a way out of this re-circulating water (for example, by swimming to either end of the stopper or being pushed through by the main flow), this cycle will be repeated until he drowns or is rescued.*

OPEN WATER AND SEA PADDLING

Kayaks and canoes are ideal for paddling over a great distance, or across exposed areas of open water. Indeed, both types of craft originated precisely because their builders needed to use them in this way, for hunting, trading and migration. The kayak is eminently suited to coastal and ocean travel, and the open canoe to exploring large rivers and great lakes.

The demands of long-distance paddling are quite special, and are unlike most of the other disciplines covered in this book. The main criterion is a need for speed because the distances covered can be quite long. Directional stability is equally important because one cannot paddle far in a boat that keeps veering away from straight lines. The boats also need to be very stable and easy to paddle. Long-distance boats need good storage space for food and water, and camping and survival equipment.

LEFT *Riding an ocean wave. Surfing is now a hugely popular branch of paddle sport.*

BELOW *Two paddlers in modern traditionally-styled sea kayaks explore a rocky coastline.*

Tides and Currents

Knowing about tides and currents is extremely important if you are planning to paddle a boat out at sea or on any large body of water. Ignoring them means possibly endangering your safety.

Tides

The tide is a familiar concept to anyone living or working near the sea, but it can be exceptionally confusing to others. All over the world, the sea and other large bodies of water are visibly moved by the gravitational effect of the moon, and to a lesser extent by the sun and planets. With only a few exceptions, this results in the water rising and falling twice a day – in any 24-hour period there will be two high tides and two low tides, with the water rising and falling fairly predictably from one to the next.

The size of the variation depends on two things: where you are in the world, and the date. Every month there is a cycle of tidal variation, which sees more extreme tides (highest highs and lowest lows) around the time of the full moon and 14 days later, reducing to less extreme ones (with a smaller change in height from highs to lows) in the weeks

ABOVE *A sheltered estuary at high tide. Always remember that the tide comes in and out twice a day, with currents much faster than you can paddle.*

in between. The extreme tides are known as spring tides, and the moderate tides are known as neap tides.

There is also a yearly variation. The biggest spring tides will be those that occur worldwide around the time of the equinoxes (when the sun crosses the equator) on 21 March and 21 September, and the smallest around the solstices (when the sun is furthest from the equator) on 21 June and 21 December.

It is useful to understand how tidal variations occur but there is no substitute for getting a tide table or checking the time of high and low tide on the day you

plan to paddle. If there is no appropriate information service available in the area, look for the information on the internet. Tides can vary by up to an hour between places only 100km (60 miles) apart.

BELOW *The same estuary as above, shown here at low tide. As well as the currents, you will have to contend with difficult access over deep mud banks.*

BELOW *The high-tide level of this river is clearly visible. At low tide there is access to the grassy bank, but at high tide there is no accessible landing spot.*

Currents

Although we describe the tide as rising and falling, there is a dramatic flow of water associated with it in many areas. The sea can exhibit strong tidal currents that are, in many cases, faster flowing than a river's. This is dangerous because you could set off when the water is slack at high or low tide, and find yourself a few hours later in a raging torrent like Skookumchuck in British Columbia, Canada, the Bitches in Wales or the Falls of Lora in Scotland, a situation for which you might be totally unprepared.

In most cases, the effects of a sea current are much the same as on a river. Good paddling technique will help you deal with the possible eddies and waves. There is, however, a special type of current called a rip that can be found in coastal areas. This can be dangerous to swimmers, but is a mixed blessing to paddlers who can use it to their advantage, as long as they know how.

The rip is a current most often found on surf beaches. The ocean swells breaking on the shore push a lot of water onshore, and this water has to run back

BELOW *The directional pull of the current. A rip takes water out to sea, while the longshore drift moves around the land.*

into the sea. Usually, it flows back in one or two spots, dictated by the shoreline, creating currents flowing back out through the waves. Anything in the area will be drawn towards the rip, and towed out to sea through the surf. You can see where they are from a cliff top, because the waves look flatter, but they are almost impossible to see at sea level. If you want to get out through the waves, a rip can

ABOVE *This exposed beach could be prone to strong currents. Find out about local currents before launching out to sea.*

offer a welcome free ride. If you are in trouble or are trying to stay inshore, you must get out of the rip by paddling or swimming straight across it to water that is going inshore. Never try to fight against it, which is exhausting and futile.

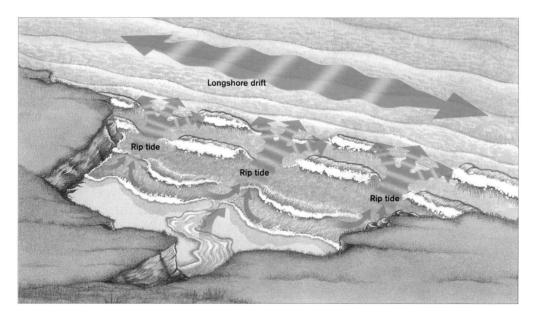

Longshore drift

Rip tide

Rip tide

Rip tide

Wind and Waves

When paddling on the open sea, winds and waves are important features, and they can have an immediate effect on what you are trying to do. It is crucial that you appreciate their power, and the way in which they work.

Wind Types

It does not take a strong wind to affect a boat. Even a light breeze, which you would barely notice on shore, can have quite a dramatic effect. Surprisingly, it is not paddling into the wind that causes most people problems, because this merely slows you down. A following wind is the one to look out for.

When it strikes, your boat will constantly try to turn around to face upwind, and most of your energy is used to keep the boat pointing the way you want to go. Kayaks suffer the worse from this; canoes a little less so, especially if a solo paddler is sitting in the back. It happens because the centre of drag of the boat (the deepest part of it, where most of your weight is) is usually quite far forward, and the tail half of the boat slews around quite easily. Boats are often designed this way to make them easy to

ABOVE *The wind has a huge effect on waves, which should never be underestimated.*

turn. The solution is to have a skeg, or rudder, at the back, or even to move your weight back if you can, to make the tail a little heavier. Some short boats as short as 3m (10ft) long, are very difficult to paddle in a following wind.

A cross-wind has much the same effect, blowing the tail away and making the boat turn towards the wind. It is less annoying and more predictable than a tail-wind because you know which way it wants to turn, but it is still very tiring as you constantly have to sweep stroke to

keep the boat on track. Many of the design features of sea kayaks are specifically intended to combat the effect of wind, but they can never eradicate it completely without rendering the boat impossible to manoeuvre.

When planning your trip, get accurate weather forecasts to see what conditions are likely, and remember that wind directions can change very suddenly. In warm weather, there is a tendency for winds to blow offshore at night as the land cools and the air over it flows out to sea. As the temperature rises through the day, the wind blows increasingly strongly onshore towards the warmer land. It is possible to experience winds swinging a full 360° in one 24-hour period. Mariners refer to a wind blowing onshore as lee shore conditions; an offshore wind creates a weather shore.

Waves

On the open sea, waves are caused by the wind unless the water is moving quickly over submerged rocks. In the latter case, the effect is exactly the same as a white water river. Wind-blown waves are another matter, and they fall into two categories: chop and swell.

BELOW *Waves without wind. This shore is catching a big ocean swell, but there may still be places to launch and land.*

ABOVE *Onshore wind. Wind on its own isn't a danger, but the effect it has on the swell makes for heavy surf conditions.*

Chop

Random small waves, created by variable winds over a short distance, are known as chop. A calm sea can become choppy in a matter of minutes when the wind strength increases. Chop can be confusing for paddlers because waves seem to come at them from all directions. The best thing is to ignore the waves as much as possible – try to relax and trust your balance. Sometimes it can help to surf the waves, if only for a few seconds.

Swell

Winds blowing in the same direction for a long distance create a swell. The longer the wind pushes, the bigger the waves get. Winds blowing around the outside of a storm system commonly send 6m (20ft) waves radiating out across the ocean. Once these waves are made, they do not diminish unless they meet an oncoming wind, which reduces them. They will still be very large even after travelling 1,000km (620 miles) without any further power from the wind that created them.

Swell only ever occurs over oceanic distances, and is rarely a concern in small enclosed seas such as the Mediterranean.

Small swells of 1m (3½ft) can occur, for example, in some of the larger lakes in the North American and Canadian Great Lakes, but they do not rival the swells of the Pacific or Atlantic, which commonly reach 10m (33ft) high.

When paddling in the sea, you could experience chop and swell at the same time, and in fact this is very common. If you can think of the two as separate features, superimposed on each other and to be treated independently, you will not find them difficult to deal with.

Wind with Waves

A combination of wind and waves can occur in a variety of ways. Since choppy water is always associated with a local wind, you will have the latter to contend with as well. When the conditions become severe, with a 1m (3½ft) chop, you might find yourself in a trough, but when you go over a wave you will be hit by a savage gust that might even capsize you. Be ready for this. Anticipate, and lean into the wind, keeping your paddles low to stop the wind catching them.

Swells are affected by the wind direction. A following wind (onshore) will blow the tops off the waves and make them crumble rather than pitch. Offshore winds will steepen the faces of the waves, and make them rear up and crash down as they break.

One of the most notable effects of winds, waves and currents is the difference between wind blowing in the same direction as the tide and wind against the tide. If the tide creates a current flowing strongly downwind, the water might be smooth despite quite windy conditions. When the tide turns and the water is flowing against the wind, there might be a dramatic worsening of the conditions at sea until the area resembles a rapid, with large standing waves as well as chop.

BELOW *The effects of swell and wind-chop superimposed on one another.*

Navigation and Distance

It is easy to think of touring and sea paddling as placid activities, far removed from the demands of white water, but a river flows in only one direction, and this makes it hard to get lost. On the sea there is a far greater chance of ending up in the wrong place, and the demands on your physical strength and stamina mean that you will tire more easily. No matter how confident a paddler you are inland, at sea you need to be able to navigate and chart your position, and accurately gauge how far you and your group can paddle without tiring.

Navigational Equipment

Different types of open water paddling call for different pieces of navigational equipment, but you should always take a compass with you whenever you paddle on the sea, on large lakes or on estuaries. The most important point with any equipment is that you know how to use it correctly, otherwise it will be useless.

BELOW *Maps can be laminated to make them waterproof. Some spraydecks (skirts) have an accessory to hold maps in place.*

Compass, Charts and Maps

If you are planning to spend the duration of your trip within easy reach of the shore, there is little need for sophisticated navigational equipment, but whenever you paddle on large lakes, rivers and the sea you should always have a compass with you, just in case. You also need to be sure that you know how to use the compass properly. At sea, a chart is extra insurance and will help you to identify onshore landmarks.

If you intend to make a significant open-water crossing, you must study basic nautical navigation. It is important that you can decide what compass bearing to paddle on to reach your goal, and that you can pay attention to it during your trip. It is rarely a case of pointing your boat where you want to go – at best this usually results in paddling much further than necessary, and at worst you might never get there.

If you are at sea and a fog descends unexpectedly (as it so often can do), a compass and a good knowledge of your locale make the difference between getting ashore safely and needing to be rescued by the emergency services. Paddling in the dark is great fun, and navigation at night can often be easier than by day if you can identify the onshore lights. Even so, you still need to be equipped with a compass.

Global Positioning System

For adventurous paddlers planning longer trips out at sea, more sophisticated navigational equipment is now available. The high-tech gadget known as the global positioning system (GPS) will provide you with a definitive position (a grid reference), and indicate which way you are travelling and how fast, which is invaluable information when the land is out of sight. The GPS is now becoming increasingly popular and affordable. If you can afford one, and want to use the very best navigational technology, it is a brilliant acquisition, although you will need a chart and a compass to use with it. Make sure you know how to use it correctly before you set out to sea.

ABOVE *A compass mounted securely on the front deck hatch of a sea kayak. This is invaluable equipment for open water.*

Lighting

Not only is it important that you can identify your location with accuracy on open water, you also need to be well lit yourself. If you ever need the help of a rescue crew, they won't be able to find you unless you are visible. There is also a very real chance that you could be hit by a larger boat that cannot see your tiny craft. Always find out in advance what kind of shipping uses the water you are planning to paddle on, and plan the route of your trip accordingly.

Even if you are planning to paddle only 1km (½ mile) offshore, you need to make sure you can be seen clearly. Many paddlers use chemical glow-stickers attached to their boats and their helmets and clothing to make them visible at night. Glow-stickers do not ruin your night vision, and they have the advantage of needing no batteries or precautions against soaking. They are available from most boating suppliers and some large DIY stores.

It always pays to be prepared for all eventualities, just in case you ever do need to take evasive action. If paddling out at sea, include a strobe light and flares as part of your safety and rescue equipment. For emergency use – for example, if you think a larger boat may collide with you – a strobe light is extremely bright and eye-catching, and your best chance of attracting attention. If you do not have a strobe, use a flare.

ABOVE *Younger children can paddle in double boats with an adult; they should always wear a flotation aid.*

RIGHT *Your personal limits can vary. If you feel less than 100 per cent on the day, your stamina will be affected.*

Know Your Limits

It is important to know how far you and the rest of your group can paddle before tackling the open water. Bear in mind that your range on sheltered flat water will be greater than out at sea, where conditions are more demanding: paddling against a wind or current can make a big difference to your range, as can the roughness of the sea. Your response and strength can only be learnt from experience, so don't present yourself with too much of a challenge to begin with.

Children can run out of energy quite suddenly; when they do, they may refuse to co-operate, and towing them will be essential. The best solution is to have them in a double boat with an adult. This way they will not tire as quickly because the adult will do most of the paddling.

OPEN WATER EQUIPMENT

Open water, sea and long-distance paddling has special demands, and the boats usually differ dramatically from those used for inland day boating. There is also a variety of other accessories that can make touring in a kayak or canoe that much safer and more enjoyable. The key issue is self-sufficiency.

If you are likely to be away from any possible assistance for much of your journey, you will have to carry everything with you. You might end up using a fully equipped, expedition sea kayak. If, on the other hand, you are going to be a short distance from populated areas for the whole journey, your only considerations are comfort, and a credit card may be all you need.

Finally, it is important that you have everything you need to be safe and comfortable, but equally important that you can carry your boat. Do not attempt to take every gadget that could possibly come in handy. The emphasis should be on keeping it light. If you cannot carry the boat, how well can you paddle it?

LEFT *Paddling on the open sea is awesome, but make sure you are sufficiently equipped.*

BELOW *Open water gear can be stowed on the boat in waterproof compartments.*

Boats for Open Water

The range of open-water boats available can be divided into sea or inland, and kayak or canoe. Many of the key issues that need to be accommodated for by the boats' design are the same, whether it is a kayak or a canoe, to be used on inland waterways or the ocean. There are a variety of first-rate boats that can be used for both touring and open and sea-water paddling, and these will give you maximum flexibility.

Kayaks

Sea kayaks are intended for coastal and open-sea touring, but they can be used for touring inland and can negotiate simple rapids up to Grade (Class) 2 as easily as ocean waves. There are also light, fast, narrow sea boats suitable for day trips, and bigger, heavier ones aimed at trips and expeditions lasting several days. Both have waterproof bulkheads and hatches to contain essential equipment. They can be used with or without a rudder; purist paddlers object to

BELOW *An open canoe is an ideal platform for exploring marinas such as this.*

rudders because they think the kayaker should be able to control the boat without one, but do not let that put you off. Some boats have small, traditional cockpits, and others modern keyhole ones.

Double kayaks can be a faster and more sociable way to travel. Some have provision for carrying children in their mid-section. They have most of the features found in solo kayaks, but will also have a rudder because the boats are too long to manoeuvre without one.

ABOVE *Open boats are a popular choice for one or more paddlers taking excursions on inland lakes and waterways.*

Touring kayaks are usually less comprehensively equipped than the sea boats, but often have many of the same features. The hull design tends to be the main difference, the emphasis being on manageability in more restricted conditions on inland water rather than sea-worthiness in extreme conditions.

ABOVE *Modern touring kayaks suitable for inland, coastal or open sea use.*

Canoes

Except for those canoes used on challenging stretches of white water, canoes tend to have fewer fittings and features than their counterpart kayaks. This belies the fact that subtleties of hull design can make a huge difference to the way the canoe behaves.

Touring canoes are built to cope with tracking and windage, which is the deflection of the boat off its route by the wind. They have a significant keel, and more balanced seating positions than other kinds of canoe. However, there is less specific provision for storage in a canoe than a kayak, despite its greater load-carrying capability.

Some canoe models have air tanks for flotation. These are usually small, forming seats in the bow and stern. They can be used for additional storage, and are reached through a waterproof hatch. However, they are not very common in touring boats, the very boats in which you might want to carry bulky camping or other equipment. Usually you will have to store gear in large dry bags or drums, which can be lashed to the seats to keep them securely in place.

Touring canoes are sometimes used for coastal paddling, but you should rarely venture far away from the shore in one because they are much more susceptible to the wind than sea kayaks, making them less easy to control. However, they do have one advantage: even if you cannot roll a touring canoe you can still right it, re-enter it, and bail out in the event of a capsize. For a full description of this method of self-rescue, see the technique, *Right Boat and Re-enter.*

BELOW *Paddling a sea/touring kayak. Note the waterproof hatches and the deck lines for attaching gear, safety and rescue equipment and spare paddles.*

Deck Fittings

Touring kayaks usually have deck lines, which are ropes running along and across the deck for handling the boat, and under which you can store equipment. Some of the cross-lines might be made from shock cord for securing a map or other item.

Canoes, clearly, do not have a deck on which to stow things but, if you need to lash down a lot of gear, a good solution is a cargo net, which can also be used for tying or hooking on quick-access items.

Pumps

Inevitably, you will ship water if paddling for a long time. A hand pump can be used to bail out a kayak or canoe. Some kayaks come equipped with hand pump and/or foot pumps, which means you can pump out water with your spraydeck still attached. As a rule, hand pumps move more water, but you need one or both hands free to operate them. The foot pump is a slower way to get the water out, but at least you can carry on using your paddle, which might be essential in rough seas. When choosing a pump, think about what you are likely to face in your paddling. After a capsize and re-entry (canoe or kayak), you will definitely have to pump out water, but this is an extreme case. If you're not going to be doing anything like this, the money might be better spent on a really good spraydeck to keep the water out, and a sponge for the annoying splashes you ship while getting in and out.

Paddles for Open Water

There is a wide choice of paddles for use on open water and the sea, from wing to split kinds. Paddles for touring and open water need different design features to paddles for general-purpose flat and white water paddling. Here we look at some of the popular advanced styles of touring paddles.

The most important issue when deciding which kind of paddle to buy is weight. If you are going to paddle for a long time, you need blades which are as light as possible. This means that modern high-tech composite materials are most people's first choice, but many paddlers still like wooden paddles, too.

Long paddles are also important to achieve a low paddling angle. This is especially true for kayaking, but even touring canoeists tend to use longer paddles with narrower blades.

Whatever paddle you choose, inspect it carefully before each use, and remember that your ability to move the boat, steer and roll relies on the integrity of your paddle. A damaged blade might break off just when you need it most.

BELOW *Symmetrical bladed paddles work very well for touring and open water.*

ABOVE *A replica of a traditional Greenland paddle, as used by Inuit paddlers. It is so narrow that it gives little support, but it propels the kayak well.*

Symmetrical Blades

The simple, symmetrical paddle is perfectly adequate for touring despite the undoubted benefits of more specialized designs. Make sure that your symmetrical blade is curved and spooned, or has a dihedral face, or it will flutter and will be difficult to paddle with over any distance.

Asymmetrical Blades

Paddle blades with an asymmetrical edge are more efficient than the equivalent symmetrical kind, and they make less splash in the water. The reasons for this

are clear when you look at how a paddle blade enters the water for a stroke. The disadvantage is that you must pick it up the right way round to get the full benefit.

Paddle Shafts

One notable feature of open water paddles is the shaft design. Many touring paddlers use bent paddle shafts. Kayak paddles are available with ergonomically curved shafts, which are very helpful in preventing some of the repetitive strain injuries that long-distance kayaking can cause. Canoe paddles are also available with these ergo shafts, or with a simpler

BELOW *The bent paddle shaft is less likely to strain the wrists over long distances.*

BELOW *Symmetrical bladed paddles work very well for touring and open water.*

BELOW *Asymmetical blades are less splashy and more efficient for forward paddling.*

Spare and Split Paddles

If you are planning to paddle a long distance, or a long way from the shore, you might want to take spare paddles with you in case any member of the group loses or damages their paddle. In a canoe it is easy to store a spare paddle under the seat, but this is a little more difficult in a kayak. The usual solution is to have a set of split (break-down) paddles that can be secured under the deck lines of your kayak, so that they do not get in the way of your paddling. By storing them here, it is possible to access them to roll with half a paddle if you lose your main paddle when knocked flat by a wave.

Spraydecks for Touring

These spraydecks (spray skirts) are not necessarily different to those worn for flat or white water, but few paddlers want to have a tight neoprene tube around their waist when paddling over a long distance and for several hours. Some paddlers choose to wear nylon spraydecks to avoid this, but these will let in water and allow water pools to form on the deck. A good solution is a combination touring deck. This comprises a neoprene deck with a fabric body tube, and will sometimes have braces to hold it up. With this deck you will have the advantages of both systems.

ABOVE *Though it is rare to break a paddle, the consequences can be dire if you are a long way from the shore. Split (break-down) paddles are carried on deck or stowed in the boat as insurance in case this happens.*

bend, so that the blade is at an angle to a normal, straight paddle shaft. The latter simply allows the blade of the paddle to address the water at a more efficient angle, rather than altering the ergonomics of your physical movement.

Wing Paddle

The wing paddle was invented for kayak racing, but many of its benefits make it useful for touring. The wing paddle is supremely efficient and it helps to stabilize the boat. The blade moves through the water in an arc, which utilizes many more muscle groups than does a conventional paddle, thereby making each stroke far more powerful.

Greenland Paddle

The Greenland paddling technique is described in *Stroke Variations*. The actual Greenland paddle acquired its long thin shape because the Inuit peoples who designed it did not have the right materials to make wider, flatter blades. There are some advantages to the design, such as low windage (deflection caused by the wind), and the fact that you can use the paddle as a club, or can wind your fishing tackle around it, although these are dubious benefits for today's kayaker. Those who use this paddle do so because they enjoy using traditional equipment and mastering the same challenges as the Inuit.

BELOW *This touring spraydeck features a neoprene deck with a fabric body tube and represents the best of both worlds for long-distance paddling.*

Open Water Clothing and Accessories

It is vital that you make the right choices with clothing for open water and the sea, not least so that you feel comfortable and warm. There is a wide choice of clothing available, and newcomers might feel slightly bewildered, but these guidelines will point you in the right direction.

Clothing for open- and sea-water paddling varies much more than that for white water because the emphasis is on versatility, due to the changing nature of the conditions. It is quite usual to take a choice of clothing with you in the boat.

Insulation

Though this is usually the same as for any other active sport, it is vital that you have a number of layers so that you can adjust your insulation level to suit the changing conditions. If you stop paddling you will notice a dramatic drop in your perceived temperature, unless you use a combination of fairly expensive layers.

Breathable Shells

It is usually necessary to have a wind- and waterproof shell garment with you, even if you do not wear it all the time. This should always be made from a breathable fabric that allows the vapour from perspiration to

ABOVE *A cagoule may not be necessary in fine weather but it is useful to have one with you if you become chilly.*

ABOVE *You may want to remove your cagoule, but you should always keep on the flotation device.*

escape, otherwise it will condense and you will become increasingly cold and wet. Some paddlers prefer a shell that they can put on over a buoyancy aid (personal flotation device) while they are afloat. Be aware, though, that capsizing with a cagoule over your head

ABOVE *A kayaking jacket for use on open water and the sea.*

can be a frightening experience: it would be very difficult to free yourself or to remove your spraydeck if you became tangled up in your garment underwater! In fine weather, a cagoule may be unnecessary, but it is very useful to be able to put one over your buoyancy aid if your thighs turn chilly. No matter how warm the weather, it is absolutely essential that you wear your buoyancy aid when paddling on the sea.

There are jackets and cagoules specially designed for paddlers. They are much better, and cheaper, than using a breathable walking jacket, which would fall apart very quickly if used for boating. In more extreme sea paddling conditions some kayakers wear cagoules. These are not quite as good as dry tops, but they have the advantage that they offer a little more adjustability and ventilation. They usually come with a hood, and are modern versions of the Inuit tuvilik or paddling jacket, which was made from sealskin. In Arctic and sub-Arctic conditions it is necessary to wear survival or drysuits because of the extremely short survival time should a paddler fall into the water.

Trousers

Many open water paddlers prefer salopettes, which are trousers with braces attached to hold them up, because they are more versatile, and provide a bit of upper body protection when worn without a jacket. Basic over-trousers are also popular, and these will keep the wind out when you are not in the boat. The choice of lower body wear for kayaking depends on how much time you will spend on land: whereas the canoeist will have his or her lower body exposed to the elements the whole time, the kayaker is relatively protected from the elements and has little need of extra insulation when paddling. Wetsuits are not appropriate for this type of paddling because they are fairly restrictive, can become hot and clingy, and are generally too uncomfortable to be worn for long periods.

ABOVE *Durable polyethylene containers, known as BDHs, are ideal for storing small items that need to be kept dry.*

BELOW *A roll-top dry bag is useful for carrying items such as mobile (cell) phones and car keys.*

Headgear

It is unusual to wear a helmet while touring, but you may need to keep your head warm. It is well known that most of your body's heat loss is from the head so, if you are getting cold, wear a hood or a hat. Any hat will do; a woollen hat is a popular choice because it is very warm, but it can get heavy when wet.

In sunny conditions a hat with a peak or brim is invaluable. If your hat does not stay firmly on your head, you might want to tie it on, or attach it to your collar; if you don't, it is likely to blow away in a strong gust of wind. Of course, in colder weather you may be wearing a paddling shell with a hood, and this can serve the same purpose as a hat, without the likelihood of it falling off and blowing away.

ABOVE *Two sea kayakers appropriately dressed for the conditions. Despite the sunshine, sharp sea winds mean that warm headgear may still be needed.*

Additional Gear

Many items such as mobile phones, car keys and first aid kits need to be kept dry. The dry compartments of a sea kayak are not 100 per cent waterproof and, in any case, it is better to have really important items on your person.

Dry bags are a good way to protect your essentials from the water. There are different types, but the most common is the roll-top variety. For dryness and more protection, use screw-top polyethylene jars, known as BDH containers after the chemical company that invented them. These are available from paddling stores. They are only 100 per cent waterproof if used with a rubber seal inside the lid.

Safety and Rescue Equipment

You can meet all kinds of problems, from being injured and requiring a tow back ashore to attracting sharks drawn by your flailing legs as you attempt to swim for safety. The following equipment should help to guarantee your safety.

Flotation

The buoyancy aid (personal flotation device or PFD) should be worn at all times when paddling on open water or the sea. Styles of buoyancy aid vary but the emphasis for most sea and touring paddlers seems to be on having pockets in which you can carry certain essential items. Apart from this, the important thing is comfort. You will see many touring paddlers wearing a buoyancy aid that is incorrectly adjusted or unzipped, simply because it is not designed for long-term comfort. If they were to capsize, they would have difficulty doing up the buoyancy aid in the water, and would

BELOW A typical buoyancy aid (personal flotation device) for sea paddling. It has bright panels and retro-reflective tape for visibility, and a selection of pockets for survival essentials.

experience all kinds of problems through not being able to keep hold of the boat and paddles.

Many buoyancy aids have some retro-reflective material, making them and the wearer more visible in poor light. This safety feature is not so visible when you are swimming though, in which case consider retro-reflective cuffs on your jacket, or a strobe light.

Whistle

A whistle is very useful if you need to attract attention in open water. Sound carries a long way over open water, and it could be that it is the only way to alert rescuers to your position.

Strobes and Beacons

A specialist strobe light is essential for anyone going offshore. When switched on it will flash at a rate that is quickly recognized by the rescue services, and be visible over a long distance. If attached to the shoulder of a buoyancy aid it will be seen even when you are swimming. Some offshore paddlers also take radio or satellite

ABOVE Additional items for a sea trip might include a hand pump, knife, compass, VHF radio, transistor receiver, sunscreen and a mobile (cell) phone.

beacons with them. When activated they send out a signal that is detected by special receivers, or even satellites, which alert the emergency services, giving them your exact position. The disadvantage is that they can be accidentally activated.

Flares

Flares are a common piece of safety kit to ensure that you can attract attention in case of an emergency. They can be

ABOVE Many types of flares are available commercially; these flares are a popular choice for offshore paddling.

ABOVE *Using a waist-towline to recover a kayak after a capsize.*

BELOW *The towline packs away neatly into a pouch worn as a belt.*

BELOW *Pumping water out of a sea kayak using a hand pump. Excess water in the boat can be a real discomfort.*

spotted over greater distances than a strobe, and without many of the problems of radio beacons. You will need to carry a minimum of three flares. Always check that your flares are within their "use-by" date, otherwise they may not work.

Towline

A towline is a useful piece of equipment for helping other paddlers. You might need to tow a boat back to a swimmer, an injured or tired paddler ashore, or help a slower one keep up. The line is usually worn around the waist, but some paddlers have towing systems built into the deck of their kayak.

A simple tow can be attached to the front of the boat you are helping. If more paddlers are on hand to help, it is worth considering a husky tow, which means that two or more paddlers pull.

The most important point about towing is to ensure that you can release the tow, using the quick release buckle, if you get into difficulties yourself.

Bivvy Bag

This is possibly the best piece of safety kit ever made. If you have nothing else, an orange plastic bivvy bag can be a lifesaver. It is light, takes up little space, and can be used in four ways:

• To keep a victim warm when back on land: put them in the bag and, in extreme cases, get in with them to add your own body heat and increase their temperature.

• To keep yourself alive in the water. If you get into a bivvy in the water, it dramatically reduces the rate at which you lose heat. You can extend your cold-water survival time tenfold because while your body will heat up the water around you, you will keep the warm water in the bag, rather than constantly exchanging it for more cold water. You may also be less likely to get unwanted attention from predators such as sharks, because you will be big and orange and wafting gently rather than small, flailing and behaving like an injured seal.

• To attract attention by waving it around.

• To build a shelter from the sun, wind or rain when stranded ashore.

ABOVE *A waterproof first-aid kit suitable for all kinds of outdoor activities, including paddling. The orange plastic bivvy bag (right) is invaluable.*

OPEN WATER PADDLING SKILLS

People who only paddle canoes and kayaks on flat or open water often pay less attention to the basic paddling skills than those involved in white water or other specialist disciplines. This is understandable because they think that precise manoeuvring skills and technical strokes are wasted on flat water, or water with a lot of room to move around on. What these paddlers do not understand is that the better and more efficiently you can paddle, the farther and faster you will go on flat and sea water with the same amount of effort.

   If you take up open water paddling or touring, having reached a level of proficiency in a general-purpose boat, you may well find that you have to modify your approach. In a short, simple kayak, many strokes are even more effective if done aggressively and explosively. But in a longer touring kayak, or when countering the effect of the wind, you may need more finesse and subtler leans to make the stroke work, and this can be very satisfying. The same applies to canoes – perhaps even more so. That is why it is so important that you respond sensitively to your boat and your paddle.

LEFT *Setting out to sea in a boat gives an overwhelming sense of freedom.*

BELOW *Sea kayaks offer plenty of opportunity for camping and touring trips.*

Stroke Variations

When paddling long distances in touring boats, or in the windy conditions often found on open water, you will need to adopt a different paddling style and in some cases learn new techniques.

Slide Hand

As we have already mentioned, kayak paddles for touring tend to be longer than a general-purpose or white water paddle. This is partly so that you can paddle with a lower stroke, reducing the effect of the wind, the chance of being blown off course or being capsized. A high paddle stroke is more efficient in still air, but a low stroke can be essential in a breeze, and is certainly more relaxing if you are paddling a long way.

One excellent low-stroke technique, called the Greenland slide hand, originated with the Inuit people of Greenland. They recognized the benefits of a narrow blade and a small overall paddle size in a strong wind. The technique involves holding the paddle with one hand, close to the middle, and the other near, or holding, the blade. You can then make a stroke with an extended reach, which allows a lower paddle angle, as well as more leverage to keep a wayward boat on track.

As the paddle goes across to make a stroke on the other side, slide the hands to use the same grip at the other end of the paddle. The action is almost one of throwing the paddle across, and catching it in the required grip just as the stroke begins. The technique can be used

continuously while paddling forward, or just to increase your reach in order to turn difficult boats more easily.

The picture below shows a paddler using a traditional Greenland paddle, but the technique can be used with any kayak paddle that does not have a bent shaft.

Assisted Turns

Another way to make a touring boat turn more easily is by using a dramatic outside lean. Whether moving forward or stationary, most straight-running boats, which have a long keel to assist tracking, will be much easier to turn if you lean them over to reduce the effect of the keel. Leaning to the inside or the outside might work, but an outside lean is better when going forward because you can then lean on your sweep stroke which, with an extended grip, can be very supportive indeed.

Sculling for Support

The concept of using a blade in a sculling action was described in the basic kayak and canoe paddling skills chapter. Sculling for support was deliberately

LEFT *Using a slide hand for forward paddling with a Greenland paddle. The top hand is holding the paddle at the blade. As the stroke ends, the paddle is slid across to be held at the other end. It feels odd but works surprisingly well.*

ABOVE *Sculling for support is a skill that can prove very useful in a long, narrow closed cockpit kayak.*

omitted because it is a more advanced skill and much more difficult to achieve. In most general-purpose kayaks sculling for support is ineffective, and it is best avoided altogether in canoes. In a long, narrow boat such as a sea kayak, however, it can be very useful.

The sculling support stroke can help the paddler to avoid a capsize. It uses essentially the same action as the sculling draw, but the paddle blade is placed face down on the water. If the boat is at a dramatic lean angle, sculling can support it there indefinitely, whereas a low or high brace would only provide lift for long enough to recover to an upright position. An expert can scull with the boat laid completely on its side, provided his body is in the water and effectively supporting itself.

Many people find it easier to lie back while sculling for support, and this is recommended by many older books and instructors. However, it is safer and more effective to maximize your reach by remaining perpendicular, particularly once your body is immersed. The danger of lying back while sculling or high bracing is that it strains the shoulder, which can lead to injury, and the position makes it difficult to control the boat.

ABOVE *Sliding the hands to one end enables the paddler to lean over for much of the stroke, which helps the boat to turn.*

Knifed-J and Figure Eight

These two strokes are peculiar to open canoeing, and though fairly obscure, they are worth mentioning because they are useful in windy conditions. Sometimes, particularly when paddling solo in a single-seater boat, it seems that every time you take your blade out of the water the boat blows off line. The solution is not to take it out at the end of the stroke, but to turn it flat to the hull and slice it forward to where the stroke started. In its simplest form this is called a knifed-J. The blade rotates at the end of the stroke and is ready to knife forward through the water, controlling the tracking without slowing down the boat.

A more complex version is the figure eight. It is a powerful stroke for controlling inside turns and is sometimes called an Indian stroke. It is similar to the knifed-J stroke, except that after the blade slices forward the T-grip is rotated in the palm of the top hand so that the next stroke is made with what was the back of the paddle. The figure eight is only suitable for fairly flat paddles.

Both the knifed-J and the figure eight are also very useful for sneaking up on wildlife, when taking the blade out of the water would make audible splashing and dripping sounds.

Re-entry and Roll

If you are paddling a sea or touring kayak on open water, this is a skill that will give you great confidence. If conditions are bad and you have had to swim, your companions may be struggling to rescue you. Or you might have ignored all advice to the contrary, and gone paddling alone. If you can re-enter your boat while it is upside down, and roll up, you will have the ultimate self-rescue skill at your disposal.

You may be tempted to right the boat first, and then try to climb in. This is possible in an open canoe, but a narrow kayak is too unstable. You will also find that righting the boat allows water into the cockpit. If you re-enter and put the spraydeck on underwater, you may be able to roll up with less water aboard.

The technique for re-entry and roll is non-specific. You need to try it for yourself and work out the best way for you, but obviously, being able to roll already is a pre-requisite.

RE-ENTRY TIPS
• Put your paddles through the decklines of the kayak sideways. This helps to keep the boat upside down as you get in.
• Get right under the boat before trying to put your legs in. Start off by facing the stern, then back somersault into the cockpit. Think of it as a capsize drill in reverse.
• Remain calm and move slowly, so that none of your actions are wasted.

Re-entry Technique

1 Hold either side of the cockpit rim, push yourself down under the boat, and allow your legs to float up between your arms.

2 Push your feet into the cockpit, concentrating on staying directly under the boat. Try not to float up to one side.

3 Once your legs are in, get into the seat and put on your spraydeck (spray skirt). Grab your paddle and roll up.

Launching and Landing

Launching and landing skills are rarely required, but nonetheless are important because you are most likely to need them in an emergency situation. Practise them, and note the rules that apply in what can often be testing and difficult conditions.

While all paddlers should learn and practise how to seal launch into water from a height, touring paddlers will have less need of this skill, except in an emergency. Instead, sea paddlers need to be able to get afloat through waves on the sea, or a big lake or river that is large enough for the wind to produce some chop or swell.

In any type of boat it is important that you can launch and land effectively. In a touring boat, such as a sea kayak, that might be relatively fragile and

ABOVE *A double sea kayak setting out to sea from a public beach.*

LEFT *Even small waves require good technique and can upset the unwary.*

heavily laden with supplies and rescue equipment, it is particularly important that you can do the job correctly. If a wave catches you sideways, you may lose control of your boat and capsize. Quite apart from it being a bad start to your fun day out, capsizing in very shallow water can cause you difficulties, and may even prove dangerous.

Launching Through Waves

Make sure that the boat is ready to launch, and that you have put in a drain plug (if required), secured the hatch covers, and tied down and protected your kit from the elements.

Next, put the boat down at the water's edge, pointing directly at it. If you are in a tidal area, remember that the tide might be coming in or going out, which could affect matters. If it is a heavy or tandem craft, make sure that you can move it towards the water without having to lift it, otherwise, once you get in, you might be stuck fast. And do not put the boat in

Launching Technique

1 Get into your kayak and attach the spraydeck when you are well above the waterline. Most paddlers find this easiest to do at the water's edge.

2 Move the kayak into the water, using your hands to lift yourself off the ground and push yourself along.

3 As soon as you are afloat, pick up the paddle and head out into the deeper water, propelling yourself forward with the paddle.

deep water where it can float because if you do it will be turned sideways by the waves, and can possibly knock you down or capsize. Once sideways to even small waves in shallow water, any boat becomes difficult to control. If you must manhandle it while afloat, stand on the seaward side.

Next, get into the boat quickly, and secure your spraydeck if you have one. Do not put your paddle down because it might be washed away. If you need both hands, secure the paddle under the deck-lines. If there are two of you, get into the boat one at a time.

Once in the boat, push it into the waves using your paddle on one side and hands on the other. Concentrate on keeping the boat at 90° to the waves, and then grab your paddle and get moving. Do not stop until you are so far out that the waves are not breaking. In particular, try to avoid capsizing in shallow water.

ABOVE *Holding sea kayaks stready in preparation for landing.*

LEFT *This double kayak is preparing to land through waves.*

Landing Through Waves

The important point about landing a boat is to make sure you do not surf in on the front of a wave. Paddle in as close as you can while still allowing waves to pass underneath you. Even in small waves you might have to back-paddle to make sure they do not propel you shorewards, especially if the wind is onshore.

When you are as close to the shore as you can get, or are in danger of touching the bottom, paddle in on the back of a wave until your boat runs up the beach. Leap out as quickly as you can before the boat is sucked back with the returning wave, or before another wave comes in to turn your boat sideways. From here, you may be able to push yourself up the beach, using your hands, without getting out of the boat. Otherwise, jump out of the boat and pull it up through the shallow water on to the beach. Take care not to drop your paddle, or else it might be washed back into the sea.

Landing Technique

1 Wait for a wave to pass under your boat, then paddle in towards the shore on the back of the wave. Do not surf on the front of the wave.

2 As the water gets too shallow for the boat to float, paddle on to the wave to get as far ashore as you can.

3 Push yourself safely ashore and jump out of the boat before any more waves come along. Keep hold of your boat, so that it doesn't get swept away by a wave.

ADVANCED PADDLING

SPECIALIST DISCIPLINES

Paddlers who achieve a high level of all-round skill and fitness tend to specialize in one or two disciplines: no one has the time to be an expert in more than a couple of fields. If you are looking for a speciality, the choice is wide – kayak or canoe, sea or inland, paddle or sail, freestyle or race. To help you make your decision, here are some key considerations. Two points to note are that, firstly, those disciplines with a competitive element are covered in more detail in the next section of this book. And secondly, with the possible exception of IC10 sailing, it will not be possible to attempt any of the following activities safely, with any hope of real success, until you are proficient at the skills covered so far.

LEFT *Play paddling is the aquatic equivalent of skate-boarding on land.*

BELOW *Using a kite to power a double sea kayak. This technology is still in its infancy.*

Extreme White Water Paddling

It is probably a lot more sensible to read about extreme kayaking than to try it, but if you really are tempted, the following gives a graphic description of what is involved. Danger is the key note, and the risks of serious injury are extremely high.

Extreme kayaking began around the 1970s, when paddlers first attempted white water descents so severe that if they fell out of the boat they were unlikely to survive. Usually listed as Grade (Class) 5+ or Grade 6 type waters, extreme paddling is characterized by large vertical drops or waterfalls.

The first practitioners were slalom paddlers because they already had the highly developed skills needed to tackle the difficult conditions. They were badly limited by their equipment, however. There was a limit to the volume of water or the size of drops they could tackle before their fibreglass boats disintegrated and pitched them into the water.

In retrospect, we know that the boats could have been made stronger then, but there was an obsession with light weight among performance-orientated paddlers. Perhaps this was justified

because they invariably used 4m (13ft) long kayaks that became increasingly unwieldy as they got heavier.

As more boats were made from plastic, there was a significant shift in the world of extreme kayaking. First, the paddlers were able to attempt much more difficult conditions knowing that their boats were strong enough to withstand the water. Second, the foremost extreme white water paddlers were freestyle paddlers who had honed their skills doing the three-dimensional white water acrobatics that smaller, stronger boats made possible.

Assessing the Risks

The modern extreme kayaker is attempting water on which drowning or serious impact injuries are a constant threat. To stand any chance of survival he must use a boat that has been reinforced to prevent it from collapsing under the enormous pressure it must withstand, and have plate footrests with shock absorbers. Usually the boat will be very short.

Most kayakers now recognize that acceleration and manoeuvrability are far more important than outright speed. The boat will tend to be fairly rounded, and able to withstand impacts and potentially lethal pinning to which more pointed boats are susceptible. Extreme kayakers sometimes wear full face helmets such as those worn by motorcyclists, and even elbow pads and reinforced gloves. For instance, paddlers attempting long vertical drops might wear back supports to prevent spinal injuries.

Usually, tackling water this extreme is a team effort. While it is unusual for the paddlers to be able to help each other on the water, a rescue and support team in place on the banks will provide invaluable safety cover. All members of the team should be trained in first aid, and usually there will be at least one fully qualified doctor on hand. Climbing skills and equipment are often required to get paddlers to the top of a descent in order

LEFT *An open-boat canoeist running an extremely large waterfall.*

to inspect the river beforehand. In some of the more extreme cases, when the geography makes climbing too difficult, helicopter support is used to inspect and gain access to the location.

Using all the skills and support at their disposal, modern extreme kayakers have successfully negotiated Grade 6 rapids that were thought impossible only a few years ago, and have paddled waterfalls more than 30m (100ft) in height without injury. However, there is always a fine line between success and failure, and a number of paddlers have died in far less extreme conditions. It is, therefore, hugely important to understand that such extreme and dangerous kayaking is only for a talented few who are supremely skilful, athletic, experienced, confident, determined and well-equipped.

BELOW *Steep and technical, this rapid holds all kinds of dangers. A moment's loss of control could lead to entrapment by the rocks or powerful hydraulics.*

ABOVE *This rapid looks so big and turbulent that even a big kayak is hurled end over end out of control as the kayaker battles with the might of the river.*

ABOVE *A Grade 5+ river with water seething over and around submerged rocks. To be upside down or swimming here would lead to certain injury.*

Play Paddling

As the name suggests, play paddling is the out-and-out playful side of paddling, where practitioners practise all kinds of fantastic tricks in what is the boating world's answer to roller-skating.

Play paddling began in slalom boats because skilful paddlers enjoyed trying to stand their boats on end in waves and stoppers. It was good practice for white water river running because it taught paddlers to cope with anything that the river could throw at them.

It was not until the plastic revolution of the early 1980s that play paddling gripped the imagination of the average recreational boater. Paddling these new and apparently indestructible boats, boaters were able to expose their craft to extraordinary feats and a level of pounding that had never before been possible. This was probably the most significant development in the history of paddle sport.

Today, play paddling and its competitive discipline, freestyle, means being so skilled at using a kayak or canoe in white water that all safety and survival considerations become second nature. In effect, the paddler is playing – frolicking in the waves and hydraulics, surfing, and performing acrobatic tricks using the power of the river.

Since the 1980s, nearly all white water paddlers have used play to exploit the power of the river. Their antics led to the development of kayaks and canoes that were specially designed for play paddling, and it subsequently transpired that experts could negotiate harder rapids in

ABOVE *A play paddler makes a wave-wheel down a rapid. Acrobatic tricks such as this are the main focus of play boating.*

these boats than they could in boats originally designed for more serious river running. This led to more people using play boats for all types of paddling and the development of new skills, spawning yet another generation of play boats.

This trend continued for the best part of 20 years. At the end of the twentieth century, play boats were relegated to what is known as park and play. This is a kind of extreme play paddling that revolves around taking your boat to a specific spot, playing there the whole time, and then going home without having run any rapids in the play boat.

The core play paddling activities are surfing river waves, and using hydraulics to perform vertical tricks, flipping the boat from end to end. These are the key skills, but the range of manoeuvres the expert can perform is bewildering. Virtually every river feature now facilitates some form of boat gymnastics. Many of the tricks are influenced by skate- and snow-boarding, and there is a culture of kayakers with their own music, dress code and jargon.

BELOW *A twenty-first century play boat. This kayak is only 1.9m (6¼ft) long. It is designed to be dynamically unstable to facilitate aggressive acrobatic and aerial manoeuvres.*

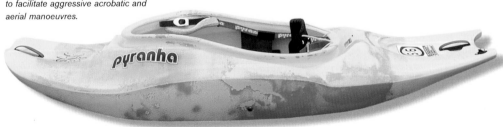

Play-paddling Equipment

The essential equipment for play paddling is virtually the same as for any other white water routine. There are special park and play kayaks that resemble squirt boats, but they are made from plastic and have more volume in the centre to ensure that they are held by powerful hydraulics, while also having many of the safety features of a normal white water kayak. They are not terribly safe for general white water use but you can make good use of a general white water boat (especially a fairly recent one), for play paddling. A 1999 competition freestyle boat was still regarded as a good all-round white water kayak two years later, for instance.

It helps to have shorter paddles for play and freestyle paddling, but any strong white water paddle will do. A flexible shaft is a useful feature because this

RIGHT *A big three-dimensional aerial manoeuvre, called a "kick flip", performed by the author, Bill Mattos.*

BELOW *The open canoeist, European Freestyle Champion, James Weir, paddling a massive stopper wave.*

ABOVE *A play boater performs a cartwheel in a decked C1 freestyle canoe.*

type of paddling is quite hard on the wrists. Most play boaters use a 45° feather on their paddles (feather is the term used to describe the angle between the two blades on a kayak paddle), a good compromise between the higher feather angles for long-distance paddling and the very low angles used by squirt boaters. Play paddling tends to wear down the paddle blades from paddling upstream in shallow water, and constantly scraping them across the boat.

What to Wear

Clothing is an important consideration for play paddlers because you will be regularly rolling and getting fully immersed in the water. Most play paddlers have the best spraydecks (spray skirts) and drytops money can buy. Safety, on the other hand, is less of an issue. Despite the undoubted danger of white

water, the play paddler tends to wear a fairly minimal buoyancy aid (personal flotation device, or PFD) because anything more would interfere with the flexibility needed for the play boater's gymnastic body movements. Helmets, unfortunately, often err on the side of fashion rather than total protection because play boaters try to avoid being thought of as too serious. It would be rare to find a play-boater with a throw-line or any other safety equipment in the boat, and many remove the end grabs from their boats, perhaps to improve the hydrodynamics, but more likely just to make the point.

This is the less responsible side of the sport. The appeal lies in the absence of many of the restrictions seen elsewhere, and the emphasis is on fun and dare-devil feats. It is worth adding, though, that play boating has a low accident rate, perhaps because of the extremely high skill level of the participants. It is not for novice paddlers.

BELOW *Paddling into a stopper wave from downstream. The paddler's bib denotes permission to paddle on a commercial artificial white water course.*

Play Paddling Etiquette

There is an accepted etiquette among play paddlers that differs from some of the rules normally observed on the river. White water paddlers usually focus on safety, which means giving way to anyone coming downstream, and letting other people join the front of an eddy wherever possible. However, these rules don't work very well for play paddlers. If a boater is playing on a wave or in a hole, they will not want to get out when another paddler approaches, but will expect the other paddler to be able to go around them. Similarly, play boaters tend to queue in the eddies to wait their turn on the wave, so to join the front of the eddy is jumping the queue, and not acceptable.

These variations work fine among like-minded individuals, because play paddlers are usually highly skilled, and they tend to stick to familiar sections of water that they can handle easily. The problems arise when paddlers of a different standard play on the same stretch of water, and when confident paddlers become impatient with others who are finding it a challenge just to survive. Whenever this situation occurs, both parties should be aware of the

other's needs and accommodate them as much as possible. If this can't be achieved, one of the parties should agree to move to another stretch of water. Confrontations in the water are never acceptable because of the risk that someone will be hurt.

ABOVE *A canoeist attempting a cartwheel stopper. Open canoes can perform amazing acrobatics in expert hands.*

BELOW *A play boater cruising around on a broken river wave before planning his next move.*

Squirt Boating

Squirt boating is a radical and very special type of paddling which appeared in the early 1980s, and had a profound influence on all kinds of white water boating. It added new levels of fun, especially when dipping the end of the boat under water.

A squirt boat is an extremely low-volume, lightweight kayak or canoe. In fact, squirt canoes are fairly rare, but should not be ignored. Most of the development of the squirt movement took place in kayaks, but the slalom canoeists contributed perhaps the most important idea of all, that of sinking the end of the boat in a controlled manoeuvre.

How It Developed

Slalom paddlers learnt to dip the ends of the boat, usually the stern, so that they could squeeze under the poles when negotiating difficult gates in a race or practice session. They quickly realized that this technique could also give them a dramatically quicker brake, turn and acceleration. It feels as though the water is storing up the energy carried into the

BELOW *This squirt kayak shows just how flat and surfboard-like these low-volume boats are. The paddler's feet fit in the two bumps near the bow, and the knees in the two either side of the cockpit.*

LEFT *Bob Campbell, 1995 World Champion, surfing a wave on a cross-bow rudder. The unusual blade shape gives low resistance under the water.*

turn, which then feeds back into the boat as it accelerates away from the gate. And this is, indeed, how it works; the kinetic energy is stored as hydraulic energy, which converts back to kinetic energy. Paddlers quickly realized that swooping around the rapids, using these invisible dynamic forces, can be tremendous fun.

C1 (single-seater competition canoe) slalom boaters developed stern-dipping until they could easily get the bow above head height. Their K1 (single-seater

competition kayak) counterparts were not far behind, despite having less leverage and the weight of their legs in front of them. At the time, the move was called a pivot turn. In the United States in the 1980s, kayakers experimenting with cut-down race boats likened the feeling to a wet bar of soap squirting out of the hand, and the name stuck. From then on, any move that involved sliding the end of the boat under the water was known as a squirt, and boats specifically designed to do it became squirt boats.

The American Influence

Largely because of the influence of two American brothers, Jim and Jeff Snyder, who were experts at the sport, the boats rapidly became smaller until they had to be custom-built to fit the paddler. The Snyder brothers were convinced that, as long as you had the requisite skills, a squirt boat could be used on any stretch of water provided it was not trapped on the surface by its own buoyancy. They called this the dense boat theory, and they proved their point by running some of the roughest white

squirting techniques have been absorbed into the repertoire of the expert white water paddler.

These new techniques, and the evolution in boat design that they spawned, have been the driving force behind the transition from what is called old school white water paddling to the new school. They have made much of what was written or taught on the subject before about 1990 largely redundant. More importantly, though, it helped turn the sport of white water boating from one surrounded by issues of danger to one featuring fun, and for that we owe the founders a great debt.

Squirt Appeal

So why do squirt boaters choose to paddle these relatively dangerous boats. Why deliberately use a kayak that barely floats in green water, and take it into an aerated environment, where it will almost certainly spend most of its time underwater? This comes back to the aforementioned "dense boat theory".

A paddler who is comfortable with the white water environment finds that, so long as he can remain in control, a

LEFT *Top British squirt-boater Hazel Wilson doing a past-vertical cartwheel in the World Freestyle Championships, 2001.*

BELOW *A squirt-boater deliberately swipes at a rock in a flamboyant aerial move.*

water in the world in boats so small that they looked more like surfboards. They cartwheeled end over end on flat water, and performed the hallmark squirt boat trick, called the mystery move, where the paddler disappears completely below the surface to re-emerge at another place.

Shaping the Sport

Squirt boats are handmade in fibreglass or similar composite materials, and they have to be very strong to survive immersion in powerful water. Because of the way squirting has influenced white water boating, plastic play boats now bear a closer resemblance to squirt boats than they do to general-purpose boats from the pre-squirt era. Indeed, many play boats can now do cartwheels, and many

• Squirt boats are about 2.5m (8¼ft) in length. The volume is designed to match the weight of the paddler, so that the boat is just above the point of neutral buoyancy.

• The boat is so flat that it needs special "tunnels" to accommodate the legs, and "bumps" for the feet.

• The paddler must be able to roll whenever necessary because getting out of the boat in an emergency is completely impractical. Most squirt paddlers use what is called a suicide block between their legs to stop undue body movement in the boat. This dramatically increases the wet exit time.

• Squirtists use very small paddles so that they can move them around easily underwater, constantly sweeping the blades across the deck. The paddles also have very low feather angles so that they can be turned to present no resistance to the current while underwater.

• The spraydeck (spray skirt) must make a perfect seal because the boat will become unmanageable, or even sink, if it ships any water at all.

• The paddler must always do a seal launch into the water because otherwise the boat is so low that it will fill up with water immediately, before the paddler has time to attach the spraydeck deck.

ABOVE *A squirt boater resurfaces from the water after momentarily disappearing in the so-called mystery move.*

RIGHT *Although squirt boaters invented the cartwheel, to perform one in a stopper like a conventional play boater, as here, is an extremely difficult feat.*

squirt boat is actually less likely to fall victim to hydraulics and other powerful water features. With minimal volume, the boat is almost "invisible" to aerated water, and responds only to the call of the green, allowing the pilot to navigate the solid currents of the river's heart without fear of turbulence and random transients.

ABOVE *Vertical gymnastics are another hallmark of the expert squirt boater. The boats themselves are low-volume and are highly sensitive to shifts in the paddler's weight.*

RIGHT *The surfboard-like shape of the squirt boat lends itself to fast surfing and carving through the waves.*

Being made from stiff composite materials also makes the squirt boat a joy to paddle, compared to relatively soft and unresponsive plastic kayaks. The problem arises when things get out of control. To collide unexpectedly with a rock underwater is a nightmare for a squirt boater. Quite apart from the damage and injury it can cause, the loss of control can set off a chain of events that could end in disaster. So squirt boating is always practised in what are, for the expert paddler, extremely familiar and safe waters, so that the unexpected can never occur. Within the relatively safe confines of familiar rapids, the squirtists play unhindered by boat volume and the other limitations imposed on the more usual, surface-bound craft.

Squirting Safely

Paddlers should not attempt squirting until they are confident and quite expert at paddling an ordinary kayak. On top of this it is essential that they are able

to roll. Squirt boats are very sensitive to shifts in the paddler's weight, and this makes them prone to capsize. While squirt boats have performance advantages over other, high-volume designs, the consequences of any white water mishap are extremely serious. Entrapment, where part of your body or the boat gets stuck beneath the surface of the water, is the main danger for all white water paddlers because the strong currents can quickly pull you under. This is an even greater risk when paddling a squirt boat because

you are deliberately putting your boat in more precarious positions. These kayaks are physically difficult to get out of at the best of times, and to be seriously pinned in one would almost certainly prove fatal. In addition, the squirt boat is more prone to becoming pinned, and to planing to the bottom, by virtue of its wing-like shape. Drowned squirt boaters have been found still in their boats, with zigzag scratches on the hull a testament to their desperate attempts to lift an edge and unstick the craft from the bottom.

Kayak Surfing

In the latter part of the twentieth century, the explosion in the popularity of all kinds of surfing has meant that kayak surfers need to put some thought into how they go about taking a kayak out in the surf. Undeniably exhilarating, kayak surfing carries risks, and before you rush in, you need to practise in safe conditions. You must also learn the surfer's etiquette that respects the enjoyment and safety of other paddlers. Incidentally, surfing is one of the few disciplines that is not practised at any serious level in a canoe, despite the fact that the concept was almost certainly invented by canoe paddlers, thousands of years ago in Polynesia.

Riding the Waves

In most cases a wave will start to break at one point, and this breaking part will rush along the face of the wave until the whole wave is broken. The surfer takes off next to the breaking part, and rides along the wave on the green, unbroken face of the wave. He attempts to ride in the shoulder, or power pocket, where the breaking wave is at its steepest. Riding here provides the energy that gives the surfer enough speed to remain in control. If you are too far from the shoulder, you will not be able to ride fast enough and will be overwhelmed by the break. If you are too deep in the pocket, the same thing might happen. It is a balancing act that can only be learned from experience.

An inexperienced kayaker cannot go out in the surf safely unless he can roll repeatedly and well, and there is no one to collide with. After a little practice you can learn how to get off the wave when it has broken, and avoid being carried ashore by the soup, which is the broken white water that tumbles shorewards after the wave has collapsed. However, even a good paddler may have problems,

ABOVE *A kayak surfer hurtling along a steep, barrelling wave-face. This is skilful wave-riding at its best.*

and while you are bouncing in the soup you cannot ensure the safety of anyone paddling through the waves. If you hit them, it can mean serious injury. Do not attempt to come ashore where there are other people until you are experienced.

Spin Sequence

1 The kayaker is riding in the shoulder of the power pocket of a small wave. The breaking shoulder is on the left, the green part of the wave to the right.

2 The paddler uses the paddle and his edge control (which in this case comes mostly from the legs) to spin the boat around without losing any momentum.

3 The kayak continues to ride along the wave, still in the power pocket but now travelling backwards, ready to perform another trick.

ABOVE *An example of an aggressive top turn in a high-performance kayak. The wave is moving from right to left. The paddler is riding the power pocket towards the camera, and has turned (known as a cut-back) so as not to get too far from the shoulder of the wave.*

Tricks of the Trade

A good surf kayaker can get fantastic rides, every bit as good as most board surfers, with the possibility of trying more tricks. Early surf kayaks were, unsurprisingly, based on slalom boats, and there is still an international competition class which has a minimum length limit of 3.5m (11½ft). These boats can be paddled fast, out through the waves, and can race incredibly quickly along the face of a wave, and perform long, carving turns rather like long surfboards.

More recently, many paddlers have taken to using white water play boats in the surf. Typically about 2.5m (8¼ft) long, these boats are not very fast between waves, but they do have the advantage of being able to jump over some very large broken waves, enabling the paddler to get more rides. The disadvantage of these boats is that they do not have enough speed to ride along the face of an ocean wave ahead of the breaking wave.

Wave Skis

Wave skis, a type of sit-on-top surf craft, had a spate of popularity in the 1980s. They were the first craft to provide spectacular leaping, aerial manoeuvres, but have now been replaced by the high-performance surf kayak – a 2.5m (8¼ft) boat which combines the best features of a wave ski boat, an international 3.5m (11½ft) boat, and a play boat. Surf kayaks often have surfboard-style fins to improve their grip and performance.

Essential Equipment

Kayak surfers use short paddles, usually about 1.85m (6ft) in length. They also need an extremely tough spraydeck (spray skirt) because the power of waves as they break is enormous, and will pull off all but the strongest decks. A helmet and flotation aid should be worn at all times, unless you are absolutely certain of your safety. They are recommended because swimming in the surf is unthinkable. An empty kayak is a dangerous projectile that could seriously injure you or other water users. Airbags can be used to fill up any space in the boat in case of a spraydeck implosion. Airbags prevent sinking and will make it easier for you to get the boat ashore: a boat that is full of water is heavy and difficult to move when totally submerged.

Taking Up Kayak Surfing

The best way to start is by watching the experts. When you try it, remember that you need good all-round kayak skills, and the ability to roll well. It helps considerably if you can first become proficient at white water paddling on rivers because, contrary to appearances, they are a good place to learn the basic boat skills from others who can coach from the eddy. In the surf, no one can really help you.

Once you are good at controlling the boat, lifting your leading edge, and surfing small river waves, you can practise these skills at sea, building up the size of the wave as you progress. Aim for a quiet spot, where there are few people around.

ABOVE *Twice World Kayak Surfing Champion Tim Thomas hurls a play boat into a spectacular exit manoeuvre.*

LEFT *Riding in the shoulder of a wave in a long International Class 3.5m (11½ft) surf kayak.*

TIPS

• Do not go surfing in a kayak unless you can roll and have basic white water skills. Use a soft-foam wave ski craft to learn the principles.
• Notice how other surfers ride along the wave in the shoulder.
• Learn to get off the broken waves as soon as you can.

ABOVE *A cut-back move in a play boat. These boats are widely used in the surf, despite being designed for river waves.*

BELOW *A classic surfing shot. The author, Bill Mattos, riding in the power pocket under the breaking lip of the wave.*

SURFING RULES

• Before you get into the water, sit on the beach and watch how other surfers ride it.

• Do not paddle out where other people are surfing. Wait until they have moved or paddle out elsewhere.

• Do not ride the soup unless there is no one between you and the shore.

• Do not take off on the same wave as someone else, unless you are on the other side of the break and you are sure you are going to ride away in opposite directions. Taking someone else's wave is called dropping in, and it is a surfing sin. The wave belongs to the first person to take off on it. If someone drops in on you, get off the wave, and afterwards explain the etiquette.

• If the surf is really crowded, go somewhere else, no matter how good a surfer you are.

Canoe and Kayak Sailing

Using sails on canoes or kayaks is a new and challenging aspect of the sport. Still in its infancy, there are few dos and don'ts, but what you will need most of all are strong arms and plenty of confidence as you get whipped along at high speeds.

It is perfectly possible to use sails either to assist paddling or as the sole means of propelling a canoe or a kayak. It is not a formalized discipline because it is still in its experimental stage but it does, however, have a long history. Many books and drawings from the late nineteenth century feature canoes and other narrow craft with a sail being used to help propel it along.

Sails for canoes tend to have a swinging gaff-type rig. This can emulate a square rig, but tracking is a big problem. Kayaks are often fitted with a small Bermuda-style Delta-sail, which can help to support a paddled kayak, but it does

not offer any significant propulsion by itself. Some double sea kayaks are fitted with two of these sails. This is more effective because the sails are small enough that there is little likelihood of the craft being blown over by the wind,

ABOVE *A traditional sea kayak with the mast and sail stowed along the deck. When required, the mast can be stepped in a recess just in front of the cockpit.*

and the double boats are so long that tracking is extremely good no matter what the weather is like.

Kites

A kite can be harnessed to a boat to support paddling. Kites are extremely powerful, and can pull a boat along at speed even in a light wind. Contrary to appearances, it is possible to sail at most wind angles provided the boat tracks quite well, but you need confidence in your ability as well as strength.

Now that two- and four-line kites have become commonplace, their use with canoes and kayaks has proliferated because the canopies have become more controllable. With a big 7.3sq m (24sq ft) kite or larger flexifoil design it is possible to make a double sea kayak plane along, but because the lateral force is considerable it would be very difficult to control a solo boat in this way. The advantage of a double is that one person can fly the kite, and the other can steer and brace with the rudder and paddle.

Experiments have been carried out with powerful kites and smaller, planing hulled kayaks. Still in its early days but demonstrating considerable potential, in kiting the emphasis is on excitement and aerial acrobatics.

Launching a Kite

1 When the wind is up, inflate the buoyant chambers of the kite.

2 DO NOT tie the kite lines to the boat or to yourself: this is potentially lethal.

3 Pay out the lines. This kite is designed to be launched from the water surface.

4 As the wind fills the canopy, hang on tightly. It could be a wild ride!

ABOVE *Two sea kayaks with small sails. There is a batten near the top, so that a square sail becomes more like a gaff rig with a mini topsail.*

RIGHT *Sailing downwind. The paddle is being used as a rudder here, but could equally act as a keel when reaching, i.e. sailing across the wind.*

TIPS

• Small sails can be used to assist while paddling a kayak manually.
• Larger sails will require that you concentrate on steering the boat using the paddle.
• Make sure that if the kayak capsizes, you will be able to unstep the mast and roll up.
• The sail can be rolled around the mast, and both mast and sail can be stowed on the deck when the kayak is being paddled.

Sailing IC10

This obscure and eccentric feature of the competitive canoeing scene is included here more for its historical than its contemporary relevance. Many people wonder why it counts as canoeing at all because the boat requires a sailing dinghy and paddles are not necessary. But canoeing it is, and if it is excitement that you are looking for, sailing IC10 really does have it all.

BELOW *Two IC10 boats racing on Lake Windermere in England. The boat bears little resemblance to a canoe.*

What Is IC10?

The International Canoe 10 Square Metre was, until recently, the fastest single-handed sailing craft in the world. Nowadays, a variety of sail-boards and a handful of high-tech modern dinghies go faster, but it is still an amazing craft both to sail and to watch, requiring an incredible degree of skilful handling, balance, athleticism and agility. There is probably nothing else like it in the sports of sailing and paddling when it comes to the wide range of talents required for good control and handling.

The IC10, as it is sometimes known, is a sophisticated boat in a traditional form. Its name comes in part from its 10sq m (100sq ft) sail area, but how it resembles a canoe, except in the narrowness of its hull and consequent instability, is more of a mystery. The IC10 has a 5.2m (17ft) long hull weighing 63kg (139lb). The helmsman has a sliding seat on rails that can be extended up either side of the boat, allowing him to shift his body weight in and out. It replaces the wire trapeze system found on more modern dinghy designs. This, in combination with the narrow hull and relatively large sail area, allows the boat to reach speeds in excess of 30km per hour (19mph) in a stiff following breeze.

How It Developed

The sliding seat concept has its origins in the Native American open canoe. While there is no evidence that sailing these boats was ever commonplace, the paddling technique involved sitting outside the up-wind gunwale on a plank of wood, to stop the high-sided boats being blown over by the wind. The strength of the wind would be described as "it's a two-plank day" or a "three-plank day", depending on how many people had to sit out on the plank to keep the boat stable. This appears to be the tradition that led eventually to the development of the sailing canoe as we know it.

Perhaps not surprisingly, given its American origins, the sport of IC10 is especially popular today in the United States. In competitions in the United States, there used to be a so-called "paddling leg", in which the canoe would be sailed around the course for one lap and paddled for the next. The paddling aspect is new rarely included.

The shape of the IC10 hull is strictly determined by competition regulations, but competitors are at liberty to adjust the sail and rig design to optimize the boat's performance, as long as the total sail area does not exceed the stipulated 10sq m (100sq ft). In the latest high-performance sailing dinghies, the sail is usually fully battened from top to bottom.

ABOVE *A wooden sailing canoe. The sliding seat system can be clearly seen.*

RIGHT *Two IC10s on a reach. Note the narrow hull design, and the sailors with their weight right outside the boat.*

As a championship discipline, overseen by the International Canoe Federation (ICF), IC10 boats are sailed by men or women of 69–95kg (152–210lb) in weight, and of 19–60 years of age. To win, sailors must have all the skill and determination of motor-racing drivers, knowing how to use the wind and tides, while being tactically aware, and knowing how to prepare and tune the rig to give the best possible performance.

The racing of IC10 boats is governed by the ICF and national canoeing bodies. World Championships are held tri-annually, and national championships annually in many countries worldwide.

COMPETITION EVENTS

After World War I European skiing enthusiasts, who were starting to paddle white water for sport, came up with a new idea – the format for slalom and down-river racing that we see today. And much later, towards the end of the twentieth century, developments in boat design became the prime movers behind a whole range of more recent competitive events such as polo, kayak surfing and freestyle.

In turn, these events have led to an increasing emphasis on training, coaching and, in particular, psychology in order to improve performances. It would now be very difficult for even a talented individual to compete without attention to these issues. While theory is certainly important, there is no substitute for time spent paddling your boat as a way of increasing your experience.

What follows is general information on the nature of, and requirements for, today's major competitions. The best way to get involved in a competition is to approach your local kayak or canoe supplier, who will recommend a club that practises your chosen discipline. For all of the events mentioned in the following pages, you will need to be skilled with the paddle and, in some cases, will have to acquire better techniques and more experience before you can begin to compete, but do not let this put you off.

LEFT *A paddler performs his manoeuvre on a rapid while other competitors wait their turn.*

BELOW *Competitive paddling makes excellent spectator viewing for the whole family.*

Slalom

For plenty of spills and thrills, you cannot beat slalom. Racing downstream, through a series of gates, it tests racers on three levels, demanding great technical skill, strength to manage the boat, and superb concentration because highly accurate decisions about which stroke to make have to be made at fantastic speed.

Inspired by the sport of slalom skiing, which is a race downhill in which the skier must negotiate a large number of gates, European skiers came up with the idea for kayak and canoe slaloms. They needed something to replace their own sport in summer when the snow melted.

Racing the Clock

The sport is a time trial. One paddler at a time attempts to negotiate a predominantly downstream course on a white water river, marked out using gates through which they must pass. Each gate consists of two vertical poles suspended from wires. All the gates are numbered; green and white gates must be paddled in the downstream direction, while red and white gates must be paddled upstream.

The object is to paddle the course as quickly as possible without touching the gates or missing any. If you do either, penalty seconds are added to your time by the gate judge. Each competitor will

BELOW *A British duo racing a double-seater competition canoe, or C2, in France.*

have one or more practice runs, and then two timed runs. The best of the two times counts towards the final result.

Competition Categories

There are a number of categories, including men's and women's kayak (K1) classes, and single and double-decked canoe (C1 and C2) classes. There is no separate women's class for canoe events. The kayaks must be 4m (13ft) in length and at least 60cm (2ft) in width; in the C1 class they must be the same length and at least 70cm (28in) wide. The C2s are 4.58m x 80cm (15ft x 31½in). Juniors classes use the same size boats as the adults. There is also often a team event in which a team of three paddlers negotiates the course at the same time. The team is timed from the first to start to the last to finish. All three paddlers must finish within 15 seconds of each other, and all their penalties are added to the time.

ABOVE *Manoeuvring skills and stamina are the key to the slalom paddler's success.*

BELOW *A K1 slalom paddler. The bent paddle shaft is popular among slalom kayakers.*

If you want to become involved in slalom, you will need to join a club that has some members who are interested in this field. Not all canoe clubs have slalom paddlers as members, let alone a slalom coach. It would be very difficult to get to grips with it on your own, so seeking out the society of fellow slalomists is pretty essential if you wish to progress.

There are no skill pre-requisites, since the techniques for paddling a slalom boat are the same as for flat water paddling, and can be learnt in a competition craft, even if you have never paddled any kind of canoe or kayak before.

There are also divisional systems in most countries, which means you do not have to compete against national champions unless you are at that level!

Slalom Kayaking

Slalom kayaks are extremely lightweight boats made from carbon and/or Kevlar™. Hence, they are fragile considering the environment they are used in, but slalom paddlers are adept at dodging obstacles.

Slalom used to be the natural choice for anyone skilful at white water paddling and who had the urge to compete but, sadly, participation has declined since the introduction of plastic kayaks. The plastic boats have allowed more people, and in particular less skilful ones, to go paddling white water without fear of the consequences. However, slalom has been included in the Olympic Games intermittently since 1972, and it remains one of the few paddling disciplines to be well known to the general public. It is an extreme test of strength, skill and concentration, and is unlikely to be dislodged from its position as the world's premier canoeing and kayaking discipline, because of it's profile, status, and the fact that the whole family can enjoy watching the competition events in a controlled and safe environment.

ABOVE *Using a stopper wave to help make the fastest line between gates.*

RIGHT *This kayaker has exited a wave so fast that his lightweight boat is almost launched clear of the water.*

BELOW *A C2 slalom crew competing at World Championship level.*

Specialist equipment is not required - the same basic equipment that you would use when you first start paddling is fine for slalom initially, although you will find that most slalom paddlers aspire to close-fitting garments and gear that emphasizes light weight, and acquire such items as soon as possible. The boats themselves are relatively expensive compared to plastic recreational canoes and kayaks, but you do not need to have a top-flight slalom boat right away. In fact, you will usually be able to borrow boats for the first few seasons from a club that offers coaching in slalom. Contact your local paddling stockist for information.

ABOVE *This paddler has just cleared a gate but is careful not to touch the pole with his elbow or paddle blade.*

LEFT *Note the intense concentration on the face of this Italian slalom competitor.*

SLALOM FACTS

• Slalom is the original white water sport, and is still one of the few Olympic paddlesport disciplines.

• The following are the only classes available to the slalom racer:

MK1 – men's single kayak
LK1 – ladies' single kayak
C1 – single canoe (unisex)
C2 – double canoe (unisex or mixed).

• Top slalom paddlers train in the boat every day as well as gym- and cross-training.

• In an entire event, a racer might have only three two-minute runs down the course.

• Slalom boats are 4m (18ft) long, which makes them almost twice as long as a white water playboat. In addition, the slalom boat weighs only half as much as a modern plastic white water boat.

• A slalom course is designed to test all of the basic white water skills, such as breaking in and out, ferry glide, S-cross, and using currents and water features to full advantage. It is also a test of the fitness and power of the athlete.

River Racing

River racing, which includes wild water and rapid racing, is another competitive class that was first promoted primarily by European skiers. If slalom equates to slalom skiing, then river racing is the equivalent of downhill racing on skis.

Like slalom, the sport has strict regulations governing the design and dimensions of the boat, and the way the races are held.

Rules and Boat Shapes

Wild water racing (WWR) regulations are laid down by the International Canoe Federation, paddle sport's regulating body. These require the boats to have a maximum length of 4.5m (15ft) and minimum width of 60cm (2ft) for the K1 class, 4.3m x 70cm (14ft x 28in) for C1, and 5m x 80cm (16ft x 31½in) for C2. These maximum lengths are necessary because, generally speaking, the longer a boat is, the faster it is; similarly, the narrower the boat, the faster it is. These lengths in turn have led to homogeneous designs where all the craft are identical in dimensions and are extremely similar in overall shape.

River racing boats have a deep, vertical bow for slicing through waves, a narrow hull for speed, and a wide deck, which creates the minimum width while also

ABOVE *A white water racing C1 and K1. The boats are extremely similar but for the kneeling/sitting issues and the paddles used. The easiest way to tell the boats apart is by the fact that the canoe has a smaller, rounded cockpit.*

LEFT *These racers are preparing for a practice run. Note the high bow and flared hips of their boats.*

providing the necessary volume to stop the boat rearing up when punching through hydraulic water. The wide back deck tapers rapidly again to a pointed, vertical tail to give a clean, turbulence-free passage through the water. That is why the racing boat looks very strange, and quite different from any other canoe or kayak around today.

ABOVE *The downstream speed of the river racer is apparent in this photograph.*

They are usually made from high-tech composite materials such as carbon and/or Kevlar™, and are therefore extremely light and fragile. Some manufacturers produce plastic replica river racing boats that are suitable for learning and training in.

Handling the Boat

Wild water boats are quite unstable compared to slalom or play boats, but are not as wobbly as flat water racing boats.

BELOW *Breaking in and out of the current at speed is not easy in a river racer.*

They turn fairly responsively when leant to the outside of the turn, and can make dramatic changes in direction, using what is called a wave top turn, but with the full length of the hull in the water they are more directional than manoeuvrable.

Reading the water is an important skill for any white water paddler, but in racing it is absolutely essential to spot the fastest line down a rapid.

All steering must be done with leans, or with strokes that drive the boat forward rather than slowing it down. There is a rhythm to the forward paddling which attempts to make all the strokes when the boat is going up a wave, and not down. This helps a lot with speed and endurance, and stops the nose of the boat from getting buried in white water, and slowed down, any more than is absolutely necessary.

The most important part of river racing is to avoid both rocks and eddies. Hitting a rock in a lightweight Kevlar™ racing boat would almost certainly result in damage, and may well sink the boat. Clipping an eddy can cause the boat to spin round and out, which results in lost time. With practice and observation, you will find the best and fastest way down, and make no mistake, it is a wild ride.

River Races

Wild water races are run as time trials over a section of Grade (Class) 3, or higher, rapids. Rapids up to Grade 5 have been used for top-class events. The rapids rarely demand special skills, however, because of the length of the boats and their lack of manoeuvrability. The course takes 20 minutes to complete, and competitors start at one-minute intervals. This means that sometimes racers will overtake each other, which makes for extra excitement.

Rapid racing is identical to wild water racing, except that the course is more of a sprint, only one or two minutes long. It was designed for spectator appeal, and at some venues two boats at a time race each other. Rapid racing represents an attempt by the organizers of river racing events to attract interest, from the media and potential participants, to a sport which, like slalom, has declined dramatically since the growth of informal play paddling.

Taking up River Racing

The best way to get involved in river racing is to join a club that has a strong tradition of the sport. Get into a WWR boat and paddle it regularly to get used to the way these strange beasts behave.

Freestyle

Freestyle kayaking or canoeing is a spectacular modern form of whitewater paddling competition. It may perhaps be little more than a formalized play paddling competition, but since its inception in the 1970s, it has grown to become a significant force in canoeing and kayaking in many countries around the world, and could be said to have profoundly influenced the design of all whitewater craft for at least two decades.

The original concept came from the common practice of taking turns to show off your best trick on a wave or any other whitewater feature. Informal freestyle get-togethers, or "rodeos" as they were often known, sprang up pretty much anywhere there was an eddy next to an interesting feature, and paddlers vied with each other to perform the biggest, hardest or most consistent tricks.

Scoring and Competitions

In the early days, judging was ad-hoc and usually completely subjective, and often consisted of the competitors simply voting for who they thought the best paddler that day! However, the skill levels of participants in these events soon improved to the point where impartial

ABOVE *A British Junior competing in the 2000 Pre-World Championships.*

or independent judges were required, and more formal competitions were commonplace throughout the '80s. For most of this period, however, the sport was not taken very seriously by the more

established sporting bodies and competitors, largely because the freestylers themselves didn't take it too seriously either.

At the end of the twentieth century, freestyle became almost as rigidly formalized as other whitewater events such as slalom. There is now an accepted structure insofar as paddlers always have a set period of time (typically one minute) in which to perform as many high scoring tricks as possible on a given feature or set of features. What varies, however, is the type of tricks and the way in which they are scored. As a very young and dynamic sport, the actual content of the competitive freestyle repertoire seems to evolve so rapidly that at times there seems very little in common from one year to the next.

The first World Championships were held in 1991 at the Bitches tidal race in Pembrokeshire, Wales. Unusually, the competitors were required to perform various stages of the competition in identical boats supplied by the organizers – this meant that none had any particular

LEFT *An overview of an international competition scene. The competition stopper (hole) is clearly visible.*

advantage of boat design, but also made it easier for the participants, who didn't need to fly in their own boats from all around the world. The event was somewhat experimental, but two years later a much larger and more "conventional" event was held in Tennessee, USA, and there has been a World Championship every two years since then, hosted by a different nation every time.

Evolution of the Sport

Back in the beginning, the possible tricks fell into two categories – wave-surfing tricks like front-surfing, back-surfing, and

BELOW *Kayak paddler midway through a helix – a very complex manoeuvre involving a 360 degree rotation of the kayak in two planes simultaneously! The move is intitiated after a big bounce on the wave to release the kayak from the water.*

transitions between the two, with paddle tricks like twirling and throwing added for effect and good measure, and spectacular attempts to stand the boat vertically on end and perhaps spin it around on end in a sort of pirouette. As the design of the boats evolved, the former became absurdly easy, and vertical moves performed in hydraulic features (holes/stoppers) became the focus of the entire sport.

In the mid nineties a freestyle competition was little more than a challenge to see how many end-over-end cartwheels the canoeist or kayaker could do in a minute. It had all become rather boring and inexplicable to watch, so the rules of competition were changed to encourage variety, and freestyle entered perhaps it's most exciting phase to date, as paddlers were forced to become more inventive, instead of merely concentrating on how fast they could perform certain high-scoring tricks.

Influence on Boat Design

Freestyle paddling has been extremely influential upon boat design, as manufacturers constantly vie with each other to make craft that will enable their athletes to perform a wider variety of tricks ever more spectacular than the season before. For a while, the vast majority of white water boats that were sold to the public were identical to, or based upon, the latest freestyle designs. Interestingly this had also happened to slalom twenty years previously.

In the 1970s nearly all the boats used for whitewater paddling of any kind were essentially based on slalom kayak designs. Unlike slalom boats, however, freestyle kayaks soon became too specialist and extreme to be used for everyday whitewater paddling. This has led some manufacturers to reconsider their support for freestyle research and development, as the sport runs the risk of becoming marginalized by its own rigid

paddle used in the kneeling position. The performance of freestyle canoes has recently overtaken that of the kayaks in whitewater skills such as cartwheeling. It is now common to see the overall score of a canoeist exceed that of the top kayakers in a freestyle event.

Open C1 (Solo Open Canoe) – The freestyle open boat is usually the class least subscribed to. The rules ensure that the boat must be fairly close in design to a traditional open canoe. This makes it absurdly difficult to do any of the latest freestyle tricks. Because of its minority and marginal nature there are often calls for event organizers to drop this class from competitions, but so far it has continued to endure, probably because of the tenacious nature of those competitors who enjoy this particularly challenging style of paddling.

Squirt C1 and K1 – The definition of a squirt boat is that it will ship water if you remove the spraydeck (spray skirt) even on flat water. Squirt boating is responsible for the invention of many of the whitewater skills we see used today. It is rare to see one paddled canoe style, but nevertheless there are still occasional events for this class. Squirt boats do not

adherence to a competitive structure and deviates further and further from the latest thinking in recreational paddling.

As soon as it becomes a competitive discipline only, rather than a fun pastime, it may, like slalom, become a sport for a limited number of special enthusiasts. Luckily, many of the proponents of freestyle recognize this danger and have begun to merge the play paddling skills repertoire with the downriver skills of extreme racing. This type of paddling is sometimes known as "freeride".

The Classes

Freestyle competitions usually have separate classes for Men, Ladies and Juniors and these are subdivided into different boat types as well. The main boat classes that you might expect to find included in a freestyle event are as follows:

K1 (Solo Kayak) – Typically the largest entry class in a freestyle competition. There are no limitations on boat design

ABOVE *A freestyle competitor performs an aerial manoeuvre (often called a blunt) on the face of a wave, and uses the paddle to effect a vertical transition as he lands.*

RIGHT *A C1 competitor performing a loop in a hole or stopper. He will throw himself forward so that the boat performs a somersault and remains in the hole.*

except that the competitor must paddle kayak style (sitting and with a two bladed paddle) and the kayak must be a float boat not a squirt boat. The loose definition of a float boat is that you can get in one on flat water with no spraydeck (spray skirt) without the boat shipping any water, but the final decision will be up to the event organizers. The difference between float and squirt can be marginal.

Decked C1 (Solo Decked Canoe) – These boats are usually identical in design to the competition kayaks, or K1s, except that they are propelled by a canoe

ABOVE *A C1 paddler front surfing a combination wave/hole feature and setting himself up for his next move. The point where the green wave becomes a breaking hydraulic is the "sweet spot" in which most freestylers like to work.*

excel at the same tricks that float boats do. The lack of buoyancy makes it less retentive in a hydraulic and their typically greater length is a limiting factor on a wave. However, these minimal volume craft still entertain the crowds with their smoothness, style and their signature manoeuvre, the mystery move, where the paddler disappears from view below the water and emerges at another place!

Types of Freestyle Tricks

At present, in freestyle the emphasis is on aerial moves performed on a wave. The majority of competitions are held only on a wave-type feature which might at most have an element of breaking foam pile. This means that the play paddler's

repertoire of "hole" tricks go mainly unused. However, some events do still use a hole or stopper type hydraulic.

Wave Moves – These moves vary from the basic surfing, back-surfing and spinning tricks, through blunts (a type of elevated transition on the green part of a wave) to aerial transitions like front-flips, back-flips and barrel rolls. Moves performed without using the paddle usually score extra points, but are both more high risk and more time consuming to achieve.

Hole Moves – These are typically vertical transitions like cartwheels achieved with or without paddle strokes, including the splitwheel which is a cartwheel with a change of axis in mid-trick, and the loop, which is a kind of end over end somersault. Some rules allow extra points for certain extremely complex sequencing of moves. Although it is rare these days for an even to use only a hole rather than a wave feature, it is very possible that a wave will have a

breaking lip or foam pile section that will enable versatile competitors to mix and match their hole and wave tricks to achieve the most efficient and high scoring ride possible.

The Future of Freestyle

It may be true to say that freestyle competition has had its heyday, and that it no longer represents the interests of most white water canoeists and kayakers. However, it still reflects the highest level of three dimensional boat control and spatial skills that can be achieved by paddlers. For this reason, if no other, it will inevitably continue to be a powerful influence on the sport of white water paddling as a whole. In particular, because its competitors are relatively young (in common with most freestyle sports), freestyle canoeing and kayaking will continue to feed highly skilled practitioners into the white water paddling world for as long as it remains in existence.

Extreme Racing

Extreme racing is, at the time of writing, the newest form of specialist competitive discipline to gain widespread publicity. Though it sounds incredibly dangerous, it is not that alarming, though you will need high skill levels to try it.

Usually run over a section of Grade (Class) 4 rapids, extreme racing is a modern incarnation of what white water racing used to be – a race down rapids which, though extreme for an inexperienced paddler, is well within the capabilities of an expert. Perhaps because of its perceived danger level, it is now mainly practised by professional boaters. It is not, however, as extreme as the descents attempted by those who push the limits of extreme kayaking.

ABOVE *This paddler's face shows the effort as he sprints a fairly flat section during an extreme race.*

LEFT *The power of the hydraulic at the base of this fall makes the bow of the boat rear up, and the paddler has to fight for control of the boat.*

History of Extreme Racing

Extreme racing as we know it today grew out of the shortcomings of freestyle as a media flagship for canoeing and kayaking. In fact, people had been racing down rapids for many decades, whether in specialist racing boats or in informal competitions using general-purpose craft. This probably attracted more media attention than most paddle sport events, but in the mid-1990s top freestyle paddlers, already established as the most skilful and extreme boaters in the world, began to look at the fun race events that often ran alongside freestyle get-togethers with renewed interest.

These events were more popular with the crowds and the media than any freestyler gyrating inexplicably in a hydraulic, so people began to organize races down what was, for them, quite manageable white water, but which could be billed as extreme. This 1990s buzzword attracted big crowds and advertising. At first, these races were by

invitation only, and just a few paddlers competed but, as the idea began to catch on, more people participated.

How to Take Part

To consider participating in extreme racing, you need to be totally confident at paddling Grade 4 and 5 rapids, and tackling waterfalls (albeit fairly safe ones) up to 10m (33ft) in height. There are currently no rules about the type of kayak you should use. Unlike white water racing, the emphasis is on what is possible and not the best time achieved by a boat

LEFT *This paddler has taken an unusual and very risky line to try to stay on the top flow of this folded drop.*

BELOW *Sprinting through turbulent rapids in a European extreme race.*

within set rules. Most paddlers use river-running or crossover play boats that are equipped for extreme paddling with full plate footrests, airbags, and plenty of padding.

The best extreme racers in the world currently seem to be top freestyle paddlers, but this may well change as more people begin to train specifically for racing. This is the likely trend because extreme racing seems the most likely kind of paddle sport to attract major sponsorship and prize money. In the meantime, however, you cannot simply go along to your local canoe club and tell them that you want to get involved in extreme racing. Instead, go white water paddling and freestyling, and get plenty of valuable experience. If you see an event advertised in the paddling press, you will have an opportunity to test out your skills.

Sprint and Marathon

Paddlers are always looking for new thrills and ways of racing, and sprint and marathon provided plenty of action. The two disciplines are accessible and attractive to all ages and abilities.

Paddling fast boats on flat water, or sometimes moving water has been a part of the canoe and kayak scene from the very outset. Pick any sports activity, and there will always be lots of people who want to adapt it for racing, and paddle sport is no exception.

Sprint racing is incredibly popular, and is a time trial over a fixed distance from a standing start. There are categories for K1 (solo kayak), K2 (double kayak) and the spectacular K4 (four-seater kayak), and races are over 500m, 1000m or 10,000m. The maximum for a Ladies race is 5,000m. There are similar categories for canoes with C1, C2 and C4, all paddled with a single blade in a high drop-knee position, which is half kneeling, on one foot and one knee.

Marathon is very similar to sprint, but the distance could be anything from 10km (6 miles) to the mammoth 200km (125 miles) Devizes to Westminster race, which is held every year in the United Kingdom, or the Arctic Canoe Race that is over 1,000km (620 miles) long.

LEFT *An older and more stable K1 still shows a fair turn of speed.*

ABOVE *A paddler holds on to the jetty as he adjusts the spraydeck (spray skirt) in his unstable racing kayak.*

The fundamental difference between sprint and marathon is that sprint boats usually race on a lake and in a straight line, whereas the marathon is a journey, and might involve negotiating bends and getting out of the boat to carry it around weirs, rapids or other impassable sections of river. In some races, such as the British Exe Descent and the Irish Liffey, competitors might even tackle large drops and rapids in their wobbly racing boats in order to avoid walking around them.

Race Criteria and Skills

Single racing boats are about 5.2m (17ft) long and 50cm (20in) wide, although the double boats are longer to accommodate two paddlers, at about 6.5m (21ft).

You have to get in fairly carefully, putting your feet squarely in the middle of the boat and keeping some weight on your hands, but once you get moving it will be more stable. Marathon kayaks are fitted with a rudder, which is operated by the feet, because, while the boats are good at running in straight lines, nothing you do with the paddle seems to make much difference to the course. This is unlike most kayaks in which you expend a great deal of energy trying to make them run straight ahead.

While the rudder is effective at steering the boat, it does interfere with the rhythm of paddling, and is actually much more useful for offsetting a constant veer caused by a cross-wind, for example, than for making any changes in direction. Luckily the boats are responsive to slight leans: lean a little to the left, and it veers quite dramatically to the right, and vice versa. This allows you to do a lower, more sweeping stroke on the outside of the turn and a good high stroke on the inside. Because the boat is so narrow that it encourages a vertical paddling action, with lots of body rotation without too much effort from the arms, it is highly efficient for long-distance paddling.

The racing boat is quite unresponsive to most kayaking strokes apart from a really good forward paddling action. A low brace will be required to keep the boat balanced; placing the back of the blade flat on the water provides some support. Otherwise, you will not need to do much except paddle and lean, and anticipate when to turn, because large circles are the rule for these courses.

BELOW *This K2 marathon crew uses the rudder to approach the bank for a portage. The stern paddler is trailing a low brace to keep them stable.*

Equipment and Safety

You need very little additional equipment except for the paddle, which should probably be a modern asymmetric design to facilitate a fast, long paddling action.

The usual test for paddle length is to stand the paddle up in the shop – you should just be able to reach and grip the top of the blade without having to stretch. It is worth spending a lot on a paddle to make sure that you get a good one that is light with slightly less than a 90° feather (the angle between the two blades of a kayak paddle). A full 90° will eventually place quite a strain on the wrists, but because much less causes a lot of wind resistance, settle for 70–80° if you can. The rule with paddles is try before you buy. Serious racers use wing paddles, a specialist type that provides high efficiency and lift, but these are initially very difficult to use and you will need a lot of practice before you can use one effectively.

A spraydeck (spray skirt) is sometimes used as small waves splash into the cockpit even on flat water, or you could simply opt for a decent sponge. And,

generally speaking, racers do not wear buoyancy aids (personal flotation devices) unless they are juniors, but this is because rescue is always at hand at the course. You should wear a flotation aid when training for a race because it can be fairly difficult to recover a swamped racing boat alone, and your friends will not be able to offer much apart from moral support. Furthermore, hardly anyone ever drowns while wearing a buoyancy aid. Unless you have taken other steps to ensure your safety, you should use one.

You should also wear shoes that you are not too heavy amd are safe to swim in, and take a drink of water or energy drink in the boat. You can end up quite dehydrated paddling a kayak, and when you are racing a boat it is very easy to forget how long you have been in the water. Being thirsty over a short period of time will not kill you, but it will negate many of the benefits of doing exercise.

The best way to get involved is to attend a club that specializes in sprint or marathon racing and training. Ask your local kayak supplier to recommend one.

Canoe Polo

Canoe polo is an aquatic ball game similar to water polo. Despite its name, it is not played in canoes but in kayaks that are known as polo boats. It is a fast, lively team game, nearly as good to watch as to play.

You need two teams of five players who endeavour to pass or carry a football-sized ball and throw it in the opposing goal, a square net that is 1.5m (5ft) wide by 1m (3½ft) high, suspended 2m (6½ft) above the water. The goals are placed at each end of a stretch of water, which is marked out to form a pitch, the dimensions of which can vary. The pitch can be delineated on any stretch of water, but will often be in a swimming pool. Canoe polo originated separately in a number of different places and in different ways.

Chasing and playing with a ball is an excellent way of learning good boat control skills while focusing on the ball rather than on the boat. This sub-conscious learning is a terrific way of developing and reinforcing the skills required to pilot a kayak successfully,

ABOVE *A polo player scoops up the ball to pass. Note the flotation aid and helmet.*

LEFT *Two players face off. The wire face guard is absolutely essential.*

and because it was commonly used as a learning tool by instructors, it developed into a game, particularly in Britain, France and Australia. In 1989, the International Canoe Federation (ICF) accepted polo as one of its recognized paddle sports, and merged and adapted the different rules from various countries to create a set of international rules common to all ICF member nations.

Rules and Regulations

The game now has a strict set of regulations. Crash helmets are compulsory, as are buoyancy aids (personal flotation devices) that give the torso all-round impact protection. Although there are rules against dangerous play, quite a high level of

ABOVE *Polo flotation aids have additional padding in the sides to protect the torso against injuries caused by heavy impact from other boats and paddles.*

BELOW *A polo player about to shoot for a goal. He has simply dropped his paddle across the deck to free both his hands.*

protection is necessary. Helmets have wire face guards, and paddles have a minimum blade thickness and radius to minimize injuries that might occur with a sharp edge. Ramming and other aggressive play is not allowed, although, like ice hockey, the game is a contact sport with plenty of pushing and shoving. Since the paddles and hands can be used to control the ball and to block opponents' shots and passes, it is inevitable that there will be firm contact and clashes of boats, paddles and heads. It is quite common to be pushed in by an opposing player while trying to play the ball, although there are strict rules on where on the body the player can be pushed (shoulders and arms only).

Being an explosive sport it is incredibly good exercise with plenty of sprinting, braking, accelerating, rolling and hand-rolling, as well as ball handling. Play

regularly and you will be incredibly fit. You do need to warm up and stretch before playing, though, otherwise the severe physical demands you place on your body may result in injury. The best thing about playing in an indoor pool is that it will be heated.

Although there are specialist polo boats, most clubs will have a selection of pool training boats and paddles, which are often used. If you join a local canoe club that plays polo, you will probably be able to take part without buying any gear. If you take only one piece of kit, make it a nose clip. You can only enjoy getting chlorine up your nose for so long.

For more information or the address of your local club, contact either your national governing body for paddle sport, or a local kayak or canoe store in your area that may be able to put you in touch with a relevant organization.

Dragon Boat Racing

The phenomenally popular sport of dragon boat racing dates back to early China. With boats powered by up to 20 paddlers they charge through the water, and make a fantastic sight when decked out in traditional colours.

How It Developed

Dragon boat racing originated in China more than 2,000 years ago. According to legend there was a warrior-turned-poet by the name of Qu Yuan. A loyal subject of the emperor, he was overcome with sorrow at the poverty and corruption that was then rife in the country. He protested by committing suicide, throwing himself into the Mi Lo River. When his followers heard of his death, they took to the river in their boats, beating the water with their paddles, and threw rice dumplings into the river to feed his spirit.

From that time onwards, the Chinese people commemorated the death of the heroic Qu Yuan by holding the annual Dragon Festival. Since then, dragon boat racing has become a widespread sport. In fact, some sources claim it is the

BELOW *Dragon boating hosted as a fun event by the British Army's Royal Marines.*

second largest participation sport in the world, after soccer. This may be due to its enormous popularity throughout China, and its more widespread use as a commercial adventure sport in other parts of the world. Anyhow, the sport of dragon boat racing only really came to the West in the early 1980s. Since then it has grown steadily, and thousands of people now take part each year.

ABOVE *A ladies' dragon boat team in action. Synchronized paddle strokes are vital.*

Taking Up Dragon Boating

The first step is to find a club, or go to a session run by an outdoor centre. You can find them extremely easily on an internet search engine by typing in "dragon boating" for whichever country you are in.

Paddles for dragon boating are like canoe paddles, but they are shorter because of the lower sitting position. Serious practitioners use traditional wooden paddles, but centres and club boats more usually use plastic ones. Women often use paddles that have a thinner shaft and T-grip. With a really strong crew of 20 the boat practically lifts out of the water with every stroke, and can be powered at more than 4m (13ft) per second. In a race, there is always a drummer at the front who beats in time with the stroke paddler. This is an important job because if the drum is out of time the crew will be too.

For training and individual performance comparison, dragon boat racers paddle the racing K1s with an outrigger attached for balance, and they use a dragon boat paddle. Competitions are held in most countries, with national and world championship events held regularly.

Traditionally, a dragon boat is decorated with a colourful dragon's head and tail, and has scales painted all over the sides.

ABOVE *This team's optional warpaint matches the livery of their dragon boat and adds enjoyment to the ride.*

BELOW *A hard-charging dragon boat crew, with the drummer in the front and the steersman aft.*

Kayak and Ski Surf Competitions

If you want to go in for kayak and ski surf competitions, you have got to learn the special rules and techniques. Incredible fun, they are well worth trying on a good beach with first-rate surf.

Competitive kayak surfing is managed by national governing bodies for kayaking in many countries, and there may also be a governing body for wave-ski paddling. There are regular local and national events in many countries, and bi-annual world championships in both of these surfing disciplines.

Scoring System

Surfing is very much a freestyle discipline, but unlike freestyle kayaking in white water, points are awarded for riding a particular part of the wave rather than for tricks performed *ad hoc*. The usual format is for a heat of four paddlers at a time going out in the surf for a set period, usually of 20 minutes. Judges on the shore will award points (typically out of a total of 20) for the length and quality of the rides of each surfer on the wave. At the end of the heat, the two highest scoring paddlers out of the four will go through to the next round.

BELOW *A short, high-performance class kayak charges a steep section of surf.*

ABOVE *A 3.5m (11½ft) International Class surf kayaker in action.*

Eventually, there will be a final heat of four paddlers, who will be scored in the same way as in the earlier rounds. Sometimes there will be a head to head, with only two paddlers going out in the water at a time, to make the competition more dramatic. This sort of drama is often added for the benefit of television.

To score highly in a surf competition, you need to be good at selecting waves that will give you the best possible ride. You then need to take off in just the right place to make your position in the power pocket as perfect and dynamic as possible, and use all your skills and manoeuvres to maintain that position throughout the ride, before exiting the fading wave with a flamboyant and impeccably controlled manoeuvre.

BELOW *Straight take-off on a wave-ski. The paddler focuses on his balance.*

What the Judges Look For

On a wave-ski, you can carry on riding the wave after it has broken and the judges will carry on increasing your score for the length of ride, and for every impressive manoeuvre you make. In a kayak surfing competition, you will lose points for riding in the broken wave, unless you regain a shoulder and revert to riding in a power pocket. This reflects the different ways in which skis and kayaks handle the breaking wave; the finned and lightweight ski is a safer craft to ride in the broken wave because it is less inclined to go sideways out of control, and is easier to move off the wave.

To enter a competition you should be a member of the national governing body for your discipline (which will often provide insurance). You will be made aware of the regulations for your craft and equipment, which includes a leash for skiers, and a flotation aid and helmet for kayakers. Kayaks must be fitted with airbags, footrests and end toggles because end loops can be very dangerous in the surf.

ABOVE *A women's ski competitor on a custom, composite wave-ski craft.*

BELOW *Driving a ski through a carving turn on a beautiful, glassy shoulder.*

PADDLING AROUND THE WORLD

Many paddlers see their boat as a way to travel and to explore areas that might be less accessible by any other means. Others see paddling as an end in itself, and travel in order to experience their sport in a different country, or in a different way. Travelling with a canoe or kayak is extremely fulfilling. You will often find that you are warmly welcomed by local boaters, who are usually only too pleased to show you the best paddling in their area. If you travel to a place where there are few indigenous paddlers, you will experience the ultimate fulfilment of being one of the few people who has navigated there. The canoe or kayak is accepted in most parts of the world, since it leaves no traces of environmental impact. With the right knowledge and preparation, you can paddle just about anywhere there is water.

The best way to get up-to-date information on paddling in any country is from the Internet. Just use a search engine site to find out about guidebooks, local tourism, rafting companies, and anything else related to paddling worldwide.

LEFT *Breathtaking scenery and exotic wildlife are some of the bonuses of paddling abroad.*

BELOW *Travellers in search of white water need to be aware of seasonal water levels.*

Europe

Broadly speaking, Europe consists of
Scandinavia, mainland Europe, and the
United Kingdom. The entire continent
offers a mixture of white water rivers,
inland waterways, open water (inland and
sea) and reasonable proximity to coastal
paddling and surf. In northern and central
parts of Europe, the winters are snow-
and ice-bound. In the far south, around
the Mediterranean sea, it is extremely
hot in summer and moderate in winter.

Scandinavia

In Scandinavia, which consists of Iceland,
Norway, Sweden, and Finland, every kind
of paddling imaginable is available, but
the season is short since the whole area
is ice-bound for at least half the year.
White water paddling derives entirely
from snowmelt, so the rivers tend to be
biggest in the spring (April and May),
dropping off to a low in August. The local
geography is very rocky and mountainous,
and tends to result in white water that is
steep and full of waterfalls, but there is
also a wide variety of more placid, mature
rivers and estuaries (locally called fjords)
for the touring paddler. Some of the
Scandinavian lakes are enormous,
resembling inland seas.

BELOW *A kayaker carries his boat down
a tranquil street in a Swiss village.*

ABOVE *A medieval bridge over Grade
(Class) 2 white water in France.*

LEFT *Typical Alpine white water: the
river is bouldery and not too steep.*

Mainland Europe

Central continental Europe is dominated
by a number of large mountain ranges,
which offer Alpine white water paddling
in Germany, the Czech Republic, Austria,
Switzerland, southern France, Spain,
northern Italy, Croatia and Yugoslavia.
This varies in character from generally
small and technical rivers in most areas,
to a few very high-volume ones in
Germany and Austria. River guidebooks,
which are kept up to date, are available
in local languages and in English.

ABOVE *Paddlers navigate their way down a steep and narrow gorge.*

RIGHT *Entering a committing gorge, three paddlers line astern.*

United Kingdom

Considering its small size and maritime climate, it is perhaps surprising to find that the United Kingdom offers excellent paddling of all kinds, and has possibly the largest number of paddle sport enthusiasts per capita in the world.

White water paddling in the United Kingdom is entirely rainfall dependent, but such is the reliability of the British climate that the rivers are sure to be fast-flowing throughout the autumn and winter (October to January), and often during rainy spells in the spring (March to April). However, a peculiarity of British law dictates that, unlike most other countries in the world, it is illegal to navigate rivers without permission from the landowners. Luckily, most interesting sections of river have some sort of agreement negotiated on them, which means that paddling is allowed at least during the "closed" season for fishing. Nevertheless, it may still be necessary to apply for a licence, or some other kind of permit. The best way to find out about this is to contact the British Canoe Union (BCU), who have a comprehensive database and will tell you what you need and how to apply for it. Assume that white water paddling at least will be allowed only from October to March in most areas. This is the best time for the water anyway.

There are no such restrictions on Britain's extensive coastline, which offers excellent sea touring and estuary paddling, and the West Coast (Scotland, South Wales and Cornwall in particular) offers world class surfing. The sea is warmest in September and coldest in April.

The Alpine paddling here is almost entirely glacial or snowmelt, but it is often bolstered up in some areas by rainfall in the summer. The season therefore runs from April to August. In Portugal, exceptionally, the white water mostly comes from rain, so the season is October through May, although with luck there will still be decent white water during the summer.

The island of Corsica, off the coast of France, offers spectacular, big-volume and steep white water from April to June.

There is also an extensive network of very large inland waterways, which provide spectacular opportunities for the touring canoe or kayak. These are available throughout the Alpine countries and also in the low countries of Holland, Denmark, and Belgium.

Switzerland contains some huge and beautiful lakes, while coastal paddling in mainland Europe is plentiful wherever there is a coast. Surf, however, is mainly found on the west coast of Europe. France and Portugal face the best of the Atlantic swells. The Mediterranean does not provide rideable waves except after storm conditions.

North and Central America

The North American continent is the spiritual home of modern paddling. The traditional open canoe of course originated there, and the kayak as we know it today is descended directly from the Inuit craft that hails originally from the northern shores of what is now Canada, as well as from neighbouring Greenland and Siberia.

The United States and Canada together form an enormous continental land mass. The sheer geographical size of these countries means that there is inevitably a wide variety of paddling, but there are also great distances to cover. Whereas in Europe one might have a number of rivers within a few minutes drive of each other, it is common in the United States and Canada to travel for several hours, if not days, to find the water you are looking for. At least this way, you get to see more of the country.

BELOW *A big drop on the South Fork of the river Yuba in California.*

The United States
It is commonly believed that most of the white water paddling is restricted to the mountain ranges down the East and West coasts, but in fact almost every state in the United States boasts quality white water. However, the size of the country means that American paddlers tend to be either an East Coast paddler, or a West Coast one: zipping across the country from one side to another is not feasible for most people, and they prefer to stick to the coast nearest to where they live. This way, the United States even manages to field two separate teams for international competitions: one from the East and one from the West.

As well as its world-class white water, there is an enormous following for the more placid open water boating on flat water rivers and lakes. Open canoes are widely used for hunting and fishing as well as being recreational craft in their own right. It is probably true to say that open canoeing is bigger in America than

anywhere else, with whole families packing up their boat and heading down to the water, dog and all.

The coasts of North America are popular destinations for sea kayaking, and they offer good quality surf at most times of year. In particular, the Pacific coasts of California and Mexico are, perhaps not surprisingly, very well attended surfing locations. The east-facing Gulf of Mexico also catches some very good swells.

Central America
Guatemala, Belize, El Salvador, Honduras and Nicaragua all have spectacular white water and excellent surf on both the Pacific and the Caribbean coasts. However, these are not the safest or the most politically stable countries you could visit as a tourist. Further south, Costa Rica is a better bet, with world-class tropical white water paddling, great surf, and sea kayaking too. It is best visited from November through February, but

ABOVE *Huge white water: the National Falls, Upper Youghiogeny, Maryland.*

is so popular with tourists that if you try to fly in around Christmas time it can be expensive, if not impossible.

Further south again, the narrow land-bridge that is Panama boasts some excellent touring in its beautiful National Parks, and sea kayaking on both of its coasts. From there we reach Colombia, part of the South American continent.

Canada

Canada is famous for big-volume white water. Although there are a variety of different rivers to explore, it is the mighty rapids of the Ottowa and St. Lawrence in the east, and the Slave, Peace and Fraser in the west that have captured the imagination of white water paddlers since the 1970s. These rivers are fed almost entirely by snowmelt, but because of the lakes, which act as reservoirs for the colossal amount of meltwater, the season is quite long – the water levels tend to be (too) high in April and May, dropping

slowly through the summer. They are still supplying big-water fun into September.

There are many enormous lakes scattered across the Canadian landscape, as well as the almost Scandinavian coastlines of Newfoundland and British Columbia. Alaska, which is the northern-most state of the United States although entirely within Canada geographically, has much in common with Canada. It is dominated by the splendid Yukon river and the often ice-bound Bering Straits that separate it from neighbouring Russia.

The Canadian Great Lakes, Superior and Huron, border with the American states of Minnesota, Wisconsin and Michigan. These inland seas are bigger than a small country, and because of this, sea kayaking has a strong following in the area; the local paddlers often use full-on ocean kayaks. Sea kayaking in Canada is big business, and commercial trips are widely available. Adventure tourism is huge in Canada anyway, and opportunities to go paddling with seals, dolphins and killer whales are irresistible for tourists and paddling fanatics alike.

BELOW *Running a sloping drop into an eddy on the Maryland National Falls, USA.*

South America

South America is a rather different place from its northern neighbour. Composed of 13 independent nations, each with a far less developed economy than the United States, it is inevitably less affluent, and this is reflected in the poor state of the continent's transport and communications network. Travelling with boats must be done mainly through bus travel, and anyone who has paddled here will have stories of epic ten-hour bus journeys in oppressive heat.

River Paddling

By far the largest of the countries is Brazil, which is dominated by the vast network of Amazon tributaries. The Amazon itself, the greatest river in the world, starts in Peru, in the west of the continent, and stretches right across to its equatorial delta in the east.

All the South American countries have great rivers and, with the exception of Paraguay and Bolivia, hugely interesting and extensive coastlines, but the popular kayaking destinations are Ecuador, Peru and Chile. Each of these countries has a mixture of indigenous native Indian cultures, and Spanish influence, courtesy of the medieval Spanish *conquistadores*. Living and travelling is inexpensive, but all three countries are dangerous places in wilderness areas, both medically and because of a widespread risk of theft, mugging and corruption.

White Water

Classic white water runs abound in Ecuador and Chile. The white water season throughout South America runs from October through to February.

There is more and more commercial kayaking and rafting in South America, especially in Chile. At the same time, however, many classic and beautiful white water runs are being dammed for hydro-electric power and are lost to paddlers forever. This is one of the problems facing white water rivers in developing countries.

ABOVE *River gorges form beneath clear blue skies and steep mountainsides in Peru.*

LEFT *Casa Nova Falls and Land of the Giants, Rio Misahualli, Ecuador.*

Open Water

The Pacific coast features excellent surf, and is a popular destination for surfers. The sea kayaking opportunities, too, are plentiful, as one would expect from such extensive coastlines and tropical climate, but the infrastructure isn't really there to support anything more than the self-sufficient adventurer.

To the far south of the continent, the climate changes dramatically. By contrast with the tropical climes further north, the south of Argentina and Chile, culminating in the Tierra del Fuego and Cape Horn, are close to Antarctica. Severe bleak weather, combined with savage ultra-violet penetration because of damage to the ozone layer, make this an inhospitable place. The stormy seas around Cape Horn are famously the roughest in the world. They are not suitable for kayaking, although some intrepid expedition paddlers have rounded the cape and much of Tierra del Fuego in sea kayaks.

ABOVE *A team meeting on a river beach on the Rio Cassanga in Ecuador.*

RIGHT *Huge white water: the Lost Yak rapid on the Rio Bio Bio in Chile.*

BELOW *Typical boat transportation in South America: the going is slow, but at least you have time to appreciate the sights.*

Australia and New Zealand

The enormous continent of Australia has relatively little in the way of white water, but with its incredible and extensive coastline makes up for it in sea kayaking and surf. The relatively diminutive islands of New Zealand, on the other hand, feature enormous paddling opportunities, and for this reason among others is beginning to be hailed as the adventure tourism capital of the world.

Australia

Of course, Australia does have its white water rivers, and the artificial white water course at Sydney, which was built for the Olympic Games in 2000, has done a great deal for the profile and the popularity of white water kayaking among Australians. But the sheer size of the country and the relatively large distances to be travelled between runs has dictated that Australia has not, as yet, become as popular a destination among white water tourists as neighbouring New Zealand.

The surf, on the other hand, is spectacular, and its close proximity to major cities makes it a very good reason to go there. Wave-ski paddling is far more popular than kayaking at the moment, although this may change as the global shift towards surf kayaks makes more

LEFT *Horizon line: a kayaker about to take the plunge on New Zealand white water.*

ABOVE *The Australian coastline offers some excellent surf and wave-ski opportunities.*

exciting kayaks available to wave enthusiasts down under. Sea kayaking is big business in Australia, with such large sections of coastline commercially exploited, and tourism being one of the stronger industries in coastal areas.

New Zealand

From the point of view of an outdoor adventure enthusiast, New Zealand is an astonishing country. Not only does it boast some of the most spectacular white water on the planet (such as Huka Falls on the Waikato, North Island) but also some of the best play waves (Kaituna, Falljames) and famous surf breaks, such as Raglan point, one of the best left-handers in the world.

New Zealand has a great deal packed into a small country, but despite this and its enormous popularity, overcrowding and overuse of resources is not yet a problem. The relatively low population and the nature of the geography mean that, although you will always see and meet other paddlers, it won't be frustratingly busy. A lot of New Zealanders do paddle, but you will be surprised to find that many of the boaters you meet there are foreign visitors.

The white water rivers seem to run for much of the year, although most are primarily spring/summer rivers (from October through to May). Some of them, however, are dam-controlled and have year-round water. There is a wealth of information available on the Internet, because New Zealand is one of the most popular destinations for paddling tourism and a lot of help and guidance has been written and provided.

Commercial rafting on white water is widespread, as are jet-boat rides on the rapids and any other adrenalin-pumping activity the New Zealanders can sell to the tourists. Commercialism is one reason why there is an excellent infrastructure and information network for anyone who wants to paddle there.

Surfing and sea kayaking are equally well catered for by the commercial sector, but you will have no trouble getting off the beaten track and finding solitude if that's what you are looking for. New Zealand has more than its fair share of beaches and beautiful coastline, and sea touring in

particular is very popular. Inland touring is less available than in many countries, but what there is makes up for this with the beauty of its surrounding countryside.

Because of its maritime and temperate climate, New Zealand isn't particularly cold in the winter. The mountainous regions in the centre of the islands get snow, which provides much of the spring white water, but in low-lying areas and nearer the coasts the temperature is unlikely to be less than 10°C (50°F).

New Zealand is a relatively expensive place to fly to, even from mainland Australia, but in particular from the rest of the world because of its otherwise remote location. Once there, however, the cost of living and of travelling is one of the lowest outside the Third World. This makes for a tempting combination of a cheap trip with a highly civilized infrastructure and a truly excellent range of commercial resources.

ABOVE *A kayaker going deep on the Kaituna river, New Zealand.*

BELOW *A kayaker makes a spectacular blunt on the Falljames river, New Zealand.*

Asia

This is rather a big place to try to describe in one small section, but in fact Asia is probably the continent whose paddling we know least about. Although intrepid expedition paddlers have penetrated almost every part of the Asian continent, there are still many rivers left to run, and all but a tiny minority of the vast land area is as yet untouched by adventure tourism.

If you plan to holiday in Asia, the Internet is by far your best way of finding out about the paddling possibilities. It is probably fair to say that this part of the world is changing faster than any other in terms of its potential for adventure tourism, although, with a few exceptions, it has a long way to go to catch up with countries such as New Zealand. However, the jewels in its crown are

RIGHT *Porters carrying kayaks towards a Himalayan river.*

BELOW *Overnight stopover on the beach of the river Sun Khosi in Nepal.*

RIGHT *Enormous white water on the Indus, the river that gave India its name.*

Nepal for white water, and Indonesia for surf and sea paddling. Both destinations are unmatched worldwide in quality for their respective types of boating.

Nepal

This tiny, land-locked country is one of the most popular destinations in the world for white water kayaking. Extensively rafted and kayaked commercially, it is accessible and cheap, and until recently it enjoyed relative political stability. The surrounding countries all feature incredible white water, but it is less commonly paddled. India, Pakistan and Tibet have all enjoyed a fair amount of attention, but none of them are popular paddling destinations as yet.

South-east Asia

China is now a developing tourist destination, but although there are many white water rivers and beautiful coastlines, very few people have paddled there. Thailand has some white water that is commercially rafted, and is popular with a great number of inland and sea touring specialists: the Asia-Pacific region in general is tropical and has a tourist-friendly coastline.

Both kayaking and canoeing are huge in Japan. The number of Japanese people who regularly go white water, touring or sea paddling is enormous, although only a small number of foreign tourists paddle there. This is perhaps a result of the high costs associated with this small country, or it may be that the language barrier makes it difficult to get information about it. Most Japanese websites are in the Japanese language, and hence illegible to most foreigners.

Indonesia has white water that is now just beginning to be paddled regularly, although it is most renowned for its world-class surf. In fact, almost all of the Pacific island chains, Tahitian islands and Hawaii (which really counts as America) have the most fantastic surf imaginable, and these are key destinations for kayakers.

RIGHT *A Nepalese mountain gorge. Scenes like this make for exhilarating paddling.*

Africa

The enormous continent that is Africa is a hugely popular tourist destination because of its natural beauty and the sheer scale of its geography.

Almost all of Africa is either tropical or sub-tropical, so it is characterized by its extreme heat for most of the year. The continent is a good paddling destination: inexpensive and with a good infrastructure for tourism in many areas. Health issues must be considered – consult your doctor before you go, and explain what you will be doing there. It is a beautiful continent, but not one to be taken lightly.

Northern Africa

The desert countries of the northern sub-tropical areas (Morocco, Tunisia, Algeria, Libya, Egypt) have few paddling opportunities, although there is good surf on the west coast, and the Atlas Mountains have potentially exciting white water (though no-one ever seems to catch good water levels there).

Central Africa

The central tropical African nations have a wealth of rivers, both white water and mature. Access to these is fairly difficult, however, and the long-term political instability of many of these countries must be a concern. The Nile and Niger, Africa's biggest rivers, are still a draw for many tourists, and commercial paddling is available in many regions.

The white water of the Congo, Uganda and Zambezi is world-famous, and is becoming increasingly popular as a result of developing commercial tourism. This is enormous white water, and should not be attempted by the complete novice. However, there will often be expert guidance on hand in these areas from the local rafting companies and professional kayakers, and if you want to paddle the most amazing white water in the world, it should be possible – subject, of course, to adequate technical skills, fitness and strength.

ABOVE *Getting airborne in an African sunset. The scenery here is breathtaking.*

BELOW *An absolutely colossal stopper (hole) in Uganda, Central Africa.*

Southern Africa

South Africa is a popular destination for all kinds of paddling, while neighbouring Namibia and Botswana are less popular. South Africa is sought-after for its surf and sea kayaking: wave-ski paddling is huge. The south-west coast of South Africa, around Cape Town, and Durban on the coast, are perhaps the two most popular and versatile location choices.

Coastal Areas

Africa is blessed with good surf. The entire west coast faces on to massive Atlantic swells, and Morocco, Senegal, the Ivory Coast, Cameroon and Gabon are all popular with surf fanatics. On the east coast, the waves are less consistent, but the Indian Ocean and Madagascar still provide some thrills and spills as well as beautiful coastal touring.

ABOVE *Playing on a big rapid. Central Africa has some world-famous white water.*

BELOW LEFT *Play boating on white water in South Africa. The country offers good opportunities for all kinds of paddling, and is a favourite with paddling tourists.*

BELOW *Safety kayakers with their raft on an eddy on the White Nile, Uganda.*

KEEPING SAFE

Safety and Rescue

While good planning and appropriate equipment can prevent many difficulties, accidents will still happen. This section is intended to tell you about the safety and rescue techniques that all kayakers and canoeists need to know, whatever type of water they are paddling on. More detailed advice, including essential equipment, aimed at specific types of paddling is given in the flat water, white water and open water sections of this book.

Practise the following techniques to a proficient level, and make sure you know how to use the equipment you have with you. In a situation where every second counts, it is vital that you know what to do.

Communication
The biggest part of safety and rescue on the water is communication. Make sure you know your paddling group's level of ability and experience, so that you will be better prepared if an incident occurs. If you come across a situation involving people you don't know, start a dialogue immediately. You can't bring your skills to bear on the situation until you have understood what is happening.

BELOW *Attempting a chase boat rescue to help a swimmer out of the water.*

Rescue and Recovery
If someone in your group is unable to re-enter their boat after a capsize, you may have to rescue them by paddling over and helping them to get back in. If they are unable to paddle due to injury or tiredness, you may need to tow them and their boat back to safety.

The following rescue and recovery techniques detail how to do this. Learn them all so that you can use the most appropriate for the situation on the day.

ABOVE *Talking through the plans for the trip in advance can eliminate confusion later.*

Chase Boat Rescue
If a paddler is in the water and unable to re-enter their boat, you may be able to get them to hold the front or back of your boat, or even get on to or into your boat, so that you can carry them to shore. It is slow progress, and often better to get to shore and use a throw-line to pull them in.

When you attempt to rescue someone who is upset or panicking, they may be irrational and can unwittingly put you in danger by clinging to you or clambering on to your boat. Don't let a victim get hold of you until you have established verbal and eye contact, and you are sure they are not going to put both of you in more danger than you are already in.

SAFETY RULES
- Always wear a flotation aid, and put it on before you get into the boat.
- Learn how to capsize as a priority.
- It is more important to rescue the victim than the boat.
- Never undertake a rescue that puts you or the victim in more danger than you were already in.
- Only ever practise rescue procedures in a safe environment.

ABOVE *A shoulder belay is one way to pull a swimmer or boat from the water.*

Throw-line

A throw-line consists of a length of rope that will float tied to a bag. The bag will often have some foam buoyancy to keep it afloat as well. In order to rescue a swimmer when you are standing on the bank, take the throw-line, open the bag and grasp the loose end of the rope, and throw the bag to the victim. Aim to land the bag beyond the swimmer, so that the rope falls across him, and he can grab it and be pulled to safety.

Shoulder Belay

This is an efficient way to maximize your strength when using a rope to rescue a paddler or equipment from the bank against a fairly strong current. Wrap the rope around your back and over your shoulder to get your whole weight behind the pull. This way you can apply a force to the rope equal to about 110 per cent of your body weight. Pulling with your arms will only give you about 80 per cent.

Pulleys for Mechanical Advantage

If you are trying to recover a swimmer or a boat against a current that is too strong to resist manually, you can set up a pulley system from the bank to increase the strength of your pull.

Karabiners can be used with a sling to make a pulley. Karabiners are strong metal devices used for connecting ropes and slings to each other, or to boats and rescue equipment. They can also be used as improvised pulleys. You can attach a karabiner to a tree or rock with a sling, then put a throw-line through it to apply some braking to a swamped boat as it hurtles downstream. A boat full of water is a heavy projectile and you will not be able to control it otherwise. Karabiners are not as good as real pulleys because they apply a lot of friction, but this can be used to your advantage if you need to brake or control a descent or rescue.

If you use a pulley to double the force you apply to the boat, you will have to pull 2m (6½ft) of rope through the system for every 1m (3½ft) that the boat moves. With two pulleys, in a system called a Z-drag, there will be three times more force, but you will need even more rope. You also need to ask yourself whether you want to carry hardware such as pulleys every time you go on the river, and whether it might not be safer to abandon the boat and concentrate on rescuing only the swimmer.

Towing

A waist tow is a useful technique to operate from your boat. It can be used for towing a boat or a swimmer. It can also be used by two or more paddlers in a yoked or husky tow, which is invaluable for towing over long distances or in difficult conditions.

Using a proper towline, which will have a shock absorber to prevent spinal injury, loop the towline over your shoulder so that it can be quickly released if you become entangled with something in the water, or if you capsize, which would put you and the victim in further difficulties.

A simple 2m (6½ft) sling can be used in place of a towline for towing a boat or paddle. Put the sling around your elbow or shoulder. Never put it around your waist or body: you must be able to get rid of it easily if you capsize, even if the tow is keeping it under tension.

Modern flotation aids for white water incorporate a quick-release rescue belt as part of the design. This provides a stronger attachment for the towline.

Air Sea Rescue

Helicopters are often used to rescue kayakers from the sea or from remote wilderness rivers. You are unlikely to have experienced a helicopter rescue before, and it pays to know what to expect.

Helicopters make a lot of down-draught with their rotors. If you are afloat in a boat and one hovers overhead, it is like getting a trashing in a hole or in the surf. You will be blown over, and may not be able to roll up. It has been known for sea kayaks to be blown end over end across the water by the power of a helicopter's down-draft.

If a winchman or unmanned strop is lowered to you from a helicopter, you may need to allow for the strop to be earthed to ground on water before you try to grab it. Helicopters can generate a potentially lethal amount of static electricity which must be released to earth.

If an Air Sea Rescue helicopter is called out to recover you, they will not transport your kayaks and equipment. In fact, at sea they will deliberately sink your kayak to prevent potential false call-outs when an empty boat is spotted by shipping.

BELOW *Most countries have an Air Sea Rescue service that will come to the help of paddlers in trouble at sea.*

Medical Knowledge for Paddlers

Kayaking and canoeing are very safe sports when compared to most other adventure activities, and much safer than team contact sports such as football, basketball, rugby or cricket. However, minor injuries are commonplace in all sports, and in addition to knowing how to cope with them, you must also be aware of problems that are specific to paddlers.

The skills required to tackle serious and/or life-threatening injuries in a remote environment cannot be learnt from a book. If you intend to paddle in situations where such threats are possible, it is vital that you go on a registered first-aid course to practise the techniques involved.

Of the few injuries that do occur, most happen while actually paddling, and not while capsizing, rolling or swimming.

The most common mechanism of serious injury is striking an object such as a rock, paddle or another kayak. The next most common are traumatic stress injuries caused by the impact of water against the body or equipment, and overuse injuries such as tendon problems, particularly in the wrists, and chronic back problems.

BELOW *A bivvy bag can be used to retain heat and prevent wind chill. Note here the buoyancy aid being used as a pillow to stabilize the head position and maintain clear airways.*

ABOVE *Rolling up with the head tucked on to the front deck can save you from knocks to the head and facial injuries.*

Minor Cuts and Bruises

Cuts, bruises and splinters are far more likely than fractured limbs. Immersion of the affected area in cold water and/or wind chill ensures that minor cuts and bruises will not usually become painful until you get off the water. If there is an open wound, however small, be aware that it might get infected and decide whether to close or cover the wound before the wound gets wet, if you still have a choice. Clean water (fresh or sea), should be used to clean the wound, and this will temper any pain. If you suspect the water is dirty, keep the wound dry.

Hypothermia

If you become excessively cold you will slowly succumb to hypothermia unless you are able to warm up your body. The victim is unlikely to realize it themselves, but early symptoms may be noticed by other paddlers. These include:
- Irrational behaviour.
- Loss of co-ordination.
- Loss of communication skills.
- Memory lapse.
- Loss of motivation and will to move.

Hypothermia can be caused by sudden cooling, for example taking a swim in cold water, or by slow progressive cooling through the onset of exhaustion and/or inadequate insulation over a period of hours. The cause might even be a combination of the two. With the former, it is correct to warm up the victim quickly, when back on land, using a warm bath or shower, or switch on the car heater.

In the case of profound hypothermia caused by slow heat loss, this would be ineffective, extremely dangerous and could result in heart failure. Instead, get the victim dry and insulate them as much as possible with clothing, a hat, gloves, sleeping bag or anything else to

hand. If you are carrying a bivvy bag as part of your first aid kit, you can put the victim into it. If necessary, you can get into the bivvy bag with them to increase the temperature. Check constantly that their air passage is clear, and get professional medical help as quickly as possible. The victim will not be able to do anything to help himself.

Remember that prevention is better than cure. If you or anyone in your paddling group is exhibiting the normal signs of getting cold, for example shivering, and loss of feeling in the extremities, while on the water, act immediately before hypothermia can set in. Get the person away from the water, and get them warm.

Hyperthermia

The opposite of hypothermia is heatstroke, also known as hyperthermia. The symptoms are loss of colour, a high temperature but not necessarily sweating, and shallow breathing. The victim will feel faint and nauseous. Cool down the casualty gently by moving them into the shade and giving them lots of cool fluids.

By far the most common cause of hyperthermia in paddlers is moving around off the water when it is hot, while still wearing all the insulation that was intended for the colder conditions on the water. The best immediate treatment is to remove as many levels of clothing as necessary to enable them to cool down before they overheat.

Shock

Traumatic injury or a frightening experience can lead to shock. Similar symptoms to those of hypothermia occur. The victim may be disorientated and not capable of looking after themselves. Shock can be treated as follows:
• Treat the cause if it is physical.
• Make the victim comfortable, and place them in the recovery position if possible.
• Keep the victim warm, and provide warm drinks if there is no reason to preclude this (if the victim is unconscious or has a head or facial injury).
• Watch the victim constantly in case they stop breathing or fall in the water.
• Provide professional medical attention as soon as possible.

EMERGENCY ACTION

A realistic attitude towards personal safety on the water is essential, and a few common sense precautions will ensure you are as prepared as you can be for an emergency. Attending a registered first-aid course will give you confidence in your ability to react swiftly, and can help save lives. Contact your local kayak or canoe club for details of appropriate courses in your area.
• Drowning poses an ever-present threat to paddlers of all levels and on all types of water. Knowing how to treat a drowning person can mean the difference between life and death. First aid treatment for drowning always begins with cardiopulmonary resuscitation, and while it is beyond the scope of this book to teach this, it is recommended that you attend a first-aid course to learn what to do. The threat of drowning can be minimized by following three basic rules:
    1. The ability to swim 50m (170ft) in light clothing.
    2. Personal flotation aids should be worn at all times.
    3. A minimum number of three people in any paddling group.
• Anyone who is unconscious or semi-conscious must be placed in the recovery position to ensure that their breathing remains unobstructed. Make sure your first-aid training includes the recovery position.
• If you need to telephone the rescue services for help, find out your exact location before you call so that they know where to look for you. Include an up-to-date 1:50,000 map and a compass as part of your safety equipment, as well as a torch to help you read it if the light is poor, and give accurate map co-ordinates for where you are when you make the call.
• Keep your first-aid training up to date, and practise safety and rescue procedures with your group on a regular basis. Practising in conditions where the emergency is likely to happen – such as on a river bank in wet and windy weather – is particularly useful.

Head Injuries

These can be caused by anything from low-hanging tree branches to rocks in the water when you capsize. Anyone suffering a severe blow to the head or who becomes unconscious for any reason needs professional medical advice as quickly as possible. If this happens when the group is out on the water, return the victim to the shore, and put them in the recovery position until help arrives. Do not move the victim unless it is absolutely essential.

BELOW *Improvise an effective stretcher using two kayak paddles and flotation aids.*

RIGHT *Warming up and stretching properly before paddling is a good way to prevent injury and mishap on the water.*

Cramp

Cramp is a painful muscle spasm that occurs when the blood supply to the affected area is impaired. It commonly affects paddlers because of their sitting or kneeling position, especially in cold weather conditions.

The condition is not serious but the pain can be severe. The best treatment is to try to stretch the muscle, counteracting its contraction, and to massage the whole area to improve the circulation. Cramp can occur in any muscle but it is particularly common for boaters to get it in the calves and the feet.

Cold Hands

Paddling in very cold water can cause extreme discomfort in the hands and particularly in the fingers. Unfortunately, the instinct to stop and warm up the hands can prolong the time you are on the water and the discomfort. A good solution is to carry on paddling and getting wet, ignoring the fact that your

BELOW *A group of kayakers venturing out to sea with a qualified instructor.*

fingers are getting cold, until they really begin to hurt. If, at this point, you continue to exercise quite hard, you can provoke a reaction from your blood vessels which, though initially painful, will after a few minutes stop the discomfort. You will then be able to use your hands normally and can continue paddling.

Surfer's Ear

Surfer's ear, also known as exostoses, is an increasingly common complaint among paddlers who regularly get completely wet. The complaint is the growth of bony lumps in the inner ear as a result of the ear canal being constantly exposed to cold water and wind chill. After a several years of regular exposure, the lumps can impair the hearing, and will cause constant ear infections by preventing the inner ear from drying out as quickly as it normally would. The best preventative measure is to protect the ears whenever you paddle by wearing a skull cap or earplugs. These are available from most paddling suppliers. Consult your doctor if you suspect you might have surfer's ear.

Shoulder Dislocation

One of the most common traumatic injuries experienced by canoeists and kayakers is shoulder dislocation, and in particular anterior dislocation (where the upper arm is forced up and back beyond its normal range of movement until the shoulder joint is dislocated). In rare cases the joint is able to relocate on its own, but more usually it will have to be repositioned by an expert medical practitioner. The injury is extremely painful, precluding further activity of any sort, and usually requiring evacuation. All you can do is to try to stabilize the injury to prevent further pain and damage. It usually takes months to rehabilitate from a dislocation, so prevention is the way to go. Avoid high bracing, reaching too far behind you, and paddling without first warming up.

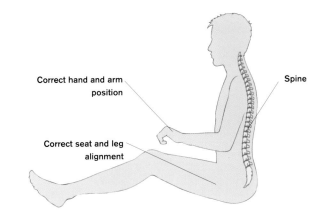

Correct hand and arm position

Spine

Correct seat and leg alignment

FIRST AID KITS

Always carry a basic first aid kit and include the following items. Look through the equipment in your kit, and make sure you know how to use it. Better still, attend a first aid course so that you can practise the theory.
• First aid manual.
• Sterile bandages.
• Sterile plasters.
• Sterile gauze and burn patches.
• Mild relief tablets for headaches, nausea, and bacterial infection.
• Surgical tape.
• Scissors and tweezers.
• Thermometer.

Tendonitis

Paddlers are prone to tendon problems, particularly in the wrists and elbows. This tends to be a chronic (ongoing) complaint, which can best be addressed by using paddles with low angles of feather, and simply not overdoing it. Gripping the paddle too tightly when anxious can exacerbate the problem, as can paddling aggressively with a poor or jerky technique.

Back Pain

Back pain is common for kayakers and canoeists alike. Back problems can be minimized by good all-round training,

BELOW *A dislocated shoulder or arm injury can be stabilized very effectively using a flotation aid in this manner.*

warm-up and stretching routines, but you must also concentrate on maintaining a good body posture.

The spine needs to maintain a correct curvature, with particular attention given to the curve in the lower back. A kneeling canoeist can more easily maintain this posture while paddling, while a kayaker will find it almost impossible. Failure to maintain correct lower back posture while working hard can result in severe back pain. The problem is compounded if you get into a car without adequate lumbar support to drive home. Lying in the bath at home will further aggravate the condition, as the bath floor is sloping and not flat.

BELOW *An awkward capsize can easily lead to injury if there are any rocks or boulders beneath the water surface.*

ABOVE *Perfect posture, with the spine in the shape of a letter S, reduces pressure on the invertebral discs in the lower back.*

Perfect Posture

All back pain should first be tackled by checking the posture. Perfect posture is the position of the seated spine when there is the least amount of pressure on the intervertebral discs in the lower back. Every spine has it own unique shape. When this shape is preserved the posture is perfect. However, the human spine is a vertical flexible column that was not designed to be seated. Perfect posture is nearly impossible to attain for long periods: it must be supported. Holding the spine in the shape of a letter S when kneeling, sitting or standing will support the spine and maintain perfect posture.

SAILING

Introduction

Sailing began as a sport for wealthy gentlemen at the end of the 19th century, at a time when steam and diesel were making sails redundant for both commercial and naval use. A historic race was staged around the Isle of Wight off the south coast of England on 22 August 1851 with sixteen yachts taking part, and The Royal Yacht Squadron's Hundred Pound Cup made by Garrard of London as the prize. Its name was changed to the America's Cup in honour of the winning schooner *America*, and this was the start of international yacht racing as we know it today.

Since those early beginnings the rich have continued to enjoy the sport at racing events such as Antigua Race Week, the Aga Khan Cup at Porto Cervo or La Nioulargue Regatta for vintage racing yachts at St Tropez, while at the other end of the spectrum the growth of dinghy sailing and affordable cruising has made the sport available to all. You don't even need to own a boat to experience sailing, since willing crews are in

demand at every level of the sport, and time rather than money is the commitment that is required.

So why sail? It all comes down to experiencing the exhilaration of two elements – wind and water – and learning to contain and control them. The basic skills are easy enough to acquire, but beyond that a lifetime of experience awaits.

OPPOSITE **The twin wire skiff represents the ultimate expression of what was first conceived at the end of the 20th century – the high performance racing dinghy.**

RIGHT **Twin-hulled catamarans are a modern re-working of an ancient concept that provides an unrivalled combination of stability, power and performance.**

ABOVE **Sailing a modern dinghy can be an athletic and challenging pastime, with crews using their skills to balance the power of wind and waves.**

ABOVE **The challenge of mastering the elements under sail reaches its full potential in an event such as the Vendee Globe Race.**

DINGHY BASICS

For many people, the first introduction to sailing comes via small open dinghies that provide an immediate and thrilling response to wind and waves. Dinghy sailing began to establish itself as a popular concept in the 1950s, when a new breed of relatively light, fast and responsive, marine plywood designs began to make sailing widely available at reasonably low cost. The sport prospered mainly as a competitive pastime, and clubs were established wherever there was sailable water and racing was organized on a regular basis.

Learning the basics – including how dinghies are constructed, what to wear, how a sailboat moves, where and when to sail and safety measures – is sufficient knowledge to provide endless hours of fun and pleasure. However, for those who want more, modern technology has also made high performance sailing readily available, with dinghy and small boat racing providing the bedrock of an international sport that ranges up to the heights of Olympic competition.

LEFT *Small sailing dinghies are ideal for people who are learning the basics.*

BELOW *It is important that you learn how a dinghy is constructed.*

Taking up dinghy sailing

A sailing dinghy can be defined as a small, open boat powered by sails, which is usually crewed by one or two people. Unlike a sailing cruiser, it has no cabin to provide any kind of overnight or foul weather shelter and, unlike a keelboat, it lacks a weighted keel to help keep it upright. More than any other type of sailing craft it relies on the skills of the crew to keep it balanced against the force of the wind, sailing forwards efficiently rather than leaning on its side, and heading where the helmsperson directs it.

A century of design evolution has ensured that modern dinghies are as user-friendly and easy to sail as is possible. At one end of the scale internationally popular boats such as Optimists, designed for children's use, or Toppers, perform an entry-level role, and are just about perfect so long as you accept that the business of learning to sail must start well before you even think about launching on to the water.

ABOVE **Nothing can beat learning to sail in an open dinghy as it brings the crew into the closest possible contact with the elements.**

Harnessing the forces of nature

Sailing is all about learning how to harness the natural forces of wind and water, and a small dinghy brings you closer to them than any other kind of sailing. Dealing with the forces of nature should never be undertaken lightly, particularly when the combination of too much wind and cold water temperatures can threaten life. To deal with them efficiently and ensure that sailing is both enjoyable and safe, all sailors have to accept that learning to sail is a lifelong process in which experience is built on basic knowledge.

LEFT **Different sizes of boat suit different sizes of people. The International Topper is small, light and forgiving, ideal for younger sailors.**

RIGHT **The Laser Pico is a modern, slightly scaled up rival to the International Topper.**

Why take up sailing?

The reasons for enjoying sailing are many, but the following points cover most of them:

Healthy for you
Lots of exercise and clean, fresh air make it a top choice for children and adults alike.

Meeting people
It's a camaraderie sport, where half the fun is enjoying sailing with others and talking about your experiences.

Seeing new places
There are all kinds of options for travelling and viewing places from a different perspective.

Inexpensive
While the sky is the limit for those indulging in offshore racing in keelboats, costs can certainly be kept reasonable with a small dinghy. At dinghy sailing level the costs of the sport compare favourably with other pastimes.

Challenging
That's what is so good about it. While virtually anyone can kick a football or even jump on and ride a bike at a basic level, almost no one could just get in a dinghy and sail without some help. The skills required and the time spent learning them are all part of the attraction of the sport.

Feeling great
The wind in your hair and the sun (sometimes) on your face contributes to an indefinable feeling of wellbeing as you skip across the water.

Continual learning
There is so much to learn, and the continuous learning process, which owes so much to experience, invariably makes sailing a sport for life.

Variety
There are all kinds of boats and types of sailing available. The choices range from state-of-the-art, knife-edge performance to traditional, relaxed cruising. Just pick whatever suits you best.

Competitive satisfaction
If you are that way inclined, dinghy racing is widely available at all levels and for all ages from seven onwards.

A safe sport
It is rare for anyone to drown or get seriously injured while sailing, and properly organized schools and clubs, which are backed by national authorities, can boast a near unblemished record. It is however vital to start by getting proper tuition; while experience is built up you can continue to enjoy the sport in a controlled environment such as a sailing club.

ABOVE **Capsizing is all part of the fun of sailing, and modern equipment and clothing allows the crew to stay safe and warm.**

ABOVE **The Topaz continues the Topper/Pico theme, with a blow-moulded plastic hull, which is virtually unbreakable, and the option of different rigs.**

Starting to sail

Children can learn many things quicker than adults, and the 10–14 age range is an optimum age for fast learning. Some children – often from hard-core sailing families – are encouraged to start much younger, which is acceptable so long as parents realize that they run the risk of putting them off. Six is the youngest realistic age to sail a small dinghy such as an Optimist, and then only in perfect Force 2 conditions or less with close supervision at all times. Do not take chances as the child may feel out of control and become scared if the wind blows harder.

Adults can take up and enjoy dinghy sailing at any age, including those who are well into their retirement years. A modicum of physical fitness is necessary, and the level required is directly related to the type of sailing being pursued – hanging from the trapeze while controlling the power of a 49er bears little resemblance to enjoying the staid comforts of a family-style dinghy such as a Wayfarer or Laser 16.

It is also important to accept that factors such as fitness, strength, maturity and experience, which age may or may not confer, have to be compromised with sailing conditions. Ideal conditions for learning probably mean warm air and sea temperatures, light winds and flat water, none of which are demanding, while colder, windier conditions will require considerably more resilience and hardiness if you are to enjoy the experience.

Join a sailing club

When it comes to dinghy sailing, the ideal solution is often to join a sailing club where you can enjoy organized activities, exchange views with like-minded people, learn about racing, sail with safety cover available, and have a permanent launching and boat storage facility.

It is not even necessary to own a dinghy to join a club. Many successful dinghy sailors, such as boat designer Phil Morrison who has boats such as the Laser 5000 and

ABOVE **A club provides an opportunity to meet and socialize with fellow sailors, to sail in company and enjoy the camaraderie that the sport offers.**

RS 400 to his name, learnt their skills by offering to crew for local dinghy owners. This can be an excellent and very cheap way to gain experience, so long as the owner is a good sailor who will actually pass on the right way to do things. A phone call to a local club, a word with the secretary, or a look at the notice board is the best way to find people seeking crew.

Geographical location can pose problems, and the cost and hassle factor will obviously increase if you have to drive long distances to find a suitable club. Most well-populated areas with good sailing waters are well served by sailing clubs, but in some cases over-subscription and high costs of membership can put up a barrier for newcomers.

The boat

Dinghies are widely available new or second-hand. A new boat comes with all the usual guarantees, but the second-hand supply means that boats are available at all prices and really start very cheaply.

ABOVE **The Topper Sport 14 provides an ideal modern mix of learner-stability combined with gennaker-performance. This medium-size dinghy is suitable for both adults and teenagers.**

Buying a second-hand boat is considerably less dangerous than buying a second-hand car, but there are still plenty of pitfalls with rigging, sails and hull materials, all of which suffer from wear and tear, and replacement parts are generally expensive. This means that good advice is necessary for anyone considering buying second-hand.

Boat accessories

Your boat will probably require a launching trolley to push it to and from the water. It may also need a road trailer or roof rack bars depending on size, and a boat cover for protection and storage.

Personal accessories

A buoyancy aid (personal flotation device) is the most vital accessory. It must be the right size for the sailor's weight and allow maximum freedom of movement. In most conditions the crew will need a minimum of a wetsuit and spray top to keep warm.

As in most sports you can pay a lot of money for the very latest technical clothing. As a minimum requirement, you may also need to buy special dinghy shoes or boots, which are recommended for good grip, warm feet and ankle protection, a woolly hat in a synthetic

ABOVE **Find opportunities to talk to more experienced sailors to gain more knowledge and learn by your mistakes, which will take your skills to the next stage.**

thermal material to prevent heat loss in colder weather and reinforced sailing gloves for hand protection.

Maintenance

Modern mass-produced polypropylene dinghies, such as the Pico and Topper, should require little more maintenance than cleaning and the very occasional replacement of fittings. Otherwise, the

great majority of modern dinghies are built in fibreglass, which is virtually maintenance-free when new but can present problems in an older boat when faded colours, cracks, splits and delamination may all require preventative maintenance. More traditional wooden built dinghies may require a great deal of time and money by comparison, but these tend to appeal to the kind of sailor who actively enjoys the upkeep of his boat and regards it as a source of pride.

Insurance

In a litigious society, third party insurance is vital for dinghy owners and mandatory for most racing. Comprehensive cover, which insures against theft, fire or serious damage, is wise.

Clubs

The costs of belonging to a sailing or yacht club vary enormously, as do the associated costs of boat storage. One advantage of belonging to a club with active fleets is that they are good outlets for second-hand equipment, whether buying or selling.

Other costs

These may include launching fees, harbour dues and winter storage.

ABOVE **Where are you going to keep it? A dinghy needs secure storage both in and out of the sailing season. This is often provided by a sailing club boat park.**

Sailing schools

Sailing schools in general are governed by national sailing authorities. They are highly organized when it comes to teaching both children and adults and generally make a pretty good job of what they set out to do. As a rule, sailing schools should guarantee that all tuition is done safely, and at an all-inclusive price, which should include the necessary equipment and clothing.

Courses should be run according to detailed principles laid down in national authority logbooks, and the time span is important. A weekend beginner's course may be adequate time enough for adults to enjoy casual sailing, but depending on the area's general climate may not necessarily allow for unsuitable weather conditions. The time span may also be too short a period for children to discover an interest in the sport. A five- or six-day course, by contrast, can become a real group adventure as well as improving the odds on good weather. Time spent on the

ABOVE **Learning to sail in a sailing school should involve a carefully structured course, which provides the right mixture of knowledge, safety and fun under good supervision – preferably in the sun.**

water is what counts when learning to sail and, with luck, a week at a sailing school can provide as much as 25 hours of quality sailing time, which is the

equivalent of a great many weekends of occasional summer sailing, ample time enough to learn the basics.

During a sailing course, students will have the opportunity to overcome various hurdles placed in their way, such as learning to rig up, get afloat, sail the boat upwind and downwind, tack, gybe, try capsizing and then progress beyond. They learn at their own pace, but if the school knows its job that pace will be fast, the course will be fun, and should clearly be experienced as a holiday.

Teaching children

If parents know little or nothing about sailing, it obviously makes good sense to send the children to a school.

Sailing school induction for children should be run according to the detailed principles laid down in logbooks, such as the International Optimist Logbook or the RYA Young Sailors Logbook, whose requirements are shown here.

ABOVE **Children will soon build confidence if they are taught correctly and learn to enjoy the sport on their own. It is best for parents in general to leave the teaching to qualified instructors.**

Instructor qualifications

National sailing authorities require that their sailing instructors are qualified to a certain level. The basic level required by the Royal Yachting Association in Britain states that an RYA Instructor must:

- Register with the RYA.
- Hold a valid RYA Powerboat Level 2 certificate – this includes safe powerboat driving skills and the use of kill cords to eliminate any danger from propellers.
- Hold a valid first-aid certificate.
- Pass a pre-entry assessment sailing test which includes sailing without a rudder, sailing backwards, man overboard drill and coming alongside, using the Wayfarer in difficult, windy conditions.
- Complete a five-day training course plus a one-day assessment administered by an external RYA coach assessor.

In addition, any instructor must have the rapport and communication skills to get on with the students, keep them in order and pass on a love of sailing.

International Optimist Logbook

Includes personal details, boat details (if you own one), awards divided into five grades (covering practical technique and theory) and the Coastal Bar, major racing achievements, a complete equipment breakdown and diagram of the Optimist, detailed syllabus for passing each grade with space for certificates, tips and diagrams, and suggested further reading.
Grade 1 This should be within the reach of most beginners after a six-day course.
Grade 2 Usually reached after about 12 days' instruction.
Grade 3 You need to be a confident and experienced sailor.

Coastal Bar To achieve this you must learn to sail in tidal waters. A minimum of 20 hours' sailing experience is required to achieve this level.
Grade 4 You should be racing regularly at club level and occasional open meetings.
Grade 5 To make this grade you should be racing regularly in open meetings.

RYA Young Sailors Logbook

This is a detailed booklet that includes an introduction and instructions aimed at parents, a summary of all the requirements for the awards, a personal logbook, and a record of achievement. It divides the RYA Young Sailors Scheme into a total of nine different awards with a clear progression from novice to expert:
Start Sailing Stage 1, 2 and 3 certificates.
Advanced Sailing Blue, white and red badges.
Racing Blue, white and red badges.

TOP **The International Optimist is the classic children's single-handed dinghy, and enjoys highly competitive fleet racing worldwide.**

LEFT **Children learn rapidly when blessed with enthusiastic instructors. Helmets are one solution to save small heads from getting hurt by the boom.**

LEFT **Three teenagers get to grips with a gennaker hoist at dinghy school.**

How much do children learn?

The popular image of a sailing school is that you spend the whole of the first day in a classroom learning about sailing theory before you are allowed anywhere near the water. Apart from being boring this simply does not work with children. If they have never been sailing before there is no way they will understand the theory of it, and the first priority for any sailing school that knows its business should be to get the children on the water as soon as possible and make sure they stay on the water, which is the ultimate classroom, throughout the course.

The ideal should be to have a dinghy such as an Optimist for each child, with two instructors teaching 10 children (minimum 1:5 ratio) from two rescue boats. If the wind is more than Force 2 the children may start to find things difficult, so then the instructors can use half the number of Optimists to let half the children take a breather in the rescue boats at any one time. This is all part of the fun, as children enjoy roaring around with the instructors as much as sailing.

Once they are on the water, children will do what they are told without asking instructors why, and soon develop an automatic and instinctual reaction to things such as moving the tiller. On the whole children pick up the basic skills much faster than adults.

Safety first

When sailing, safety is of course a primary consideration. A specific safety problem for everyone is getting banged on the head by the boom. Schools are obliged to take a child to the local casualty department (emergency room) if there is any sign of concussion. Some schools have solved this by providing children with lightweight helmets, a good idea but not necessarily the most ideal. They can also give the wrong impression that sailing is a dangerous sport. A better solution being used by schools recently is customized dinghies featuring padded booms and high clews that eliminate the dangers of head injury.

LEFT **Young sailors can have a lot of fun, and gain important experience, by going offshore in small cruisers, which may also offer the opportunity to live on board.**

Teaching Adults

Adults, juniors and children tend to learn very differently in terms of what they accept as worthwhile, how quickly they assimilate information, the amount of hardship they will put up with and the kind of experiences they enjoy. This means that adults should always be taught dinghy sailing in separate groups from youngsters. They tend to benefit from more dedicated tuition which can be given in large, stable dinghies of which the Wayfarer is a favourite. This allows the instructor to sail with up to three students while they learn the rudiments of handling a boat as quickly and safely as possible. The instructor can then move to an accompanying safety boat when the confidence and sailing skills of the students has increased to the point where they feel comfortable enough to take physical charge of the boat.

Beyond the basic introductory levels (Adult level 1 and 2 on the RYA syllabus) adults should learn in groups of similar ability so students can progress at the same pace. Intermediate level tuition (Adult level 3) should extend beyond the basic skills of sailing in order to improve both knowledge and techniques, which is often best done by incorporating elementary racing into a five- to six-day course.

The next stages of Racing and Advanced Sailing (Adult levels 4&5) are both recommended as full six-day courses. Even if you have no desire to compete, learning to race is particularly useful for sharpening your boat handling skills and making quick assessments of on-water situations. Tactics, boat tuning, roll tacking and fast manoeuvres are all covered and a single-hander such as the Laser 1 is ideal for adult tuition. An Advanced Sailing course requires the highest level of sailing skills and is only recommended to students with real commitment and who have several years of experience. The course is designed to test sailing abilities to the limit and can only be assessed in strong winds when all boat manoeuvres must be performed to the highest standards, including specialist skills such as sailing backwards and sailing without a rudder.

LEFT **Learning to sail on a holiday in a warm climate brings all the advantages of a relaxed environment combined with predictable warm waters and reliable, mellow winds.**

Short course tuition can also be a real benefit for learning specific skills such as trapezing, spinnaker and/or gennaker techniques, as well as catamaran sailing. These are ideally run with a small group, and with suitable equipment and good winds should enable fast progress over no more than a weekend.

Learning yacht sailing

Cruising skills are also well served by a professional syllabus. The RYA National Cruising Scheme for instance ranges from a basic introductory Competent Crew five-day course, which is largely practical and aims to provide sufficient knowledge of basic seamanship for a novice to become a useful crew member. The course syllabus includes: understanding sea terms

and boat parts; sail handling; rope work; fire precautions; man overboard; emergency equipment; manners and customs on board; flag etiquette; rules of the road; loading and rowing a dinghy; basic meteorology; dealing with seasickness; helmsmanship; sailing and general duties on board.

Beyond that, the next stages are Day Skipper, which is divided between shore based and practical to provide enough ability to skipper a small yacht in familiar waters by day. Coastal Skipper is also shore based and practical, and should provide the ability to skipper a yacht on coastal passages by day and night, while the very top qualification of Yachtmaster Ocean is, as its name implies, sufficient to skipper a yacht across oceans.

ABOVE **Theory is a vital part of any sailing course, covering subjects such as sailing dynamics, the effects of wind and weather, tides, first aid and safety.**

Dinghy construction

There is a massive choice of dinghy and catamaran classes, with construction and components that vary from the very simple, as found on classes such as the Topper, to the downright complex on boats at the top of the performance range such as a 49er. However, all classes regardless of size and performance will share some of the principal features.

Wooden boats

Boats with wooden hulls have been almost completely superseded by modern plastics, and they are now a rarity reserved for traditionalists. Carvel and clinker are alternative methods of horizontal planked construction, with carvel planks laid flush to a frame while clinker planks overlap. Clinker, which was once widely used on small rowing boats, enjoyed a period of great popularity for racing classes such as the National 12 and Merlin Rocket, until it lost popularity to fibreglass. Clinker is still used to build the occasional modern traditional class such as the Salcombe Yawl.

Fairey Marine pioneered the art of moulding sheets of laminated wood around a frame to provide a lightweight skin, using techniques that they originally developed to build aeroplanes. Famous classes built in this way included the

ABOVE **The 49er uses a modern sandwich laminate to provide the optimum mix of light weight and rigidity in a severely stressed platform, which has to cope with both waves and an exceptionally powerful rig.**

Firefly, Finn and Flying Dutchman, all of which were Olympic classes. This building technique has been completely superseded by modern plastics.

The simplest and cheapest wood construction used sheets of laminated marine plywood to give a box-like shape, and was extremely popular with many of

the new generation post-war dinghies such as the Optimist, OK, Enterprise and GP14. The Mirror, for many years one of the most popular small dinghies in the world, helped pioneer the home-built technique. It was constructed with plywood panels held together by stitches of wire and fibreglass tape.

ABOVE **The International Cadet class for children was one of the first postwar designs with a simple plywood box shape and flat pram bow.**

ABOVE **Labour of love: a wooden boat can look very beautiful, but requires a considerable amount of care if it is to stay that way.**

ABOVE **The Salcombe Yawl is a modern racing class based on a traditional design, which still uses clinker planking in its all-wood construction.**

ABOVE **A fibreglass yacht requires rather more maintenance than a small dinghy, with an annual application of anti-fouling paint below the waterline and possible use of varnished fittings.**

Fibreglass boats

GRP (glass reinforced plastic) began to replace wood for dinghy building in the 1960s. Despite years of development, construction principles have remained the same.

Sheets of woven glass fibres are laid in (or sometimes on) a hull or deck mould, and layers are built up to the required thickness. The fibreglass sheets are laminated by brushing or spraying on a liquid catalyst, which is usually a polyester (sometimes called Vinylester) resin. When the resin cures, the fibreglass sheets provide a hard-skinned hull, which can be removed from the mould with the help of a release agent. Hull rigidity is usually formed by using plywood frames, and a gelcoat (polyester paint finish) is used to give a smooth outer and inner finish to the hull. The deck may be plywood, but on a modern dinghy it is more likely to be moulded fibreglass as well, and features such as the thwart and centreboard case made from additional moulds.

The attractions of fibreglass are threefold. First, it is economic to set up a production line using the same mould or set of moulds, which will guarantee a virtually identical series of mouldings. Secondly, the skills required to produce mouldings are likely to be considerably less than those needed to build a wooden boat and the raw materials are much

ABOVE **Modern fibreglass dinghies put fun and function first with an easy-to-clean hull and deck that requires minimal maintenance over the first few years.**

cheaper. Finally, fibreglass requires virtually no upkeep. It does not need the rubbing down, painting and varnishing that wooden dinghies used to require annually, but it does need cleaning, and over the years the gelcoat may be prone to cracking and fading and will then need painting to restore its appearance.

Serious problems on older fibreglass boats may include: osmosis (bubbles

forming on the hull when the skin delaminates); the hull soaking up water between laminates and putting on weight; and the seams between hull and deck coming apart. However, fibreglass remains the number one choice for dinghy construction, and modern materials and techniques help to ensure that the long-term problems that afflict many earlier boats have become less prevalent.

LEFT **The effects of salt, sun and dragging up the beach will degrade fibreglass over a number of years. Once you get to the stage of having to paint the hull, the advantages become less obvious.**

ABOVE **The Laser Pico has a rotomoulded and foam sandwich hull, which makes it rigid, giving better performance. It has become a favourite with sailing schools and holiday operators.**

ABOVE **The Dart 16 has rotomoulded hulls that combine high volume, light weight and durability.**

Plastic boats

Rotomoulded plastic hulls were developed for the mass production of simple dinghy hull and deck shapes, at the same time as the boom in windsurfing technology. The first and best known rotomoulded dinghy is the polypropylene Topper, while other more recent designs include the Pico and Dart 16 catamaran moulded in Techrothene, a polypropylene variation that is combined with a plastic foam sandwich.

The principal advantage of rotomoulding is that it is one of the most economic means of ensuring high volume production using a material that is highly durable (though prone to scratching) for beach use. However, initial tooling costs are very high, which restricts rotomoulding to a very small number of strongly marketed classes, and the skin material is likely to be too flexible and/or too heavy for a really high performance.

Advanced laminate boats

Basic fibreglass technique has led on to a variety of materials and skills that can provide greater rigidity combined with a much lighter weight. These requirements are reserved for the high performance end of the dinghy market where cutting edge construction is likely to feature foam sandwich and advanced laminates.

Foam sandwich construction utilizes a layer of superlight foam, such as Airex, sandwiched between two fibreglass skins. This makes it possible to produce thicker, more rigid hull walls at considerably lighter weight than pure fibreglass. The building technique is considerably more advanced and more time consuming, which tends to add significantly to the cost. With older boats there is also the possibility of the sandwich delaminating, and the foam deteriorating and soaking up water, all of which may spell the end of the road for an old (or not so old) hull.

Foam sandwich may also be used in conjunction with more advanced materials than basic polyester with fibreglass. Epoxy resin produces a stiffer and stronger moulding than polyester, but is more expensive and difficult to work with,

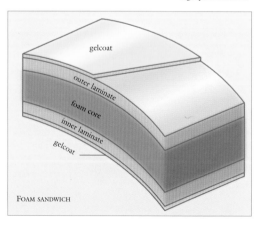

FOAM SANDWICH

gelcoat

outer laminate

foam core

inner laminate

gelcoat

LEFT **A typical section of foam sandwich. Hull walls can be made much thicker with this, and therefore more rigid, while the superlight foam filling ensures that they also remain light.**

RIGHT **Aluminium tubing is a popular material for racks, and can also be incorporated to stiffen up the hull with a space frame structure.**

ABOVE **Advanced sandwich construction, which makes use of epoxy and carbon, is favoured by large-scale, high-performance boats where weight is at a premium. This is a big catamaran under construction at Multiplast in France.**

and the critical curing times may require intensive techniques such as vacuum bagging to suck out excess air or hot oven curing to ensure a consistent finish. More resin equals more weight, so pre-preg fibre is impregnated with exactly the correct amount of epoxy resin for the optimum strength/weight ratio before it is oven baked.

Fibreglass comes in a variety of specifications, and may be replaced by a higher performance woven material, of which black carbon cloth is most widely used. Carbon can only be laminated with epoxy resin and has the potential to produce the lightest, stiffest boats of all. There is a considerable price penalty in both materials and construction technique, which ensures that carbon is mainly reserved as a reinforcing material in critical hull areas.

Extra hull reinforcement may be provided by a tubular space frame that gives lateral support. This allows heavy deck areas to be removed, increasing working space for the crew and cutting down weight. Aluminium is the favoured material as there are likely to be too many complex joins for effective use of carbon.

High performance dinghies such as the Laser 4000 and .eps feature wings that increase righting moment and can provide a weight equalization system – this is used on the widest setting for the lightest crews and narrowest setting for the heaviest crews. Favoured materials for wings are foam filled fibreglass, which provide a solid rack (Laser.eps), or aluminium tube, which may have nylon mesh that you can both sit on and trapeze off (Laser 4000). The possible disadvantages of wings include increased weight, and catching a wing end in the water, which can lead to capsizing when the boat heels too far.

ABOVE **A large, modern sportsboat such as the Mumm is an all-out racer that demands sophisticated construction.**

LEFT **The Laser.eps uses foam filled fibreglass wings to allow the crew to exert more leverage. The wings require maximum rigidity and minimum weight for top performance.**

Foils

Centreboard, daggerboard and rudder foils have to be rigid with maximum resistance to sideways pressure, though some twist in the tip may be built into the design to help promote lift to windward.

Foils generally need to be as light as possible for ease of use and high performance. The exception is a ballasted centreboard, which is weighted to keep the boat stable while sailing or at a mooring. Ballasted centreboards are mainly found on traditional pre-war dinghies, with a cast iron plate weighing as much as 50kg (110lb) and requiring a drum winch to lift it.

Laminated plywood This is the simplest material for a foil. This type of foil can be relatively light, but is likely to be prone to flexing and impact damage, while the constraints of the material are likely to limit it to a basic foil shape with parallel rather than tapered sides, which will inhibit performance.

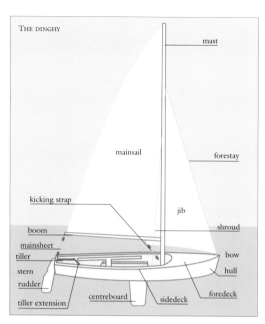

THE DINGHY

mast

mainsail

forestay

kicking strap

jib

boom

shroud

mainsheet

tiller

bow

stern

hull

rudder

foredeck

tiller extension

centreboard

sidedeck

LEFT **This shows a typical two-man dinghy that is easily handled and does not require a high level of sailing expertise. It has most of the basic common features of the majority of dinghy designs.**

ABOVE **The centreboard or daggerboard has to be strong enough to withstand one or both crew using it as a righting lever during a capsize.**

ABOVE **Rudder foils are prone to impact damage if the tips hit the bottom. Most sailors have to make simple repairs at the end of a season.**

Moulded plastic This is the most price-effective foil material for mass-produced dinghies such as the Topper and Pico. The foil can be moulded in any shape using a strong and durable material, but is likely to be too heavy for really high performance sailing.

Solid fibreglass This is moulded round an internal frame and is a popular choice for an overall improvement in weight and rigidity characteristics. Refinements on this system may use more exotic materials such as self-skinning epoxy foam that expands inside the outer skin to produce a super-light, super-rigid core to help ensure the foil will not bend or break on impact. At the top of the scale in price, performance and beauty, glass sheathed wood-laminate foils are hand built and shaped on a one-off basis using a variety of materials.

Hiking aids

Dinghy sailors hook their feet under webbing straps so they can hike over the side and use their weight to hold the boat upright. Over a period of more than a few minutes the experience may range from moderately enjoyable to downright

painful, depending on the ergonomics of the boat and the fitness and dynamism of the crew.

A more efficient alternative is to stand out from the boat, a technique pioneered by Sir Peter Scott in the 1930s. The modern variation uses a trapeze wire, which is attached to the mast next to the shrouds, and has a handle and ring to hook on to with the free end secured to the boat by an elastic shockcord.

ABOVE **The skipper has his feet hooked under the straps for hiking, while the crew stands out on trapeze, and both working to hold the boat down.**

Masts

Aluminium masts Classes such as the Topper and Laser have a very simple mast made up of two parallel sided, sealed (to prevent water ingress during a capsize) aluminium tubes with a round section. These are sleeved together and it is vital to ensure that the sleeved area is free of sand or grit, and to take the mast apart regularly to ensure the two halves do not fuse together. The mast is supported at the base and at the deck of the boat, but is otherwise self-supporting and requires no forestay or shrouds. The mainsail is pulled over the mast using a luff sock, similar to the system used on windsurfers.
Pros. Low cost, easy storage and roof racking, with very little to go wrong.
Cons Relatively heavy, with unsophisticated bend characteristics.

A more refined alternative is a one-piece, oval section, tapered, aluminium mast. The taper at the top is designed to provide bend characteristics that match the curved luff of the mainsail, and the lighter weight reduces pitching moment. An aluminium mast should ideally be sealed to prevent sinking and inversion during a capsize, but using internal

LEFT **The Pico has a simple, unstayed aluminium mast that is cheap and highly functional. The sail can be stowed by wrapping it round the mast.**

halyards to reduce wind drag may prevent this. In some cases a compromise is possible, using a foam-filled top section to provide sufficient buoyancy.
Pros Good performance and weight characteristics are possible, though tapered aluminium masts come in all sizes and shapes, so this varies.
Cons Tends to be complex and heavy.
Carbon masts These offer the greatest performance potential in terms of light weight, strength and resilience, and the best available bend characteristics. Carbon is equally suitable for both fully supported masts (forestay, shrouds and spreaders) and unsupported use as on windsurfers, and can be combined with a glued aluminium or plastic track and riveted fittings. A lower cost compromise is a carbon top mast, which combines a carbon top section with an aluminium bottom section.
Pros Lightest possible weight makes rigging and righting easy, and reduces pitching moment. Precise bend characteristics can be built into carbon to provide potential top performance.
Cons The most expensive option at present, but price differences will fall and carbon masts will gain in popularity.

Catamarans tend to have masts with a wide oval section that look like a tear drop when viewed from the top. The mast rotates at the base to keep in line with the mainsail, and plays an aerodynamic role as a part of the sail when the catamaran sails at high speeds. Due to its shape, a

catamaran mast will bend sideways with little or no movement fore and aft, and doesn't require any spreaders because the shrouds are spread over a wide base.

Carbon masts are gaining in popularity for catamaran use due to their much lighter weight, while extreme high performance catamarans have for many years experimented with full-sized wing masts – these may completely supplant the conventional sail in terms of performance, but are impractical for regular use.

ABOVE **This skiff's masthead gennaker and powerful mainsail relies on the lightweight strength and resilient, pliable characteristics of its carbon mast.**

ABOVE **The 470 has a tapered aluminium mast for high performance. The support from shrouds and spreaders can make the mast relatively complex.**

Booms

On the majority of dinghy classes the boom is an aluminium tube whose sophistication matches that of the mast. A carbon boom is the luxury, lightweight choice for high performance.

The boom is attached to the mast by a gooseneck, which allows it to swing freely from side to side in a near 180 degree horizontal arc to the limit imposed by the shrouds. The gooseneck will also allow the boom to swing in a vertical arc. When sailing, the boom is held up by the pull of the mainsail and held down by the combined forces of mainsheet and kicking strap.

Until the 1990s most dinghy booms featured a slot for a bolt rope in the foot of the mainsail. On modern dinghies this has been superseded by a loose-footed mainsail simply held at the tack and clew.

While aluminium is the traditional material for spinnaker poles, carbon has become a popular alternative for gennaker poles due to its superior stiffness and weight characteristics.

ABOVE **The bolt rope, which is built into the luff of the mainsail needs to be guided carefully up the mast slot. The Dart 16 catamaran shown here has no boom and therefore relies on a loose footed mainsail, which is secured by the tack at the mast and clew by the mainsheet.**

RIGHT **Shrouds and spreaders are used to support the mast and control how far it bends sideways. Sail controls such as the mainsheet, downhaul and kicker tension also affect the degree of mast bend. A great deal of extra stress is created by sailing with a gennaker, a feature of the Laser 3000.**

Shrouds and spreaders

A tapered aluminium or carbon mast, which supports both mainsail and jib, will usually need to be upheld by a wire forestay at the front and wire shrouds at the sides. Shrouds are generally made from 3mm (⅛in) wire, and may be covered in plastic to help prevent wear when the mainsail is let out against the leeward shroud on a downwind course.

An una-rig dinghy has only a mainsail and may not require shrouds or forestay despite its bendy mast. The Finn and Europe, both Olympic classes, are typical examples. Some boats such as the Laser.eps feature a mini-shroud system that only supports the bottom of the mast.

Spreaders are used to increase the angle at which the shrouds join the mast in order to give greater side-support. Due to the width of the platform, spreaders are not used on catamarans.

The length of both forestay and shrouds should be adjustable using chainplates. This enables the mast to be raked forward and back to tune the boat's handling characteristics.

Mainsails and jibs

The mainsail is the main powerhouse of the boat, and is usually held to the mast by a bolt rope, which is pulled vertically up the mast slot by the main halyard. Problems maintaining sufficient luff tension led to a period when locks at the top of the mast became popular, but the advent of 2:1 halyard systems featuring non-stretch braids (synthetic woven lines) such as Dyneema (Spectra) made the halyard lock unnecessary.

The mainsail roach (the outer edge beyond a simple triangle shape, see diagram right) must be supported by battens. The old style of wooden battens have been completely supplanted by modern, superlight, tapered, laminate fibreglass battens, which allow precise flexing characteristics to be incorporated. Catamarans and some high performance

RIGHT **All modern dinghies have similar features. Note the large roach shown here, which must be supported by full length battens.**

dinghies such as the 49er and International Canoe feature full-length battens that run from mast to luff, emphasising the aerodynamic concept of a wing style sail to maximise high speed sailing. Fibreglass battens that are moulded in a round section may give a better stiffness to weight ratio for this application.

The role of the jib is primarily to help drive the boat upwind, while the size of the slot between jib and mainsail needs to be carefully adjusted for optimum performance.

The luff of the jib is traditionally attached to the forestay with small plastic hanks, or cloth snaps, which replaced the brass hanks of long ago. Aerodynamically sophisticated alternatives include a

THE MAINSAIL

batten · mast · roach · luff · leech · mainsail · foot · jib · boom

zippered luff, which closes over the forestay and is often found on high performance catamarans. However, most modern dinghies have dispensed with any attachment to the forestay. They rely instead on non-stretch halyards to provide sufficient luff tension, which are combined with a luff wire that gives enough strength to dispense with the forestay altogether.

Roller systems are a useful feature for jibs, allowing them to be furled for storage onshore or when sailing with a gennaker or spinnaker.

Sail materials

Woven polyester replaced cotton as the leading sail material in the 1950s and, in terms of numbers of sails produced, seems likely to continue as the most popular material. Dacron™ is the best known brand name. In some aspects of performance, however, woven polyester sails have been left far behind by sails made from laminate materials of which the best known brand name is Mylar™.

The main advantage of woven polyester is that it is tough and hard wearing over a long period of time, as well as being relatively cheap. Apart from being on the

LEFT **Most catamarans use a fully battened mainsail, which acts like a rigid foil when set on a rotating mast with an elliptical section. This type of mast is aero-dynamically extremely efficient for high speed sailing, but considerably heavier than a normal dinghy mast.**

RIGHT **The Laser.eps has a novel system that features "mini shrouds", which support the lightweight carbon mast on three sides at boom height.**

RIGHT **Dinghies for regular use, such as the Sport 14, are most likely to use hard-wearing woven polyester sails with traditional horizontal panels.**

ABOVE **The Hobie 17 uses a radial cut mainsail combined with full length battens, that help create a rigid wing effect. Note the furler, which is a slick method of stowing the jib away.**

BELOW **High-performance racers like the 29er opt for laminate sails which combine light weight with maximum stability, and also look smart.**

heavy side, the major disadvantage is that it is prone to stretching. Woven polyester is a woven cloth in which the fibre yarns snake or crimp over and under each other. Under tension the crimp will pull straight, which is why there will always be a small amount of stretch in a woven polyester sail. The warp fibres run down the cloth, and have to bend round the fill fibres, which run across the cloth. The fill fibres therefore have less crimp (less potential stretch), so the cloth stretches less across the fill than down the warp. This makes woven polyester most suitable for traditional cross-cut sails where the joins between the sail panels are virtually horizontal with most of the load across the cloth.

The amount of stretch in a woven polyester sail should not be exaggerated. In most circumstances it is likely to be invisible to the eye, and a woven polyester sail will provide maximum durability combined with excellent performance for most dinghy uses. The exception is dinghy classes which are looking for ultimate performances. In these classes it is common to combine a laminate mainsail with a woven polyester jib since the flogging of a jib can soon destroy a laminate.

In terms of ultimate performance, woven polyester has steadily been overtaken by the use of plastic laminate materials, of which the best known is Mylar™. The laminate can be used in a number of ways, but the basic principle is that two sheets of clear plastic form the outside of a sandwich, which is filled with a flat lattice scrim made of polyester, kevlar or carbon fibres. Everything is then bonded together to produce sail panels that are glued together, and the use of conventional stitching is reserved for reinforcement at the corners. Variations on this formula include the use of hybrid laminates for cruising, which combine woven polyester with a rigid scrim.

The final result is a sail cloth that is considerably lighter and more stable than woven polyester. Laminate sail material will not distort when hit by a gust, and can be used to create radial cut sails where the predicted load that radiates from the corners will travel along the length of the cloth. The result is a highly efficient sail that looks smarter than woven polyester, but the downside is that laminate sails are more expensive. Most importantly they are likely to be considerably less durable as well as suffering from UV degradation in strong sunlight. This will lead to cracks in the plastic and a less than aesthetically pleasing sail. However, development in laminate materials is so rapid that these problems may soon be overcome.

Spinnakers and gennakers

The spinnaker is the traditional downwind sail, cut very full and primarily suitable for running downwind. It is supported by a pole or boom, which must be hoisted on the windward side and makes hoists, drops and gybes a relatively complex affair. A spinnaker can be launched from a bag or chute and will tend to collapse and pull sideways if the wind comes on the beam (from the side).

The gennaker is a modern downwind sail that seems set to supersede the spinnaker. It is much simpler to use.

LEFT **The 49er opts for a huge gennaker to maximize its reaching performance. Gennakers – usually rather smaller than the one shown here – are generally fairly simple to control. They lack the complexity of a spinnaker, and can be treated like a massively oversized jib set with a loose luff.**

BELOW LEFT **The 470 has a traditional spinnaker to aid downwind performance. It may look easy, but spinnakers can take a lot of knowledge to control.**

The gennaker is like an oversize, over-full jib with a very loose luff, and is designed exclusively for broad reaching. This has generated a new style of fast sailing in which sailors tack downwind to optimize their speed, aiming to keep the boat planing while bearing away on the apparent wind to sail as deep downwind as possible.

Gennakers are cut much flatter than spinnakers in order to promote fast reaching, and are not at all suitable for sailing straight downwind. They are supported at the tack by a bowsprit, which is launched at the same time as the gennaker is hoisted from its bag or chute, and have a single continuous sheet, which makes hoists, drops and gybes comparatively easy.

Spinnakers and gennakers need to be as light as possible so that they pull easily and stay filled with minimal support. The favoured material is woven nylon or polyester cloth. Both have a light weight to tear strength ratio combined with excellent stretch stability and zero porosity – for obvious reasons it is important that the sail does not hold water when stored in its bag or chute.

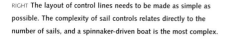

ABOVE **The RS300 single-hander has an uncluttered cockpit with all sail controls in easy reach of the front hand for easy adjustment on either tack while the sailor concentrates on hiking and steering.**

RIGHT **The layout of control lines needs to be made as simple as possible. The complexity of sail controls relates directly to the number of sails, and a spinnaker-driven boat is the most complex.**

Sail controls

The mainsail is built with a pre-determined amount of camber and luff curve that must be matched to the natural bending characteristics of the mast. Sail controls are used to adjust the depth and position of the camber with the outhaul simply flattening the camber of the foot of the sail, while the downhaul and/or kicking strap both flatten and pull the camber forward for sailing upwind and better control in stronger winds.

Mainsheet This is used to control the angle of the attack of the mainsail.

Centre mainsheet Favoured by most dinghy classes, despite some obvious disadvantages: it clutters up the boat and

as it is closer to the mast it requires more sheeting movement and has higher loadings than a transom mainsheet. This requires a multi-purchase sheeting system with extra blocks and extra expense.

The most obvious advantage of a centre mainsheet is that the sheet won't lasso the back of the boat every time you tack or gybe, or worse still lasso other boats during a race. A less obvious advantage is that many sailors prefer to handle the boat with their sheet hand held forwards, in particular when tacking.

When centre mainsheets first appeared they were mainly used with a full length traveller. However, apart from use on

catamarans, the traveller has been replaced by a much simpler strop or hoop, and the role of the traveller has been superseded by sail development and sailing technique, which makes use of maximum kicking strap tension.

Transom mounted mainsheet Found on the Topper and Laser 1, this is altogether a simpler system, which gives greater power for less sheeting purchase than the centre mainsheet. However, it frequently suffers from the lasso effect, catching round the transom or rudder stock when you tack, and is otherwise not fashionable.

The loading on the mainsheet will determine the number and complexity of blocks being used. This may range from a

RIGHT Many modern dinghies feature an open transom, which immediately drains water from the boat, but makes a transom mounted mainsheet impractical. The crew can adjust the sail controls from both side decks.

simple 2:1 purchase of the most basic single sheave blocks on a Topper, to a heavily loaded 16:1 purchase on a Tornado catamaran with complex twin block systems that allow the sheet to be led through eight sheaves to a high load auto-ratchet jammer.

All blocks should feature low friction, precision machined components, which can flourish in a marine environment. Acetal (plastic), stainless steel and

LEFT The NACRA 6.0 features a multi-purchase mainsheet led to a traveller, which runs the full length of the aft beam, allowing the mainsail to be let out, but still sheeted in, when sailing offwind at speed.

anodized alloy are favoured materials. The most efficient blocks have sheaves mounted on ball bearings for smooth running under load. Most mainsheet systems require an on/off auto-ratchet, which will lock the sheet while giving the crew up to 14:1 holding power for use with the mainsheet, jib sheets or spinnaker and gennaker sheets.

Downhaul and/or cunningham This control is used to increase luff tension, flattening the camber of the sail and bringing the draught (draft) forward to maintain control in stronger winds. On all but the smallest dinghies it relies on a multi-purchase system to maximise control.

Kicking strap or boom vang This system forms a triangle that links the underside of the boom to the base of the mast. It holds the boom down at a constant angle, and is used to tighten the leech and control power in the mainsail using a multi-purchase system. The alternative **GNAV** was pioneered by Laser as an upside-down vang. It has a rod-on-roller mechanism mounted above the boom, which provides extremely powerful luff tension control, as well as opening up the area below the boom for much better crew movement.

LEFT With three sails on a gennaker-driven boat it is vital that all controls are easy to use and identify, and within easy reach. The RS200 provides a lesson in control ergonomics.

LEFT The downhaul plays a major role in mainsail control on a high performance dinghy or catamaran. A multi-purchase system is needed to exert maximum leech tension.

Cleats

Four main types of cleat, produced in glass filled nylon, anodized aluminium or stainless steel, are used for sheet controls. **Cam cleats** feature two, spring-loaded, swivelling jaws, which lock on the rope or line. The cam cleat is the most sophisticated cleat design, combining maximum holding power with easy rope entry and exit while under load with minimum rope wear. The cam cleat is the number one choice for mainsheet and jib sheets. It may also be used in smaller sizes for secondary uses with high loading such as the spinnaker/gennaker halyard, where a combination jamming fairlead is sometimes used.

Open cleats are based on the traditional style of cleat where the rope is criss-crossed over a horn. Available in a number of different designs, but only suitable for securing ropes that are not under load. It is superseded for dinghy use by the Clamcleat and V cleat.

The outhaul stretches the foot of the mainsail and is usually led along the boom. It plays a secondary role to the downhaul/cunningham and kicking strap when flattening and moving the flow in the mainsail, and on some boats may be left in a fixed position.

Controls for the jib are generally kept to a minimum. The angle of attack is adjusted by jib sheets on either side of the boat, led through fairleads or blocks (ratchet optional for high loadings) to cleats where they can be locked off. On some dinghies and catamarans it is possible to adjust the lead block fore and aft or sideways to flatten the luff or foot, as well as fine tuning the angle of attack.

RIGHT The outhaul is led to the end of the boom. Note the loose footed mainsail that has superseded the use of a bolt rope led through a slot in the boom. When used with modern, stable sail materials it is an equally effective solution to controlling the foot of the sail, and one that allows lower manufacturing costs and makes rigging just that bit faster.

LEFT **The Clamcleat is a simple and clever design which will not slip if used with the correct diameter rope. The alloy version shown here on a Dart 16 allows the mainsail halyard to be pulled up and locked off by the side of the mast.**

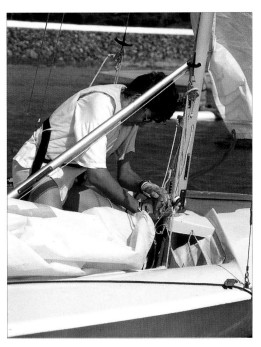

V cleats offer the simplest solution to very low load application for small diameter ropes such as the outhaul on a Topper dinghy.

Clamcleats are a refinement of the V cleat and offer a more precise lead, better grip and more efficient entry and exit for small diameter ropes while under load. They are particularly suitable for in-line, mast-mounted applications such as halyards and downhauls.

RIGHT **Rigging demands a certain amount of care and attention to ensure everything is set up correctly. Once you are out on the water, it is difficult to put things right. Always check for wear and tear before setting off.**

LEFT **The role of cleats in high performance sailing is to catch and hold a control line with a fail-safe grip, and immediately free the line when required. This provides the right kind of back-up for sailing on the edge, such as allowing this catamaran to perform wildthing (the lifting of one hull) while sailing fast downwind, a manoeuvre that requires nerve and firm control.**

What to wear

Part of the fun of sailing a small open boat is being exposed to the elements. In the early days enthusiasts had to make do with the most basic protective garments, but modern high-performance clothing has transformed the sport and made sailing a pastime that can be enjoyed year-round in most corners of the world.

DRYSUITS

The modern drysuit is a descendant of the all-enveloping diver suit with a brass helmet and is the first choice for committed dinghy sailors who have to cope with cold water. Sailing ceases to be fun if you get cold and, worn with a thermal fleece base layer, a drysuit provides the best protection available. It is designed to keep all the water out and has the following prime benefits:

- Jumping in and out of a drysuit, particularly one with a front entry zip (zipper), is quick and easy when compared to the horrible, soggy hassle that often has to be endured when struggling in and out of a wetsuit.
- Unlike a wetsuit, a precise fit isn't necessary or even desirable. A drysuit should be big enough to allow easy movement but not so big that it flaps and gets in the way. A drysuit is also excellent for growing children and will accommodate at least three years' growth.
- A good quality drysuit may be expensive, but it is a hard-wearing item that will last over several seasons. The stretchy latex rubber of the neck, wrist and ankle seals or socks will eventually tear or perish, but can be replaced with a proprietary do-it-yourself kit. Tears in the main fabric of the suit can be patched, and if the suit eventually leaks it can be returned to the manufacturer for re-proofing.

HOW TO PUT ON A DRYSUIT

1 Slide the foot gently into the foot of the suit, ensuring that you do not snag the rubber ankle seal on anything.

2 Pull the rubber seal up over the ankle. Dusting your foot with talcum powder makes this easier and is kinder on the seal.

3 The seal guard is made of stretchy latex rubber that will ensure minimum entry of water at that point.

4 Before attempting to put the top of your drysuit on, remove your watch and any other items that may snag the wrist seal.

5 Next, slide the suit over your head, stretching the rubber around the neck so that your head can fit through.

6 When you have put your hand into the sleeve of the drysuit, ensure that the rubber seal around your wrist fits properly.

7 The diagonal front zip means that the whole suit can be done up easily without needing any outside assistance.

8 The seal around the neck and flap over the zip means that you should remain well protected against the elements.

9 A well-fitting drysuit, although it can be expensive, is well worth the investment for the comfort it gives you.

Choosing a drysuit

The lighter the material the easier it is to wear, but it is no good having a drysuit that is prone to tearing and there must be a compromise with durability. Favoured drysuit materials tend to feature PVC (vinyl)/polyurethane coated nylon fabrics in the 115g (4oz) weight range.

The areas that are in most contact with the boat, mainly the seat and knees, need to be heavily reinforced. If you spend a lot of time sliding around on your seat, a trapeze harness or hiking pants will provide extra protection.

When trying on a drysuit, remember to bend and stretch in all possible directions to ensure the suit really is the right size for you.

Seal guards These are like reinforced cuffs, offer valuable protection against inadvertently snagging the wrist or ankle seals, and if made of neoprene may give some thermal advantage.

Storm collar This adjustable collar around the neck has a measurable effect on limiting heat loss.

Internal braces These help to keep the drysuit sitting correctly on your body and can be invaluable if you overheat and want to "drop the top" for onshore activities such as rigging in the dinghy park.

Diagonal front zip This means you can get in and out of the drysuit without an extra pair of hands. The more traditional style of drysuit zip is aligned horizontally across the shoulders, and may be preferred by trapeze crews if a front zip clutters up their harness. The more heavy duty the zip, the more robust the zip handle or puller needs to be. If the handle comes off in your hands, you'll have to use wire or rope as an emergency handle!

Drysuit variations

Breathable drysuits for dinghy sailors have been developed from drysuits for offshore sailors where the no-sweat concept is of particular importance when suits are being worn for long periods. These are likely to be the most expensive drysuits available and the concept will only work properly if your other clothing allows the suit to breathe. This makes it

ABOVE **The drysuit is recommended for children sailing in colder weather. It is comfortable, easy to wear and should provide many years of use for an extended family.**

imperative to wear performance-based thermal underwear, which draws perspiration away from the skin without retaining any moisture. It is also important to realize that any part of the drysuit that is covered – for instance by a buoyancy aid and trapeze harness – will not be free to breathe correctly. In general terms, the more physically demanding your style of sailing is, the more desirable a breathable drysuit becomes.

Most drysuits offer a choice between ankle seals or integral socks in the same latex material. Both have their pros and cons. Wearing ankle seals makes it easier to get in and out of dinghy shoes, and gives you the option of being able to walk around the dinghy park in bare feet. Latex socks can be worn with neoprene boots and are the best choice for sailing in water at freezing winter temperatures. Slipping your feet in and out of a latex sock is also much easier than dealing with an ankle seal, but the unprotected sock is very vulnerable to being damaged by a rough surface such as shingle or concrete.

Variations on the conventional drysuit also include the two-piece drysuit, which joins at the waist with two pieces of latex rolled together to create a perfect seal. This dispenses with the need for a zip (zipper), and means you can also wear the top on its own with a wetsuit or shorts.

Another variation is the combi-suit, which combines a loose drysuit-style top with a tight wetsuit-style bottom. This gives a trimmer fit and may provide better thermal protection.

Drysuit care

A drysuit is an expensive garment and care and a small amount of maintenance will be repaid.

Latex seals are one size, which means they often need to be cut down to achieve a comfortable fit. Take great care when you do this because there is no going back if you cut too far. Use very sharp scissors and cut slowly and carefully round one ring at a time before trying each seal for comfort. Remember that the neck seal in particular will stretch when you are using the suit on the water. A perfect seal must be tight enough to keep out the water without choking you at the same time.

Be as gentle as possible when pushing the various parts of your body through the seals. Give the seals a regular dusting with talcum powder to keep them supple and prevent them going sticky, which happens when the chlorine residue from the manufacturing process wears off. Remember that a ring or watch can easily snag and tear a latex seal.

Check your boat over for anything like split pins, screw ends or frayed wire, which could snag and tear a drysuit. At the very least, wrap them with tape.

Clean and lubricate the zip regularly. Rub candle wax on both sides of a metal zip, and very briefly melt the wax into the teeth with a hair dryer. Never allow salt residue to build up on the teeth.

Do not store the suit while it is still wet. Wash it out in fresh water and allow

FEATURES OF THE DRYSUIT ....

1 Some drysuits have zips across the back. This creates less clutter when wearing a harness, but you will need help opening and closing the zip.

2 Once zipped up, the dry suit will be full of air, so squat down to force the air out of the legs.

3 Pull the neck seal open to let all the air out and deflate the drysuit round your body.

4 Stretch to make sure you have a good fit and can move easily in the suit.

5 Be very careful of snagging latex socks on rough ground. A good way to get dinghy boots on is to fill them with water first.

it to dry completely. Be sure to lubricate the seals with a proprietary solution before storing. A drysuit is best stored out of full light on a plastic hanger. Drysuits are easily damaged by overexposure to direct sunlight or heat. Leaving a drysuit on the rear shelf of your car is never a good idea.

WETSUITS

The neoprene wetsuit is the popular choice for keeping warm and comfortable when dinghy sailing in all but the hottest sea and air conditions. The principle is that the neoprene traps a thin layer of water, which warms up to the temperature of your body. This is fine so long as the wetsuit is a perfect fit and doesn't let any more cold water flush through that layer.

A close-fitting wetsuit is therefore critical to warmth and comfort and, when buying off the rack, it is important to differentiate between male and female suits and accept that suits for children will only work for as long as they fit correctly. An option is to buy a made-to-measure wetsuit provided by specialist manufacturers.

Choosing a wetsuit

The tight fit of a wetsuit means that the neoprene must stretch in all the right places to provide maximum freedom of movement. In this respect modern neoprenes are far lighter and more supple than their predecessors, and laminate materials such as woven titanium can allow thinner, and therefore lighter and more supple, neoprene to maintain the same body heat. In general, the thicker the neoprene the warmer, heavier and bulkier the suit will be, and the current

ABOVE **Perfectly fitted wetsuits are generally favoured for the kind of performance summer sailing in which a drysuit would simply overheat.**

norm is to have a 5mm (³⁄₁₆in) body and 5mm (³⁄₁₆in) legs used in conjunction with flexible 3mm (⅛in) arms for the coldest sailing conditions, while a 3mm (⅛in) body should suffice for summer use.

The system used to hold the neoprene panels of a wetsuit together will have a major impact on how much water can flush through. The cheapest, most basic form of stitching is the mechanical overlock, which punctures the neoprene with hundreds of tiny holes that will allow water through. This may be acceptable for a short summer suit, but is no good for serious cold weather sailing. By contrast, flatlock and blindstitching use a stitch that only pierces one side of the edge of the panel, which is also bonded and taped with neoprene glue to produce a virtually failsafe watertight join.

Neoprene is usually lined with lycra on the inside (single lined) to make it easy to pull on and off your body. It may also be lined on the outside (double lined), which increases both abrasion and tear resistance, but is thought to reduce the thermal

effectiveness of the neoprene as the lycra holds cold water on the outside of the suit instead of running straight off a plain neoprene surface. The compromise solution is to have strategically placed double-lined panels in a predominantly single lined suit, providing a hard wearing surface where needed, and the added advantage of incorporating bright primary colours.

ABOVE **Modern wetsuits combine single or double lined neoprene in different thicknesses to ensure a warm body with flexible limbs.**

LEFT **The steamer style wetsuit creates its own closed weather system, but the fit must be body hugging to keep cold water ingress to a minimum.**

The right fit

A good fit at the neck, wrists and ankles is vital to prevent cold water flushing through the suit, while the zip (zipper), which normally runs straight up the spine, should feature some kind of water barrier such as two overlapping neoprene flaps or a single C-Flap that folds over. An alternative solution is to have no zip at all, which has become possible with the most modern flexible neoprenes, and is the direction in which wetsuit development seems likely to go. It is considerably easier to get in and out of a wetsuit with ankle zips, but they can be expensive and they do let water flush through. When trying on a wetsuit, remember to bend and stretch in all directions to ensure it is both tight fitting and comfortable.

Reinforcement

Whether a wetsuit is single or double lined, knee pad reinforcement, which is built into the suit, is vital for any style of sailing that involves the crew going down on their knees, for instance on the mesh trampoline of a catamaran or on the deck of a high-performance gennaker-driven monohull. Depending on your style of sailing, a trapeze harness or hiking shorts may also be necessary to protect the seat.

Steamers

The steamer was first used by surfers who needed a warm, watertight wetsuit, which allowed them to sit in cold water and wait for waves for long periods. Modern steamers are one-piece, full-length suits featuring watertight seams and watertight or fully protected zips. A super-flexible neoprene suit may have no zip at all.

Long john and bolero

The long john is a traditional style of armless, one-piece suit, which can be slipped on without a zip and is therefore very easy and cheap to manufacture. It can be worn in conjunction with a bolero-style neoprene jacket, but this tends to be a poor thermal solution and a loose-fitting dry top with a watertight seal at the waist should provide better flexibility and warmth.

FEATURES OF THE WETSUIT ....

Knee reinforcement is vital for any high performance dinghy in which the crew may have to kneel to launch and retrieve the gennaker.

Most wetsuits have a zip, which is pulled vertically up the back. Care must be taken to ensure that neoprene flaps behind the zip fold in correctly to keep water out.

Convertibles

The convertible is a full-length suit, which has to a large extent outdated the traditional long john and bolero. It has removable single-lined neoprene sleeves, which can be peeled off in seconds to create a short sleeve/bare arm suit for warmer days. The concept works well, making a 3mm (⅛ in) convertible the ideal summer companion to a 5mm (³⁄₁₆in) winter steamer in your wardrobe.

A steamer may be suitable for three or four seasons' use, depending on the thickness of the neoprene, but will overheat in warmer weather.

Short sleeves give much greater upper body freedom for summer sailing, while long legs help protect knees and shins from the hard edges and non-slip surfaces of a modern performance dinghy.

ABOVE **The convertible wetsuit is a clever answer to the overheating problem – pull off the sleeves and enjoy the breeze. The concept can effectively add another season.**

ABOVE **The shortie is for the warmest weather, when it will help protect your body from the ravages of salt and sun as well as providing a barrier to wind chill.**

Wetsuit care

A quality wetsuit will last for many years provided a few basic care and maintenance principles are adhered to:

• Always wash the wetsuit inside and out in clean, fresh water after use, ensuring that salt does not build up on the zip.

• Allow the suit to dry, and then store in a cool, dark place on a plastic hanger.

• Do not leave the suit folded or lying around in a crumpled heap for long periods of time.

• When not in use do not leave the suit exposed to sunlight.

• Make a regular inspection for damage to the neoprene or frayed stitching. Single-lined neoprene is prone to small tears, which are easily repaired with super-glue.

It is worth remembering that since the wetsuit is worn next to your body, personal hygiene should be a general consideration. Some people tend to assume that being in and out of water automatically cleanses the wetsuit. This is not at all true, and a neglected or maltreated wetsuit can easily become a bacteria-ridden garment.

Shorties

For warm sailing conditions, a short sleeve, knee-length wetsuit allows maximum agility while heat loss from the central body core is still protected by 3mm (⅛in) neoprene.

Rash vests

The seams of a wetsuit can chafe against bare skin, which is why some sailors choose to wear a nylon rash vest as an accessory. Rash vests are also available in thermal material to provide extra insulation.

LEFT **Made out of flexible, super-stretch neoprene material, wetsuits are a sailor's favourite item of choice for use in the modern action-packed style of dinghy sailing and racing, which requires plenty of continual body movement to and fro.**

ABOVE One-piece (centre) or two-piece (right) dinghy suits can be more comfortable and easier to wear than a wetsuit. Braces (left) help keep trousers in position.

DINGHY SUITS AND OTHER EQUIPMENT

The dinghy suit affords sufficient protection for any type of open boat sailing where the crew needs to stay warm and dry from wind, spray and rain, but does not expect to fall in, capsize, or spend time in the water when launching or retrieving. Most dinghy suits are made in proofed nylon and feature a separate smock with a tight-fitting neoprene waistband and velcro-adjustable wrist and neck closure, which is worn over chest-high trousers with an adjustable ankle closure or, more unusually, a pair of matching dinghy shorts.

Features to look out for include reinforced knees and seat for longevity, a short zip (zipper) at the neck of the smock, full length zip on the trousers to make them easy to get on and off, and one or more pockets. The fit should be loose, light and comfortable allowing thermal layers to be built up underneath. Breathable outer materials are available at the top end of most ranges. One-piece dinghy suits are also available and are likely to be lighter and more comfortable to wear at the expense of being a single garment.

Dry tops

The dry top bridges the gap between the dinghy smock and drysuit, using latex seals at the neck and wrists plus a deep, neoprene waistband to create a fully waterproof top that can effectively be worn with dinghy trousers, a long john or a convertible-style wetsuit.

Thermal underclothing

In cold weather, thermal underwear should always be worn beneath drysuits and dinghy suits. Using stretch fleece materials that are light and quick drying when wet, such as Polartec, enables layers of internal warmth to be built up with minimal bulk. When used with a breathable outer suit they can draw perspiration away from the body so that sweat can be dissipated rather than trapped on the surface of the skin where it becomes cold and leaves the wearer feeling clammy and wet.

For general use, the most user-friendly base layer tends to be thermal trousers or salopettes worn with a matching, long-sleeved thermal zip-top polo- or turtle-neck jersey. One-piece thermal suits may offer marginally better thermal protection.

Boots and shoes

Sailing a dinghy barefoot is seldom a good idea, as there are fittings that can bruise or cut your feet, bare skin won't grip as well as rubber, and there may be something sharp and unpleasant when you come ashore and put your feet over the side.

For all-round use, the dinghy boot combines a neoprene sock, to provide warmth and comfort, with a hard-wearing rubber sole, plus extensive PVC (vinyl) rubber reinforcement at the heel and over the top of the foot to allow for tucking the boot under footstraps and hiking out. The traditional height is high enough to give complete protection to the ankle bones, with zips or laces for easy access. A pull-on boot with neither will be cheaper as well as more thermally efficient, but can be a pain to put on (fill it with water or use talcum powder) and pull off.

The optional choice for warm water sailing is a slip-on rubber or neoprene shoe such as the Okespor Beachsurf. These shoes are light and comfortable, grip like limpets, and are much cheaper than boots – they can also fall off your foot at inopportune moments such as during a capsize.

ABOVE Neoprene boots have a tendency for unpleasant odour after a period of time. Wash them in fresh water and air regularly. To clean them properly, use a little soap or soak them in a solution of sterilizing tablets.

ABOVE Thermal base layers are available in different weights and for various degrees of cold. From left to right: short-sleeved top; long Johns and long-sleeved top; and a thick one piece suit.

RIGHT Modern high-performance sailing requires clothing that controls body warmth during periods of relative physical inactivity interspersed with furious activity.

Gloves

Modern dinghies have a battery of synthetic ropes and control lines, which can be hard on the hands, particularly heaving on a downhaul or taking the strain of the gennaker sheet when a slip could cause a serious burn. For this reason gloves are now widely worn in all seasons.

Summer gloves consist of a reinforced palm made in a synthetic leather material, which can cope with being wet and won't harden when dry (popular materials include Amara and NASH), combined with lightweight mesh backs, which let spray drain through, velcro wrist straps for a precise fit, and the option of short fingers so that relevant ropes can be picked out more easily. Synthetic DIY knitted

gloves covered with a PVC lattice provide a lower cost alternative that works as well, even if they don't have the same style rating.

Dinghy gloves for winter pose more of a problem. A glove that is both warm and waterproof tends to be bulky and lack feel. It is no doubt only a matter of time before a winter glove that really works becomes available, but in the absence of anything better most sailors opt for a wet solution, which combines Amara style palms for grip and feel with 3mm (⅛in) double-lined neoprene backing for warmth.

Headwear

An unprotected head is a major source of heat loss in cold weather, which is easily and very effectively protected by a

beanie-style hat made in a quick drying thermal material. With the right fit these hats are extremely resilient, offering basic protection against knocks by the boom, and they generally stay in place even during a capsize.

For more extreme cold weather conditions it may help to resort to a neoprene hood or balaclava, but they tend to inhibit hearing and are not particularly pleasant to wear.

Hiking shorts

A long, hard hike off the deck of a small performance dinghy like a Laser or Optimist can be tough and uncomfortable. The role of hiking shorts, similar to cycling shorts, is to provide a soft layer between you and the deck. Made with a combination of mesh, neoprene, straps and padding they may look bizarre but they do the job well and should be very hard wearing.

Knee pads

These are yet another extra that make the modern dinghy sailor look like a medieval knight dressing up for battle. They are necessary on the type of high performance dinghies and catamarans where the crew have to drop to their knees, as when stowing the gennaker in its bag, and therefore need all the extra knee protection that materials such as neoprene and kevlar reinforcement provide.

LEFT Variations on all-seasons headgear. The peaked cap will help keep the sun off your face but has no thermal properties; the "bush ranger" hat looks good, but stands a good chance of going over the side; balaclavas in fleece or neoprene are the best choice for keeping cold winds out, but not particularly comfortable to wear.

Buoyancy aids

The buoyancy aid (personal flotation device) is considered the most vital item in a dinghy sailor's wardrobe. It is only designed to provide sufficient (50 Newton) buoyancy in the water to float a fully conscious person, and should not be confused with a full lifejacket, which is a much bulkier item that has considerably greater (inflatable) buoyancy and is designed to roll an unconscious person on to their back so they can continue breathing. The bottom line is that if you knock yourself out and fall face down in the water, you will continue to float face down when wearing a buoyancy aid. However, this type of accident rarely happens in dinghy sailing and usually there is someone to provide an immediate rescue.

A modern, vest-style buoyancy aid is the top choice for dinghy sailors because it is lightweight and compact, providing maximum freedom of movement in the boat and in the water. Padding provides extra thermal insulation and protection against the kind of knocks and bashes that can occur in a fast-moving capsize.

ABOVE **Capsize is all part of the fun of dinghy sailing. A good buoyancy aid will ensure that you can enjoy the experience in a relaxed frame of mind.**

ABOVE **The waistcoat style buoyancy aid (left) is simple to wear and provides good protection. The buoyancy aid (right) that slips on like a vest, allows freedom of movement with a harness.**

Price will to some extent depend on the type of foam used. PE (polyethylene) foam is both lighter and cheaper, but is layered in sheets that will degrade in time. PVC (vinyl) foam is heavier and more expensive, but will last much longer and provides better thermal insulation.

Always be sure and check that the buoyancy aid fits with your wetsuit or drysuit. Ensure that it is a close, comfortable fit, which allows unrestricted arm movement and will not ride up if you go down in the water. If you intend to sail wearing a trapeze harness, it is important to ensure as well that the buoyancy aid leaves the hook area unobstructed.

Trapeze harnesses

The number one feature to look for in a trapeze harness is comfort. Do not buy a harness unless you can give it a dry land test. A precise fit, which moulds to the body, is vital and, although there is nothing that can simulate the reality of trapezing on the water, you should at least seek answers to these four questions when selecting a harness to buy:

- Is the harness quick and easy to get in and out of, with failsafe buckles that are simple and fast to adjust?
- Is it comfortable and user-friendly when worn with your wetsuit/drysuit and buoyancy aid?
- Does it still feel good when you're bending and stretching?
- How does it feel hanging off a line and what is the pull like on your hips and groin area?

Harness styles

The most popular style of harness is the Nappy, which features a full back with padded straps, padded waist flaps either side, and a padded crutch strap that passes between the legs. An alternative style replaces the nappy element with twin thigh straps that need to be well padded as they pass either side of the groin.

Back support has always been considered vital to help maintain a straight-out stance in a harness, but the newer skiff-style of sailing requires more of a sit-up stance plus maximum upper body mobility. Therefore for short course racing many skiff sailors favour the windsurfer type of harness that has no upper back support at all. Lower back support can still be provided by padded foam inserts and hip tensioning points.

An aluminium spreader bar spreads the load across the hips and prevents crushing. Adjustable hook height is a useful feature as some people require extra lumbar support, which means they like to wear the hook higher.

Shoulder, hip and thigh straps should feature a quick and easy adjustment system using velcro or buckles. When sailing, the ends of webbing straps must be tidied away so they do not interfere with the hook.

Trapeze sailing tends to involve a lot of sliding in and out on your bottom. A tough reinforcement material such as Cordura is vital for durability in the seat area. Custom made-to-measure harnesses that provide a virtually perfect fit, are available from specialist manufacturers.

ABOVE **The harness should give full support tailored to the individual. Size is chosen to give a close fit round the hips and tuning the shoulder and leg straps ensure that the harness stays put.**

Sailing bags

A large sailing bag is a vital accessory for stowing all of your dinghy sailing kit. It is important to get the right size for your personal requirements, and the best bags should have the following features:

- Built in hard-wearing, water-resistant fabric, with a reinforced waterproof base that will cope with wet changing room floors or dinghy decks.
- Separate wet and dry compartments.
- Large cargo pockets for small extras.
- Heavy duty zips (zippers) all round.
- Shoulder and hand straps.
- A built-in name tag so that the bag won't go missing.

ABOVE **It is worth investing in a top-quality sailing bag that is tough and water resistant.**

ABOVE **Daring young men on the flying trapeze. It looks good, but a trapeze harness must be as comfortable as possible to actually enjoy trapezing over long periods of time.**

Sunglasses for sailing

The combination of blue sea and white water provides a brilliant reflective surface for the sun, which can make sailing both trying and tiring without sunglasses. It is also potentially dangerous, since the effects of ultraviolet (UV) light on a person's eyes are cumulative throughout their lifetime. When choosing sunglasses for sailing, consider the following:

- Good quality sunglasses should block out both UVA and UVB sunlight to at least 99 per cent.
- For dinghy and small boat sailing it is vital that sunglasses fit comfortably and securely and stay in position come what may. The wrap-around, face-hugging style tends to be more secure and has the advantage of having no protuberances to catch on a flailing rope or line. A good security back-up for an expensive pair of sunglasses is an adjustable eyewear retainer.
- The main disadvantage of wrap-around sunglasses is that they tend to reduce the field of vision.
- Top quality lenses and frames for sailing should be virtually unbreakable, and manufacturers should provide a repair service.
- If you wear corrective lenses, check the availability of prescription sunglass lenses or consider using daily disposable contact lenses with sunglasses.
- Investing in the best will reduce potential eyestrain.

BELOW **You can simulate the feel of a trapeze harness on dry land, and ensure that the fit is right and the straps provide the necessary support.**

How a sailboat moves

At its simplest, wind pushes a sail from behind, which is known as running downwind. Sailing a few degrees either side of downwind was the only direction in which the old-fashioned square-riggers could go, and if the wind was blowing in the wrong direction they would simply have to wait days or weeks for it to change. Thankfully the modern style of Bermudan rig came along to change all that, and now sailboats can sail in almost any direction with the obvious exception of straight into the wind; the more sophisticated and performance-oriented the sailboat, the closer to the wind it will be able to go.

The ability to sail towards the wind rather than just away from it is achieved by the airfoil effect of modern sails. Wind flowing over the sails is composed of a moving mass of air particles that separates when it hits the front or leading edge of the sail. From there it accelerates around both sides, following the curved shape of the sail to produce positive high pressure on the windward side (the side the wind is blowing on to) and negative low pressure on the leeward side (the side the wind is

ABOVE **With sails pulled hard in, a modern sailboat can sail towards the direction the wind is coming from. The sails and daggerboard provide a lift to windward.**

blowing away from). The difference between this positive and negative pressure creates the aerodynamic force that sucks the sail forwards and drives the boat along, generating sufficient force to overcome the natural resistance of water

against the lower part of the hull as well as air resistance against the top of the hull, sails, rigging, fittings and crew.

Sail camber and incidence

The cross-sectional shape of a sail will help determine its performance. The degree of curvature (camber) must be correctly aligned with the apparent wind (the angle of incidence) to produce maximum drive. The optimum angle of incidence is widely held to be at 15 degrees between the chord (an imaginary straight line connecting both ends of the sail) and the apparent wind. If the angle of incidence is greater, airflow will detach from the leeward side creating turbulence and reducing drive. If the angle of incidence is smaller, the sail will stall as positive air flow ceases to flow over the windward side.

The amount of camber and its position in the sail will greatly effect performance characteristics. All modern

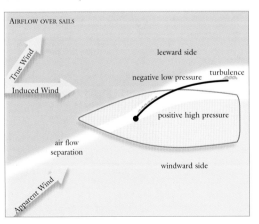

AIRFLOW OVER SAILS

True Wind

Induced Wind

leeward side

negative low pressure   turbulence

positive high pressure

air flow separation

windward side

Apparent Wind

LEFT **Airflow over sails separates on to the windward (high pressure) and leeward (low pressure) sides, and turbulence is created at the leading and trailing edges. The sails must always be adjusted to make maximum use of the speed and direction of the apparent wind.**

high performance dinghies provide adjustment systems to alter luff (leading edge) and foot tension, which will maximize or minimize camber as well as changing the position of maximum camber fore and aft from the midpoint of the sail.

True wind and apparent wind

The wind's force in a sail is concentrated in an area known as the centre of effort (CE) while the outer area of the sail plays a secondary role in keeping the power of the wind under control. This concept can be directly experienced by windsurfers who hold up the rig and can effectively feel the centre of effort pulling between their hands.

Windsurfers also have the most direct experience of the difference between true wind and apparent wind, a concept that is particularly important with all types of high performance dinghy and keelboat sailing, particularly skiff-style, gennaker-driven dinghies and catamarans.

True wind is the real wind. In terms of speed and direction it is the wind experienced by a stationary observer.

Apparent wind is the wind experienced by any moving object. For instance, if a cyclist is cycling at 16kph (10mph) directly into an oncoming wind, which has

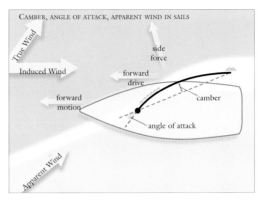

CAMBER, ANGLE OF ATTACK, APPARENT WIND IN SAILS

True Wind · Induced Wind · forward motion · Apparent Wind · side force · forward drive · camber · angle of attack

LEFT **The main sheet or jib sheet is the primary control used to control the angle of incidence or angle of attack, which is adjusting the position of the sail relative to airflow. Adjusting the deepest point or camber is equivalent to tuning the sail to maximize performance.**

a true speed of 16kph (10mph), the apparent wind he has to contend with will total 32kph (20mph). Conversely, if the cyclist is cycling in exactly the same direction as the wind, and both are moving at 16kph (10mph), the apparent wind will be zero. The speed of true wind and apparent wind will never be the same when a boat is moving. Apparent wind is at its lightest when a boat is travelling in exactly the same direction (running dead downwind) as true wind, and becomes progressively stronger as a boat sails closer to the wind. This phenomenon also has a marked effect on the difference in temperature when sailing downwind and upwind.

The direction of true and apparent wind will only be the same when a boat is travelling in the same direction (running dead downwind). On any other course the apparent wind will come from further forward (the direction the boat is heading towards) than the true wind. This is the induced direction of the wind as a result of the boat's forward progress. The greater the speed of the boat, the more the direction of the wind will move forward, which is why the fastest sail-powered craft for their size – windsurfers and catamarans – must always have their sails pulled hard in when they are sailing at speed in order to maximize the apparent wind.

ABOVE **Rapid forward movement transforms the true wind into apparent wind. This is the wind the sailor actually sails in, and may be stronger and from a different direction than on dry land.**

ABOVE **As a boat accelerates, the direction of the apparent wind changes and comes from further ahead. To keep up speed, the helmsman must steer away from the wind.**

Slipping sideways (leeway)

Because of their design, sails cannot achieve a pure forward force. Instead, most of the force is sideways, and becomes progressively more as a boat sails closer to the wind. The sideways force must be converted into forward speed instead of driving the boat sideways or blowing it on to its side. This is largely achieved by the use of a centreboard or daggerboard to provide leeward resistance, combined with minimizing hull and air resistance to allow the boat to move forwards and the crew's skills to keep the boat upright.

Centreboards and daggerboards

While displacement yachts have a fixed keel to prevent them being blown sideways, dinghies are fitted with a centreboard or daggerboard foil which prevents side-slip and also helps lift the boat to windward when it is being driven hard. Both are housed within a case inside the boat – a centreboard swivels through

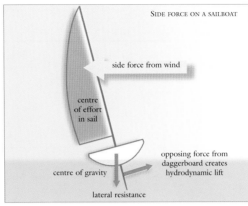

SIDE FORCE ON A SAILBOAT

side force from wind

centre of effort in sail

centre of gravity

opposing force from daggerboard creates hydrodynamic lift

lateral resistance

LEFT **The side forces on a sailboat act on the rig, sails and hull, which are pushed one way, while the centreboard, daggerboard or keel provides a counter balance. It helps to transform the sideways movement into forward movement, as well as providing resistance against the sailboat heeling.**

90 degrees to its down position while a daggerboard drops vertically.

The centreboard is a neater system and has the major benefit of kicking back without damage if the boat hits the bottom. The daggerboard is a simpler system and cheaper to manufacture, and

can be made in a longer, narrow foil shape to optimize both lateral resistance and lift to windward. However, a long, fixed foil can cause serious problems when sailing at speed in shallow water because it is difficult to lift this type of daggerboard quickly.

RIGHT **A catamaran has a smaller surface area in contact with the water and a wide platform that provides sufficient leverage to carry an over-size rig. The Tornado shown here is wider than any racing catamaran of a similar size. The disadvantage of such a large catamaran is that in most countries its platform has to be dismantled or tipped on its side to be able to transport it legally.**

A centreboard or daggerboard foil will work with the rudder foil to maximize leeward resistance. The shape and area of the foil is critical to performance, which will depend on the length to thickness ratio, the position of maximum thickness and the radius of the leading edge.

Hull and air resistance

These are related to the speed and course of a boat, the wind speed and direction, and water conditions. Resistance due to friction under the boat is known as skin friction, and is created by individual layers of water passing beneath the boat. The solution is to reduce the amount of boat in contact with the water (wetted surface area) to a minimum, which is first achieved by design and second by the crew trimming the boat correctly.

Resistance due to the shape of the hull (form resistance) is mainly caused by hitting waves, plus the turbulence created by the imperfect shapes of bows, stern and centreboard or daggerboard and rudder foils. Form resistance decreases in proportion to the weight of the boat, and

ABOVE **All modern dinghies need to be sailed virtually flat on the water to minimize friction and optimize performance. A slight degree of heel, as shown here, is almost inevitable.**

ABOVE **Once a dinghy is allowed to heel over, its underwater shape changes and form resistance increases dramatically. At the same time its foils cease to function as efficiently.**

is the factor that prevents displacement boats such as heavy keelboats from accelerating beyond a specific point.

However, with the kind of planing hulls found on most dinghies, resistance stops increasing once the boat rises off its bow wave, leaves its stern wave behind and begins planing. A displacement boat will create a single wave, from bow to stern, from which it cannot escape, but planing boats can break out of that wave and plane over the waves. This is a sensation akin to skimming over the sea, which feels like a great leap forward. It is the fastest form of sailing on a monohull or windsurfer, but the speed of the pencil-slim hulls of a catamaran is due to the combination of minimum wetted area with maximum sail area.

Means of reducing form resistance include: producing a boat to minimum weight at the design stage, sailing with minimum weight, trimming the boat correctly both fore and aft and sideways, and ensuring the stern does not drag and create turbulence, which may also be created by an incorrectly profiled rudder.

Resistance due to heeling of the boat increases in form resistance in direct

relation to the angle of heel. The solution is to sail dinghies absolutely flat at all times, while most yachts should be sailed as upright as the given conditions will possibly allow.

Resistance due to leeway (induced drag) builds up turbulence on the leeward side of the boat as form resistance increases. This can be cured by sailing the boat as flat as possible, ensuring the centreboard is fully down, and driving the boat forwards, which is a specific skill.

Wind resistance on hull, rigging and anything else that stands out is most apparent when sailing close to the wind. The solution is to make the outline of a boat as clean as possible, using internal halyards, which do not break up airflow round the sail, combined with minimalist rigging and no unnecessary protuberances. Wind resistance caused by the physical bulk of the crew is likely to be minimal, and it is more important for the crew to sit in the right place to trim the boat correctly.

Resistance caused by sailing through rough water is best solved by technique to keep the boat driving and prevent it stalling on waves.

ABOVE **Wind resistance on mast and rigging can be kept to a minimum by using the simplest possible fittings, as on this catamaran mast.**

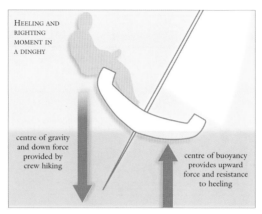

HEELING AND RIGHTING MOMENT IN A DINGHY

centre of gravity and down force provided by crew hiking

centre of buoyancy provides upward force and resistance to heeling

LEFT **The heeling and righting moment of a dinghy is determined by the crew acting as the centre of gravity, while the centre of buoyancy lifts the opposite side of the hull. The more the boat is allowed to heel, the less responsive it will be to the down force exerted by the crew.**

Keeping upright

All sailboats are designed to be sailed virtually upright, particularly dinghies that have nearly flat bottoms, to maximize their planing ability.

Unlike a yacht, which has a fixed keel weighted (ballasted) with lead, the centreboard of a modern dinghy is not ballasted and totally relies on the skills of the crew to keep the boat sailing upright. How easy or difficult this is will depend on the stability of the hull and the power of the rig. A sturdy, wide-bottomed cruising dinghy with a modest rig such as the Wayfarer will be slow to heel over and easy to control. An ultimate high performance dinghy such as the 49er combines a superlight, minimum wetted surface area hull with a powerful rig that its crew can control using racks and trapezes for maximum leverage. It therefore demands lightning responses and the very best technique to keep it upright.

The skills used by a crew to keep a dinghy upright are a combination of depowering the sails as necessary and using weight to counteract the pull in the sails. This is achieved by using their own centre of gravity as a lever that pulls against the boat's centre of buoyancy, which is directly related to its wetted surface area. The power of that lever is increased by hanging over the side of the boat (hiking) or standing out using a trapeze.

When a dinghy heels over a number of things happen: the angle of the centreboard allows greater side-slip, the angle of the rudder foil can lead to loss of control with the foil leaving the water in extreme cases. As the wetted surface area increases it creates extra drag and prevents effective planing. This change in the wetted surface outline can lead to loss of control. The sails become less efficient and drive is reduced. The righting effect of the crew is diminished as their centre of gravity lifts towards the centreline of the boat. Once a dinghy heels beyond a certain angle its centre of gravity (the crew) will pass over its centre of buoyancy (the wetted surface area). At this point its natural righting moment is transformed into positive heeling moment as the weight of the rig helps pull the boat over into unavoidable capsize.

ABOVE **Hiking or trapezing is the lever that helps keep a performance dinghy upright. Hiking on a Laser can be an extremely physical pastime that demands determination.**

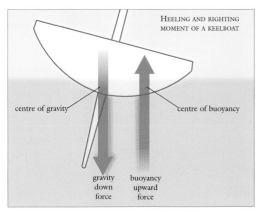

HEELING AND RIGHTING
MOMENT OF A KEELBOAT

centre of gravity

centre of buoyancy

gravity
down
force

buoyancy
upward
force

ABOVE **The heeling and righting moment of a keelboat will depend on the position of the centre of gravity. This is much lower than in a dinghy and will depend on the length and relative weight of the fully ballasted keel.**

ABOVE **Getting all the crew to sit up on the windward (weather) deck of a yacht will help keep it upright, but the effect is slight when compared to a crew hiking out on a dinghy. Sitting outside the guardrails is not allowed.**

The behaviour of a keelboat is different since its centre of gravity, principally the weight of the yacht itself – is much lower down and will remain lower than the centre of buoyancy which is within the yacht. The righting arm between the centre of gravity and centre of buoyancy actually gets longer as the angle of heel increases, which means that the yacht's resistance to heeling increases. So while a yacht may be blown almost flat, there will be minimal heeling moment induced by the sails, and the ballasted keel will soon bring her back upright, albeit with her bow slewing into the wind. There are exceptions. If a yacht is held down by an out of control spinnaker or knocked down by waves, its cockpit could fill with water. This has caused a few sinkings, but it is a rare occurrence limited mainly to small, open keelboats racing on inshore waters or yachts caught in extreme conditions. These can occur in confused waters on a coastal shelf after a storm, as in the open wilds of the southern oceans where well publicized capsizes have been the result of racing yachts losing their keel.

LEFT **In normal conditions a yacht will not capsize, since the righting arm between the centre of buoyancy and centre of gravity gets longer as the yacht heels further, while the effect of wind on the sails is reduced. This means that a yacht can only be capsized by a wave, or an accumulation of waves, in very extreme weather conditions.**

Where and when to sail

Dinghy sailing probably qualifies as a risk sport, although the risks are so minimal for those who take care that fatalities or serious injuries are extremely rare. However one should always have great respect for the elements of wind and water, particularly when sailing near a coast.

Safe locations

When starting out, the ultimate safe sailing location would probably be a fresh water lake or reservoir of no more than 1.6 km (1 mile) diameter, with an even depth, warm water, a regular, steady wind of Force 4 maximum, a club to sail from

and non-stop rescue cover. Look for a gently shelving beach or easily accessible pontoons or launch ramps from which to launch. There should not be any overhead powerlines in the locality, no obstructions such as moored boats, no swimmers and absolutely no powered craft except for rescue boats in case of emergency.

The shoreline

The suitability of where you launch and land on the shoreline will depend on its composition and location, how you launch and how it is affected by the prevailing wind. A gently shelving launch ramp with

a hard surface is ideal if you have a trolley, but beware of any slippery areas. Grass or soft sand is fine to launch from if you don't mind dragging the boat, otherwise you may need a trolley with oversize wheels. Shingle makes for hard work when it comes to pulling a boat up. It can also be unforgiving on your feet and even worse on the smooth, shiny bottom of your dinghy.

Launching or landing on mud is to be avoided at all costs. It is most often found in harbours and estuaries that dry out at low water, and can grab your feet and act like glue. Apart from being very messy,

LEFT **With an easily accessible shoreline and no difficult tides to deal with, a lake or reservoir may often be more user-friendly to beginners, with the added bonus that fresh water does not sting like sea water.**

ABOVE **Choose level ground to rig up on. Try not to disturb sunbathers or people having a picnic, and beware of all overhead lines.**

it can also be potentially dangerous if a boat and its occupants get stuck in the mud and are unable to extricate themselves.

Steeply shelving beaches can cause a lot of problems as well. First, the angle of the beach may make it difficult to manage and control the boat on the way down, followed by a struggle to pull it back up. Secondly, you will soon find yourself in deep water, which is difficult when launching and landing. Thirdly, if there is an onshore wind, a steeply shelving beach will encourage waves to build up and crash, and cause heavy undertows that follow.

Lee shores

A lee shore (a shoreline that the wind is blowing on to) was a terrifying prospect for all the old square-rigged ships. It was a lee shore in Ireland that became the wrecking ground for the Spanish Armada. Their captains often found themselves in an impossible position, blown on to inhospitable lee shores with no ability to sail upwind and escape the danger. To this day a lee shore in strong winds can still be extremely dangerous for modern yachts sailing offshore, as was demonstrated by the loss of the famous racing yacht *Morning Cloud* (owned by the former British Prime Minister, Edward Heath) together with two of her crew off the south coast of England in 1974.

ABOVE **When launching, make sure the water is deep enough to get the rudder down, but not so deep that the crew struggles to hold on to the boat.**

By contrast a lee shore can be a positive advantage for dinghy sailors and deserves a five-star rating for most windsurfers (who spend a lot of time drifting downwind when they are learning). A U-shaped bay with the wind blowing across becomes an ideal location to sail in if it provides a lee shore for a capsized boat to drift down on rather than being blown out to the open sea. This assumes that the shoreline is easy to land on, and is not being battered by waves.

Crowded water and shores

It is a fact of modern life that all popular pastimes attract crowds, and sailing is no exception to the rule. Always be aware of beach users and swimmers when launching and landing. In an ideal situation swimmers and dinghies should be separated by lanes, but there are times when swimmers will still cross your path and get in the way. Furthermore, they probably do not realize that they are causing an obstruction, and have little idea

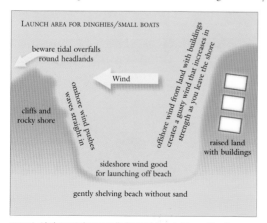

ABOVE **A sideshore wind is generally favoured for launching and landing. Both offshore and inshore winds require care and consideration.**

ABOVE **Keep clear of other boats when launching or landing. Take your turn, help others and, if necessary, tell people what you are going to do.**

RIGHT **The Topper is easy to launch owing to its light weight and a shallow hull moulded in extremely tough polypropylene. Touching the bottom should cause few problems.**

that the dinghy you are sailing may be difficult to manoeuvre and unpredictable in waves. Take extreme care in these situations, particularly with children, and consider giving a friendly call to the swimmers to clear the way.

Be thoughtful and considerate towards other boat users. There is plenty of pushing and shoving in real life, and no need to follow such behaviour when pursuing a pastime. When launching or landing wait your turn; leave plenty of space for other boats to manoeuvre; help others and they will help you. Beware of boats that are anchored or moored close in to the shore when you are launching. Give them a wide berth and if in doubt always aim to pass downwind (or down tide if applicable) of them.

Beware of powercrafts. Power gives way to sail, but some powerboat owners are unaware or oblivious to this, go much too fast, and often have very little comprehension of the problems of manoeuvring a small sailboat. Jet-skis have a particularly bad reputation, but large powercrafts can be equally lethal.

Safety first

- Make sure that the dinghy is correctly rigged, ready to sail and properly buoyant.
- Wear buoyancy aids whenever you and any other crew members are on the water.
- Take suitable clothing for yourself and your crew. Dress up not down, and always allow for the weather worsening.
- Take a paddle in case the wind drops to a flat calm, and a spare rope in case you need to be towed.

RIGHT **Fibreglass dinhies such as the Topper Sport are heavier and more prone to scratches, and require extra care when launching or landing.**

EXTREMES OF TEMPERATURE AND WEATHER

Dressing correctly for the conditions, in particular wearing an efficient drysuit with thermal underwear and protecting your head from heat loss, is essential when sailing in very cold weather.

Sailing in cold water

Exposure to water temperatures below 20°C (68°F) needs to be treated with progressive seriousness as the temperature decreases and the time increases. Very cold water below 10°C (50°F) may be experienced when sailing on freshwater lakes and reservoirs, where temperatures are potentially at their lowest in spring. This is just when many people start to sail after winter, and a sunny spring sky is all that is necessary to lull them into a false sense of security.

Hypothermia

Prolonged exposure to cold water causes hypothermia (acute heat loss) and is eventually fatal. The timescale is very short. Tests have shown that an average person in normal clothes loses consciousness after 20 minutes of floating in water of 10°C (50°F), and death usually follows. If they attempt to splash around to keep warm, the heat loss will be even faster.

ABOVE **There can be a lot of standing around, sometimes in cold conditions, when learning. Instructors must keep a watch for any signs of the first stages of hypothermia, and be ready to take action.**

Before losing consciousness there are two phases. During the first phase, the person in the water is alert and has the will and ability to participate in his or her rescue; during the second phase, the person's will to survive is effectively lost and rescue becomes totally dependent on outside assistance.

ABOVE **A delicate balancing act is required for sailors to be able to sail to their full potential in cold water areas. Advances in clothing design tailored for cold conditions has made a tremendous difference.**

Treating hypothermia

First stage Shivering, looking cold, complaining of cold. Time to head for the shore without delay.
Second stage Lethargy, drowsiness or confusion followed by numbness, cramp, nausea, slurred speech and eventual loss of consciousness.
Action If a person complains of the cold or shows any symptoms of moving towards the second stage of hypothermia, keep them warm and get them ashore as soon as possible. Get them out of the wind and provide them with dry clothing/coverings. If their condition deteriorates or fails to improve, seek urgent medical attention.

ABOVE Sitting in a cold shower is fine so long as the body core keeps warm. With the added effects of wind chill, a leaking drysuit or ill-fitting wetsuit could help kick-start hypothermia.

ABOVE Catamaran sailors know they have to dress correctly to enjoy whistling along at high speeds in all weathers. The faster the boat, the more you need to dress up.

Wind chill

It's always warmer out of the wind, and the stronger the apparent wind on a boat the more it will chill the crew. This is why catamaran sailors always need to dress for colder sailing conditions than those who sail at slow speeds. As an example, an air temperature of 20°C (68°F), rated as warm in zero wind, will become progressively cooler as the wind passes a Force 2 breeze (3–6 knots) and be rated cold at a Force 6 (27 knots). By comparison a very cold air temperature of 5°C (41°F) will become icy cold at Force 6 (27 knots).

Wind chill is dependent on what you are wearing, how much of your body is exposed, whether you are wet and your general fitness and body temperature.

Wind chill is not so important in air temperatures of 30°C (86°F) and beyond when a warm wind is guaranteed, but beware the possibility of a thunderstorm or heavy rainfall, which can make the temperature drop dramatically.

RIGHT When sailing in hot climates the effects of wind chill may become irrelevant due to the warmth of the wind, so that sunburn combined with dehydration becomes a more pressing problem. However, if a thunderstorm occurs the temperature will lower dramatically, and hypothermia becomes a real possibility.

ABOVE **The cooling effects of wind and water can easily deceive about the strength of the sun. Maximum protection should be applied to prevent sunburn.**

ABOVE **The reflection of water combined with the white hull and super-structure of a dinghy or yacht provides a medium in which the effects of the hot sun are magnified. Stripping your shirt off could be hazardous.**

Beware the sun

Sailors in cold climates can seldom get enough of it, but when sailing in hot temperatures the sun needs to be treated with caution. The effect of a cooling wind can be very misleading and, when combined with the effect of strong sun reflected off the water, can lead to severe sunburn, which is exacerbated by the drying effect of a salty sea. Sailors are always advised to use sun block (SPF 15 or higher) on exposed body parts in strong sunlight, and if they burn easily to ensure that their body is suitably covered with lightweight protection and to wear a hat.

A secondary effect of strong sun is dehydration. It is easy to ignore or even not to notice the effects of drying out while sailing, until symptoms, which include a parched mouth and a muzzy, tired, headachy feeling, become apparent. The best cure is prevention, making sure

to drink plenty of liquid and regularly to ward off the onset of dehydration. Plain water is as good as anything and on most dinghies you can store it quite easily in large plastic bottles.

If dehydration does begin to get to you, the first thing to do is to seek protection from the sun. Head for the shore and shade, or take refuge behind or even under a lowered sail.

LEFT **The proliferation of skin cancer has struck a chord in countries such as Australia where the sun ethic is being tempered by the need to avoid full exposure.**

Lost in the fog?

A sea fog or sea fret is a common phenomenon in early summer at the start and end of the day. It relies on the heat of the land to burn off as the morning progresses, but frustratingly fog may linger on the coastal stretch where the warm land meets the cold sea. Fog should be avoided at all costs for the following reasons:

- There will be zero or very little wind at all.
- It will be cold, clammy and unpleasant.
- Getting lost in fog is very easy and the chances of collision are high. Be wary of sound signals such as hooters and horns, it can be difficult to tell where they are coming from.
- You need to keep well clear of shipping lanes and out of the way of powercrafts who are relying on radar unable to detect a small boat and that are travelling too fast.
- Persistent fog has a habit of clearing, and then rolling back in to envelop the sea. It is better to wait until all fog has cleared before launching.

ABOVE **Murky conditions can deteriorate and if fog drops down it becomes an unnerving experience. With minimum visibility racing would certainly be cancelled.**

RIGHT **Inland lakes surrounded by high mountains can be prone to violent thunderstorms in warm weather. Be prepared for high winds, and make sure you have sufficient clothing to cope with a considerable drop in temperature.**

Thunderstorms and lightning

It is rare for yachts or dinghies to be struck by lightning, particularly when out on the water. All you can do is be philosophical; lightning must strike somewhere, but the chances of being injured or killed by lightning while sailing are remote.

However, being caught in a thunderstorm while sailing a small dinghy can be an unnerving experience. Following a period of humidity and light winds, there will be a sudden drop in temperature accompanied by fierce gusts of wind fanning out from the leading edges of the storm. If you are unprepared in terms of technique or clothing, capsize and hypothermia become real possibilities.

Most thunderstorms are created inland when the ground becomes overheated. A thermal low leads to falling pressure over the land and rising pressure out to sea, and as the unstable air from the thermal low shoots high into the sky it forms massive cumulonimbus clouds along with thunder and lightning.

If the thunderstorm is moving offshore against an onshore wind, it will suck up this wind and throw back a downdraught (downdraft) gale, creating violent gusts, which are often followed by heavy rain or hailstones. The effects can be most extreme on inland lakes surrounded by high mountains, with downdraughts of Force 6 (27 knots) or more tearing into the surface of the lake and kicking up a violent sea. Some Italian and Swiss lakes

in Europe are so prone to this phenomenon that storm warning lights and flags are on regular stand-by.

The most obvious sign of an impending thunderstorm is a heavy and oppressive feeling in the air, while on land everything, in particular the birds, appears to go silent. The first rolls of thunder can be heard up to about 16km (10 miles) away and, if the thunder is clearly coming your way, you can reckon that the usual rate of progress is about 19kph (12mph). This allows only a modest time to prepare yourself by putting on waterproof and windproof clothing, or to seek shelter on land. Needless to say it is prudent to avoid standing alone on the shoreline, and keep well away from solitary trees.

LEFT **Never sail too far offshore or out of sight of land in a dinghy. The wind may increase beyond your capabilities or drop to nothing and leave you stranded, or its direction may transform what was to be a fast reach home into a slow, cold and very wet upwind grind.**

UNDERSTANDING WINDS

Without winds you cannot sail, but it is exceptionally rare to have no wind at all. This is when you are totally becalmed, a state which seldom lasts for more than a few hours as eventually the wind will fill in from some direction.

Wind direction

The direction and speed of the wind will be graphically displayed on all visual weather forecasts. The wind blows along the isobars, keeping low pressure to the left and high pressure to the right. However the isobars show the wind direction at about 600m (2,000ft), and the surface wind over the coastline will back (move anti-clockwise) about 15 degrees from the isobar direction due to friction on the earth's surface. The most reliable way to check wind direction and speed before you launch is to consult an anemometer (wind speed indicator). Less precise methods include looking at flags or smoke, watching boats out on the water, and feeling the wind on your ears, it sounds loudest when you face directly into the wind.

The ideal wind direction for launching is sideshore, when the wind is blowing parallel to the shoreline. This should allow you to sail out on a reaching course, turn round, and sail back in on the opposite reach, before turning parallel to the beach to come head to wind and slow the boat to a stop before landing. The more onshore (blowing on to the shore) the direction of the wind is, the more problems you are likely to have. A side-onshore wind of Force 2+ (4–6 knots) may start stacking up waves, but should still allow you to sail straight out from the beach. A dead-onshore wind will push in waves that drive the boat back, and mean that you have to sail out at an angle across the waves. Offshore winds, blowing away from the shore, should be treated with particular caution. An offshore wind, which appears zephyr-like close in by the beach, will gain strength as you move away from the shore. This effect can be extreme if you sail off a shoreline protected by high ground. The light, gusty wind will soon pick up and, if you can't handle the

ABOVE **This Enterprise with hoisted mainsail and jib is being launched in crowded surroundings that require extra vigilance. Once off its launching trolley the boat can easily become a handful should the wind speed suddenly increase.**

LEFT **It is always necessary to have a fairly accurate idea of wind speed and direction before you leave the shore. Most sailing clubs will have anemometers (wind speed indicators) for this purpose. Otherwise, if in doubt, you can always consult with other sailors.**

LEFT **Launching on a sideshore wind will allow the crew of this 29er to sail on a reach straight out from the beach and back in again. This boat is the high performance small sister to the Olympic 49er, and is particularly suitable for teenage crews.**

conditions and start to capsize, your boat will be driven further offshore where the wind gets progressively stronger and your difficulties increase.

Lulls and gusts

These are caused by rising and sinking air on days when cumulus clouds indicate an unstable wind pattern. Because the gusts come straight from above they will veer (turn clockwise) in a direction more closely aligned with the isobars. The gust may last for a few minutes, followed by a lull when the wind backs to its original direction. The difference in the wind shift direction is an important tactical consideration in all yacht racing, and no more so than in dinghy races inland, which are often decided on playing the wind shifts.

Wind speed

On a weather map closely spaced isobars generally indicate strong winds, while wide spacing mean light winds. If the gap between the isobars halves, the wind speed will double.

The perfect sailing breeze will depend on ability. Beginners will prefer a light wind, but not so light that it is difficult to assess where the wind is blowing from or keep the boat moving. For most beginners winds between Force 1 and 3 (1–10 knots) wind should be suitable. Those with more experience will enjoy sailing in stronger winds. Force 3–4 (7–16 knots) represents perfect sailing conditions for most dinghies, though catamarans and windsurfers perform best when the wind is even stronger. Force 5–6 (17–27 knots) becomes considerably more demanding, but should be viewed in the context of the sailing location. Low air temperatures, cold water and the effect of tides and waves are likely to make such winds considerably more challenging than when sailing close to the shore in a warm, tideless location.

There are plenty of tall tales told by dinghy sailors of braving Force 8 (30–40 knots) winds, but most are down to exaggeration. Despite Force 6 (22–27 knots) being described by Admiral Beaufort as merely a strong breeze it is in effect very windy. Beyond Force 6

ABOVE **Wind shifts play a major role in deciding tactical success in dinghy racing. They become particularly important in classes such as the Laser, which can be tacked with minimal loss of speed.**

conditions become extremely unpleasant and controlling a dinghy can become a matter of survival.

Summer winds

Seabreezes are created by the sun warming up the land ahead of the comparatively cold sea, and are mainly a coastal, summer phenomenon that will continue to blow no more than 48km (30 miles) inland. They are most effective when the change from cold night to hot day is reliable and pronounced, but will not work if the land is shrouded by cloud. A typical seabreeze

location is the eastern Mediterranean where the afternoon summer wind turns on like clockwork on most days.

A regular coastal pattern is for the seabreeze to gradually cancel out the effect of any night wind that has been blowing offshore. A period of calm and irregular wind ensues, before the seabreeze is established in the early afternoon and provides a steady onshore wind of Force 4 (10–15 knots); perfect for summer sailing. The seabreeze will then die away to a calm as the land starts to cool in the early evening.

ABOVE **Piles of cumulus clouds indicate a weather pattern with frequent gusts and lulls creating wind shifts. The timing of the gusts can be critical when racing.**

Lakes that are surrounded by mountains can also be affected by summer winds. A well known example is Lake Garda, a popular sailing location in northern Italy that benefits from this. There, the normal pattern is for a fairly light mountain wind (named the Ora on Lake Garda) to blow from the mountains during the night and early morning, and be replaced by a much stronger valley wind (the Vento on Lake Garda), which blows in the opposite direction from the lake towards the sunny side of the mountains. This will blow from midday to late afternoon, and is at its strongest at the leeward (onshore) end of the lake (the Torbole on Lake Garda).

ABOVE **Waiting for the wind. The summer seabreeze is a delightful phenomenon, which relies on a marked difference in night and daytime temperatures. These Dart 18 catamarans are ready to start racing with the afternoon wind.**

ABOVE **Lakes or coastal waters which are surrounded by high mountains can experience strong thermal winds. These often turn on like clockwork, but are never 100 per cent reliable.**

LEFT **Beware the end of the summer seabreeze. By late afternoon the wind will start to die again, so make the most of it while the wind is up.**

Admiral Beaufort's scale of wind force

Distances over the sea are measured in nautical miles (1 nautical mile equals 1,853.27 metres, 2,025 yards or 1.15 statute miles), and wind speed is measured in nautical miles per hour or knots. These knots are divided into wind forces, which describe the speed of the wind. This system, invented by Admiral Beaufort in the 18th century, is still in use today with modern updates, describing likely conditions both inland and on the open ocean. Conditions on protected coastal waters will generally be less marked, but in some instances may be more extreme if there is a tidal influence.

Force	Description	Velocity
0	**Calm**	**Less than 1 knot (less than 1kph)**
	Smoke rises vertically.	
	Sea like a mirror.	
1	**Light air**	**1–3 knots (1–5 kph/1–3 mph)**
	Direction of wind shown by smoke drift, but not by wind vanes.	
	Ripples like fish scales form on the sea.	
2	**Light breeze**	**4–6 knots (6–12 kph/4–7 mph)**
	Wind felt on face. Leaves rustle. Ordinary vane moved by wind.	
	Small wavelets, still short but more pronounced.	
3	**Gentle breeze**	**7–10 knots (12–19 kph/8–12 mph)**
	Leaves and small twigs in constant motion. Wind extends light flags.	
	Large wavelets. Crests beginning to break.	
4	**Moderate breeze**	**11–16 knots (20–29 kph/13–18 mph)**
	Raises dust and loose paper. Small branches are moved.	
	Small waves become longer. Fairly frequent white foam crests.	
5	**Fresh breeze**	**17–21 knots (30–39 kph/19–24 mph)**
	Small trees in leaf begin to sway. Crest wavelets form on inland waters.	
	Moderate waves taking more pronounced long form. Many white foam crests. Chance of spray.	
6	**Strong breeze**	**22–27 knots (40–50 kph/25–31 mph)**
	Large branches in motion. Whistling heard in telegraph wires. Umbrellas used with difficulty.	
	Large waves begin to form. White foam crests are more extensive. Probably some spray.	
7	**Near gale**	**28–33 knots (51–61 kph/32–38 mph)**
	Whole trees in motion. Inconvenience walking against the wind.	
	Sea heaps up and white foam from breaking waves begins to be blown in streaks along the direction of the wind.	
8	**Gale**	**34–40 knots (62–74 kph/39–46 mph)**
	Breaks branches off trees. Impedes progress.	
	Moderately high waves of greater length. Edges of crests begin to break into spindrift.	
9	**Strong gale**	**41–47 knots (75–87 kph/47–54 mph)**
	Slight structural damage such as chimney pots and slates blown away.	
	High waves. Dense streaks of foam along the direction of the wind. Crests of waves begin to topple, tumble and roll over. Spray may affect visibility.	
10	**Storm**	**48–55 knots (88–101 kph/55–63 mph)**
	Seldom experienced inland. Trees uprooted. Considerable structural damage occurs.	
	Very high waves with long overhanging crests. The resulting foam is blown in dense white streaks along the direction of the wind.	
11	**Violent storm**	**56–63 knots (102–117 kph/64–73mph)**
	Widespread damage.	
	Exceptionally high waves sometimes concealing small and medium ships. Sea completely covered with long white patches of foam. Edges of wave crests blown into froth. Poor visibility.	
12	**Hurricane**	**64+ knots (118+ kph/73+ mph)**
	Widespread damage.	
	Air filled with foam and spray. Sea white with driving spray. Visibility bad.	

UNDERSTANDING WAVES

Waves come in all types and sizes. They can either increase power on the water, or seriously tax a sailor's skills.

Ground swell waves These are generated by far off storms and can travel thousands of miles across an ocean, steadily growing in size. They approach a coastline in long, even and well-spaced parallel lines, until they hit shallow water and break. Ground swell is only experienced on open waters, and is most relevant to offshore yachts.

Wind swell waves These are wind-blown waves created by local conditions, which travel at about three-quarters of the speed of the wind. They are unlikely to get bigger than 1.5m (5ft) high, and tend to break in shallower water close to the beach. Wind swell is directly relevant to small boat sailing. The behaviour of wind swell waves will depend on the wind, tides, shoreline and other obstructions. It will also depend on the angle at which wind swell meets ground swell. If wind swell is blowing across ground swell, it can produce confused waves. If wind swell flows with or against ground swell, it can create occasional oversize waves.

Wave height The height of a wave is proportional to its length. A wave that is 7m (23ft) long can be no more than 1m

ABOVE **Playing the waves is an important skill when racing dinghies, which accelerate rapidly on wave faces. Avoiding ploughing into the back of the next wave is just as important.**

(3ft) high. When it exceeds this height as it is pushed up by contact with the bottom in shallow water, it will break.

Refraction This is a phenomenon that turns waves in towards the shoreline and helps create a wave current that runs one way along the beach.

Rip This is a surface current where water that comes into land with the waves is allowed to flow back out to sea. A rip can

be a fast-moving outgoing piece of water between incoming waves, and is potentially dangerous. When closely spaced waves prevent the water landing on the beach from returning to the sea via rip currents, there will be an outgoing undercurrent known as the undertow that runs seaward beneath the incoming surface water. When waves break on steeply shelving beaches at high tide an undertow can be extremely powerful.

ABOVE **When racing offshore the waves are likely to become much bigger, and may become confused and dangerous when wind swell and ground swell cross one another.**

Wave height international scale

The height of the face of a wave is measured by doubling the height of the back of the wave.

Code	Sea	Height
0	Calm	0m (0ft)
1	Rippled	0–0.2m (0–½ft)
2	Good	0.2–0.5m (½–1½ft)
3	Slight	0.5–1.25m (1½–4ft)
4	Moderate	1.25–2.5m (4–8ft)
5	Rough	2.5–4m (8–13ft)
6	Very rough	4–6m (13–20ft)
7	High	6–9m (20–30ft)
8	Very high	9–14m (30–46ft)
9	Huge	14m+ (46ft+)

UNDERSTANDING TIDES

With the exception of seas such as the Mediterranean, which are surrounded by land, most seas are influenced by the tide, which is directly related to the gravitational pull of the moon. The tide ebbs (flows away), turns and then floods (comes back again) in a regular cycle. How long this process takes depends on geographical location. There are three major types of tide.

Diurnal tides Mainly confined to the Tropics where they experience just one high and one low tide per lunar day. The tidal range (the difference in height between high tide and low tide) is usually small.

Semi-diurnal tides These are experienced on the Atlantic shoreline and round much of the European coast. The tide cycle takes approximately 12½ hours between successive high or low tides. For instance, if high tide (also called high water or HW) is at 6 a.m., low tide (low water or LW) will be shortly after midday with the next high tide following at 6.30 p.m. From then on the times of high or low tide will be about 50 minutes later every day.

Mixed tides Experienced along the Pacific coast of North America and on much of the Australian shoreline. These areas also

ABOVE **Be prepared! The difference between high and low tide can be extreme, with yachts left stranded and open sea replaced by a huge expanse of sand or mud at low tide.**

have two high and two low tides in a full lunar day, but there are noticeable differences in height between the first high and low and the second high and low, which becomes higher high water (HHW) and lower low water (LLW).

Tidal flow

Tides are measured in vertical height using feet or metres, and the difference between high and low tide is known as the range. The greatest range is experienced during the period known as spring tides. This is when the gravitational pull of the sun and the moon coincides, and is usually experienced around the time of a new moon and a full moon. In between this phase the range of the tide dwindles, with the smallest range experienced during a period known as neap tides, when the moon is in its first or last quarter. The timing is never precise; the spring tide with the greatest range may take place from one to three days after a new moon or a full moon. This phenomenon is also true of the neap tide, with the smallest range following the first and last quarter of the moon.

Tidal currents relate to the flow of the tide and the direction in which it is heading. The rate of flow is not consistent. As the tide approaches low or high water the current slackens before ceasing during a period known as slack water. This is when the tide turns from flood to ebb or vice versa.

ABOVE **Tidal flow will have a marked effect on racing tactics, with the most tide usually in deep water channels and the least tide in shallow water close inshore.**

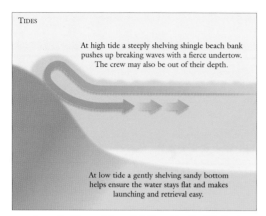

TIDES

At high tide a steeply shelving shingle beach bank pushes up breaking waves with a fierce undertow. The crew may also be out of their depth.

At low tide a gently shelving sandy bottom helps ensure the water stays flat and makes launching and retrieval easy.

ABOVE **Beware the difference between high tide and low tide. If the beach shelves steeply at high tide, it may create large crashing waves and a fierce undertow, which makes landing dangerous and may roll the boat.**

ABOVE **Knowledge of the state of the tide is vital when racing, particularly when the course is near to the shoreline where yachts will venture into shallow water to minimize the effects of tidal flow.**

The twelfths rule

To determine how far or fast the tide has risen or dropped at any given time the normal method is to use an approximate system known as the twelfths rule. The twelfths rule divides the tidal range into twelve, and in the first hour after high or low water the tide falls or rises by one-twelfth. This is the period when the tide flow is slowest. In the second hour it falls or rises a further two-twelfths. In both the third and fourth hours it falls or rises a further three-twelfths. This is the period when the tide flows fastest, beween half and three-quarter tide. In the fifth hour it falls or rises a further two-twelfths as the tidal flow begins to slow. In the final sixth hour the tide once again falls or rises by one-twelfth in the approach to slack water. This is the period when the tide flow is once again slowest.

The times and heights of tides can be found by consulting the relevant tide tables, which are widely published, sold by all good boat shops, and are on display at sailing clubs.

Tides and launching

Understanding tidal heights and times is important when launching in a tidal area. You should know in advance what happens at the opposite end of the tide. If you don't you might, for example, launch

at high tide, land at low tide, and discover you have to drag the boat two miles over flat, soggy sand to get back to your start point, or discover that the rapidly dropping tide has brought rocks, reefs, wrecks or groins within striking distance of your centreboard.

You might, on the other hand, launch at low tide in a light onshore wind, then return in a much increased wind to

discover that the incoming tide has advanced from the gently shelving beach where you launched to the steeply shelving shingle at the top of the pile. The sudden change in the angle of the bottom increases the force of the waves which crash down on the shingle. The only way home is to sail straight through the surf and up the shingle; you'll survive the experience, but damage your boat.

ABOVE **High performance boats such as the 49er are likely to be least affected by tides, but the crew must still beware of being pushed into or away from a racing mark when their boat slows down.**

ABOVE **A shingle beach could turn into a nightmare if the wind turns onshore and the tide comes right up. As well as consulting charts and tide tables, local knowledge is required for safe sailing.**

Obstructions

Check for submerged and semi-submerged obstructions before you sail. These may range from the most obvious reefs and rocks through to wrecks, sand banks and sea defences, such as groins. Problems are most likely to occur when these obstructions cover and uncover at different states of the tide, and something that wasn't there an hour earlier suddenly meets your precious daggerboard with a sickening impact.

Tidal acceleration

The behaviour of the tide can be affected by land configuration. A narrow channel will concentrate and accelerate the tidal flow, which will be fastest in the deepest area. In extreme cases the current may flow at 10 knots or more, making it impossible to sail against the current and potentially dangerous to sail through it. A headland or closely spaced islands may also concentrate and accelerate the tidal flow, particularly when combined with a shelf of shoal water. This can accelerate the tidal flow so violently that it becomes a race, producing an unpleasant series of closely spaced waves, which are at their most chaotic and violent when the directions of wind and tide are opposed. The headland may also feature a mass of underwater rocks, which produce equally violent overfalls. Further problems can occur when a headland produces a reverse eddy that sends the tidal flow back in the wrong direction as it rebounds off the next part of the coast.

The direction and strength of the wind can also have a marked effect on tides. Strong winds combined with low barometric pressure can play havoc with tide heights and times, but of more concern to sailors is the effect of wind against tide. When the wind blows in the same direction as the tide it will calm the waves and make for a smooth passage. However, when the tide turns and flows against the wind, the combination of strong wind and fast flow can push up an ugly series of tightly packed waves. In such conditions sailing against the tide is likely to be a long and unpleasant process, while sailing with the tide could resemble a scary roller-coaster ride.

Capsize

This is probably the most common form of trouble for dinghy sailors. Some boats are generally easy to right after a capsize while others are more difficult. All capsizes sap the energy of the crew due to the physical exertion required to get into a position to pull the boat upright and climb back on board. Depending on the sailing location, there can also be the added effect of being in cold water, which saps energy even further. Multiple capsizes cause a lot of problems, particularly when associated with problems such as the crew becoming separated from the boat and having to swim to make contact or the boat coming up and flipping over through a full 180 degrees. Each capsize progressively saps strength as the crew enters a vicious circle in which the attempted recovery gets harder every time.

Don't leave the boat. A capsized dinghy is easily spotted and provides the crew with something to hang on to and, depending on the type of dinghy, they may even be able to get some protection from the wind and water. Leaving the boat and swimming for land is normally a recipe for disaster but there could be rare instances when it proves the best course of action. Otherwise, always stay put.

ABOVE **Capsizes can be fun, as long as you don't do them too often. A huge amount of energy can be lost through physical exertion combined with the effects of too much cold water.**

Safety measures

The sport of dinghy sailing is as safe as you choose to make it. For sure there are many potential hazards, but these can generally be avoided if you think ahead, take care and accept that you have embarked on a process of continuous education. Accidents may happen and emergencies may occur, but the well prepared sailor will always be able to minimize the damage through a process of common sense and knowledge.

The following safety measures will help ensure that you still have fun while practising safe sailing:

• Never sail on your own until you are suitably experienced. It is also best to never sail alone in a solitary area. If possible, only sail in an area where there is a rescue boat on call.
• Tell someone when you are going, and when you expect to be back.
• Never risk sailing after sunset. Always aim to return to the shore in plenty of time and don't wait until you get tired.

• Always check that there are no overhead powerlines when you are launching or sailing. Touching one with any part of the mast can easily result in fatality.
• Get a weather forecast and assess the strength and direction of the wind before you launch. Don't overestimate your abilities. If the conditions don't look right for you, leave it for another day.
• Consult charts and tide tables when launching in a tidal area. Make sure you know where and when the tides and currents are flowing.
• Avoid any fast flowing tidal race, and ensure that you find out about underwater obstructions such as rocks and sand banks, which may be covered at high water.
• Offshore winds must be treated with the greatest respect.
• Always keep clear of shipping lanes and commercial vessels.
• Learn the Rules of the Road and abide

by them (see Basic Sailing Rules), but don't assume that everyone will possess the same knowledge as you have.
• Never sail in a dinghy too far offshore or out of sight of land. In France it is a legal requirement for dinghy sailors to stay within two miles of a suitable point of refuge on the coast. However, two miles is considerably further than we would recommend to any dinghy sailor without specific safety support. Be sure to check the local sailing regulations wherever you are.
• Beware the effects of cold and tiredness. They are cumulative, particularly if you capsize. Consider heading home after the first capsize, and if you start to capsize consistently make every effort to get to the nearest land without delay. If necessary sail under jib alone or accept outside assistance.
• Drink plenty of liquids when sailing on a hot day. The effects of dehydration are marked.

LEFT **So much to play for and so much to go wrong. The combination of strong wind, cold air, powerful waves, strong tides and freezing water is a potential killer. However, armed with sufficient knowledge, common sense, the right equipment and an appreciation of personal safety, a sailor can turn all those negatives to a positive experience and have a great time.**

INSURANCE

As sailing areas become more crowded and attract too many inexperienced people, the risk of collision grows. Hitting and injuring a swimmer or running into another boat and causing damage could result in litigation, and it is vital to ensure that at the very least you have sufficient cover for third party liability.

In some cases a household insurance policy will provide adequate cover, but it may be preferable to seek out a specialized dinghy insurance policy that will operate on a number of levels with premiums tailored to the value of the dinghy and associated equipment. The most important aspects of a specialist policy might include:

Third party liability The most vital component, with a comparatively cheap premium as a stand-alone policy. The amount of cover is tailored to satisfy all legal possibilities.

Liability cover while racing This is mandatory when taking part in most organized events.

Accidental damage cover Normally subject to a policy excess. A specialist insurer should be able to evaluate the claim fairly, help arrange repairs and speed up the entire process.

Accidental cover while racing As for the previous.

ABOVE **Basic liability cover is likely to be mandatory while racing. As speed increases, so does the danger of boats becoming damaged in close-fought situations.**

Cover for theft Normally subject to a policy excess. Check that the cover is sufficient for associated equipment such as clothing, which can sometimes cost almost as much as the boat itself and is easily stolen from a sailing club changing room. Be sure to check the insurance requirements as well, which may stipulate keeping the boat in a locked compound or building.

Roadside rescue and recovery Very useful if the wheels of your trailer decide to seize up due to too much salt water, but this may be covered by your motor insurance policy.

Worldwide cover If you plan to tow your boat abroad, ensure that it has sufficient cover for the relevant countries.

Fire damage A rare occurrence with a sailing dinghy, but occasionally the result of vandalism.

Medical expenses and transfer These are useful features if you are not already covered by a household insurance. Note the maximum amount of cover being offered.

Dealing with an incident

If you are involved in an incident that is likely to lead to a claim, don't waste time and effort getting angry with the other party. Ensure that everyone is safe and that there is no imminent danger. Be as courteous and logical as the conditions permit, and make a sensible appraisal of both the incident and the damage. Record the time, date and place, take notes and, if possible, make a sketch showing details such as direction of boats, wind speed and direction and conditions on the water. Take a photo of the damage if you can.

Find witnesses to the incident and note down the relevent addresses and sail numbers/boat names for all concerned. Lastly, do not forget to exchange insurance information with the other party involved in the incident. Contact your insurance company at once and deal with sailing experts preferably. Be honest and truthful with your claims.

ABOVE **When a mass of crew are engaged in sailing a high performance boat with associated high risks, it's important to ensure that everyone is covered against accidental injury.**

Basic sailing rules

It is vital to know the rules of the road when sailing. If you don't, your attitude is akin to someone driving on the wrong side of the road. The basic right-of-way rules are comparatively simple, unlike racing rules, which can become incredibly complex and deserve a book (of which there are many) in their own right.

Port gives way to starboard Nothing could be clearer. A sailboat on starboard tack has right of way over all sailboats on port tack.

The windward boat keeps clear If two sailboats meet on the same tack, either port or starboard, the one that is to leeward (downwind) has right of way. This means that a boat that is beating to windward has right of way over a boat that is reaching or running on the same tack.

The overtaking boat keeps clear When cruising, a boat that is behind keeps clear of a boat ahead; a matter of common sense and courtesy. The rule changes somewhat in racing.

LEFT **Whether racing or cruising, the whole purpose of sailing rules is to avoid collisions and ensure that skippers and crews know how to avoid them.**

Keep to the right in a channel This applies to all powercraft and should be borne in mind by small sailboats. In some cases it may be safe and feasible for sailboats to tack from side to side in a channel, but they must leave plenty of space for all craft that need to use the main deep water area and are best advised to keep to the shallower water at the sides.

Right of way rules cover all sailing craft, but they sometimes need to be overruled by common sense. It is a courtesy to give way to a yacht that is racing when you are cruising, but not mandatory. The racing yacht has no right to force a passage if you have right of way. But, if you meet a large yacht in your small sailboat, it is often much easier for you to give way.

Don't stick rigidly to "power gives way to sail" either. There are times when it is easier for a small sailboat to give way. Some powerboat drivers show little regard or respect for sail, which could lead to tragic consequences if a sailboat insists on enforcing its rights.

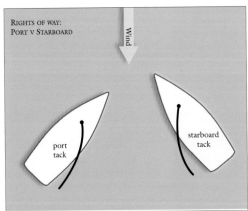

RIGHTS OF WAY:
PORT V STARBOARD

Wind

port tack

starboard tack

ABOVE **Port must always give way when crossing tacks. In this instance the port tack boat can either tack on to starboard, or bear away below the stern of the starboard tack boat.**

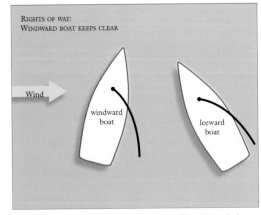

RIGHTS OF WAY:
WINDWARD BOAT KEEPS CLEAR

Wind

windward boat

leeward boat

ABOVE **When boats are on the same tack, port tack in this instance, the boat that is on the side the wind is coming from must alter course to keep clear of a boat that is sailing higher.**

RIGHT **Racing rules make overtaking a more complex affair, and rely on the inside boat gaining an overlap before it reaches the turning mark.**

Rules definition

The use of the rules of the road depend on where your boat is positioned at the time of an incident, what it is doing, where it is going and what is in the way.

Position A boat may be clear ahead, clear astern or have an overlap. This can be determined by running an imaginary line from the stern and bow, set at right angles to the centreline of the boat. If another boat crosses either line, there is an overlap. If no boat crosses either line, your boat is either clear ahead or clear astern.

Movement Many of the rules refer to a type of movement or change of course.

- Luffing is altering course towards the wind.
- Tacking is from the moment a boat is beyond head to wind until she has borne away to a close hauled course.
- Bearing away is altering course away from the wind.

- Gybing is from the moment the foot of a boat's mainsail crosses the centreline with the wind aft, until she completes her gybe when the mainsail has filled on the other tack.

Something in the way An obstruction is any object that is large enough and close enough to require a boat to make a substantial alteration in course to pass to one side. This could include buoys and anchored vessels.

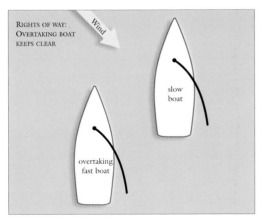

RIGHTS OF WAY: OVERTAKING BOAT KEEPS CLEAR

Wind

slow boat

overtaking fast boat

ABOVE **Overtake to either side without forcing the slower boat to alter course. You cannot barge another boat from behind. Overtaking to windward, as shown here is generally the easiest way to get past.**

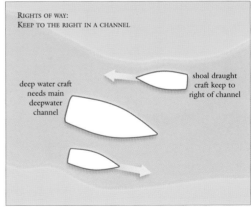

RIGHTS OF WAY: KEEP TO THE RIGHT IN A CHANNEL

deep water craft needs main deepwater channel

shoal draught craft keep to right of channel

ABOVE **Boats with shallow draught must not obstruct deep water craft, which have priority in a channel. Always be courteous and sensible, and be prepared to give way to larger craft whether under sail or power.**

DINGHY SAILING TECHNIQUES

All sailing techniques start from a set of basic principles that govern the skills required to utilize the wind. At their most basic, the skills of sailing towards the wind and away from the wind are very simple, but that statement relies on perfect conditions, flat water, a steady breeze and no obstacles. Real sailing is seldom like that, the wind yo-yos up and down, waves form, tides run and other boats get in the way. Neither are sailing boats so simple that you just steer and pull a piece of string. The desire for improved performance is natural, and with it comes the potential for more complex rig and sail controls, such as those used on the Olympic 49er, where maximum power set on a superlight platform has tobe controlled.

The message is that sailing technique is an exceptionally wide-ranging subject that can be learnt at all levels. It can also be learnt quickly, but there is nothing like practice combined with experience to ensure that the lessons are learnt well.

LEFT *Having mastered sailing techniques, you will be able to derive hours of pleasure on the water.*

BELOW *Trapezing enables crew to keep a dinghy level, and it is also great fun.*

Points of sailing

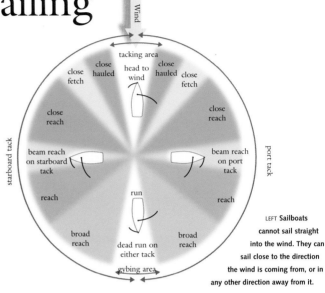

The angle between a sailboat's heading and the true wind is referred to as points of sailing. The points of sailing can be divided into three main categories: running, reaching and sailing upwind – with various subcategories within them.

Running

A dead run describes sailing with the wind blowing from behind, when the true angle of the wind exactly matches the heading of the boat. In reality a boat will seldom stay perfectly aligned to a following wind, nor is it desirable, as the dead run can be a very unstable point of sailing. Maximum wind pressure on one side of the sails, combined with minimal rig-induced stability when a boat sails through waves, leads to poor forward drive as well.

It is most efficient to let the mainsail out at 90 degrees to the centreline, but on many dinghies this is impossible as the leeward shroud gets in the way. With an unstayed or mini-shroud rig, letting the sail right out can make the boat very unstable: power increases in the top of the sail, the boat rolls to windward, and a

ABOVE **Running with the wind behind is a relaxed form of sailing in light air conditions that allows the boat to travel in a virtual straight line.**

regular rolling motion is created that can lead to a death roll, in which the boat capsizes, usually to windward.

On a run the mainsail will tend to obscure or blanket the jib and steal its wind. This can be solved by goose-winging the jib (going wing on wing), which means holding it out on the other side, but it will not pull consistently until you bear away and sail by the lee.

Sailing by the lee is sailing with the wind blowing onto the leeward side of the stern while near to dead downwind. Get it just right and the boat will be better powered with the jib pulling hard. Bear away too far, usually due to a lull in the wind or an untimely wave, and the wind will catch the back of the mainsail, force it into an unwanted gybe, and all too easily lead to immediate capsize.

Reaching

A reach is sailing with the wind blowing across the boat. This ranges from a broad reach (wind from behind), through a beam reach (wind straight in from the side) to a close reach (wind from ahead).

From a dead run the tiller can either be pushed away to luff on to a broad reach on the same tack, or pulled in to gybe (change tack downwind) on to the opposite run, and from there luff onto (head up to) a broad reach. On a broad reach the wind blows at an angle of around 45 degrees over the transom. This is potentially the fastest point of sailing in

Downward variations

To optimize performance, a sailboat may make rapid changes to its point of sailing, particularly when sailing downwind. For instance the direct course may be a beam reach, but when a gust hits, the boat bears away on to a broad reach to keep control. If however the wind drops, it luffs on to a close reach to accelerate wind over the sails and build up speed. These changes may be combined with the use of waves, steering the boat to make it sail downhill on the faces while avoiding sailing uphill on the back of waves.

Sail sheeting angles

The point of sailing does not always dictate the sheeting angle of the sails, which also depend on the speed of the boat and consequent angle of the apparent wind. On a dinghy with slow or modest performance, apparent wind will not differ greatly from true wind, and the sails will be conventionally sheeted to match the wind angle. However, on a high performance sailboat – windsurfer, catamaran or skiff-style monohull – the apparent wind will get closer to the centreline of the boat as speed increases. The sails have to be sheeted to match the apparent wind, and so are pulled hard in for almost all points of sailing.

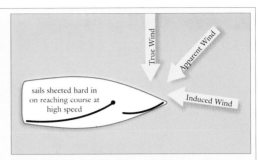

ABOVE **When sailing at speed the apparent wind direction can be very different from the true wind direction and sails need to be sheeted hard in.**

a strong wind in which the rig produces maximum power combined with minimum side-pressure.

Luffing (pushing the tiller away) from a broad reach changes the course to a beam reach, with the wind blowing at about right angles to the boat. The sails will be sheeted further in to accommodate the change in wind angle, and side-pressure increases so speed through the water will be slower, but still remain rapid.

Luffing from a beam reach changes the course to a close reach, with the wind blowing at around 45 degrees over the bows. The sails will be sheeted even further in, and greater side-pressure slows the boat still further.

Sailing upwind

Luffing from a close reach leads to a point of sailing known as a close fetch when the boat is sailing towards the wind, but not so critically close as for close hauled or beating. Luff a little further, and a close hauled or beating course is as close as you

can sail to the wind – at best about 30 degrees away from the true wind direction. The object is to point the boat as high as possible towards the wind, known as pointing, without the sails luffing and losing power, which is indicated when the telltales (see Basic Manoeuvring) start to lift on the windward side of both mainsail and jib.

To sail to an area that is directly upwind, a sailboat must sail to windward on alternate tacks (this is known as beating). Changing tacks avoids the head-to-wind or no-go zone where the wind blows from bow to stern directly down the centreline.

BELOW **On a reaching course the wind comes from the side and the crew may need to balance the boat to prevent it from heeling over.**

ABOVE **When beating upwind the wind comes from ahead and it is on this point of sailing that the boat is most likely to heel over.**

Which tack?

- Port tack (red) is when the wind blows on to the port (left) side of the boat and sails. This is the windward side that you normally sit on.
- Starboard tack (green) is when the wind blows on to the starboard (right) side of the boat and sails.

Rigging, knots and preparation

All dinghies are rigged using the same basic principles, but there is likely to be an enormous leap in complexity between an unstayed single-hander and a three-sail, skiff-style dinghy.

Unstayed single-handers

The Pico, Topper and Laser are typical of very simple una-rig dinghies, which are great for solo sailing but can also be enjoyed with a crew on board. In all three cases the mast is made of parallel aluminium tube, and is sleeved in two halves to make storage and rigging as easy as possible. The sail has a luff tube, which fits over the mast like a sock, and sail controls consist solely of a downhaul, outhaul, kicking strap and mainsheet.

BELOW **The traditional butterfly-shape cleat is still often used to secure halyards. Start with a full turn followed by a half turn and a final locking turn. Never use a locking turn if you need to let a line off in a hurry.**

The result is a small dinghy that is simple, efficient and very easy to put together. The lack of sophisticated rigging and sail controls, however, means that the shape of the sail cannot be very effectively dictated by the crew, which leads to a consequent relative downturn in performance with increased winds.

Time taken to rig 10 minutes
User-friendliness 10/10

Three-sail dinghies

A three-sail rig, such as an RS200, or Laser 3000 generally requires full support for the mast in the form of shrouds, a forestay or reinforced jib luff wire, and possibly spreaders. Consequently it is much more complex both to set up and use, but enables an experienced crew to shape the sails to combine maximum performance and control in the prevailing conditions with more ease. With the addition of a spinnaker or gennaker, the amount of rope required to act as sheets and control lines

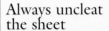

Always uncleat the sheet

Never leave a mainsheet (or jib sheet) cleated on dry land. If you need to leave a boat unattended with the mainsail up, ensure all sail controls are let right off. If possible unclip the outhaul or disengage the clew so the mainsail is not attached to the mainsheet or boom. Better still, and for complete peace of mind, drop the mainsail altogether and stow it neatly inside the boat with the mainsail halyard secured or removed.

becomes even more complex, which is a very good reason why everything should be colour coded.

Time taken to rig 40 minutes plus
User-friendliness Becomes easier with greater familiarity

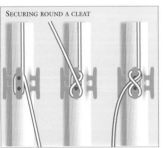

SECURING ROUND A CLEAT

JAM CLEATS

LEFT **Most halyard and control ropes on modern dinghies are locked securely with a mixture of jam and clam cleats. Pull the rope through the cleat under load and it will lock automatically, but the angle and diameter of the rope must be correct to securely jam it. To let the rope off pull it in a fraction tighter while at the same time lifting it away from the locking jaws.**

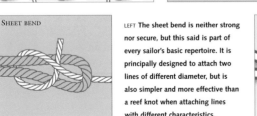

SHEET BEND

LEFT **The sheet bend is neither strong nor secure, but this said is part of every sailor's basic repertoire. It is principally designed to attach two lines of different diameter, but is also simpler and more effective than a reef knot when attaching lines with different characteristics.**

REEF KNOT

LEFT **The reef knot can only be used to attach two identical lines. Beware of getting the ends the wrong way round, or of using a reef knot on small diameter lines, which can pull very tight and become difficult to undo. In this instance a sheet bend provides superior performance.**

RIGGING A DINGHY WITH AN UNSTAYED MAST

1 Slot the two halves of the mast together, then slide the luff tube of the sail onto the mast before pushing in with the sail furled.

3 Attach the boom fitting to the mast. On a Topper or Laser Pico this is a plastic jaw that simply clips around the mast.

4 Secure the end of the mainsheet to the transom, and lead it up so it runs through the block on the outer end of the boom.

2 Clean sand or dirt off the mast base before pushing it down, and ensure the mast is held firmly in position by the deck lock.

5 Pull the mainsheet through the blocks. The sequence will depend on the boat, with small differences between Pico and Topper.

6 Lead the inner end of the mainsheet through the main central block, and secure the end with a figure-of-eight knot.

7 Unfurl the mainsail. This should be done with the bows of the boat pointing into the wind, to prevent it from blowing over.

8 Pull the clew of the mainsail out to the end of the boom, and attach it to the boom outhaul line, which can then be tensioned.

9 Attach the downhaul to the tack of the sail and pull down to remove wrinkles. Then attach kicking strap between mast and boom.

10 When attaching the rudder ensure the tiller passes under the mainsheet strop. This is much easier to do on dry land.

11 Drop the rudder on to the pintles and ensure it is locked on and will not fall off in a capsize. Lift the blade before launching.

BOWLINE

LEFT **The bowline is possibly the most useful knot in sailing. It can take as much load as a rope is designed for without pulling into a hard lump and is therefore always easy to undo. Ideal for all uses when a rope is under load, such as securing mainsheet and gennaker sheets.**

FIGURE-OF-EIGHT

LEFT **The figure-of-eight is the sailors' top stop knot, used to prevent jib and mainsheet ends from pulling out through fairleads and blocks. It is also relatively easy to undo, unlike the overhand knot, when used with a modern soft rope or control line.**

RIGGING A THREE-SAIL DINGHY

1 On modern dinghies halyards are secured with a simple loop system that has replaced the use of fiddly shackles.

2 A plastic ball is enough to lock the halyard to the head of the sail, and is easy to undo when it comes to de-rigging.

3 When hoisting the mainsail, ensure the boat points into wind and all battens are tensioned. One crew feeds the bolt rope, while the other hoists the sail.

4 The mast slot should be a tight fit. If the bolt rope jams in the slot, ease the halyard off enough to clear the jam.

5 The inner end of the boom is pushed on to a gooseneck pin. The kicking strap is secured to the base of the mast and underside of the boom.

6 When hoisting the jib, attach the tack and sheets first and ensure that the head of the sail is kept clear of the spreaders.

7 On modern boats a simple loop knot tied halfway along the soft, thick sheet will be adequate to secure it to the clew of the jib.

8 You can tie the ends of the jib sheet together, so the crew can always grab an active sheet. This helps when making fast tacks.

9 It's wise to make sure that everything works while still on dry land. Make sure all sheets and control lines are secured yet run free.

10 Check that bungs and hatch covers are properly closed or you may sink the boat.

11 Ensure that the rudder retaining clip clicks shut, or it may drop off (and sink) during a capsize.

Raising the mast

Also known as stepping the mast, this procedure can be done by one or two people. Before you start, lay the mast lengthways along the boat, and sort out halyards, shrouds (and trapeze wires if fitted) to ensure they are not tangled, then attach the lower ends of each shroud to the shroud adjuster plates on either side of the boat.

Except on small, light single-handers such as the Optimist, Topper or Pico, two people are needed to raise the mast. One stands in the boat astride the centreboard case and lifts the mast, while the helper guides the mast heel into the mast step.

Depending on the type of boat, the mast is stepped into the bottom of the boat (keel stepped), or onto the foredeck (deck stepped). The helper then pulls the mast upright with the forestay, which is then attached to the bow fitting. Some performance dinghies have no forestay, which requires an alternative means of pulling/holding the mast up, such as the gennaker halyard.

Before you raise a mast or wheel a dinghy along the ground, check for overhead powerlines. Although rare, fatal accidents have occurred through this oversight.

RIGGING A THREE–SAIL DINGHY WITH A GENNAKER LAUNCH SOCK ....

1 To rig the gennaker, pull the end of the continuous halyard through the sock and tie it to the centre of the gennaker using a secure bowline knot and the loop provided.

2 Ensure sheets run outside the shrouds and round the forestay. They should be pulled tight enough to hold them up around the sides of the boat.

3 Most gennaker boats use blocks with a ratchet lock to help the crew to hold the load. Make sure the sheet is led through in the right direction.

6 Attach the tack of the gennaker to the tack line, which emerges from the end of the pole. This acts as a gennaker boom outhaul when the sail goes up.

4 The halyard must run outside everything and should be attached to the head of the gennaker with a bowline. Part hoist the sail to get a clear view for rigging.

5 Tie one end of the sheet to the clew, lead the other end through the gennaker blocks, round the outside of the boat and back to the clew.

7 Use the continuous halyard to pull the gennaker back into the sock, then relaunch to check all is well and that the sail sets on both sides of the boat.

Sail numbers

Attaching sail numbers is a fiddly job that requires care and preparation, and should never be hurried. Read the instructions with care. There are different methods of attaching numbers to a sail, but the following are good general rules:

- Prepare a clean, flat space for the area of the sail to be worked on.
- Sort the numbers into the correct order, carefully cutting them out if required.
- Lay the numbers on the sail, make sure everything is totally smooth, and mark the positions in pencil.
- Correct number spacing is vital. Numbers should start at least 75mm (3in) from the clew, and often look best when set at right angles using a batten as a guide. Allow at least 65mm (2½in) between each number.
- Do not make the mistake of putting the numbers back-to-back on either side of the sail. This makes the number impossible to read, and is illegal under ISAF racing rules. Allow at least 200mm (8in) of vertical height between the row of numbers on either side of the sail.

Launching and coming ashore

A boat is most vulnerable to damage when launching and coming ashore; banging or dragging on the ground and maybe colliding with other boats. So always think through the sequences before you start, discuss it with your crew and be patient and courteous.

LAUNCHING

Traditionally it was always considered best to hoist the mainsail and jib after the boat was launched, with the crew standing in the water and holding the forestay while the helm sorts out the sails.

The advantage of this method is that it is much easier to push or carry the boat down to the water without the wind taking control of the sails, and it can save possible damage to the hull when rigging on a trolley.

However, this method assumes that the crew can hold onto the boat in fairly flat water, which is just the right depth. If the crew is in too deep, it's too rough or the back of the boat is banging on the bottom, getting sails up on the water can be a nightmare.

Dinghies with luff tube systems, such as the Topper and Laser, can only have their sails hoisted and dropped on dry land. Many high performance dinghies

LEFT **Beware of other boats and people when launching. There may be no problems in light winds, but things can get difficult when the wind increases.**

must also have their mainsails hoisted and dropped on dry land, due to bolt rope feeds and halyard locking systems, which can be difficult to manipulate on the water. To hoist or drop the mainsail on dry land, the boat must be sitting firmly on a trolley or a soft surface such as grass, and turned to face directly into the wind to prevent it rocking from side to side. The mainsheet or boom must be disengaged from the mainsail until the boat is in the water, with sail controls such as downhaul, cunningham and kicker let right off so there is no chance of powering up the sail prior to the launch.

Guiding a rudder onto its pintles can be extremely frustrating when the boat is moving around on the water. It is usually easiest to fit and remove the rudder on

ABOVE **Rigging on the water is fine so long as the water is flat, not too windy, the boat stable, and it is easy for someone to hold on at the bow.**

dry land. Make sure that the rudder foil stays lifted and does not drag on the ground. Check that the centreboard is fully retracted or the daggerboard removed before you launch or retrieve the boat.

RIGGING ON DRY LAND

1 When rigging on dry land, ensure the boat points more or less into the wind and is stable and won't rock when sitting on its launch trolley.

2 Take care when attaching the outhaul, which will have the effect of powering the sail up on an unstayed boat like the Pico or Topper.

3 The rudder blade must be securely locked in the upright position to ensure the tip does not catch on the ground.

ABOVE **This is a virtually perfect launch spot operated at a beach-based sailing club, complete with a gently shelving sandy beach and rescue boat immediately to hand.**

STEEPLY SHELVING BEACH

launch area suddenly shelves

beach

If the water is too deep, the crew rapidly gets out of depth and cannot hold boat

ABOVE **Beware the steeply shelving beach! While the shoreside end of the boat may be scraping the bottom, the other end may be in very deep water for the crew.**

The best place to launch

Choose a launch spot that is clear of boats, rocks, swimmers and any other obstructions. Remember that you may have poor steerage control when you set off or come in to the beach if the centreboard or daggerboard and rudder foils have been lifted in shallow water.

● Keep well upwind of obstructions to leeward, and allow room for sideslip.

● Keep clear of breaking waves (surf) if possible. The windward end of a beach will generally have the least surf.

● With an onshore wind a gently shelving beach pushes up small waves; a steeply shelving beach pushes up big waves.

● Avoid steeply shelving launch places where you will soon be out of your depth when holding the boat in the water.

● Check that the gently shelving beach that you launch from at low tide does not become a steeply shelving mass of shingle when you return at high tide.

Getting to the water

All boats are heavy. On a gently sloping sandy beach it requires less effort to carry a boat to the nearest water and pull it round to your favoured launch spot.

If you have the mainsail hoisted and are carrying the boat or pushing it on a trolley, you must ensure the wind does not catch the sail and flip the boat. This means keeping the bows pointing more or less into the wind when you launch or retrieve. The bows are angled towards the water in an onshore wind and away from the water in an offshore wind. You obviously need to

bear off from this course to get where you want to, and how much you can do so will depend on the strength of the wind and how the boat reacts to gusts. Be prepared to spin the boat into the wind and push down on the windward side. In a sideshore wind, you may need some dry land tacks to get to and from the water, in which case it is probably better to launch where you can and pull the boat to a more suitable place.

Push the trolley into the water until it is deep enough for the boat to slide off with a shove. One crewperson should hold the boat head to wind by the forestay, while the other takes the trolley ashore and carries it above the high water mark. If you are launching single-handed, you may need to enlist help.

GETTING TO THE WATER WITH A PICO ....

1 Keep the boat facing downwind when you wheel it backwards. Avoid launching with the wind blowing side-on to the boat.

2 Push the trolley into the water until the hull begins to float off. The rudder blade must be fully up with the daggerboard out of its case.

3 Hold the trolley, lift the bow and push the boat away. Keep holding the bow with one hand, and the trolley handle with the other.

Launching in offshore winds

In an offshore wind the water should be flat, and the boat lie with the transom pointing out to sea. The extra depth should allow the helmsperson to lower and lock the rudder foil, ensure the mainsheet is attached and active, and put slight tension on the sail control lines preparatory to starting.

The 180 degree turn needed to sail out will require plenty of space to allow for poor initial steerage and control. The helmsperson must ensure everything is clear while choosing which tack to start on. The crew then pushes the bow away from the shore. The helm steers the boat through an arc, and the crew hops on just after the boat has started to turn out to sea. Acceleration from this beam reach position may be rapid, so the crew must get on board without delay.

On a single-handed boat the distance between mast and bow is usually small enough for the crew to stand by the front of the cockpit, get everything ready and still hold the boat head to wind.

SAILING OFF WITH A PICO ....

1 You don't need to push the boat in any deeper than this to get sailing.

2 When ready, move back along the boat and push down and lock the rudder.

3 Move alongside to insert the daggerboard in its case and push halfway down.

4 On the Pico you can let the bow blow downwind and hop in over the stern.

Trolley guide

Pneumatic tires make pushing a trolley much easier – the softer the surface, the bigger the tyres need to be. Ensure that they are correctly inflated throughout the sailing season.

A basic A-frame trolley has a padded cross-member between its two wheels, which is fitted with two long arms that reach forward along the sides of the hull

LEFT **The standard A-frame trolley gives sufficient support for smaller dinghies like the Pico. Note the padding on the trolley to protect the hull along the sides.**

with a curved or right angle finish at the bow. It can be adapted to fit most dinghies, but the arms tend to rub the side of the boat and the load is spread over one small area of the hull, which could cause long-term damage.

A gunwale-hung trolley supports the boat beneath the deck and hull overlap. This spreads the load and completely removes pressure on the hull. The gunwale-hung trolley has to be fitted to a specific class of boat, and there is potential for scratching the sides of the boat if it is pulled on at an odd angle. In a few cases over-enthusiastic crews have split the hull/deck seam by jumping into a boat standing in a gunwale-hung trolley.

The most sophisticated twin cradle trolley supports the hull through two

ABOVE **The best trolleys have supports that provide an exact fit for the bottom of the boat, and are dedicated to a specific design.**

padded cradles, which are moulded for an exact match to the hull. This dedicated design gives perfect support for the hull with minimal risk of scratching. Critics claim there is potential for a warm film of water lying between the padded cradles and hull, which will eventually penetrate the gel coat. This can be cured by using rubber slots or coarse carpet, which gives the water space to evaporate.

Launching in sideshore winds

A sideshore wind is often perfect for launching or landing, because the boat can sail out and back on an easily controlled beam reach. When setting off the boat can be held parallel to the beach. It only needs a small push from the crew to turn through 90 degrees and sail out on a reach with minimum sideslip (leeway) and maximum control. However in a side-onshore wind things may be more difficult if the boat is being being rolled from side to side by incoming waves.

Launching in onshore winds

In anything more than a light wind, launching from a lee shore in an onshore wind poses problems. Clear thinking, good communication and a carefully rehearsed plan are necessary to get away.

If the beach curves, you may be able to pull the boat round to a point where you can sail away on one tack, rather than having to tack out through waves, which is much more difficult.

There may be waves driving into the shore. While the crew struggles to keep his or her feet in deep water at the bow, the transom crashes up and down in shallow water, which prevents the rudder being fully lowered. Without the rudder fully lowered, and with the centreboard or daggerboard only partly down, the boat will suffer from a great deal of sideslip combined with poor steerage control. This cannot be cured until the water is deep enough to drop the rudder.

To get away from a lee shore, the crew should hold the boat so it is angled for the tack that leads most directly out to sea. The crew gives a push, jumps on board, lowers the centreboard or daggerboard as far as possible without grounding as the boat pitches through waves, and sheets in the jib to help accelerate and bear away. The main requirement is to get the boat moving fast to gain maximum steerage as soon as possible. If the boat stops moving it will be driven back by the waves. It is much better to sail free and fast and edge away from the shoreline, rather than attempt to point high, which will slow the boat and drive it sideways.

SAILING OFF WITH AN RS200 ....

1 Helm and crew ensure it is deep enough to get the rudder down. The crew gets in over the stern while the helm holds the bow of the boat.

2 The crew moves forward and gets the centre-board halfway down, while the helm moves aft to the stern and lets the bow blow downwind.

3 The helm grabs the tiller and steps in at the stern, sheeting in the mainsail while the crew sheets in the jib to help power up the boat.

4 As the boat accelerates from the shore, the helm uses his weight to level it out before sheeting in on the mainsail and sitting down inside the boat.

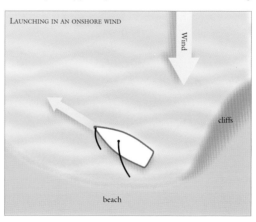

LAUNCHING IN AN ONSHORE WIND

Wind

cliffs

beach

LEFT **Do not attempt to point high when launching in an onshore wind. You need to sail free and fast, but you may have to luff into oncoming waves.**

At this stage it will be impossible to sail any higher than about 75 degrees to the wind. In a half-down position the rudder will feel very heavy and will constantly try to turn the boat towards the wind (weather helm). Do not attempt sheer physical power to overcome this, or you may tear the rudder off its pintles. Instead, make the boat bear away by heeling it to windward, moving crew weight back, and easing the mainsheet. The opposite, heel to leeward, mainsheet in, weight forward, will turn the boat to windward. As soon as the rudder can be put fully down, luffing will be controlled more easily. From then on drifting to leeward is the result of pinching to windward (pointing too high), over-sheeting the mainsheet, or not powering up the jib to help the bows bear off.

COMING ASHORE

When heading in to the beach to land, there are three essential rules: slow down, be cautious and take it easy.

Speed control

If the wind is offshore or sideshore, you can slow down the boat by depowering the sails or luffing (turning upwind). To slow to a full stop, the helmsperson must turn the boat until it is head to wind. Check for swimmers, following boats, or any other obstacle before you do this.

It may be impossible to depower the sails when coming ashore in an onshore wind. If possible, luff and drop the mainsail before entering the surf line, and from there sail straight in under jib alone.

Coming ashore in an onshore wind, the boat may pick up and accelerate on breaking surf with following waves taking control of the wide transom and slewing the boat side-on to the waves. This is a great way to have an unpleasant and very public capsize, with the boat rolling in the surf, breaking its mast, tearing its sails, and causing widespread misery.

Lifting the foils

It is bad practice to let the centreboard or daggerboard or rudder hit the bottom. At best it will put dents in a perfect smooth finish; at worst it may completely destroy a centreboard and its case. Be prepared to lift the foils in plenty of time to prevent grounding, but not so soon that you lose

steerage. If the daggerboard/centreboard does touch the bottom, you will at least know it is shallow enough for the crew to jump over the side. Note though that this rule may not apply to performance craft with high aspect daggerboards.

When coming ashore in an offshore wind, a steeply shelving beach will allow you to keep the foils down until you are virtually on the beach. Don't stop or jump off too soon, or you may find yourself in deep water and unable to hold a boat that is being blown back out to sea.

Holding and retrieving

The crew should be ready to lift the centreboard or daggerboard completely when the boat has almost stopped, then

COMING ASHORE WITH A PICO

1 Luff the boat, let the mainsheet go, lift the daggerboard halfway and hop off windward side.

2 Grab the side of the boat and move forward quickly while lifting out the daggerboard.

3 Make sure the boat keeps pointing into the wind as you walk it into the shore.

COMING ASHORE WITH AN RS200

1 Coming into shore, the crew lifts the centreboard and prepares to drop over the windward side.

2 The helm balances the boat, while the crew drops in at just the right depth about hip-high.

3 The crew grabs the forestay and lets the boat swing downwind, watching for any obstacles.

4 The helm moves aft to lift and lock the rudder blade. The centreboard should be right up.

5 The helm stays in the boat or drops over the side and begins to lower the mainsail.

6 The crew fetches the trolley, which is pushed under the boat with the handle fitting tightly against the bow.

7 The boat can then be pulled up on shore safely without risk of damage to the hull.

8 Pulling up the shore can be difficult if it gets steep, and the jib should be furled if it is windy.

immediately hop over the windward side and grab the forestay. Never jump to leeward, between the beach and the boat, which can be particularly dangerous, and even fatal, in an onshore wind when waves may push and drive the boat on top of you.

In an offshore wind The boat will blow away from the beach, making retrieval easy. The helm disengages the mainsheet and frees off the primary sail controls, having ensured the rudder is fully lifted. He or she then runs ashore for the trolley while the crew holds the forestay.

In a sideshore wind The boat may be side-on to the waves, requiring a rapid retrieval with the mainsail lowered when the wind is side-onshore.

In an onshore wind The boat will be

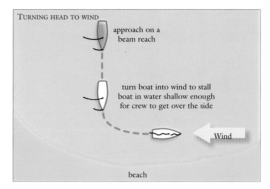

TURNING HEAD TO WIND

approach on a beam reach

turn boat into wind to stall boat in water shallow enough for crew to get over the side

Wind

beach

LEFT **You need to turn the boat head to wind to come to a halt close by the shoreline. The daggerboard or centreboard must be at least part way down for the boat to turn.**

transom-on to the beach, with the crew standing in deep water and possibly being buffeted by waves. Getting help to carry the boat out of the water and onto its

trolley may be the best option. If the boat feels heavy, it's wise to unscrew the bungs once it is out of the water in case it has taken in water.

Trailer guide

- Combi-trailers, which have a combined trailer-trolley unit are an excellent concept for those who use trailers regularly. Both trailer and trolley should be galvanised for rust protection, with efficient rollers so the trolley-borne boat can slide off and on with ease.

- Never tow a boat with the mast up, even for the shortest of distances. Lay the mast along the boat, using the crutch to lift the front with minimum overhang at the rear. Secure all shrouds and halyards with tape, and secure the mast to the boat. Beware of pulling down on unsupported areas that may kink the aluminium.

- The load should be evenly balanced. Beware of too much nose weight, which may end up steering the car.

- Use webbing straps to secure a boat to its trailer, the most effective come with ratchet adjusters. Straps should be long enough to secure to both sides of the trailer base. Beware of using ropes that can fray or cut into the gunwales. If in doubt, use small pieces of carpet for protection.

- Maximum legal dimensions for a boat trailed by a car (in Europe) are 7m (23ft) long by 2.3m (7½ft) wide, with a maximum cumulative trailer and vehicle length of 18m (59ft). Any overhangs such as the mast must be made highly visible. Maximum weight for an unbraked trailer is 750kg (1653lb), which is more than enough for most dinghies. By EU law trailer tires must have a minimum of 2mm (⅛in) tread depth over two-thirds of the width.

- Check speed limits, lane and motorway restrictions for trailers. In some countries a special driving test is mandatory to tow a trailer.

- Check wheel nuts, tire pressure, lights and fastenings before each journey. Leave enough space between trailer and car socket for turning.

- Always use a safety wire in case the tow hook fails. Always carry a fully inflated spare tyre together with a wheel brace that fits.

- Salt water eats bearings, and salty bearings love to seize up halfway down a motorway. The best rule is never launch a dinghy on its road trailer. The second best rule is never

ABOVE **Trailers range from the simple to the more complex, such as this double catamaran trailer carrying two Hurricane 5.9s.**

launch immediately after driving when the hubs are warm, the grease thin, and the bearings poorly protected. If you do get salt on the trailer, hose it down with fresh water as soon as possible.

- At the end of each season check the trailer coupling for wear and make sure it is securely attached to the trailer. If a trailer is out of use for long periods, use chocks or axle stands to take the weight off the tyres.

- Boat insurance should cover any trailer claims. You may be required to fit a wheel clamp to secure your trailer.

Basic manoeuvring

If you have never sailed before, then take the boat out on a day when the water is flat and the wind blowing at no more than Force 2 (4–6 knots). Begin by practising basic exercises such as making the boat stand still, which will help you understand how the sails work in relation to the wind, before moving on to sailing forwards on a beam reach (when the wind is blowing straight across the side of the boat). This is the easiest way to get started in sailing.

Standing still

The way that sailors conventionally make a boat stand still is by heaving-to. The boat is stalled by sheeting the jib hard in on the windward side. The jib will then blow backwards, and tend to push the bow away from the wind and drive the boat backwards. This can be counteracted by sheeting in the mainsail, which will push the bow towards the wind and drive the boat forwards.

If you sit in the middle of the boat and let go of the sails, the boat will lie side-on to the wind. It will be slowly blown to leeward (sideways), but how far and how fast will depend on wind strength and the amount of resistance put up by the centreboard or daggerboard. The mainsail will seldom blow at exactly 90 degrees across the boat, since it is usually held back by the leeward shroud or insufficient mainsheet length. The boat will therefore drive slowly forwards while being blown sideways.

This exercise works well in a light or moderate wind up to about Force 3 (7–10 knots), if it's windier the amount of leeway (sideways slip) will get progressively greater, and you may need to sit on the

ABOVE **In a light to moderate wind the RS200 makes good progress on a reach. Note how the sails are already sheeted quite hard in to allow for the wind angle of the apparent wind.**

side of the boat to balance the natural windage of the sails and rig. In addition to being an annoyance, the flapping of the sails will also destroy the sailcloth.

The RS200 (ABOVE) and Laser Pico (BELOW) are both very stable with the sails let out and with only a light wind blowing across the beam. They will move slowly sideways and forwards in this position, until the sails are sheeted in and they accelerate straight ahead.

ABOVE **The Pico is relaxed and easy to sail on a broad reach with the daggerboard two-thirds retracted. Note how the helmsperson trims the boat to keep it level without the stern dragging.**

Moving forwards

Pull in the sails until they stop flapping, and the boat will start to move forwards. If there is enough wind the boat will also begin to heel to leeward (away from the wind). This can be counteracted by moving your weight out on the windward side, or easing the sails until the boat comes back upright.

The boat must also be trimmed fore and aft so that the stern does not drag in the water. If the wind increases the extra power in the sails will start to push the bow down, and the crew will need to move their weight back in order to compensate for this.

ABOVE **The RS200 heads up from a reach to a beat. Note how the crew keep the boat in perfect trim, almost flat on the water, with their weight moved forwards to lift the stern.**

Rudder balance

The rudder should feel light and well balanced at all times, whether steering straight ahead, luffing up (pushing the tiller away) or bearing away (pulling the tiller in). If there is any pull on the tiller, it should be slight weather helm, where the tiller pulls slightly away from you, reflecting the boat's natural tendency to steer up towards the wind. You should however still be able to steer with just two fingers.

Something is wrong if the rudder feels heavy and the tiller keeps pulling away from you as it tries to steer the boat into the wind. This is called heavy weather helm and there are three likely causes:

• The rudder is unbalanced due to the centre of effort of the rig being too far aft. The probable solution is to lengthen the shrouds and shorten the forestay. It may also happen if you try sailing a two-sail boat to windward without the jib, which is needed to balance the boat.

• The boat is being allowed to heel too far. This gives a different shape to the boat under the water and reduces the area of rudder that is in contact with the water. Easing the sails will immediately solve the problem.

• The rudder is not fully down. People often forget to ensure the rudder is down vertically, and that it is held down securely. If it lifts a fraction, there will be immediate weather helm. The more you push the rudder, the more you will brake the boat and slow it down. Only small rudder movements should be needed, particularly when luffing towards the wind.

Trimming sails

Both mainsail and jib need to be trimmed to the correct angle to produce maximum forward power. As you luff (head up) from a beam reach, the sails will need to be pulled in to reflect the changing apparent wind angle. The jib should be trimmed ahead of the mainsail, since it creates the slot that accelerates wind over the leeward side of the mainsail and determines how the mainsail is sheeted.

Sail trim needs to be precise. If a sail is flapping or backing (the front of the sail blowing inwards) it is likely to be too far out. If a sail is not flapping at all it is likely to be too far in (over-sheeted) with a reduction in power as the wind stalls on the trailing edge of the sail. The most precise indicators of perfect sail trim are likely to be telltales. Windward telltales start to lift if the sail is too far out or if the boat is pointing too high; leeward telltales start to lift if the sail is too far in or if the boat is sailing too low. Perfect sail trim is often indicated by a slight flutter on the leech of the jib with all the telltales flowing straight back. This should be coupled with slight backing in the front part of the mainsail where the bottom telltales are just starting to lift, indicating that the slot between main and jib is working.

TRIMMING THE JIB BY TELLTALES..

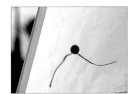

1 If the leeward telltale drops you need to ease the sheet.

2 If the windward telltale drops you need to bear away.

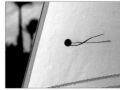

3 When the telltales flow aft the jib is perfectly trimmed.

4 If not quite straight, then bear away or sheet in just a little.

ABOVE **With more wind the boat goes faster, so the helmsperson moves a little further aft and gets his body further outboard to balance the boat.**

ABOVE **A gust hits and the crew of the RS200 lean right out to flatten the boat. This position is physically tiring, but need only be used for short periods.**

Hiking/Sitting out

In stronger winds the heeling force created by the sails is much greater, and it is normal to hike (lean out over the side) or use a trapeze to keep the boat upright.

All performance dinghies are fitted with toe straps that allow the crew to hike, increasing righting moment by moving their centre of gravity away from the centreline of the boat. It is an effective, if tiring, means of holding the boat level.

Both crew in a two-handed boat must be able to hike in enough comfort to be able to adjust sail controls, steer the boat and concentrate on sailing.

The Laser 1 is a typical example of a boat that may be excellent in many respects, but is desperately uncomfortable to hike over long periods. This is due to wide, flat side-decks and narrow gunwales providing minimal ergonomic advantages for the crew.

It was only in the 1990s that dinghy designers began to wake up to the fact that with carefully sculpted decks and correctly positioned toe straps it would be possible to hike in relative ease. However, crews with different length legs will always pose a problem for perfect ergonomic design, and the fact remains that hiking over a long period is a tough pastime that requires physical training and a relentless mind-over-matter attitude.

Rights of way

- Port tack always gives way to starboard tack.
- Windward boat keeps clear. If three boats are all on the same tack, the boat sailing upwind has right of way over the boat on a beam reach, which in turn has right of way over the boat on a run.

RIGHT **Sailing upwind in a moderate breeze. Note the relaxed stance with both feet close together under the footstraps and the helmsperson looking ahead. The excellent ergonomics on the Laser Pico allow this position to be comfortably maintained for long periods.**

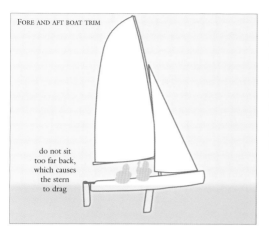

FORE AND AFT BOAT TRIM

do not sit too far back, which causes the stern to drag

LEFT **Sailing upwind the crew must ensure the stern does not drag in the water – they need to keep their weight forward to drive in the bow. This also increases the boat's waterline length and its resistance to leeway.**

The wind is seldom constant, blowing harder one moment and lighter a few seconds later. Lulls and gusts should be balanced by the helmsperson's skill in driving the boat forward and keeping it flat on the water, rather than by the crew constantly moving their weight in and out, which is particularly tiring when hiking.

If a gust makes the boat heel, the helmsperson can steer up into the wind and luff, depowering the sails while maintaining forward momentum; this also allows the boat to sail higher upwind. A gust will often be quickly followed by a lull, and when the sails start to back and the boat begins to heel to leeward the helmsman must respond immediately by bearing away to power up the sails and bring the boat back upright.

If the wind veers, it changes to a more side-on direction. This frees the boat, allowing the helmsperson to push the tiller away and sail towards a higher point. If the wind backs, it changes to a more bows-on direction. This "heads" the boat, which means that to avoid stalling and coming head-to-wind the helmsperson must pull the tiller to bear away and sail towards a lower point. Identifying windshifts becomes vital in a race. Tacking just before a heading windshift will immediately put a boat on a better course for the windward mark.

SAILING UPWIND

Knowing how to sail towards the wind is an essential skill for sailing a modern boat.

Basic skills

Sailing upwind (to windward) is a precise skill. Since you are sailing towards the wind, the apparent wind is at its strongest, causing the boat to want to heel over more. The closer you sail towards the wind, the greater the effect will be. If you sail too high you will stall the boat with the sails flapping in the head-to-wind position; sail too low and you will make negligible progress to windward. Most

dinghies perform best when crew weight is well forward for sailing upwind. This lifts the stern to reduce drag and increases effective waterline length giving better resistance to leeway.

Changing winds

A reach or run can be sailed in a virtual straight line on flat water, although in reality the effect of wind and waves makes a true straight line impossible. With the exception of sailing on a close fetch, sailing upwind in a straight line is neither possible nor desirable, and it is necessary to sail a course like a wavy line.

RESPONDING TO GUSTS ON AN RS200

1 Both crew watch for gusts coming from ahead. Note how the boat is trimmed with the stern lifted out of the water.

2 When the gust hits the crew hike out in unison, using their weight to maintain the same angle of heel.

SAILING OFFWIND

Steering away from the wind is more difficult than steering towards the wind, which is the way a modern sailboat naturally wants to go. Sailing offwind relies on trimming the angle of both the boat and the sails, as well as steering, to work effectively.

Bearing away

As you bear away from a beam reach to a broad reach, the sails need to be let out to allow the boat to steer off downwind; if you keep the sails sheeted hard in, the boat will constantly keep trying to turn up into the wind. Heeling moment on the sails becomes less as the apparent wind starts to blow from the stern so, unless it is windy, the crew will need to move their weight inboard.

Apparent wind decreases as you bear away downwind. (However in stronger winds the speed and angle of the apparent wind will stay constant if the boat is travelling fast enough.) With less apparent wind the boat may slow down. Leeway will also decrease when bearing off on a reach, and the boat may sail slightly faster with the centreboard or daggerboard lifted halfway.

Dead downwind

Bear away some more on to a run, and the sails should theoretically be let out so that they are at an angle near 90 degrees to the boat.

The apparent wind will decrease still further as you bear away from a broad reach to a run and sail dead downwind. If the wind increases, or the boat starts to surf on a wave, the crew will need to move their weight back. Otherwise they should trim the boat in order to prevent the stern from dragging.

Without any wind blowing from the side stability will be compromised. To balance the boat and prevent rolling, it may be best for the helmsperson to sit on

ABOVE **The RS200 bears away from a broad reach to a run. Note how full the mainsail becomes when the mainsheet is eased and the mast straightens. If the helmsperson bears away further, the jib will need to be goose-winged to the other side.**

the leeward side where he or she can hold the boom out against the shroud, while the crew sits on the leeward side and holds out the jib in a goose-winged (wing-on-wing) position.

When sailing dead downwind, a burgee or wind indicator at the top of the mast is vital to show the exact direction of the apparent wind. It is very easy to start sailing by the lee, with the wind blowing from the leeward quarter.

Sailing by the lee

This can be the most efficient way to sail goose-winged or with a spinnaker, since the mainsail will not blanket the headsail. It is a straightforward skill in light winds, which becomes more challenging as the wind gets stronger and the potential for uncontrolled rolling or unexpected and violent gybes increases. The skill is to bear away just far enough and no further to sail a few degrees by the lee, while watching

RIGHT **Bearing away from a broad reach, the sailor lets out the mainsail to allow the boat to turn. He needs to move his weight a little inboard and forward to trim the boat.**

SAILING DEAD DOWNWIND ON THE PICO ....

1 Sailing dead downwind the Pico is beautifully trimmed with daggerboard lifted and boom parallel to the water.

2 A roll to windward can be corrected by pushing the tiller away to turn towards the wind and pulling the sheet in.

3 The crew can also use body weight to keep the boat even. Note how he places his feet either side of the centreline.

for gusts and windshifts, which could power up the top of the mainsail or hit it on the wrong side.

- A roll to windward can be corrected by heading up and sheeting in the sail.
- A roll to leeward can be corrected by bearing away and sheeting out the sail.
- Anti-roll corrections should be small, precise and very carefully done on waves. The idea is to eliminate the roll altogether, rather than helping build up a pendulum momentum.

Avoiding involuntary gybes

Involuntary gybes while sailing by the lee can be prevented by:

- Watching the burgee/wind indicator very closely.
- Steering very carefully, particularly on waves, to keep the boat sailing dead downwind.

- Looking for any sign of the mainsail backing. This will be most obvious on the leech near the top of the sail. The helmsperson should luff immediately but carefully to bring the wind further astern and to windward.
- Remember that the stronger the wind, the faster and more deadly an involuntary gybe will be.

When the boat gybes it is essential that the crew ducks their heads to avoid being hit by the fast-moving boom. Then, when the boom and sail come to a sudden stop as they hit the leeward shroud or run out of mainsheet the helmsperson needs to have a firm hand on the helm to steer the boat downwind, while the crew leaps up on the new windward side. Otherwise, the boat is likely to slew through 90 degrees to a beam reach position, and the momentum will create an inevitable capsize.

ABOVE AND BELOW **An uncontrolled roll can soon build to a violent momentum when sailing by the lee, as the crew of the RS200 discover.**

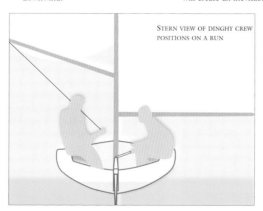

ABOVE **When sailing dead downwind a two-up dinghy can be balanced by the crew sitting on the windward side and the helmsperson on the leeward side.**

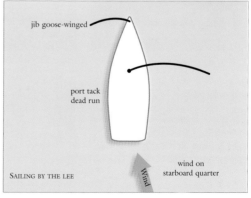

STERN VIEW OF DINGHY CREW POSITIONS ON A RUN

jib goose-winged

port tack dead run

wind on starboard quarter

SAILING BY THE LEE

Wind

ABOVE **Sailing by the lee the wind blows over the leeward quarter. If the boat bears away further, or rolls to windward, the wind may promote a gybe.**

Tacking

If you wish to sail directly towards the wind, you will have to sail a zigzag course using a number of tacks. During each tack the boat will luff from close hauled to turn through the head-to-wind area (often called the no-go zone), and immediately bear away on to the new tack. A successful tack requires momentum as the sails will produce no power when they are head to wind, and if you do not bear away quickly the sails will start to blow the boat backwards. In this position the boat will stall, which is traditionally known as "getting into irons", and was a nightmare for skippers of old sailing ships.

Tack preparation

Before you tack, ensure there are no boats bearing down from behind and that you have time and space to tack and sail off without getting in anyone's way. A boat that is tacking has no rights of way over a boat sailing a course. Choosing when and where to tack is a matter of experience. A rough estimate used by dinghy sailors is that the heading on the next tack will be at about 90 degrees to your present direction. Consider that optimistic unless you know your boat well.

The boat should be upright and under control before entering the tack, and must be travelling at good speed to get through the tack. If waves are likely to stop the boat you should wait for a suitable flat patch of water.

The helmsperson prepares the crew for the tack by saying "ready about" or "prepare to tack". When the moment comes he or she gives the traditional cry of "lee-oh!" ("helm's alee!").

Tack technique

The helmsperson pushes the tiller away, but not too hard or fast or the rudder blade will act like a brake. With the sails sheeted in, the boat will naturally want to turn into the wind, and requires minimal help. The boat may heel to leeward due to turning upwind, so both crew stay on the windward side. The crew keeps the jib sheeted in until it starts to back. This will help bring the bow round on to the new tack when the boat is in the head-to-wind position. It is vital not to let the jib go too quickly. The boat will level out in the head-to-wind position, so both crew move to the middle with the boom in the centre of the boat. The helmsperson must continue to steer through the turn. If he or she allows the rudder to centre itself, the boat will stall in the head-to-wind position.

TACKING THE PICO FROM PORT TO STARBOARD ....

1 The helmsperson chooses a flat spot to tack.

2 He pushes the tiller away to steer through the wind.

3 At "head to wind" he ducks under the boom.

4 He twists his body through 180 degrees.

5 Passes the sheet to the tiller and changes hands.

6 Then sheets in hard and hikes out.

TACKING THE RS200 FROM PORT TO STARBOARD..

1 The helmsperson says "ready about!" then "lee-oh!" ("helm's alee!") as he starts the tack.

2 Note how the helmsperson pushes himself across the boat as it tacks round.

3 The helmsperson is first up followed by the crew, with both sheeting in to power up the boat.

As soon as the jib has pulled the bow round on to the new tack, the crew lets go of the old sheet and pulls in rapidly on the new sheet to power up the jib. He or she may need to move smartly to the new windward side to prevent the boat heeling.

The helmsperson may need to ease the mainsheet during the tack. This may be necessary for keeping control if it is windy. However, make sure not to ease the mainsheet so far that the sail is depowered prematurely. On a fully battened sail this helps to pop or invert the battens so that they are the right way round.

LEFT **An uncontrolled roll on the Pico leads to a capsize. The helmsperson has got to the windward side too late, with the sail already powered up for the new tack.**

Changing hands

The helmsperson must change hands for tiller and mainsheet while changing sides. The normal method is to spin round through 180 degrees facing forwards while in the middle of the boat.

On many boats a centre mainsheet can be left cleated, and makes changing hands easier. As the helmsperson turns, he or she passes the tiller from the back hand to the front hand, and the sheet from the front hand to the back hand. With an uncleated centre mainsheet an alternative method is to move to the new side with the tiller held in the old hand behind your back, then bring the old mainsheet hand across the front of your body to grab the tiller and change hands. With a transom mainsheet both tiller and sheet can be held temporarily in the back hand, transferred to the front hand, and then the sheet can be handed forward. This technique will require some practice in order to ensure a smooth transition.

Finishing the tack

With his or her weight moved to the new windward side, the helmsperson bears away on the new tack and sheets in carefully to power up the boat without stalling it. It may be necessary to bear off a few degrees to build up speed, before luffing on to the proper close-hauled beating course. Do not confuse this with oversteering and bearing away too far on the new tack, which can lose valuable upwind ground.

Tacking should be like a smooth, continuous movement that can be executed almost without thought. Regular tacking drill is necessary to ensure that you can always tack when and where you want, no matter how hard the wind is blowing.

Roll-over

Changing tacks should feel like a smooth, continuous movement. It is possible to help the boat by rolling it through the tack. As the helmsperson pushes the tiller away, both crew lean out to heel the boat to windward and help accelerate it through the tack. They then move quickly to the new windward side in order to power up the sails and flatten the boat on its new course.

ABOVE **Just before the boat starts to turn, the crew lean out to roll it to windward. They need to get back in and over to the new side without delay.**

Gybing

A gybe enables you to change tacks while sailing downwind. If a boat is sailing directly downwind, and wishes to bear away, it will have to gybe. Tacking gains distance to windward as you turn upwind; gybing loses distance to windward as you turn downwind. When rounding a mark in a race you may need to gybe from a reach to a reach (requiring a full 180 degree change in direction between two beam reaches), or even from a reach to a beat.

Boats with gennakers, and catamarans are generally much faster on a reach than on a dead run. It is therefore quicker for them to sail a zig-zag course so they can reach downwind, tacking from gybe to gybe. Calculating gybing angles when tacking downwind requires experience and skill.

During a gybe the mainsail and boom describe a complete arc from full-out on one side to full-out on the other. This can create sufficient momentum to throw the boat out of control and into a capsize. A successful gybe requires a great deal of practice, particularly in strong winds.

Gybe preparation

A gybe is a fluid manoeuvre during which the boat keeps moving forwards, unlike an upwind tack during which the boat virtually stops moving forwards. Therefore a gybe requires a wide turning arc, so before you gybe ensure that there is plenty of space downwind and that there are no other boats in the way. A boat that is gybing has no rights of way over a boat sailing a course.

The boat should be upright and under control before entering a gybe. It must also be travelling at good speed to survive the gybe. If you let the boat slow down, the apparent wind will increase, put more power in the sail and send it crashing across the boat with greater force. If you keep the speed up the apparent wind will be kept to a minimum, putting minimum power into the sail and making the gybe much easier to control. The ultimate target is to exit the gybe with the boat travelling as fast as when you enter it. A strong wind gybe can be intimidating because the boat goes fast into the turn. Practice makes perfect.

The helm prepares the crew for the gybe by saying "Ready to gybe". When the moment comes he or she gives the traditional cry of "Gybe-oh!".

GYBING THE PICO ....

1 Note the tiller position and slight heel to windward as the helmsperson starts the gybe.

2 The helmsperson moves inboard as the boat bears away on to a dead downwind course.

3 He then ducks across the middle of the boat as the boom swings through an arc to the new side.

4 Then he changes front and back hands to sort out steering and sheeting.

5 He powers up the Pico on a new reaching course, with the boat flat as it powers away.

GYBING THE RS200 ....

1 The helmsperson stands to steer through the gybe. The crew ensures the arc of the gybe is clear.

2 In this position the helmsperson can balance the boat and trim the sail, before ducking for the gybe.

3 The crew pulls the boom across by the kicking strap and the boat points downwind.

4 Both move smartly to the new side so they are sitting out as the boat starts to heel.

5 They flatten the boat and allow it to bear away on the new reaching course.

Gybe technique – light winds

The helmsperson first bears away onto a dead downwind course, then bears away a little further until the crew can goose-wing (wing on wing) the jib. The helmsperson bears away some more to initiate the gybe. He or she flips the tiller extension so that it points to the new side, and moves across the boat at the same time turning through 180 degrees, facing forwards to see ahead. He or she changes tiller and mainsheet hands while in the middle of the boat.

The gybe will be more controlled if the helmsperson pulls in some mainsheet before the boom starts to move across the boat. The further out the mainsheet is, the further you have to turn before the mainsail will gybe. Pulling in the mainsheet will not only start the gybe movement, but also limit the arc the boom can travel through and reduce the shock when it stops at the other side. The mainsheet can then be run out for the new course.

As the boom crosses the boat, the crew changes side. Watch out for the boom and kicking strap, which can be equally dangerous as they swing to the new side.

If the helmsperson is not in full control the boat may start heeling, and the crew must be prepared to jump to the new windward side to level the boat.

Gybe technique – stronger winds

Everything happens much faster in a gybe as the wind increases, and all mistakes are more costly. If the mainsail is well powered up it will need a tweak to encourage the gybe. This can be vital when gybing onto a reach. If the boat turns onto the new reaching course before the sail gybes, the build-up of power will send the boom across the boat like a sling-shot. You need to gybe the boom while the boat is still heading downwind, by either tugging on the top part of the mainsheet or using the kicking strap as a pulling handle.

Steering through the gybe becomes more important as the wind increases, and it's a common mistake to let the boat follow its natural inclination, which is to turn into the wind once the sail has gybed. A fast gybing boat can spin through almost 180 degrees in a second, and comes to a grinding halt as rapidly increased apparent

wind hits side-on and knocks the boat flat. Always bear away onto the new course as soon as the gybe is completed and keep the boat flat to maintain maximum steerage.

Keeping the boat flat can be very difficult in a strong wind, but if the boat tips it is vital that the boom end doesn't catch the water, which can trip the boat. The kicking strap should be tight enough to control the mainsail and prevent rolls to windward, but not so tight that the boom end is bound to catch. Sheet-control will also help prevent the boom end catching.

Different boats react in different ways to their centreboard or daggerboard when gybing. Modern skiff-style designs with narrow, high aspect foils can generally gybe with the foil fully down. More conventional dinghies with wide, low aspect foils need more careful treatment. The traditional advice is that you need the foil about halfway down to provide sufficient resistance to rolls to windward when going into the gybe, but not so far down as to act as a deep water pivot during the gybe, spinning the boat round and capsizing it to leeward.

Managing the rig

Hiking out or using the trapeze will help keep the boat level, but will inevitably be insufficient beyond a certain wind strength. When that happens, you have three choices, which can be summarized as basic response, reefing and rig tuning.

Basic response

A gust hits, the boat heels, and no matter how hard you hike out the boat continues to heel. To bring the boat back upright you have three options:

Bear off with the gust An old-fashioned seaman's response of "running before a storm", meaning to head in the direction the wind sends you, which is not very practical when sailing a dinghy.

Let the sheet out The sail will flap, the boat will slow down and it will come back upright. This is an uncomfortable way to continue sailing, frightens the crew, creates a great deal of drag and could damage the sails.

Luff to windward If you're sailing to windward and a gust hits, you can ease your grip on the tiller and let the boat turn further into the wind. This will depower the front of the mainsail, while still leaving enough drive in the back of the sail to

ABOVE **The Pico helmsperson is at full stretch in a comfortable hiking position. He can react to gusts by sheeting out or luffing.**

REEFING A PICO ....

1 The Pico uses a similar system to the Topper, which has rolls round the mast acting as reefs.

2 Having lost more than 30 per cent of its area, the sail still provides good performance.

push the boat forwards. Used in conjunction with easing the mainsheet, it is likely to be the best solution for survival in comfort if there is too much wind.

Reefing

Some dinghies will sail well with the jib dropped or furled; others may prove impossible to sail to windward. This is a matter for experiment.

Reefing the mainsail is only possible on a limited number of dinghies, mainly cruiser and cruiser-racer designs such as the Wayfarer or Laser 2000. Roller-reefing is a basic mainsail reefing system. The mainsail is rolled around the boom, and when the area is sufficiently reduced the boom can be locked onto its gooseneck and the halyard tensioned. However roller-reefing only works with a transom

mounted mainsheet, it is difficult to fit an effective kicking strap, and the shape and performance of the sail is often severely compromised by the effect of rolling the sail.

Slab reefing, reducing the size of the sail panel by panel, is a more sophisticated reefing system. The mainsail is marked into

ABOVE **The Wayfarer helmsperson and crew look comfortable as the helm eases the mainsheet and sails free and fast through choppy water.**

SLAB REEFING THE MAINSAIL ON A WAYFARER

1 Secure the new tack position at the junction of the mast and boom.

2 The new clew position is pulled down and along the boom.

3 Excess sail is tidied away along the side of the boom.

4 The Wayfarer handles well with the first of two reefs in.

one, two or even three parallel slabs. These can be pulled down onto the boom one at a time, using a hook and cringle to secure the new tack position by the junction of the mast and boom, and using a pennant (reefing line) to pull the new clew down and out along the boom. The excess sail can be rolled into a neat sausage, which is secured by shockcord along the boom. This system can produce an effective sail shape, and allows the use of a centre mainsheet and conventional kicking strap.

Prevention is better than cure, and reefing the mainsail is best tackled ashore. With practice it is certainly possible on the water, but it will always be tricky in a strong wind and while completing the reef the boat is likely to be blown a long way downwind.

RIG TUNING

Many modern dinghies have sophisticated rigs that can be tuned both on the beach and while sailing to maximize their performance in different wind strengths. The principal aims of rig tuning are to vary the amount and position of camber (fullness) and twist (leech shape) in the sails by using various controls.

All dinghies need to be tuned and set up in different ways, and are often provided with excellent tuning manuals, but the following are general rules for all classes.

Camber

A full sail is usually preferred for light winds and a flat sail for strong winds. However

in very light winds a comparatively flat sail may perform best. The point of maximum camber tends to be blown aft in stronger winds, and needs to be pushed forward to maintain control.

Sail twist

A sail will naturally curve off at the top and act like a twisted wing. In light winds the twist may suit a slightly more open wind angle at the top of the mast. In moderate winds the twist needs to be tightened up and the leech straightened to power-up the sail. In strong winds the twist at the top will help exhaust excess power over the leech, while the bottom of the sail is effectively sheeted in at a closer angle.

ABOVE **The Pico sail twists from top to bottom, with excess power exhausting over the leech.**

ABOVE **The cunningham is used to control mainsail luff tension while sailing, and is pulled half-down on the RS200 shown here. If the wind increases the crew will increase the tension to flatten the sail.**

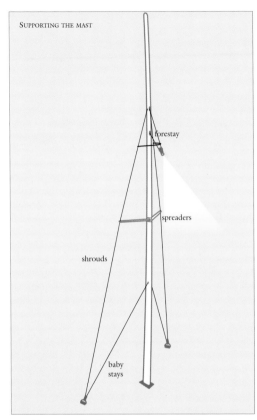

SUPPORTING THE MAST

forestay

spreaders

shrouds

baby
stays

ABOVE **A heavy crew sails with a stiffer, more powerful mast than a light crew, who need to depower the rig when sailing upwind. Spreader length dictates how much the mast bends sideways, the longer the spreader the less bend. Not all boat types have baby stays, which help support the mast's lower half.**

ABOVE **The RS200 is heeling much too far, slipping sideways and slowing down due to increased hull resistance. The crew need to depower the rig with cunningham and kicker tension, and could even try hiking a bit harder.**

ABOVE **Note the clean mast bend of the RS200 and the lack of any major creases in the sail. In this instance the crew should definitely be hiking harder.**

Mast rake

Raking the mast forward by shortening the forestay and lengthening the shrouds will move the centre of effort forward improving control in stronger winds. Raking the mast back can improve pointing performance in lighter winds.

Mast bend

A heavier crew can sail with a stiffer rig than a lighter crew. The stiffer rig will hold more power and support a heavier crew; the softer rig, which bends sideways and backwards will exhaust more power and be manageable by a lighter crew. Mast bend can be tuned by spreader length (longer equals stiffer) and mast gate position (a wider gate lets the mast bend more). Lower shroud tension can be increased to stiffen the bottom half of the mast and power up the rig in medium winds; and reduced to allow the bottom half of the mast to flex and lose excess wind in gusts, as well as creating a wider slot and less power between mainsail and jib.

Luff tension

Increased luff tension, using the downhaul or cunningham controls, flattens the camber in the mainsail and keeps it well forward. On modern rigs this is a key control to sail power, and on some high performance boats the downhaul can be played or adjusted by the crew while sailing upwind. A vertical crease near the mast indicates too much tension.

The wrong tale

Due to turbulence around the mast, the lower mainsail telltales nearest the luff will not function correctly when sailing upwind. The lower leeward telltale should always be horizontal; if the lower windward telltale is horizontal, the sail needs easing until it begins to lift.

LEFT **Creases appear in the luff panel next to the mast when the unstayed rig of the Pico becomes well powered up, but the sail still provides good control and drives the boat forward.**

Sailing in very light winds

- Getting the best performance out of a boat in very light winds requires intense concentration.
- Don't rock the boat. Keep as still as possible, with your weight trimmed so the stern is lifted and the boat heeled enough to keep the sails filled.
- Do not oversheet the sails, particularly after a tack. The aim is to slowly build up speed without stalling the airflow.

Outhaul tension

Increased outhaul tension flattens the sail, but is very much a secondary control and much less effective than adjusting luff or kicker tension. A horizontal crease near the boom indicates too much tension.

Mainsheet tension

Modern rigs are designed around maximum mainsheet tension to bend the top of the mast, flatten the top of the sail, reduce twist, increase jib luff tension and provide maximum pointing ability and power when sailing upwind. Easing the mainsheet promotes fullness and twist in the sail, unless balanced by kicking strap tension.

Kicking strap/Vang/Gnav tension

The original role of the kicking strap was to hold the boom down. On modern rigs it has become a far more sophisticated depowering sail control, which plays a dual role with the mainsheet. It bends the top of the mast, flattens the top of the sail, reduces twist, increases jib luff tension and provides maximum pointing ability and power on all points of sailing.

Jib sheets

Easing the jib sheet to open the slot can be the most immediate and effective way of temporarily depowering the rig. Moving jib fairleads forward flattens the jib, closes the luff, reduces twist and narrows the slot between jib and mainsail. Moving jib fairleads aft increases jib twist, opens the leech and widens the slot, which will help if the crew is overpowered. The performance of the jib will also depend on whether the jib is new and in good condition or old and blown out of shape.

RIGHT **The slot between the jib and the mainsail plays an important role in driving a two sail boat forwards. Easing the jib, and so opening the slot, has the effect of immediately depowering the rig.**

ABOVE **Modern rig controls coupled with sophisticated sail materials allow relatively simple boats such as the Pico to cope with a wide range of wind conditions.**

Sailing in waves

On the sea, sailing with the waves can make a huge difference to both speed and controlling the boat when sailing downwind.

- Watch the waves coming up from behind the boat.
- Bear away to catch a wave face at about 90 degrees to your transom, so you are travelling directly with it.
- As the boat accelerates down the wave, sheet in to match the new wind angle as the apparent wind moves forward with your increased speed. You may need to move crew weight quickly forward to help initial acceleration on the wave face, and quickly back to avoid a nose dive into the next wave.
- Luff across the face to stay with the wave for as long as possible.
- Look for gaps, and avoid ploughing into the back of the next wave.

Capsize and recovery

Capsizing is all part of the fun of dinghy sailing, and should hold no fears. A capsize used to be a long, cold, messy business during which crews got freezing cold and boats were swamped and had to be painstakingly bailed out. Modern crews have the advantages of highly efficient clothing coupled with dinghies that are designed to float high and drain any water immediately once they are righted. That should make capsizing less of a worry, but it can still pose problems.

CAPSIZE TO LEEWARD

This is the conventional capsize, when the boat is simply blown over due to a combination of too much wind and the crew failing to ease the sheets or luff to windward.

LEFT **Modern dinghy designs allow capsizes to be a relatively relaxed affair, and the RS200 floats at just the right height to make things easy. If the helm rights the boat now, the crew can simply roll into the bottom of the boat.**

Going over

The boat will be blown on to its side. It reaches a point of no return, after which the final stages of the capsize are a relatively slow and graceful process.

Do not throw yourself on to the sail. You may break battens or rip the sail, and your weight may sink the mast (few masts are completely buoyant) and turn the boat upside down. As the boat goes over on its side, try to step over the top of the hull so you can sit astride the gunwale ready to stand on the centreboard or daggerboard.

Different boats behave in different ways as they go over. If the boat starts to invert, get on to the centreboard or daggerboard immediately. If there is only room for one on the centreboard or daggerboard, it should be the helmsperson.

If the mainsheet or jib sheet is still cleated, the crew will need to uncleat them so they run free when the boat is righted. It may also be necessary to push the centreboard or daggerboard in or down.

RIGHTING THE RS200 AFTER A CAPSIZE ....

1 The helmsperson stands on the centreboard, facing the wind with both hands on the gunwale.

2 As he pulls back and the boat comes up, he lifts himself on to the side of the boat.

3 The helmsperson goes in head first while the crew simply rolls in on the downhill side.

4 The wind (blowing from the right) blows the boom across.

5 So the crew gets out smartly to prevent a complete 180 degree roll.

GETTING THE CREW ON BOARD AFTER A CAPSIZE ON THE RS200 ....

1 A more conventional method is for the crew to get back in over the stern.

2 Once the boat is righted, it sits in a stable position beam-on to the wind.

3 The crew gets on without tipping the boat, and is ready to go sailing.

Blowing downwind

It is important to right the boat as quickly as possible. Give it time, and the capsized boat will turn so the hull (windage) is blowing downwind of the rig (drag). This is true of most modern dinghies that have high buoyancy and float very high in the water. Once the hull is downwind of the rig, righting the boat becomes more difficult. As you pull the boat upright, the wind will help it on its way up. However as can often happen, it may also be too helpful so that the mast tip describes a complete 180 degree arc, which means the boat comes up and capsizes on top of you and you have to start all over again. If the boat is starting to turn downwind, the crew should get in the water, grab the forestay and swim the bows around so that it points upwind.

Righting

The helmsperson should be able to stand on the centreboard or daggerboard and lean back with one or both hands on the gunwale lip. Try stepping back as far as you dare for extra leverage, but don't risk breaking the foil. Try leaning back while holding onto a line so you can get further outboard, but don't use the mainsheet. Some dinghies have special righting lines attached along the hull. If the boat still won't come up, ask your crew to hang on the centreboard or daggerboard tip from underneath (very tiring) or clamber up on the foil behind you if it will take the weight.

You can feel the boat come up. As the mast tip breaks free of the surface of the water the rig will start to accelerate.

ABOVE **Once a boat goes this far, capsize is often inevitable. The helm is in a perfect position to hop onto the top side, and should be able to get on the centreboard and right the boat without getting wet.**

Getting back into the boat

This can be a difficult manoeuvre with the crew in the water. There are two methods:

- When the helmsperson is on the centreboard or daggerboard and ready to right the boat, the crew lies in the water alongside the cockpit area. Providing all goes well he or she will be scooped up and dumped in the bottom of the cockpit as the boat comes upright.
- An alternative method is for the crew to lie in the water parallel to the forestay, while keeping the boat pointing into the wind. As the helmsperson pulls the boat upright, the crew lifts his or her feet up onto the deck either side of the forestay, stands up and steps back into the cockpit.

You must control the rate of lift so it doesn't build up enough momentum to throw the rig into a 180 degree capsize. Step off the centreboard or daggerboard as soon as you can get on to the windward deck, and prepare to balance the boat. If your crew is still in the water, he or she should be ready to hold down the leeward side. You can then help the crew to get in over the stern.

Recovery

Once righted the boat will sit side-on to the wind with the sails flapping. Capsize can be tiring and disorientating, so take a breather, look around, decide what to do next, indicate to any would-be rescuers that you are OK and, if you need to start bailing, roll up your sleeves. Most modern dinghies will self-drain as soon as you get the boat moving.

CAPSIZE TO WINDWARD

A capsize to windward (backwards) normally results from a windward roll while sailing on a broad reach or dead downwind. It can happen when travelling fast, and is likely to be fast and unexpected, as opposed to the slow and graceful leeward capsize.

Going over

As the boat goes over grab something, such as the mainsheet or footstrap, so you don't get left behind. The boat will capsize with the hull downwind of the mast. In a light or moderate wind it should be possible to right the boat from the leeward (top) side.

Capsize rules

- Try to stay with the boat as it goes over. Modern dinghies float high and can be blown downwind faster than you can swim wearing a buoyancy aid, dinghy boots and hi-tech clothing. Catch a rope as the boat goes over.
- If you find yourself under the sails or tangled in sheets and lines, don't panic. Your buoyancy aid will keep your head well clear of the water, and you have plenty of time to extricate yourself.
- Beware of highly buoyant dinghies that float very high. Some float so high that it is very difficult to get up onto the centreboard or daggerboard once you are in the water.
- Try to prevent the boat turning turtle. You may bury the mast tip in the mud at the bottom, which makes righting difficult and can lead to a broken mast.

- If the boat turns turtle and you are underneath, don't panic. There will be plenty of air in the cockpit, so when you are ready you can take a deep breath, duck down and escape from the transom or side.
- When things go wrong avoid a pattern of repeat capsizes. Each attempt to right the boat becomes more physically draining, and all the time you may be being blown further out to sea. Don't hesitate to accept outside help.
- If you can't right the boat, grab hold of something and stay with the boat until rescue comes. Never leave the boat and attempt to swim to shore – an upturned boat will float and is much easier to spot than a sailor lost in the sea.

LEFT **No hope. The boom is pressing on the water, keeping the sail powered up and the boat pinned down. Think where you are going to go, and make sure you grab something and do not lose the boat.**

EASY UP WITH A WAYFARER

1 The Wayfarer is a stable and fairly heavy boat, and not prone to capsizing.

2 But if it does go over, it comes up more sedately than any lightweight flyer.

3 The water will drain out through the stern flaps once the boat gets moving.

UN-TURTLING THE RS200..

1 A turtled boat can be brought upright by the helmsperson standing on the gunwale and pulling on the tip of the centreboard.

2 The crew helps by swimming the bows into the wind, which will blow under the deck rather than on to the hull.

Recovery

You need to scramble aboard very quickly as the boat comes up. Be prepared to throw your weight to windward in order to prevent the boat performing a complete 180 degree flip. In stronger winds it will be necessary to swim the bow round until it points almost into the wind, and then right the boat from the windward side.

Turning turtle

If the boat turns turtle, try standing on the underside of the lip of the gunwale with your back to the wind and lean back with both hands holding the end of the centre-board or daggerboard. Having the crew hold on to the bow will help spin the boat into the wind.

LEFT **Either the result of sailing by the lee unsuccessfully or pulling out of a strong wind gybe, the RS200 is about to roll all the way over to windward. The crew can expect a speedy capsize.**

Capsize tricks

If the capsized boat is lying downwind of the rig, try a San Francisco Roll (a variation on a kayak Eskimo Roll) to prevent the rig doing a 180 degree flip on top of you. One of the crew hangs on to the tip of the daggerboard or centreboard as the boat comes upright, is pulled through an underwater arc beneath the hull, and shoots out and breaks surface on the windward side. He or she can then immediately grab the windward deck and weigh down the boat to prevent it tipping any further.

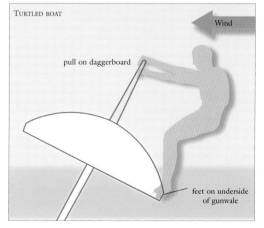

TURTLED BOAT

Wind

pull on daggerboard

feet on underside of gunwale

LEFT **Turning turtle is unusual with a monohull, but may happen if the crew push the rig down and the mast sinks. Getting the boat up again requires a little time and patience, and the crew must take care not to dig the mast into the bottom.**

Trapeze techniques

The trapeze is the most effective lever for keeping a dinghy level. It is generally much less tiring than hiking, and a lot more fun as you fly across the water.

The trapeze handle should be easy to grab, which usually means around eye level when you are sitting on the side of the boat. The handle has to carry all your weight in short bursts, so make regular checks that it is up to the job.

Trapezing in bare feet is seldom a good idea. You need grippy, lightweight boots that allow maximum movement but also give good protection to the ankles.

Modern trapeze hooks only stay hooked under tension. If you dangle from the trapeze wire by hanging on the handle, the hook will probably fall off.

If the boat capsizes while you are on the wire, try to avoid dropping into the mainsail from a great height. It's much better to squat down, unhook and drop in by the centreboard or daggerboard before the boat starts to turn right over.

If you're hooked on under the sail after a capsize to windward, don't panic.

Knock the ring off the hook, moving your hips forwards or up to give a little slack if necessary.

Getting out

Make sure there is enough power in the rig to support your weight before going out on the wire. The helmsperson may need to ease the mainsheet while the crew is getting prepared.

Sit on the side deck, sheet and cleat the jib, and hold it with your back hand. Then hook onto the ring with your front hand and grab the trapeze handle to lift yourself off the deck – all in one smooth movement. Slide out over the side in a semi-hiking position with the trapeze wire taut. Do not ease your weight, or the ring may drop off the hook. To get out into the trapezing position, bend your front leg and lift your front foot onto the side of the boat then push your front leg straight. At the same time push off from the side of the boat with your back hand while lifting your back foot onto the side and straightening the back leg. Let the jib sheet

ABOVE **On the wire, feet close together, looking ahead, staying relaxed, that's the way trapezing should be.**

run through your hand as necessary. Keep both feet as close together as possible and lean back until your shoulder straps start to pull taut. You can then let go of the handle.

TIGHTENING UP A TRAPEZE HARNESS ....

1 Pull the leg straps of your trapeze harness tight first.

2 Then tighten the shoulder straps until your body starts to bend.

ABOVE **The trapeze allows the crew to greatly increase leverage on the 29er, but will require good technique on such a short and frisky boat.**

Newcomers to trapezing often find letting go of the handle a major challenge, but it soon becomes a delight to swing free with the jib sheet in one or both hands.

Staying there

You may feel unsteady on your feet as the boat pitches through waves and the trapeze wire pulls you forwards. Try bracing your front foot against the shroud plate, and keep the back leg flexed so that you are leaning slightly back towards the transom – do not stand straight out at 90 degrees to the boat. Your front leg supports most of your body weight, while your back leg is used for balance. Get used to moving your weight in and out on the trapeze by bending your legs so the helmsperson can respond to lulls and gusts without the boat tipping to windward. If the wind is fluky you may have to come in and go out like a jack-in-the-box and adopt an ungainly crouching attitude on the side deck.

The traditional style of trapezing requires a dead straight body for maximum leverage. However, on modern skiff-style boats this has been superseded by a more comfortable, sit-up posture in which the sailor sits upright in the harness. This provides increased vision and allows better control and faster responses when sailing a fast moving, gennaker-powered boat at the expense of slight loss of leverage.

On a fast and gusty reach – particularly with a gennaker – the crew needs to keep well braced to avoid being thrown round the forestay if the bows go down. This will

GETTING OUT ON THE WIRE

1 Grab the hook and handle.

2 Hook on with the back hand.

3 Take the weight and move out.

4 Use the back hand for support.

5 Step out with the front foot.

6 Follow with the back foot.

almost certainly result in a major wipeout, and the sling-shot effect can cause damage to crew or equipment. If it helps, the crew can grab the helmsperson's shoulder to hold back; or use a special restraining line that clips on to the hook as when sailing a performance catamaran.

Coming in

Take the jib sheet in your back hand. Grab the handle with your front hand, and pull up so you can slide your back leg in over the side deck. Bend your front leg, using the handle to lift your backside onto the deck. Unhook for the next manoeuvre.

STAYING OUT ON THE WIRE

1 Brace the front leg and hold the jib sheet with your back hand.

2 Angle your feet so that you can lean and look forwards.

3 If conditions are marginal, then bend your legs and move in.

Trapeze height

For upwind sailing the trapeze ring should generally be adjusted so it is just clear of the deck. It is theoretically most efficient to trapeze parallel to the deck of the boat. However at that height waves will almost certainly hit your body, so you need to lift the trapeze ring enough to clear them. Do not lift the ring too high, or you will topple into the boat every time it heels.

All good trapezes need a system to lift or lower the ring, which can be used while on the wire. This is normally an adjustable length, two-part purchase led through blocks and locked by a friction cleat. Unless you are strong and experienced, adjusting ring height is a two-handed job. Cleat the jib, take your weight on the handle with your front hand, and use your right hand to pull the line through the adjuster. Be very sure that the line is firmly locked before you let go.

"Moon walking"

In stronger winds and on reaching courses, the crew will need to move back along the side deck to stop the bow burying. The more you move back, the greater the forward pull on the trapeze

ABOVE **On modern trapeze boats such as the 29er an upright sitting position is common. It allows maximum control of the sails, plus a good view of the surroundings.**

wire becomes, and the more you need to lean back towards the stern with your back leg well bent and the front leg straight. You also need to set your feet

wider apart for greater stability. Moving back effectively shortens the length of the trapeze wire. You will need to lengthen it for a reaching course, or risk being pulled forward into the boat.

Trapeze tacks

When you are ready to tack, pull up on the handle in order to take your weight, and let the rig slide off the hook, with the pull of the shockcord retainer helping it. As the boat goes through the tack, wait until the last moment before coming in over the side and uncleating the jib. Cross to the new side taking the new leeward jib sheet with you – a continuous jib sheet makes this much easier.

Newcomers to trapezing will want to hook on before going out on the wire on the new side. Once you become more experienced, you can grab the handle on the new side with your new front hand, and push yourself straight out in the trapezing position. Sheet in and cleat the jib, while still hanging on the handle. Use your back hand to grab the ring, hook on and let the trapeze harness take your weight.

GETTING THE HEIGHT RIGHT ....

1 Take your weight on the back hand and shorten or lengthen the height of the hook.

2 Make very sure that the adjustment line is firmly locked in position.

HELMING OFF THE WIRE

This is a skilled art, whether on a two-handed or single-handed boat requiring plenty of practice. In most cases the helmsperson will have to manage both rudder and mainsheet and is unable to move in and out as quickly or easily as the crew. The crew will generally go out on the wire first and come in last, and should take responsibility for weight trim and respond to lulls and gusts, while the helmsperson stays out and concentrates on keeping the boat powered up.

When tacking the helmsperson will normally come in off the wire ahead of the crew, using the mainsheet hand to knock off the trapeze ring.

When the wind goes aft of a beam reach, helming from the wire becomes extremely difficult. It's much faster to be in control and hike, than out of control and on the trapeze.

Getting in and out

Before the helm goes out on the wire, he or she needs to hold both mainsheet and tiller in their back hand, in order to grab the trapeze ring and hook on. There is a natural tendency to pull the tiller with you when going out on the wire. This makes the boat bear away and can throw the crew forwards at an inopportune moment. To avoid it happening, try crooking your tiller

TACKING ON THE WIRE ....

1 Cross quickly to the new side, grabbing the handle with your front hand.

2 Go all the way out on the handle, while sheeting in with the back hand.

3 Bring the sheet hand into your body and use it to hook on.

4 Easy on dry land – not as easy on the water with the wind and the waves.

arm so you can hold the tiller by the side of your head. Straighten your arm as you go out on the wire, and the rudder will stay centred. Avoid pushing the tiller away and luffing the boat as you come in off

the wire. Slide your hand as far down the tiller extension as it will go, and then bend your arm as you come in to keep the rudder straight.

Tricks and tactics

The helm needs to trapeze from a slightly higher position than the crew to get an unobstructed view forwards.

Your front hand can manage small sheeting movements while on the wire. If you need to take in or let out a lot of mainsheet, you will need to use the back hand, which is holding the tiller, as a mainsheet clamp.

Do not let the tail end of the mainsheet drop in the water and drag. Lay the amount of slack that's needed for mainsheet adjustments over your thighs, with the remainder of the sheet thrown down in the cockpit.

LEFT **Helming off the wire is a refined but very satisfying skill, particularly when out on the racks of a demanding single-hander such as the RS600.**

Gennaker techniques

A gennaker is a general term for an asymmetric spinnaker that is a pure reaching sail. Many people would agree that gennakers are a lot simpler and a whole lot more fun than conventional symmetric spinnakers, which are primarily for downwind sailing. Most gennakers have a clearly defined triangular shape: the leech is shorter than the luff and the mid-girth (halfway measurement) is shorter than the foot. The sail tapers from foot to head, unlike a spinnaker, which gets wider in the middle.

A gennaker can be effectively used on any point of sailing between a broad reach and close reach. However on a close reach in light winds there comes a point where a gennaker will drive a boat more sideways than forwards.

The key technique on a gennaker-driven boat is to luff to build boat speed. This creates a stronger apparent wind and closes the apparent wind angle so the sailor can bear off with the wind. If it's windy a fast boat such as a 49er or International 14 can sail a blistering close reach on a course that's almost dead downwind.

Hoisting, gybing and dropping the gennaker requires excellent co-ordination and communication between the crew. The object is to keep the boat level and sailing fast throughout these manoeuvres. Ratchet blocks and gloves are necessary to handle the loads generated by a gennaker. Travelling at speed helps reduce loads, which could otherwise overpower the crew.

Socks and bags

The main difference in technique for hoisting and dropping the gennaker is likely to revolve around whether the boat is equipped with a bag or a sock (also known as a chute) to stow and launch the sail.

A sock stows the gennaker neatly and automatically. It also allows the gennaker to be hoisted and dropped on either tack, so long as the mouth of the sock is in front of the forestay.

A bag on the other hand is able to hold a larger size gennaker and there is no friction in the hoist. However, the gennaker has to be gathered and packed manually every time it is dropped, and the sail must be hoisted on the same side as the last drop.

ABOVE **The gennaker looks great and is brilliant fun to sail with, adding a lot of downwind power to a boat like the RS200.**

SOCK VARIATIONS ....

The Laser 4000 has a moulded bridge at the mouth of the sock.

On the RS200 the sock is simply laid along the foredeck.

SAILING WITH A BAG ....

1 The 29er uses a gennaker bag, mounted behind the mast, with an elasticated opening.

2 When not in use, the bag shuts like an oyster and is held together by velcro.

HOISTING FROM A SOCK ON AN RS200 ....

1 It's often a good idea to talk through the sequence before you start.

2 On the RS200 the crew launches the gennaker while the helm sails the boat.

3 The pole pulls right out before the gennaker starts to go up and fill.

4 The helmsperson bears away to blanket the gennaker behind the mainsail.

5 The crew cleats the gennaker halyard when he is sure it is all the way up.

6 The helm luffs to help power up the gennaker while the crew sheets in.

Standard hoist

Bear away well downwind before the hoist. If the helmsperson does not bear away enough the gennaker may become wrapped round the forestay. During the hoist the helm can stand with legs astride to balance the boat and keep it level. A slight luff lifts the windward side; a slight bear-off lifts the leeward side.

The crew usually launches the gennaker by pulling in the halyard very fast, hand over hand. On some boats this action will automatically pull out the gennaker pole, which comes out of its hole in the bow rather like a torpedo; on others the pole may need to be pulled out separately before the halyard. The hoist needs to be as fast as possible to avoid the sail dropping and being run over, or the boat slowing to a crawl while sailing downwind.

The point where the gennaker is fully hoisted should be clearly marked on the halyard. Once the gennaker is sheeted and

fills, it is very difficult to hoist the halyard further in anything other than a light wind, and performance and control will be compromised. The crew takes in the sheet and moves out to the windward side, or goes straight out on the trapeze if fitted. At the same time the helmsperson locks the pole at a suitable angle to windward, and luffs onto a reaching course to build up speed and apparent wind as the crew sheets in. If the helm wants to get out on the trapeze, the crew may need to depower the gennaker for a couple of seconds to help him or her onto the side.

Bag hoists

A leeward side hoist is easiest from a bag. The crew can manage the hoist from the windward side, and the helmsperson can sail a reaching course.

If a windward side hoist is necessary, most likely after dropping the gennaker on the wrong side for the next hoist, the helm

7 The boat accelerates and they bear off on the apparent wind.

must bear off downwind to ensure the gennaker goes up cleanly. Don't stay downwind too long – a fast hoist and a slight luff will help ensure the gennaker floats around the front of the boat without wrapping its luff around the forestay.

DROPPING INTO A SOCK ON THE RS200 ....

1 The helm bears away to blanket the gennaker, while the crew lets go of the sheet.

2 The crew pulls in hand over hand on the retrieval line.

3 The gennaker is drawn into the bag without wrapping or snagging it around the bow.

Standard drop

The helmsperson temporarily takes the gennaker sheet as the crew comes inboard, and bears off dead downwind as the crew moves to the middle of the boat.

The helm keeps the boat trimmed, while the crew prepares to uncleat the halyard. On some boats, particularly catamarans, you can throw the bundle of excess halyard over the bag so it streams out in a straight line. This guarantees it will run free.

Sock system

The crew uncleats the gennaker halyard and pulls hand over hand on the retrieval line, which will drag the gennaker into the sock and the pole into the bows. The helm may need to uncleat the pole angle controls to allow this.

Bag drop

Unless the wind is very light, the drop is best done on the windward side so the crew does not have to move down to leeward and risk heeling the boat. It is also very uncomfortable trying to retrieve the gennaker when you are squashed under the boom. The long, continuous gennaker sheet must be tensioned and cleated when not in use, to prevent any chance of it falling off the bows and under the boat.

For a windward drop the crew grabs the windward sheet, lets the leeward sheet fly, pulls the sail round the forestay or jib luff and gathers in the foot while letting go of the halyard. Within a few feverish seconds he or she drops the sail in the cockpit, rapidly bundles it into the bag, and finally secures the top with velcro straps so that none of the corners pull out while sailing. The helmsperson may need to uncleat the pole launch system to let the pole slide back into the boat while this is going on.

If dropping to leeward, bear away enough to prevent the sail blowing back and catching on the ends of the battens. The helm may need to stand and grab the leeward sheet to get it within the crew's reach. The crew then pulls in the foot with the leeward sheet, taking great care to bring the sail under the leeward jib sheet.

A gybe drop lets you drop the sail to windward, without having to bear away and pull it round the forestay. As the boat gybes, the crew crosses to the new windward side but keeps pulling in on the old sheet. As the boom goes across, he or she grabs the gennaker clew, lets go of the halyard, and catches the sail as it drops on the windward side.

Gennaker gybing

Gybing requires good balance and trim, with the boat travelling at maximum speed to reduce apparent wind and potential overloading of the sails. The faster the gybe, the smoother and more effortless it should be. Both crew come inboard as the helmsperson begins to bear away. The helmsperson keeps the boat level as the boat turns past dead downwind ready to give a tug on the mainsheet to help gybe the mainsail.

DROPPING THE GENNAKER IN STRONG WIND ....

1 The helm bears off and lets the main flog as the crew prepares to let go the gennaker sheet.

2 The crew pulls it down and into the sock at top speed. Any wraps or snags would be a disaster.

3 On a gusty day, the helm needs to sheet in and head up straightaway to keep the boat upright.

The crew waits to let the old gennaker sheet run free. If it is let go too soon it may blow forwards and wrap round the forestay. Sometimes it will unwrap with a tug; at other times it is necessary to gybe back onto the old course. The crew lets the sheet off so both boom and gennaker cross to the new sides together, with the clew of the gennaker just brushing the forestay.

The helmsperson continues to steer through the gybe. If the jib is set, a good trick is for the crew to cleat the gennaker on the new leeward side before moving to the other side of the boat. The crew then sheets in fast, and goes out on the side or wire.

Once the sail is powered up on the new gybe, the helm starts to luff to build up to full speed and the crew sheets in to match the apparent wind angle. If the boat heels over and does not power out of the gybe, the gennaker must be eased off by letting out the sheet slightly. If the boat loses speed at the end of the gybe, the helmsperson must luff before bearing away on the apparent wind and a suitable downwind course.

GYBING WITH THE GENNAKER ON THE RS200

1 The helmsperson stands up to bear away and grab the boom.

2 He flicks it across, while the crew moves across and lets go of the gennaker sheet.

3 The helm balances the boat with his feet while the crew pulls the gennaker round the forestay.

4 The crew then sheets in, powers up and flattens out the boat on the new course.

GYBING WITH THE GENNAKER ON THE RS200 IN STRONGER WIND

1 The boat is moving fast on a broad reach as the helm starts to bear away.

2 The helmsperson stands to give the boom a flick to the new side as the boat turns downwind.

3 The helmsperson ducks while the crew lets the gennaker sheet fly and pulls in on the new side.

4 The helmsperson concentrates on steering and levelling out the boat on the new course.

5 The helmsperson luffs to build speed while the crew sheets in.

6 As apparent wind increases they start to bear away at full speed.

Gennaker trimming

With the apparent wind coming from ahead, a gennaker tends to be more stable and easier to trim than a spinnaker, but there is skill in getting it powered up to maximum advantage. As with the mainsail and jib, the trick is to sail with the gennaker on the edge. Let the sheet out until the luff starts to curl inwards near the top, and from there trim it back in until the curl is just hovering on the edge. If the gennaker keeps collapsing, it could be that the halyard is not fully up or that the helmsperson needs to sail a lower course. If the boat lacks power in light winds, the probable solution is to head up. If the pole can be trimmed to either side, a task performed by the helmsperson, it should be trimmed a few degrees to windward. The further downwind you are heading and the lighter the apparent wind, the further to windward it needs to be so it is kept well clear of the mainsail. Pole trim will also need to be adjusted every time the boat gybes.

When a gust hits, the gennaker sheet is eased to compensate for the apparent wind shifting forward, as the helmsperson bears

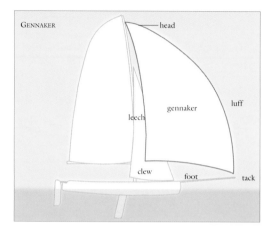

GENNAKER — head

leech — gennaker — luff

clew — foot — tack

LEFT **The gennaker is essentially a free floating, overlapping jib (genoa), which has a very full shape owing to its loose luff. It retains the same clew, head and tack as any headsail.**

away to maximize downwind course and prevent the boat from heeling. As the boat accelerates even faster the sheet must be trimmed in. In strong winds, the helm can steer the boat to keep the gennaker on a finely tuned edge, bearing off when the luff curls in and luffing when the luff lifts outwards. The crew may need to ease the gennaker to help the boat bear away in gusts.

The jib can be sheeted for a close reaching course, easy with a self-tacking jib as on the 49er. Other dinghies may have self-furling jibs, so on a more downwind course it is easier to furl the jib leaving the area between the mast and gennaker totally unobstructed. This gives a better view when trimming the gennaker. The jib can then be unfurled just prior to dropping the gennaker and changing course upwind.

TRIMMING THE GENNAKER ON A 29ER

1 The crew bear off on a gust with everything pulling hard.

2 The apparent wind drops and swings aft, collapsing the gennaker.

3 The helm luffs and the crew sheets in to power up the sail.

TACKING DOWNWIND AND REGAINING CONTROL

1 The boys in the RS200 are on a blast, sailing flat out downhill on the apparent wind.

2 Time to put in a downwind tack, so the helmsperson says, "let's go for it!".

3 All's well as the boat slews round onto the new course.

4 But they have a few problems getting the boom across.

5 The momentum of the gybe looks set to flatten the boat, but the helm keeps the tiller up.

6 The helm can now bear away while the crew helps flatten the boat.

Tacking downwind

A gennaker should never be used for sailing dead downwind. The object of a gennaker is to be able to sail a downwind course on a succession of very fast broad reaches, with gybes in between. The skill is to be able to build up apparent wind on a beam reach, and then bear off and head downwind holding the same speed. The exception is in very light winds, when it may pay to sail a more direct downwind course without luffing.

All gennaker boats have an optimum velocity made good (VMG) downwind sailing angle, which is determined by different wind speeds. The difference between optimum VMG and being slightly off the angle, either sailing too high or too low, will be proportionally greater as a boat becomes lighter, faster and starts to plane. The angle between a luffing course to build speed and bearing off with a gust can be as much as 90 degrees. A gennaker boat therefore sails a kind of slalom course, luffing and bearing off to maximize its downwind VMG.

Gybing angles are more difficult to guess than tacking angles on a course sailed in gusts and lulls. As an average rule, the gybing angle needs to be about 45 degrees or more to the course of the boat.

ABOVE **Judging how deep you can sail downwind and when to tack is largely a matter of "seat of the pants" experience and watching other boats. There is a constant trade-off in the search for maximum velocity made good (VMG).**

Spinnaker techniques

The spinnaker is a traditional symmetrical sail for downwind sailing. Most spinnakers are fuller than gennakers and considerably more full than the mainsail or jib. The amount of fullness or flatness helps determine how efficient a spinnaker is on a dead run, and how close to the wind it can be carried on a reach. A spinnaker is only useful when the wind is aft of the beam. If the wind goes forward of the beam, the fullness of a spinnaker will heel the boat over and pull it sideways. It is also likely to become less controllable than a gennaker. Unlike a gennaker, the velocity made good (VMG) of a spinnaker can be maximized by taking the shortest course downwind, when the difference between true wind and apparent wind is less critical than when tacking downwind with a gennaker.

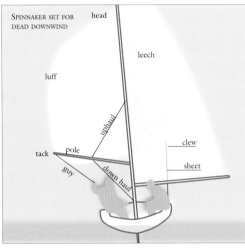

SPINNAKER SET FOR DEAD DOWNWIND

head
leech
luff
uphaul
tack
pole
guy
down haul
clew
sheet

LEFT **The clew and sheet of a spinnaker are to leeward and the tack, pole and guy are to windward. Both sides of the sail are interchangeable unlike a gennaker where tack and clew are in fixed positions.**

ABOVE **Both tack and clew of the spinnaker are level as the Wayfarer runs downwind, and the spinnaker is pulled well round to the windward side so it is not blanketed by the mainsail.**

Spinnaker controls

A spinnaker has control lines to both sides of the sail, unlike a gennaker, which has sheets led to a single clew and is closer in use to an oversized jib. The control line on the leeward side of the spinnaker is the sheet. This is attached to the clew and controls the leech by means of constant trimming. The control line on the windward side of the spinnaker is the guy. This is attached to the tack and is also clipped into the outer end of the spinnaker pole. The guy controls the luff, and once a course is set is cleated in a fixed position. Since the spinnaker is symmetrical, the luff/leech, tack/clew and guy/sheet swop roles every time the boat changes tacks.

To avoid being blanketed by the boat, crew or mainsail, the spinnaker is held out to windward by a spinnaker pole while sailing downwind. The vertical angle of the spinnaker pole is adjusted by an uphaul and downhaul line. The more downwind the course, the higher the end of the pole should be. The horizontal angle of the

spinnaker pole is adjusted by the guy. The pole should be set at approximately 90 degrees to the apparent wind.

Spinnaker hoists

A spinnaker will begin to fill the moment it leaves its bag or sock. If you hoist while bearing away and are still on a beam reach, the top of the spinnaker may fill and capsize the boat; if you wait until the boat is dead downwind, lateral stability becomes poor and the boat may start rolling as the spinnaker goes up.

The centreboard or daggerboard needs to be lifted at least halfway. This is a compromise between providing enough resistance to windward rolls and letting the boat slide leeward rather than trip on its board; the side pressure from a partly filled spinnaker can capsize a boat with the board fully down.

To start the hoist, the crew rigs the spinnaker pole, which has identical clip fittings at both ends. The outer end is clipped over the guy and then the inner

SPINNAKER HOIST ON A WAYFARER

1 The helmsperson bears off downwind. The crew picks up the spinnaker pole.

2 The crew clips the outer end of the pole to what will be the guy.

3 She clips the uphaul/downhaul to the middle of the pole, and clips the inner end to the mast.

4 The spinnaker is hoisted from its bag, and goes up on the leeward side of the sail.

5 The crew pulls in on the sheet after the helm has pulled back the guy.

6 The spinnaker sets perfectly.

end is clipped to the mast with the vertical angle of the pole pre-set for the course. On many boats, the helmsperson stands and faces forward while pulling up the halyard. In this way the person can use their legs to balance the boat, as well as pulling in a lot of halyard with each heave. Meanwhile, the crew pulls in on the guy to get the pole round to windward. The guy should be locked with the pole at 90 degrees to the wind, pointing across the boat for a dead downwind course, and in line with the boat for a beam reach. Never let the pole push against the forestay on a beam reach. The crew sheets in and trims the spinnaker for the course.

Trimming the spinnaker

As with a gennaker, the spinnaker should always be sheeted so that it is on the edge of collapse with the top of the luff starting to curl inwards but not collapsing. If the spinnaker collapses the crew needs to sheet in or the helmsperson needs to bear away, with the pole eased forwards for the new course.

Running with a spinnaker

As the boat bears away, the crew pulls the pole right back. This lets the spinnaker lift and fly as far forward as possible, so it can

pull the boat with minimal effect from wind shadow or turbulence. The helm usually sits to leeward on the same side as the mainsail boom, with the crew to windward on the same side as the spinnaker pole. Both crew need to move aft where the hull is flattest and most stable. The crew must keep trimming the boat, laterally and longitudinally, when sailing

and surfing with following waves. Beware of a sudden death roll caused by a clumsy crew movement or sudden rogue wave.

To provide roll resistance the centreboard or daggerboard should be part-way down. The mainsail should be sheeted in a short way off the shroud, and the spinnaker slightly over-sheeted to prevent it swinging from side to side.

TRIMMING THE SPINNAKER

1 If the luff of the spinnaker collapses, the crew needs to sheet in or the helm has to bear away.

2 The spinnaker is just on the curl. A quick tug on the sheet will bring it back and halt its collapse.

Reaching with a spinnaker

The pole should be at around 90 degrees to the wind with the tack and clew as level as possible to maintain the sail's symmetrical shape. Pulling in the sheet for a reaching course will automatically pull the clew down, and the tack needs to be pulled down to the same height.

In anything more than a light wind, the crew will need to hike or trapeze to keep the boat flat. The guy is pushed out of the way under a clip by the windward shroud, which also holds the boom down.

The difference between true and apparent wind poses more problems with a full bellied symmetric spinnaker than a flat bellied asymmetric gennaker. If the boat accelerates and drives the wind forward, the helmsperson must bear away to continue to carry the spinnaker and keep the boat level. On a reaching course a spinnaker will start to collapse or pull the boat sideways well before a gennaker, and it is an important skill to be able to judge when a spinnaker ceases to be an advantage and should come down.

A boat that is well powered up and flying with a spinnaker will make the rudder seem finger light, exerting only

ABOVE **When reaching, the spinnaker pole is let forward, but must always be pulled back off the forestay. The pole should be pulled down a little harder than is shown here. The jib should either be furled or sheeted in and cleated, even though it will produce negligible drive.**

marginal control. If the boat suddenly heels and goes into an involuntary luff, the top of the spinnaker will power up and take control of the boat. It is a top priority for the helmsperson and crew to keep the boat flat, with the crew depowering the spinnaker to let the helmsperson bear away in gusts.

GYBING THE WAYFARER WITH A SPINNAKER ....

1 The helm bears away, pulling in the guy while the crew eases the sheet.

2 The helm pushes the tiller over to gybe the boat, while the crew gives a sharp pull on the kicker.

3 Both crew move to the new side while the helm centres the rudder to keep downwind.

4 The crew unclips the pole from the mast, and clips this end of the pole onto the new guy.

5 She pushes the pole forward, releases the old guy, and clips the pole's new inner end to the mast.

6 The crew sheets in as helm pulls in on the new guy and heads up onto the new reaching course.

Spinnaker gybes

The spinnaker gybe is more complex than the gennaker gybe, and provides more opportunity for getting things wrong.

The centreboard or daggerboard must be raised at least halfway; down enough so it won't roll going into the gybe, and up enough so it won't trip and heel the boat when luffing out of the gybe. The helmsperson plays a major role, steering the boat through the gybe, balancing the boat and managing the spinnaker controls all at the same time.

The helmsperson bears away until the boat is sailing by the lee, with the spinnaker pulling well out to the windward side and the clew floating close to the forestay. The helm steers the boat through the arc of the gybe, standing in order to balance the boat, holding the spinnaker sheet in one hand and guy in the other, and steering with the tiller between his or her legs. This allows the crew to unclip the inner end of the pole from the mast, and clip this end (the old inner end) to the new guy (old sheet). He or she then quickly unclips the old outer end from the new sheet (old guy) – there is usually a line along the spinnaker pole to facilitate this – and supports the pole with both hands for a second before pushing it out towards the new tack and clipping the new inner end to the mast. Meanwhile the helm steers the boat through the gybe, keeping the boat level and the spinnaker filled so no speed is lost and the apparent wind does not power up at an inopportune moment.

In light to moderate winds the main boom will gybe of its own accord; in stronger winds the momentum may throw the boat on its side, so the crew will need to yank the boom across by pulling the kicking strap just before clipping the pole to the new side. As the boom comes over and the boat powers up, the crew is ready to hike or trapeze the boat, having taken the guy and sheet from the helm who has already set them for the new course.

Spinnaker drops

The traditional spinnaker drop is on the leeward side, with the sail coming down the same way that it went up. With the

LEFT **When gybing there is no need to let the downhaul and spinnaker go up in the sky. Keep them down with the pole level or the boat will go out of control if a gust hits.**

spinnaker blanketed by the mainsail, the crew lets off the guy and halyard, then pulls the spinnaker in from the clew (via the sheet) to bundle it into its bag; or alternatively pulls it back into its sock or shute with a retaining line. Once the spinnaker is stowed with halyard and sheets tensioned and cleated, the crew can unclip and stow the pole.

If the next spinnaker hoist is on the opposite tack, the crew will need to drop the sail on the windward side of the boat. Having let go the sheet and halyard, the crew grabs the tack via the guy and pulls the sail down into its bag. Care is needed to ensure that the spinnaker and all associated lines are pulled in under the jib sheet to avoid a mess at the next hoist.

SPINNAKER DROP ON THE WAYFARER ....

1 The crew passes the sheet to the helm, unclips the pole from the mast and lets go of the guy when the spinnaker is blanketed by the mainsail.

2 She drops the pole into the cockpit, having unclipped the downhaul/uphaul line, and stows it ready to drop the spinnaker halyard.

3 The spinnaker is dropped on the leeward side of the mainsail where it is kept under control.

4 The crew sits inboard to cram the spinnaker into its bag, letting the three corners protrude.

Sail care and maintenance

Direct, strong sunlight is your worst enemy. It will degrade all sail materials, especially Mylar™ style laminates and windows, the most vulnerable. Sails should always be stored out of the sun and never near direct heat. Always keep laminate sails away from solvents such as fuel and cleaning agents that can dissolve the glue and cause separation.

Avoid flogging

Try to prevent sails flogging (hard flapping in the wind), which will degrade the material, especially laminates. A flogging sail may also damage anything around it – a clew hitting someone in the face can knock a tooth out. Never dry a sail by leaving it to flap like a flag in the boat park. Allow it to dry where there will be minimal movement. Avoid letting the jib flog while launching, landing or waiting on a start line. It is better to back the jib if you don't want it powered up. If you have a roller, always roll the jib away. Learn to sheet the jib in quickly and efficiently when tacking. If the spinnaker or gennaker starts to flog repeatedly, it means your ability doesn't match the conditions. Avoid explosive refillings, drop it and stow away.

Go easy on the tension

On a high performance woven polyester sail it's common to put a lot of weight on the downhaul or cunningham to increase luff tension, take out the stretch and move draught forward. A more stable laminate sail should require considerably less luff tension to get the same effect. Pull the downhaul or cunningham until any horizontal wrinkles disappear, then don't pull any more or you could damage the sail.

Tears and repairs

Small tears can be temporarily taped over with sailmakers' tape, but the tear should be professionally repaired as soon as possible. Never sail with a torn spinnaker or you'll find a new meaning to the word ripstop. Laminate sails are prone to impact damage. If you capsize, try to avoid falling into the sail and never do so feet-first or head first.

Avoid rough contact

Try to keep the mainsail pulled back off the leeward shroud and spreader when running downwind. This will leave unsightly marks on the sail and will start to rub through

ABOVE **Letting a sail flog in the wind is not the best way to care for it as it will degrade the material.**

the outer surface of the cloth. Plastic-coated shrouds give some protection.

Never drag a sail over a hard surface like a concrete slipway. Avoid rolling or folding a sail away on a rough surface. Check the boat for any sharp or rough edges that sails may catch on. The relatively fragile material of a spinnaker or gennaker is vulnerable to snagging on untaped cotter pins, screw threads or hooks, while the foot of the jib may get damaged by dragging across the deck when you tack.

LEFT **The laminate sails are all pumped up on a 29er. They look great and give brilliant performance, but need a certain level of care and attention, even more so in a sunny climate.**

ABOVE **Salt is the enemy. It scratches and holds moisture that will damage your sails, so wash it off after every outing.**

Wash sails regularly

Sails don't like the corrosive crystals of salt, which may cause long-term damage if allowed to build up on the cloth. So if you sail on the sea, give your sails a regular hose down with fresh water.

Dry them well

Always let sails dry thoroughly before you put them away, and never leave a wet sail in a bag. Given time a damp environment will promote mildew, which can be difficult to remove from the cloth, and dark colours on a nylon spinnaker or gennaker can bleed into lighter colours.

Check the corners

The head, tack and clew have to cope with high loadings on high performance dinghy sails. Check that all reinforcement, plates, cringles and stitching are intact before you put sails away, if not, take them to the sailmaker for repairs.

Free up the battens

Let the tension off battens before putting sails away. Depending on the way the sail is cut you may be able to leave the battens in, but battens that obstruct a nice tight roll or fold must be removed. Check

ABOVE **The traditional way to pack a woven polyester sail is to "flake" it in zigzag folds. Try to avoid permanent creases by not folding along the same lines every time.**

ABOVE **All laminate sails should be rolled. Use a plastic pipe if there aren't any full length battens to support the sail, and remove battens as necessary.**

the batten end pockets for wear and abrasion, and send the sail to a sailmaker if reinforcement is required.

Roll them up

Never stuff a sail into a bag. The exception is a spinnaker or gennaker which, due to its light material, can be stored in a loose bundle. The traditional method of storing woven polyester sails is to fold them from head to foot, holding the luff and leech to make horizontal creases, which are folded

in a concertina pattern. Don't fold along the same creases every time, or the creases may become permanent. Laminate sails must be rolled into a tube as any creases can crack the laminate. If you have the right sausage-shaped bags this is the easiest and most efficient way to store sails, whether laminate or woven polyester. You may also find it convenient to roll the mainsail around the boom, or to roll the sails around the length of a plastic drainpipe, and remove when necessary.

ABOVE **Sails get a lot of stress. Make a regular check of the head, tack and clew for any signs of wear or fatigue.**

ABOVE **Battens have a nasty habit of wearing holes in the ends of their pockets. Make sure it is not happening to your sails.**

ABOVE **It's often easiest to roll the jib, whether laminate or woven polyester. Roll it around the luff wire, starting at the head.**

Boat maintenance

If you sail on salt water make a regular practice of washing your boat with fresh water. This will help keep the boat looking good for longer, and ensure that everything works by flushing salt out of spars and fittings.

Household cleaning products, such as washing-up liquid, can be used to clean a fibreglass or plastic boat quite adequately, but beware of leaving an undesirable super-slip finish on the deck and in the cockpit. If in doubt, it's worth paying the price of proprietary boat cleaners, which include specially packaged shampoos, polishes and rubbing compounds to burnish the hull plus aluminium cleaners for spars and fittings.

Laying up

When laying up a boat for a long period such as a winter lay-off, take time to ensure it will not deteriorate.
Ensure that you do the following:

- Wash everything down thoroughly with fresh water.
- Remove all ropes and lines that may retain moisture.
- Check over all blocks, cleats and other fittings. If you have washed them regularly in fresh water, they should stay in perfect working order. Be wary of using any lubricants that may lead to slipping lines.

ABOVE **Salt can degrade everything, so wash it off the bottom of your boat.**

ABOVE **High performance sailing depends on reliability; and that depends on taking care of your equipment.**

- Remove all hatch covers and bungs to promote circulation of air.
- Leave the boat fully supported so that air can circulate under the hull. The trolley or trailer should be ideal for this.
- If possible store the boat under cover. If the boat has to be left outside, make sure it has an effective cover that drains water off and raise the bow so any water that gets inside will run out from the transom.
- Spars should be supported so they are horizontal to the ground, but never lying on the ground. Inspect shrouds and forestay, and replace any broken wires. Inspect rivets, and if any need replacing use Chromite paste to prevent corrosion between aluminium and stainless surfaces.

ABOVE **Boats take in water. Make sure it gets regularly drained and dried out, and arrange to leave the hatch covers off when the boat is laid up and out of use.**

ABOVE **Control lines will abrade and eventually break under stress. Check and replace them on a regular basis.**

Foil repairs

Denting foils, particularly in the bottom and leading edge, is very common. Most dent repairs can be accomplished by using a proprietary gelcoat of the correct colour. Only if the dent is on a large scale will fibreglass need to be added. The best way to repair the damage is to:

- Thoroughly wash and dry the repair area.
- Grind out the dent to solid material.
- Mask the repair area.
- Pour liquid gelcoat into the hole, and build up layers as necessary.
- Once the gelcoat has cured, rub the surface to a smooth finish with wet and dry sandpaper.

ABOVE **Rig fittings can suffer from corrosion and stress damage. It is vital that shrouds do not fail, so check both the terminals and shroud wires themselves.**

proprietary fibreglass paint. It is vital that all release agents from the original moulding process and any build-up of grease are removed by using a fibreglass cleaner before starting.

Polypropylene repairs

In the unlikely event of holing the hull or deck of a boat made from polypropylene or a derivative, a special gun is required, which places the repair outside do-it-yourself abilities.

Avoid dragging polypropylene boats as the resulting scratches can only effectively be removed by professional repair.

Polypropylene boats with dark decks are prone to fading. There is no solution, beyond ensuring your boat is protected from strong sunlight. Use a cover or store it indoors when possible.

Fibreglass hull and deck repairs

A small surface dent in the hull is primarily a cosmetic problem, which can be repaired with the right colour gelcoat. If a dent goes right through the boat:

- Thoroughly wash and dry the repair area.
- Grind out the damage to solid material, cutting back and chamfering the edges.
- Lay in fibreglass and resin, and build this up to about 2mm(⅒in) below the surface of the hull.
- Dab on the right colour gelcoat with a brush, building up two or three layers until it is above the surface.
- Rub the gelcoat flat and smooth with wet and dry sandpaper.

- To completely disguise the repair area, dab on a final layer of gelcoat with an extensive overlap, and rub down to an acceptable finish.

If there is damage to a foam sandwich, contour foam can be moulded to any size or shape and inserted between fibreglass layers during the repair.

Gelcoat fade

Exposure to UV sunlight causes the colour of a fibreglass gelcoat to fade over a number of years, and the surface eventually breaks down to a powdery appearance. Polishing with wax may delay this, but if the appearance worries you the only real solution is to paint the hull with

Time well spent

- All do-it-yourself repair and refurbishment jobs require time, care and patience. Allow as much as 80 per cent of total job time for preparation. This is the key to a successful finish.
- Gelcoats, resins, catalysts, solvents and fibreglass are volatile materials that all need careful and precise handling. Read the instructions right through before starting to use them, and pay particular attention to personal safety such as ventilation and protection from splashes.

REPAIRING A HULL ....

1 Preparation is 80 per cent of the job. Leave enough time to make it perfect.

2 Cut out all the damage and make sure it is totally dry before going further.

3 Endless burnishing of the gelcoat is the key to a perfect finish.

CATAMARAN SAILING TECHNIQUES

Catamarans go fast because they have a wide, stable platform that can support a big and often oversized rig, combined with pencil-slim hulls that create minimal wetted surface area. The result is a very different boat from a monohull; it is invariably wider, frequently faster and usually requires a very different style of sailing.

Not everyone likes catamarans, which are very much in a minority compared with monohulls in most countries – notable exceptions are Holland and France. Catamarans are ungainly and take up a lot of space on land, can be rather slow and unresponsive in light winds, do not sail well when heading dead downwind and may lack the super-sensitive feel of a finely tuned dinghy. But in return they can be brilliant fun, fast and tremendously powerful, with rudder foils that literally hum with glee as the wind passes Force 3 (10 knots). From there on a catamaran's sensational performance really kicks in, with the promise of the windiest, wildest and wettest rides of them all.

LEFT *In the right conditions, catamarans skim extremely quickly across the water.*

BELOW *Using a trolley makes launching a catamaran much easier.*

Rigging and tuning

Most aspects of assembling, rigging and tuning a catamaran are similar to those of monohull dinghies though there are important differences.

The platform

The hulls, beams and trampoline of a catamaran form a platform that is equivalent to the hull and deck of a monohull. The main problem for designers and builders is to ensure the platform is as rigid as a monohull, with minimal amount of flex and perfect parallel alignment between the two hulls. The platform also needs to be light, and the correlation between light weight and speed is more marked in catamarans than monohulls.

Each hull is an individual sealed unit accessed by inspection hatches. The platform is created by joining the hulls with two crossbeams, which are usually bolted to the top of the hulls or slide and lock into moulded slots. Crossbeams are invariably made from aluminium extrusions, while carbon fibre is a much more expensive option. The front crossbeam may have a dolphin striker – a V-shaped brace – to help support the load of the mast without bending. The rear beam carries the mainsheet loads, and will usually incorporate a full length track for the mainsheet traveller.

The self-draining, mesh trampoline forms the deck of the boat, and has to be rigid enough to support the crew as well as helping to stiffen the whole platform. Most trampolines are fed into slots along the beams and sides of the hulls, and tensioned with lashings at the rear beam.

The rig

All catamaran masts are stepped on the front beam, and most can rotate through an arc so they line up with the mainsail. This is achieved by a shaped cup at the mast base, which fits over a raised ball that is similar to a towball on a car. A pin locks the mast cup securely onto the ball, and the mast is held up by a single forestay that splits into a V-shaped bridle leading to each bow, and conventional shrouds allow enough twist for the mast to rotate from side to side.

Most catamarans have an elliptical wing shape mast with zero or minimal taper. The mast will bend sideways, but not fore and aft, and due to its size is considerably heavier than the mast of a comparable monohull. Catamarans also have mainly aluminium masts, but carbon fibre is increasingly taking over despite being more expensive:

- Carbon is considerably lighter, which makes the mast easier to hoist or lower when rigging and reduces pitching when sailing.
- It is also more likely to float, which prevents a catamaran turning turtle when capsized.

All high performance catamarans are fitted with flat-sided, square-section booms, and they had loose footed mainsails long before the trend became accepted by monohulls. Aluminium is the favoured material; carbon fibre is the lightweight option.

LEFT **Formula 18 catamarans such as the Dart Hawk can carry a big, powerful rig thanks to the righting moment leverage created by wide-spaced hulls and both crews on trapezes.**

ABOVE **The platform of a catamaran features a quick-draining mesh trampoline suspended between the two main beams. On the Dart 6000 the beams slot directly into the hull mouldings.**

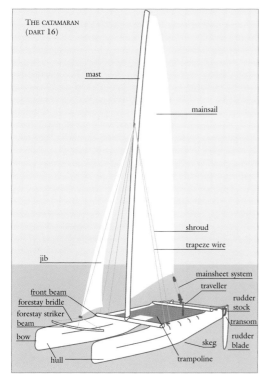

THE CATAMARAN
(DART 16)

mast

mainsail

shroud

trapeze wire

jib

mainsheet system

traveller

rudder
stock

front beam
forestay bridle
forestay striker
beam

bow

transom

rudder
blade

skeg

hull

trampoline

ABOVE **Formula 18s charging upwind. Long, deep daggerboards that give
tremendous lift to windward are only practical for sailing in deep water.**

LEFT **Catamarans have several design features not found on other high
performance boats. Twin hulls make the trampoline and twin foils necessary
while the sails are flatter, and the mainsail has full length battens (not
shown) to keep it tensioned to help the sailor cope with the higher speeds.**

The foils

Catamarans can be fitted with centreboards
or daggerboards to provide resistance to
sideslip and upwind lift. Long, narrow,
straight-sided daggerboards are favoured
for top performance, and are used on
classes such as Formula 18 and A Class
single-handers. They are not advised for
the faint-hearted or inexperienced sailing
in shoal waters – if you hit the bottom at
20 knots, you will certainly smash a foil
and possibly rip open the entire hull.

Another disadvantage is that they are
clumsy to put in and take out, and protrude
way above the deck when retracted.
Centreboards, which are used in the
Tornado, are more user-friendly since they
flip up inside the hulls and barely protrude
above the deck line when lifted. However,
they do not give the same upwind lift as a
high aspect daggerboard, and, unfortunately,
they increase the difficulty and cost of
manufacturing a catamaran hull.

Beware of sand, grit or pebbles getting
into the cases and jamming the tightly
fitting boards when you pull the boat on
to the beach.

Another option is to have no boards at
all and rely on the speed of the catamaran
to ensure that it still makes reasonably
good upwind progress. Cats in this
category include the Hobie 16, which
relies on the flat outer sides of its
asymmetric hulls to prevent leeway, and
the Dart 18, which has small, built-in keels
known as skegs running under its hulls.

All catamarans have twin rudders, twin
tillers, and a single tiller bar and tiller
extension. Aluminium is the favoured tiller
material. Rudder alignment is critical on a
catamaran when the effects of weather
helm (tiller pulls away from you) or
lee helm (tiller pushes towards you) are
pronounced since the leeward rudder is
effectively doing all the work. The rudders
should feel balanced and light at all speeds.

If there is an uncomfortable pull:
• Check that both blades are locked
  fully down. Most catamarans have a
  tiller-lock, which lets the rudder flip
  up if it hits the bottom.
• Check the blades are aligned. Measure
  between the leading edges and trailing
  edges, and adjust the tiller bar to
  equalize any difference.

ABOVE **The transoms of a catamaran need protecting
when left on its trolley on rough ground. This French
built Diam Formula 18 has a beautiful set of
Sailworks wood and laminate rudders from Sweden.**

Mainsail

All catamarans have fully battened mainsails that act like semi-rigid aerofoils. Since the battens push against the luff there is a great deal of friction inside the mast track, and it can be difficult to hoist or lower the mainsail unless guidelines are followed:

- The leading edge of the mast must point directly into the wind with the trailing edge correctly aligned for the sail.
- Hoisting is often a two-person job. One feeds the sail into the track from the front beam, while the other pulls the halyard from wherever gives as straight a lead as possible.

Catamaran controls

The size of the catamaran mainsail, combined with the power generated from sailing at speed on the apparent wind, requires sophisticated controls to handle the boat when you are out in winds of up to Force 4 (11–16 knots).

Mainsheet

A catamaran mainsheet needs to be sheeted in whenever the apparent wind is forward of the beam.

The mainsheet controls sail twist in the top of the leech. For normal sailing and maximum pointing ability, it should be pulled in hard enough so the leech points backwards without curling to windward. If the sail is overpowered and the boat starts

Righting lines

Most catamarans need a righting line to pull the boat back up after a capsize. At its simplest, a righting line is a rope that is about 3m (10ft) long, thick enough to be comfortable on the hands, but thin enough to take a hitch round a trapeze hook. Secure one end to the base of the mast or dolphin striker, and stow the rest in a trampoline pocket where it comes easily to hand.

ABOVE **A righting line is a critical requirement when attempting to right the majority of cats. The Dart 16 shown here will come up easily.**

ABOVE **The very wide trampoline of an Olympic Tornado is left relatively uncluttered, allowing the crew more room to move, because the boat has no gennaker.**

ABOVE **The Tornado control lines are led down from the boom, under the trampoline and out to the sides of the boat so they can be adjusted while the crew is on the trapeze.**

to heel, easing the mainsheet will open the leech and promote sail twist with excess wind spilling out of the sail. The mainsail will need to be sheeted in and out continuously to keep the boat flat and moving fast on a gusty day. This is hard

work. To make it easier, the 17sq m (183sq ft) mainsail of a Formula 18 has an 8:1 multi-purchase mainsheet complete with ratchet-block control, and most catamarans are fitted with similarly powerful sheeting systems.

HOISTING A CATAMARAN MAINSAIL ....

1 The headboard of the mainsail is reinforced for high loadings.

2 The bolt rope must be carefully fed into the mast slot.

3 Keep the mast pointing directly into the wind. This is vital to ensure the fully battened mainsail, which is under tension, will slide freely up the mast slot.

Halyard locks

Most catamarans feature a halyard lock that locks the sail to the top of the mast, of which the two following examples are typical. The Hobie 16 has a V-shaped cleat on the leading edge of the mast and a ferrule (basically a lump on the halyard) that fits over it. The Dart 16 has a hook on the trailing edge of the mast and a ring on the end of the halyard that fits over it. Both systems require a similar technique for hoisting:

- With the downhaul let right off, the halyard is pulled to the top using maximum tension.
- On the Dart the ring rises onto the hook, while on the Hobie the ferrule has to be dropped into its cleat.
- Easing the halyard will drop the top of the sail enough to lock the ring onto the hook and the ferrule into the cleat, so long as they are correctly aligned.
- Tensioning the downhaul ensures the halyard is totally locked.

A similar technique is required for dropping the mainsail:

- With the downhaul let right off, the halyard is pulled to the top of the mast using absolute maximum tension.
- On the Dart the ring rises above the hook, while on the Hobie the ferrule rises above its cleat.
- Rotating the Dart mast through 90 degrees should pull the ring away from the hook. Hold the mast in that position and pull the sail down hard until the ring is definitely below the hook. You can then let the mast rotate back to its in-line position, and drop the sail.
- On the Hobie the halyard needs to be pulled forwards and to the side, to lift the ferrule away from the cleat. Keep the halyard in that position while pulling the sail down to get the ferrule above the cleat, and then drop the sail.

ABOVE **The black mast rotation spanner can be seen just above the boom on this Tornado. The red control line is used to lock the angle between mast and sail.**

ABOVE **The 1–10 calibration gives precise outhaul control on this Tornado. The mainsheet is led forward along the boom and back under the trampoline to a small cut-out, saving mess and clutter for the crew.**

Jib and jib sheets

The primary role of the jib is to accelerate airflow through the slot between mainsail and jib. The size of the jib is generally small in relation to the mainsail, but speed and the effect of apparent wind means that sheets will often need a 2:1 purchase system. Due to the width of a catamaran, the jib sheet fairleads may be mounted on barber-haulers, which are used to pull the clew of the jib outwards, opening the slot for offwind sailing or strong winds. Jib fairleads may also be adjustable fore and aft to tighten or open the leech.

Traveller

This controls the angle of attack of the mainsail, with the traveller control line usually attached to the end of the mainsheet so that it comes easily to hand. The traveller is generally set in the centreline for beating, and moved out for sailing offwind. It can be let right out to the inner edge of the leeward hull for

downwind reaching. The traveller can also be eased away from the centreline to feather the main and make the boat more comfortable, but point lower, while beating in stronger winds.

Mast rotation

The mast rotation spanner usually has a control line led to the boom, which limits the amount of natural rotation. The rotation can be locked at a specific angle, either in-line to flatten the sail and direct wind over the leeward side, or side-on to increase fullness in light winds and downwind.

Downhaul

The downhaul is widely recognized as one of the most important sail controls on a catamaran. Pulling hard on a multi-purchase downhaul will compress and bend the mast, flattening the sail and opening the leech for conditions when the crew are overpowered and cannot keep the windward hull down.

Outhaul

Tensioning the outhaul helps to pull the bottom of the sail flat for when sailing upwind. Easing the outhaul in contrast increases camber for offwind sailing in light wind conditions.

Diamonds

Some catamarans have diamonds (diamond-shaped spreaders) that support side-bend in the mast. Lighter crews need a bendier mast to help depower the mainsail, and can adjust the amount of tension while rigging up. This is used to produce predictable pre-bend for the expected wind speed, after which downhaul and mainsheet are used to control gusts out on the water.

Launching and coming ashore

Most aspects of launch and retrieval are similar with catamarans and monohulls, although catamarans have the advantage of much better stability. There are some important variations.

Trolleys

A simple catamaran trolley comprises an axle, two wheels and two moulded cups to support the hulls. Big wheels with oversize tires make a catamaran considerably easier to push across shingle or soft sand. To get the trolley under the catamaran, one person lifts one bow. This will raise the front enough for a second person to slide the trolley cups beneath each hull. To move the catamaran, the trolley cups need to be pushed just behind the main beam. When it is perfectly balanced fore and aft, one person should be able to walk it across smooth ground.

Do not leave the catamaran with the trolley in the pushing position. Lift the bow and pull the trolley forwards about a metre (yard), so it is approximately halfway between the main beam and bow. In this position the catamaran will sit tail-down. Some catamarans have box-shaped tail protectors to save the gelcoat from scratches. If you leave the catamaran for an extended period, it is best to remove the

ABOVE **With the trolley pulled forward the Formula 18 Diam will rest on its sterns. It is vulnerable to wind, so it is unwise to leave a catamaran unattended for long periods like this.**

trolley so the hulls lie flat on the ground. If there are strong winds forecast, it is a wise precaution to lash the boat down to some suitable anchor since there is considerable windage on the wing mast and trampoline.

Big-wheel catamaran trolleys tend to hold fast on to catamaran hulls due to their own buoyancy, but will float out

when given a tug by the crew. They are easily carried up and down the shore.

Launching in onshore winds

When launching in side-onshore or onshore winds, it is important to drive the catamaran free and fast, luffing into the waves as necessary and bearing away to regain speed between crests.

LAUNCHING A DART 16 WITH A CATAMARAN TROLLEY ....

1 The helm lifts one bow, which is sufficient for the crew to push the trolley aft of the mast.

2 In this position the catamaran is perfectly balanced and can be wheeled backwards or forwards.

3 When the catamaran is in deep enough to float, the trolley can be pulled out from underneath.

Coming ashore in onshore surf

When coming ashore in breaking surf, the wide turning circle and twin hulls of a catamaran can make it difficult to turn the boat into the wind without being rolled before the 180 degree turn is complete.

One option is to run the catamaran straight up the beach with the rudders kicking up on impact, a trick that boats such as the Hobie 14 and 16 were originally designed for. In extreme conditions the crew will let off the sail controls and lift the boards, drive the catamaran in on the top of a wave, then leap off, pull the boat clear of the water and spin it round into the wind before the next wave hits. This is not for the faint hearted, or for catamarans with relatively fragile hulls and rudders.

A second option is to drop the mainsail and come in under jib alone. With a ring and hook system you can drop the mainsail by heaving-to so that the head of the mainsail turns at 90 degrees to the mast and automatically lifts off the ring. You can then drop the mainsail and roll it up on the trampoline, before heading into shore. This is a technique that requires practice.

Launching in offshore winds

Push the boat into the water with rudders and boards raised. As soon as it's deep enough, approximately shin height, both crew choose a bow and hop on with feet dragging either side. Let the boat blow offshore, pushing down on the starboard bow will turn the catamaran to starboard and vice versa. When it's deep enough, walk back, drop the foils, and bear off downwind.

Coming ashore in onshore winds

Turn the catamaran head to wind. Lift the boards and rudders, and depower the sails. Sit on the bows and steer them towards the beach with the sterns lifted. Hop off at the last moment and grab the bows before the sterns touch the beach.

Catamaran tricks

The stability of two hulls means you can steer the boat downwind without rudders. This feature is useful when launching with offshore winds or coming ashore with onshore winds.

COMING ASHORE ON A DART 16

1 Make sure the mainsheet is unclipped and the downhaul loosened right off to depower the mainsail.

2 In this situation one crew may need to pull from the sides (using a shroud) to stop the boat slipping.

Tacking, gybing and capsize

Catamarans share the same principles as dinghies and use sailing techniques closest to gennaker-driven skiffs. However, there are a number of specific skills for two hulls.

TACKING

Owing to its width and twin hulls, a catamaran is likely to be considerably slower to tack than a monohull, and the tacking circle is wider as the outer hull has further to turn. Stalling is a particular problem with some older catamarans such as the Hobie 16, which are prone to come to a stop halfway through the tack due to their slab sides.

In general catamarans with daggerboards or centreboards will tack more easily since they have something to pivot around. All catamarans need to be kept moving through the turn, with particular attention to weight distribution, which on some classes may involve lifting the bows.

Tacking technique

The helmsperson steers into the tack, but does not slam the rudders over, which would make them act like two brakes. He or she must keep steering through the tack and not let the rudders centralize halfway, which will stall the boat.

On some catamaran classes both crew need to keep on the windward hull until the boat has passed through the eye of the wind. This lifts and lightens the leeward hull, so that the boat can spin round on the inside. Other catamarans tack faster if the bows are lifted – don't do this on a Hobie 14 or 16, which can quite easily capsize backwards.

The crew may need to keep the jib sheeted in until the boat starts to bear away on the new tack. This helps pull the bows round. The helm lets the mainsheet out enough for the battens to pop round, while continuing to steer through the tack, bear away, power up the catamaran and luff onto the new beating course.

If the catamaran stalls just as you've got onto the new tack it will soon start to move backwards. Try reversing the rudders and pushing against the boom, which will reverse the boat into the right position to start sailing forwards.

TACKING A CATAMARAN ....

1 The Dart 16 sails free at good speed as the crew comes in off the trapeze wire.

2 The crew crosses the trampoline as the catamaran turns, keeping forward and away from the helm.

3 Backing the jib helps pull the bows round. Care is needed to prevent stalling at head to wind.

4 The helmsperson crosses to the middle and concentrates on steering the boat round onto the new tack.

5 The helmsperson moves out while the crew sheets in, still keeping his weight forward on the trampoline.

6 The crew goes out on the wire while the helm gets the boat back up to speed before luffing.

GYBING

Catamarans are generally less intimidating to gybe than dinghies since the platform is so stable. However, you may be moving at considerable speed in a strong wind, and this speed must be maintained throughout the turn to keep the apparent wind, and the amount of power in the sails, to a minimum. The danger area during a gybe is when the boat swings dead downwind and starts to slow right down. If the catamaran is fitted with daggerboards or centreboards, the leeward board may need to be lifted halfway to prevent the boat tripping.

Beware of nose-diving during a gybe in strong winds. The leeward bow will go down if you accelerate into the gybe, and down again if the mainsail and boom crash across onto the new gybe. Keep your weight well back and help the mainsail across.

Gybing technique

The helmsperson turns to face aft during the gybe, kneeling by the rear beam in order to grab the falls of the mainsheet

ABOVE **If a catamaran stalls mid-way through a tack, you can back the jib and mainsail and reverse the rudders to pull the bows round.**

and help pull the mainsail over as the catamaran passes downwind. Avoid letting the mainsheet crash across of its own accord as the length of the traveller may generate enough momentum to throw the boat into a violent luff on the new gybe.

The helm must keep steering through the gybe and not let the rudders follow their natural tendency to straighten up. Once the mainsail has gone across the rudders must be straightened for the new gybe to prevent luffing.

GYBING A CATAMARAN

1 As the helmsperson bears away the bows tend to go down, so keep weight aft.

2 Both crew move inboard as the helmsperson starts bearing away.

3 The helmsperson turns to face aft and lifts the tiller extension.

4 The helmsperson then flicks the tiller extension onto the new side.

5 At the same time he moves across and pulls the mainsheet falls over.

6 Then he sheets in and powers away on the new gybe.

CAPSIZE

Righting a capsized catamaran presents considerably more of a challenge than righting a monohull, since you have to lift the combined weight of the rig, which with an elliptical mast and fully battened mainsail is heavy anyway, and the upper hull that will have tipped past the vertical.

Capsize technique

A catamaran can be sailed with the windward hull high in the sky, but will reach a point where capsize is inevitable.

Try not to throw yourself into the mainsail, which may break battens or push the boat into a complete inversion. Just slide down the trampoline into the water, and grab a line so you do not get separated from the boat – a capsized catamaran presents a lot of windage, and can blow away quickly. Once in the water, both crew should pull themselves round to the bottom, and clamber up on the side of the lower hull. This is a surprisingly comfortable place to take a breather, with time to assess the situation.

A pitchpole – when the bows drive down and the catamaran goes tail-over-nose – is likely to be considerably more violent than a conventional capsize when the boat blows over sideways. It will happen at speed, both helm and crew will be thrown forwards, and the crew may shoot round the forestay if he or she is out on the wire with the potential for cracked ribs on the gennaker pole. Both crew may also be thrown well clear of the capsized boat, so grab something as you go.

Capsize retrieval

To get a catamaran up, you often need to line up the capsized boat so the platform is lying downwind from the mast top. The wind will then blow directly against the topside of the trampoline, which helps push the platform vertical, and start to blow under the mainsail as soon as the rig lifts from the water. A capsized catamaran

CAPSIZING AND RIGHTING A DART 16 ....

1 A catamaran will usually go over slowly. Do not throw yourself into the mainsail.

2 The helm swims round to the back of the boat while the crew swims to the front beam.

3 The crew gets up on the lower hull and grabs the righting line, which is stowed by the mast foot.

4 He flips it over the top hull and passes the end to the helmsperson.

5 The crew leans out on the righting line while the helmsperson pulls from the main beam.

6 The boat starts coming up slowly, and then as the mast lifts accelerates.

7 Watch out when the top hull comes down. The crew must grab the dolphin striker in the middle.

8 From this position it's easy for the crew to get back on the trampoline.

9 The crew and helmsperson make sure everything is OK, then sail away.

will generally blow round into this position given time, but you can accelerate the process by standing on the lower bow. This lifts the stern and helps the boat pivot downwind.

Make sure all sheets are free and, if it's windy, let off the downhaul to fully depower the mainsail. With both crew standing on the lower hull, grab the righting line and throw the free end over the top of the upper hull. One crew leans back on the righting line until there is enough leverage to start lifting the mast off the water. Leverage can be increased by taking a turn round the harness hook, with both crew leaning out together – the crew can even sit on the helm's shoulders.

The rig will start to lift slowly, and then accelerate as it comes clear of the water. Stay under the trampoline as it comes upright, and watch out for the upper or leeward hull, which will come down with an almighty crash – don't let it fall on your head. The crew must be ready to grab the dolphin striker on the lower or windward side to prevent the boat blowing right over. The helm still holds the righting line so as not to be separated from the boat – a catamaran with a fully battened mainsail may try to sail off. The helmsperson can then climb in over the rear beam, and help the crew up over the front beam, ready to sort out the boat and sail away.

Turning turtle

If a catamaran turns turtle (upside down) it is still possible to get it upright.

Get up on the underside of the trampoline and take a breather. Make sure all control lines are free. Lead the righting line over the windward hull, then stand on the back of the leeward hull and pull.

Capsize problems

In some cases it is virtually impossible to right a catamaran without outside assistance. A rescue boat can aid retrieval by lifting the mast tip until the wind gets under the mainsail and your leverage is enough to pull the boat upright.

- If you are sailing single-handed there may not be enough wind blowing onto the trampoline to help lift the rig from the water.
- If you opt to sail a two-person boat single-handed, you may not have enough weight to lift the mast.
- The mast of a Tornado has internal halyards and will sink rapidly. Combined with its extreme width, this makes the Tornado prone to turn turtle and difficult to right.

This should raise the bows of the windward hull clear of the water, encouraging the mast to float upwards. Walk your weight forward to level out the leeward hull as the windward hull lifts above you. Continue to right the catamaran as normal.

PITCHPOLING AN OFFSHORE CATAMARAN...

1 An 8 metre (26ft) long racing catamaran will pitchpole if pushed too hard offwind.

2 Firebird *Orion* drives her bows down so hard that the sterns come right over.

3 Past the point of no return she turns turtle with the crew thrown into the sea.

Sailing upwind

Most catamarans with centreboards or daggerboards perform well with both boards fully down, but on some it pays to lift the windward board, which means the crew has to do a down-up sequence with the board during each tack.

The narrow, twin hulls of a catamaran will tend to stick to the water in light winds, when it is vital to move weight forward, so the crew sits on or even in front of the forward beam. This will lift the sterns and help prevent them

dragging, while the crew sit close together and as still as possible in order not to disturb water flow over the hulls or wind flow over the sails. It may pay to heel the catamaran slightly to windward, increasing waterline length while lifting the windward hull if possible. The most important thing is to keep the boat sailing free and moving, with light mainsheet tension.

As the wind picks up the catamaran should be sailed with the windward hull just skimming the surface of the water, if it is

lifted any higher the leeward hull will start to dig in and slow you down. Weight still needs to be well forward to lift the sterns. The crew typically trapezes with one leg in front of the shroud, and the helm is directly next to him or her. The mainsheet should be well tensioned without going so far as to hook the leech to windward.

In stronger winds, the crew will need to move far enough back to prevent the leeward bow making a nose dive. Both crew have to work to hold the windward

UPWIND VARIATIONS ON A DART 16

In light winds it's vital to prevent the sterns dragging by moving forwards.

In light winds it also helps to take weight off the windward hull by moving inboard.

Never pinch a catamaran by pointing too high. It's best to go for speed as shown.

The catamaran should be sailed with the windward hull just skimming the water.

Let the hull get this high and you dig in the leeward hull and slow right down.

As the wind increases the crew can move back, but not so far that you sink the stern.

hull just clear of the water, with the crew setting the downhaul to depower the mainsail until it's at maximum tension.

From then on the helm will need to ease the mainsheet from its hard-in setting while sailing into gusts, which can be both tiring and difficult when the helm also has to contend with directing the boat through waves. On some smaller catamarans it pays for the crew to play the jib, which opens the slot and depowers the boat enough to bring the windward hull back down. On larger catamarans the crew may need to cleat the jib and take the mainsheet, trimming to the helmsperson's call. If the boat is still overpowered, easing the mainsheet traveller away from the centreline will make it easier to handle.

Strong arm tactics

If you can't point as high as the next catamaran, it's probably because you are not pulling in enough mainsheet. Try pulling in the mainsheet as hard as you can, and set up a test to discover if you pull in less on port tack (the left arm is the weak arm for most of us) than starboard tack. You can do this on shore:

- Point the catamaran into the wind.
- Hike or trapeze as if sailing to windward and sheet in as hard as you can on one side. Get your crew to mark where the sheet exits from the blocks.
- Repeat the process on the other side, but this time close your eyes so you don't attempt to compensate. Get the crew to mark the sheet once again and you are likely to be amazed at the difference.

The next stage is to get the mainsheet right in on the water. Pull it in as hard as you can when hiking or on the trapeze, then tuck the tiller under your back arm so you have both hands free to haul the mainsheet in some more.

ABOVE **On the Tornado it's normal for the crew to play the mainsheet, which requires a lot of strength while the helm plays the traveller.**

ABOVE **The helm has his hands full getting the mainsail hard in on this Formula 18 while his crew sorts out packing the gennaker.**

Weather helm

This will be most pronounced when sailing upwind, and is usually caused by poorly adjusted rudder blades. There should be no backward movement when the blades are locked fully down – the slightest tilt is enough to cause weather helm.

If you have weather helm on one tack and lee helm on the other, it is probably caused by a twisted rudder blade, which will affect the boat upwind and offwind. You can diagnose the problem by sailing the boat in a moderate wind on a broad reach, lifting first one and then the other rudder, and repeating the process on both tacks. If one rudder is clearly at fault, it may need to be replaced.

Sailing offwind

On a reaching course you should aim to fly the windward hull, with the leeward board down and the windward board retracted. The traveller should be eased away from the centreline to remove twist from the leech, keeping the sail powered up to the maximum when sheeted hard in.

The helmsperson needs to bear away in gusts and luff in lulls to maximize apparent wind and keep the boat moving at full speed, as well as using waves to help acceleration. In survival conditions bear away and sail low to reduce the apparent wind. Keep bearing away in big gusts until you are effectively dead downwind or even by the lee, but luff when the gust has passed.

Tacking downwind

Most catamarans will sail downwind fastest when they gybe from reach to reach with both boards fully retracted, using the apparent wind to build speed, which is substantially faster and more fun than sailing on a dead downwind course. The only time when a dead downwind course might be faster is in very light winds.

An effective method of judging downwind angles is to use a wind indicator mounted on the bridle, and steer a course at 90 degrees to the apparent wind. If the wind indicator points back, bear away to sail lower; if it points forward, head up to build speed.

Preventing a nose dive

All catamarans are prone to nose dives when sailing on a fast reach in moderate to strong winds. A leeward nose dive can lead to a cartwheel on any reaching course; a double nose dive can lead to a pitchpole, and only occurs on a very broad reach typically when the apparent wind has suddenly swung aft due to the boat stopping. Nose-dives in general can be caused by:

- Crew weight too far forward.
- Not easing the sheets when you bear away.
- Too much power in the rig, which is the result of failing to bear away in a gust.
- Driving the boat into the back of a wave where it comes to a dead stop.
- An uncontrolled gybe when the bow goes down due to gybing too tightly in strong winds, letting the boom crash across, or letting go of the tiller.
- Insufficient buoyancy in the bows, which is a design problem.

ABOVE **The Hobie 16 enjoys a wild ride on a downwind course, while the wind indicator shows that the apparent wind is on the beam.**

Keeping the crew weight back is the best way of preventing the catamaran from nose diving. If it's a twin wire boat, the helmsperson will have better control sitting in by the rear beam. The crew can

DOWNWIND VARIATIONS ON A DART 16 ....

Sailing in a light wind of Force 1-2 the crew need to concentrate on lifting the windward hull so that it does not stick to the surface.

When the wind picks up to Force 3–4 (7–16 knots) the crew moves aft and stands by the helmsperson to prevent the bows burying.

Deep downwind in a strong wind, with the traveller right out, the crew sits inboard to help lift the windward hull.

ABOVE **A wildthing variation is possible on the Dart 16 although, with no centreboard or daggerboard to push against and help hold the hull up, it's less effective.**

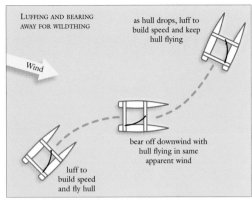

LUFFING AND BEARING AWAY FOR WILDTHING

Wind

as hull drops, luff to build speed and keep hull flying

bear off downwind with hull flying in same apparent wind

luff to build speed and fly hull

ABOVE **Wildthing means following a course like a snake, with constant repetitions of luffing to fly the hull and bearing away to go deep downwind.**

move right back and straddle the helm, using a rear foot loop for security, or clipping onto a retaining line attached to the rear beam, which will prevent him or her being pulled forwards. If the leeward bow goes down:

• Let off the jib.
• Move your weight back.
• Let the jib fly.
• Let off the mainsheet.
• Do not luff or bear away, which can make it worse by holding the leeward bow down or accelerating the boat.

Wildthing

Australian catamaran champion Mitch Booth – Tornado winner of Bronze and Silver Medals at the 1992 and 1996 Olympics – is credited as the inventor of wildthing.

The object of wildthing is to sail as deep as possible while flying downwind on a single hull. If you get it right it is the fastest way to go downwind, depending on the catamaran you are sailing it can be effective in winds from about Force 3 (10 knots) upwards. The trick is to build

apparent wind by luffing, hold it when you bear away, and with the reduced wetted area of one hull streak away from catamarans that are sailing downwind with both hulls stuck to the water. To keep the boat flying the crew must sit down to leeward, which requires plenty of nerve and firm control in strong winds, with the leeward centreboard or daggerboard down to give the windward hull something to push against.

The helmsperson sets the main traveller close to the leeward footstrap, sheets in hard, luffs, flies the hull and accelerates. As this happens the helmsperson bears away quickly and smoothly so that the boat keeps flying and accelerating, easing the mainsheet if the boat fails to bear away. When the hull begins to drop, the process is repeated, resulting in a kind of tightly spaced slalom on a dead downwind course.

Whistle-stop

The sound of rudder blades whistling at speed pleases some people and convinces others that turbulence is slowing them down. If it displeases you, try lightly filing and flattening the trailing edge of the blades at 90 degrees; if that doesn't work, try the same treatment at 45 degrees both sides.

ABOVE **Wildthing was first used on the Tornado. Despite the sails being sheeted hard in, this boat is sailing downwind.**

Gennaker basics

The principal difference between sailing with a gennaker on a catamaran and most monohulls is that the gennaker can only be launched from behind the jib – normally from a bag on the trampoline.

Chutes and gennaker poles

Some catamarans have a chute, but this has to lie down one side of the trampoline where it gets in the way and doesn't have the advantages of a monohull chute that launches with the gennaker in front of the forestay. Another important difference is that the gennaker pole is permanently rigged between the front hulls and bridle, and not launched from the boat as on most monohulls. To avoid having to use an oversize section, the pole is usually pre-bent to stiffen its middle section and inhibit flex when pulled by the gennaker.

Slow upwind

With a fixed pole and bag there is a lot of extra clutter on a catamaran fitted with a gennaker, and it will be slower upwind than an identical catamaran sailing with mainsail, jib and no gennaker. This has been proven by trials with Tornados, with and without gennakers. The gennaker slows the boat for various reasons:
- Extra weight and windage.
- The halyard breaking up air flow round the elliptical mast.
- Clutter on the trampoline slowing down tacks.
- Pole length making manoeuvres, such as pushing in on the start line or crossing tacks, more difficult.

Fast downwind

A gennaker is certainly more effective downwind, allowing the catamaran to sail deeper even if it doesn't go faster. However time lost hoisting and lowering the gennaker, as well as dealing with the

LEFT The gennaker is a mixed blessing when sailing a catamaran as the additional clutter and weight of a fixed pole and bag slows the boat down going upwind.

problems that an out-of-control gennaker can cause, means that it needs a very long downwind leg for a gennaker-driven catamaran to win back lost ground. The conclusion is that, unless courses are predominantly downwind, a gennaker adds both hassle and expense to a catamaran in return for a marginal improvement in performance. However, broad reaching with a gennaker is considerably more fun than with jib and main alone, and for that reason the gennaker seems destined to become a common accessory on most catamarans.

Gennaker techniques on catamarans are virtually the same as on gennaker-driven skiffs fitted with a bag, but some points need to be highlighted.

ABOVE **Offwind the gennaker is a total blessing: it looks great, feels great, is a lot of fun to sail with and helps the catamaran go deeper downwind.**

ABOVE **The skipper lifts both windward foils to maximize offwind performance on the Hobie Tiger.**

Hoists and drops

The gennaker can only go up on the same side as it comes down, which makes it important to drop the gennaker on the right side for the next hoist during a race.

Hoisting to leeward is favourite. The gennaker goes up on the correct leeward side of the mainsail, and the helm bears away from a beam reach in anything more than light winds. Hoisting to windward requires turning well downwind to let the gennaker blow out to the end of the pole, before the helmsperson luffs to blow it

RIGHT **This Hawk looks neatly controlled as it sails a gybe-to-gybe downwind leg.**

across the forestay onto the leeward side. All this must be done quickly to avoid the gennaker taking a wrap.

Dropping to windward is favourite, but the helm has to turn well downwind to float the gennaker round the forestay to the windward side. Allowing the gennaker to drop between the hulls and then running over it is a disaster. The sail must be pulled in fast and the halyard must run free; if in any doubt, throw the coiled halyard over the rear beam and let it stream astern.

Dropping to leeward has the disadvantage of putting the crew down on the leeward side of the catamaran. In anything more than very light winds the helmsperson would need to bear right away to manage this without the windward hull lifting. Beware of catching the gennaker round one of the mainsail batten ends.

A drop-gybe lets you drop the gennaker on the windward side of the catamaran, without having to bear away and pull it round the forestay:

- Reach in on port tack.
- Helm bears away and gybes mainsail.
- As the boom comes across, the crew moves to the new windward side of the boat (starboard side), drops gennaker, which is immediately to hand and on the right tack for a port tack hoist.
- Always remember to pull the gennaker and all its ropes in under the jib sheet during the drop.

ABOVE **You can only sail so high with a gennaker. Any more wind, and the helm will need to bear away to maintain control.**

Reaching control

Keeping control of a catamaran and its gennaker follows the same main principle as on a monohull, if the sail collapses or a gust hits you need to bear away and go with the apparent wind.

You will need both centreboards or daggerboards right down to minimize leeway on a reach. To maximize leeway when sailing downwind, pull them right up. If you are bearing away to absorb a gust on a reach and the boat trips on the leeward board, you need to half-raise both boards, although the windboard could be further down to allow for lift out of the water.

In extreme conditions the elliptical mast of a catamaran will pant – flex rapidly from side to side – when you let the gennaker flog in a hard gust. This is a clear indication that the time has come to get it down.

Capsizing with a gennaker

If you capsize with a gennaker, do not attempt to right the boat with it up unless the wind conditions are very light. Lower the gennaker while the catamaran is on its side, and bundle it on top of its bag where it will sit while the catamaran is being righted.

RACING AND REGATTA SAILING

Many sailors respond to the thrill of dinghy and small boat racing, which is without doubt the best way to improve all high performance sailing techniques. Those who race learn to sail faster, tack faster, gybe faster and keep their boats under perfect control, as well as developing the instinct for tactical superiority that puts them in the right place at the right time.

Anyone who wants to get to the front of a fleet will need to develop finely honed skills, combined with a real determination to win, but this does not exclude less committed sailors who quite rightly view their sport as a means of relaxation and fun. While Olympic racing has evolved into a totally dedicated, full-time career, which is only accessible or even desirable for a very few, local club racing should provide the opportunity for sailors of all abilities and inclinations to get out and have a good time on the water and it really doesn't matter if you come last.

LEFT *Racing enables you to practise and improve your sailing skills and builds team spirit.*

BELOW *Picos are a good introduction to competetion as well as being fun social events.*

Racing courses and rules

Dinghy and small boat racing makes use of a comparatively simple format revolving around crossing a start and finish line, sailing a course with marks to indicate each turn, and abiding by rules so that everyone races fairly and safely together.

Triangle and sausage

The triangle and sausage is the traditional style of course that offers beating, running and reaching in equal measure, though the beating legs take at least 50 per cent of the time. There are three marks of the course – a windward mark (1) at the top of the course, a wing mark (2) out to the side of the course, and a leeward mark (3) at the bottom of the course. On the old Olympic course the upwind leg could be as long as 3km (2 miles), with a total distance round the course of 11km (7 miles) equivalent to about 19km (12 miles) sailed. For club racing, the distances need be no more than a few hundred metres.

The start line is laid at the bottom of the course and, at club level, may incorporate mark 3 as an end marker. The line is angled close to 90 degrees to the wind to give a dead upwind beat to windward off the line, but should have a slight bias in favour of the port end of the line. This will prevent starboard tack boats from all bunching up at the starboard end of the line, where the start/committee boat is normally situated. The finish line is laid at the top of the course and, at club level, may incorporate mark 1 as an end marker. The line is angled at 90 degrees to the wind to give a perfect beating finish.

The traditional triangle and sausage course is laid as an equilateral triangle, which provides two broad reaches from marks 1–2 and 2–3. The wing mark can be moved closer to the beating/running line to provide more variety, with a close reach followed by a broad reach.

Sausages and triangles can be used in any order and with any number of laps, but always with a start and finish to windward. All marks are rounded to port. The pattern of a typical race might be:
- Start
- Beat to 1
- Bear off for a reach to 2
- Gybe for a reach to 3
- Head up for a beat to 1
- Bear off or gybe for a run to 3
- Gybe or head up for a beat to 1 and finish

Trapezoid

The three-sided triangle and sausage course is confusing and very boring for spectators when boats are scattered all over the water, some sailing the triangle and others the sausage, a huge beating area and no easily identifiable leaders. A new four-sided trapezoid course was therefore introduced at the 1996 Olympics, which

LEFT **Lasers can lay claim to being the perfect sailboat racing class, offering the keenest competition in a simple low cost boat with a total one-design format. They are extremely physical at top level, requiring a level of commitment that makes Olympic standard racing a virtual full-time occupation.**

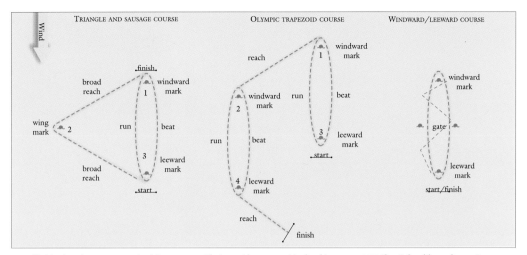

TRIANGLE AND SAUSAGE COURSE   OLYMPIC TRAPEZOID COURSE   WINDWARD/LEEWARD COURSE

ABOVE **The triangle and sausage course, involving long beats and dead downwind runs, is a traditional favourite, but confusing for spectators.**

ABOVE **The trapezoid course was introduced to offer better spectator interest, with a reach to the end to provide a thrilling finish.**

ABOVE **The windward/leeward course is very simple, and relies on the fastest racing boats, which tack from reach to reach, going downwind.**

was designed to be more compact and easier to understand, as well as providing more high speed reaching to thrill spectators and competitors and win better TV coverage.

The trapezoid course has two windward and two leeward marks, and all boats sail the same course throughout the race. There are beating and running legs

on either side of the course between marks 4 and 1 and marks 3 and 2, separated by reaching legs across the top and bottom of the course between marks 1 and 2 and marks 3 and 4.

Course marks can be used in different orders, but races always start with a beat to sort out competitors on the start line

and end with a reach to show which boats are leading on the last leg to the finish line, as well as displaying them at their fastest and most impressive.

The trapezoid course is used for the slower Olympic classes such as 470s, Finns and Europe dinghies, and variations can be used for dinghy racing at all levels.

Windward/leeward

The windward/leeward course is specifically designed for gennaker-driven dinghies and catamarans, which tack downwind by gybing from reach to reach. In the Olympics it is used for the 49er and Tornado that are the two fastest boats in the event. The course is simplicity itself, with just a beat and a run, which is always sailed as a series of fast reaches. The length of the course varies enormously and will depend on where the event is being sailed, with a maximum distance between top and bottom marks of about 2½km (1½ miles).

The boats start from a conventional start line, which is normally 50m (165ft) or so to leeward of the bottom mark of the course. After a 6-5-1 minute starting signal sequence they start the race. The first leg is straight to windward, beating up to the

ABOVE **The 470s now race round a trapezoid course in both men's and women's Olympic classes, offering close-quarters beat to reach racing.**

ABOVE **These two 49ers are at the start of the downwind leg on a windward/leeward course, ready to gybe all the way down to the bottom.**

ABOVE **The windward boat keeps clear rule means the overtaking Laser 4000 must stay upwind until it is clear ahead of the other boat.**

top windward mark, which competitors leave to port. From there they gybe back down to the bottom of the course. Some courses use a mid-way gate on the downwind leg, which keeps the boats together, stops them sailing far out to the sides of the course, and helps ensure spectators can follow the action.

At the bottom of the course there may be a single leeward mark, which competitors round to port, or a two mark gate, which is the more interesting option. Competitors can turn round either side of the gate but it is usual for starboard tack

boats to turn round the starboard side marker and port tack boats turn round the port side marker, before starting the beat back up the course. The finish line is at the bottom end of the course and is a straightforward downwind reaching finish when competitors do not have to round the bottom mark.

Races are usually based on a time factor. Depending on wind conditions, the race management fixes the number of laps calculated to come closest to a target time of one hour for Olympic classes – four laps is about average.

Rules

Racing rules were originally drafted to prevent collisions and ensure racing was safe. However over the years they have become more and more complex as a direct result of competitors pushing the limits and finding loopholes in the rules. In some cases this has led to a style of racing far removed from the ideal of sporting enthusiasm, and sailors, who play the rules rather than the game, resorting to sailing rule litigation and long, acrimonious and frequently incomprehensible protest deliberations.

A minority of sailors will continue to enjoy this type of racing where mental cunning and subterfuge is at a premium, but most just want to get on and enjoy the race. There has been a backlash against wanton rule exploitation and an attempt to simplify the rules and, as gennaker-driven boats go faster and the dangers of collision become greater, more competitors stick to a basic principle of keeping out of trouble and finishing the race.

Port gives way to starboard but not without fail. The starboard tack boat has a duty to avoid a collision and give the port tack boat a route of escape, and cannot alter its course to catch a boat on starboard. Common sense and seamanship also plays a role, and it is not unusual for a starboard tack boat to dip behind a port tack boat on a windward leg, and expect to have the favour returned next time they cross tacks.

Windward boat keeps clear applies to two boats on the same tack. In essence it means that a boat that is overtaking a slower boat to leeward must keep clear once

ABOVE **Competition in a class such as the 470, is so close that skipper and crew must understand the racing rules and how they affect them.**

ABOVE **Championship fleet racing requires a strategy of scoring a consistent level of low points, without any high numbers, in order to win.**

its bows have overtaken the stern of the other boat and established an overlap. This can apply to a beating, reaching or running leg of the race. It also allows the boat that is being overtaken to luff to windward, but when doing so it must give the overtaking boat room to keep clear in order to avoid any possibility of collision.

A boat clear astern must keep clear When coming up from behind a boat is not allowed to run into one in front, sailing instead to either side.

Overlap at the mark If two boats are turning round a mark together on the same tack, the inside boat has right of way if it has established an overlap before

getting within two boat lengths of the mark. This should prevent anyone trying to crash in at the last second.

Protests and penalties

We all make mistakes, and it is easy to infringe one of the basic racing rules, particularly in the hurly-burly of bearing off or gybing round a mark. Racing rule verdicts are designed to be black and white, and in most cases it should be fairly easy to make an instant decision if you were right or wrong.

If you were wrong Most instructions will absolve you from blame if you do a 360 or 720 degree spin (720 for infringement with another competitior and 360 for hitting a mark), which must be completed as soon as is possible and practical. If you chose to ignore this, you can expect a protest from the other boat.

If you were right You can protest if the other boat does not do the appropriate 360 or 720 degree spin. To do so you need to fly a red protest flag, look for witnesses, and be prepared for a long protest meeting with the race committee once racing is over. Whoever loses the protest will be disqualified.

ABOVE **After a long beat, Lasers bear off round the top windward mark. The inside boats have right of way so long as overlaps have been established before they get within two lengths of the mark.**

Race scoring

The scoring in most race and regatta series is based on the Olympic system of awarding first place to the competitor with the lowest number of points. Each race counts as follows:

- First: 1 point
- Second: 2 points
- Third: 3 points, etc
- Did not start/compete (DNS/DNC): number of entries plus 1
- Premature start (PMS): number of entries plus 2
- Disqualified (DSQ): number of entries plus 1
- Retired (RET): number of entries plus 1

Sailing instructions will typically allow one discard in a five-race series and competitors will count the best four races for their overall total.

Starting a race

In many ways the start is the most stressful part of a race. Competitors are crammed into close company and theoretically have an equal chance of making a good start. In reality only a minority will leave the start line first and fastest; they will have an enormous advantage due to sailing in clear wind; and they are in a good position to maintain that advantage throughout the race.

Allow plenty of time before the start of a race. You cannot rush rigging and launching and expect to be in a winning state if you reach the start area with 30 seconds to go. Allowing too much time is better than too little. You can then do some exercises and loosen up, or have a sandwich and a drink but no coffee or beer, which are both diuretic.

If there is a skippers' meeting before the start you need to go to it. Information provided will include types of courses, starting times and sequences, and specific local difficulties. You must read and understand the sailing instructions, which should be issued at the start of any series race or regatta. Check carefully whether the sailing instructions require extras such as a tow rope, anchor or flares to be carried while racing. If you fail to carry the right equipment, you may be disqualified. Most regatta organisers will operate a safety system, which ensures that all starters return to the beach. The sailing instructions will tell you whether you are expected to sign on or sign off or post a tally at the start or finish of each race. If you fail to do so, you may be disqualified. You may also need to put an entry number on your boat.

Rig the boat methodically, checking for wear and tear and replacing and repairing as necessary. Check the weather forecast, and rig the boat for the expected conditions. Consider the sea and air temperature and how wind chill will effect your own body, and dress accordingly. Dress up, not down, and make sure you go to the lavatory before struggling into a wetsuit or drysuit. Check tides in the race area, and where and when they are running. Local sailors will normally help out with advice.

If you are going to be a long time on the water, perhaps doing two races back to back, you will need to take food, drink and maybe suntan protection. The aim of food

ABOVE **Know your boat. In a big event you need to know where you left it, and be prepared to get on to the water and out to the start before the main rush.**

ABOVE **Racing is not all about Olympic standard sailing. It is possible to have a lot of fun in a Pico, which can offer a perfect introduction to competition.**

ABOVE **Make sure you understand the layout of the course, how many times you have to go round, which way to leave the marks and the starting sequence.**

ABOVE **Preparation is all. If you have the facility to tune the rig for specific conditions, such as with adjusting the length of the spreaders, you need to be prepared to do so as the wind changes.**

and drink is to rehydrate and energise, and whatever you choose needs to be compact and easily stowed.

Start signals

In the hurly-burly of the start it is vital to understand start signals. These will be set out in the sailing instructions or at the skippers' meeting, and may vary in timing and style. Start signals at a mixed regatta should go something like this:

Ten minutes before the start Sound signal (gun or horn) from the starter or race officer who will hoist the class flag for the next start. A red flag or sign will indicate that you should leave marks to port; a green flag leave marks to starboard. If there are different courses the course number will be posted in an easily visible position, and will have to be checked off against course maps in the sailing instructions.

Five minutes before the start Second sound signal (gun or horn) from the starter who will hoist the Blue Peter (International Code P) alongside the class flag to indicate prepare for the start.

The start Third sound signal (gun or horn) from the starter who will drop both the Blue Peter and class flag at the exact moment of the start. In some regattas this may also be the ten-minute signal for the next class.

RIGHT **The flags you might see flying on the committee boat at the start line. A for Alpha is just one possibility for the class flag, while all the other flags are standard. PAPA = Preparatory flag (5 minutes to start).XRAY = Individual Recall. First Substitute = General Recall. INDIA = One Minute Rule (Boats on course side of start line within 1 minute of start must sail back round either end before starting). AP Code and Answering Pennant = Postponement. ZULU = Z Flag Rule (Boats in triangle between start line and windward mark within 1 minute of start receive 20 per cent scoring penalty if there is a general recall). SIERRA = Shortened course. YANKEE = Buoyancy must be worn (though this is invariably mandatory). BLACK = Black Flag (Boats in triangle between start line and windward mark within 1 minute of start are disqualified). NOVEMBER = Abandon race. CHARLIE = Change of course.**

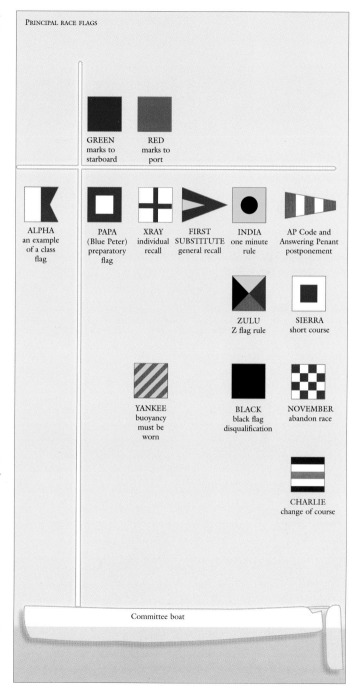

PRINCIPAL RACE FLAGS

GREEN
marks to
starboard

RED
marks to
port

ALPHA
an example
of a class
flag

PAPA
(Blue Peter)
preparatory
flag

XRAY
individual
recall

FIRST
SUBSTITUTE
general recall

INDIA
one minute
rule

AP Code and
Answering Penant
postponement

ZULU
Z flag rule

SIERRA
short course

YANKEE
buoyancy
must be
worn

BLACK
black flag
disqualification

NOVEMBER
abandon race

CHARLIE
change of course

Committee boat

Start line bias

If a start line is laid at exactly right angles to the wind, it will give a clear advantage to starboard tack boats that start to windward on the starboard end of the line. The start line should ideally be laid with an 80 degree bias in favour of the port end of the line – theoretically all boats hitting the line at the same moment will then be equal.

In practice it is extremely difficult to lay a perfect line, particularly in the morning when the wind is likely to back and veer before it settles down to a more consistent direction. The race officer may be forced to keep postponing and re-laying the start line, which is frustrating for competitors. Or he or she may decide to start them regardless, in which case it is vital to assess how the line is biased. If the wind veers and comes from further to starboard, boats at the starboard end of the line will have an advantage and be able to point higher while sailing off the line, while port tack and port end boats point lower. If the wind backs and comes from further to port, boats at the port end of the line will have an advantage and be able to point higher while sailing off the line, while starboard tack and starboard end boats point lower. It may even be possible to start with a port end, port tack flyer, which means sailing so fast and high on

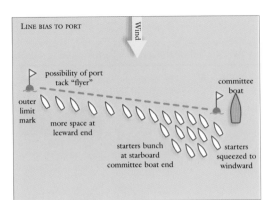

LINE BIAS TO PORT

Wind

possibility of port tack "flyer"

committee boat

outer limit mark

more space at leeward end

starters bunch at starboard committee boat end

starters squeezed to windward

LEFT **If the start line is exactly at right angles to the wind, all boats will want to start at the starboard end. Laying the port end marker angled towards the windward mark gives a more equal chance all the way along the line.**

port that you can sail across the course clear of all the boats on starboard.

You can assess line bias by watching boats sailing off either end of the line. If a boat sailing off the port end of the line on port tack can clearly point higher than a starboard end and starboard tack boat, the line is biased to port. A more accurate method of assessing line bias may be to use a compass. The standard method is to sail straight along the line and take a compass reading (A). Then point the boat straight into the wind from the middle of the line and take a compass reading (B). If the difference between A and B is greater or less than 90 degrees, the line is biased by the same number of degrees.

A start line may also be biased due to tides when tidal flow is stronger at one end or the other. This is difficult to assess without prior experience and will also depend on how flow relates to the time of day.

Countdown

Get out to the start line at least five minutes before the ten-minute signal. Assess line bias and from there decide from which end and on which tack you want to cross the line. If the line is crowded it may be impossible to see the end markers, and therefore difficult to tell if you are behind or over the line when there is a recall immediately after the start signal. It may help to sight down the line and pick a

ABOVE **The Laser class flag and Blue Peter are up, as Lasers line up along the line in the five minutes before a race start.**

ABOVE **Second row boats are already breaking away on port tack in an attempt to clear their wind after this Laser 4000 start.**

LEFT **Hobie 16s nudge up to the start line. It's an anxious time with boats pushing and shoving and, to make things even more difficult, the Hobie is impossible to steer if it loses momentum.**

fixed transit, which will provide this information – a solitary tree or large block of flats on the shoreline could be ideal.

Before the ten-minute gun, allow time to sail off the line as you would for the start. Beat to windward for 200 metres or so to check the boat is set up properly, and also look for the first marker if it is in sight. Put your watch into countdown mode,

ready to start it at the ten-minute signal. It's optional whether the crew or helmsperson (or both) takes this responsibility.

Check that your watch countdown is set correctly at the five-minute gun.

The start

The theory of a good start is to cross the line at maximum speed as the gun goes, so

you have clear wind with no boats ahead to windward or to leeward. The reality is rather different. At Olympic standard sailors tend to be so closely matched that they all sit on the line before the start and then accelerate off the line together. At lower standards, a handful of sailors who are more clever and experienced, or simply lucky, will get away first and fastest, while the rest are stuck in dirty wind.

Unless there is plenty of room on the line, most sailors will choose to move into a pre-start position where they will sit and reserve their space in the last three or four minutes before the starting gun. On a crowded line boats may be stacked two or three rows deep, those at the front having a major advantage of clean air after the start. You can only sit on starboard tack, which has right of way over all port tack starters, and cannot bear down on boats to leeward. If a boat to leeward luffs head to wind, the windward boat must keep clear. If you are pushed over the line, the only way out is to sail round one end of the line

Dirty wind

This is caused by the turbulence or blanketing effect of another boat's sails when it is anything less than three or four boat lengths ahead. It may be caused by:

- A boat that is ahead and to windward, when you will fall directly into its wind shadow.
- A boat that is directly ahead, when you will be affected by both wind shadow and turbulence off its sails.
- A boat that is ahead and to leeward, when you will be affected by the turbulence off its sails.

In all cases your boat will sail more slowly and point lower until you are at least level with the other boat. The most likely solutions out of the situation are to luff and sail through to windward, which will only work if you have superior technique, or to change tacks. Sailing through to leeward is seldom possible.

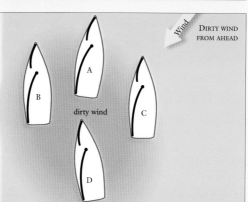

LEFT **49ers bunch up in the final countdown to the start. Those in the second row have little chance of winning.**

LEFT **Dirty wind can come from ahead or from both sides. The result is always the same, the boat getting the dirt goes slower and won't point so high. Leading boat A creates dirty wind for B to leeward, for C to windward and for D behind. They will not point so high or foot so fast.**

and join the back of the queue – with plenty of dirty wind to look forward to on the first beat. When moving into your parking position, aim for a spot that is several lengths up the line from where you want to start since your boat will drift sideways. It is possible to hold your position by carefully luffing, and even backing the sails, moving slowly sideways down the line at the same pace as all other boats using this stratagem.

Beware of getting stuck at one end of the line in the last three minutes. If you are to windward of the start mark at the starboard end, it may be impossible to bear away and get in on the line. If you are to leeward of the outer end mark at the port end, it may be impossible to get in on the line without tacking onto port. Aim to be about three lengths behind the line as your watch counts down to the last ten seconds. Leave enough space to leeward so you can bear off, accelerate for the line, and hit it going fast.

At all costs avoid pinching or pointing too high into the wind at the start, which will allow other boats to sail over you and get ahead.

WHEN THE GUN GOES ....

1 49ers reach down to the port end of the line in the moments before the start ready to power off the line at full speed.

2 The gun goes and the Norwegian boat gets away first, but the leeward British boat is squeezed out by dirty wind.

Port or Starboard

- Starting on starboard tack is the safe option in a crowded start since you have right of way over any port tack boats. However, the disadvantage is that most boats will probably start on starboard as well, and the only way you can beat them is to cross the line first and fastest.
- Starting on port tack is a potential high risk option, which can pay handsomely if there is clear bias to the port end.
- If there is an advantage in sailing out to the right side of the course – due to an obvious wind bend, which will let you sail higher, or an advantageous tidal flow – it may pay to start on the starboard tack at the starboard end of the line, with a view to tacking onto

port within seconds of the start signal. This stratagem can also be used to get clear wind from the rest of the starboard tack fleet.

ABOVE **A venue with very strong tides and crowded waters, may dictate that all racers start on port tack in order to keep close inshore and cheat the tide as this fleet of Dragons are doing.**

Penalties

If there is only one sound signal at the start, everyone has started correctly.

If there are two sound signals, one or more boats are over the line and must sail back and recross the line without getting in the way of any other competitors. This is marked by the XRAY flag. Any boat that fails to restart will be disqualified, which is why it is important to be able to assess if you have started correctly.

If there are three sound signals, the majority of the fleet is over the line and there is a general recall for another start, marked by the First Substitute flag. After a general recall, the race officer will generally enforce a one minute rule marked by the INDIA flag. Any boat that gets pushed over the line during the minute before the start is black flagged, and must go round the outer ends of the line to rejoin the start or be disqualified.

If you cross the finish line in a winning position, but the finish boat appears to ignore you with no gun or hooter to signal your achievement, you can assume you have been disqualified

from the start. It pays to be very careful on the start line, or risk the frustration of sailing a winning race for a score equivalent to the number of entries plus one.

Leaving the line

The immediate requirement on leaving the start line is to sail as fast as possible in clear wind. Ideally the helmsperson should have allowed space to leeward to bear off a few degrees and get the boat going flat out. The crew need to put particular effort into powering up the boat, with hiking done in the most effective straight legs position, which can only be held for a short time. The crew should watch boats all round, and tell the helm if the boat is sailing into a wind shadow.

If luffing or bearing away fails to solve the problem of being blanketed, then the crew must look for the first possible opportunity to tack onto port and sail with clear wind. When tacking you have no rights over boats sailing a course on port or starboard, and must wait for a suitably large hole to windward. To make the move worthwhile you should also allow enough space to clear boats coming up on starboard once you are on port

tack. The alternative to tacking back onto starboard is to dip behind them by bearing away round their transom.

Gate start

This start is sometimes used in a big fleet of identical boats. One competitor is chosen as the "pathfinder" who, as the gun goes, leaves the port end of the line on port tack, sailing as high and as fast as possible with the option of an official starter's boat known as the gate boat following close behind. The rest of the fleet have to pass behind the pathfinder or gate boat on starboard tack in order to start.

The major advantages of this system are that no one is over the line so there are no recalls or false starts, and every boat has a good chance of starting in clean air. The main problem is that the pathfinder cannot sail a dead straight course or at a speed that matches every other boat in the fleet and, if the differences are great, when and where you start will be important. If the gate boat is relatively slow and/or being headed, it pays to start as early as possible. If the pathfinder is relatively fast and/or being lifted, it pays to start as late as possible.

Racing upwind

A race is traditionally won or lost when racing upwind by fast sailing, quick tacking, tactical use of wind shifts, covering opponents and choosing the right side of the course as the fleet spreads out en route to the windward mark.

When and where to tack

The crew should feed information to the helm since he or she is likely to have a better view of the course, particularly from a trapeze. He or she can comment on the position of the windward mark, boats in the immediate vicinity, approaching waves that may stall the boat, approaching gusts that may require easing the main-sheet to keep the boat flat, signs of wind when drifting on an otherwise windless course, and whether boats on the opposite side of the course are heading any higher or lower on the same tack.

At a certain level, many competitors will be able to sail their boats at virtually identical speeds upwind. What sets them apart is where and when they tack. This is governed by how quickly you tack. A small single-hander such as a Laser can tack with minimal loss of ground; a big boat like a Tornado catamaran tacks slowly, and may lose several boat lengths in the process.

A compass is a useful tactical weapon when considering when to tack, and much more accurate than judging wind shifts by the seat of your pants or watching other boats. If your mean course is 180 degrees while sailing on starboard, a course change to 175 degrees indicates that you have been headed by five degrees, a header that scarcely warrants a tack.

ABOVE **The purple Laser 4000 has all the advantages, but needs to be flatter for optimum speed. Both 4510 and Team Unlimited should be slowed by dirty wind, but with dynamic sailing 4510 could climb out of it.**

ABOVE **Laser 2s race in close company upwind. The leeward boats will have to wait until there is a big enough gap to escape on port tack.**

The rhumb line

The direct line from the start to the windward mark is called the rhumb line. If the wind is shifty and there is no obvious advantage to be gained from sailing on either side of the course, it is generally safest to keep close to the rhumb line and sail up the middle of the beat. In certain circumstances a wind bend or tidal flow may favour sailing out to one side of the course.

In most races the upwind leg is repeated two or three times. After the first time, you should be able to work out if boats have done better by sailing up one side of the course. If they have it is likely to be due to more favourable winds and tides, but these conditions will not necessarily be repeated.

Why tack?

The first reason to tack is to clear your wind. The longer you are blanketed by another boat, the more time the leading boats have to pull away. The second is to capitalize on a wind shift. If you sail into a header, your course will alter so you point further away from the windward mark. However, it is important to ascertain how long the change in course will last before the wind reverts back to its mean direction. A gust or lull can have the effect of a temporary lifter or header due to the change in apparent wind direction. If the change in course lasts for seconds rather than minutes, the time spent tacking may lose more than it gains. The third is to get over to better wind, usually when there is very little wind but you can see ripples forming out to the windward side of your course.

Tacking does rely on confidence and skill. You need to know you will be able to tack quickly and effectively, are doing so at the right time, and can get back up to speed with minimal delay.

RIGHT **Close racing for Finns with 21 (2000 Sydney Olympics Gold medalist Iain Percy) just nudging ahead while the boat at the back of the bunch breaks away on port. It is extremely difficult to find clear air in such crowded conditions when tactical moves become as complex as a game of chess.**

ABOVE **Hobie 16s beat up to the windward mark in light winds. Stacking up for the turn before rounding the mark to head downwind requires a cautious approach under these circumstances.**

Port v starboard

When crossing tacks port always gives way to starboard, but starboard must maintain its proper beating course and not change direction in an effort to run down the port tacker. In reality, when two boats close on port and starboard, both crews will make a concerted effort to sail their boats as fast and high as possible. This is fair sailing and not to be confused with a wanton change of course – most likely bearing away – by the starboard tacker, which is not allowed.

If the port tack boat (A) is ahead, but not confident of clearing the starboard tack boat (B), it may tack just before crossing. If the tack is fast and effective, boat A will be able to accelerate ahead of B on the same tack, and far enough ahead to feed boat B with dirty wind, which is also known as the lee bow effect. From this position boat A can point higher and sail faster than boat B, moving directly in front and then to windward. In such circumstances boat B would have been better advised to slow down and let boat A cross tacks in front.

If the port tack boat (A) is likely to hit the starboard tack boat (B) amidships, bearing off to sail round B's transom is likely to lose less ground than throwing in an ill considered tack.

Lay lines

These are defined as the direct courses a boat would sail on port and starboard to reach the windward mark in a single tack. Tacks should become progressively shorter as a boat approaches the windward mark, and always kept within the lay lines. If a boat sails beyond the lay lines, it will have to bear off onto a fetch or even a reach to the mark, losing valuable ground to competitors who have stayed inside the lay line.

Windward mark

The final approach to the windward mark should be made on starboard tack to ensure right of way. Approaching on port is a high risk venture. This means that the final approach will follow the lay line on the starboard side of the course. However, this final approach should be kept to less than 100m (330ft) to minimise the effect of wind shifts. If the wind lifts, you will have to bear away for the mark having lost time and distance. If the wind heads, boats approaching on the opposite tack (port) will be lifted and be able to tack ahead of you, giving you dirty wind to help push your course below the lay line.

A late approach to the starboard lay line reduces the chances of being adversely caught by a wind shift. However, unless you are leading, you may have to dodge a procession of boats following the lay line on starboard tack. Do not tack to leeward of them even if you reckon you could lay the mark in ordinary circumstances, since their dirty wind is likely to push you to leeward (downwind) of the mark. Find a way through the procession by dipping behind boats as necessary, and tack as soon as there is clean air to windward.

Leave plenty of space to get round the mark without hitting it (which is a rule offence) when you let the boom out to bear away. If you are sailing in undisturbed

ABOVE **Lasers race up to the windward mark in stronger winds, and a capsized boat blocks the turn, probably causing confusion.**

ABOVE **49ers round the leeward mark at the bottom of the course. GBR422 has AUS409 well covered, having gone in wide and come out tight.**

wind, it may be fine to cut your rounding so tight that you have to pinch for the last few metres approaching the mark. If there are other boats coming in at the same time, be prepared to lose speed and pointing ability, as their dirty wind may send you drifting sideways into a general mêlée. In such circumstances it is far better to go high and overstand or sail above the mark, and have reserves of speed, power and space to get round without trouble. If a boat has established an inside overlap before getting within two lengths of the mark, you have to keep clear and give it space while going round the mark.

Be aware that tides can make a big difference by lifting you upwind towards a mark, or pushing you downwind away from a mark. If you are close enough to clearly see the water round a marker buoy, the tide will push up small waves on the side it is flowing onto, with smooth water on the side it is flowing away from.

Covering

The purpose of covering is to ensure that a rival boat cannot overtake you on the beat. It is usually most important in the final stages of a race, and particularly in the final stages of a championship when you might want to ensure that one boat stays behind you, at the cost of allowing other boats to get ahead.

Cover is most easily imposed at the bottom (leeward) mark of a course. Boat A turns the mark and rounds up from a reach to a beat ahead of boat B. Boat A immediately luffs hard, moving into a position that is both to windward and ahead of boat B, which is now firmly in her wind shadow. From this point boat A aims to "sit" on Boat B for the rest of the race.

Every time boat B tacks to clear her wind, boat A follows suit in order to immediately reinstate the cover. This strategy presumes that the helmsperson of boat A is at least as proficient, if not better, than the helmsperson of boat B. If boat B has the better sailor, he or she will be able to break cover by tacking faster, sailing faster or pointing higher than boat A.

Racing offwind

On traditional courses offwind legs often became a procession. All that changed with windward/leeward courses and gennaker boats that tack downwind. Offwind racing has become as tactical and demanding as racing upwind.

From reach to reach

On a triangle or trapezoid course, the upwind leg is followed by a reaching leg to the wing mark:

Triangle (60 degree) close reach
Trapezoid beam reach
Triangle (squashed) beam reach
Competitors then gybe round the wing mark for the second offwind leg to the leeward bottom mark:

Triangle (60 degree) broad reach followed by beat
Trapezoid downwind (run) followed by beam reach across the bottom of the course
Triangle (squashed) beam reach followed by beat

On a windward/leeward course, the upwind leg is followed by a downwind leg (gybing from broad reach to broad reach) to the leeward mark.

Rhumb line reaches

The direct rhumb line route on a reach is a straight line between the marks. Wind and waves will make this impossible, and also undesirable as boats need to follow a wavy course either side of the rhumb line, luffing and bearing away to maximize performance. In reality most boats on reaching legs follow an indirect and considerably longer route, which follows a big curve to windward. The reasons are simple. Boats coming up from behind will invariably try to overtake to windward. Boat A which is overtaking will therefore luff to windward, which is also likely to build speed by increasing apparent wind, while boat B which is defending will luff to try to hold boat A back. The result is

ABOVE **Lasers head off on a reaching leg with the leeward boats already starting to head low and the windward boats heading high. Few manage to sail a straight course to the next mark.**

RIGHT **Boats invariably sail in an arc on reaches because they are either being pushed upwind by leeward boats, or bearing away to get clear of windward boats.**

ABOVE **Olympic gold medalist Ben Ainslie uses waves and broken surf to outsail the opposition. He looks relaxed and his boat is absolutely flat.**

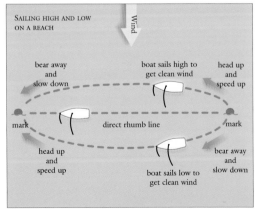

SAILING HIGH AND LOW ON A REACH

Wind

bear away and slow down

boat sails high to get clean wind

head up and speed up

mark

direct rhumb line

mark

head up and speed up

bear away and slow down

boat sails low to get clean wind

"Keep clear!"

On a reach it is possible to protect your position by luffing any boat that attempts to overtake to windward. The overtaking boat must keep clear, and be given room to keep clear and avoid collision. If a boat is attempting to over-take to leeward and is within two lengths of the defending boat or has an overlap, the windward boat may not sail below its proper course.

ABOVE **The modern racing rules are primarily aimed at avoiding collisions.**

ABOVE **A tight reach with a spinnaker gives the 470 fleet an edge. No one can bear away because there's a mark to make and they are all being held up by the leeward boats.**

that both boats begin to arc to windward, a phenomenon that may be repeated many times on a reaching leg.

All the boats that have sailed in a windward arc will then have to bear way to round the wing or leeward mark. This becomes a particular problem if boats have to bear away from a broad reach to a run, and then slow right down in their final approach to the mark, while boats that have followed a more direct course get to the mark first and have all the advantages of an inside overlap before the wing mark gybe.

An alternative stratagem is to bear off and sail low on a close reach or beam reach, keeping clear of windward boats with the advantage of being able to luff and build speed on the final approach to the mark and getting there on the inside. You have to go far enough to leeward to avoid all wind shadow and turbulence, and may lose a lot of ground having slowed

down while bearing away. However, if the majority of boats have been sucked into sailing an arc to windward, the leeward arc is likely to be shorter and more direct.

Spinnaker and gennaker tactics

Plan ahead when flying a spinnaker or gennaker on a reach. If the reach is close enough to the wind to be marginal, it may pay to rely on the mainsail and jib. An alternative solution may be to sail to windward on a two-sail reach for a few hundred metres after rounding the windward mark, in order to provide enough downwind space to bear away with the spinnaker or gennaker. You should then get to the wing mark without problems, ready to gybe the spinnaker onto the opposite reach for the next leg of the course.

If a spinnaker or gennaker is overpowered on the reach, you will need to bear away to keep the boat flat and

moving forwards. Adjust to luffing in lulls and bearing away in gusts as you sail a course that snakes across both sides of the rhumb line, but make sure you leave enough space downwind to bear away if a gust hits on the final approach to the mark.

In light winds a spinnaker becomes inefficient when sailing dead downwind. You need to luff to build up speed, the helm relies on information from the crew about too much (bear away) or too little (head up) pressure on the spinnaker sheet. The same technique can be used for gennaker sailing in all conditions. If gennaker sheet pressure builds, the helmsperson can bear away with the apparent wind. If the pressure drops he or she must luff to build apparent wind.

If you are overtaking to windward with a spinnaker or gennaker, you will not be able to bear away in a gust. This becomes particularly important on a reach when attempting to overtake a non-spinnaker or gennaker boat and can easily lead to capsize and chaos. However, once in a clear ahead position, you can use a gust to bear away and open out a gap.

With superior technique it may be possible to overtake to leeward with a spinnaker or gennaker. On a reaching leg this will depend on being able to react more positively to gusts, lulls and waves in order to accelerate fast enough to draw level with your rival, from where you can luff and accelerate past. On a downwind leg you will need to use gusts and waves to sail deeper and push through; if this ploy fails the solution may be to gybe onto the other tack.

RIGHT **Sailing with the big gennaker of a 49er is a balancing act at the best of times, and some crews will be better at driving the boat through gusts than others.**

ABOVE **The perils of racing hard downwind. An International 14 digs in the nose and goes end for end while its rivals zip by.**

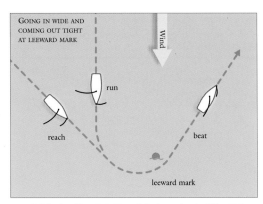

ABOVE **Both boats sailing offwind towards the leeward mark will be able to round close enough to start the beat with maximum windward advantage.**

Tacking downwind

Downwind gybing angles with a gennaker are best determined by:
- Experience of your boat as well as the conditions.
- Seat-of-the-pants style sailing, which tells you when it is right.
- Watching the downwind speed and heading of other boats.

Getting the right angle will always be a compromise between speed (and fun) and a good downwind course, with continuous luffing and bearing away required to maximise apparent wind. Watch for gusts coming up from behind – it may pay to gybe over to meet them – and be aware of tidal flow pushing you, which can help increase apparent wind and promote deeper downwind angles.

Mark rounding

Any boat that has established an overlap before getting within two lengths of the mark, must be given room at the mark. This includes allowing boats with an inside overlap to bear away or gybe round the wing mark with space for the boom to describe a full arc from side to side, or to head up from a reach or run onto a beat at the leeward mark. In practice a number of boats may stack up with overlaps at the wing mark. This can push some boats far to the outside, force them to postpone their gybes, and put them at a disadvantage by being to leeward on the next reach to the leeward mark.

Boats may also stack up with overlaps at the leeward mark, where the effects of being pushed to the outside will leave no escape until there is room to break tacks with the boat in front. It is therefore critical to try to maintain your windward position on the approach to the mark, and if necessary slow down to keep close in to the mark.

The length and turning circle of the boat will require you to allow enough space to go in wide and come out tight at the leeward mark, rather than going in tight and coming out wide. Coming out tight with the crew almost brushing the leeward side of the mark gains maximum upwind advantage while luffing onto the new windward course. The centreboard or daggerboard must be lowered before rounding, and the boat kept flat while sheeting in and powering up to windward.

Port v starboard

On a port-hand course starboard tack boats have right of way in the final approach when tacking downwind to the leeward mark, but will need to gybe before luffing onto the new upwind course. One solution is to approach the leeward mark

ABOVE **Flying machines. The crew of the 49er gets the gennaker up at the start of the downwind tacking duel that is about to commence with the boat ahead as they zig-zag from gybe to gybe.**

Chaos at the mark during a women's 470 race. The Swedish boat on the inside and the American boat to leeward are having the kind of confrontation that makes it vital to understand the rules.

Racing tactics

- Gybing on major wind shifts will enable you to sail a shorter course to the leeward mark.
- Beware of windward leg boats when you are on the downwind leg. If you are on port tack, you must give way to all boats sailing to windward.

on starboard tack, before doing a drop-gybe in the final approach. Aim to leave enough time for the gybe to be completed before you start to luff – a half-filled gennaker causes all kinds of problems with the crew struggling to tame it – but keep the gybe distance from the mark to a minimum so starboard tack boats will have minimum impact. If it is windy you will need to gybe early during the final approach to the leeward mark, so you can bear away and keep the boat downwind and under control. If the wind is light you will need to gybe late, so you can luff and maximize speed. In both cases aim above the mark, so you can bear away to drop the spinnaker or gennaker.

RIGHT **Laser 157130 is having a hard time trying to cut in on port tack to join a high speed mass of starboard tack boats about to round the mark.**

The end of the race

- Sail for the nearest end of the finishing line.
- Make sure your finish has been logged by the race boat.
- Head for shore and do not crowd the finish area.
- Park your boat away from the crowded shoreline.
- Post a tally or sign off as required.
- Get changed and warm up.
- Eat and drink sensibly and healthily to replenish lost energy.
- Discuss and analyze the race with your crew, but relax and accept that this is a sporting pastime.
- Fix anything that needs fixing on the boat, and make a checklist for next time.
- Pack up the boat, put everything away and prepare your clothing and equipment for the next race.
- Congratulate the winner.

49ers head for home at the end of a race. Time to reflect on what happened, what went wrong, and how you could do better, but remember it's only a game.

DINGHY AND CATAMARAN CLASSES

The following selection does not aim to be fully comprehensive, but includes many well-loved favourites, which give some idea of the breadth of contemporary dinghy sailing. There is of course a good deal of crossover between the categories of the various classes (specific dinghy designs) and we can only apologize to those whose personal favourites have been left out.

There are three types of classes: one design, restricted and development. In a one design class every boat must be as identical as possible in every detail down to ropes and cleats. Careful policing by class authorities ensure consistency among the small numbers of licensed builders. Restricted classes allow a certain amount of freedom in choice of fittings, sails or construction, but are still restricted by rules that ensure the boats remain similar. Development classes allow a wide degree of latitude in important areas such as hull shape and sail plan. The most open-ended development classes have rules that govern little more than maximum length and sail area. Other details on each class featured includes the overall length (LOA) and the maximum upwind sail area, which generally relates to the mainsail and jib, or mainsail alone.

LEFT *International Lasers prosper at all levels of competition and are sailed in over 100 countries.*

BELOW *Picos are ideal starter boats as they are both easy to sail and to right after a capsize.*

Classic racing dinghies

What makes a classic class? Longevity combined with continuing enthusiastic support is the obvious answer, and while those qualities can be found in dinghy classes that date as far back as the end of the 19th century the popular post-war classes designed by Jack Holt are likely to be among the first classics in any dinghy sailor's mind.

Enterprise

The Enterprise is one of Jack Holt's finest racing classes, immediately recognizable by its pale blue sails. Despite its age the Enterprise enjoys continuing popularity with sail numbers in excess of 23,000. The early marine ply Enterprises have been joined by modern foam sandwich alternatives, with restrictions on the class ensuring it remains an effective one-design that keeps pace with the times. As such it is a great favourite with inland clubs where it is an excellent boat for tactical racing, and while the class remains strongest in Britain the 1999 World Championships were hosted by South Africa.
Designer Jack Holt (UK)
First launched 1956
Type Restricted
Length overall (LOA) 4.04m (13ft)

LEFT The Fireball was born out of a scow design, and appeared radically different when it first appeared in the 1960s. Its low, narrow, skimming hull was ideal for marine ply construction, but fibreglass has since become the norm for modern Fireballs.

Beam 1.6m (5ft)
Minimum hull weight 94kg (207lb)
Upwind sail area 10.5 sq m (113 sq ft)

Fireball

The Fireball caused a sensation when it was first introduced with its futuristic, skimming dish style of design and a hull that proved ideal for low cost, marine ply construction. Modern Fireballs are mainly built in foam sandwich fibreglass and, thanks to updates to the rules, the class has stayed popular with traditionalists. Sail numbers are around 15,000, with fleets scattered throughout Europe.

Designer Peter Milne (UK)
First launched 1961
Type Restricted
LOA 4.93m (16ft)
Beam 1.37m (4½ft)
Minimum hull weight 79.4kg (175lb)
Upwind sail area 11.43 sq m (123 sq ft)
Spinnaker 13.01 sq m (140 sq ft)

LEFT **The Enterprise can always be recognized by its pale blue sails, which are mandatory throughout the class. It is considered a great boat for tactical inland racing.**

ABOVE **The Firefly has always been distinctive for beautiful, varnished hulls, but the spread of fibreglass has invaded even this classic class.**

Firefly

The Firefly is one of the great Uffa Fox classics. It was originally built in moulded ply, but modern boats are built in fibreglass. Its history as a racing class is long and noble, starting as the Olympic Monotype in 1948 when the great Danish sailor Paul Elvstrom won his first Gold medal and continuing as a favourite for team racing with class restrictions ensuring it is an effective one-design.

Designer Uffa Fox (UK)
First launched 1947
Type Restricted
LOA 3.66m (12ft)
Beam 1.25m (4ft)
Minimum hull weight 74kg (163lb)
Upwind sail area 10.5 sq m (113 sq ft)

International 505

For many years the 505 enjoyed tremendous popularity as the ultimate high performance dinghy and its star only began to wane with the advent of skiff-style sailing in the 1990s. It has remained one of the most elegant boats on the water with a turn of speed that puts it on par with a modern equivalent such as the Laser 4000. The 505 remains one of the great design classics, with a committed, if limited, following in Britain and France.

ABOVE **The 505 was considered the supreme high performance dinghy for many years, and had a much bigger following than the Flying Dutchman.**

Designer John Westell (UK)
First launched 1954
Type Restricted
LOA 5.05m (16½ft)
Beam 1.88m (6ft)
Minimum hull weight 127.4kg (281lb)
Upwind sail area 13.56 sq m (145 sq m)
Spinnaker 23.3 sq m (250 sq ft)

International Flying Dutchman

The Flying Dutchman was designed and developed to meet the need for a new, high-performance Olympic dinghy, and filled that slot for a total of 40 years and 11 Olympic Games. For most of its Olympic years the Flying Dutchman reigned undisputed as the fastest dinghy on the water, with its long waterline length and massive overlapping genoa making it unbeatable on any upwind course. As foam sandwich replaced moulded plywood construction it also became increasingly expensive to compete, and the restricted rule that allowed slight variations in hull shape and rig tuning devices to tame its power became highly complex. The Flying Dutchman will remain one of the most elegant dinghies of all time, and is still raced by an elite group of enthusiasts in Europe and the USA.

Designer Uwe Van Essen (Holland)
First launched 1952
Type Restricted
LOA 6.06m (20ft)
Beam 1.78m (6 ft)
Minimum hull weight 130kg (286lb)
Upwind sail area 18.6 sq m (200 sq ft)
Spinnaker 21 sq m (226 sq ft)

ABOVE **The Flying Dutchman enjoyed a 40-year reign as the longest international dinghy and the fastest of them all upwind.**

International 470

The 505 was such a big success in France that André Cornu designed the 470 as a more accessible, scaled-down version with the same brief to provide thrilling racing. Despite the class being mainly confined to France the International Yacht Racing Union (IYRU) chose the 470 as the second two-man class at the 1976 Olympics, and 20 years later the 470 was also adopted as an exclusive women's class at the 1996 Olympics.

Designer André Cornu (France)
First launched 1964
Type Restricted
LOA 4.7m (15½ft)
Beam 1.68m (5½ft)
Minimum hull weight 120kg (265lb)
Upwind sail area 13.9 sq m (150 sq ft)
Spinnaker 14.3 sq m (154 sq ft)

LEFT **The 470 was France's popular answer to the 505 and must be considered one of the most successful racing classes of all time, and the only one with entries for both men's and women's class at the Olympics.**

LEFT **The GP Fourteen continues to provide keen fleet racing with a spinnaker. This stable and well behaved design is equally well suited to cruising and family sailing.**

GP Fourteen

With a distinctive bell sign on the sail, Jack Holt's General Purpose 14 footer was introduced as one of the first post-war all-round dinghies that could be cheaply built and enjoyed by the family or raced with enthusiasm. Its narrow, boxy design has been left far behind by modern trends, but with its predictable stability it remains a popular club class with over 13,500 boats registered and the 2000 World Championships was held in South Africa.

Designer Jack Holt (UK)
First launched 1950
Type Restricted
LOA 4.27m (14ft)
Beam 1.54m (5ft)
Minimum hull weight 133kg (293lb)
Upwind sail area 12.85 sq m (138 sq ft)
Spinnaker 8.4 sq m (90 sq ft)

ABOVE **The Laser 2 provides the thrills and challenge of sailing with a spinnaker on a comparatively simple platform. The Laser 3000 is based on the same hull.**

Laser 2/3000

The Laser 1 was a difficult act to follow, but the Laser 2 has proved successful in providing one-design, trapeze and spinnaker, two-person racing at the lowest possible cost. With more than 10,000 boats sold the class has become established worldwide with World and European championships and other big events held on both sides of the Atlantic. While it may have been overtaken by skiff-style dinghies, its cost for performance rating has made it a firm favourite for colleges, universities and the armed forces.

The Laser 3000 is based on the Laser 2 hull, but brings the boat more up to date with gennaker-driven power and a new deck layout, which makes it a good funboat for lightweight sailors, but still retains essential Laser simplicity.

Designer Frank Bethwaite (Australia)/Laser
First launched 1980/1995

RIGHT **Scores of different designs have been produced for the Merlin Rocket, which has grown wider over the years. It is a supreme tactical boat with excellent upwind performance.**

Type One-design
LOA 4.39m (14½ft)/4.4m (14½ft)
Beam 1.42m (4½ft)/1.46m (4¾ft)
Minimum hull weight 75kg (165lb)/ 79kg (174lb)
Upwind sail area 11.52 sq m (124 sq ft)/ 11.6 sq m (125 sq ft)
Laser 2 Spinnaker 10.2 sq m (110 sq ft)
Laser 3000 Gennaker 12.6 sq m (136 sq ft)

Merlin Rocket

As one of Britain's most celebrated development classes, the Merlin Rocket with its wizard's cone on the sail enjoyed its heyday between the 1950s and 1970s, when designers ranging from Ian Proctor to Phil Morrison made their name in a class where the rules encouraged non-stop development. Many of those Merlins were absolute classics, exquisitely built in wooden clinker construction with a trend towards vast beam and fathead sails, a trend in design that other classes would eventually follow. The Merlin remains a beautiful boat to race on confined waters, and one that is still enjoyed by purists who are willing to pay the price of continual change.

Designer Various (all UK)
First launched 1946
Type Restricted/Development
LOA 4.27m (14ft)
Beam 2.2m (7½ft)
Minimum hull weight 98kg (216lb)
Upwind sail area 10.2 sq m (110 sq ft)
Spinnaker Variable

Mirror dinghy

Designed in collaboration with do-it-yourself expert Barry Bucknell, the Mirror is probably Jack Holt's best known dinghy, with more than 70,000 of the little red-sailed craft built in its first 40 years. With sponsorship from the Daily Mirror, the Mirror dinghy was intended for home building using a simple method of stitch-and-glue (wire stitches and fibreglass tape) to hold the plywood panels together. Despite its tubby appearance, the Mirror is a surprisingly lively boat to sail, and by no means a children's boat as some people imagine. The Mirror is a boat for all ages and can be raced, cruised and rowed. It remains a common sight around Britain.

LEFT The International 12 Square Metre Sharpie is a wonderful looking classic boat, though one that has become comparatively rare and is now maintained and raced by small numbers of enthusiasts.

ABOVE The Mirror dinghy can be recognized by its bright red sails. It is a potential bargain buy second-hand.

Designer Jack Holt & Barry Bucknell (UK)
First launched 1962
Type Restricted
LOA 3.30m (11ft)
Beam 1.39m (4½ft)
Minimum hull weight 45.5kg (100lb)
Upwind sail area 6.5 sq m (70 sq ft)
Spinnaker 4.4 sq m (47 sq ft)

Thames A Rater

With only 23 boats built in its first 100 years, the Thames A Rater is a classic for the select few. It is typical of a local design that is unique to local conditions. A Raters race solely on the River Thames from Upper Thames and Bourne End sailing clubs on the outskirts of London. While A Raters are certainly obscure, these three-crew, high performance, Victorian river racers are magnificent to see in action.
Designers Various (all UK)
First launched 1898
Type Restricted/Development
LOA 8.23m (27ft)
Beam Open
Minimum hull weight 340.5kg (750lb)
Upwind sail area 32.5 sq m (350 sq ft)/ 35.3 sq m (380 sq ft)

International 12 Sq M Sharpie

The 12 Sq M Sharpie was originally designed as a hot performer, with a narrow hull and low freeboard, hard chine mahogany construction, steel centreboard and a high, peaked, gunter mainsail with large overlapping genoa giving a minimum sail area of 12 sq m (129 sq ft). The class gained international recognition in 1933 and was selected for the 1956 Olympics in Australia, which established its reputation worldwide.
Designers J. Kroeger (Norway)
First launched 1931
Type Restricted
LOA 5m (16½ft)
Beam 1.43m (4½ft)
Minimum hull weight 230kg (507lb)
Upwind sail area 12 sq m (129 sq ft)

LEFT The Thames A Rater is a highly specialized design, which is raced on a narrow stretch of the River Thames where mainly light and gusty winds, and a constant tidal flow dictate a very stylized form of racing.

Cruising dinghies

A cruising dinghy needs to be roomy, stable and above all seaworthy. It should be able to undertake extensive coastal cruises in comfort and safety, and be the perfect boat for family sailing with the option of propulsion by oars or a small outboard. Any cruising dinghy worth the name should also provide enough speed and performance to be satisfying to sail, and the potential for good racing is a bonus.

Laser 16/13

Bruce Kirby of Laser 1 fame designed the Laser 16 as a comfortable and very stable cruising dinghy. With modern, handsome lines and a big, reefable rig it delivers good performance and can carry four adults in reasonable comfort. Due to its ballasted centreboard, the Laser 16 can be safely left on a mooring during the sailing season and bridges the gap between a dinghy and keelboat.

The Laser 13 was introduced as a smaller sister to the Laser 16, following the same concept for a smaller number of crew. It had the bonus of being considerably lighter with a conventional dinghy centreboard, and therefore much more appropriate for dry sailing with a trolley.

ABOVE **The Laser 13 provides comfortable cruising in a modern package.**

Designer Bruce Kirby (Canada)
First launched 1980/1982
Type One-design
LOA 5.19m (17ft)/4.05m (13ft)
Beam 2.06m (6¾ft)/1.72m (5½ft)

Minimum hull weight 250kg (551lb)/ 132kg (291lb)
Upwind sail area 14.02 sq m (151 sq ft)/ 10.4 sq m (112 sq ft)
Spinnaker 11.54 sq m (124 sq ft)/ 10.5 sq m (113 sq ft)

LEFT **The Laser 16 is a considerably bigger boat than the Laser 13, and is stable and heavy enough to be safely left on a mooring during the summer season.**

Laser Stratos

Both the Laser 16 and 13 enjoyed a comparatively brief period in production before being replaced by the Laser Stratos, a novel approach to the concept of a cruiser-racer dinghy designed by Phil Morrison. In its cruising mode the Stratos can be fitted with a ballasted centreboard to provide stability on a mooring; in its performance mode a conventional centreboard coupled with optional gennaker and trapeze gives racing-dinghy-style sailing. In between

ABOVE **The Drascombe Lugger and associated range of different length Drascombes are modern cruising classics that sail far and wide. Cruises in company are very popular, and crews adapt their boats to live on board.**

ABOVE **The Laser Stratos is a multi-package approach to modern dinghy design, which can be optimized for racing or cruising according to requirements. The race version shown here is fitted with trapeze and gennaker; the cruiser version has a ballasted centreboard and can be left on a mooring.**

those two extremes the Stratos retains room to go sailing with the family, and features a unique capsize safety system. This floods the down-side of the hull during a capsize to ensure the boat floats low enough for the crew to get on the centreboard and right with ease, after which the water drains out again.

Designer Phil Morrison (UK)
First launched 1999
Type One-design
LOA 4.94m (16ft)
Beam 2m (6½ft)
Minimum hull weight 170kg (375lb)
Upwind sail area 14.53 sq m (156 sq ft)
Gennaker 12.54 sq m (135 sq ft)

RIGHT **The Wayfarer has proved exceptionally successful as a dinghy that is equally suitable for cruising, racing or teaching novices to sail. With a history spanning more than 40 years, it is also widely available second-hand.**

Drascombe Lugger

The Drascombe Lugger started a popular trend for traditional dayboats built in modern materials, and was followed by a range of different size Drascombes and similar craft from other designers, which can be either trailer-sailed or left on a mooring.

The double-ended traditional design is both seaworthy and handsome, with loose footed tan sails, sliding gunter rig and small mizzen, all designed for ease of handling. It has a short wooden mast and no boom. A sprayhood and boat tent can be used to convert the Lugger into a fair weather cruiser with room for two to

camp on board. If the wind fails, alternative propulsion is provided by an outboard in the transom, or rowing.

Luggers and similar craft have enjoyed a long period of success for all kinds of small boat cruising: adventure sailing along open coastlines, fishing and exploring backwaters, as well as running up on deserted beaches.

Designer John Watkinson (UK)
First launched 1965
Type One-Design/Restricted
LOA 5.72m (18½ft)
Beam 1.9m (6ft)
All-up weight 340kg (750lb)
Upwind sail area 12.26 sq m (132 sq ft) including mizzen

Wayfarer

Having over 10,000 boats registered, Ian Proctor's Wayfarer has enjoyed a long life as a well established cruiser-racer dinghy. It is stable and roomy enough to have been a firm favourite with both sailing schools and families, but also possesses a good enough turn of speed for enjoyable and competitive racing. A Wayfarer World Championship is held once every three years and the 1998 event was held in Denmark.

The Wayfarer has also enjoyed a great deal of fame as a long-distance cruising dinghy, and many Wayfarer sailors dream of emulating the feats of Frank and Margaret Dye who cruised their wooden Wayfarer (number 48) over thousands of miles around Norway and Iceland in the years soon after the design first appeared. The class association holds an extensive library of cruises undertaken by members all round the world, as well as organizing regular cruises in company.

Continuous updates in construction have ensured that the tough, seaworthy and versatile Wayfarer keeps pace with the times. The design was brought right up to date by the all-fibreglass Wayfarer World in 1996, which featured a self-draining floor through to the transom. A 17 sq m (183 sq ft) gennaker is optional and, while not class legal for racing, has proved extremely popular for cruising and learning.

ABOVE **The Wanderer gives a good turn of performance, while maintaining good sea-keeping qualities when cruising.**

Designer Ian Proctor (UK)
First launched 1957
Type Restricted One-Design
LOA 4.82m (16ft)
Beam 1.85m (6ft)
Minimum hull weight 168kg (370lb)
Upwind sail area 8.8 sq m (95 sq ft) mainsail plus 4.3 sq m (46 sq ft) genoa or 2.8 sq m (30 sq ft) jib
Spinnaker 13.5 sq m (145 sq ft)

Wanderer

Ian Proctor designed the Wanderer as a little sister to the Wayfarer. It has less capacity, lower weight and a much smaller rig, which is easier to handle when sailing, as well as when it is on a slipway or on a trailer. In that role it has proved popular for family sailing, cruising and gentle racing.

Designer Ian Proctor (UK)
First launched 1978
Type Restricted
LOA 4.27m (14ft)
Beam 1.78m (6ft)
Minimum hull weight 129kg (284lb)
Upwind sail area 10.68 sq m (115 sq ft)
Spinnaker 9.94 sq m (107 sq ft)

Dinghy cruising

With skill and a certain amount of daring, it is possible to undertake extended inshore cruises in a stable and roomy dinghy. The advantages over a yacht cruise are that you can trail the dinghy to an ideal starting point and from there explore anchorages and landing places that are too shallow or confined for bigger sailboats. Careful planning combined with good weather are essential for enjoyment, and for those who get it right the experience of pulling up on a remote, isolated beach is likely to be unforgettable.

As with any land-based camping trip, trim the amount of gear being carried to a practical minimum, store it with extreme care and ensure that everything that needs it has waterproof protection.

Routes must be planned with great care, taking note of weather forecasts and tidal streams and ensuring every landfall is made at least two hours before sunset.

Dinghies for young sailors and learners

Children can start learning to sail properly from about the age of eight, and this selection primarily spans the 8–18 period during which a nervous first-timer out in an Optimist can be transformed into a full-on skiff sailor blasting in a 29er. However, while the Optimist and Cadet are specifically for young sailors, classes such as the Topper, Pico, Laser Radial and Topaz are equally suited to adult use.

International Cadet

This is a classic junior two-up racing class for under-18 sailors of optimum crew weight of around 86 kg (189 lb). Originally designed by Jack Holt in 1947 for low-cost, marine-ply construction. The design, concept and performance are now very dated, but with World and European championships, competition up to international level remains extremely tough.

Designer Jack Holt (UK)
First launched 1947
Type Restricted
LOA 3.22m (10½ft)
Beam 1.27m (4ft)
Minimum hull weight 54kg (119lb)
Upwind sail area 5.16 sq m (55 sq ft)
Spinnaker 4.25 sq m (46 sq ft)

LEFT The International Optimist has worn its years well, and has even bounced back to become undisputed as the world's top racing class for young single-handed sailors involving racing that is extremely tactical.

International Optimist

The Optimist is an old timer that has bounced back to become the number one worldwide racing and learning class for young single-handed sailors, and the calibre of international championships ensures that top sailors frequently move on to contest the Olympics. Racing is restricted to under-16s with an optimum crew weight of around 50kg (110lb), but it is common to find sailors of half that age learning to sail in these boats. The Optimist was originally designed for plywood construction, but is now widely available with both marine ply and fibreglass foam sandwich hulls, while the quaint looking sprit rig remains the same.

Designer Clark Mills (USA)
First launched 1947
Type Restricted
LOA 2.3m (7½ft)
Beam 1.13m (3¾ft)
Minimum hull weight 35kg (77lb)
Upwind sail area 3.5 sq m (37.7 sq ft)

International Topper

The Topper is a hugely popular one-design with more than 40,000 boats on the water. Originally designed to be carried on a roof rack, the Topper was re-designed for rotomoulded polypropylene construction, and is the epitome of a low-cost, super-durable, zero upkeep funboat. The Topper can be sailed by one or two children from about the age of ten upwards. It is also an excellent solo boat

LEFT The International Cadet was once renowned for producing future world champions in all of the leading adult classes. Although it can no longer claim that role, the level of competition remains extremely keen.

LEFT **The International Topper combines maximum durability with an extremely user-friendly design. It is at its best when sailed single-handed by lighter weight sailors, but can also be enjoyed by two children or a heavier adult.**

ABOVE **The Topaz is an ultra durable, multi-purpose boat which can be sailed both as a single-hander, or two-up complete with trapeze and gennaker.**

for moderately agile adults and is very popular for learning as well as providing excellent competition.

Designer Ian Proctor
First launched 1976
Type One-design
LOA 3.4m (11ft)
Beam 1.2m (4ft)
Minimum hull weight 43kg (95lb)
Upwind sail area 5.2 sq m (56 sq ft)

Pico

Laser introduced the Pico as an all-round funboat for learners and families, with special appeal for sailing schools and holiday centres that need a boat that is very easy to sail and even easier to right after a capsize. The Pico's tecrothene construction combines rotomoulded plastic with foam sandwich for the best combination of durability and rigidity and, with all that foam, the Pico has enough buoyancy to carry two (not too large) adults or four children – at a squeeze. Design features include an excellent

ergonomic cockpit, with a small jib available in Pico Plus mode.

Designer Jo Richards (UK)
First launched 1996
Type One-design
LOA 3.5m (11½ft)
Beam 1.37m (4½ft)
Minimum hull weight 60kg (132lb)
Mainsail 5.9 sq m (63½ sq ft)
Optional jib 1.09 sq m (12 sq ft)

Topaz

The Topaz is a clever triple concept design that was introduced as a direct competitor to the Laser Pico. The hull is produced using similar rotomoulded, foam-sandwich polyethylene construction to maximize low cost and durability, with three rig options to suit different requirements. Topaz Uno has a simple, unstayed una-rig for learning and general fun sailing in the style of the Topper. Topaz Duo has a much more sophisticated two-sail rig with tapered mast, fully battened mainsail, shrouds and trapeze wires. Topaz Tres includes a full gennaker.

Designer Ian Howlett (UK)
First launched 1998
Type One-design (three versions)
LOA 3.86m (12½ft)
Beam 1.42m (4½ft)
Minimum hull weight 60kg (132lb)
Upwind sail area 5.2 sq m (56 sq ft)/ 8.35 sq m (90 sq ft)
Gennaker 9 sq m (97 sq ft)

International 420

The 420 was first introduced as a junior partner to the 470, and adopted by the French as their principal youth trainer for teenage crews. It maintained that role for more than 30 years and over 50,000 boats were sold worldwide and, despite its age and dated design, it became the automatic twin-crew choice when the ISAF Youth World Championships were

LEFT **The Laser Pico has become established as a great favourite with sailing schools since it is durable, simple, has good performance and is an excellent weight carrier for all ages.**

ABOVE **The International 420 has enjoyed over 30 years as a junior racing class, but is being challenged by more modern designs.**

first held in the late 1990s. The class also holds annual World and European championships where the competition is intense.

Designer Christian Maury (France)
First launched 1964
Type Restricted
LOA 4.2m (13¾ft)
Beam 1.62m (5½ft)
Minimum hull weight 80kg (176lb)
Upwind sail area 10.25 sq m (110 sq ft)
Spinnaker 9 sq m (97 sq ft)

International Hobie 405

The single trapeze Hobie 405 was conceived as a high performance youth trainer that would bring dinghy sailing up to date, appealing to young sailors with an optimum crew weight of around 100–120kg (220–265lb), and replace elderly designs like the 420. It was adopted as the official twin-crew youth trainer by the Royal Yachting Association (RYA) in Britain and enjoyed a period of moderate popularity, but by the end of its first decade the design seemed ready to be outphased by even more modern concepts such as the 29er.

Designer Chris Benedict (Canada)
First launched 1991
Type One-design
LOA 4.05m (13ft)
Beam 1.38m (4½ft)
Minimum hull weight 68kg (150lb)
Upwind sail area 7.98 sq m (86 sq ft)
Gennaker 8.8 sq m (95 sq ft)

29er

The 29er is no less than a junior 49er, aimed at giving the same state-of-the-art skiff thrills in a twin crew, single-trapeze package that's ideally suited to experienced teenagers with an optimum crew weight of 110–135kg (242–298lb). The 29er was due to receive international status for the year 2000, with its first World Championship in the same year and, with performance matched by appearance, looks set to become established as a major high performance youth class.

Designer Julian Bethwaite (Australia)
First launched 1998
Type One-design
LOA 4.45m (14½ft)
Beam 1.77m (6ft)
Minimum hull weight 65kg (143lb)
Upwind sail area 12.5 sq m (134 sq ft)
Gennaker 15 sq m (161 sq ft)

International Laser Radial

The optional Laser Radial rig has a different lower mast section and smaller, radial-cut sail compared to the International Laser, but in all other respects is exactly the same. The rig delivers approximately 15 per cent less power, and was introduced as an alternative for lightweight and young sailors who find the Laser's 7.06 sq m (76 sq ft) sail physically too demanding in stronger winds. The Radial has its own keenly fought international race series, culminating in events such as the ISAF World Youth Championships.

Designer Bruce Kirby (Canada)
First launched 1971
Type One-design
LOA 4.23m (14ft)
Beam 1.37m (4½ft)
Minimum hull weight 60kg (132lb)
Radial sail area 5.76 sq m (62 sq ft)

LEFT **The Hobie 405 was introduced at the start of a decade that saw rapid change in dinghy designs and by the end its appeal was eroded by even more modern dinghies.**

ABOVE **The radial rig makes the International Laser much easier to handle for lighter weight and less able sailors. An alternative 4.7 sq m (50 sq ft) sail is available with a shorter mast, and is ideal for learning or for younger teenagers.**

The gennaker generation

The Australian experience combined with rapid developments in the International 14 class spawned a whole host of gennaker-driven dinghies with Phil Morrison the most popular designer. These boats are great fun to sail and seem destined to make the old spinnaker classes obsolete, but come in much more user-friendly packages than the mega-light, monster rig ideal of the true skiff.

Laser 4000

The Laser 4000 has been a huge success, combining modern single trapeze, gennaker-driven, skiff-style sailing in a user-friendly accessible package. It features the Laser crew power equalisation system, with sliding racks and weight correctors, that is designed to provide level racing for a range of crew weights between 118–188kg (260–414lb). Well over 4,000 boats were

LEFT **The Laser 5000 was originally conceived as a new Olympic class, but was beaten by the 49er. It is known as a powerful boat that is a real challenge when the wind gets up.**

sold in the first four years of production, with a high profile in Europe for the annual Audi Laser Eurocup – a major series of events in France, Italy and the UK.
Designer Phil Morrison (UK)
First launched 1995

Type One-design
LOA 4.64m (15ft)
Beam 1.5–2.3m (4½–7½ft) maximum
Minimum hull weight 80kg (176lb)
Upwind sail area 14.7 sq m (158 sq ft)
Spinnaker 17.1 sq m (184 sq ft)

RIGHT **The Laser 4000 looks great and is a huge amount of fun to sail. Part of its attraction lies in the weight equalization system which allows different weight crews to race on a level basis. The sliding racks are pushed in for heavier sailors.**

Laser 5000

The Laser 5000 was introduced as an early Olympic contender to replace the aging Flying Dutchman. It is a super-powerful and almost brutal boat with its gennaker pole extending the overall length to a mighty 11.2m (37ft) but, with a comparatively heavy hull, the 5000 lost out when lined up against the lean and lightweight 49er. Failing to get Olympic selection is no bad thing for a class, and the 5000 has continued as a powerful boat for heavyweights, using the same weight equalisation system as the Laser 4000 and the same EuroCup series.
Designer Phil Morrison (UK)
First launched 1992
Type One-design
LOA 5.0m (16½ft)
Beam 1.9–3.05m (6–10ft) maximum
Minimum hull weight 109kg (240lb)
Upwind sail area 21.16 sq m (228 sq ft)
Gennaker 33 sq m (355 sq ft)

LEFT **The RS400 was originally designed with a spinnaker, but the gennaker was chosen as a more popular option and gives the boat exceptional broad reaching performance. The RS200 is a smaller sister.**

ABOVE **The Laser 2000 was introduced as a stable and well behaved club racer with the appeal of a modern replacement for the Enterprise or GP14.**

RS400/200

The RS400 has rapidly become a modern British classic, with a design pedigree honed on the National 12, Merlin Rocket and International 14 classes and a huge turnout at major championship events in the UK and on the Italian lakes. It is a powerful, gennaker-driven, non-trapeze class that requires a fairly heavy crew weight in the 135–165kg (298–364lb) range for stronger winds. It has impeccably designed ergonomics and sail controls that make it a real delight as a race boat.

The RS200 was introduced in 1995, using the same Phil Morrison design concept but with a much smaller rig for lightweight crews in the 112–137kg (247–302lb) range.

Designer Phil Morrison (UK)
First launched 1993/1995
Type One-design
LOA 4.52m (15ft)/4m (13ft)
Beam 2m (6½ft)/1.83m (6ft)
Minimum hull weight 85kg (187lb)/78kg (172lb)
Upwind sail area 14.76 sq m (159 sq ft)/11.52 sq m (124 sq ft)
Gennaker 13.94 sq m (150 sq ft)/8.29 sq m (89 sq ft)

Laser 2000

Laser introduced the 2000 as their new club racer, aiming to convert the owners of more elderly classic boats with a design that bears comparison with the RS200 as a rival. The difference is that the Laser 2000 is heavier and likely to be more stable, with more appeal to the cruiser-racer type

of user who wants a combination of club racing, family cruising and enjoyable but predictable performance.

Designer Phil Morrison (UK)
First launched 1998
Type One-design
LOA 4.44m (14½ft)
Beam 1.85m (6ft)
Minimum hull weight 100kg (220lb)
Upwind sail area 10.78 sq m (116 ft)
Gennaker 9.86 sq m/106 sq ft

Weight equalization

As boats have become lighter and rigs more powerful, crew weight has become a major influence on the relative speed of boats in a one-design class. In light winds lighter crews have less dead weight to carry, while in stronger winds heavier crews can exert more leverage and keep on more power. But in general light crews have the overall advantage – regatta winds are more often light than strong and, when the wind picks up, lighter crews can use advanced rig control techniques to stay in touch, while heavy crews can never compensate for too much weight.

Laser was first to tackle the problem of light crews making a potential mockery of one-design racing. Their crew power equalization (CPE) system was initially introduced on the Laser 4000 and Laser 5000 using adjustable racks and weight correctors to equalize the weight of crews. At each major

ABOVE **Adjustable racks and weight correctors allow different weight crews to race on a level playing.**

Iso

The Iso was conceived by John Caig, a multi-championship winner in Fireballs and Toppers. Iso means equal, and his idea was to produce a new high performance dinghy in which a range of crew weights would be equal by using detachable wings. The design was based on an International 14 by Ian Howlett, and as the first of the new style gennaker-driven dinghies the Iso was an immediate

regatta the crew must be weighed in sailing gear, and this produces a total weight and leverage figure that determines which rack setting and correction weights must be used. Random checks are carried out to catch anyone cheating.

ABOVE **The ISO was among the first of the new generation of gennaker dinghies, and proved an immediate hit.**

and rapid success before popularity started to decline in the face of challengers such as the Laser 4000.

Designer John Caig/Ian Howlett (UK)
First launched 1993
Type One-design
LOA 4.74m (15½ft)
Beam 1.75m–2.25m (5¾–7ft)
Minimum hull weight 100kg (220lb)
Upwind sail area 14.3 sq m (154 sq ft)
Gennaker 18.8 sq m (202 sq ft)

Topper Buzz/Spice

The Topper Buzz was introduced as a bouncing baby skiff, which would provide an introduction to high performance sailing in a simple, single trapeze, gennaker-driven package, which could be enjoyed by sailors from teenagers and upwards. The Spice is a big-rig, twin trapeze variation on the same International 14 style hull that takes the boat into pocket rocket territory.

ABOVE **The launch of the Topper Spice coincided with the Spice Girls' early successes and its popularity has lasted just as long as its namesake.**

Designer John Caig/Ian Howlett (UK)
First launched 1994/1997
Type One-design
LOA 4.2m/4.25m (13¾ft)
Beam 1.92m/1.9m (6½ft)
Minimum hull weight 90kg (198lb)/ 85kg (187lb)
Upwind sail area 12.85 sq m (138 sq ft)/ 15.93 sq m (171 sq ft)
Gennaker 17.4 sq m (187 sq ft)/ 21.68 sq m (233 sq ft)

RS800

The RS800 was introduced in late 1999 as an exceptional high performance racer featuring a twin mode form of weight equalization that is usable by a wide range

ABOVE **The RS800 is reckoned to be one of the fastest of the new generation dinghies on the water, with a unique single trapeze or twin trapeze weight equalization concept.**

of crews. The boat can be raced with single trapeze or twin trapeze, with weight equalized by weights and the racks. The RS800 is built from epoxy foam sandwich and uses carbon spars.

Designer Phil Morrison
First launched 1999
Type One-design
LOA 4.8m (15ft 9in)
Beam with racks 1.88m–2.89m (6ft 2in–9ft)
Minimum hull weight 78kg (172lb)
Upwind sail area 16.5 sq m (178 sq ft)
Gennaker 21 sq m (226 sq ft)

Boss

A carbon reinforced sandwich hull and carbon spars make the Boss a super-light flying machine and a 2.7m (9ft) pole extension and massive gennaker give a blistering performance offwind. The hull is based on Ian Howlett's world championship International 14 designs, and the rig is designed by Jon Turner to ensure that maximum power is combined with a boat that remains manageable. The Boss was originally conceived to outpace the Laser 5000, though both boats had to give second best to the 49er when it came to Olympic selection.

Designers Ian Howlett and Jon Turner
First launched 1997
Type One-design
LOA 4.9m (16ft)
Beam with racks 2.37m (7¾ft)
Minimum hull weight 85kg (187lb)
Upwind sail area 17.85 sq m (192 sq ft)
Gennaker 33 sq m (355 sq ft)

ABOVE **The Boss is the biggest sister in the Iso/Buzz/Spice family, aiming at the ultimate end of twin wire sailing with performance on par with the Laser 5000.**

Single-handers

The most obvious advantage of sailing single-handed is that you don't need a crew. Beyond that, all decisions and the control of the boat are down to you alone, which can make single-handed sailing the purest and most satisfying form.

International Laser

With over 165,000 boats sold worldwide, the Laser is the most successful sailboat ever. The key to its success is absolute simplicity combined with very low cost, plus challenging performance and the strictest possible one-design rules to ensure that race success is purely down to the sailor. Robert Scheidt of Brazil took the first gold medal at Savannah in the USA in 1976, and the Laser has continued to prosper at all levels of competition with active fleets in over 100 countries.
Designer Bruce Kirby (Canada)
First launched 1971
Type One-design
LOA 4.23m (14ft)
Beam 1.37m (4½ft)
Minimum hull weight 60kg (132lb)
Standard sail area 7.06 sq m (76 sq ft)

ABOVE **The International Finn is one of the most graceful boats on the water, a heavyweight classic that hails from another era but has been kept alive by the Olympics.**

International Finn

The Finn replaced the Firefly as the men's Olympic single-handed class in 1952, and remained the only single-hander until 1996 when it was joined by the Laser and Europe. With a massive 120kg (265lb) hull weight the Finn remains a heavy classic that demands the services of heavyweight sailors, and 90kg (198lb) is the optimum weight for best performance. As such its appeal is very limited and it is slow by modern standards. Having won a gold medal sailing a Firefly in the Olympics in 1948, the great Danish sailor, Paul Elnström, went on to win three more golds sailing the Finn in 1952, 1956 and 1960, an unsurpassed record.
Designer Rickard Sarby (Sweden)
First launched 1949
Type Restricted
LOA 4.5m (14¾ft)
Beam 1.52m (5ft)
Minimum hull weight 120kg (265lb)
Upwind sail area 10 sq m (108 sq ft)

International Europe

The Europe became the first ever women's single-handed Olympic class at Savannah, USA in 1996 when Kristine Roug of Denmark took the gold medal. Since the boat first appeared as a Moth design in 1960 it has evolved into a small, high performance single-hander, which offers excellent racing for sailors in the 50–70kg (110–154lb) weight range. The class is particularly strong in northern Europe.
Designer Alain Roland (France)
First launched 1960
Type Restricted
LOA 3.35m (11ft)
Beam 1.38m (4½ft)
Minimum hull weight 45kg (99lb)
Upwind sail area 7 sq m (75 sq ft)

ABOVE **The International Europe provides the best possible racing for women, using a design that has been greatly refined since its first appearance.**

ABOVE **The International Laser has been a massive success, based on the winning formula of the best possible racing combined with absolute simplicity.**

OK dinghy

The OK was originally introduced as a smaller, lighter alternative to the Finn, which would appeal to a wide range of sailors in the 70 kg (154 lb) range and be cheaply available in basic, box-shaped marine ply construction. Despite there being little more than 2,000 OKs registered, the class enjoys popularity in many countries with World and European champions drawn from nations as diverse as Australia (which hosted the 1998 World Championships), Poland, Denmark and Sweden.

Designer Knud Olsen (Norway)
First launched 1957
Type Restricted
LOA 4m (13ft)
Beam 1.42m (4½ft)
Minimum hull weight 72kg (159lb)
Upwind sail area 8.5 sq m (91 sq ft)

ABOVE **As a restricted class the OK has been steadily brought up to date, with carbon fibre masts being allowed from the year 2000.**

International Contender

The Contender was designed by Bob Miller, who confusingly changed his name to Ben Lexcen. Great things were expected of the Contender which, with a single-handed trapeze, was extremely radical for its time, and was widely tipped to supplant the aging Finn in the Olympics. Despite winning IYRU trials to find a new single-hander the Contender never made it to the Olympic slot, and its appeal has remained limited with less than 700 boats registered in almost 40 years.

Designer Bob Miller/Ben Lexcen (Australia)
First launched 1962
Type Restricted
LOA 4.87m (16ft)

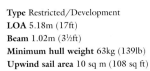

LEFT **The International Contender is the original single-handed trapeze boat. Despite being a difficult boat to sail, a committed band of enthusiasts continue to race it, and the best fleets are found in the UK and Germany.**

Beam 1.5m (5ft)
Minimum hull weight 83kg (183lb)
Upwind sail area 10.8 sq m (116 sq ft)

International 10 Sq M Canoe

The International 10 Square Metre Canoe is one of the most radical craft of them all with the narrowest beam of any one-design/restricted dinghy the world has ever known. This helps to give it a tremendous turn of speed upwind, making it undisputed as the world's fastest single-handed monohull for more than 50 years. It has a small but dedicated international following and has strong fleets in the UK, USA and Sweden, and regular World and European championships.

Learning to control an International Canoe is a skill that is reckoned to take an experienced sailor three or more years to perfect. Much of the difficulty is due to the enormous sliding seat, which projects more than 3m (10ft) from the centreline of the boat, where the crew hikes off the outside edge. Every tack is an exceptionally tricky manoeuvre.

Designer Nethercot (UK)
First launched 1946

RIGHT **Despite being among the oldest dinghies of them all, the International Canoe remains in a class apart when it comes to upwind speed.**

Type Restricted/Development
LOA 5.18m (17ft)
Beam 1.02m (3½ft)
Minimum hull weight 63kg (139lb)
Upwind sail area 10 sq m (108 sq ft)

International Moth

The International Moth is the boat for radical lightweights. There is no minimum hull weight, which encourages featherweight construction, and the basic rules cover little more than maximum length, beam and sail area. This has helped to take the International Moth design in very extreme directions, with the norm being a super-narrow hull coupled with maxi-wings. The result is a boat that is incredibly unstable and specialised to sail, but a lot of fun for the small band of enthusiasts who frequently build and design their own boats.

Designer Various
First launched 1939
Type Development
LOA 3.35m (11ft)
Beam 2.35m (7½ft)
Minimum hull weight No minimum.
Upwind sail area 8 sq m (86 sq ft)

ABOVE **With super-wide wings mounted on an extra narrow hull you can see why the International Moth is such a tricky boat to handle, but although it is very wobbly, it is also a lot of fun.**

RS600

The RS600 revived the single-handed trapeze concept of the Contender 30 years later in a much lighter, wider and more powerful package. The option of racing with wide or narrow racks provides a weight equalization system that allows technically able sailors across the 65–90kg (143–198lb) weight spectrum to enjoy racing in a single-hander, which is acknowledged as one of the fastest and most demanding dinghies on the water.

Designers Chris Everest and Nick Peters (UK)

First launched 1993

Type One-design

LOA 4.47m (14½ft)

Beam 1.93m (6½ft)

Minimum hull weight 52kg (115lb)

Upwind sail area 12.14 sq m (131 sq ft)

RS300

The RS300 is a very modern, club racing single-hander with a super-wide design concept borrowed from the International Moth, but used in a much more sailor-friendly way. The result is an exciting boat, which has wings spread wide over a narrow waterline, an unstayed carbon mast fitted with a GNAV, and the choice of two sail sizes for weight equalization.

Designer Clive Everest (UK)

First launched 1997

Type One-design

LOA 4.25m (14ft)

Beam 2m (6½ft)

Minimum hull weight 53kg (117lb)

Upwind sail area 9.25 sq m (99 sq ft)/ 10 sq m (108 sq ft)

Laser.eps

The Laser.eps was introduced as a direct challenger to the RS300 in a bid to establish a new, state-of-the-art small single-hander. Designed by Yves Loday, the Laser.eps introduced the mini-stay system with a short forestay and stub shrouds supporting the carbon mast at the gooseneck in order to control the rig while letting the boom right off downwind. The .eps also continues the Laser weight equalization philosophy, with a choice of two rigs for different weight helms and sliding aerowings which are adjusted to equalize leverage.

ABOVE **The RS300 is an innovative single-hander, which features wide wings with a surprisingly user-friendly hull design and carbon spars for fast tactical racing.**

Designer Yves Loday (France)

First launched 1998

Type One-design/Weight equalization

LOA 4.3m (14ft)

Beam 1.85–2.4m (6–8ft)

Minimum hull weight 53.5kg (118lb) plus 9kg (20lb) aerowings

Upwind sail area 9.3 sq m (100 sq ft)/ 8.4 sq m (90 sq ft)

ABOVE **The RS600 is a single-handed trapeze skiff, faster than most two person dinghies and featuring a unique reefing rig system.**

ABOVE **The Laser.eps features weight equalization adjustable aerowings and a mini shroud system, which supports the lightweight carbon mast. It also has two rig options.**

Skiffs

Skiff racing was first held in Sydney Harbour in 1827, and over the next 150 years developed a strong public following due to the spectacular size of the enormous rigs being used. However, it was not until 1975 that skiff development really began to race ahead and change the face of performance dinghy sailing. Dave Porter won the 18 Foot World Championships with KB, the first skiff to be helmed from the trapeze with a three-man crew replacing the conventional four-man crew, and the first boat in the world that would plane continuously on all points of sailing in nine knots of wind.

From then on there were two decades of intense development in lightweight hulls, wings, asymmetric spinnakers and flex-top masts, increasing the speed of the Australian skiffs to the point where they were unchallenged as the fastest boats in the world for round-the-buoys racing. This led directly to the development of

the 49er, a miniaturized 18 Foot Skiff with a blistering performance which at a single stroke took Olympic sailing into the 21st century.

Cherub

Despite first appearing almost half a century before the 49er, the Cherub is a clear forerunner of the modern gennaker-driven skiff concept. Just 3.5m (11½ft) long, weighing around 73kg (160lb) fully rigged and with plenty of canvas, it still combines spectacular downhill performance with on-the-edge handling that is only found in true lightweight skiffs and makes them so much fun to sail. The design was originally a one-off commission by John Spencer in New Zealand, which got its name when the owner referred to her as a perfect little cherub to sail. The new class rapidly spread to Australia and from there to Britain, and had rapid development until

ABOVE **A long bowsprit, a big gennaker, a fast ride and the front of the boat flying clear of the water mark out the Cherub as a forerunner of the modern skiff.**

The spinnaker/gennaker connection

In the 1960s the Cherub sported a primitive kind of asymmetric spinnaker mounted on a long boom with tremendous reaching performance, but the concept was soon shelved in favour of a more conventional spinnaker and did not resurface until the 1980s when Julian Bethwaite claims to have invented the asymmetric spinnaker or gennaker.

At the time Julian was looking for ways to simplify his Sydney Harbour 18 designs, which had become so over-complex that the skills required to sail them were overloading the crews. One of his answers to the problem was to replace the conventional gybing spinnaker pole with a fixed bowsprit, and flatten the leech of the spinnaker to give it an asymmetric shape, which would allow the boat to go downwind like an ice yacht. As downwind speed increased, it was found that speed depended on the luff length of the spinnaker rather than its area, with a single continuous sheet controlling the balance of the sail from tack to head with comparatively light sheet loads.

LEFT **Julian Bethwaite's development work on asymmetric spinnakers for the Sydney Harbour 18 class led directly to his design for the 49er more than a decade later.**

ABOVE **Flying high with the front half of the boat lifted clear of the water is the hallmark of an International 14 fully powered up by its gennaker. The class has experienced massive evolution since the trapeze was first introduced and then banned as being an unfair advantage.**

1984 when rules for UK Cherubs and Australian and New Zealand Cherubs went their own separate ways (the UK allowing a bigger rig and a considerably bigger gennaker).

Designers Various (New Zealand, Australia and UK)
First launched 1951
Type Development
LOA 3.7m (12ft)
Beam 1.8m (6ft) maximum
Minimum hull weight 50kg (110lb)
Upwind sail area 12.5 sq m (134 sq ft) (UK)
Gennaker 15 sq m (161 sq ft) (UK)

B14

The B14 is a wonderful little flying machine, which has become popular in the UK. Super-wide racks replace the trapeze for crew power, giving this lightweight boat performance that is both demanding and rewarding, and a phenomenal speed round a race course rated on par with the International 14.

Designer Julian Bethwaite (Australia)
First launched 1985
Type One-design
LOA 4.5m (14¾ft)
Beam 3.05m (10ft) (including wings)
Minimum hull weight 62kg (137lb)
Upwind sail area 17.2 sq m (185 sq ft)
Gennaker 29.2 sq m (314 sq ft)

International 14

The International 14 is a development racing dinghy with a very long and illustrious history, which has kept it at the forefront of small boat technology. Two British designers, Uffa Fox and Morgan Giles, proved that light is fast, and the first weighed less than 100kg (220lb) in the 1920s. In 1938 the class pioneered the use of the trapeze, then banned it for the next 30 years due to protests from the light wind, inland fleets.

In 1984 the class took a big step forward with the introduction of twin trapezes to increase sail carrying power and performance, and in 1988 unlimited asymmetric spinnakers were allowed,

ABOVE **Old meets new. Europe and Australia met head-on to resurrect the International 14, and turned it into a modern classic that rates as one of the most challenging boats on the water.**

following the lead of skiff sailors in Australia and New Zealand. Carbon hulls and masts soon followed.

The parallel development of the Australian 14 Foot Skiff class over a similar period of time led to the two classes merging in 1996, with the first combined World Championship held at San Francisco the following year. Despite being an expensive boat to race the International 14 continues to be one of the most desirable high performance boats the world has to offer and has international fleets in Australia, Canada, Denmark, Germany, Japan, New Zealand, Switzerland, the UK and USA. It had no less than 130 boats on the start line at the 1999 World Championships in Melbourne.

Designer Various
First launched 1908
Type Development
LOA 4.27m (14ft)
Beam 1.83m (6ft) maximum
Minimum hull weight 74.25kg (164lb)
Upwind sail area 18.56 sq m (200 sq ft)
Gennaker Unlimited

LEFT **The B14 has extra-wide wings instead of trapezes. Despite being a comparatively old design, it is a brilliant boat and is a real buzz to sail.**

16 Foot Skiff

The 16 Foot Skiff is a uniquely Australian dinghy, which has seen many developments over more than 100 years. The latest designs feature three crew, with two on trapeze wires, and massive masthead gennakers. Despite being highly demanding, they are one of the most popular high performance dinghies in Australia with more than 150 boats scattered through 12 clubs and 70-strong fleets at major regattas. To prevent costs escalating and provide closer racing, strict design rules were introduced in 1997/98, which fixed hull design and construction for eight years. The rules also limited competitors to having two masts, three jibs, two mainsails and two gennakers, which can be used in different combinations for optimal performance.

Designer Various (Australia)
First launched *c.* 1900
Type Restricted/Development
LOA 4.9m (16ft)
Beam 1.52–1.78m (5–6ft)
Minimum hull weight no limit
Upwind sail area 22 sq m (237 sq ft) maximum
Spinnaker 45 sq m (484 sq ft) maximum

LEFT **Popular modern classes such as the Iso and Laser 4000 have all the hallmarks of skiff development, but lack the super light weight combined with a powerful rig and knife edge handling, which is the hallmark of a true skiff.**

18 Foot Skiff

The Sydney Harbour 18 Foot Skiff is the ultimate triple trapeze development class, and probably the most spectacular dinghy on the water with a racing history that extends back to the 1890s. The first World Championship was held in Sydney in 1938, and Australia remains the home of the class although there are smaller circuits in the UK, USA, New Zealand and Japan as well as individual boats from France, Sweden, Holland, Italy and Canada.

Despite the exotic and extreme nature of the boat, class rules are framed to uphold the original philosophy of a boat within the means of the average man, which provides good competitive racing and attracts public interest. To this end the class currently uses a one-design hull, and an Iain Murray design replacing one by Julian Bethwaite and a list of approved materials that includes epoxy resin and carbon fibre. The maximum sail inventory allowed is two mainsails, two jibs and two gennakers, with mains and jibs constructed from Mylar, Dacron, Aramaid or Spectra at a minimum weight of 38g (1½oz). Each boat is allowed two masts of 10.2m (33½ft) and 9.2m (30ft) built in 6000 Series aluminium with optional fibreglass tops, and a maximum of one boom. In this class, there is also a maximum of one gennaker pole with a maximum length of 3.8m (12½ft) built in 6000 Series aluminium, while the most unlikely rule is a minimum age of 14 for crew members.

Designer Julian Bethwaite, Iain Murray (Australia).
First launched *c.*1890
Type Development
LOA 5.41–5.48m (17¾–18ft)
Beam 1.82–2.44m (6–7½ft)
Wings Not to exceed 2.13m (7ft) from the centreline.
Minimum hull weight 82.5kg (182lb)
Upwind sail area Unlimited
Gennaker Unlimited

ABOVE **Australia's 16 Foot and 18 Foot Skiffs push the limits where other classes dare not go, and provide a unique spectacle of humanity battling against extreme forces.**

ABOVE **It's difficult to believe that the 18 Foot Skiff first appeared in 1899, though there have been a few changes since then. This must be the ultimate fun machine for a three-man crew.**

International approval

International recognition is conferred on leading racing classes by the International Sailing Federation (ISAF, formerly known as the IYRU). The ISAF licenses class builders and administers and polices class rules, ensuring that all boats in a class race to a consistent formula wherever events are held in the world.

LEFT **The Europe is one of many internationally recognized classes, policed by the ISAF, which ensures consistency in construction and class rules.**

49er

The 49er set the dinghy world alight when it was selected as the new Olympic high performance dinghy within little more than a year of first taking to the water, making its Olympic Games debut in Sydney in 2000. It is a miniaturized development of the Sydney Harbour 18 Foot Skiff but, with a lower drag factor, is reckoned to need 85 per cent of the 18's relative power to achieve the same speed. In real terms it is rated almost as fast as the 18, despite giving away a tremendous amount in sail area.

With licensed builders around the world, the 49er is built in an epoxy woven cloth laminate with a PVC core using a glass epoxy space frame to handle loads from the rig. It has proved popular and extremely demanding, but while fun on flat water, sailing in wind and waves has a tendency to make it nose dive.

Designer Julian Bethwaite (Australia)
First launched 1995
Type Restricted
LOA 5m (16ft)
Beam 3m (10ft)
Minimum hull weight 62kg (137lb)
Upwind sail area 46.4 sq m (499 sq ft)
Spinnaker 29.2 sq m (314 sq ft)

RIGHT **The 49er brought the skiff story up to date and gave it worldwide respectability, even though it is rated as an exceptionally difficult, and sometimes downright unpleasant, boat to sail.**

Ultra 30

The Ultra 30 is in a class of its own as the
biggest one-design dinghy class in the
world. It was inspired by the Ultimate 30
development class in the USA, designed
by Rob Humphreys, and enjoyed a high
profile, fully televised circuit in Britain
during the 1990s.

The Ultra 30 class is 9.14m (30ft)
long with a 13.7m (45ft) mast, and has a
5m (15ft) long carbon gennaker boom to
fly its 150 sq m (1614 sq ft) gennaker. Six
identical boats were first built by Richard
Faulkener in Southampton in 1991,
followed by a seventh in 1999. All seven
feature a super-light epoxy laminate foam
core hull structure, and rig loads are
supported by an aluminium space frame.

Apart from sheer size, the feature that
really sets the Ultra 30s apart from other
skiffs is the number of crew needed to sail
them. Having no less than nine crew
crammed into an over-sized, over-powered
dinghy makes the Ultras an extraordinary

and spectacular boat to sail, particularly
when fitted with racks and nine trapeze
wires (introduced as an added attraction in
1999) in order to keep the boat level.

The Ultra 30 Crew

The boat is designed so that all nine crew
play a vital role in getting it around the
short, tight race course and, if they lack
perfect team work, they are likely to go
swimming. The crew are numbered from
1–9, and this is what they have to do:

Bow team:
*No 1 Bowman, No 2 Mastman, No 3
Halyard Tailer*
The bow team are in charge of getting the
gennaker up and down, which requires
skill, agility and timing combined with a
good deal of nerve when they drop the
sail in the last seconds before rounding a
mark. Any mistakes will result in a capsize
or a shredded sail.

RIGHT **The Ultra 30 circuit is more about fun than outright speed. Compared to an 18 Foot Skiff or 49er the boats are relatively heavy and ponderous and probably have too many crew for their own good, but they do provide a magnificent team building spectacle when sailing at full tilt.**

Mid-boat team:
No 4 Jib Trimmer, No 5 Gennaker Trimmer, No 6 Vang Trimmer, No 7 Mainsheet Trimmer

The mid-boat team must tweak the sail controls to keep the boat at performance boiling point. They also provide the main central ballast to keep the boat upright using brute force.

The afterguard:
No 8 Tactician, No 9 Helmsman

The afterguard plot tactics around the course and co-ordinate the crew. Communication is the key to success, as the tactician watches rival boats, looks for windshifts upwind and down, yells encouragement and orders at the crew, and feeds the helmsman with constant updates while he or she focuses on steering the boat to its ultimate performance. The final decision in all matters rests with the helmsperson, but when a boat is often in semi-control with the gennaker he or she can do no more than the skills of the crew allow when racing these magnificent dinosaurs, which appeared to be threatened by extinction when the circuit collapsed in 2000.

The Ultra 30 course

The Ultra 30s use the simplest possible upwind and downwind course, with just 0.8 km (½ mile) between the top and bottom marks and three intense races held on each day of a two-day regatta. The start line is a gate between two marks at the bottom of the course, from where the Ultras tack upwind to the top mark, which they can round in less than two minutes. From there it's gennakers up and gybe downwind to get back to the gate, choosing the best angles and watching gusts from behind, with the option of rounding either mark.

From there on the Ultras keep blasting round and round the course, until the 30 minute gun goes after which the leading boat through the gate is declared the winner. Boat-on-boat tactics and tight manoeuvring skills are vital when the one-design Ultra 30s can all sail at the same speed. With plenty of potential for collisions and not a little danger, a team of on-water umpires is on-hand to issue

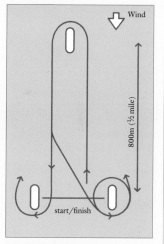

ABOVE **The upwind-downwind Ultra 30 course is simplicity itself, and similar to the race course used by a Tornado or 49er.**

immediate penalties for any rule infringements.A red flag means that a boat must do a complete 360 degree turn without delay, while a black flag spells instant dismissal from the race.

Catamarans

While the best gennaker-driven dinghies may push catamarans hard, two hulls are very fast and top catamarans such as the Tornado remain in a class of their own. Catamarans also provide a different style of sailing and competition, and are recommended to sailors who adore the thrill of speed.

International A Class

The A Class catamaran is the fastest small single-handed sailboat in the world, with a blistering performance that puts it close to the 49er despite its diminutive size. It is a largely unrestricted development class built to a super-light rule, and is at its fastest and most potent when racing inland in light to moderate winds. There is a small but dedicated following for the class led by Germany, Switzerland, Italy, Australia and the USA, while in Britain the Unicorn – a 1967 vintage A Class design by John Mazzotti (UK) – is established as a more popular and less extreme restricted class racer.

Designers Various
First launched 1962
Type Development
LOA 5.5m (18ft)
Beam 2.3m (7½ft) maximum
Minimum platform weight 30kg (66lb)
Upwind sail area 13.94 sq m (150 sq ft)

LEFT **The International Tornado has proved a difficult act to follow. It is exceptionally fast, a delight to sail, and Olympic competitors always rate it as their number one choice.**

International Tornado

The Tornado swept the board at the first ever trials for an Olympic catamaran, and has been an Olympic class at every Games since 1976 in Canada, when Reg White and John Osborn won the first gold medal. More than 30 years of intense competition among the best sailors in the world continuously refined the Tornado and ensured it seldom had a problem proving that it was the fastest racing catamaran in the world. However by 1996 it had become refined to the point where it was turning into a virtual one-design, with almost all boats built by Göran Marström of Sweden. Attempts to introduce a Tornado Sport with twin trapezes, bigger mainsail and gennaker failed. The ISAF may try to replace this catamaran classic with a more modern and potentially more popular alternative.

Designers Rodney March (UK)
First launched 1967
Type Restricted
LOA 6.1m (20ft)
Beam 3.05m (10ft)
Minimum platform weight 127kg (280lb)
Upwind sail area 21.8 sq m (235 sq ft)

ABOVE **The International A Class catamaran has an exceptional power to weight ratio, and is likely to be the fastest boat on the water upwind in a light or moderate breeze.**

ABOVE **Formula 18 is a tightly drafted measurement rule that prohibits the use of carbon. The class has flourished in Europe where it is the top choice for gennaker catamaran racing.**

Formula 18

This was originally a French concept for a restricted measurement class of twin trapeze, gennaker-driven catamarans. Support for the rule spread through Europe, with France, Britain, Italy and Germany leading the way in national and European racing circuits.

The Formula 18 rule was very carefully drafted in an effort to limit an arms war attitude to sailing and premature obsolescence. In this it has been highly successful, and leading designs, primarily the Dart Hawk, Hobie Tiger and Nacra 18 – have stayed competitive over a long period of time and rely on the crew's skills to decide who wins the races.

Designers Various
First launched 1993
Type Restricted
LOA 5.5m (18ft)
Beam 2.6m (8½ft)
Minimum overall weight no limit
Upwind sail area 20.45 sq m (220 sq ft)/ 21.15 sq m (228 sq ft)
Gennaker 19 sq m (205 sq ft)/ 21.8 sq m (235 sq ft)

Dart 18

Following straight on from his design for the ultra elite Tornado, Rodney March demonstrated the breadth of his design skills by introducing the Dart 18 – a single trapeze, performance catamaran that is as simple as possible to own and is suitable for everyone. The Dart 18 has skegs rather than daggerboards, no boom and the most fundamental sail controls, but the result is that it has enjoyed non-stop popularity as an exceptionally user-friendly one-design. It also provides some of the very best class racing on a scale that ranges from club to international championship events in many countries. To help bring it in line with modern skills it can be sailed for fun with an optional gennaker package.

Designer Rodney March (UK)
First launched 1976
Type One-design
LOA 5.5m (18ft)
Beam 2.3m (7½ft)
Minimum platform weight 130kg (286lb)
Upwind sail area 16.072 sq m (173 sq ft)

Hobie 16

Hobie Alter designed his first Hobie 14 as a boat to get out and sail in waves, using distinctive asymmetric banana-shaped hulls with no daggerboards or skegs so it could sail straight up the beach, and a raised trampoline to keep the crew clear of the waves. The 14 became a worldwide success as a fun-racing, single-handed cat, and was soon followed by the two crew, twin trapeze Hobie 16. This was a scaled-up, and even more successful version and is the best selling catamaran of all time selling thousands of boats worldwide and sales still going strong.

The appeal of these early Hobie designs is that they define the phrase beach cat, have an image that has remained attractive, are tough and very durable if somewhat heavy, and still have formidable reaching performance, plus a tendency to indulge in sensational pitch-pole capsizes. While the Hobie 14 has become rather dated, the Hobie 16 has built up and maintained a huge international racing circuit, and even made an unsuccessful bid to replace the Tornado

ABOVE **The Hobie 16 has proved equally successful as a beach catamaran for recreational use and as a racer, which has been selected for major ISAF championships.**

in the 2000 Olympic Games. Both Hobie 14 and 16 have been built in the USA, South America, Australia, South Africa and France, reflecting a worldwide enthusiasm for sailing and racing the original Hobies.

Designer Hobie Alter (USA)
First launched 1970
Type One-design
LOA 5.11m (16¾ft)
Beam 2.4m (8ft)
Minimum platform weight 145kg (320lb)
Upwind sail area 20.26 sq m (218 sq ft)

ABOVE **The Dart 18 is a one-design racing catamaran that is almost as simple to own and race as a Laser. Events for the class are held worldwide and the 2000 World Championship was staged in South Africa.**

OTHER CATAMARAN CLASSES

With the noble exceptions of Holland and France, catamaran sailing and racing tends to be a minority interest when compared to monohulls. Most countries support their own favourite classes, and the following brands are among some of the best known names.

Dart (UK)

Apart from the Dart 18 one-design and Dart Hawk Formula 18 racer, Dart's best known catamaran is the Dart 15, a little sister to the 18, which was designed by Rodney March in 1979. The 15 can be sailed either with two lightweight crew or single-handed.

A more recent arrival to the range is the Dart 16, which was launched in 1997, and designed and developed by Yves Loday and Reg White (both Tornado Gold medalists) who also produced the Hawk.

RIGHT **The Hurricane 5.9, shown here in optional sport mode with a gennaker, has slim, sharp hulls like the Tornado, but is slightly shorter. It is also a lot narrower to make it more practical, with twin trapezes to make up for the loss of leverage.**

White Formula (UK)

Having won the first Tornado gold medal, Reg White was for many years a famous builder of Tornados, before concentrating on the Hurricane 5.9, which he developed as a more user-friendly catamaran offering nearly as good performance. It is narrower than the Tornado, for easy trailing and storage, but has twin trapezes to compensate for loss of crew power. The Hurricane 5.9 built up a popular and very competitive circuit in the UK, with occasional incursions into France, Holland and Italy.

White Formula has also made attempts to produce and market an ultimate catamaran. The 6.5m (21ft) Hurricane 6.5 sported massive racks and a huge rig, but proved too ponderous to sail consistently fast and was very expensive. The Tornado Sport left the standard Tornado in its wake thanks to twin trapezes, bigger mainsail and gennaker, but was rejected by the International Tornado Association. The 6m (20ft) Storm was introduced in prototype form in 1999, and was due for series production in 2000.

Prindle/Mystere (USA/Canada)

The Prindle 16 followed the design style of the Hobie 14 and 16, but with more volume in the hulls for all-round fun use. It proved a big success, and was followed by totally different models such as the Prindle 18.2 and 19. Both of these slim, swift catamarans owed their style to the Tornado, as did the similar Mystere 6.0 from Canada.

Nacra (USA)

The Nacra catamaran range is manufactured alongside Prindle in California, and has replaced it for high performance competition use. Much of the design input and demand for Nacra comes from Holland, a small country that boasts more catamarans and more Nacras

LEFT **These young sailors are having a good time on a Dart 15, but this catamaran has proved equally successful as an adult single-handed racer. It was originally introduced as the small sister to the Dart 8.**

ABOVE **The Dart 16 combines beach friendly moulded plastic hulls with design development led by Yves Loday and Reg White. The result is a catamaran that belies its appearance and is easily controlled and fun to sail. The crew displaying a rather unconventional trapeze stance here.**

LEFT **A fleet of Prindles line up for an offshore marathon. The Prindle 18.2 and 19 were well regarded as high performance racing cats, but the range then switched to the recreational market in favour of Nacra.**

RIGHT **The Nacra (named after the North American Cat Racing Association) enjoyed a period of popularity with the 5.0, 5.5 and 6.0 models before the introduction of the Inter 18 (Formula 18), Inter 20 (Formula 20) and single-handed Inter 17.**

ABOVE **Fast and stately. The Hobie 21 Formula is the biggest Hobie of them all, and a magnificent boat for long distance sailing.**

Marström Sailworks (Sweden)

Göran Marström was the Tornado bronze medal winner at the 1980 Olympics, and became established as the world's most popular Tornado builder over the next 20 years. With the ISAF keen to replace the Tornado for the 2004 Olympics, Marström launched an all carbon 6m (20ft) prototype in 1999 designed to take over from the Tornado as the undisputed fastest catamaran in the world.

ABOVE **The Inter 18 soon established itself as one of the fastest boats in the Formula 18 class, racing with the Hobie Tiger, Dart Hawk and Diam at venues such as the Italian lakes.**

than anywhere else in the world. The Nacra line-up is committed to high performance and includes:

- The Inter 18 is a Formula 18 designed by Gino Morelli of PlayStation mega-cat fame.
- The Inter 17 is a scaled-down, single-handed variation on the 18.
- The Inter 20 is a scaled-up, self-styled Formula 20 suitable for heavier sailors.

Hobie (Europe and USA)

Following the initial success of Hobie Alter, the Hobie business was sold and split between Hobie USA and Hobie Europe, both of which have manufactured the original 14 and 16. Other top Hobie models include the Hobie 17 single-hander (single trapeze with wings), the Hobie 18 and 18 Formula (twin trapeze with optional wings), the Hobie Tiger Formula 18 and the mighty Hobie 21 (twin or triple trapeze).

ABOVE **The Tornado Sport was a big rig, twin wire, three-sail, variation on the Tornado developed by Reg White, Yves Loday and Mitch Booth, but rejected by the International Tornado Association.**

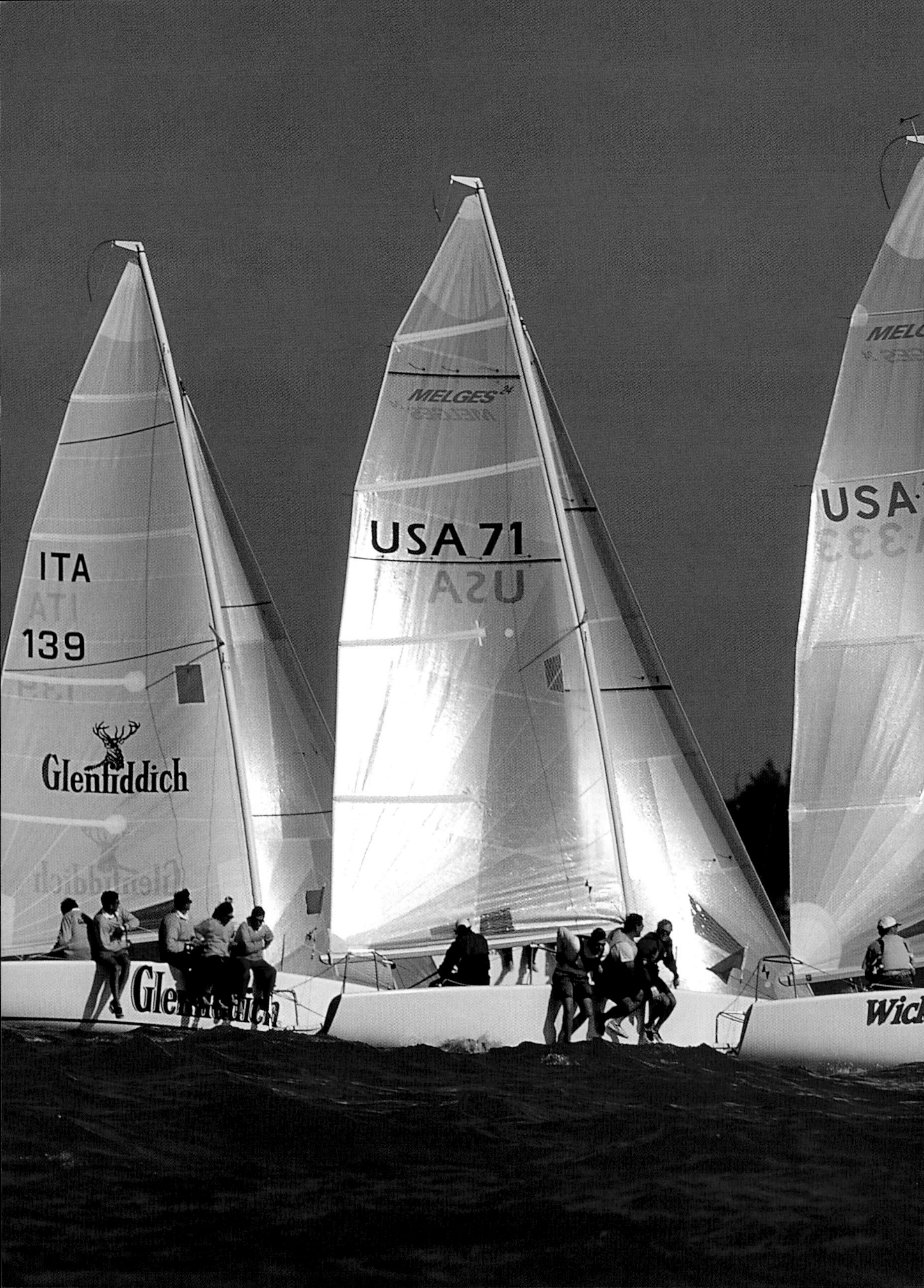
ITA
139
Glenfiddich
MELGES 24
USA 71
USA
MELGES
Wick

KEELBOAT
BASICS

Yachts that have ballast hanging beneath the boat come in all shapes, sizes and styles. The keel is there to ensure that they cannot capsize – except in rare and extreme circumstances – and the levels of performance range from sedate cruising to blue ocean racing. Pure cruisers and cruiser-racer yachts comprise by far the biggest category of keelboat, with out-and-out racing boats such as W60 round-the-world racers only accounting for a very small but highly publicized sector. In contrast to the spartan demands of pure racers, cruising yachts aim to combine the best possible accommodation with excellent seakeeping and performance, as do many yachts that can be cruised or raced with equal enjoyment.

An important sub-category among keelboats consists of the smaller open racing boats, many of which have become classic designs, epitomized by the beautiful Dragon, Etchells and Soling, which are all designed for a three man crew. Sportsboats provide a newer thrill in racing keelboats, needing four or five crew to handle a vessel that behaves like a performance dinghy.

LEFT *Sportsboats are small, fast, and provide excellent competition around the world.*

BELOW *It is important that crew check ropes regularly for abrasion.*

Types of keel

The traditional full-length keel has been almost totally superseded by variations on the fin keel. This removes the after part of a full length keel, leaving the ballasted equivalent of a dinghy daggerboard to provide the necessary righting moment and resistance to leewards side-slip, and is likely to offer the best performance in all its forms.

The more performance-oriented the yacht, the deeper and narrower the fin profile is likely to be since hydrodynamic force is proportional to the area of the keel. However, a deeper, narrower fin may prevent the yacht from sailing and mooring close inshore. Drying out on the bottom when the tide goes out is particularly difficult, and the boat is likely to be more sensitive under sail. Most cruising yachts will therefore compromise with a shoal (shallow) draught fin keel, which provides a high level of stability combined with a long, straight bottom for the yacht to rest on. This type of keel is frequently used with a skeg – a mini keel at the back of the yacht that helps balance the rudder.

Bulb and fin keels

These combine a slim, narrow keel with a large lump of ballast fixed to the bottom. This may appear to be a good solution for

LEFT **Even under perfect conditions, careful preparation and a basic knowledge is needed to ensure that cruiser sailing is safe and enjoyable.**

maximizing the righting moment of the keel due to having all the ballast on the tip, but the bulb offers poor performance compared to a tapered fin when it comes to cutting through the water with minimum resistance and maximum lift.

A bulb and fin profile is sometimes used for lifting keels, which retract into the

hull. The fin lifts into a housing inside the boat and the bulb lies flush under the hull to minimize draught.

The disadvantage is the complex mechanical or hydraulic lifting system and a keel case that takes up considerable room inside the boat. Apart from being able to lift the weight of the keel into the hull, the

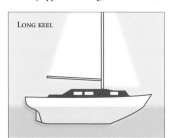

ABOVE **The traditional long keel yacht tends to be very stable, but more slow and ponderous than a fin keel yacht.**

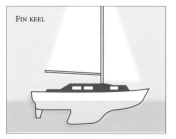

ABOVE **A fin keel that is similar to a dinghy daggerboard gives a yacht maximum performance with very sensitive handling.**

ABOVE **This W60 round the world racing yacht has deep fin keels that provide maximum lift to windward and resistance to leeway.**

design needs to ensure that the keel stays totally rigid and locked down while sailing. A compromise solution is to have a centreboard that lifts into a shallow, stub keel. The centreboard combats leeway and provides lift when fully down and, when retracted, the boat is able to negotiate shoal waters under motor, or possibly under sail with plenty of allowance for leeway and poor response.

Bilge keels

These provide a clever solution for yachts that have to dry out frequently on a mooring or at anchor in tidal waters, and require shoal draught. The identical twin keels protrude from the bilges, and allow the boat to sit upright rather than resting on its side when aground. Due to much greater hydrodynamic resistance the performance of a bilge keeler

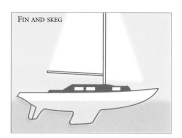

ABOVE **The fin and skeg is a popular modern compromise, which effectively removes most of a long keel, but retains the after part as a skeg to enhance stability and ensure the rudder remains well balanced.**

is inferior to a yacht with a single fin keel, but cruising performance may be more than adequate when only a small percentage is lost in terms of absolute speed and pointing ability.

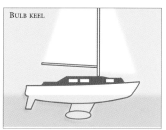

ABOVE **A torpedo shaped bulb on the end of a fin keel helps concentrate the centre of gravity lower down, allowing stability to be combined with a comparatively short keel for shoal draught sailing.**

LEFT **This Dufour yacht has a large bulb at the end of its short keel with plenty of weight to ensure maximum righting moment and stability. The bulb is extended towards the stern to produce a sufficiently long base for the yacht to dry out in tidal areas.**

LEFT **The bilge keeler provides unrivalled stability when drying out in a tidal location, with two stubby keels resting on the bottom and the ability to sail or motor into shallow anchorages. The downside is that performance is compromised due to the much greater wetted surface area.**

Capsize impossible?

The ballasted keel of a keelboat ensures that it cannot capsize in a conventional sense like a dinghy. The more the boat heels, the more effective the righting moment of the keel becomes, until there comes a point where it is impossible to heel any further. However, in extreme cases a keelboat may be knocked flat on the water by the combined effects of wind and waves. Thankfully this is a rare occurrence. Early problems with open racing keelboats and sportsboats filling with water have largely been solved by the use of self-draining cockpits and better buoyancy distribution. Even short-handed yachts that get knocked down while racing through the Southern Ocean tend to remain afloat even when they lose their keels and turn turtle.

ABOVE **This knock-down on a Hunter 707 looks horrific. However, the centre of gravity has swung in an arc, which takes it further and further from the centre of buoyancy, and it is impossible to tip any further. Only the spinnaker is holding it down.**

Cruiser size

Bigger is better is not necessarily true of yachts where big will almost certainly entail proportionally greater expense in the costs of buying the boat, annual maintenance and everyday running. Additional disadvantages include not being able to get into anchorages, which are delightful but small, due to length or draught, plus the hassle and effort of signing on extra crew to sail the boat. It's not much fun for a husband and wife with two young children to have to manage everything on an 18m (59ft) boat, where big starts to mean heavy and hard to handle.

The obvious advantages of going big are that you get far more space both on deck and below deck with the possibility of large, double berth cabins; the boat will probably go faster due to its extra waterline length; and there is plenty of scope for on-aboard luxuries such as a fridge, central heating, computer and TV.

However, on top of being cheaper to buy, smaller cruising yachts have a lot going for them. They are cheaper and

LEFT **Racing yachts of this size demand a crew that is 12 or 13 strong. Running them becomes a complex management task, which demands considerable expense.**

simpler to own, as well as sail, and will often enable those on board to experience a style of sailing that gets as close as possible to the pure sensation of a dinghy. Luck with the weather may be required to enjoy cruising in company on a small yacht, but it is likely to be far more important to keep the boat ship-shape and prevent the depressing build-up of cramp conditions caused by clutter.

6m (20ft) cruisers

This is about as short LOA (length overall) as you can go for comfortable cruising. Two good friends can have a great time if the weather is fine, especially if they have a cockpit tent to provide extra shelter in rainy weather. Facilities for cooking and personal hygiene are likely to be very basic, but a small cruiser of this size should be easy to handle and, if fitted with a lifting keel, will be able to get right into the beach and go where larger yachts dare not follow. Auxiliary power is likely to be provided by oars or an outboard motor.

LEFT **Big is magnificent, but comes at a price. This purpose built 32m (105ft) record-breaking catamaran** Playstation **is very fast, expensive and not practical for everyday use.**

BELOW **Less impressive for sure, but a simple, small yacht can give a great deal of hassle-free pleasure. The most important ingredient may well be the sun, with fair or foul weather making all the difference to the level of enjoyment when sailing.**

RIGHT **The Dragonfly 800** trimaran provides a great deal of space for fair weather sailing, with wide trampolines between the main hull and floats on both sides. It also has cracking performance, with no need for a heavy yacht keel owing to the stability of its platform.

LEFT **The Bavaria 46** provides all the luxuries a larger yacht offers with a teak deck and sun awning for use in the Caribbean or Mediterranean, while roller reefing headsails and mainsail help ensure it can be handled by a family size crew.

6–9m (20–29¹/₂ft) cruisers

The tendency for designers to produce small cruisers with all the characteristics of a caravan – maximum accommodation with awful looks and even more awful sailing performance – has thankfully been overcome and replaced by more thoughtful creations. A modern yacht in the middle of this range should accommodate up to four adults in comfort on a one or two-week cruise, while a 9m (29¹/₂ft) boat could possibly accommodate up to six adults. In both cases this presumes fine weather – if it is foul and freezing and the crew are forced to spend a lot of time below deck, it will be wise to reduce their numbers by one or two.

Most modern yachts from about 7.5m (25ft) upwards will feature a reasonable fixed galley with a small sink and two-burner stove, a heads (lavatory) compartment complete with a door for privacy, and may also have a fixed navigation area. Boat handling will

become progressively heavier as the size of the boat increases and inboard diesel engines take over from outboards as the preferred auxiliary option.

9–14m (29¹/₂–46ft) cruisers

Yachts in this range can pack in a lot of extra space, which is often used to provide double berth cabins and complete owners' suites. Everything is on a bigger scale and include luxury fittings such as ovens, fridges, hot and cold pressurized running water and heating. The galley, heads compartment and navigation centre become progressively grander as the general level of comfort increase, but eight adults on a cruise for an extended period may still feel like a crowd despite the increased size of a 14m (46ft) boat. The rig, sails and anchor also become larger, and are consequently heavier and more difficult to handle. Heavy duty winches are needed to wind up and wind in the sails, and an electric windlass to let down and pull up the anchor.

14m (46ft) plus cruisers

At this level a yacht passes what many people might consider a sensible size for a family cruiser used for coastal pottering. It enters the realm where size may help to make long distance sailing and ocean passages an enjoyable possibility, presuming the crew are experienced and have a yacht that is well set-up for the task in hand.

Wheel or tiller?

Tillers are normally found on smaller cruisers 9m (29¹/₂ft) or less in length where they are a simple, low cost solution to steering the boat. The tiller gives direct feedback from the rudder, which must be balanced so the tiller stays light in the helmsperson's hands with no excess weather or lee helm. The main disadvantage is that the tiller sweeps across the cockpit and uses up valuable space.

Wheels are likely to be standard on any cruiser much bigger than 10.5m (35ft), either fitted with a cable linkage or a hydraulic mechanism, which makes steering easier on bigger yachts. The wheel leaves an uncluttered cockpit for the crew, and enables the helmsperson to change position, steering from either side, or in the middle where he or she can watch the compass. Apart from greater cost, a possible disadvantage is that a wheel system is more complex and therefore more likely to fail than a tiller. An emergency tiller should therefore be carried at all times.

ABOVE **The X-412** aims to combine top performance with cruising luxury. Note the roomy and well protected cockpit, stern ladder for swimming and boarding, and wide teak decks comfortable for bare feet (but don't risk bare toes when sailing).

ABOVE **When a yacht heels** the rudder will pull to windward, and a geared wheel is necessary for comfortable control on mid-size yachts and upwards. The bigger the wheel the better the leverage and response. The helmsman of the Corel 45 has a fine view forwards standing to windward.

Types of rig

The rigs on the majority of modern yachts follow the Bermudan sloop format, either fractional or masthead. In addition there are still plenty of traditional yachts fitted with a wide range of delightful rig variations, which may be less practical, but seldom fail to delight the eye.

Traditional style

A gaff, gunter or lugsail rig may look very fine but, when compared to a modern sloop rig, is likely to be heavier, have more windage and drag, be considerably less efficient upwind and probably more difficult to handle. A possible plus-point is that a shorter mast is required, which, with a quickly lowered gaff, is a useful feature for sailing on rivers with low bridges.

Mizzen style

Yawls and ketches have a mizzen mast and sail aft of the mainmast. This mast is either sited behind the helm (yawl) or in front (ketch), and in most cases is considerably smaller than the forward mainmast. The exception is a two-masted schooner on which the mizzen mast is taller, and therefore becomes the mainmast supporting the mainsail.

The object of a mizzen is to produce a rig that is more balanced fore and aft, with an overall reduction in sail and spar size for easier handling, particularly in very windy conditions when the boat can

LEFT **Wooden boom, mast and blocks add to the weight of a vintage racing rig, with the complexity of running backstays (windward side on the right) to hold it all up.**

be sailed without the mainsail. The principal drawbacks are lost deck space taken up by the extra mast and sail, plus considerable extra cost and complexity. As such the concept is only likely to be found on very large yachts of 27m (88½ft) and more, where it is desirable to reduce the height of the mainmast and sails and constraints of cost and space are less likely to matter.

GAFF

GUNTER

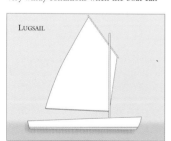

LUGSAIL

YAWL

KETCH

RIGHT **The fractional rig also allows controlled mast bend which is used to vary the amount of camber in the mainsail of a racing yacht as well as tightening the forestay and headsail luff.**

ABOVE **The Sunsail Venezia 42 catamaran has an easily handled, fractional Bermudan sloop rig complete with roller furling headsail, making it an ideal yacht for Caribbean charter.**

Sloop style

The Bermudan sloop rig with a single main mast and a sail wardrobe built round two principal sails – mainsail and headsail/jib – is the number one choice for most modern sailboats including dinghies and keelboats of all kinds. Heavy wooden masts have been totally replaced by lightweight, tapered aluminium (and occasionally carbon) masts. High aspect rigs, which do not compromise performance or safety when a boat is heeling or pitching, have been developed. These use sails that can be reduced or increased in area with relatively little effort in order to match changing wind conditions.

There are two principal types of sloop rig. The more traditional masthead rig has a forestay that goes right to the top of the mast and can be used with a full-height genoa. This is suitable for most cruising requirements, but in many cases has been superseded by the fractional rig in which the forestay only goes a certain height up the mast. The fractional rig is a direct development from dinghy sailing and dedicated cruiser racing and has a number of plus and minus features that sets it apart.

The fractional format allows a smaller section, lighter mast, which can be bent or straightened, making the sail flatter or fuller for different conditions. It has the potential for far superior windward performance than a masthead rig, as well as being lighter and more aerodynamically efficient. However, the lighter and bendier the mast is, the more complex the rigging will need to be to prevent it from failing. It may also require considerable input and skill from the crew, who will use the combination of top and bottom runners (running backstays), adjustable backstay and kicker to progressively bend the mast and flatten the sail to their requirements, while maintaining a taut forestay for maximum pointing ability. The additional cost of a high performance fractional rig will of course be considerable, and the concept is not recommended for relaxed cruising.

SLOOP MASTHEAD

SPRITSAIL

SLOOP FRACTIONAL

SCHOONER RIGGED YACHT

LATEEN

STANDING RIGGING

The standing rigging, which holds the mast up, is generally made of cable using twisted wire strands. The greater the number of wire strands the more flexible the cable becomes. A cable with 259 strands of 0.5mm (⅟₅₀in) wire bends so easily that it can be used for applications such as runners and be pulled around blocks, but because the strands are thin they will wear through. At the other end of the scale a cable with 19 strands of 1.14mm (⅟₂₀in) wire is very strong, relatively cheap and ideal for straight pull applications such as stays and shrouds. A single strand 8mm (⅟₃in) rod with a smooth outer surface is lighter and more aerodynamically efficient but is generally considered an expensive solution for fixed shrouds, which only racing boats need indulge in.

Sail inventory

A typical cruising yacht might carry the following sail wardrobe:
Mainsail Slab reefing is most common on small to mid-size cruisers. Sail size is reduced by pulling equivalent points on the luff and the leech down onto the boom.

Boom roller reefing is a more old-fashioned option. The sail is rolled around

LEFT **Standing rigging on a Trintella 51, which sports a fairly complex rig with triple spreaders and running backstays to allow a comparatively slim and lightweight mast.**

RIGHT **Bottlescrews allow precise adjustment of the length of the shrouds and inner stays, which help control mast bend. Tape is used to cover the ends of split pins to prevent snags and tears.**

the boom to reduce sail area, but normally sets very poorly due to insufficient leech and foot tension.

Mast roller reefing is a highly sophisticated system mainly used on large, luxury yachts. To reduce sail area the mainsail is wound onto a roller inside the mast. This produces an efficient sail shape with plenty of leech and foot tension, but the mechanics for rolling the sail are complex and expensive.

Headsails Genoas have the clew behind the shrouds when sheeted hard in, and may be either a number 1 (large) or a number 2 (small). Jibs have the clew in front of the shrouds when sheeted hard in, and may also come in different sizes: number 1 (also known as the working jib), number 2, and so on as they get smaller. A storm jib is for use in severe gale force conditions. It is the smallest possible headsail, cut from the same heavyweight

cloth as a mainsail and has robust reinforcement and fittings, with a very short chord and high clew almost halfway up the sail to ensure the flattest possible shape. Modern storm jibs may be coloured bright orange for maximum visibility.

Many cruising yachts are now fitted with a genoa mounted on a roller in the pulpit, which allows the size of the sail to be progressively reduced by roller-reefing. This eliminates the need for filling the interior of the boat with bulky, heavy sails, and is much simpler, and often safer, than sending crew up onto the foredeck to change sails. However, as the size of the headsail is reduced it may progressively loses its shape, becoming baggy and inefficient to windward. Therefore many yachts with roller-reefing genoas carry a separate storm jib to ensure they can make ground to windward in severe conditions.

ABOVE **An in-mast mainsail system allows the mainsail to be rolled into the mast for reefing or total stowage. It is most often used in a powered application on luxury yachts. In some instances the mainsail is rolled inside the boom.**

RIGHT **The overlapping genoa is the powerhouse of most modern high performance yachts. The slot funnells the wind over the leeward side of the mast and mainsail to help drive the rig forwards.**

ABOVE Spinnakers always look great and can be a lot of fun to sail with. However, if the wind's up, they demand commitment and skill, with the wide top half of this powerful sail taking over control of the yacht when the crew gets things wrong.

Spinnakers The conventional spinnaker is a relatively complex sail to use, which demands a high level of expertise from the crew and enough spare hands to manage the sheet, guy, pole, hoist and drops.

For cruising use the spinnaker has therefore been superseded by the asymmetric cruising chute, which requires

ABOVE The spinnaker on a racing yacht is launched off the foredeck. The crewman wears a harness, ready to go up the mast or out to the end of the spinnaker boom if required.

no pole, and is flown from a tack-strap with a permanent clew in the style of a dinghy gennaker. The cut of the sail normally combines radial head panels with horizontal lower panels to maximize how easily the sail floats or flies with the wind, and thanks to a dousing sock (a sausage-shape bag that pulls up and down over the sail) the sail can easily be launched and dropped by a short-handed crew.

Materials Woven polyester cloth has long been the favoured material for cruising sails, with heavier cloth up to 23g (1oz) used for mainsails and stormsails and progressively lighter cloth down to 13g (½oz) for genoas and other headsails.

The rapid development of lightweight laminates for racing sails has had an indirect effect on the cruising market, where laminate sails can claim several advantages over woven polyester despite the considerable extra cost:

- Laminates are lighter, which makes them easier to handle, and to a minor extent creates less heel and pitching.
- Laminates are more stable with less stretch. They can be carried higher up the wind scale, and are likely to maintain their shape better when used with a furling system.
- Laminates claim similar durability, if they have woven polyester bonded to both sides of the reinforced scrim for maximum protection.
- Cruising spinnakers and asymmetric chutes are generally made from woven nylon. The best materials combine optimum tear strength, stability and light weight.

What is a laminate?

A traditional polyester sail is made from a solid mass of woven cloth. A laminate sail is made from a layered sandwich of materials, which at its most basic will consist of an open lattice-shaped scrim of fibres held together with resin, with a layer of film bonded to each side. The film prevents air blowing straight through the laminate, the load is taken by the scrim, and the result is a sail material that can be considerably lighter and less prone to stretch than woven polyester, but with greater cost and poorer long-term durability.

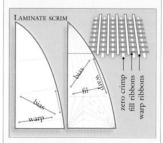

ABOVE A laminate scrim uses bonded warp and fill ribbons, which lie completely flat, to provide maximum resistance to stretch and loading in both horizontal and radial cut sails. Materials used may range from an economical polyester such as Dupont Dacron to top performing High Modulus Twaron combined with Spectra.

Ropes and hardware

Winches, blocks, cleats and ropes all contribute to making it possible for a short-handed crew to handle a relatively powerful rig in safety. With modern design and technology, ropes and hardware are also becoming lighter, more powerful and more efficient.

Ropes and lines

All modern ropes have a synthetic fibre base and are supplied in various diameters that are suitable for specific breaking loads. There are four principal applications listed as follows:

Sheets These need to be easily handled, soft on the hands, flexible and non-kinking. Rope diameter for cruising use will range from about 10–16mm (around ½in) for mainsail and headsail sheets depending on the size of yacht, and upwards from 8mm (¼in) for spinnaker sheets. Colour coding helps to differentiate between spinnaker and headsail sheets and other control lines.

Halyards and control lines These need the best possible strength-to-weight ratio with minimum stretch. They should be non-kinking and easily coiled, with colour coding as well to help differentiation. Rope diameter is likely to range from 8mm (¼in) and upwards.

Anchoring and mooring lines These should be soft and flexible on the hands and non kinking. When choosing lines, suitability for splicing and good abrasion resistance are added factors to look out for. The breaking load of anchoring and mooring lines should relate directly to the displacement (weight of water displaced by a floating boat, same as that of the boat) of the yacht.

General purpose lines These include narrow diameter lines for uses such as burgee halyards, leech lines, outboard starter cords and whipping twine.

Rope care

- Ensure ropes are correctly sized for all deck hardware.
- Make regular checks for chafing against rough surfaces.
- Beware of sharp edges on blocks, cleats, winches and other hardware.
- Ropes should be periodically hand-washed with mild soap to remove salt crystals.
- Unlaying (coming apart) of rope ends can be prevented by applying quality whipping twine or tape.
- Damaged rope must be completely replaced, or where possible cut out and spliced with a new section.

ABOVE **Winches, cleats, clutches and tracks have been designed for minimalist simplicity on the racing yacht Arbitrator, ensuring the weight of hardware is kept to a minimum and is centred in the boat, with plenty of open space for the crew to work at maximum efficiency.**

LEFT **The running rigging of a yacht relies on a wide range of modern synthetic ropes, which have been designed for specific applications. While these ropes are very tough, the crew should make regular checks for abrasion, which is bound to occur at stress points.**

Rope safety

Beware of rope burn. Never let a rope run quickly through an unprotected hand. Any rope with a synthetic content is potentially dangerous; the cheap kind of floating, brightly coloured nylon rope that fishermen use is the most dangerous of all. If a rope wants to run, take a turn round a cleat to hold it quickly or let it go.

When handling rope, it makes sense to wear protective sailing gloves with reinforced palms that grip well and provide an important level of protection.

Rope clutches

The rope clutch (spin lock) is a unique rope holding system that has superseded the use of cleats for many applications in racing and cruising yachts. The clutch allows the line to be pulled in under load, and the line will lock firmly in position immediately the pulling stops. When there is no load the clutch can be unlocked to let the line run free, and on many designs the clutch will also allow controlled release when the line is at full holding load.

Rope clutches are particularly useful for halyards and control lines such as the outhaul, cunningham, topping lift or genoa furler, and can be used for virtually every cruising application with the exception of headsail and spinnaker sheets.

The clutch is a mechanical device, and care needs to be taken to ensure that it functions correctly. A regular flushing through with fresh water will prevent the build-up of corrosive salt, and small applications of silicone or Teflon lubricant occasionally will help the release action of the axle handle.

Rope slip

This is an occasional problem with clutches; probable causes include:
- The load is in excess of the amount the clutch was designed for. Beyond that amount the clutch will automatically slip rather than damage and possibly break the rope.
- The line is the wrong size or too soft for the clutch. All clutches are designed to operate with specific rope sizes. If the line is smaller, the maximum holding load will be reduced. A top quality hard-cored line will always hold better than a soft-cored line with a loose cover.
- The cam in the clutch may be worn or unsuitable for a new style of modern rope, but can normally be replaced or upgraded.

ABOVE **A mass of rope clutches is used to lock off control lines and free up winches, although this yacht has clearly gone for safety in numbers with such an array of pedestals.**

ABOVE **Sheets need to be soft and easily handled with minimal stretch. Always use bowlines when attaching sheets to the clew of a headsail.**

Winches

Geared winches are required to wind in all ropes with high loadings. A typical small cruising yacht will have two primary winches for the genoa and headsail sheets. As yachts get bigger, additional winches may be needed for other uses such as halyards, mainsheet, control lines, spinnaker controls, runners and in the guise of a windlass for the anchor chain. However, winches are heavy, expensive and can get in the way of your mobility on deck. The secret of a successful deck layout is to keep the number down to an absolute minimum, and ensure that they are carefully positioned and able to serve in a variety of roles.

All winch manufacturers recommend winches for specific uses and loadings. On a medium-size cruiser it is normal to have a couple of small, single-speed winches mounted on either side of the coachroof that are used in conjunction with a battery of clutches for halyards and control lines, plus two larger two-speed primary winches on either side of the cockpit for genoa sheets, which can double for spinnaker sheets or guys. Three-speed winches are

ABOVE **A self-tailing winch has a feeder with adjustable jaws, which grip the rope as it rolls off the drum. It is an extremely useful feature that allows one person to wind and winch, but is slower than having one person wind and a second person pull in the tail.**

available for use on larger yachts, with the option of electric and hydraulically driven winches.

Many cruising yachts favour self-tailing winches that have a feeder and spring-loaded jaws to hold the rope as it is wound in. This makes winching a one-person operation, and the only disadvantage over conventional tailing – in which one person winds while another pulls in the rope hand over hand – is that it is considerably slower.

Winch care

Modern winches are reliable, but periodic maintenance will increase their efficiency and minimize the chance of a breakdown.

- Clean your winches every time you sail in salt water. Simply hose down the winches to flush out any salt which will degrade the grease and corrode the metal structure.
- Make a regular five-minute check on each winch by lifting off the drum and removing the main bearings. Use solvent on a rag to wipe away grease on exposed surfaces, and examine for wear or damage to the pawls and gear teeth. Re-lubricate the bearings and gear teeth before reassembly, using all lubricants sparingly.

Winches are generally constructed using a bronze, one-piece centre stem fitted with stainless steel shafts and gear spindles. A rigid nylon case holds the stainless steel bearings, with bronze gear

RIGHT **"Coffee grinders" are linked under the deck on the racing yacht Nicorette, and can be used to drive a selection of winches with one or two crew winding from either side.**

ABOVE The mainsheet traveller on the Dragonfly 1000 runs across the back of the cockpit, with the double ended sheet led to self-tailing winches on both sides in case it needs to be freed off in a hurry.

LEFT **Lifting off the drum of a winch reveals the gear train. Maintenance is comparatively simple and should be undertaken on a regular basis to ensure top performance.**

ball car, with the tail of the mainsheet led through a jamming cleat. This gives a 4:1 purchase, which is suitable for many sub-9m (29½ft) cruisers. For higher loads a top triple-sheave block will give a 6:1 ratio, with the use of ball-bearing blocks optional for smoother running.

Genoa systems Headsail sheets are usually led through a car. This is a block mounted on a track attached to the side deck, and it can be moved fore and aft to adjust foot and leech tension for different sail sizes.

Most cars are adjustable with a simple pull-push plunger, which locks into holes on the track. It is also possible to adjust the car with control lines led back to the cockpit, but in both cases the sheet will need to be eased to allow the car to move.

Vangs and preventers The boom vang or kicking strap on a yacht will generally use similar size blocks as the mainsheet. It may be fitted with snap-shackles at both ends, allowing the bottom to be clipped to the toe rail when sailing downwind. This helps to prevent the boom from involuntary gybes.

Halyard and control line systems These lines are usually led from the base of the mast to a bank of multi-tasking clutches on the coachroof. They can be routed through stainless steel organizers, which are similar to cassettes holding two, four or six sheaves for the lines to run through.

train and stainless steel pawls to prevent the winch from unwinding. The drum itself can be alloy, which is the lightest option, chrome, bronze or even stainless steel.

A good quality handle makes winding a winch much more pleasant. A heavy, chromed bronze handle with a long arm is much easier to use than a flimsy, lightweight aluminium handle, and is even easier to use with a double grip for both hands fitted with roller bearings. The handle should also have a lock to ensure it stays attached to the winch.

Other hardware

Mainsheet traveller Most yachts are fitted with a mainsheet traveller that fits across the full width of the cockpit or coachroof. This enables the mainsail to be sheeted in and maintain a flat leech when away from the centreline, enhancing performance, helping to keep the boat flat, and removing mainsheet falls from the cockpit area when sailing offwind. The traveller normally comprises a sliding ball car mounted on a track, with control lines led to either side.

Mainsheet block systems A simple cruising application will feature two double sheave (the rollers) blocks. The top block is attached to the boom; the bottom block is attached to the main traveller

LEFT A car-mounted block on a sliding track enables the angle of the headsail sheet lead to be moved fore or aft to allow for different sail sizes.

Offshore clothing

A challenge for clothing designers and manufacturers is to produce offshore clothing that works as an interactive system. It must be flexible enough to keep you warm and dry in the prevailing conditions, as well as being lightweight, comfortable to wear and quick to dry.

The theory of layering

The layering system comprises three layers: base, mid and outer.

Base layer When energy is expended through activity, heat is generated. The body's reaction is to produce sweat. This must be dissipated quickly as it will chill on the surface of the skin, which gets colder faster because moisture conducts heat approximately 30 times faster than air. Dry skin maintains its warmth better than damp skin, thus a base layer worn next to the skin must allow sweat to pass through to the mid and outer layers, without absorbing the moisture or allowing it to return to the skin.

ABOVE **All ready for a wet ride. The W60 Brunel Sunergy shows her pace during the Whitbread Round the World Race, an event where yacht clothing is tested to its ultimate limits.**

OUTER LAYER FOR INSHORE SAILING ....

1 Chest-high trousers are worn over a fleece mid layer and a light base layer.

2 The disadvantage of a smock is that it can be a struggle to put on and take off.

3 Once on, though, it provides a tight, snug fit, which is a lot less bulky than a jacket.

Mid layer Dry skin surrounded by warm dry air conserves body heat, with personal warmth controlled by air insulation. The greater the volume of trapped air there is, then the greater the insulation of the clothing system will be. This is the main function of the mid-layer. It's secondary function is to help transfer moisture away from the body to the outer layer and enable the base-layer to draw sweat away from the skin.

Outer layer This is essentially foul weather gear. By using a breathable fabric, such as Gore-Tex™, the outer layer should be able to exhaust any moisture created inside the system while simultaneously keeping out all wind and water with special waterproof properties and sealed seams, with neck, wrists, ankles and zip (zipper) fastenings completely secure.

Outer layer

Fabric technology has made rapid progress, and materials that combine a totally waterproof finish with breathability are becoming commonplace. This is an important concept for yacht sailing, where long periods of comparative inactivity – sitting in the cockpit or up on the side deck, while dressed against the chilling effect of a cold wind – are interspersed with short periods of intense physical activity.

Tacking, reefing or dousing a spinnaker can all create a lot of body heat in a short space of time, and cold, clammy perspiration may be the result if your clothing cannot breathe. This can be so bad that sailors assume their waterproof jacket or trousers have been leaking, when in fact the problem has come from their own body.

Breathable waterproof clothes will never be 100 per cent efficient. Even if you wear the correct breathable base and mid layers, items such as reflective patches, harness and life jacket will compromise the efficiency of your outer layer, which cannot rely on conventional ventilation if you are to remain dry. Expense is also a problem, top-rated breathable outer layers sell at prices that may limit their use to those who plan to spend a great deal of time on the water. Occasional cruising sailors may manage almost as well with much cheaper, conventional waterproof clothing.

As a rule, the following features should be found on the very best outer layer clothing:

Jackets

- Flexibility and light weight.
- Bright colours with reflective patches.
- Adjustable storm collar with hood and visor combining precise fit with good visibility.
- Heavy-duty two-way zip (zipper) covered by double storm flap with integral drainage channel.
- Storm cuffs with Velcro adjustable sleeve ends.
- Fleece-lined hand-warmer pockets with storm flaps. (Fleece should be removable for drying.)
- Bellow pockets with mesh drainage and inner zipped pockets.
- Adjustable waist and hip belts.
- Optional integral safety harness.
- Optional integral life jacket.
- Optional zip-in fleece for extra warmth.

LEFT Winding winches is hot work that requires an unobstructed swing of the handle. In marginal conditions, when the risk of waves breaking over the cockpit is negligible, the crew will be much more comfortable without a jacket.

Trousers

- Flexibility and light weight.
- Bright colours.
- Ankle storm cuffs with Velcro adjusters to close over boots.
- No lining for easy entry and exit combined with fast drying.
- Strong, heavy-duty zip with high waterproof gusset.
- Wide elasticized braces plus waist adjustment to keep trousers secure and comfortable.
- Strongly reinforced patches on both seat and knees.
- Chest-high fleece-lined hand-warmer pockets.
- Thick pocket with storm flap and mesh drainage.

ABOVE **A lightweight, breathable smock is ideal for small keelboat racing where body movement is at a premium and time on the water is of comparatively short duration.**

ABOVE **The storm hood has a high, fleece-lined collar, which protects the lower part of the face.**

ABOVE **For truly extreme conditions with freezing cold, salt water spray, this must be the solution.**

CHANGING UP TO A FULL OFFSHORE DRYSUIT ....

1 The offshore drysuit is a heavy duty version of the dinghy drysuit, which may need to be put on rapidly.

2 Internal braces hold up the chest-high trousers at the waist to ensure maximum comfort.

3 Like any drysuit, care needs to be taken pushing hands and feet through the wrist and neck seals.

4 Total protection, but you need a long offshore passage to make this gear worthwhile.

Smock This has the same upper body features as a jacket, but is cut short at the waist with a blouson-style adjustable neoprene waistband to give a more fitted feel and appearance. A blouson therefore looks good, feels less bulky and should be more efficient at keeping the water and wind out. If it is an over-the-head style garment with no front entry zip, it will be considerably more of a struggle to get in and out of, which may be unpleasant down below on a heaving yacht.

Full offshore drysuit This is an extreme garment for extreme sailing conditions – most likely used by round the world sailors. It combines a one-piece waterproof suit with latex neck and ankle seals and integral feet, plus a full-length dry zip across the shoulders. Added to this are the more usual features such as a collar/hood system, ankle and wrist storm closure, reflective strips, pockets and a comfort zip to satisfy calls of nature.

Mid layer

The clothing for this layer is based on synthetic, deep pile, fleece materials such as Polartec, which combine light weight with warmth, breathability and a fast drying capability to give considerably superior performance over natural fabrics such as wool

or cotton. The only real drawback of the material is that it is very flammable, and will melt if touched by flame.

Mid-layer choice is normally divided among jackets, blousons and waistcoats (vests) worn over trousers or salopettes. A fleece jacket or blouson with a rip-stop nylon outer shell will provide sufficient wind- and water-proofing plus durability for times when you don't need to wear an outer layer jacket.

Base layer

This layer is made from a lighter weight fleece than the mid layer, combining maximum wicking with comfort and warmth. The most comfortable and practical solution for sailing is likely to be provided by close-fitting thermal trousers with elasticized waist and ankles, worn with a thermal long sleeve jersey that has a zippered neck to aid insulation and ventilation.

Short-sleeve, turtle-neck and crew-neck variations are all possible, as well as complete one-piece base layer suits.

RIGHT **A heavier duty smock will have similar features to an offshore jacket with storm collar and full hood, but because it has no zip it is likely to be more comfortable for crew work.**

These are theoretically more efficient, but make a considerable addition to the hassle of dressing and undressing on a moving boat.

BUILDING UP THE LAYERS FOR MAXIMUM PERFORMANCE..

1 A fleece base layer using a material such as Polartec 200 is warm and comfortable, does an excellent job of drawing perspiration away from the skin, and dries quickly when wet.

2 The middle layer may feature trousers or salopettes, using fibre pile or fleece lining to trap the maximum amount of warm, insulating air combined with an outer shell.

3 A jacket or waistcoat completes the middle layer, which can be worn on deck until the weather deteriorates to the point that foul weather gear has to go on.

4 High trousers and a jacket provide the third outer layer, which will provide full protection from wind, rain and cold while sailing.

ABOVE **The three-layer breathable system combines minimum weight and bulk with maximum performance for the crew to function in comfort.**

ABOVE **Windproof clothing and strong sailing gloves for handling synthetic control lines are part of the armoury of modern yacht clothing. This level of gear is ideal for a fresh day when you don't expect to get wet.**

Extremities

Socks Sailing socks should reach well above the shin, stay up with elasticized grippers, and have cushioned soles to provide extra insulation when worn with yachting boots or shoes. Synthetic materials such as polypropylene combine maximum warmth and durability with minimum moisture absorption and are quick drying. Breathable, waterproof socks may potentially be worn for longer without odour, and are there to satisfy the top end of the market.

Footwear Rubber boots need deep cleated soles that grip like limpets and help provide an insulating barrier between your feet and the cold surroundings. Do not wear them ashore any more than you have to, as the alien elements of tarmac and concrete will soon wear down the soft rubber. Boots should have a warm,

ABOVE **Thermal, long sailing socks made from polypropylene yarn provide the right combination of maximum warmth and durability having low moisture absorbency and a quick-drying quality.**

ABOVE **Waterproof trousers should fit snugly round boots to prevent water washing up inside. Note the reinforced sides to the boots, which are required for bracing against the toerail and other parts of the boat when moving forwards.**

comfortable lining, be easy to get on and off but fit well enough to stay on when hanging over the sides of the boat. They must also be light and comfortable when worn for long periods, and provide a snug fit over trousers or under the outer layer. Leather yachting boots, sometimes combined with Gore-Tex™ breathable material, provide a classy alternative for those who want only the best.

Dockside-style leather mocassins are the most popular deck shoes, although some prefer trainer style shoes that provide the same level of grip and protection from

ABOVE **A fleece-lined waterproof storm cap, which covers the back of the neck, is likely to be an excellent performer. It will keep your head warm and dry, is comfortable to wear and the peak helps deflect spray and sun.**

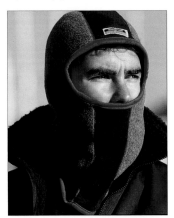

ABOVE **If it is truly cold, a neoprene balaclava worn beneath an outer layer hood will make a tremendous difference to keeping warm.**

snubbing on uncompromising deck hardware – sailing a cruiser barefoot is seldom a good idea. Some care is needed to preserve leather against the ravages of salt, which may be little more than a hose-down with fresh water. As with yachting boots, the soft soles of deck shoes will wear rapidly if worn ashore.

Headwear About 40 per cent of your body's heat loss can be avoided by wearing the right hat. Nowadays, the simple woolly of yore has been replaced by the modern alternative of a fleece hat, which combines light weight with moisture

ABOVE **Neoprene-backed gloves with full length fingers will provide good protection for colder conditions, but for exceptionally cold sailing nothing can beat a pair of waterproof and breathable fleece-lined mitts.**

ABOVE **Gloves with short fingers are ideal for easy handling of small diameter control lines, but only in relatively warm conditions.**

resistance and is shaped to grip your head no matter how hard the wind blows. A fleece balaclava worn below an outer layer hood is recommendable for really cold weather, while fleece-lined storm caps do a good job of combining thick warm fleece with a waterproof outer shell and peak, and can even be found in the style of the old fashioned oilskin fishermans's hat.

Gloves and mittens. Modern synthetic ropes and lines can be hard on the hands, and dinghy-style gloves with mesh backs and padded leather palms can be recommended for general use in full-finger and short-finger variations. If the gloves are to provide any cold weather insulation they will need neoprene backs, while the only real answer for serious winter sailing is to wear full length, fleece-lined mitts made from a breathable, waterproof shell fabric with adjustable closure at the wrists.

Fair weather sailing

Always wear shoes on deck when sailing. They grip better than bare feet and you won't damage your toes.

You owe it to your yacht to stay smart. If it's hot, wear shorts and a comfortable T-shirt, polo-shirt or crew-shirt. If it's cooler, crew pants should be made from a quick-dry material, have large useful pockets, and may benefit from knee and bottom reinforcement patches if you can live with a bizarre appearance.

During summer a peaked cap will provide your face with useful protection against the sun, but take care to protect the back of your neck as well. Wear sunglasses to cut out associated glare and prevent possible UVB damage.

Luggage

Invest in the best possible luggage made in a strong coated fabric for maximum water resistance with suitably sturdy plastic zips (zippers). Beware of over-size crew bags, which can be a nightmare to carry. It is better to have two small ones, plus a matching backpack if required. Use a navigator's case or document case to keep all your paperwork together.

LEFT **Sailing luggage should be lightweight, durable and water resistant. This style of navigator's case is ideal for taking paperwork on board.**

BELOW **In fair weather the crew still needs deck shoes to protect their feet and polo shirts to help keep off the sun. Note that the crewman forward is wearing waterproof trousers as the foredeck is likely to take a few waves.**

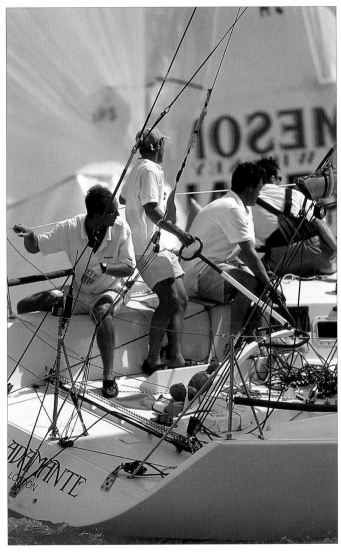

Safety

The sea can be a very treacherous and dangerous place. However, modern equipment and survival techniques help to make it as safe as possible.

LIFE JACKETS

Every yacht should carry enough life jackets for the number of crew on board. One size should fit most adults, with smaller children's sizes provided as required. The life jackets should be easily accessible. Every member of the crew should know where they are and practise how to put them on before setting sail. Many cruising sailors will only don a life jacket for night sailing or rough weather, but it is good practice to encourage crew to wear a life jacket whenever they go on deck, particularly for those unable to swim.

International regulations

International standard have a number of basic requirements with minor variations. Regulations for Europe are typical:
- A life jacket must be a distinctive colour.

- The life jacket should allow freedom of movement on deck and in the water, where there should be adequate head movement without interfering with hearing or breathing.
- Donning a life jacket should be obvious, simple (except for young children who will require assistance) and not unduly affected by adverse conditions such as poor light, cold or wet.
- The means of adjustment must be obvious and easy to carry out to ensure a secure fit. After reading the instructions printed on a life jacket, the wearer should be able to don and securely adjust it within one minute.
- Auto-inflation systems must inflate the life jacket sufficiently to float the wearer within 5 seconds of being triggered. Oral top-ups must be possible when in the water.
- The force required to operate the pull-toggle for the inflator should be between 20 and 120 Newtons (5 to 25lbs).
- A wearer should be able to leap into

ABOVE **A floating strobe light attached to the life jacket is a useful feature. It will activate as soon as the life jacket hits the water and inflates.**

the water from a height of up to 1m (just over 3ft) without displacing the jacket, causing injury or effecting its performance.
- The life jacket must self-right the wearer face-up within 5 seconds, without any voluntary movement. This is particularly important if the wearer is unconscious.
- A life jacket should provide lateral and occipital (back part of the head) support so the mouth of a well relaxed

ABOVE **The combined harness and life jacket is neat and comfortable to wear, and not at all bulky. The lungs of the life jacket are neatly stowed inside the red covers.**

ABOVE **Once inflated by the CO_2 cartridge, the lungs can be orally topped up if required. In most instances they should not be inflated while on the boat, since they will clearly restrict movement.**

ABOVE **The harness should be adjusted for a close but comfortable fit, and be provided with a nylon webbing safety line that has easy-to-use clips at both ends.**

individual is held clear of a still water surface with the trunk of the body inclined backwards at an angle between 30 and 90 degrees.

- A life jacket wearer should be able to swim 10m (33ft) and easily climb a vertical ladder.
- The wearer must not show any tendency to slip out of the life jacket while in the water.

Buoyancy

Life jackets with a buoyancy of 150 Newtons (33lb) are suitable for coastal and offshore uses; 275 Newtons (63lb) is recommended for long-distance passage.

Most modern life jackets are worn with the air chambers deflated to eliminate cumbersome bulk. Inflation is usually a two-stage process with an automatically fired CO_2 cylinder (one-time use) followed by oral back-up if required. The standard automatic inflation trigger for life jackets is activated when a salt-water tablet is fully immersed. An alternative hydrostatic system based on water pressure has been introduced to eliminate the possibility of a salt-water tablet activating due to damp or very wet conditions. All automatic life jacket systems need to be re-armed at specific service intervals.

HARNESSES

A harness must always be worn – and used – when going on deck at night. Disappearing over the side is most likely to occur when a member of the crew goes forward in rough weather, and has to unclip his or her harness to change position. Therefore, if a crew member needs to wear a harness he or she must also wear a life jacket and vice versa. A combination life jacket and harness makes good sense, and is faster and less fiddly to put on. If you wear a separate harness and life jacket, always put the harness on first to ensure it is fully secure.

As with life jackets, every yacht should carry enough harnesses to fit the number of people on board. They should be easily accessible, with every member of the crew knowing where they are and how to put them on before setting sail.

Yacht basics

Sailing on a yacht can mean anything from a day out with the family visiting a nearby bay, to a round the world tour spread over several years. Most of us are able to experience the former while only dreaming of the latter, for even if you can't afford to own a yacht there is always plenty of demand for crew – and the more experienced the crew, the more rewarding their role will be.

Whatever type of cruise you wish to undertake you must cruise within your capabilities, which includes the following:
- Good planning and preparation.
- A cautious attitude to sailing and cruising that always puts safety first.
- Maintaining a yacht that is tidy and ship-shape at all times.
- Courtesy to other members of the crew, and an understanding of their needs, requirements and concerns.
- Courtesy towards all other vessels, and a precise knowledge of rights of way.
- Sufficient knowledge of navigation (reading a chart, taking a bearing, and understanding weather forecasting and tides).
- The ability to change plans rapidly and decisively to meet changing circumstances, particularly in deteriorating weather.
- A relaxed, confident and knowledgeable attitude to yacht handling, which inspires respect in the crew.

A harness should have an adjustable waistband and shoulder straps, with a front opening stainless steel buckle and robust D-ring for the safety line. The safety line should be made from a 1–2m (3–6ft) length of nylon webbing with a minimum 2080kg (4,586lb) breaking strain, and stainless steel carbine clips at both ends. Some stretch lines incorporate a third hook in the middle.

Get used to moving around the deck with a harness and learn where and what is safe to clip on to. The traditional jackstay – a wire safety cable running along the coachroof or side decks – allows the crew to slide fore and aft, and the webbing provides a 1–2m (3–6ft) reach either side. Never clip to the lifelines running between the stanchions, which are comparatively flimsy.

ABOVE **Bashing to windward can be a cold and wet affair. The crew on the lead boat looks vulnerable with deck shoes rather than boots.**

KEELBOAT SAILING TECHNIQUES AND CLASSES

Learning to handle a cruiser is rather different from learning to handle a dinghy. You can move around the deck of a cruiser without it tipping over, everything should happen in virtual slow motion (at least while you learn), and there should be absolutely no chance of a capsize. However, the stakes are considerably higher when you skipper a large, sometimes unwieldy and often rather expensive craft, and have the responsibility for a number of crew on board. The subject also becomes considerably wider as it encompasses areas as diverse as marine engines and electronic navigation.

As with dinghy sailing, basic cruiser handling can be learnt in a reasonably short space of time and will open the door to one of the most delightful pastimes. However, knowledge that is learnt so easily is little more than a prelude to a lifetime of gaining experience, and nothing is more important than learning to respect the unpredictable power of the elements. Wind and sea can turn when you least expect it and catch out the expert sailor as readily as the novice, and will continue to do so for as long as we love to sail.

LEFT *Skill is required to manoeuvre a yacht in a confined space.*

BELOW *Sweating up the mainsail is a good way of quickly raising the halyard.*

Handling the mainsail

The primary power source of a yacht
sailing to windward is the mainsail.
This is also the most easily controlled sail
on the yacht because it is accessible from
the cockpit, and a powerful multi-purchase
mainsheet provides relatively quick and
effortless adjustment.

Preparation

- Undo the mainsail cover and fold it
  along the boom, working aft from the
  mast. Stow in a cockpit locker.
- Free off the main halyard and attach
  the shackle to the head of the mainsail.
  Take up the slack, ensuring the halyard
  is not caught round the shrouds.
- Undo the sail ties. Many modern
  yachts have a spider made up of a
  single length of shockcord below the
  boom with numerous legs that fasten
  round the sail. If using conventional
  shockcord ties, be very careful that
  loose ends do not fly off – serious eye
  injuries have been caused this way.
- Free off the mainsheet, traveller and
  kicking strap. Before hoisting, make
  sure the wind is well forward of the
  beam, ideally the yacht should point
  head to wind.

LEFT **Attach the halyard to the head of the mainsail
with the shackle, which has a pin that will turn
and lock. Make sure the halyard does not lasso
the spreaders, and keep it taut at all times.**

TAKING OFF THE MAINSAIL COVER

1 Start from the mast, and unclip and untie to the
vertical overlap of the cover.

3 Lift the shockcords off the hooks as you
go along.

2 From this point you can start to fold the cover
back along the boom while you work aft.

4 If the wind takes control you may need another
pair of hands.

Hoisting the mainsail

There are various methods of hoisting the
mainsail, which one you use will largely
depend on the size of sail and how much
effort is required to get it up. On a small
to medium-size yacht the main halyard
will normally be led aft through a clutch
on the coachroof, allowing for one crew
to stand in the cockpit and pull it in hand
over hand.

The helmsperson keeps the yacht head
to wind, and may need to keep a hand on
the falls of the mainsheet to stop the boom
from moving around. While the mainsail is
being hoisted, the helm's vision is likely to

be drastically reduced. If the yacht is under
way a lookout must be kept at all times.
The helmsperson should also watch that
the batten ends don't catch on lazy-stays
(if used) or get caught on the wrong side
of the shrouds.

As soon as the halyard starts to feel
heavy, it's time to take a turn round the
relevant coachroof winch. You can then
spin in a few more handfuls of halyard. If
a second crew sweats up the halyard – he
pulls a triangle of rope outwards from the
mast or coachroof which the other crew
can then pull in on the winch – it helps get
the sail up faster. Once pulling becomes
slow and difficult, it's time to wind the
mainsail to the top of the mast, which will
require three turns round the winch.
Either use the self-tailing mechanism, or
get another crew person to tail (pull the

LEFT **Undo the sail ties that are used to hold the mainsail in a neat bundle along the boom. Beware of old fashioned shock-cord ties, which can fly round and hit you in the face; beware also of obscuring the helm's vision if you let the sail fall down off the boom.**

ABOVE **The mainsail can be rolled tight to the boom or flaked as shown here. Sail ties are the traditional way of securing the sail, and safer than shockcord ends flailing around.**

rope in hand over hand), which is considerably faster. The halyard should be wound in until the luff appears sufficiently taut. Before pulling in on the mainsheet, the topping lift, which holds the boom up, must be slackend off or removed and taken forward to the base of the mast.

Once the sail is sheeted hard in the kicking strap can be tensioned. Check how the sail sets. Horizontal creases indicate that the luff should be tighter – you will need to free off the mainsheet and kicker to wind up more halyard. Vertical creases indicate that the luff is too tight, and you need to ease the halyard.

Dropping the mainsail

When dropping, the helmsperson's view is likely to be severely obstructed for a few minutes. It is generally safer to drop the mainsail at anchor; if under way, a careful

lookout must be maintained. The wind must be well forward of the beam to drop the sail. The mainsail slides will drop down the track most easily when the yacht is head to wind.

Free off the mainsheet and kicker, and take up on the topping lift to ensure the boom does not drop on anyone's head. It may be necessary to wind in the main halyard to free off the clutch or cleat.

When ready, the crew should be prepared to let the halyard run in a controlled fashion, ensuring there are no snarl-ups in the tail. A second crew may need to pull the slides physically down the track, and start bundling the mainsail into a roll starting at the mast. The crew in the cockpit can then let the halyard run, and jump onto the side deck or coachroof to help roll the mainsail into a bundle that is tight to the boom. At this stage, it is vital

that the helmsperson pulls in on the mainsheet to prevent the boom swinging from side to side. He should also ensure the yacht points into wind so the sail falls between the lazy-stays (if fitted).

The crew removes the main halyard, which should be secured away from the mast to prevent clattering caused by wire cable beating against alloy. Attach the sail ties, put on the sail cover if required, and coil the tail end of the mainsheet to make everything ship-shape and tidy.

Knotting sail ties

Conventional sail ties without a loop can be secured with a reef knot. Learn to get it right; there is a 50:50 chance of tying it the wrong way.

SWEATING UP THE MAINSAIL ....

1 Sweating is a good technique to get the mainsail halyard up fast.

2 One crew pulls a length of halyard out from the mast. The other pulls the slack through the clutch.

3 Winding need only be used to achieve final luff tension.

Handling the headsails

Yachts with conventional headsail systems rely on a choice of headsails to match wind conditions. Minimum requirements are likely to be an overlapping genoa for light to moderate winds, a working jib for moderate to strong winds, and a storm jib for excessive winds.

Many cruisers still use traditional bronze or stainless steel hanks with a piston closure to attach the luff to the forestay. The alternative headfoil system uses a special forestay fitting, which has one or two full length grooves that hold the boltrope of the luff. This is potentially much lighter and aerodynamically more efficient than hanks and, with a double groove, allows two headsails to be hoisted at the same time for fast sail changes when racing. The downside of the headfoil is that it is more prone to damage, and there is limited scope for do-it-yourself repairs while at sea.

In anything more than a light wind, it is generally easiest to hoist or change a headsail offwind. The boat has a kinder motion and is less likely to heel over, while the headsail will be partly blanketed by the mainsail and is less likely to put up a fight.

Hoisting a headsail

Pull the relevant sail bag up on deck. The most direct route may be through the forehatch, but this is not recommended if the boat is under way and pitching with water coming onto the foredeck. Secure the sail bag to the leeward side toerail so it remains inside the guardrail and you can work from the windward side. If there is any question of personal safety, wear a life jacket and harness and clip on.

Modern headsail bags are shaped like a sausage with a full length Velcro-sealed opening along the side. Locate the tack of the sail and clip it to the snap-shackle tack fitting. If using hanks, start from the bottom hank and work up the luff, ensuring all hanks are the right way up – it's surprisingly easy to twist them through 180 degrees. Push the hanks down the forestay to ensure the sail does not start to fill and blow over the side. If using a headfoil, the head of the sail must be fed into the foil guide, a little metal triangle that feeds in the luff to ensure that it does not jam when the halyard goes up. A headfoil generates greater friction than hanks. Windward and leeward sheets should be attached to the clew with tight bowlines. The sheets are led aft through blocks to the primary winches where figure-of-eight knots secure the ends.

When the crew is ready to hoist, the halyard must be given plenty of slack so the snap shackle can be taken forward and attached to the head. Beware of allowing the halyard to blow back round the spreaders or forward round the forestay. The halyard should be pulled up hand over hand and as fast as possible. Only begin winding when you can pull no more. It is vital that the leeward sheet is free, so the sail doesn't power up before it is fully hoisted. Secure the halyard with the clutch or cleat. Sheet in, and check the sail

ABOVE **Use sail ties to hold the headsail to the guardrails or toerail when not in use. Remove the halyard, clip the end to the pulpit and take up the slack.**

for horizontal or vertical creases, indicating the luff is too slack or too tight. Check the shape of the foot and leech, which should match each other in smooth, flat curves. If the foot is too full, the car on the fairlead traveller needs to be moved aft; if the leech is too full, the car needs to be moved forwards. The sheet must be eased off to accomplish this.

Dropping a headsail

If the yacht is sailing upwind, it may be pitching, heeling and taking waves over the foredeck; all of which can make sail changing a difficult task. In order to remove any potential problems for the crew on the foredeck, the drop must be precisely controlled by the crew in the cockpit.

One crew should let off the halyard, and control the rate of descent so that the headsail doesn't blow over the side and dump in the sea. Keeping the leeward sheet hard in will ensure the sail drops inside the guardrail, but the foredeck crew may need to call for slack if the hanks won't slide down the forestay. If the sail bag is on deck it should be securely attached to the leeward toerail. The foredeck crew bundles the sail as low as it will go on the forestay, before unclipping and securing the halyard, and the cockpit crew keeps enough tension to prevent it blowing around the spreaders or forestay. Let off the hanks from the top, and feed the top of the sail into its bag with the tack going in last and on top. Undo the sheet ends, which can be tied together or onto the pulpit for temporary security, and bundle in the clew end of the sail before closing the sailbag. If it's dry you can

SETTING THE HEADSAILS ON A LUFF FOIL ....

1 Attach the tack by a snap shackle.

2 Loosely flake the sail with the head at the top.

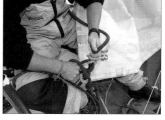

3 Lead both sheet ends to the clew of the sail.

4 Attach the sheets using bowline knots.

5 Tie each bowline tight to the cringle.

6 Attach the halyard to the head of the sail.

7 Push the top of the bolt rope through the feeder.

8 Pull 1m (3ft) of the bolt rope up the luff foil.

9 Ensure the bolt rope feeds without snagging.

10 Sweat the halyard to help get it up fast.

11 Wind in the halyard for final luff tension.

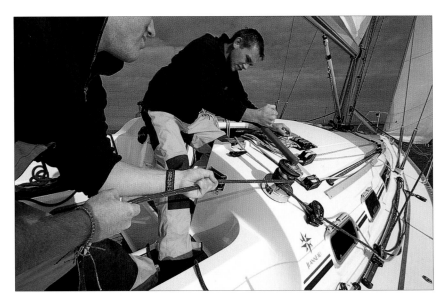

RIGHT **The winch being used to wind in the headsail has a self-tailing facility, but it is quicker and more powerful if one crew tails by pulling in the sheet hand-over-hand as shown here. The tailer should keep well clear of the winder whose hands whirl round in a 360 degree circle. The tailer should also watch the leech of the headsail, advising on progress and judging when it is time to stop winding.**

bundle the bag below; if it's wet you may prefer to leave it on deck. An alternative is to bag the sail later and leave it secured temporarily to the guardrails by sail ties.

Beware that, when a headsail is being lowered for a sail change, the yacht will lose forward momentum and steerage. Always make sure there is sufficient sea room to allow for leeway and loss of manoeuvrability during any headsail change, when the mainsail may need to be eased to make handling more responsive.

When changing headsails it saves a lot of time if the car controlling the headsail fairlead position is moved to the right place on the track before sheeting in. The track can be marked to show the correct position for each sail.

Using a winch

All winches turn clockwise and the rope is wound round them in a clockwise direction. You should put on just enough turns to hold the rope around the winch without slipping. Any more, and you risk jamming the winch with a riding turn.

When starting to pull in a rope, you just need a single turn round the winch. Any more turns will slow down the process of pulling in a rope and risk a riding turn. Put on

a second turn when the pull of the rope starts to get heavy, followed by a third turn just before you need to insert the handle and start winding. You should always be able to hold the sheet on the winch drum. If it slips, you need another turn.

To ease the sheet use your free hand to physically move the turns round the drum. To remove the sheet completely – as when tacking – take enough turns off the drum so you can just hold the rope, then spin the rest vertically off the drum.

Riding turns If the bottom turn on the winch rides up on the second turn – usually when you have too many turns and are

pulling in hand over hand – it will jam and create a riding turn, which jams the sheet so it cannot be eased off. If you see the bottom turn start to ride up, you should immediately let the turns slip round the drum, which should cure the problem. If you are too slow and the riding turn jams on the winch, the solution is to take tension off the pulling end of the rope and lift the free end straight off the winch.

Using a handle Beware of flailing around with a winch handle while transferring it from winch to winch. It is surprisingly easy to smack a fellow crew member in the face with this uncompromising object.

USING AS SELF-TAILING WINCH ....

1 When ready to wind, take enough turns to fill the body of the winch, pulling the sheet over the feeder and round the jaws.

2 Wind in steadily, and the free end of the rope will be thrown clear by the self-tailing mechanism.

LEFT **Furling headsails are ideal for charter and flotilla yachts, and remove the need for handling bulky, heavy sailbags or stowing them in the cockpit lockers or down below. The downside is that these permanently hoisted sails may tend to degrade more rapidly when left hoisted in harsh sunlight, but can be protected by a sausage-like cover.**

It is important to find a comfortable and effective position for winding, where you can swing the handle round its arc with minimum effort, and without hitting fellow crew members with your elbows. The ergonomic design of the cockpit will reflect how efficiently you can wind, as will the weight and length of the handle. A double-handhold delivers the most

potential power. Ensure that the winch handle is firmly locked into the top of the drum before you start winding. On a two-speed winch you wind one way for the high gear, then reverse the winding direction for the low gear. The skill is to get the sail sheeted home before you need to use the low gear, and then use its slow speed for fine tuning.

WINCHING TRICKS

1 Beware of the riding turn, which will appear if too many turns are put on too rapidly. If it locks solid, the only solution is to remove all the loading.

2 When winding you need a comfortable position and room to swing the handle. How easy it is will also depend on how far the boat is heeling.

Roller-reefing headsails

These combine a luff foil with top and bottom rollers and allows sails to be changed using the same technique as any headfoil system, with the choice of at least one heavy and one light air sail to cover all conditions.

The windier it is, the flatter a headsail needs to be. Roller-reefing systems with tack and head swivels independent of the foil allow the centre of the sail to furl before the tack and head to produce a flatter shape for reefed sailing.

Many owners leave a roller-genoa hoisted for the whole season. A sun cover should be used for protection from the effects of ultra-violet light.

Roller technique Furling and unfurling a roller headsail is essentially a simple operation with a single control line led from the coachroof to the stem-head drum. The line must be fully wound round the drum when the sail is full out, and fully unwound when the sail is full in.

Problems can be caused by the reefing line taking riding turns or dropping off the drum. To prevent this, the line must always be kept under tension.

Never let the reefing line go with a bang if there is enough wind to power up a partly unfurled sail. On any medium-size yacht the line should be eased off from a winch, with careful use of the leeward sheet to encourage the sail to unfurl. When reducing sail in stronger winds, the reefing line will often need to be winched in with the sheet eased off. The reefing line must always be securely held by a self-tailer, human tailer, clutch or cleat.

Reefing the mainsail by rolling it around the boom is relatively inefficient, and has been superseded by slab reefing for both racing and cruising use. The option of rolling the sail inside the mast is reserved for larger, more exotic cruising yachts.

- Always reef early – it is much easier to reef before the going gets tough.
- Make sure the crew know what they have got to do.
- Reefing needs to be done quickly, as the mainsail is prone to damage while it is flogging in a heavy breeze and can be dangerous with crew struggling on deck.

Slab reefing The helmsperson steers the yacht so the wind is forward of the beam. It is difficult to reef if the mainsail is pressed against the shrouds. Mainsheet and kicker must be eased right off, with the topping lift made up so the boom will not drop into the cockpit.

BELOW **The luxurious Wauquiez 43 cruiser boasts twin furling headsails and a mainsail that furls on an internal boom roller for maximum cruiser-friendliness.**

ABOVE **This Harken furling drum clearly shows the strongly engineered, heavy duty nature of a piece of equipment that has to withstand extremely high loads without any chance of failure.**

RIGHT **Despite very light winds, this yacht has its mainsail pulled down to the first reef. It also has the No2 and No3 reefing pennants led through the leech of the sail. These control lines are used to pull the leech down to the outer end of the boom, creating a new clew position for the second and third reefs in the mainsail. On a cruising yacht they can be left permanently in position, which is useful in area such as the Aegean where afternoon winds of Force 6 (22-27 knots) are quite common during the summer.**

One crew takes responsibility for the halyard, which will most likely be controlled from the cockpit. He or she eases the halyard so the foredeck crew can pull the relevant tack cringle down to a hook on the side of the boom – luff slides may need to be removed to accomplish this. The cockpit crew re-tensions the halyard, and pulls the relevant clew pennant tight so the new clew position is hard down and full out along the boom. It is vital that the mainsheet is free when doing this. Finally, the clew pennant is locked off, the topping lift is released, the helm brings the boat back on course, and the mainsheet and kicker are pulled in. Excess sail can be rolled into a tight bundle on the windward side of the boom and tied off as necessary.

Shaking out a reef To reverse the process and take out a reef, the kicker and main-sheet need to be eased off and the topping lift made up. The crew then lets off the tack pennant, and drops the halyard to unhook the tack cringle, before re-hoisting the sail to its full extent.

PUTTING A SLAB REEF IN THE MAINSAIL ....

1 With the topping lift supporting the end of the boom, the cockpit crew eases off the halyard.

2 The foredeck crew has pulled the luff cringle down to the first reef point and takes the halyard.

3 The luff must be fully tensioned using the halyard before the leech can be pulled down on the boom.

4 The No1 reefing pennant pulls the leech down and out along the boom. Excess sail can then be rolled into a tidy bundle secured by sail ties.

Using auxiliary engines

Auxiliary power plays a vital role when manoeuvring in confined spaces, when it is impractical to sail and when charging battery-powered electrics.

Inboard engines

Most cruising and racing yachts over about 7.5m (25ft) are fitted with inboard diesel engines. They are practical, reliable and economic to run. In addition, they can be sited low down in the yacht where their weight contributes to the righting effect of the ballast and the propeller will always stay underwater.

Unlike petrol (gasoline) engines, the fuel of diesel engines is not affected by temperature, will not produce explosive vapour and requires no electric spark for ignition, which has the added benefit of making diesel engines considerably more resistant to the effects of damp or water. The safety disadvantages and greater fuel consumption of petrol engines make them a non-starter for inboard use, even though they are lighter and quieter.

Most modern inboard engine installations feature a variation on the Saildrive (see below), which has an integral propeller

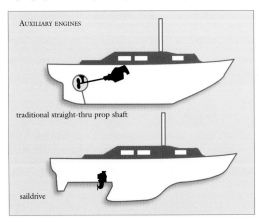

ABOVE **An auxiliary diesel engine gives effortless power and control at the touch of a button. It is highly effective in this kind of light wind situation, but the windage on the rig of a yacht may make handling under power considerably more difficult in a strong wind.**

unit sited directly beneath the engine. This is considerably simpler than the traditional full-length propeller shaft, is entirely suitable for fin keel yachts, and tends to make steering more precise and predictable.

Outboard engines

Smaller yachts are sometimes fitted with outboard engines, with 4-stroke power providing a heavier but quieter and

smoother running option than 2-stroke. Outboards are considerably cheaper than inboards to buy and install, and occupy very little space inside the yacht. They can also make the yacht very manoeuvrable if the motor can be moved through 180 degrees to execute tight turns.

Outboards are often fine for auxiliary use at an anchorage or in a marina, but do not provide the consistent performance

RIGHT **The saildrive style of propeller-to-engine coupling was a great step forward, placing the engine directly over the propeller for easier installation and superior handling.**

AUXILIARY ENGINES

traditional straight-thru prop shaft

saildrive

ABOVE **On most small or medium-size yachts engine access is behind the companionway ladder, with everything easily to hand for everyday maintenance and excellent sound insulation.**

ABOVE **Multihulls such as the Dragonfly 800 (top) and F-24 (bottom) will generally only use their outboards for auxiliary power when berthing, and mainly rely on pure sail power.**

Diesel engine controls

ABOVE **The instrument panel is located in the cockpit coaming for easy access by the skipper. The combined throttle/gear control (black handle) is shown in the full astern position, and the nearby pull lever is used to stop the engine. Before starting, always ensure the gear button is in neutral.**

Before starting an inboard diesel engine, check there is sufficient fuel, oil and fresh water coolant, and that the salt water inlet and outlet is open.

Most modern diesel engines use a simple key-start, with a push button, puller and/or key stop. The standard throttle and gear control is a combination lever with a central red button for neutral.

- Button in: engine is in neutral, pushing lever forward or back increases revs.
- Button out: engine is in neutral when the lever is only in the upright position.

- Engine is in forward gear with lever in forward position: push to full forward for full revs.
- Engine is in reverse gear with lever in backward position: push to full backward for full revs.

Always pause in neutral when changing from forwards to reverse and vice versa, it's kinder to the gearbox.

Run the engine at no more than half power for a few minutes while the engine is warming up, and before shutting off in order to let the engine cool down. Never run the engine flat out. It will use a lot more fuel for a negligible increase in speed.

required for extended running in adverse conditions. An engine requires an output of 4–5 horsepower per ton of displacement if it is to function as an effective auxiliary. The ultimate test is being able to drive a yacht straight into a strong wind or tide, while maintaining a speed of at least 5 knots. In such conditions an outboard powered yacht may perform better under sail, which removes the additional risk of a wave drowning the ignition.

Most outboards are transom-hung and may need to be sited to one side of the rudder. The propeller may be lifted from the water when the boat heels away from the outboard, with the result that the yacht loses forward momentum. This problem can be exacerbated if the yacht is pitching, or crew have to go on the foredeck. If it is persistent the engine will keep over-revving with possible damage to the transmission. It may also overheat due to the water inlet lifting clear of the water.

On many yachts, dropping and lifting the outboard is a real hassle. The helmsperson has to bend over the transom and fiddle with the motor, looking aft

when he or she should be looking forwards. Left on its transom bracket, the outboard is prone to theft. Lifting it off and locking it away in a cockpit locker is a gut-wrenching operation that can be tricky as you balance on the back of the boat. You should also beware of petrol leaking out of the outboard when it is laid on its side in the cockpit or in a locker, which should be water tight and air tight to contain petrol and its fumes.

An outboard has a limited fuel supply compared to the inboard tank of a diesel. Outboards with integral fuel tanks have the most limited running time, and are difficult and potentially dangerous to refill when under way. A remote fuel tank located in the cockpit or a cockpit locker is a more practical and safer option.

Hot engines

Overheating is a common problem with both inboard and outboard engines, and will become obvious if an audible alarm goes off (fitted on modern diesel engines) or if no cooling water is being pumped from the outlet. The likely cause is a blockage in the sea water inlet, which prevents sea water from being sucked in to cool the sealed fresh water cooling system. Stop the engine, and check for debris.

Mooring and anchoring

Nowadays many yachts are berthed side-on to a floating pontoon or dock in a marina, or have a swinging mooring attached to a buoy. A few yachts may be berthed to a quay or harbour wall, generally in non-tidal areas.

MARINA BERTHING

Most marina pontoons and the yachts alongside them go up and down with the tide in a protected environment. Other marinas have locks and are accessible only a few hours either side of high water. Yachts will normally be secured by the following lines:

- **Bow line** Led forward from a cleat on the foredeck to a cleat, ring or bollard on the pontoon.
- **Stern line** Led aft from a cleat on the aft deck to a cleat, ring or bollard on the pontoon.
- **Springs** Fore and aft springs pull against the bow line and stern line to keep the yacht snug alongside the pontoon without the stern or bow swinging out. They can either be led from the middle of the pontoon to the bows and stern of the yacht, or from the middle of the yacht to equivalent positions on the pontoon.

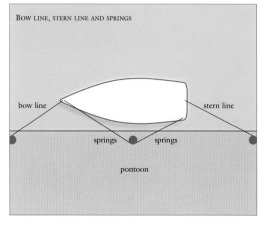

BOW LINE, STERN LINE AND SPRINGS

bow line   springs   springs   stern line

pontoon

LEFT The bow and stern lines hold a yacht fore and aft, with springs to hold it in tight alongside. The springs should be led fore and aft from the middle of the pontoon or quay, as shown, with all lines adjusted so the yacht is aligned alongside with sufficient space for fenders.

Securing the lines

Mooring lines should be led through the appropriate fairleads, which are cut into the toerail. Each line from the yacht may be secured to its cleat by a tight bowline.

A full turn, half turn and locking turn should be used to secure the line to a cleat on the pontoon; a bowline or round turn and two half hitches should be used to secure the line to a bollard or ring. An alternative solution is to make a slip rope, passing the line through a suitable ring or

slot in the cleat, and leading it back to the yacht. The advantages are that all excess line is removed from the pontoon, the line can be adjusted from the yacht, and it is possible to cast off without going ashore.

If a bollard or mooring ring is being used by other yachts, it is courteous to pass your lines underneath so they can remove their own lines easily.

ABOVE **A pre-tied bowline can be used to hold the yacht to its berth while manoeuvring alongside.**

ABOVE **Variations on the conventional cleat provide the simplest solution to mooring.**

Round turn and two half hitches

A quick and easy knot for attaching a mooring line to a ring, bollard or post.

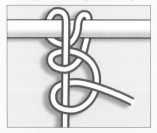

GETTING FENDERS IN POSITION ....

1 Fenders are mainly needed to protect the wide part of the yacht. They can be tied to the toerail or guardrail as shown here.

2 A simple overhand knot allows each fender to be untied quickly. Alternatively, use a round turn and two half hitches.

3 Coming alongside all the fenders are out, with the crew holding bow and stern lines and ready to jump onto the dock or pontoon.

Attaching fenders

Fenders are used to protect the side of the yacht. They can be hung from a suitable cleat or from the toerail. They should be concentrated at the wide point of the yacht and any other areas that may be vulnerable. Fenders must hang straight down between the yacht and the pontoon, and be down far enough so they do not ride up and pop out, which can happen when the yacht is pulled in tight to the pontoon and is rocked by the wind or passing traffic. Once underway and free of potential obstructions, the fenders should always be removed and stowed away.

ENTERING A MARINA BERTH ....

1 If there is tide flowing, always come in against the tide to stop the boat.

2 You could either take a pre-tied bowline round the cleat, and allow the skipper to take in the slack.

3 Or use the tail-end of the stern line as a spring led forward to the bow.

4 Adjust the bow and stern line to approximate equal lengths.

Entering a marina berth

A yacht should come alongside a pontoon as slowly as possible, with all fenders in position. Crew must be ready at the bow and stern, holding bow and stern lines. Each line should be secured to the yacht, led through the relevant fairlead, and taken under the lifelines and back to the crew's hand, where it is held in a coil ready to take ashore.

It's normal to go in bows first, with the bow hand jumping ashore just before the bow touches. Don't be over hasty and do this too early. You may fall into the water and risk getting crushed between the yacht and pontoon. Other crew should stand by to fend off if necessary.

As soon as the bow hand drops on the pontoon he or she should run ahead to the next cleat, ring or bollard, and take a turn to stop or "snub" the line and hold the yacht, which should by now have gone into reverse gear in order to take forward way off. This enables the stern hand to jump ashore and take a turn round a cleat, ring or bollard further astern, and by sweating on both lines the yacht can be pulled in close alongside the pontoon. The crew finally makes fast, attaches springs and checks fenders while the skipper closes down the engine.

Leaving a marina berth

Before leaving the skipper checks wind and tide, assesses the proximity of nearby yachts and their rigging, decides on the most practical route from the berth, briefs the crew, informs neighbouring yachts the boat is about to leave and starts the engine.

In straightforward situations the springs will be let off first; in some instances the skipper may need to motor ahead or astern against the pull of a spring, in order to move the stern or bows away from the pontoon. One crew takes responsibility for the bow line and one for the stern line. Either may need to stay on the pontoon with their line snubbed (one turn round the cleat, ring or bollard to hold the yacht) in order to help push out the yacht. They step on board at the last moment, pushing off with the back foot. All crew should be ready to fend off other yachts if necessary. It's better to use a foot than a hand, but never let any part of your body get between boat and boat or boat

and pontoon in case they come hard together. Best of all, dangle a hand-held fender to hold boats apart.

Once clear of the pontoon and marina, the crew should coil and stow all warps and fenders, ensuring they do not obstruct the helmsperson's view while moving around the boat.

SWINGING MOORINGS

These are common in rivers and estuary harbours. A large rubber inflatable buoy is made fast to a ground anchor by chain. The yacht is either secured to a permanent strop attached to the buoy with an eye that slips over the main foredeck cleat or, on a temporary mooring, may use a slip rope through an eye or ring. Smaller mooring buoys are often lifted onto the foredeck, with the strop and chain running out through the anchor fairlead. The mooring should allow the yacht enough room to swing on wind or tide without fouling adjacent moored yachts. It will also rise and fall with the tide.

Permanent deep-water moorings are at a premium in tidal areas where moorings that dry out restrict times for access and sailing.

ABOVE **A boathook is often required to grab a mooring. The skipper must aim to stop the boat dead in the water for a few seconds while the crew gets the mooring line on board.**

REVERSING OUT FROM A MARINA BERTH...

1 Depending on wind, tide and neighbouring yachts, you may need to reverse rather than go forward from a berth.

2 The crew lets off the bow line, which is then taken aboard.

3 With the stern line also removed, he holds the yacht on the forward spring.

4 Hauling in the spring pulls the bows into the pontoon and lets the stern blow out.

5 The skipper motors astern as the crew jumps on and pushes off with his back foot.

Leaving a swinging mooring

Before leaving, the skipper checks wind and tide, assesses the closeness of nearby yachts, decides on the most practical route from the berth and briefs the crew. If the yacht is lying downwind from the mooring and there are no yachts close by, it makes sense to hoist the mainsail and prepare the headsail before leaving. An experienced skipper may opt to sail off the mooring with the headsail hoisted and backed to help the bow bear off, but if there is any doubt it is wiser to start the engine and motor off.

In most cases the bow hand will lift the mooring strop off the main cleat, and ensure it runs out cleanly through the fairlead when the skipper gives the word and will then shout, "Gone!" The skipper can then let the yacht fall back on the wind or tide, allowing the bow to fall off to one side before moving ahead without danger of running down the mooring – it is exceptionally embarassing to get the mooring line caught round the keel or rudder, and even worse if it is tangled round the prop.

Picking up a swinging mooring

Before approaching the mooring the headsail should be dropped and stowed. Manoeuvring may be considerably easier if the mainsail is also dropped and furled. The approach should always be made uptide or upwind, whichever will stop the yacht.

The skipper should aim to nudge the mooring buoy with one side of the bow, and the yacht must stop moving forwards as soon as it touches. This will enable the bow hand to grab the mooring strop, using a boathook if required, and pull it up through the anchor fairlead and onto the foredeck cleat. Getting this right requires experience and excellent timing. If the bow hand grabs the mooring buoy when it is too far off or too far astern, or the yacht is still moving forwards, starting to move backwards or blowing away from the mooring, he or she will risk being pulled in. In these circumstances it is better to let go of the buoy or strop immediately, and tell the skipper to try again, which will often require a complete 360 degree circuit.

ABOVE **There must always be sufficient room for yachts and other craft to swing on wind and tide when on a mooring. Yachts of different size and motor boats will tend to have different swing characteristics.**

Manoeuvring under power

Great care must be taken when manoeuvring under power in a confined space. A yacht is prone to being blown around by the wind, and will naturally adopt a beam-on position with the bow tending to blow offwind. Yachts react slowly to changes on the tiller or wheel, and may require a strong burst of power to turn upwind. Their steering is also affected by the propeller throwing the stern to one side – if the propeller rotation is clockwise, the stern will move to starboard.

Reversing a yacht can be particularly difficult. The effect of the rudder is limited, windage on the yacht will encourage the bows to blow

ABOVE **When motoring astern, the skipper should be able to face aft. Always keep rudder movements small when going in this direction.**

downwind, and if the helmsperson attempts to turn too fast and too tight the yacht will get locked into a tight groove and continue turning until the stern points directly into the wind.

Always try to manoeuvre and come alongside as slowly as possible, and remember that the heavier the yacht the more effort will be needed to stop it moving forwards. If there is tide running you should endeavour to come alongside facing uptide so the yacht is easy to stop; if there is no tide, choose the upwind direction. You should never need to use more than a small amount of reverse throttle to stop.

ABOVE **The skipper must have a clear view forward when motoring ahead.**

NON TIDAL BERTHING

Sailing areas like lakes, with negligible tidal flow, makes berthing a simple operation.

Bows-on

Mooring bows-on to a quay works well in non tidal areas. The yacht is held to the quay by two bow lines at an angle of about 30 degrees to each other, with a stern line holding it back off the quay. This stern line may be a fixed mooring line, which is picked up from a small floating buoy, or the yacht may have to lay out a stern anchor as it approaches the quay. Care must be taken to ensure fenders protect the boat from yachts on either side, and that spreaders and shrouds will not tangle in a rising wind. A breast line may be necessary to hold the sterns of bows-on yachts together, with each outside yacht running a long line at an acute angle from stern to quay to help prevent the group of yachts from blowing sideways.

Stern-on

Mooring stern-on to a quay uses the same techniques as bows-on. It is easier and more pleasant to hop from stern to quay, particularly if you have a gangway ladder, and to run an anchor from the bows, a larger anchor giving better holding. It is also easier to leave the berth. However, anyone walking along the quay can see the innards of your yacht, which can be a disadvantage. But the principal problem associated with mooring stern-on is that you need to be extremely confident in your ability to reverse.

Rafting

In some cases pressure of space may require yachts to raft-up when moored side-on to a quay or harbour wall. An obvious requirement is that the rafted yachts should become progressively smaller. Springs should be set between each yacht, and long lines taken ashore from the bows and stern of the outside yacht to prevent the raft bending in a downwind direction.

Leaving a raft can be tricky if you are on the inside. The best solution is to wait for everyone else to go. The second best is to tell them your plans, apologize for the inconvenience, and ensure that the new inside yacht has a stern line made up and ready to pull in, with a bow line led round the back of

ABOVE **A raft of boats can lead to all kinds of problems with bending in the middle. It's just as well that this is a light hearted, lunchtime raft in fine weather.**

your yacht. You can then move out forwards with your crew physically holding the raft close alongside, and once your stern clears, the raft's new bow line can be hauled in smartly.

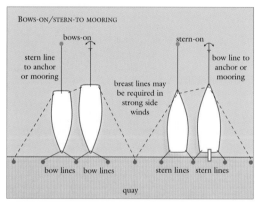

BOWS-ON/STERN-TO MOORING

bows-on

stern line to anchor or mooring

breast lines may be required in strong side winds

bow lines   bow lines

stern-on

bow line to anchor or mooring

stern lines   stern lines

quay

LEFT AND BELOW
In the Mediterranean it is often customary to berth bows-on to a quay, with a mooring or anchor line pulling the stern and holding the bows off. It is not suitable for those who find clambering between pulpit and quay difficult, but it ensures privacy and also saves having to reverse under power.

Drying out

Against a wall If you are lying alongside a fixed wall with a tidal rise and fall, lines will need to be shortened as the boat comes up and lengthened as it goes down – it is incredibly embarassing and not a little perplexing to return and find your yacht suspended in mid-air.

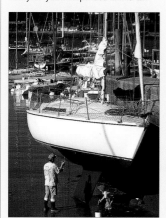

ABOVE **Drying out enables a full inspection of the bottom of the yacht, without the considerable cost of a boatyard lift. Note the rope from the quay to the mast, which prevents the yacht being lifted outwards by the tide.**

If the tidal fall is so great that your yacht will touch the bottom and dry out, it is reassuring to know that it won't fall over. A bilge keeler will obviously present few problems, while a fin keeler on the other hand will require care and consideration proportional to the length and shape of its keel. The yacht must be leaning slightly inwards to be safe, but not so far as to risk damaging the shrouds. There must be plenty of fendering along the side and, in addition to the standard

bow and stern lines and springs, a safety line should be led down from the quay and across the coachroof to the midships outside toerail.

On a mooring or anchorage Bilge keel or lifting keel yachts can dry out safely on a soft bottom such as sand or mud. A fin keel yacht, which dries out with no support, will lie on its side, and everything that is loose will slide around down below causing possible damage to the side or keel of the yacht.

ABOVE **With its daggerboard lifted, the F-24 trimaran can anchor in knee deep water and will dry out virtually level on a sand or mud bottom.**

ANCHORING

A safe anchorage should be well sheltered from prevailing wind and waves, and well away from a lee shore or rocks.

The bottom must have good holding for the anchor. Avoid areas with rocky outcrops, or underwater detritus such as old mooring chains, which may snag and trap your anchor.

There should be sufficient water under the keel at all states of the tide, but it must always be shallow enough for the anchor to hold properly. The length of the anchor chain should be no less than five times the depth of the water; if the anchor is held by a line, its length should be at least seven times the depth of the water.

Choose a spot that will allow you to anchor without fouling chains or lines from other yachts and boats, and with plenty of room to swing freely.

An anchor light should show the position of the yacht at night.

Take some bearings on landmarks to gauge if the anchor starts dragging.

If the wind changes and the holding deteriorates, be prepared to leave the anchorage and seek better protection with minimum delay.

Dropping the anchor

Drop and stow the sails, choose your spot, and slowly motor ahead. The foredeck crew should lay the anchor in the bow fairlead, and ensure the chain or anchor warp is clear for dropping.

ABOVE **A well sheltered anchorage in the Greek islands provides a delightful location for the afternoon, but may become less secure by night with the possibility of a change in the wind direction or strong gusts blowing down the hillside as the temperature falls.**

Engage neutral, and when the yacht stops moving forwards tell the foredeck crew to "Drop the hook!" while engaging reverse. The crew of a small yacht should be able to pay out the warp or chain hand over hand in shallow water. On a larger yacht, or in deeper water, the chain should be let go with the warp securely cleated or held round a windlass to ensure the right amount is paid out. Beware that a fast moving chain is potentially dangerous. Never attempt to stop it with your hands.

As the yacht moves backwards, the chain or warp will be spread along the bottom. Once a sufficient length has been dropped, the helmsperson can reverse a little harder with the chain or warp secured to its cleat or windlass to dig the anchor in. You can then line up two static objects to check it is not dragging.

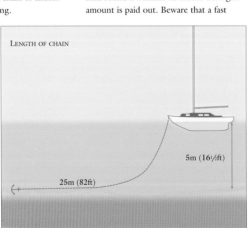

RIGHT **Multiplying the depth of water below the yacht by a factor of five gives an approximate guide to the right length of chain for a safe holding. A water depth of 5m (16½ft) for instance will require a chain length of 25m (82ft).**

LENGTH OF CHAIN

5m (16½ft)

25m (82ft)

ABOVE **In the ready to anchor position, the anchor shaft should fit snugly in the bow roller fairlead, and be securely locked so it does not fall at an inopportune moment. On most yachts the anchor should never be left in this position while sailing.**

HANDLING THE ANCHOR ....

Take great care when handling the anchor, which can easily damage the deck or bows.

The chain is also potentially dangerous and prone to bashing the sides of the anchor locker.

It is advisable to wear gloves when handling the chain, and always wear boots or shoes.

Lifting the anchor

The skipper should slowly motor ahead while the foredeck crew pulls up the anchor chain or warp, if it's a chain, he or she may need to use a windlass or crew back-up. Ensure the chain passes cleanly into the anchor locker, and keep the skipper informed of progress. When the chain or warp goes past vertical the skipper should back off to prevent it pulling back and damaging the bows. The crew should be able to feel when the anchor breaks out of the bottom, and tell the skipper who will be prepared for the bow to blow off.

Take great care that the anchor doesn't bash the bows when it comes up to the fairlead. If it's covered in mud or weed, be prepared to dunk it back in the sea for a clean-up or to give it a scrub before stowing. Always wear shoes or boots when handling an anchor.

PULLING UP THE ANCHOR ....

1 Let the skipper know as soon as the anchor breaks clear of its holding.

2 As you pull in the chain, take care the anchor does not swing back and damage the bow.

3 Brush off weed and dunk the anchor in the sea to remove any mud before you put it away.

4 Ensure the anchor goes in on top of the chain, so everything runs free next time it goes out.

Using a tender

Be very careful when leaving or returning to an anchorage or mooring in a small tender. What should be a pleasant experience can easily turn into a potential nightmare. A few precautions should be followed:

- Do not overload the tender.
- Do not rely solely on a small outboard motor for propulsion. Take oars as well.
- Make sure you know exactly where your yacht is and that you can locate it in the dark.
- Be very wary of strong offshore winds and adverse tides.
- Work out a sensible way of getting to and from the yacht or tender without falling in the sea.
- Wear waterproof clothing and encourage lifejackets all round.
- Don't even think about it if you have drunk too much alcohol.

Sailing manoeuvres

On a yacht, sailing techniques are scaled-up from dinghy practice, with two major differences. First, a heavy keel will provide considerable stability. Second, mechanical aids such as winches must be used to cope with heavier loadings.

SAILING UPWIND

While most dinghies are designed to be sailed virtually flat, keelboats will heel to leeward when sailing upwind in anything more than a light wind. Old-fashioned designs with slim, narrow hulls such as the Dragon 5.5 or 30 Square Metre were designed to heel right over at around 30 degrees or more when beating to windward, increasing their waterline length but giving a very wet ride. Modern designs are much wider and designed to sit upright, but may naturally heel to an angle past 10 degrees. The downward force of gravity provided by the weight of the keel – and to a lesser extent the weight of the crew if they sit up on the windward side – will combine with the upward force of buoyancy in the hull to prevent the yacht heeling further.

In strong or gusty winds a yacht may be knocked down, with water breaking over the leeward deck and running along the sides of the cockpit coamings. This is

perfectly safe and not a cause for panic, as there is too much resistance for the yacht to heel any further. However, it is also a highly ineffective way for a yacht to make ground to windward. Apart from being uncomfortable, with the crew clinging to

the windward side and anything loose getting thrown around down below, the yacht will rapidly lose ground to leeward as it slides on its side while the helm battles with the weather helm caused by a rudder that is half lifted out of the water.

ABOVE **Sailing on a close reach with the wind forward of the beam, the mainsail and genoa are eased and the boat at a comfortable angle of heel.**

ABOVE **When sailing hard on the wind the angle of heel increases, with the crew sitting on the deck to help increase windward leverage. If the wind increases, these yachts would need to shorten sail to maintain the same angle of heel rather than lose speed and slip sideways.**

LEFT **On this racing yacht the sails are sheeted hard in with a virtually perfect slot between genoa and mainsail. All the crew stay up to windward, with the exception of one crew who trims the genoa in and out in response to gusts and lulls.**

ABOVE **The crew needs to ease the mainsheet to break the effect of the slot and depower the rig, allowing the skipper to maintain the same course during a gust or bear away if required.**

If a yacht consistently heels too far, the crew should immediately shorten sail, while ensuring the mainsail and headsail remain balanced and the yacht has neutral helm (rudder not pulling hard in any direction). If the mainsail is too small and the headsail too large, the yacht will develop lee helm and want to bear away; if the mainsail is too large and the headsail too small, the yacht will develop weather helm and want to head up.

When a yacht is knocked down by a gust, the crew should react promptly. The helmsperson should let the yacht follow its natural inclination, which is to luff into the wind. This will help gain ground to windward, as well as bringing the yacht back upright by decreasing pressure on the sails, lifting the front of the mainsail and reducing the slot effect. Once the gust has passed the headsail will back with its windward telltales lifting, and the helm must bear away onto the old course to keep the yacht moving forwards at maximum speed. This is particularly important when

sailing upwind through waves, when the yacht should be sailed free and fast and pitching reduced to a minimum by concentrating crew weight in the middle of the boat.

When sailing on a fetch or close reach, the effects of a temporary knock-down can be reduced by easing off the mainsheet. This may be practical on a very small cruiser when the mainsheet can effectively be hand held, but will require too much

time and physical effort on a larger yacht. It is also uncomfortable and unsettling if done repeatedly, since the mainsheet and boom will tend to flog from side to side.

If the yacht has a traveller, the mainsail can be eased off the centreline to allow the yacht to stay upright during gusts without easing the mainsheet. However, if easing the traveller and letting off the mainsheet fail to keep the yacht upright, the crew must shorten sail.

ABOVE **Sailing hard on the wind, the genoa should be wound in until the leech is almost kissing the spreaders. The crew positions here provide maximum power for sheeting in.**

ABOVE **Sailing upwind on this cruising yacht is altogether a more leisurely affair. An easily handled amount of sail area for the prevailing conditions guarantees maximum comfort for those on board.**

SHEETING SAILS

The primary winches used to control headsails sheets and the multi-purchase systems for mainsheets are extremely powerful, and care must be taken not to oversheet the sails on an upwind course, which will break up the airflow and slow the boat down.

Headsail sheets

The leech of the headsail should be sheeted tight enough for the sail to be close to the end of the leeward spreader, without actually touching it. For optimum performance the crew must watch the headsail as the apparent wind changes, as when accelerating out of a tack.

As the wind increases the sail will stretch away from the leeward spreader, and needs to be sheeted in until it is once again close but not touching. If the wind or boat speed drops the sheet must be eased to pull the sail off the spreaders, while the helmsperson bears away to keep the boat moving.

Both the foot and leech should appear similarly taut when the traveller car is in

the correct position. Moving the car forwards will loosen the foot and stretch the leech; moving it back will stretch the foot and loosen the leech. Any fluttering on the leech can be controlled by pulling on the leech line. Do not pull the leech line so tight that you completely kill the flutter as this will effectively hook the sail and spoil the airflow.

Mainsheet

The mainsail should be sheeted in to match the set of the headsail, and never pulled in so tight that it is oversheeted creating a hooked leech that will kill boat speed. Sheet in the mainsail until it just starts to get backwinded by the jib. The front part of both headsail and mainsail will often backwind at the same time.

ABOVE **The leech and foot of the genoa should have a similar amount of curve as shown here. If the genoa is reduced by the rolling, the sheet lead must be moved forward.**

ABOVE **The headsail car has been moved almost to the front of the track on these First Class 8 racers, allowing their jibs to set perfectly.**

Safety first

"One hand for the boat!" is a basic law of seamanship which should be understood by both helm and crew. It is particularly important in difficult conditions when the yacht may be heeling, pitching or rolling from side to side. The most obvious application is for the crew who should use their harness safety lines as a failsafe third hand when both other hands are being used to move along the deck or pull in sails.

It is equally important for the helmsperson, as the following true story illustrates. The helmsman of an 8m (26ft) cruising trimaran was sitting on the side deck for a good view forwards, while entering the Needles Channel on a downwind course for the safety of the Solent. This is an area with a reputation for pushing up confused seas created by strong winds and fast tides, and when a rogue wave caught the yacht on its windward quarter it was spun

ABOVE **It is acceptable to stand for a better view while helming, but the maxim "one hand for the boat" should always be adhered to if there is a sea running.**

round into the wind and heeled over. In ordinary circumstances the helmsman would have hauled in on the tiller to correct the turn. However with nothing to hang onto he fell forwards into the cockpit, inadvertently pushing the tiller hard away so the boat jack-knifed side-on to the wind and was capsized.

ABOVE **A full-size geared wheel makes it possible to steer the boat from windward or leeward positions, with the latter (shown here) providing a clear view of yachts and other obstructions that might otherwise be hidden by the genoa.**

This will be clearly shown by the windward side telltales lifting in the bottom half of both headsail and mainsail, while the leeward telltales and those higher up blow back along the line of the sail.

If the leeward telltales hang down, the helmsperson needs to head up into the wind, or the crew needs to ease the sheets. If the windward telltales lift from top to bottom, the helm needs to bear away from the wind to prevent the boat from stalling, or the crew needs to pull in the sails.

CREW POSITION

Where the crew choose to sit or stand on the deck of a yacht are equally important when considering comfort and performance.

Tiller steering

The best position for a helmsperson steering with a tiller is to sit on the windward side of the cockpit, with feet braced to leeward if necessary, and with a clear view forwards along the windward deck. If the tiller has an extension, the helmsperson may opt to sit up on the windward cockpit coaming or side deck, where the view forward is much better and it is easier to watch the sails. However this position is considerably less secure if the boat heels in a gust.

ABOVE **The Mumm 36 is likely to be about the maximum size for a yacht with tiller steering, which is the preferred choice for a more responsive and dinghy-like feel.**

In either case the helm may need to move down to the leeward side of the cockpit occasionally so that he or she can see what is happening behind the headsail, but this should only be regarded as a temporary position.

Wheel steering

When steering, the helmsperson will often have exclusive use of an after cockpit that provides three possible positions: central, windward or leeward. In all cases the prime requirement is that the helmsperson maintains a clear view and full control.

In the central position a helmsperson is able to stand and get a reasonable view forward, though this may be somewhat

obscured by the mast, and the view to leeward will be completely blanketed by a genoa. The main advantage with this position is that both hands can be used on the wheel for maximum control and big movements, and should therefore always be used when sailing downwind.

In the windward position, the helm can either stand or sit. The position chosen will depend on the design of the cockpit, how the floor is sloped, and how much the boat is heeling. Its effectiveness will also depend on the diameter of the wheel and how easily it comes to hand. Good balance and good gearing is likely to be necessary for single-handed control. It should provide a clear view forward and

ABOVE **Racing upwind, the 14 strong crew of this yacht spread their weight evenly along the windward side between mast and stern away from the foredeck where extra weight would create pitching. The crew should also keep their weight to windward when they are off watch down below.**

to windward, as well as a good view of the sails, which is necessary when sailing with the wind forward of the beam.

In the leeward position, the helm will have to sit with his body braced against the guardrail if the boat is heeling, and as far as ballast is concerned is definitely on the wrong side. He or she will be able to get a view forward through the slot between

ABOVE **Sailing downwind, weight is moved aft over the wide, buoyant stern to prevent the bow being pushed down and ensure maximum effectiveness with the rudder.**

the sails as well as being able to see down to leeward behind the genoa, but the view to windward will be totally obscured.

Crew places

On an upwind course the crew should sit on the windward side of the cockpit once the boat starts heeling. For those who wish to sit up on the side deck, the most comfortable position is racing style, with your back to the centreline and legs hanging over the side of the boat. This is safe so long as you are not manoeuvring near other yachts, when legs and other body parts should be kept inboard. The crew should also concentrate their weight amidships, keeping off the bows or stern where extra weight may promote pitching.

On an offwind course the bow of a yacht will tend to go down as speed increases, and the crew should move aft to help keep the rudder down in the water. The crew should trim the boat to keep it level and the mast upright, particularly when sailing dead downwind.

TACKING

In a cruiser, tacking should be a precise, controlled manoeuvre. It cannot be done instantly, as in a small racing dinghy, and should be viewed as a fluid transition that relies on the cruiser constantly moving and not stalling while changing tacks.

Tacking technique

The helmsperson must ensure the boat is footing fast, by bearing away a touch to build speed if necessary and looking for a flat patch between waves.

The crew are prepared by the call of, "Ready about!" In typical circumstances one crew will take responsibility for the leeward active sheet. He or she will uncleat it or take it out of its self-tailer, and hold the free end until the yacht spins round. The other crew will take responsibility for the new active sheet, which is on the windward side of the boat. He or she will put one turn round the winch, and pull in the sheet until all slack is removed. The helm calls "lee-oh!"(helm's-alee!) and

TACKING FROM STARBOARD TO PORT ....

1 As the skipper puts the tiller over, the first crew lets go the headsail sheet ready for the second crew to pull in.

2 The headsail should be sheeted most of the way in before the tack is completed and the sail has filled with wind on the new side.

3 Ready for the first crew to push the handle into the winch and wind the sail hard-in, fine tuning it to the angle and speed of the wind.

turns the boat into the eye of the wind. The aim is to steer the yacht through the tack, matching the tightness of the turn to the speed and efficiency of the crew. It is a great mistake to just slam the rudder right over, because it will act like a brake. As the bows of the yacht turn through the eye of the wind, the headsail starts to back. This is the sign for the first crew to throw the sheet off the winch and let it run free. The best way to do this is to spin the sheet anti-clockwise and upwards off the top of the winch. The second crew

pulls in the new leeward sheet hand over hand, as much and as fast as possible. As soon as the sheet starts to pull hard, he or she puts a second turn on the winch and can then pull in more sheet until it is necessary to use the handle. At this point a third and possibly a fourth turn can be put on, though beware of riding turns that jam the winch if too many turns ride up. The tail end can then be wrapped round the self-tailing jaws, and the first crew can insert the winch handle and start to wind. Alternatively and more

quickly the second crew can hand hold the sheet end and pull in as the other crew winds.

One person must watch the leech and be ready to stop winding as it closes on the spreader. While this is going on the helm will have turned the yacht onto the new tack, and may need to luff to allow the crew to sheet the sail in faster. He or she can then bear away to build up speed, while the sheet is wound in as the sail stretches away from the spreaders.

TACKING FROM PORT TO STARBOARD ....

1 The leeward crew spins the sheet anti-clockwise off the winch.

2 It is vital that the old active sheet runs free and allows the new sheet to be pulled in.

3 The new sheet is then locked in place into the self-tailing jaws.

4 Allowing one crew to complete sheeting in the sail.

Tacking problems

- The sheets may catch on a cleat or winch around the mast area, which is normally the result of pulling in too slowly. If this happens one crew will need to move smartly forward to lift the sheet off the obstruction.

- If the yacht fails to tack round, it is simply going too slowly or the sheet has been thrown off too soon leaving insufficient power in the headsail to help pull the bows round.

- If the crew have difficulty winding in the sheet on the new tack, they are probably too slow pulling in hand over hand, or the helm may be bearing away too quickly. In most cases the crew should be able to pull virtually all the sheet in hand over hand reserving use of the winch handle for fine tuning.

SAILING OFFWIND

The effect of less apparent wind, coupled with a noticeably warmer airflow, frequently make sailing offwind a real pleasure after the rigours of a hard beat into the wind.

Reaching

When sailing on a beam or broad reach, the headsail should be eased until the windward telltales are just lifting. The mainsheet traveller should be let off to the end of the track, and the mainsheet eased until the mainsail's windward telltales are just lifting. The kicking strap or vang should be pulled hard down. If the yacht heels too far it will start to slip sideways, and the speed of a reaching course will exacerbate the tendency to weather helm with the result that the helm has to strain to hold the tiller or wheel. The solution is to shorten sail or bear away further downwind to reduce side-on sail pressure.

Running

On a downwind course the mainsheet should be sheeted in enough to hold the sail off the shrouds and spreaders, which will damage the coating on the sail and leave an unsightly dark mark over a period of time.

LEFT **Fast and furious. The gennaker (left) and spinnaker (right) give tremendous power when sailing downwind on a reach, and are recommended for those who enjoy knife edge thrills in this kind of close quarters situation.**

On a dead downwind course a standard headsail will be blanketed by the mainsail. It will be considerably more effective if it is goose-winged (wing on wing) to windward, but will require some kind of pole to hold it out. A genoa may be too large and low to be flown effectively, even when used with a topping lift to hold the pole clear of the water. If the pole end persists in catching, probably the best solution is to change to a smaller headsail.

Sailing under mainsail alone, a yacht will tend to luff to windward. A goose-winged cruising chute or spinnaker will help keep the yacht in balance and add to speed.

Spinnakers

For cruisers, spinnaker principles are as on dinghies, except that everything is scaled up with larger poles that require topping lifts, and downhauls, and sheet and guy controlled by the primary winches.

ABOVE **Holding out the headsail with the boat hook may be OK in very light winds, but is not recommended when sailing downwind.**

Rolling downwind

If there are waves, a yacht will be prone to roll downwind. A wave that hits on the windward quarter (side of the stern) will make the yacht luff and heel to windward, while a wave hitting the leeward quarter will make it bear away and heel to leeward. The pendulum effect of the keel can rapidly build up a rolling motion. This motion will be exacerbated by natural imbalance in the sails. On a beat or reach the sideways force in the sails will press the rig down and prevent the boat rolling. On a run the wind is directly behind, and the force in the sails will tend to see-saw from side to side. A primary control is to ensure the kicking strap is pulled tight, reducing twist in the top of the sail, which would otherwise encourage the yacht to heel to windward.

A rudder is relatively ineffectual while the stern is being driven to one side or the other by a wave. Course

ABOVE **The effect of waves lifting the stern with the mainsail to one side and the spinnaker to the other will promote rolling, which can only be controlled by good sailing technique.**

corrections must be anticipated, and made before a wave hits and while the yacht is sailing in a trough or flat patch where rudder movements will have maximum effect. If a yacht is travelling fast in strong winds, the crew should move aft and stay off the foredeck when possible. It is vital to keep all of the rudder down in the water for maximum steerage.

To achieve perfect balance, a yacht sailing downwind with a spinnaker should be heeled slightly to windward to offset the push of the mainsail, with the centreline of the spinnaker (from head to halfway between tack and clew) vertical and the foot horizontal, which means having tack and clew at exactly the same height. The spinnaker pole should be pulled back at right angles to the apparent wind, with the inboard end of the pole raised so it is at right angles to the mast. In reality the crew can only attempt to get close to this level of perfection, and the spinnaker will always pull to one side or the other.

Letting the spinnaker blow forwards will drive the bows down and promote instability and rolling. To prevent this, the clew and tack of a spinnaker should be pulled down as low as possible to flatten the sail and bring its centre of effort aft, with both corners at exactly the same height. Sheet in the spinnaker to help the yacht luff up, and sheet out to help it bear away.

ABOVE **The uphaul and downhaul control the vertical angle of the spinnaker pole and ensure that clew and tack are virtually level.**

Cruising chutes

A cruising chute is a safer, simpler option for downwind cruising. It lacks the ultimate power of a spinnaker, but is much easier for short-handed or inexperienced crew to use. Cruising chutes are variations on dinghy gennakers, cut with an asymmetric tack and clew and using port and starboard sheets. Flat-cut chutes can be carried close to the wind on a broad or beam reach.

Coiling a line

Unused lines and the ends of lines should always be coiled so that they are neat and tidy, and will run out in the case of a sheet or halyard, or can be thrown in the case of a mooring line.

- Always coil rope clockwise, turning each loop through a half turn to avoid forming figure of eights. This is much easier with a soft rope.
- To secure the coil, take two or more turns round the top part of the coil. Then pass the free end through as a loop, which can be locked off against the coil. This will enable the coil to be hung from a winch or cleat.

BELOW **A perfectly balanced spinnaker would have an imaginary vertical line from the head to the halfway point of the foot, and an imaginary horizontal line between clew and tack.**

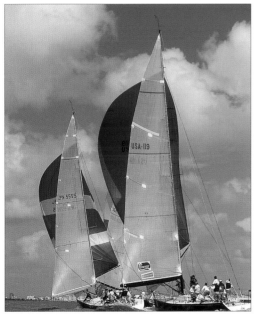

ABOVE **The Japanese racer could bear away to correct the roll to windward, but will risk sailing into the wind shadow of the chasing USA boat. Trimming in the guy and letting out the sheet would also help pull the yacht upright.**

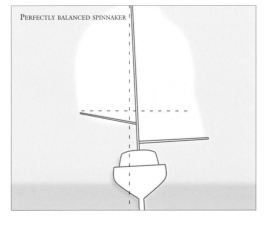

PERFECTLY BALANCED SPINNAKER

Full-cut chutes are more effective downwind, but may require a pole to goose-wing on the opposite side to the mainsail.

The tack of the chute is attached to the yacht by a variable length strop that is led into the pulpit in front of the forestay. The strop adjusts leech tension and clew height: tight and short for reaching and loose and long for running. If rolling is a problem, the strop of the chute should be shortened to bring the sail aft and the sheet should be taken in.

Sheet in the chute to help the yacht luff up, and sheet out to help it bear away.

Using a dousing sock

A standard method of launching a cruising chute is to use a dousing sock. The chute is hoisted inside its dousing sock, with the crew taking care to keep the halyard and sock clear of the spreaders and forestay. Once the halyard is fully up and made fast, the dousing sock is pulled to the top of the sail. This lets the sail blow free, and it should be smartly sheeted in to prevent it wrapping round the forestay.

As in a dinghy it is easiest to hoist and set the chute on a downwind course, using the blanketing effect of the mainsail to prevent the sail from blowing out of control. The blanketing effect should also be used when dousing and dropping the chute. The sheet must be freed off to

ABOVE **Nowhere to go. This yacht needs to bear away to avoid an imminent broach, but is held upwind by the boat to leeward.**

allow the dousing sock to be pulled back down over the sail, after which it can be dropped and fed into its bag like a sausage.

GYBING

Cruiser gybes are not as fast or furious as a dinghy, but the power of the mainsail can be awesome when the boom crosses from side to side, and the gybe must be controlled at all times.

Gybing technique

Warn the crew with a, "Ready to Gybe!", and ensure everyone is well clear of the path of the boom, it is vital that no one

pops their head out of the companionway at the critical moment when the boom comes across.

The crew must ensure that there is nothing to prevent the boom from gybing and that the kicking strap is tensioned to hold the boom down. The helmsperson or crew should centralize the mainsheet traveller ready for the gybe, so the traveller car doesn't whistle from side to side with the possibility of smashing itself on the buffers.

The helm cries, "Gybe-oh!" as he or she steers into the gybe. Once the yacht enters the dead downwind zone, helm or crew should haul in the mainsheet, taking in as much as possible so the whole lot cannot crash from side to side. The helmsperson or crew may help the boom across by handing the falls of the mainsheet, which must immediately be paid out hand over hand on the new gybe. At the same time the crew must gybe the headsail, cruising chute or spinnaker, using much the same techniques as for a dinghy.

As the yacht gybes it may have a tendency to pivot on its keel and turn up into the wind. The helm should counter this by applying rudder correction and bearing away immediately after the gybe, in order to keep the yacht heading downwind.

Gybing problems

It pays to wait for a lull to gybe, but as with a dinghy the effects of apparent wind will be minimized if the boat is sailing fast.

Broaching

This is to be avoided. It is a phenomenon in which a yacht sailing on a downwind course suddenly pivots into the wind, resulting in a total loss of control and lying on its side with most of the rudder lifted clear of the water. It causes particular problems when flying a spinnaker, as the wind will continue to blow up from the foot to the head of the spinnaker, keeping the top of the sail full and holding the yacht down on its side. Releasing the guy is the only way to depower the spinnaker and bring the boat back upright.

ABOVE **Releasing the sheet and letting the spinnaker flog is one way to bring the boat back up, but when sailing this close to the wind the solution is to drop it.**

GYBING FROM STARBOARD TO PORT

1 One of the crew begins pulling in the mainsheet while the other stands by to let go of the headsail sheet.

2 When the mainsail comes over the boom should be sheeted right in to reduce the effect of the boom crashing across to the new side.

3 Then the mainsheet is paid out and the headsail trimmed in until both sails are correctly set up for the wind direction on the new gybe.

Do not pull the mainsheet in too early when going into the gybe as this will increase the yacht's tendency to luff and possibly broach. Avoid a situation where the boom hits the new leeward shroud with a thud. Do not head up on to a new reaching course until the boom is let right out, or the boat will heel over, develop weather helm and round up further than you aimed.

Involuntary gybes

On a full downwind course there is the danger of an involuntary gybe, which must be taken seriously when the force of the boom could sweep crew over the side and cause severe injury. In fact a small number of people have lost their lives in this way.

It is vital to keep the boom pulled hard down with the kicking strap, which can be led to the toerail and used as a preventer. This will help prevent the boom starting to move through the first stages of an involuntary gybe, but should never be totally relied on. If the wind is strong and a yacht is sailing well by the lee – usually due to an uncontrolled roll to windward – the force of wind hitting the wrong side of the sail may tear the preventer out of its mounting and the speed with which the boom crashes over will be even more violent.

ABOVE **A relatively flat-cut cruising chute can be comfortably carried on an apparent wind beam reach and will behave much the same as a dinghy gennaker.**

Cruising

Life in the confined space of a yacht can be extremely pleasureable so long as a few common sense rules are adhered to. Tidiness, hygiene and consideration towards other crew members are important, particularly in less than perfect conditions.

Living on board

Take as little baggage as possible. Only use soft bags that can be shoved into cramped spaces. Stow your gear carefully and tidily, so you can find it when you need it at all times. Be considerate to the gear of other crew members. Take great care not to spread water around when changing out of wet gear. Stow waterpoofs and boots where they can drain and dry.

Choose a berth for the duration of your time on board. Pilot berths, which are outboard of the main saloon area, and quarter berths in the aft quarters may have the advantage of being out of the way if you want to lie down during the day. Berths in the forepeak are likely to be uncomfortable when the yacht is sailing.

ABOVE **Modern yacht galleys can be extremely luxurious and come complete with features such as pressurized hot and cold water. However it is important that the galley also functions in a seaway with a stove mounted on gimbals, secure storage and everything to hand.**

If a sailing trip requires alternating watches (such as 4 hours on, 4 hours off), respect the rights of those coming off watch and be prepared to take their places immediately on your turn.

Cooking

One crew person may volunteer to do all the cooking. In other cases cooking should be done on a rota, as should washing-up and clearing-up.

ABOVE **All the delights of cruising life with lunch served up on the front door.**

LEFT **The crew down on the leeward deck isn't being sick, though he could well be. Seasickness effects many yachtsmen and is nothing to be ashamed of.**

Learn to cook using gimbals and a bum strap, with fiddles to hold pots or kettles in position. The galley should be well ventilated when cooking under way. A stuffy atmosphere with the gas lit can soon lead to nausea. It is also a good idea to wear bib overalls and sea boots while cooking when under way to guard against substances such as boiling water. You should stick to food that is quick and simple to prepare, and food that can be consumed without danger of burns or spillage when under way. Variations on hot drinks and soups in half-filled mugs will suffice if all else fails. The galley is best kept clean and tidy at all times, with everything stowed in case the yacht rolls or heels too far.

If you have the luxury of pressurized water, use the power sparingly, and never throw your garbage over the side.

Seasickness

This is a complaint that many suffer from due to an imbalance of the inner ear and is nothing to be ashamed of. Furthermore, although you may feel nauseous for a time, you will normally get over it. If you are not able to take your mind off feeling sick by keeping busy, the best remedy is to get your head down, by getting into your berth and wrapping up and keeping warm in a sleeping bag. You should eat simple food, such as plain bread, and keep drinking to avoid dehydration. There are many remedies commercially available for seasickness, find one that works for you.

If you are sick, take care where you do it. The lavatory is not a very nice place to be. Throwing up over the side, always to leeward, requires care if you are not to fall over. A bucket in the cockpit may be the most acceptable solution, and it is surprising how sympathetic other crew members will be.

Personal hygiene

Keeping good hygiene standards is always important. Familiarize yourself with your marine toilet, and the workings of the sea cocks, which allow water to be pumped in and out. The lavatory can be a nauseous place in rough weather, so make sure you always leave it well pumped and clean, and ensure maximum ventilation. A few countries require yachts to have holding tanks, which are pumped out in marinas. Hopefully the rest of the world will eventually follow suit.

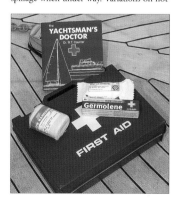

ABOVE **First aid and basic medical care for those on the boat are vital accessories for enjoyable cruiser sailing.**

ABOVE **Soggy, wet and cold, the lavatory can be a ghastly place when out at sea. Good ventilation and high standards of cleanliness are essential.**

Emergency action

Most yachtsmen spend a lifetime afloat without ever needing to put any emergency procedures into practice. But if the worst should happen, it pays to be prepared and to have a clear idea of what action is likely to be the most effective.

HEAVING-TO

This technique can be used to bring a yacht to a virtual stop, with almost no forward movement and minimal leeway depending on the strength of the wind.

Heaving-to is associated with riding out a storm, and can be used when conditions are too uncomfortable to sail upwind and there is sufficient open sea to leeward. It can also be used to stall a yacht in any conditions – to make repairs, reef the sails or allow another yacht to catch up.

The basic technique of heaving-to is to sheet the headsail (or storm jib if riding out a gale) to windward so that it is backwinded, free the mainsheet (with the mainsail reefed right down and sheeted in for a gale), and lash the tiller to leeward or the wheel hard down to windward. The opposing forces of rudder and backwinded headsail should hold the yacht in the hove-to position, though it may be necessary to adjust rudder, sheet or sail size to ensure the boat is perfectly balanced, side-on and drifting slowly downwind.

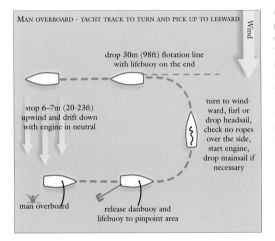

MAN OVERBOARD - YACHT TRACK TO TURN AND PICK UP TO LEEWARD

Wind

drop 30m (98ft) flotation line with lifebuoy on the end

stop 6–7m (20-23ft) upwind and drift down with engine in neutral

turn to windward, furl or drop headsail, check no ropes over the side, start engine, drop mainsail if necessary

man overboard

release danbuoy and lifebuoy to pinpoint area

LEFT **Man overboard procedure will depend on a variety of factors. This example presumes a simple situation in which the yacht can release a buoy, turn to windward, drop sails and motor back upwind of the casualty. Wind, waves, tidal flow and darkness may all make the procedure considerably more difficult.**

MAN OVERBOARD

Falling overboard is a rare occurrence that strikes in the most unlikely circumstances. Contrary to popular belief it does not always happen in strong winds and survival conditions, mostly because the crew will invariably be clipped on by a safety line. Nor is it reserved for inexperienced sailors.

Falling overboard can happen to anyone any time – getting knocked over by the boom, losing your footing while moving along the deck or when attempting to get into a dinghy.

It is generally easiest to pick up the person overboard from the leeward side, though beware of the yacht being driven over him or her in strong winds or waves. Picking up to windward removes this problem, but the yacht will be prone to blow away from the person overboard and it may be impossible for him or her to climb up or be pulled up on the high windward side. A member of the crew should have the boat hook ready to catch on to the lifejacket or harness of the person being rescued.

MAN OVERBOARD – GOOD PRACTICE ....

1 Get your crew to practise retrieving a man overboard with a fender.

2 One crewman must keep watching the "casualty".

3 Do not run over the "casualty" – approach with dropped sails.

4 Work out how you will get the "casualty" on board.

Man overboard technique

Make a habit of practising man overboard technique on a regular basis. The standard procedures are as follows:

- Yell, "Man overboard!" as soon as it happens.
- Throw the pushpit-mounted lifebelt over the back of the boat and let the line run out.
- Get someone to watch the person in the water as it is very easy to lose sight if there are waves.
- Take a compass bearing in order to be able to head back along the reciprocal (reverse) course. Start the engine.
- If the person overboard is close enough, the skipper may be able to turn into wind or heave-to without losing ground while the person in the water grabs the lifebelt and line.
- The yacht may need to tack or gybe round, whichever is quickest and most practical, to back-track for the retrieval. Keep the arc of the turn as tight as possible, and ensure the yacht does not drop too far to leeward during a gybe.
- The skipper should aim to bring the yacht to a standstill alongside the person overboard, ideally heaving-to.

Getting back on board

It can be extremely difficult to get someone back on board, particularly when he or she is unable to assist through exhaustion, shock and hypothermia, and the crew must ensure they do not fall over as well. If the crew cannot physically haul a person in over the toerail, it may be possible to use one of the following methods:

- Drop a boarding ladder over the side, or provide a knotted rope for the person in the water to hold onto.
- Launch the yacht's inflatable tender, and roll the person into it.
- Get the person round to the stern, and use the fixed boarding ladder.
- Use the main boom as a derrick supported by the topping lift, and haul the person up with the bottom block of the mainsheet attached to the harness. Or use the kicking strap in conjunction with the headsail halyard.

Basic safety equipment

Radar reflector For use when near shipping channels. The reflector must be hoisted as high as possible.

Distress flares Crew should know where they are located, and read the instructions explaining what each type of flare is for and how to operate them. Yachts must have in-date flares, but out-of-date flares can still be carried as back-up. Hand-held flares have a range of up to 3 miles and are most effective during the day. Hand-launched parachute flares can have a range of over 7 miles and are most effective at night.

Fire extinguisher This needs to be sited in the companionway for immediate use in the galley or cockpit.

Lifebelt Horseshoe-shaped lifebelts have replaced the old-fashioned circular lifebuoy. The lifebelt should be securely mounted on the pushpit so it can be removed with a one-handed throw, with a floating line of at least 50m (164ft) running free. The line may be attached to an automatic floating light.

Flashlight A powerful, hand-held flashlight should be to hand with fully charged batteries.

IOR Dan Buoy Offshore racing yachts must be equipped with a fibreglass weighted pole that floats vertically, with a flag and flashing light visible at 1.6km (1mile). This should be thrown to mark the position of a person overboard.

Radio beacons The yacht may be fitted with an emergency radio beacon that will transmit its exact position to land-based rescue organisations via the SARSAT/COSPAS satellite system. In addition crew members may carry personal radio beacons, which send out a distress signal on VHF Channel 16 and other emergency frequencies.

Life raft Most modern life rafts are mounted on the deck in a hard plastic container, with an automatic inflation system, which must be serviced by the supplier regularly. Standard features include full overhead cover plus double floor and buoyancy compartments, water stabilization to prevent capsize and a full inventory of safety and survival equipment.

Electronics and navigation

For many years conventional navigation relied on the use of land bearings with a chart, compass and plotter or parallel rules inshore, and a fiendishly complex sextant offshore. The introduction of increasingly sophisticated electronics changed all that, with early systems such as Decca, Loran and Radar soon replaced by the ubiquitous global positioning system (GPS), now established as the main navigation system for all marine uses.

The emergence of GPS

GPS provides worldwide navigational coverage via 24 Navstar satellites, which were originally launched by the US Ministry of Defense. Following the relaxation of limits imposed for non-military personnel, GPS now guarantees accuracy within a few metres when sailing between specific points, or waypoints, on a chart. It is available at low cost, with a choice of mounted or hand-held receivers that

ABOVE **The Yeoman plotter is a sophisticated instrument that links electronic navigation with the traditional chart.**

ABOVE **The GPS makes navigation seem easy, but a crew must also be able to read a chart and use a conventional plotter to find the way.**

provide immediate graphic information on a yacht's course, plus any error.

The emergence of GPS has also signalled the beginning of the end for traditional two dimensional charts, which are gradually being replaced by electronic digital charts. Electronic charts can provide features such as tidal information, showing the precise depth for a specific time and

date at any location. Multi-language electronic micro charts used with LCD plotters are already widely available for popular yachting areas. They allow the navigator to scroll through the appropriate chart on a screen, zoom in for the required amount of detail, and plot the position for the yacht, which is automatically displayed with the next waypoint, as well as having

Night lights

- A sailing vessel under way must exhibit side lights (green and red) and a stern light (white).
- A sailing vessel of less than 20m (66ft) may carry these lights as one combined lantern at or near the masthead.
- A sailing vessel of less than 7m (23ft) should carry these lights if practicable. If not, a white flashlight must be ready.
- A sailing vessel under power must exhibit an additional white masthead light.
- A sailing vessel of more than 7m (23ft) must show an all-round white light at a mooring or anchorage.

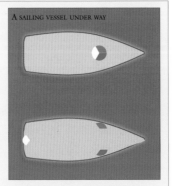

A SAILING VESSEL UNDER WAY

ABOVE **Most modern yachts are fitted with a combination tri-colour light at the top of the mast (top) rather than a separate port, starboard and stern light (bottom).**

ABOVE **Most yachts of medium size and above now boast an impressive array of electronic navigational and go fast equipment with read-outs available for skipper, crew and navigator. It's still a lot of fun to sail by the seat of your pants though.**

immediate access to speed, depth and wind information.

However all cruiser sailors must accept that electronic navigation can fail in a harsh marine environment. It is vital to be able to fall back on conventional techniques, and they can be great fun to use:

- Taking a fix with a hand-held compass.
- Plotting a course or fixing a position on a traditional chart.
- Correcting magnetic deviation, and allowing for leeway and tidal flow.
- Steering by the compass.
- Recording distance covered by the log.

Multi-function electronics

Modern electronic navigation systems provide immediate access to multiple functions, with the main unit normally located in the navigation area and LED displays for the helmsperson and crew in the cockpit. A popular system such as the B&G Hydra 2000 provides a huge amount of data on speed, depth, wind conditions and course, with a choice of three

categories and nine display pages brought up at the press of a button:

Speed/Depth Boatspeed/depth, boatspeed/speed over ground, boatspeed/apparent wind angle.

Wind Apparent wind speed/apparent wind angle, true wind speed/true wind direction, velocity made good/true wind angle.

Navigation Current heading/course over ground, heading/boatspeed, distance to waypoint/bearing to waypoint.

The IALA buoyage system

The system has been established by the International Association of Lighthouse Authorities (IALA) to create a uniform buoyage throughout the world. System A covers Europe while system B covers America, Korea, Japan and the Philippines.

Lateral marks show the way into and out of channels and ports. Starboard-hand marks (which must be left to starboard on the way in) are conical buoys or spar pillars with a cone on top. Port hand

marks are can shaped buoys or spar pillars with a can on top. Under IALA System A, starboard hand buoys are green or black and port hand buoys are red. Under IALA System B these colours are reversed.

Cardinal marks are yellow and black buoys or spar pillars, which show where it is safe to navigate round a hazardous area such a shallow water. The location of the hazard is indicated by conical pointers: for instance a cardinal mark to the north of the hazard will have two cones pointing upwards, while a cardinal mark to the south of the hazard will have two cones pointing downwards.

Isolated danger marks are sited directly over a specific danger, such as a wreck. They are black and red pillar or spar buoys with two black spheres on top.

Safe water marks, which indicate that there is navigable water all round, are red and white spherical, pillar or spar buoys.

Special marks are used to indicate specific use of an area, such as underwater cables, and are yellow with an X top mark.

Rights of way

Under sail
- Port gives way to starboard.
- Windward yacht keeps clear.
- Overtaking yacht keeps clear.

Power and sail
- Power gives way to sail.
- Sail gives way to power in restricted waters.
- Sail gives way to a fishing vessel using nets, lines or trawls, but not to a pleasure boat using trolling lines.

Under power
- Right is right! Port-side vessel gives way and must avoid crossing ahead.
- When two vessels are head to head, both turn to starboard.
- Overtaking vessel keeps clear.
- Avoid impeding safe passage of a vessel constrained by its draught.
- Keep to the starboard side of a narrow channel or fairway, where vessels of less than 20m (66ft) must give way.

UNDER POWER: RIGHT IS RIGHT

stop or change course: yacht to port must give way and should avoid attempting to cross ahead

yacht on the starboard side has right of way

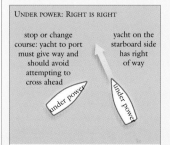

KEEP TO THE STARBOARD SIDE

under power

under power

To avoid collision both yachts must turn to starboard. If in a channel, vessels must keep to starboard side.

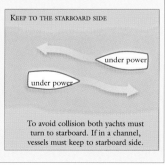

IALA SYSTEM A BUOYS.....................

1 Hazard to the north.

2 Hazard to the south.

3 Navigable water all round.

4 Starboard side of channel (entering).

5 Port side of channel (entering).

Keelboats

Open keelboats represent a traditional category, epitomised by the Dragon and a host of local classes, which can be found in yachting centres around the world.

Dragon

First launched 1929
Designer Johan Anker (Denmark)
LOA 8.89m (29ft)
Beam 1.95m (6ft)
Upwind sail area 27.7 sq m (298 sq ft)
Spinnaker 23.6 sq m (254 sq ft)

A beautiful three-person racing keelboat, which was selected for the 1948 Olympics and remained an Olympic class through to the 1972 Games. Classic wooden Dragons still race with gleaming varnished hulls, but many owners opt for lower maintenance fibreglass, which was introduced to the class in 1973. Fleets of this classic thoroughbred are concentrated in Europe and Scandinavia, as well as the USA, Canada, Japan, Hong-Kong, Australia and New Zealand.

Etchells

First launched 1966
Designer Skip Etchells (USA).
LOA 9.3m (31ft)
Beam 2.1m (7ft)
Upwind sail area 28.5 sq m (307 sq ft)
Spinnaker 48 sq m (517 sq ft)

ABOVE **The Etchells lays claim to being the most popular of modern, open keelboats with top class racing worldwide.**

The International Etchells 22 has more than fifty fleets worldwide scattered through Europe, the USA, Canada, Bermuda, Australia, New Zealand and Hong Kong. The boat is known as a fast, stable and sleek one-design that is normally dry-sailed (kept on shore) and can be raced competitively by three or four average ability sailors, although top-class professional helms also sail in the class for relaxation and pleasure.

ABOVE **The Dragon is a distinguished class which harks back to another era. With slim hull and low freeboard it can also give a very wet ride to windward in windy weather.**

LEFT **With more than half a century behind it, the Flying Fifteen is established as a modern classic and the most famous creation of Uffa Fox.**

RIGHT **The 2.4 Metre provides a unique experience in single-handed racing.**

Flying Fifteen

First launched 1947
Designer Uffa Fox (UK)
LOA 6.1m (20ft)
Beam 1.52m (5ft)
Upwind sail area 13.94 sq m (150 sq ft)
Spinnaker 13.94 sq m (150 sq ft)

A classic two-person racing keelboat, which is often raced by mixed crews, and hails from Britain's centre of yachting at Cowes in the Isle of Wight. The class has a strong international following in Australia, New Zealand, Hong Kong, Ireland and South Africa. Over 3,500 boats have been built in the first 50 years and fibreglass has replaced moulded wood as the modern building material.

International Six Metre

First launched 1907
Designer Various
LOA approximately 11m (36ft)
Beam 2m (6½ft)
Upwind sail area approximately 65 sq m (700 sq ft)
Spinnaker 85 sq m (915 sq ft)

A classic formula racing keelboat that might top anyone's list as the most beautiful class on the water. The main features of the Six are long, lean hulls with classic overhangs that find their full expression in older wooden yachts. Modern designs, built in hi-tech plastics keep taking the class forward, giving formidable upwind performance with a 60 degree tacking angle and enough sail area to keep a five strong crew fully occupied. There are fleets in Britain, Germany, Sweden, Norway, Finland, Switzerland, Argentina and the USA.

Soling

First launched 1965
Designer Jan Linge (Norway)
LOA 8.2m (27ft)
Beam 1.9m (6ft)
Upwind sail area 21.7 sq m (233 sq ft)
Spinnaker 8.75m (29ft) max circumference

The Soling took part in its 13th Olympic regatta at Sydney in 2000, and claimed to be the only gender mixed class at the 1996 Games. Its quickness, manoeuvrability and tactical effectiveness make it particularly suitable for smooth water sailing, and enabled the Soling to introduce the concept of match racing to the Olympics. Soling are sailed all over the world, and the largest fleets are found in the USA, Canada, Australia, Japan, South Africa, Argentina, Brazil and throughout Europe.

ABOVE **At Olympic level the Soling is a powerful boat, its fast response making it a perfect choice for boat-on-boat racing.**

RIGHT **There's nothing like the classical beauty of a 6 Metre racing yacht.**

2.4 Metre

First launched 1988
Designers Various
LOA 4.1–4.35m (13–14ft)
Beam 0.75–0.9m (2½–3ft)
Upwind sail area 8 sq m (86 sq ft)

The 2.4 Metre originated from Sweden, and is a miniature sister to 6 Metre, 8 Metre and 12 Metre (America's Cup) class yachts, which are all designed to a measurement formula. The helmsperson sits facing forward, and controls are within easy reach, the rudder moved by foot pedals.

The 2.4 was awarded International status in 1992, with regular World Championships attracting 60–100 boats. It was also selected as the single-handed class for the disabled sailors' Paralympics at Sydney 2000. There are large fleets in Scandinavia, Italy, England and Australia.

In 1991 the Norlin III made its appearance and has been the dominant design ever since. Rule-bending and the use of exotic materials, which could make old designs obsolete, is strongly discouraged, and the class provides a unique form of single-handed match racing.

Sportsboats

These boats are small, fast, day sailing keelboats, which aim to provide similar thrills to a high performance dinghy, with action packed racing for a crew of five or more. This selection includes half a dozen of the most popular sportsboat classes drawn from around the world, providing excellent competition.

LEFT **The Beneteau 25 may be fast and fun, but this crewman appears to be having more than a few problems with the spinnaker.**

Beneteau 25
Popular sportsboat produced by Europe's largest yacht builder.
Country of origin France
First launched 1998
Designer Bruce Farr Yacht Design (New Zealand/USA)
LOA 7.5m (25ft)
Beam 2.6m (8½ft)
Displacement 1,250kg (2,755lb)
Upwind sail area 32.5 sq m (350 sq ft)
Spinnaker 48 sq m (517 sq ft) asymmetric
Crew 4–5

BELOW **The Hunter 707 provides excellent, dinghy-style racing with its big main and small jib sail plan.**

Hunter 707
Top choice sportsboat in Britain, with total one-design specification.
Country of origin UK
First launched 1997
Designer David Thomas (UK)
LOA 7.07m (23ft)
Beam 2.49m (8ft)
Displacement 1,060kg (2,337lb)
Upwind sail area 29.7 sq m (320 sq ft)
Spinnaker 51 sq m (549 sq ft)
Crew 4–5

Bull 7000
A lifting keel sportsboat with cruiser style accommodation for four adults.
Country of origin UK
First launched 1997
Designer Greg Young (New Zealand)
LOA 7.5m (25ft)
Beam 2.45m (8ft)
Displacement 1,100kg (2,425lb)
Upwind sail area 35.1 sq m (378 sq ft)
Gennaker 55 sq m (592 sq ft)
Crew 4–5

ABOVE **The Bull 7000 boasts a lifting keel, and gennaker set from a swinging bowsprit, as well as four berths down below.**

ABOVE **The Mumm 30 is at the top of the size range for sportsboats.**

ABOVE **The 1720 comes close to the open keelboat concept without cruising accommodation.**

1720

A sportsboat targeted at a wider age and ability range than its rivals.
Country of origin Ireland
First launched 1997
Designer Tony Castro (Ireland)
LOA 8m (26ft)
Beam 2.5m (8ft)
Displacement 1,365 kg (3,009lb)
Upwind sail area 44 sq m (474 sq ft)
Spinnaker 69 sq m (743 sq ft) asymmetric
Crew 455kg (1,003lb) weight limit

Mumm 30

A sportsboat chosen for the Tour de France a la Voile and one-design racing.
Country of origin USA
First launched 1997
Designer Bruce Farr Yacht Design (New Zealand/USA)
LOA 9.43m (30ft)
Beam 3.08m (10ft)
Displacement 2,040 kg (4,497 lb)
Upwind sail area 57 sq m (613 sq ft)
Spinnaker Asymmetric and non asymmetric
Crew 525 kg (1,157 lb) weight limit

Melges 24

The Melges 24 was soon granted full international recognition as the most successful sportsboat worldwide, providing the very top levels of competition.
Country of origin USA
First launched 1996
Designer Reichel/Pugh (USA)
LOA 7.32m (24ft)
Beam 2.5m (8ft)
Displacement 780kg (1,720lb)
Upwind sail area 35.31 sq m (380 sq ft)
Spinnaker 62 sq m (667 sq ft)
Crew 360kg (794lb) weight limit

ABOVE **The Melges 24 can claim to be the most popular and successful sportsboat in the world.**

The world races

Each year sees at least one high profile round-the-world race take place, with a mixture of fully crewed, single-handed, stop-over, non-stop, west-to-east and east-to-west formats.

The Volvo Ocean Race

Originally known as the Whitbread Round the World Race. This event for fully crewed racing yachts with stop-overs was first held in 1971, when it was a fairly leisurely affair won by a Mexican crew on a stock Swan 65 cruiser-racer. It has been staged every four years since then, and has evolved into a series of full-on sprint stages. The entry was restricted to 18m (59ft) monohulls in 1997 when Paul Cayard (USA) skippered EF Language to victory, after which Volvo took over as main sponsor and renamed the event. They also created the most complex and demanding route ever. The 2001 edition of the race starts at Southampton (UK) and finishes at Kiel in Germany some 51,900km (32,250 miles) and nine months later, after stop-overs at Cape Town, Sydney, Hobart, Auckland, Rio de Janeiro, Miami, Baltimore, La Rochelle and Gothenburg.

BT Global Challenge

This race was created by Chay Blyth as a 48,279km (30,000 mile) circumnavigation

LEFT **The Whitbread (now Volvo) Round the World Race has developed into a gala event, as the start of the 1997 event in the Solent in the south of England shows.**

with stop-overs, held the wrong way round the world against prevailing winds and currents. The event takes place every four years using a one-design fleet of steel yachts, and is based on an ethos of team building using inexperienced crews. More than 200 men and women are selected

from all walks of life and, while yachting experience is not necessary, they must be able to show motivation, physical capability and mental acuity, as well as the ability to raise a sum of around $40,000, if not more, in sponsorship funds in order to take part.

ABOVE **Chay Blyth's Global Challenge found a different formula by using a fleet of identical steel yachts.**

Round the world records

1895–1898: The American, Joshua Slocum, became the pioneer of great circumnavigators when he sailed *Spray* single handed around the world.
1966: Francis Chichester (UK) 226 days solo with one stop on *Gypsy Moth IV*.
1966: Robin Lee Graham (USA) became the youngest circumnavigator of all time when he sailed *Dove* around the world at the age of 17.
1968: Robin Knox-Johnston (UK) 313 days solo non-stop in the Golden Globe Race on *Suhali*. He was the only finisher.
1971: Chay Blyth (UK) 302 days solo non-stop "wrong way round" on *British Steel*.

1973: Raymon Carlin (Mexico) 134 days fully crewed with stop-overs in Whitbread Race.
1977: Cornelius van Reischoten (Holland) 119 days fully crewed with stop-overs in Whitbread Race.
1982: Philippe Jeantot (France) 159 days solo with stop-overs in BOC (Around Alone) Challenge.
1989: Titouan Lamazou (France) 109 days solo non-stop in Vendee Globe Race.
1993: Bruno Peyron (France) 79 days non-stop in first Jules Verne Challenge.
1994: Peter Blake (New Zealand) and Robin Knox-Johnson (UK) 74 days non-stop in second Jules Verne Challenge.
1997: Olivier de Kersauson (France) 71 days non-stop in third Jules Verne Challenge. This record likely to remain intact until The Race staged in 2000.

ABOVE **An Around Alone competitor starts Leg 3 from Auckland, New Zealand in the 1998/1999 edition of the race.**

Around Alone

This race can be summarised as one person, on a sailboat, around the world, alone. It claims to be the longest race on earth for any individual in any sport, with a course spanning 43,450km (27,000 miles) including the world's roughest and most remote oceans. The race takes place every four years, and was originally known as the BOC Challenge when first held in 1982 – the inaugural event was won by Philippe Jeantot in 159 days.

Vendee Globe

While the Around Alone has stop-overs to allow competitors and their craft to rest and recuperate, the Vendee Globe goes one stage tougher as a single-handed marathon for monohull yachts up to 19.7m (65ft) with a non-stop, west-east course via all three capes. The race was first held in 1989 when it attracted 13 yachts, and was created by Philippe Jeantot who had already won the BOC Challenge twice running.

BELOW **Superwoman Isabelle Autissier streaks away from the camera during the 1996/1997 edition of the spectacularly tough Vendee Globe.**

The America's Cup

Probably the most sought after trophy in yachting, as well as being the most expensive to contest. Often known as The 'Auld Cup, it has a history that dates back to a challenge in the mid-19th century:

1844 Charter drawn up for the New York Yacht Club.

1851 New York Yacht Club invited to race in a challenge match for the Hundred Guinea Cup, named after the cup's value when it was made by Garrards of London in 1848. Following a standing start with sails and anchors down on the start line, the schooner *America* beat a small fleet of challengers, which raced once round the Isle of Wight off the south coast of England.

1857 The Hundred Guinea Cup was delivered to the New York Yacht Club, with a deed of gift designating it as a perpetual challenge cup. It was renamed the America's Cup.

1870 The British yacht *Cambria* crossed the Atlantic to attempt to win back the cup, racing round a course off Newport, Rhode Island.

1871 *Cambria* became the first of many challengers to fail, when she suffered a 4–1 defeat by the American defender in a five-race series. The "first yacht to win four races" formula has continued ever since.

1876 The American yacht *Madeline* successfully defended a challenge by the Royal Canadian Yacht Club. This was the last America's Cup event raced in schooners.

ABOVE **Paul Cayard's *AmericaOne* went down to *Prada* in the Louis Vuitton Cup, ensuring there was no American yacht in the America's Cup.**

ABOVE **The new and the old. A modern America's Cup racer sails out with a J-Class yacht. The only thing they have in common is that they were designed to race for the same trophy in different eras.**

1881 The original deed of gift was rewritten to specify that only one challenger and one defender should race for the cup, ensuring that the America's Cup should continue as a boat-on-boat match racing event. In the same year the American yacht *Mischief* won the right to defend, and saw off the next Canadian challenge.

1885 *Purita*' defeated *Genesta*, the challenging yacht sent over by England's Royal Yacht Squadron.

1886 *Volunteer* defeated *Thistle* which challenged on behalf of Scotland's Royal Clyde Yacht Club.

1893 With racing contested by J-Class yachts, the American *Vigilent* beat Britain's *Valkyrie II.* Successful American defences followed in 1895, 1899, 1901, 1903, 1920, 1930, 1934 and 1937.

1958 The first year in which the America's Cup was raced to the new 12 Metre rule, with keelboats of around 18m (59ft) length. *Columbia* (USA) beat *Sceptre* (UK), with successful defences following in 1962, 1964, 1967, 1970, 1974, 1977 and 1980 against British and Australian 12 Metre yachts.

1983 The Australian 12 Metre *Australia II* designed by Ben Lexcen became the first challenger to win the America's Cup when she beat the defender *Liberty* 4–3.

This ended the 132 year residency of the America's Cup at the New York Yacht Club, and the longest winning streak recorded in any sport.

1987 The American yacht *Stars & Stripes* beat Australia's defender *Kookaburra III.* The Americans took the cup back to a new home at the San Diego Yacht Club.

A period of relative chaos followed when 12 Metre yachts were shelved as they were thought to be too complex, heavy and old fashioned. In the absence of a precise rule a New Zealand syndicate mounted a challenge with a monster 41m (134ft) monohull. The San Diego Yacht Club responded by defending with the 18m (59ft) catamaran *Stars and Strips.* This made a mockery of the event, but the catamaran won every race with ease.

1992 With the introduction of a new International America's Cup Class (IACC) rule, the Italians made an unsuccessful challenge with *Il Moro de Venezia V* which was beaten by *America* off San Diego.

1995 With a challenge led by Sir Peter Blake, the New Zealand IACC yacht *Black Magic* helmed by Russell Coutts scored a convincing 4–1 victory over *Young America.* The America's Cup moved to a new home at the Royal New Zealand Yacht Squadron in Auckland.

1999/2000 The 30th and biggest America's Cup regatta in history was spread over a five-month period. *New Zealand's* defence attracted 11 challenging syndicates from Australia, France, Italy, Japan, Spain, Switzerland and the USA. The challenging yachts competed in three round robins, semi-finals and finals for the Louis Vuitton Cup to select the Italian yacht *Prada* as challenger for the America's Cup proper, but she then lost 0-5 to the defending yacht.

ABOVE **In 2000** *Prada* **(left) became the first European yacht to defeat all of the Americans during an America's Cup series, only to be soundly beaten by** *New Zealand* **(right), which won five straight races.**

Offshore multihulls

Big multihulls are not keelboats, since they rely on their beam for stability, with dinghy-style daggerboards to resist leeway. They are however in a class apart as the fastest ocean racing yachts of all.

ORMA Championship

The ORMA 60 Multihull Championship is a French sponsored annual series for 18m (59ft) multihulls. It consists of three inshore grand prix events, mixed with three major offshore events, which are chosen to fit the calendar for that particular season. For instance, the 1999 ORMA series included a 1,609km (1,000 mile) variation on the Fastnet Race and the five-stage Round Europe race, which totalled over 4,506km (2,800 miles) and were both fully crewed, while the final event was the two-handed Transat Jacques Vabre between Le Havre (France) and Cartagena (South America).

The multihulls that take part in the ORMA Championship are all 18m (59ft) trimarans, designed by Britain's Nigel Irens or the French team of Marc Van Peteghem and Vincent Lauriot Prevost. *Fujicolor II*, the yacht sailed to victory in the Championship in 1996, 1997 and 1999 by Loick Peyron, is typical of these carbon fibre racing multihulls. Her length

ABOVE **The big catamaran** *ENZA* **sets a new 74-day world record in 1994, having been forced to drop the main on the approach to the finish due to severe weather.**

of 18.28m (60ft) is almost equalled by her breadth of 16m (52½ft), and with a 29m (95ft) tall canting wing mast she has a combined sail area of 782sq m (8,417sq ft) driving her 6.6 tonne platform.

The Jules Verne 80 Day Trophy

This trophy, for the fastest non-stop circumnavigation of the world, was first won by the catamaran *Commodore Explorer* skippered by Bruno Peyron, which crossed the Jules Verne start line off Brest in France on 31 January 1993 and re-crossed the line to finish 79 days, 6 hours and

16 minutes later, having sailed round the world at an average 14.39 knots or 555km (345 miles) a day. A year later the 27m (88ft) catamaran *ENZA* (skippered by Peter Blake and Robin Knox-Johnston) lowered the record to just under 75 days, and then in 1997 the trimaran *Sport Elec* (skippered by Olivier de Kersauson) set a new record of 71 days on her fourth attempt at the Jules Verne Trophy.

The Race

Bruno Peyron conceived the idea of a non-stop, no limits race around the world, to begin in Barcelona on 31 December 2000 and based on the Jules Verne Trophy. Designers, skippers and sponsors were given total freedom to produce any type of yacht, and the American adventurer Steve Fossett was first to build the 32 metre (105ft) catamaran *PlayStation* launched in 1999. It immediately set a new 24 hour sailing record of 933km (580 miles) at an average of almost 25 knots. The similar sized *Club Med* then pushed the 24 hour record to 1006km (625 miles) while setting a new west-east Atlantic record. Fossett responded by lengthening *PlayStation* to 38 metres (125 ft) in his bid to break all official records with the fastest craft in the history of offshore yacht racing.

ABOVE **An amazing flying machine. Laurent Bourgnon's** *Primagaz* **shows off the fabulous performance of an ORMA 60 multihull.**

ABOVE **The monster catamaran** *Playstation* **was built to take on the challenge of The Race in 2001, pushing back the boundaries of round the world racing.**

Glossary

Abeam At right angles to the boat.

Aerodynamics The science of air and gases in motion.

Aft Toward the rear of the boat.

"ahoy!" A jolly nautical hello.

Aground When the bottom of a boat hits the ground beneath.

Amidships The middle of a boat.

Anchor A heavy steel hook used to hold a yacht to the sea bed. Popular styles of anchor include the CQR, Danforth and traditional Fisherman's anchor.

Anchor light A white light which should be illuminated to mark an anchored yacht at night.

Anchor warp A rope used to secure an anchor.

Anemometer A wind speed instrument.

Anti-cyclone A slow-moving, fair weather system based on high barometric pressure.

Apparent wind The direction and speed of the wind, as affected by the course and speed of a boat.

Aspect ratio The ratio between the length of the luff and the foot of a sail.

Asymmetric A type of paddle on which the top side of the blade is longer than the bottom side.

Back (1) A sail backs when the wind hits its leeward side.

Back (2) The wind backs when it shifts in an anti-clockwise direction.

Back-cut drops Waterfalls with an airspace or cavity behind the curtain of water.

Back stay The after stay of a yacht, which runs between the masthead and stern.

Balance A yacht is balanced when it has virtually no pull on the tiller or wheel. A perfectly balanced yacht will sail "hands off".

Ballast Weight to provide stability in a yacht, usually carried in the keel.

Barber hauler Control line to move jib or gennaker sheet inboard or outboard.

Bare poles Riding out a storm with all sails down.

Batten Fibreglass strip used to strengthen the shape of the sail.

Batten pockets Pockets in the sail into which the battens fit.

Beach Landing a boat.

Beam The maximum width of the boat.

Big water High-volume rapids.

Beam reach Sailing with the wind blowing straight from the side.

Bear away Steer away from the direction of the wind.

Bearing A horizontal angle measured on a compass.

Beat/beating Sailing as close as possible towards the wind.

Beaufort Scale A scale of wind force from Force 1 to Force 12.

Bermudan rig The modern style of rig with a jib and mainsail.

Bight Part of the rope between the ends.

Blade The part of the paddle you put in the water; can be used as a word to describe the whole paddle.

Boater Common generic term for a canoeist or kayaker.

Boils Where water surfaces from below; it gives the appearance of boiling water.

Bolt rope Thick rope attached to the front edge of the mainsail which slides up a slot in the mast. Can also be used to hold the foot of the sail to the boom.

Boof A technique for landing a freefalling boat flat on its hull.

Boom Aluminium pole attached to the bottom of the mainsail.

Bottlescrew Adjustable linkage used to control the length of stays and shrouds at deck height.

Bow The forward most part of a boat.

Bow draw A stroke that pulls the bow of the boat sideways through the water.

Bow paddler The paddler in the forward position.

Bow rudder An advanced steering stroke that is used to turn the boat quickly while it is moving forwards.

Break-in Enter the current from an area of slack water.

Break-out To exit the current into an area of slack water.

Broach When a yacht sailing downwind loses control and spins broadside on to the wind, heeling right over.

Broad reach Sailing with the wind blowing across the boat from behind.

Buoyancy aid A vest or jacket designed to give added buoyancy to a swimmer, but not buoyant enough to hinder swimming, or rolling. *See also* personal flotation device.

Burgee A small flag at the top of the mast.

By the lee Sailing downwind with the wind coming from the leeward quarter and constant risk of a gybe.

Cable Traditional measure of distance. 10 cables = 1 nautical mile.

Camber Amount of curve or belly in a sail.

Capsize To turn upside down in a boat.

Canoe A small craft propelled with one or more single-bladed paddle(s), while sitting or kneeling and facing the direction of travel.

Canoeist A person who is competent at paddling a canoe.

Catamaran (cat) A boat with two hulls.

Centreboard A big fin that swings down in the centre of a dinghy to prevent the boat from being blown sideways.

Centre of effort (CE) Imaginary point where the wind's force is concentrated in a sail.

Centre of gravity (CG) Imaginary point where a boat's weight is concentrated.

Centre of lateral resistance (CLR) Imaginary point where a boat will turn about its centreboard or keel.

Centre line Imaginary longitudinal line running through the boat from the bow to the stern.

Chain locker Small hold for the anchor chain or warp in the bows of a yacht.

Cleat A fitting to which ropes can be attached or led through and made fast.

Clew The lower aftmost corner of a sail, to which the sheets or boom is attached.

Clipper An old style of sailing ship.

Close hauled Sailing close to the wind, as for beating.

Close reach Sailing with the wind blowing across the boat from ahead.

Coachroof Exterior cabin of a yacht.

Cockpit Where you sit in a boat.

Companionway Leads from cockpit to cabin.

Composite Made from a combination of more than one material, usually resin and a fabric (like carbon fibre).

Cringle Metal eye in a sail: at the head, clew and tack, and also for controls such as a cunningham.

Crossbeams Beams connecting the hulls of a catamaran.

Cross-bow Any stroke that is performed on one side of the boat using the paddle-blade normally reserved for the other side.

Cunningham pull-down Control used to tension luff of sail.

Cushions A type of pressure wave that tends to deflect boats and swimmers from the rocks that generated it. Cushion wave See cushions

Daggerboard Fin-like centreboard which slides straight up and down.

Deck The top of an enclosed boat; another word for spraydeck or skirt; the flat surfaces on the top of a boat.

Delta Triangular type rig.

Depth The distance from the floor to the height of the gunwale measured at the boat's centre line.

Dinghy A small open sailing boat.

Displacement sailing Sailing through the water.

Downhaul Control line used to pull down on the luff of a sail.

Downstream Towards the sea.

Downwind (1) Sailing with the wind behind.

Downwind (2) To leeward of a boat or object.

Draft The vertical distance from the waterline of the boat to the lowest point of the boat; depth of the curve in a sail.

Draught The depth of a boat, including keel or centreboard.

Draw stroke A stroke that pulls the boat sideways through the water.

Drop Any change in the water level.

Dropping in Attempting to surf a wave or hole that another person is already using.

Dry-top A special type of cagoule designed for paddling, which has efficient seals to keep the water out.

Ebb When the tide goes out.

Eye of the wind Where the wind is coming from.

Eddy Area of slack water moving upstream.

End grabs Handles at each end of a boat for use when carrying or towing the boat.

Fairlead A fitting that leads a rope in the most convenient direction for pulling.

Falls Any distinct drop in the river level, but most often a vertical or near-vertical step down.

Fathom a traditional measure of depth. 1 fathom = 1.83m (6ft).

Feather To angle a paddle blade; the term usually refers to the angle between the two blades of a kayak paddle (an angle of between 30° and 90°).

Feedback (from the water) Kinaesthetic awareness of forces acting on you, the boat or the paddle.

Ferry glide A technique for crossing a current without moving up- or down-stream.

Fetch Sailing an upwind course, but not beating.

Fibreglass Glass-reinforced plastic (GRP) is the material most often used to build boats.

Flare The amount the sides of a canoe curve outward from the perpendicular; can also mean an illuminating safety device that can be used by paddlers in distress to attract attention at sea.

Flat setting a sail with as little curve as possible for sailing in stronger winds.

Flat water Water that does not have waves or currents that are strong enough to affect a canoe or kayak.

Flood When the tide comes in.

Flotation Material encased beneath the bow and stern decks that allows the canoe to float when swamped.

Foot The bottom edge of a sail.

Footstraps Straps to put feet under when the crew leans out of a dinghy to keep it upright.

Foredeck The deck at the front of the boat.

Forestay The wire at the front of the boat which holds the mast up.

Forward Toward the bow of the boat.

Forward sweep stroke The most basic form of turning stroke, which can be used while the boat is stationary or in motion.

Free When the wind direction goes aft and a boat can therefore point higher.

Free blade Any paddle or propulsion device that is held in the hands and not attached to the boat.

Freeboard The side of the hull between water and deck; the distance between the waterline and the gunwale of the canoe.

Frowny Any hydraulic with the ends (and hence the exits) upstream of, or higher than, the middle of the hydraulic.

Full Setting a sail with a lot of curve for lighter winds.

Furl To roll a sail when it is set.

Gaff A type of sailing rig wih a boom-like support at the top of the sail as well as the bottom.

Galley A yacht's kitchen area.

Gelcoat External cosmetic coat on fibreglass boats.

Gennaker Large foremost sail, hoisted only when sailing offwind.

Genoa A big sail at the bow which overlaps the shrouds on either side of the boat.

Give way Allow another boat right of way.

Go about Tack round.

Gooseneck A hinge fitting connecting the boom to the mast.

Goosewing (wing on wing) Sailing downwind with headsail on windward side.

Grade/grading The name given to the accepted system for describing the severity of rapids.

Green water Unaerated – but not necessarily flat – water.

Grip The way in which you hold the paddle, or the specific part of a paddle shaft that rests in the hand.

Gunwale A strengthening rail, running the length of the canoe on each side, which is attached to the top edge of the boat sides; the outermost edge of a boat.

Guy Control line attached to the tack of a spinnaker.

Gybe/gybing Turning the boat onto a different tack by bearing away and letting the mainsail change sides when sailing downwind.

H or HI rescue A technique for emptying another person's boat with help from another boater, while afloat.

Halyard A wire or rope used to pull the sails up.

Halyard rack A toothed rack on which a halyard can be tensioned to tighten the sail luff.

Hand-roll To right the capsized craft using only the hands, without having to get out.

Hanks Fittings which hold the jib to the forestay.

Head The top corner of a sail.

Headfoil Headsail luff groove system used in place of hanks to attach a headsail to the forestay.

Heading Direction you are sailing.

"Heads" Generic name for the toilet compartment on yacht.

Head to wind When the bow is pointing directly into the wind. If the boat gets stuck at that point, it is "in irons".

Head up Steer towards the wind.

Heave Throw a line, usually a mooring warp.

Heave-to Stop the boat so it only moves slowly sideways.

Heel When a boat leans with the wind.

Helm steer the boat The person who steers the boat.

High brace A more advanced support stroke that is to be avoided if possible since it carries a risk of injury.

Hike Lean over the side of the boat to stop it heeling.

Hitch knot Which makes a line fast.

Hoist Pull up a sail.

Hole A retentive (recirculating) wave capable of stopping and holding a boat or swimmer (also known as a stopper).

Hounds The connecting points where rigging attaches to the mast.

Hull The underside of any type of boat.

Husky tow Two or more paddlers towing a third paddler who may be tired or injured and experiencing difficulty on their own.

Inboard Towards the middle of a boat.

Inshore Near the shore.

Inshore wind Wind blowing onto the shore, also called "onshore wind".

Irons Stuck head to wind – also called "in stays" (very old fashioned).

J-stroke A special canoe stroke that keeps the boat travelling in a straight line without the need to paddle on both sides.

Jib Small sail at the front.

Jib sheets The two ropes used to pull the jib in on either side of the boat.

Jumper struts Small struts to prevent the mast bending backwards.

Jury rig A DIY rig after the mast – or part of it – falls down.

Karabiner A metal connecting device designed for climbers but much used by white water paddlers.

Kayak A small craft propelled with one or more two-bladed paddle(s) while sitting and facing the direction of travel.

Kayaker A person who is competent at paddling a kayak.

Kedge (1) Spare anchor.

Kedge (2) Use anchor to stop yacht drifting back on tide in light winds.

Kedge (3) Use anchor to pull yacht off the bottom.

Keel A longitudinal V-shape to the boat's bottom, on its centre line, to give strength, protection, and added control; weighted fin on the bottom of a boat.

Kicking strap A line, or series of lines, between the base of the mast and underside of the boom to control twist in the mainsail and the position of the boom. Also called a "kicker" or "vang".

Knots Nautical miles per hour.

Lay To be able to sail to a mark, without needing to change course or lose speed.

Lee The side the wind is blowing onto. Sailors always beware of a "lee shore".

Lee helm When the rudder wants to make the boat bear away.

Lee shore A shoreline with an "onshore wind".

Leech The back edge or trailing edge of the sail.

Leeward From the boat, the direction toward which the wind is blowing.

Leeway Drifting sideways with the wind.

Length overall (LOA) The total length of a boat including permanent fixtures such as a bowsprit.

"Lee-oh!" The call used when tacking.

Lift (1) When the wind frees and allows a boat to point higher.

Lift (2) When the wind hits the leeward side of the sail, and "lifts" the front part towards you which is shown by telltales dropping.

Log Traditional term for distance and position measurement on a yacht.

Low brace A basic support stroke.

Luff (1) The front edge of the sail.

Luff (2) To head up towards the wind.

Mainsail The largest upwind sail set on the main mast.

Mainsheet The rope used to pull the mainsail in.

Mark Racing buoy or marker.

Marlinspike Pointed steel spike used for traditional splicing and undoing knots.

Masthead rig A rig with the headsail luff extending all the way to the top of the mast. On a "fractional rig", the luff only goes part way up the mast.

Mast heel A metal casting that holds the base of the mast in place.

Mast step The position in the hull or deck where the mast step is located.

Meltdown Deliberately putting your boat underneath a wave or hydraulic.

Mizzen After mast on a yacht.

Monohull Single-hulled yacht.

Multihull A yacht with two or more hulls.

Nautical mile A nautical mile is 1.15078 statute miles or 1.852 kilometres

Neap tide When tidal range is smallest.

Oar A paddle-like propulsion device.

Offshore Generic term for sailing some distance away from the shore.

Offshore wind Wind blowing away from the shore.

Offside The side of the canoe that is opposite that on which the blade is normally used.

Offwind Sailing away from the wind.

One-design A class where all boats are identical.

Onshore wind Wind blowing on to the shore.

Open water A large expanse of usually flat water, typically a sea, lake, or very large river.

Onside The side on which a canoe is normally paddled (left or right according to personal preference).

Outhaul Control line for tensioning foot of mainsail.

Outrigger Small hull or float used to stabilize a proa or trimaran.

Overstand Staying too long on one tack when racing towards a mark.

Paddler Common generic term for a canoeist or kayaker.

PFD (personal flotation device) US description of a buoyancy aid or life jacket.

Pile Mooring post.

Pinch Point the boat so high into the wind that you depower the sails.

Pitch When the bow and stern go up and down, usually when sailing to windward through short waves.

Plane When a dinghy skims over the surface of the water on its bow wave.

Pocket/Power pocket The steepest green part of the wave, usually right next to the shoulder.

Pin spot A place where there is a natural danger of physical entrapment.

Point Heading close to the wind.

Pontoon A tethered, floating platform.

Port The left side of the boat as you face forward.

Port tack When the port side is the windward side of a boat.

Portage The carrying of a boat or its contents over land from one body of water to another.

Pourover Anywhere that water pours over a distinct drop in the river bed, but most usually water pouring over and around a boulder to form a nasty, retentive hydraulic.

Preventer Control line from boom to toerail used to prevent unexpected gybes.

Prys Strokes that are performed by levering the paddle shaft against the side of the boat (usually a canoe).

Pulpit Guardrails on bow of yacht.

Pushpit Guardrails on the stern of a yacht.

Quarter After side of yacht.

Race Very strong tidal flow, often caused by a headland.

Radial sail A sail cut with panels at odd angles.

Rake Moving the mast tip forward or back.

Rapid An area of turbulent water.

Reach/reaching Sailing with the wind blowing across the boat.

"Ready about" The call used when preparing to tack or bring the boat "about".

Recirculate To be repeatedly carried upstream and submerged by the towback of a hydraulic water feature, such as a stopper wave.

Reef Reducing the size of a sail in stronger winds.

Reverse sweep stroke A basic turning stroke that can be used while the boat is stationary or on the move.

Ribs Frames on the inside or outside of the hull to give additional strength.

Rig (1) Generic term for the mast, boom, shrouds, stays, sails and all the other bits and pieces that form the boat's "engine".

Rig (2) Prepare the boat for sailing.

Roach Curved area of sail outside a line between head and clew.

Rocker The amount a boat's hull appears to be curved upwards at the ends.

Roll To right a craft after a capsize without having to get out.

Running Sailing with the wind behind the boat.

Running backstays Backstays that can be let off on the leeward side.

Running rigging Ropes (and occasionally wires) used to hold sails in position.

Saddle An open canoe seat that is straddled by the paddler.

Sculling Imparting a force using a continuous to and fro action with a submerged blade.

Sculling draw A technique that propels the boat continuously sideways towards the paddle.

Sculling pry Like a sculling draw, but the pry propels the boat sideways away from the paddle.

Seabreeze A thermal wind which blows from sea to land.

Seal launch To slide or drop into the water while seated in the boat and holding the paddle.

Seams Where two currents converge they often fold downwards to make a seam-like feature on the surface.

Shackle A metal fitting which locks closed, used to attach sails to halyards.

Shaft The cylindrical part of the paddle, also known as the loom.

Sheet The rope used to pull in a sail.

Shoulder The edge of the breaking part of a wave.

Shrouds wires at the sides of the boat which hold the mast up.

Shuttle The vehicle used for, or the practise of, transporting paddlers or equipment by road to the opposite end of a paddling trip.

Sideslip Being blown sideways.

Siphon Anywhere the current goes under an obstruction, such as a tree, with no airspace.

Ski A sit-on-top surf craft.

Skirt See spraydeck.

Slot Gap between mainsail and headsail (or gennaker) which helps govern air flow over the leeward side of the mainsail.

Smiley Any hydraulic with the ends (and hence the exits) downstream of, or lower than, the middle of the hydraulic.

Spinnaker Large, round sail at the front of the boat.

Spraydeck (spray skirt) A device that is worn around the waist to keep water out of the cockpit.

Spray rail Longitudinal rails running slightly above the waterline on the outside, to deflect waves and chop.

Spreaders Metal struts which hold the shrouds away from the sides of the mast in order to stiffen the centre section.

Sprit rig Old fashioned style of rig used on the Optimist dinghy.

Standing rigging Wire cables to hold the rig up.

Starboard The right hand side of the boat as you face forward.

Starboard Tack When the starboard side is the windward side of a boat.

Stern The rearmost end of the boat.

Stern paddler Paddler seated in the rear of the boat (kayak or canoe).

Stern rudder A steering stroke to be used while moving forwards.

Stopper A retentive (recirculating) wave capable of stopping and holding a boat, swimmer or any buoyant object hitting it from upstream (also known as a hole).

Strainer An obstruction through which the water is forced, forming a sieve-like effect.

Surf Breaking waves (noun); to ride in control on the face of a wave (verb).

Symmetrical Of a paddle, that the blades are a symmetrical shape; it does not mean that the blades are the same.

Tack (1) The side of the boat a person is sitting on – for instance starboard tack is when the helm sits on the starboard side with the wind blowing from the starboard side.

Tack (2) The tack is also the bottom corner at the front of a sail.

Tacking Turning the boat on to a different tack when sailing upwind.

Tandem paddling Two paddlers paddling the same boat.

Technical water Usually low volume rapids with a lot of rocks and much manoeuvring required.

T-grip The handle on top of a canoe paddle shaft.

Throwline A proprietary rescue device carried by most whitewater paddlers.

Thwart A support or seat extending across width of canoe from gunwale to gunwale.

Tiller The lever by which the rudder is turned.

Tiller extension An aluminium (sometimes wood) tube connected to the tiller by a universal joint which allows the helmsperson to steer the boat while hiking out or trapezing.

Topping lift Halyard used to lift the boom.

To ship water Accidentally taking on water.

Touring Travelling by boat.

Towline A proprietary rescue device commonly used by instructors.

Tracking The term used to describe how well a boat tracks (keeps its direction) under the influence of currents and wind.

Trampoline mesh Net between the hulls of a catamaran, which the crew sit on.

Transom The flat area across the back of the boat where the rudder is usually hung on dinghies. Also the square stern in canoes, designed for stern-mounted outboards.

Trapeze A wire which enables the crew to stand out from the side of a dinghy, using a harness.

Traveller Slider to allow the mainsheet to be moved across the cockpit.

Trim To load the boat so that it is level or slightly stern-down; adjust the angle of the sails to the wind.

Trimaran A boat with three hulls.

Trimming Making the boat float level by redistributing the weight of paddlers or gear.

Tumblehome The amount the sides of a canoe curves out and then returns inward from the perpendicular.

Unstayed A boat that has no forestay or shrouds.

Upstream Towards the source of the river.

Upwind Sailing towards the wind.

Vang Another term for kicking strap.

Veer A change in wind direction.

Volume The amount of air trapped inside a boat; also refers to the volume of water moving down a rapid.

Warp Rope used for anchor or mooring.

Wave-wheel A cartwheel-type manoeuvre performed going down the back of a wave.

Weather helm When the rudder wants to make the boat head up.

Weigh anchor Traditional term for lifting the anchor.

Wet exit The procedure for bailing out from the boat while under water, following a capsize.

Wetsuit A tight-fitting suit made of soft rubber neoprene which keeps most of the water out and conserves body heat.

Whirlpools Whirling vertical vortices with a core of air that carry anything that falls into them down to the bed of the river, lake or sea. Similar to the way in which water swirls down the plughole of a bath.

White water Water that, because of the wind or the current, has become turbulent enough to become aerated and appears white and frothy.

Wilderness paddling Paddling far away from the resources of civilization.

Windage The degree to which a boat's sides are exposed to, or tend to catch, the wind.

Wind shift Change in wind direction.

Windward From the boat, the direction from which the wind is blowing.

X-rescue A technique for emptying another person's boat single-handed while afloat.

Further Reading

Books

Adlard Coles' Heavy Weather Sailing
Peter Bruce/ Adlard Coles Nautical
(2004)

Canoeing: A Trailside Guide
Gordon Grant/Norton (1997)

Canoeing Handbook
Edited by Ray Rowe/British Canoe
Union (1997)

**Complete Guide to Choosing a
Cruising Sailboat**
Roger Marshall/International Marine
Publishing Co (1999)

Complete Yachtmaster
Tom Cunliffe/Adlard Coles
Nautical (2006)

**How to Sail Around the World: Advice
and Ideas for Voyaging Under Sail**
Hal Roth/McGraw-Hill Education (2003)

**Kayaking: White Water and Touring
Basics/Trailside Guides**
Steven M. Krauzer/Norton (1995)

**Kayak: The Animated Manual
of Intermediate and Advanced
Whitewater Technique**
William Nealy/Cordee (1990)

Knots and Splices
Steve Judkins and Tim Davison/
Fernhurst Books (1998)

New Complete Sailing Manual
Steve Sleight/Dorling Kindersley
Publishers Ltd (2005)

Outdoor Pursuits Series: Canoeing
Laurie Gullion/Human Kinetics
Publishers (1994)

RYA Go Cruising
Claudia Myatt/Royal Yachting
Association (2006)

RYA Navigation Handbook
Tim Bartlett/Royal Yachting
Association (2003)

RYA Weather Handbook
Chris Tibbs/Royal Yachting
Association (2003)

Sea Kayaking
John Dowd/Douglas & MacIntyre
(1988)

**Seaworthy Offshore Sailboat: A
Guide to Essential Features, Gear,
and Handling**
John Vigor/TAB Books Inc
(2001)

**Shorthanded Sailing: Singlehanded
or Short of Crew**
Alastair Buchan/Fernhurst Books
(2006)

Squirt Boating and Beyond
James E. Snyder/Menasha Ridge Press
(2001)

Teach Yourself Canoeing
Ray Rowe/Hodder & Stoughton
(1992)

The Art of Freestyle
Brymer, Hughes and Collins/Pesda Press
(2000)

The Canoe Handbook
Slim Ray/Stackpole Books (1992)

**The Handbook of Sailing (Pelham
Practical Sports)**
Bob Bond/Pelham Books (1992)

World Cruising Routes
Jimmy Cornell/Adlard Coles Nautical (2002)

White Water Kayaking
Ray Rowe/Hodder & Stoughton (1988)

Weather Forecasting for Sailors
Frank Singleton/Hodder & Stoughton
(1981)

Magazines

Bateaux
BP 804, 60732 Ste-Geneviève Cedex
France
Tel : 03 44 62 43 54
Web: www.bateauxonline.fr

Canoe & Kayak
10526 NE 68th Street,
Suite 3,
Kirkland, WA 98033
United States
Tel:(800) 829 3340
Web: www.canoekayak.com

Canoeist
4 Sinodun Row
Appleford-on-Thames
Oxon, OX14 4PE
United Kingdom
Email: mail@canoeist.co.uk
Web: www.canoeist.co.uk

Cruising World
55 Hammarlund Way
Middletown, RI 02842
United States
Tel: (401) 845-5100
Web: www.cruisingworld.com

Kayak Session
3 Rue de la Claire
69009 Lyon
France
Tel: (472) 19 87 97
Web: www.kayaksession.com

Paddler Magazine
12040 98th Ave. NE, Suite 205
Kirkland, WA 98034
United States
Tel: (425) 814-4140 or (425) 483-0220
Web: www.paddlermagazine.com
Email: Subscribe@paddlermagazine.com

Paddles
Alexander House
Ling Road, Poole
Dorset, BH12 4NZ
United Kingdom
Tel: (01202) 735 090

Playboating Magazine
Warners Group Publications plc
West Street, Bourne
Lincolnshire, PE10 9PH
United Kingdom
Tel: 01778 391180
Web: www.playboating.com

Practical Boat Owner Magazine,
IPC Media Ltd, Westover House,
West Quay Road, Poole,
Dorset, BH15 1JG
United Kingdom
Tel: 01202 440820
Web: www.ybw.com/pbo
Email: pbo@ipcmedia.com

SAIL Magazine
SAIL, P.O. Box 420235, Palm Coast
FL 32142-0235
United States

Tel: 800-745-7245 or 386-447-6318
Web: www.sailmag.com
Email: sail@palmcoastd.com

Sailing World
55 Hammarlund Way
Middletown, RI 02842
United States
Tel: (401) 845-5100
Web: www.sailingworld.com

Voiles et Voiliers
Rédaction Voiles et Voiliers
Infos lecteurs
21, rue du Faubourg Saint-Antoine
75550 Paris Cedex 11
France
Tél. 01.44.87.87.87
www.voilesetvoiliers.com

Yachts and Yachting
96 Eastern Esplanade
Southend on Sea
Essex, SS1 3AB
United Kingdom
Tel: +44 (0)1702 582245 ext 107
Web: www.yachtsandyachting.com
Email: subscriptions@yachtsandyachting.com

Yachting Monthly
Room 2215
King's Reach Tower
Stamford Street,
London SE1 9LS
United Kingdom
Tel: +44 (0)207 261 6040
Web: www.ybw/ym.com
Email: yachting_monthly@ipcmedia.com

Useful Addresses

National Governing Bodies

British Canoe Union
Dudderidge House
Adbolton Lane
West Bridgford
Nottingham
NG2 5AS
United Kingdom

American Canoe Association
8580 Cinderbed Road
Suite 1900
Newington
Virginia
United States

Canadian Canoe Association
333 River Road
Vanier City
Ontario K1L 8B9
Canada

Australian Canoe Federation
Room 510 Sports House
157 Gloucester Street
Sydney
NSW 2000
Australia

New Zealand Canoe Association
P. O. Box 3768
Wellington
New Zealand

French Canoe Kayak Federation
17 Route de Vienne
69007 Lyon
France

German Canoe Association
Berta-allee 8
4100 Duisberg 1
Germany

Training and Education

United Kingdom
Royal Lifesaving Society
Mounbatten House
Studley
Warwickshire
B80 7NN
United Kingdom
Tel: (01789) 773 994

British Waterways
Melbury House
Melbury Terrace
London NW1 6JX
United Kingdom

International Long River Canoeist Club
Catalina Cottage
Aultvullin
Strathay Point
Sutherland KW14 7RY
United Kingdom

Advanced Sea Kayak Club
7 Miller Close
Newport
Isle of Wight PO30 5PS
United Kingdom

For details of canoe and kayak clubs in your area, please contact the British Canoe Union.

United States
Rescue 3 International
9075 Elk Grove Boulevard 200
P. O. Box 519, Elk Grove
California 95759-0519
United States
Tel: (916) 685 3066
Customer Support 800–45–RESCU
www.rescue3.com

American Rivers
801 Pennsylvania Ave S. E. Suite 303
Washington DC 20003
United States

Nantahala Outdoor Center
US 19W Box 41, Bryson City
NC 28713 United States
Tel: (704) 488 2175

A directory of state and local clubs can be found in the *ACA Canoeing and Kayaking Instruction Manual.*

SAILING AUTHORITIES

Australian Yachting Federation
Locked Bag 806, Milsons Point, NSW
2061, Australia
tel: 02 99224333
ausyacht@ausport.gov.au; www.aussailing.org

Osterreichischer Segel-Verband
Zetschegasse 21,
A-1230 Vienna, Austria
tel: 01 662 44 62-0
oesv@sailing.or.at; www.sailing.or.at

Federation Royale Belge du Yachting
Halve Maanstraat 2C, 8620 Nieuwpoort,
Belgium
tel: 058 23028

Canadian Yachting Association
1600 James Naismith Drive, Gloucester
Ontario KIB 5N4, Canada
tel: 613 7485687
sailcanada@sailing.ca; www.sailing.ca

Danish Sailing Association
Idraettens Hus, DK 2605 Broendby,
Denmark
tel: 043 262189
dan.ibsen@sejlsport.dk; www.sailing.dk

Finnish Yachting Association
Radiokatu 20, Helsinki,
FIN-00093 SLU, Finland
tel: 058 9 348121
aarne.kusi@splfsf.slu.fi

Federation Francaise de Voile
55 Avenue Kleber, 75784 Paris Cedex 16,
France
tel: 0144058112
barbierm@compuserve.com; www.ffv.fr

Deutscher Segler-Verband
Grundgenstrasse 18, 22309 Hamburg,
Germany
tel: 040 6320090
100763.105@compuserve.com

Hellenic Yachting Federation
51 Poseidonos Avenue,
18344 Moshato, Greece
tel: 01 9404825
webmaster-eio@eio.gr; www.eio.gr

Irish Sailing Association
3 park Road, Dun Laoghaire, Co.Dublin,
Ireland
tel: 01 2800239
isa@iol.ie; www.sailing.org/isa

Federazione Italiana Vela
Corte Lambruschini, Paizza Borgo Pila 40,
Torre A - 16 piano, 16129 Genova, Italy
tel: 010 5445 41
federvela@federvela.it; www.federvela.it

Yacht Club de Monaco
16 Quai Antoine 1er
MC 98000, Monaco
tel: 077 93 106300
ycm@yacht-club-monaco-mc
www.yacht-club-monaco-mc

Koninklijk Nederlands Watersport Verbond
Postbus 87, 3980 CB Bunnik
The Netherlands
tel: 030 6566550
info@knwv.nl; www.knwv.nl

Yachting New Zealand
PO Box 33 789, Takapuna,
North Shore City, Auckland
New Zealand
tel: 09 488 9325
mail@yachtingnz.org.nz
www.yachtingnz.org.nz

Norwegian Sailing Federation
Serviceboks 1, Ullevaal Stadion, 0840
Oslo, Norway
seiling@nif.idrett.no; www.nif.idrett.no/seiling

Polski Zwiazek Zeglarski
Chocimska 14, 00791 Warsaw, Poland
tel: 022 495731
pya@polbox.com.pl; www.sailing.org.pl

Federacao Portuguesa de Vela
Doca de Belem, 1300 Lisboa, Portugal
tel: 021 3647324
fpvela@fpvela.pt; www.fpvela.pt

All Russia Yachting Federation
Luchnetskaya nad.8,
119270 Moscow, Russia
tel: 095 725 4703; ilyin@yachting.ru

South African Sailing
5 Vesperdene Road, Green Point, 8051
Cape Town, South Africa
tel: 021 4391147
sailsa@iafrica.com; www.sailing.org/rsa

Real Federacion Espanola de Vela
Luis de Salazar, 12, 28002 Madrid, Spain
tel: 091 5195008
info@rfev.es; www.rfev.es

Swedish Sailing Federation
Af Pontins väg 6
S-115 21 Stockholm, Sweden
tel: 08 4590990; ssf@ssf.se; www.ssf.se

Swiss Sailing Federation
Haus des Sportes, Laubeggstrass 70
3000 Bern 32, Switzerland
swiss_sailing@compuserve.com
www.swiss_sailing.ch

Royal Yachting Association
RYA House, Romsey Road, Eastleigh
Hampshire SO50 9YA, United Kingdom
tel: 0845 345 0400
racing@rya.org.uk, www.racing@rya.org.uk

US Sailing
PO Box 1260, 15 Maritime Drive,
Portsmouth, RI 02871-6015, United States
tel: 401 6830800; www.ussailing.org

Index

Acknowledgements

ACKNOWLEDGEMENTS FOR KAYAKING
AND CANOEING

*The author, photographer and publishers
would like to thank the following individuals
for their valuable contributions to this book:*

Kevin Andriessen, Pete Astles, Dragons Alive
Team Activity Group, Duncan Eades, Nathan
Eades, Rob Feloy, Rodney Forte, Paul Grogan,
Dino Heald, Darren James, Graham Mackereth,
Malcolm at Mega Kayaks, Mark Potts, Jason
Smith and Martin Tapley.

*Thanks also to the following companies
who supplied clothing and equipment
for photography:*

AS Watersports
Kayaking and canoeing accessories.

Delta Sportswear Ltd
www.delta-sportswear.com
Kayaking and canoeing clothing accessories.

Nookie Xtreme Sports Equipment
Kayaking clothing, accessories
and safety equipment.

Perception Kayaks
www.perception.co.uk

Pyranha Mouldings Ltd
Canoes and kayaks.

River Dart Country Park
For photography locations, logistics, hospitality
and bank support.

System X
Werner and Schlegel paddles.
*Thanks also to the following models,
canoeists and kayakers:*

Alec Ashmore, Steve Balcombe, Nikki Ball,
Duncan Browne, Owen Davies, David Dean, Tim
Denson, Rob Feloy, Mark Harvey, Roger Hopper,
Mariano Kälfors, Beki King, Tom Klamfor, David
Manlow, Bill Mattos, Tim Maud, Jon Miles, Lee
Pritchard, Jason Scholey, J. Simpson, Howard
Smith, Tank, James Weir, Steve Whetman, Hazel
Wilson and Paul Woodward.

ACKNOWLEDGEMENTS FOR SAILING

*The author would like to thank the following
for their help:*

Firstly, Frazer Clark, Gael Pawson and Peter
Spence of Yachts & Yachting, followed in no
particular order by the RYA, ISAF, Rockley
Watersports and Sail France, Minorca Sailing
Holidays, Sunsail at Port Solent and in
Turkey, Crewsaver, Musto, Brian Phipps of
Windsport, Robin Smith, Roger Tushingham,
Rob and Reg White, Rodney Pattisson,
Lewmar, the Laser Centre, RS Racing,
UK Sails, Sobstad, Topper International,
Clamcleat, Hobie Cat and John Pierce plus
various dinghy and keelboat classes which
have provided invaluable information.

*The publishers would like to thank
everyone at Team Unlimited in Spain, and
Sunsail at Port Solent. This book would
not have been possible without their help.*

Thanks also to the following models:
Rob Andrews, Sonia Kirk, Ioan R. Leavey,
Andrew Moore, Mark Reynolds, Ewan McNeill,
Felix Thornton-Jones and Ben Donald.

*Lastly, special thanks to Richard Langdon
and Marie Rondoz of Ocean Images for
the specially commisioned photography,
and extensive use of their picture library.*

PICTURE CREDITS FOR KAYAKING
AND CANOEING

All photography by Helen Metcalfe except for
the following.
t = top; b = bottom; c = centre;
l = left; r = right

Action Images 205t, 206b, 207t, 207b,
216b, 217b.

Kevin Andriessen 232t.

The Art Archive 12t, 12b.

Dino Heald 28bl.

Duncan Eades 236t, 236b, 237t, 237bl, 237br.

Rob Feloy 163t, 179tr, 198tr, 199t, 199b.

Rodney Forte 13cr, 13bl, 13br, 128t, 130t,
130cr, 130br, 131ct, 170bl, 171bl, 172bl,
172br, 173br.

Dino Heald 26bl, 149b, 214t, 215b.

Martin Ording 226bl.

Mark Potts 31tr, 117b, 119t, 119b, 120bl,
121t, 121b, 135t, 135b, 137bl, 141t, 148br,
149t, 185tc, 185tr, 185b, 211t, 2230t, 228b,
229t, 229b, 230tr, 230bl, 231t, 231bl, 231br,
234t, 234b, 235t, 235b.

Jason Smith 188t, 188b, 189t, 189b, 192tl,
192br, 193tl, 226t, 226cb, 227t, 227b, 232bl,
233t, 233b.

Max Spielman 200, 201t, 201b.

Jono Stevens 222t, 222bl, 223t, 223b.

Martin Tapely 184, 187b, 211b, 214b, 215t.

Dan Trotter 198 (sequence), 241b.

PICTURE CREDITS FOR SAILING

All photography by Richard Langdon except
for the following.
t = top; b = bottom; c = centre;
l = left; r = right

Agence D.P.P.I. 249br, 489, 490b, 491bl.

C. Fevreier: 491br

Champion Photos: 400br, 401bl, 435tr.

Cherub Association: 416t.

Christel clear 429br, 434tl, 434tr, 434bl,
437c, 456t, 475tr, 477b, 478l, 479bl, 479br,
481lt, 481ltc, 481lc, 481lbc, 481rt, 481rc,
483lc, 483rt, 483rb, 485tl.

Declan Tiernan 405tr.

GP 14 Association 402t.

Jacques Vapillon 263tr.

Janet Harber 429t, 429bl, 462t, 463t, 483lb
& 484l.

Jonathan Smith: 428t, 458t.

Laser 312.

Mark Greenberg 430.

MAX 403t.

Mike O'Brien 243tr.

Minorca Sailing Holidays 294b.

Ocean Images/Richard Langdon 248,
249bl, 260t, 261tl, 261b, 263bl, 263br, 264br,
265bl, 265br, 266b, 267, 269, 270, 272b,
273b, 277t, 281tr, 283tr, 283br, 284, 285,
286, 287, 288, 289, 290r, 291b, 293b, 294tl,
294tr, 295tr, 295b, 296, 297, 298t, 298b,
299, 300tr, 302, 303, 304, 305b, 306, 307,
308, 309, 310, 343t, 343c, 356t, 360, 362l,
363tr, 373, 374tl, 375b, 376, 377, 378, 380,
381, 382, 383, 384t, 386bl, 386br, 387, 388,
389, 390, 391, 392, 393, 394, 395, 396,
397, 398, 400t, 400bl, 401t, 401br, 402bl,
402br, 403c, 404, 405tl, 405b, 406, 407,
408br, 409bl, 409br, 410, 411, 413, 414,

415, 416b, 417tr, 418b, 419, 420, 421, 422t,
422br, 423t, 425bl, 425br, 426, 428b, 430t,
431br, 432, 433r, 434br, 435tl, 435bl, 436,
439b, 440t, 443br, 445b, 447, 465bl, 468r,
469tl, 470t, 470bl, 471, 472, 474t, 474br,
475bl, 478, 479t, 483, 483lt, 483r, 485c,
485b, 486, 487, 488, 490t.

Pat Collinge/Sunsail 252t, 252bl,
254b, 258b, 261tr, 290l, 313b, 430br,
433l, 448, 455t, 457t, 464, 466t, 469br,
474bl, 478r.

Peter Bentley/Hobie Cat 425tr.

Prindle 425tl.

Richard Neal: 253bl, 282bl, 298c, 313t.

Ross Laney Photographic Ltd 371bl, 371bc
& 371br.

RS Racing Sailboats 345b, 412c.

Sue Pelling 403b, 408tr.

Written Products/Jeremy Evans 249bl,
252br, 253br, 254t, 255, 256, 257, 258, 259,
260tl, 260bc, 260br, 263tl, 268tl, 268tr, 271t,
271c, 272t, 273tr, 275, 291b, 292, 293t, 295tl,
300tl, 300b, 305tl, 318t, 318c, 319t, 320bc,
323, 362r, 363b, 364cl, 364cr, 365, 366t,
371t, 408tl, 412tl, 412bl, 417b, 422bl, 423b,
424t, 424c, 425c, 431tl, 431tr, 431bl, 438b,
439tl, 456b, 459tl, 459c, 465t, 465br, 491t.